ANCIENT ISRAEL

*From Abraham
to the Roman Destruction
of the Temple*

Revised and Expanded Edition

On the cover: The silver dome of the Al-Aqsa mosque on
Jerusalem's Temple Mount overlooks extensive excavations of the ancient remains
along the Old City's southern wall. *Photo by Garo Nalbandian.*

ANCIENT ISRAEL

From Abraham to the Roman Destruction of the Temple

Revised and Expanded Edition

Edited by
Hershel Shanks

PRENTICE HALL

BIBLICAL ARCHAEOLOGY SOCIETY

Library of Congress Cataloging-in-Publication Data

Ancient Israel : from Abraham to the Roman destruction of the Temple /
edited by Hershel Shanks. — Rev. ed.
        p.   cm.
    Includes biographical references and index.
    ISBN 1-880317-53-2 (hardcover). — ISBN 1-880317-54-0 (paperback)
    1. Jews—History—To 70 A.D.   I. Shanks, Hershel.
DS121.A53   1999
    933—dc21   98-52678
                                                                                   CIP

Co-published by: Biblical Archaeology Society
4710 41st Street, NW
Washington, DC 20016
and
Prentice Hall
Upper Saddle River, NJ 07458

Design by Auras Design, Washington, DC

ISBN 0-13-085363-1 (paperback)

Prentice-Hall International (UK) Limited, *London*
Prentice-Hall of Australia Pty. Limited, *Sydney*
Prentice-Hall Canada Inc., *Toronto*
Prentice-Hall Hispanoamericana, S.A., *Mexico*
Prentice-Hall of India Private Limited, *New Delhi*
Prentice-Hall of Japan, Inc., *Tokyo*
Pearson Education Asia Pte. Ltd., *Singapore*
Editora Prentice-Hall do Brasil, Ltda., *Rio de Janeiro*

TABLE OF CONTENTS

Illustrations

Color Plates

Maps and Charts

The Authors

JOSEPH A. CALLAWAY led the archaeological expedition to et-Tell (biblical Ai) from 1964 to 1976. He also excavated at Jericho, Shechem and Bethel. A professor of biblical archaeology at Southern Baptist Theological Seminary from 1967 to 1982, Callaway served as president of the William F. Albright School of Archaeological Research in Jerusalem. He died in August of 1988.

SHAYE J.D. COHEN is the Ungerleider Professor and Director of Judaic Studies at Brown University. From 1987 to 1991, he served as dean of the graduate school of the Jewish Theological Seminary, in New York, where he also taught Jewish history. A specialist in the emergence of rabbinic Judaism, he wrote *From the Maccabees to the Mishnah: A Profile of Judaism* (Westminster Press, 1987) and, most recently, *The Beginnings of Jewishness* (University of California, forthcoming).

RONALD S. HENDEL is an associate professor of religious studies at Southern Methodist University. He wrote *The Epic of the Patriarch: The Jacob Cycle and the Narrative Traditions of Canaan and Israel* (Scholars Press, 1987) and has just published *The Text of Genesis 1–11: Textual Studies and Critical Edition* (Oxford University, 1998). He is preparing a commentary on Genesis for the Anchor Bible series.

SIEGFRIED H. HORN directed the excavation of Hesban (biblical Heshbon), Jordan, from 1968 to 1973, after having dug at Shechem for four seasons in the 1960s. From 1951 to 1976, Horn taught archaeology and the history of antiquity at Andrews University, in Berrien Springs, Michigan. He also served as dean of the university's seminary and founded the school's archaeological museum, which was renamed for him in 1978. The author of 12 books and more than 800 articles, Horn formerly directed the American Center of Oriental Research in Amman, Jordan. He died in November 1993.

ANDRÉ LEMAIRE is *directeur d'études* at the École Pratique des Hautes Études, History and Philology Section, of the Sorbonne, in Paris. A specialist in West Semitic epigraphy, he has written several books in this field and is presently preparing a full corpus of Paleo-Hebrew inscriptions from the First Temple period. He is also the author of a short history of Israel, which has been translated from French into several languages. Lemaire has participated in excavations at Lachish, Tel Keisan, Yarmouth and other sites in Israel.

LEE I. LEVINE is a professor of Jewish history and archaeology at Hebrew University in Jerusalem, where he is also head of the Dinur Research Center for the Study of Jewish History. He has directed the excavation of an ancient synagogue at Horvat 'Ammudim and codirected two seasons of excavations at Caesarea. His numerous books include *Judaism and Hellenism in Antiquity* (University of Washington, 1998) and *The Ancient Synagogue* (Yale University, forthcoming).

P. KYLE McCARTER, JR., is the William F. Albright Professor of Biblical and Ancient Near Eastern Studies at Johns Hopkins University, in Baltimore, Maryland. He taught at the University of Virginia from 1974 to 1985 and has held visiting professorships at Harvard University and Dartmouth College. A former president of the American Schools of Oriental Research, McCarter wrote the commentaries on 1 Samuel and 2 Samuel in the Anchor Bible series. His many other writings include *Ancient Inscriptions: Voices from the Biblical World* (Biblical Archaeology Society, 1996).

ERIC M. MEYERS, professor of religion at Duke University, has directed digs in Israel and Italy for 27 years. He is currently working at Sepphoris, in the Galilee. His most recent publications, cowritten with his wife Carol Meyers, are the commentaries on Haggai and Zechariah in the Anchor Bible series and *Excavations at Gush Halav* (Eisenbrauns and ASOR, 1991). He served as editor-in-chief of *The Oxford Encyclopedia of Archaeology of the Near East* (1997) and cowrote the *Cambridge Companion to the Bible* (1997).

J. MAXWELL MILLER is a professor in the Candler School of Theology at Emory University, where he has taught since 1971. He has excavated at Arad, Beersheba, et-Tell (biblical Ai) and Zeror in Israel; Buseirah and the Moab Survey in Jordan; and Qarqur in Syria. He cowrote, with John Hayes, *A History of Ancient Israel and Judah* (Westminster, 1986), prepared a commentary on Joshua for the Cambridge Commentary series and edited *Archaeological Survey of the Kerak Plateau* (Scholars Press, 1991).

JAMES D. PURVIS is professor emeritus of religion at Boston University, where he taught from 1966 to 1989. He has participated in excavations at Dor and Gezer in Israel and at Idalion in Cyprus. An expert on the Samaritans, Purvis wrote *The Samaritan Pentateuch and the Origin of the Samaritan Sect* (Harvard University, 1968), as well as numerous articles on the sect. He has also prepared a four-part video on *Jerusalem: The Holy City* (Boston University, 1990).

NAHUM M. SARNA is Dora Golding Professor Emeritus of Biblical Studies at Brandeis University, in Waltham, Massachusetts. He is the author of the widely acclaimed *Understanding Genesis* (New York: Schocken, 1970), *Exploring Exodus* (New York: Schocken, 1986) and *Songs of the Heart—An Introduction to the Book of Psalms* (Schocken, 1993). He is the general editor of the Jewish Publication Society's five-volume commentary on the Torah and author of the volumes on Genesis and Exodus.

MICHAEL SATLOW is an assistant professor of religious studies at the University of Virginia. His book *Tasting the Dish: Rabbinic Rhetorics of Sexuality* (Scholars Press, 1995) evolved from his Ph.D. dissertation at the Jewish Theological Seminary, in New York. He has written numerous articles on gender and sexuality in the rabbinic period.

HERSHEL SHANKS is founder, editor and publisher of *Biblical Archaeology Review*, *Archaeology Odyssey* and *Bible Review*. He wrote *The Mystery and Meaning of the Dead Sea Scrolls* (Random House, 1998), *Jerusalem: An Archaeological Biography* (Random House, 1995), *The City of David* (Biblical Archaeology Society, 1973) and *Judaism in Stone: The Archaeology of Ancient Synagogues* (Biblical Archaeology Society and Harper & Row, 1979). A graduate of Harvard Law School, he has also published widely on legal topics.

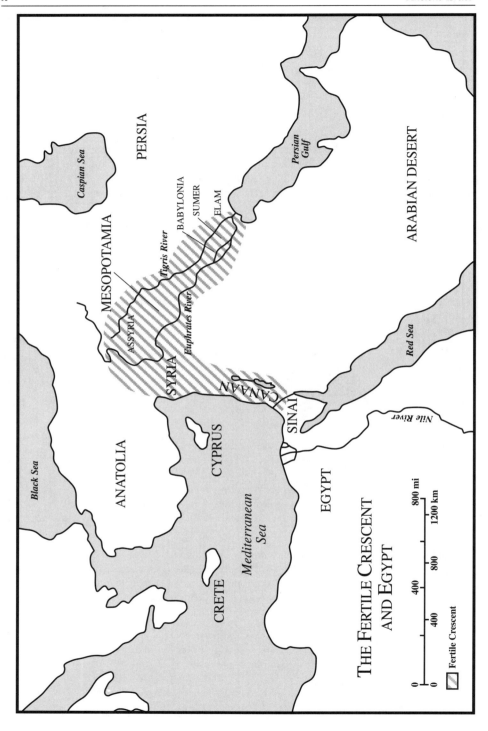

THE FERTILE CRESCENT
AND EGYPT

Fertile Crescent

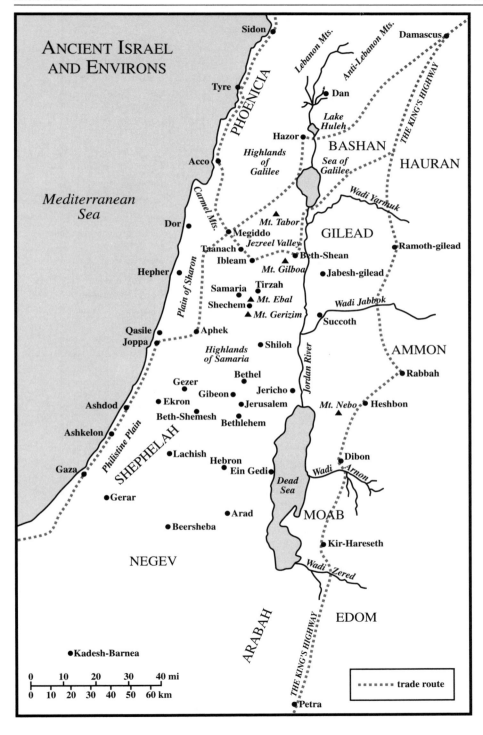

ANCIENT ISRAEL AND ENVIRONS

Sidon

Damascus

Lebanon Mts.

Anti-Lebanon Mts.

PHOENICIA

Tyre

Dan

THE KING'S HIGHWAY

Lake Huleh

Hazor

BASHAN

HAURAN

Acco

Highlands of Galilee

Sea of Galilee

Carmel Mts.

Wadi Yarmuk

Mediterranean Sea

Dor

▲ *Mt. Tabor*

GILEAD

Megiddo

Jezreel Valley

Ramoth-gilead

Taanach

Beth-Shean

Ibleam

▲ *Mt. Gilboa*

Jabesh-gilead

Hepher

Plain of Sharon

Samaria Tirzah

Shechem ▲ *Mt. Ebal*

Wadi Jabbok

▲ *Mt. Gerizim*

Succoth

Qasile

Aphek

AMMON

Joppa

Highlands of Samaria

Shiloh

Jordan River

Bethel

Rabbah

Gezer

Jericho

Ekron Gibeon

Ashdod

Jerusalem

Mt. Nebo ▲ Heshbon

Beth-Shemesh

Ashkelon

Bethlehem

Philistine Plain

SHEPHELAH

Lachish

Dibon

Gaza

Hebron

Wadi Arnon

Ein Gedi

Dead Sea

Gerar

MOAB

Arad

Beersheba

Kir-Hareseth

NEGEV

Wadi Zered

ARABAH

EDOM

Kadesh-Barnea

| 0 | 10 | 20 | 30 | 40 mi |

| 0 | 10 | 20 | 30 | 40 | 50 | 60 km |

THE KING'S HIGHWAY

· · · · · · trade route

Petra

Abbreviations

ABD	*The Anchor Bible Dictionary*, 6 vols., ed. David Noel Freedman (Garden City, NY: Doubleday, 1992)	IEJ	*Israel Exploration Journal*
		IES	Israel Exploration Society
AJS	Association for Jewish Studies	JAAR	*Journal of the American Academy of Religion*
ANEP	*Ancient Near East in Pictures*, ed. James B. Pritchard (Princeton, NJ: Princeton Univ. Press, 1954; 2nd ed., 1969)	JAOS	*Journal of the American Oriental Society*
		JBL	*Journal of Biblical Literature*
ANET	*Ancient Near Eastern Texts*, ed. James B. Pritchard (Princeton, NJ: Princeton Univ. Press, 3rd ed., 1969)	JCS	*Journal of Cuneiform Studies*
		JEA	*Journal of Egyptian Archaeology*
Antiq.	Josephus, *Antiquities of the Jews*	JJS	*Journal of Jewish Studies*
Apion	Josephus, *Contra Apion*	JNES	*Journal of Near Eastern Studies*
ASAE	*Annales du Service des Antiquités de l'Égypte*	JNSL	*Journal of Northwest Semitic Languages*
ASOR	American Schools of Oriental Research	JQR	*Jewish Quarterly Review*
		JR	*Journal of Religion*
AUSS	*Andrews University Seminary Studies*	JSJ	*Journal for the Study of Judaism*
BA	*Biblical Archaeologist*	JSOT	*Journal for the Study of the Old Testament*
BAR	*Biblical Archaeology Review*	JSS	*Journal of Semitic Studies*
BAS	Biblical Archaeology Society	MDOG	*Mitteilungen der deutschen Orient-Gesellschaft*
BASOR	*Bulletin of the American Schools of Oriental Research*	NEAEHL	*The New Encyclopedia of Archaeological Excavations in the Holy Land*, 4 vols., ed. Ephraim Stern (Jerusalem: Israel Exploration Society and Carta, 1993)
BJRL	*Bulletin of the John Rylands Library*	
BN	*Biblische Notizen*	
BR	*Bible Review*	
BS	*Bibliotheca Sacra*	NTS	*New Testament Studies*
BZAW	*Beihefte zur Zeitschrift für die alttestamentliche Wissenschaft*	OEANE	*The Oxford Encyclopedia of Archaeology in the Near East*, ed. Eric M. Meyers (New York and Oxford: Oxford Univ. Press, 1997)
CAH	*Cambridge Ancient History*, ed. I.E. Edwards (Cambridge, UK: Cambridge Univ. Press, 1981)	PAAJR	*Proceedings of the American Academy of Jewish Research*
CBQ	*Catholic Biblical Quarterly*	PEQ	*Palestine Exploration Quarterly*
CHJ	*Cambridge History of Judaism*, ed. W.D. Davies and Louis Finkelstein (Cambridge, UK: Cambridge Univ. Press, 1984)	RB	*Revue Biblique*
		REJ	*Revue des Études Juives*
		SBL	Society of Biblical Literature
EAEHL	*Encyclopedia of Archaeological Excavations in the Holy Land*, 4 vols., ed. Michael Avi-Yonah and Ephraim Stern (Englewood Cliffs, NJ: Prentice-Hall, 1975)	TB	*Tyndale Bulletin*
		TDOT	*Theological Dictionary of the Old Testament*, 5 vols., ed. GJ. Botterweck and H. Ringgren (Grand Rapids, MI: Eerdmans, 1978)
HDB	James Hastings, ed., *Dictionary of the Bible* (New York: Scribners, 1963)	VT	*Vetus Testamentum*
HTR	*Harvard Theological Review*	War	Josephus, *The Jewish War*
HUCA	*Hebrew Union College Annual*	ZAW	*Zeitschrift für die alttestamentliche Wissenschaft*
IDB	*Interpreter's Dictionary of the Bible*, 4 vols. (Nashville, TN: Abingdon Press, 1962; supp. vol. 1976)	ZDPV	*Zeitschrift des deutschen Palästina-Vereins*

Introduction to the Revised Edition

I have been criticized for heaping too extravagant praise in introductions to books I have edited. So restraint is in order. Yet, I confess, once again I am finding it difficult to contain my excitement. This new edition of *Ancient Israel* is a major advance in a text that was already excellent.

It is unnecessary to expatiate on the merits of this book, however, because the extravagant praise is already there in my introduction to the original edition—and I stand by it! The major change I would make in that introduction is to omit references to the text as "short." Indeed, we have deleted that word from the subtitle of this revised edition. Instead of calling it "A Short History from Abraham to the Roman Destruction of the Temple," it is simply "From Abraham to the Roman Destruction of the Temple."

Since its publication in 1988, this work has established itself as the leading history of ancient Israel. Yet it was clear that after a decade the text needed revision—not only because of the artifacts that have continued to emerge from the ground, but also because of new developments in scholarly perspectives. This was especially true for the earlier periods.

In a sense, however, revision is an inapt word to describe what we have done. It does not imply that we have simply eliminated errors in the original edition. For the most part, we have tried to take account of what is new since the original edition was published. Indeed, very few of our conclusions have changed. Instead, we have added new evidence, a new bibliography and, most importantly, new insights and new analysis.

Unfortunately, what is new has not clarified matters; in most cases, it has complicated the story still more. Hence, the need for expansion, rather than, as might have been hoped, a shorter text based on more definitive answers to persistent cruxes.

What has become clear is that our initial decision to enlist the expertise of a variety of scholars was the right one. It is unlikely that a single scholar will ever write a history of ancient Israel on the scholarly level of this text and covering the period from Abraham to the Roman destruction of the Temple. There is simply too much material for one person to control. The disadvantage of a multi-authored book is, of course, the bumps in style and perspective. I think we have largely eliminated these bumps, thanks to the hard work and cooperation not only of the original authors but especially of the revisers. I can only offer praise and appreciation to these revisers, all of them, in their willingness to work and rework the text in an effort to smooth out the bumps.

Only two of the chapters have been revised by the original authors—André Lemaire on the United Monarchy and Lee Levine on the Hellenistic period. Sadly, two of the original authors—Joseph Callaway and Siegfried Horn—have died. The remaining original authors chose to give other scholars a free hand to revise as needed—as needed, in the latter's judgment, I should add.

Kyle McCarter's chapter on the patriarchal period deserves special mention. It has been widely recognized as a major original contribution to the scholarship of this opaque period. I vividly remember the lunch with Kyle and his close friend Ronald Hendel at which Ron offered to revise Kyle's chapter and Kyle accepted with alacrity. At the same time, Kyle offered to revise Siegfried Horn's chapter on the Divided Monarchy, a chapter that would obviously require extensive revision and expansion, especially in light of new editions of ancient extrabiblical texts that have recently appeared, to say nothing of new archaeological finds. There is only one way to describe what I saw at that luncheon: It was beautiful. Here were two major scholars, unprepossessing and unpossessive, joyous in their scholarly endeavors. I wonder if Kyle realized then what an effort it would take to revise Siegfried Horn's chapter; the revised chapter is now a short book in itself—and a splendid one. I think Siegfried would be pleased. And Kyle's original chapter now has an added sparkle— Ron Hendel's artful new insights into such matters as the historical implications of the Genesis genealogies.

Although I substantially revised Nahum Sarna's chapter on the Exodus, I have come to appreciate even more now than when I originally edited the chapter the enormous erudition embodied in the text. It was a pleasure to build on the insights and scholarship Sarna provided. For added support, I turned to scholarly friends—Kyle McCarter, Baruch Halpern and William Hallo—who read my draft and made sage comments and necessary corrections. With the customary release, I hereby absolve them from responsibility for all remaining errors.

The emergence of Israel in Canaan at the beginning of the Iron Age is one of the most hotly debated issues in biblical history. Joseph Callaway's original chapter squarely faced the problem of balancing the biblical text against the seemingly negative archaeological evidence. Max Miller's revision is no less courageous—and equally well-balanced—bringing the latest scholarly perspectives on the issue, supported by the newest archaeological finds. We learn not only of the complexity of the archaeological evidence but also of the complexity of the biblical text. There is no sounder or more careful weaving together of the evidence than in this nuanced treatment of the issue.

André Lemaire concisely and authoritatively revised his own chapter on the United Monarchy, expanding his treatment to deal with the new attacks on the historicity of this period coming from the so-called biblical minimalists. For Lemaire (and for Lee Levine) all the credit—both for the original and the revision—goes to a single expert source.

We were unusually fortunate at being able to enlist Eric Meyers to update James Purvis's chapter on the Babylonian Exile and the return of the exiles to Israel, commonly referred to in scholarly literature as the Persian period. Meyers had excellent material to work with, and he added his own fresh insights and vast archaeological knowledge with his customary felicity of expression.

As noted, Lee Levine revised his own chapter on the age of Hellenism. Interestingly enough, it was the latest periods that needed the least revision—perhaps because so much material was already available. This is also true of Shaye Cohen's chapter on the Roman period, which was revised by Cohen's former student, now a senior scholar in his own right, Michael Satlow. Nevertheless, the chapters on Hellenism and Roman domination have been sharpened and updated so that they appear with a special new sheen.

It has been an inspiration to me—and a wonderful learning experience—to work with these great scholars. I believe that our readers will respond to this text in the same way.

November 1998   *Hershel Shanks*
Washington, D.C.

Introduction to the Original Edition

This is a unique history of ancient Israel. Obviously, there are many other histories of ancient Israel, some of them recent, but none like this one. These are the features that make this book unique:

•It is short. The text itself—from Abraham to the Roman destruction of the Temple—is only 235 pages, including pictures, charts and maps.

•The scholarship is absolutely first-rate. This is because each of its eight chapters has been written by a world-famous scholar treating his specialty.

•This history reflects the most recent developments and the latest archaeological discoveries. While thinking about producing this book, I asked experts in the field to name a first-rate short history of ancient Israel, and they invariably came up with something 25 or 30 years old and therefore necessarily out-of-date.

•This book is intended for people of all faiths—and for skeptics, too. It reflects no particular religious commitments—nor is it anti-religious. The authors include Protestants, Catholics and Jews. They live in Israel, France and the United States.

•This history of ancient Israel spans the centuries from her patriarchal beginnings to 70 A.D., when the Romans burned Jerusalem and destroyed the Temple. Almost all other histories of ancient Israel either begin later (for example, with the settlement period) or end earlier (for example, with the return to Jerusalem of the Babylonian exiles). By contrast, here the reader will face the full impact of an unparalleled historical sweep.

•This text is highly readable—written to be understood, as we say at the Biblical Archaeology Society. It has been carefully edited, so that the words of the text are an enticement, not an obstacle. All arcane academese has been purged. I must add that the eminent scholars who wrote the text have been most cooperative during the sometimes arduous editing process; their aim, like the editor's, has been maximum clarity and maximum readability consistent with accuracy.

•Although it is short and readable, the text is fully annotated, so that the interested student has the references with which to explore in greater detail any matter of particular interest. Moreover, despite the brevity of the text, we have tried to give the evidence, or at least examples of the evidence, that lies behind the historical judgments. We hope we have avoided the unsupported assertion: "Trust me; I know the answer." There is enough evidence here to let the reader make his or her own judgment.

•Finally, the text is festooned with beautiful pictures—many of them in full color—that enhance and illuminate the text.

For these reasons, I believe this is the best book available for all those who are taking their first serious look at the history of ancient Israel—religious school students, college students, seminary students, adult study groups and the intellectually curious of all ages. This book also provides a short, but comprehensive and up-to-date refresher course for those who have been here before.

There are many ways to use this book—as many ways as there are teachers, students and interested readers. But for all, I would suggest a quick initial reading. Read it like a novel from beginning to end. If you begin to bog down in too many details for this kind of reading, then skip ahead—but keep going.

It is important to get the sweep of things, the big picture. This is a remarkable story, an immensely moving passage through time—about 2,000 years of it, ending nearly 2,000 years ago. I don't mean to suggest that reading this book is like attending a Cecil B. DeMille saga. This is a serious study. But beneath the details is a panorama of historical movement that is spiritually elevating as well as intellectually stimulating. No reader should miss this scope.

Moreover, a quick reading should make the reader comfortable with the overarching structure of ancient Israel's history. The major segments in that history—the patriarchal wanderings, the Egyptian sojourn and the Exodus, the settlement of Canaan in the time of the Judges, the institution and development of the monarchy under Saul,

David and Solomon, the split-up of the kingdom, the destruction of the northern kingdom by the Assyrians, the destruction of Solomon's Temple and the southern kingdom by the Babylonians, the Exile in Babylonia and Egypt, the return to the land, the rise of a new Jewish state under the Maccabees, the Hellenization of the Jewish world, the tensions of Roman domination in the Herodian period and, finally, the burning of Jerusalem and destruction of the Second Temple that effectively ended the Jewish Revolt against Rome—will be firmly fixed in your mind. Then details can be filled in on a slower, more intensive second reading.

A word of clarification may be appropriate to explain why we begin and end where we do. Why we begin with Abraham is simple. According to the Bible, he was the first Hebrew. The first 11 chapters of Genesis, before the introduction of Abraham, are referred to as the Primeval History. They do not purport to cover Israelite history.

Moreover, the first 11 chapters of the Bible, in the judgment of modern critical scholars, are mythic, not historic. This does not diminish the power or meaning of these stories, but it does mean that from a factual viewpoint we must approach them differently. Of course, this judgment sometimes collides with the religious faith of people who are committed to the literal truth of Scripture. This issue, however, need not detain us here because even in the Bible's own terms, the history of Israel begins with Abraham, the first Hebrew.

For many scholars, the more difficult question will be why we begin so early, rather than so late—with the patriarchs rather than, say, with the Israelite settlement in Canaan. Some scholars will question whether there is any discoverable history in the Bible's stories about the patriarchs Abraham, Isaac and Jacob. There is obviously a historiographic problem here, to which we shall return. Suffice it to say at this point that the fact that the Bible recites the stories of the patriarchs as the earliest chapters of Israelite history is enough to require a consideration of the extent, if any, to which these stories reflect or contain history of one sort or another. We are not, *a priori*, committed to an answer, but we are committed to asking the question.

At the other end of the time continuum, many scholars will question our decision to end with the Roman destruction of the Temple in 70 A.D. In discussing this project with scholars, I was told several times that it would be more appropriate to continue the story to 135 A.D., when the Romans finally suppressed the Second Jewish Revolt, the so-called Bar-Kokhba Revolt.

There is substance to this contention. I nevertheless rejected it for several reasons. First, any cutoff is to some extent arbitrary. The world always goes on, or at least it has until now. And past events always influence the future. Second, the final destruction of the Jewish Temple in Jerusalem in 70 A.D. was such a cataclysmic event that it can lay claim to marking a historic termination and a new beginning. Third, the book was already long enough, especially as a short history. Fourth, and perhaps decisive, we hope to produce a subsequent volume tracing the parallel developments of Christianity and Judaism during the early centuries of the Common Era; in that book, we will cover the events both leading up to and following the Bar-Kokhba Revolt.*

I have mentioned the sweep of the story and the overarching structure of the historical development. The reader will also notice another development as the story moves along. This development relates to the nature and reliability of the sources from which this history is constructed.

Let us consider the kinds of sources on which the recovery of our history depends. From the patriarchal period through the Exile (Chapters I through VI), the primary source is the Bible. The biblical account is supplemented by what we loosely call archaeological discoveries. (They may or may not have been recovered in a scientifically controlled excavation.) These archaeological artifacts are of two kinds—the "word" kind and the "non-word" kind. The "word" kind includes inscriptions and texts. The "non-word" kind includes anything from a pollen sample to a pottery sherd to the wall of an ancient palace. In addition to the Bible and to archaeological discoveries, we occasionally have a late copy of an earlier book whose author refers to or makes use of ancient sources now lost. But this last category is relatively rare.

The reader will notice that archaeological discoveries are more helpful in uncovering the past as we move along the time line. They are least helpful and least specific in the patriarchal period. Gradually they become more helpful and more specific.

There is another kind of development—a development on the continuum of reliability. We are least sure of what happened in the patriarchal period. Gradually, we become more confident of the history we are recounting as time moves on. Where we are least sure of what happened, we are most reliant on the biblical text. This might be thought to lead to the conclusion that archaeological discoveries are what really give reliability to the biblical text. But this is not true. The biblical text is overwhelmingly more important than the archaeological discoveries. We would pretty much know what happened from the biblical text even without the archaeological discoveries. The reverse is not at all true.

Why then is the early history of ancient Israel less reliable than the later history? The answer relates not to the illumination archaeology provides but to the nature of the biblical text. The traditional, etiological

---

*We have since realized this hope, with the publication of *Christianity and Rabbinic Judaism: A Parallel History of Their Origins and Early Development* (Washington, DC: Biblical Archaeology Society, 1992).—**Ed.**

stories of the patriarchal period present far different historiographic problems than the account of, for example, the Divided Kingdom, which the biblical writers took largely from royal annals.

As a result, the reader will notice another kind of development. In the early chapters of this book, the authors devote major attention to the reliability of the biblical account and to the ways they can penetrate the text to discover what in fact happened. In the earlier periods, we are more concerned with how to deal with the biblical text than with how to interpret the history recounted. Gradually, the emphasis shifts. By the time we reach the Divided Kingdom, we can pretty much rely on the facts given in the Bible, and the historian's task is chiefly to present and interpret those facts to create a modern history. By contrast, in the patriarchal age we confront a basic question of biblical historicity. Were the patriarchs real people who lived at a particular time in history?

In the period of the Egyptian sojourn and the Exodus, we are still at an early time when we must ask whether there was an Egyptian enslavement and an Exodus, but it seems relatively clear that something like that in fact occurred. We are more concerned with placing events in a particular period and with assessing the reliability of details.

By the time we reach the period of the settlement and the Judges, we are on firm, datable historical ground. But here we are faced with a fundamental question. Did the Israelites possess the land by military conquest or by peaceful infiltration into uninhabited areas, or was there perhaps an internal revolt of the underclass that led to Israel's emergence in Canaan? This is obviously a different kind of historiographic problem from those faced by the authors of the previous chapters.

In the period of the United Kingdom, the question of factual historicity begins to fade into the background. The major historical problem is to redress the biases reflected in the text, so that we can arrive at a more objective history of the period.

When we deal with the period of the Divided Kingdom, and with the Babylonian Exile and return, less attention is paid to historiography or the question of reliability, although these questions never disappear.

For the history recounted in the last two chapters of the book, dealing with the Hasmonean period and Roman rule, only a few late books of the Bible are relevant. Equally, if not more important, is a host of classical authors, especially the first-century A.D. Jewish historian Josephus. So-called intertestamental texts, pseudepigrapha and apocrypha, such as Maccabees, as well as later rabbinic writings and the New Testament also provide evidence. The amount of archaeological material that sheds light on this period is enormous. Pride of place, of course, goes to the famous Dead Sea Scrolls, many of which are only now becoming available to scholars. But scholars must also absorb a host of other religious and nonreligious texts, as well as archaeological artifacts ranging from buildings to coins.

Another contrast: In the earlier period described in this book the relevant evidence is sparse, and we must squeeze it in a dozen different ways to get what we reliably can from it. In the later periods, on the other hand, the amount of evidence is truly overwhelming, beyond the capacity of any human being to command. Here the task is to find meaningful strands, overarching trends in a sea of material.

The differences in the various chapters of the book reflect the differences outlined above—in the nature and reliability of the sources; in the historiographic problems; in the light archaeology sheds on the particular period; and in the sheer quantity of material that must be taken into account. The result is a fascinating variety. Reading this story will be a richer experience if these differences are kept in mind.

Ancient Israel was, in the end, defeated; but it was not destroyed. It survived. And it continued to shape the world, as the Bible says, "to this day." To understand this history is to discern why its influence endured. And only in terms of this history can we truly appreciate the scriptural treasures it left us. It is a history that is at once intellectually penetrating and spiritually uplifting. Now, in the words attributed to the great first-century sage Hillel, "Go and study!"

June 1988   *Hershel Shanks*
Washington, D.C.

Acknowledgments

In the introduction, I have expressed my gratitude and indebtedness to the extraordinary scholars who revised the various chapters of this book, so I will refrain from repeating that well-deserved praise here.

The contribution of the staff of the Biblical Archaeology Society to this revised edition has been enormous—and of course they did it in addition to their usual duties and responsibilities. First and foremost among these is Molly Dewsnap, managing editor of *Bible Review* and associate editor of *Biblical Archaeology Review*. She did the bulk of the line editing, conforming notes to text and text to text, rewriting where necessary, often serving as my voice to the revisers, arranging for new pictures, writing photo captions and generally taking responsibility for turning edited drafts into a book.

The overall production and editing supervision of the project was in the able hands of Bridget Young, executive director of the Biblical Archaeology Society, and Suzanne F. Singer, longtime managing editor of our magazines and now contributing editor.

Working with grace and good humor, Lisa Josephson Straus and Sara Murphy painstakingly proofed and corrected the manuscript and obtained the illustrations. In addition, Christen Long, Kathy Jones, Allison Dickens and Gabrielle DeFord willingly lent a hand in proof-reading some of the chapters. The book was copyedited by Jean Bernard and indexed by Barbara E. Cohen. Judith Wohlberg handled the manifold details of production and manufacture, all with her customary organizational skills. David Fox and Susann Borgeest updated the original design by our longtime creative design director, Rob Sugar. Mark Colliton created the maps.

To all, our profound gratitude.

Hershel Shanks

ONE

The Patriarchal Age
Abraham, Isaac and Jacob

P. KYLE McCARTER, JR.
revised by Ronald S. Hendel

T HE HISTORY OF ISRAEL BEFORE THE EXODUS FROM EGYPT IS, AS THE
Bible presents it, a family history. The story begins with the
departure of Abram, son of Terah, from Ur, his ancestral homeland in southern Mesopotamia. He journeys to Haran, a city in northwestern Mesopotamia, and from there to the land of Canaan (Genesis
11:31–12:5). In Canaan, Abram's son Isaac is born, and Isaac, in turn,
becomes the father of Jacob, also called Israel (Genesis 32:29). During
a famine, Jacob and his 12 sons, the ancestors of the 12 tribes of
Israel, leave Canaan and settle in Egypt, where their descendants
become slaves.

This segment of Israel's history, therefore, is the story of the patriarchs: Abram or Abraham (as he is called in Genesis 17:5), Isaac, Jacob
(Israel) and the 12 sons of Jacob.

The biblical description of the patriarchal period is concerned largely
with private affairs, as one might expect in the story of an individual
family. There are only a few references to public events, and none of
these corresponds to a known event of general history. Genesis 14, for
example, describes a war in which the kings of the five Cities of the Plain
(Sodom, Gomorrah, Admah, Zeboiim and Bela, or Zoar) are arrayed
against an alliance of four kings led by Chedorlaomer, king of Elam, a
country that lay east of Mesopotamia. Chedorlaomer is said to have ruled
over the Cities of the Plain before they rebelled (Genesis 14:4). There is

no surviving extrabiblical record of these events, and neither the name of Chedorlaomer nor that of his ally Amraphel, king of Shinar (Babylonia), has been found in Mesopotamian records. Despite numerous attempts, no scholar has succeeded in identifying any of the nine kings involved in the war. The same is true of the other public figures mentioned in the patriarchal history: None can be identified from extrabiblical sources. Thus we know nothing of Melchizedek, king of Salem, apart from what we read in Genesis 14, or of Abimelech, king of Gerar, apart from what is said in Genesis 20 and 26. No external source mentions the Egyptian officer Potiphar (Genesis 39) or Hamor (Genesis 34), who was apparently a ruler of Shechem, or Ephron the Hittite (Genesis 23), a prominent citizen of Hebron. The early kings of Edom listed in Genesis 36:31–39 are known only from the Bible. We might expect to be able to identify the pharaoh of Genesis 12:10–20 or the pharaoh of the Joseph story, but neither ruler is called by name in the Bible.

When did the patriarchs live? In the absence of references to persons or events of general history, it is very difficult to determine the historical context of the stories in Genesis 12–50. The initial question, then, is a simple one: When did the patriarchs live?

At first glance, an answer to this question seems to be available from chronological indications in the biblical narrative itself. We are told that Abraham was 75 years old when he set out for Canaan (Genesis 12:4) and 100 when Isaac was born (Genesis 21:5). According to Genesis 25:26, Isaac was 60 years old when Jacob was born. Then, if Jacob was 130 when he descended into Egypt, as we read in Genesis 47:9, the full time the patriarchs spent in Canaan before going to Egypt was 215 years. Subsequently, we are told that the period of slavery in Egypt lasted 430 years (Exodus 12:40), and that the time from the Exodus from Egypt to the beginning of the construction of the Temple in the fourth year of Solomon's reign was 480 years (1 Kings 6:1). This brings us close to the period where we have secure chronological information: Scholars agree that Solomon died within a decade or so of 930 B.C.E.* According to 1 Kings 11:42, he reigned 40 years. It follows that his fourth year, the year work began on the Temple, was about 966 B.C.E. Reckoning backward from this date and using the numbers cited above, we arrive at the following scheme:

> 2091 B.C.E. Abram's departure for Canaan
> 1876 B.C.E. The descent of Jacob's family into Egypt
> 1446 B.C.E. The Exodus from Egypt
> 966 B.C.E.   The beginning of the construction
>   of Solomon's Temple

*B.C.E. (Before the Common Era) and C.E. (Common Era) are the alternative designations for B.C. and A.D. often used in scholarly literature.

According to these calculations, the patriarchal period (the time of the sojournings of Abraham, Isaac and Jacob in Canaan) lasted from 2091 to 1876 B.C.E., and the Israelites were enslaved in Egypt between 1876 and 1446 B.C.E.

Unfortunately, there are serious problems with this scheme. First, it accepts the impossibly long life spans assigned the patriarchs. Second, it is internally inconsistent. Moses and Aaron were fourth-generation descendants of Jacob's son Levi (1 Chronicles 5:27–29, in Hebrew). The 430-year period assigned the slavery in Egypt is too long for the three generations from Levi to Moses and Aaron, an average of about 143 years a generation. In any event, this is inconsistent with the notice that Joshua, a younger contemporary of Moses and Aaron, was a 12th-generation descendant of Levi's brother Joseph (1 Chronicles 7:20–27). If this were true, the 11 generations from Joseph to Joshua would average about 39 years each.

Third, the dates produced by this chronology for the Exodus and settlement do not correspond well with the evidence of history and archaeology. If the Exodus occurred in about 1446 B.C.E., then by the same chronology the conquest of Canaan must have begun 40 years later, in about 1406 B.C.E. There is, however, no archaeological evidence of a widespread destruction or change of population at the end of the 15th century. Rather, the changes in material culture that archaeologists associate with the appearance of the Israelites in Canaan may be dated, in general, to the 13th or 12th century B.C.E., and the first clear historical evidence for the presence of Israel in Canaan is the inscription on the so-called Israel Stele of the Egyptian pharaoh Merneptah, dating to about 1207 B.C.E. (see Chapter III).

The Bible's own chronological scheme, therefore, does not provide intelligible evidence for the dating of the patriarchal period. This fact, combined with the absence of references to events of general history as noted above, indicates that the patriarchal narratives in Genesis cannot be used as historical resources in any simple or straightforward fashion. They must be interpreted on the basis of an understanding, first, of their distinctive literary history and the purposes for which they were composed, and, second, of the development of the traditions upon which they are based.

Scholars generally agree that the patriarchal narratives, as we now have them, are composite. They contain at least three written strata, or strands, the earliest of which was composed during the time of the kingdoms of Israel and Judah (tenth to sixth century B.C.E.)* and the latest after the Babylonian destruction of Jerusalem

---

*This is the earliest period in Israel's history when written historiography could be expected to develop. See Chapter IV by André Lemaire on the period of the United Kingdom.

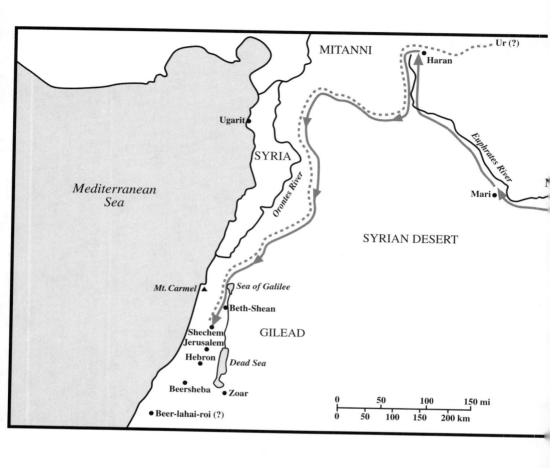

(586 B.C.E.). All of these strata were brought together and arranged in approximately their present form at some time in the Second Temple period (after 538 B.C.E.) or, at the earliest, during the Babylonian Exile (586–538 B.C.E.). On the surface, therefore, the biblical patriarchal history reflects the political and religious viewpoint of the Judean monarchy and priesthood. Thus the promise made to Abram in Genesis 12:2 is that his descendants will be, not simply a numerous people, but a great "nation."

Are the patriarchs historical individuals or eponyms?

On this level, the men and women who appear in Genesis 12–50 are less accessible as historical individuals than as typological prefigurations of the later Israelites and their neighbors. In many cases they are eponyms, that is, persons from whom the names of the later groups were supposed to be derived. Thus Jacob is also called

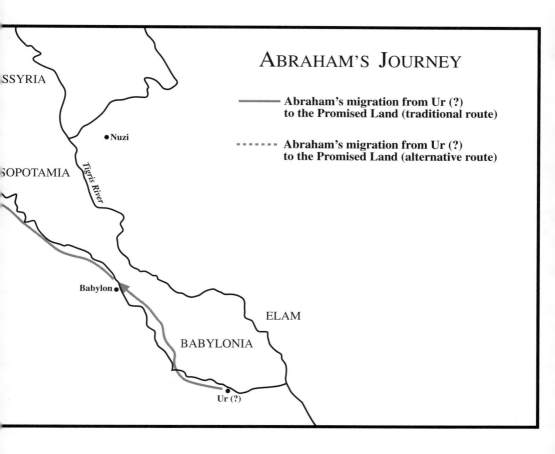

ABRAHAM'S JOURNEY

———— Abraham's migration from Ur (?)
to the Promised Land (traditional route)

······· Abraham's migration from Ur (?)
to the Promised Land (alternative route)

"Israel" (the name of the nation in later times), and his 12 sons are
the eponymous ancestors of the 12 tribes of Israel. The narratives
and genealogies characterize the various peoples of the writers' own
times and delineate the relationships among them from an Israelite
perspective. Israel's ancestors are born under auspicious circumstances, for instance, whereas the eponymous ancestors of the
Moabites and Ammonites, "Moab" and "Ben-ammi," are born of
incestuous unions of Lot and his daughters (Genesis 19:30–38).
Jacob (Israel) outwits his brother Esau, who is also called "Edom"
(Genesis 25:30, 36:1), and wins Esau's birthright and blessing.
Ishmael, the eponymous ancestor of the tribes that inhabited the
desert region between Judah and Egypt, is the child of the Judahite
patriarch Abram and Sarai's Egyptian maid Hagar (Genesis 16). This
kind of material, though of great value in considering the political

outlook of later Israel, is very difficult to use in a historical reconstruction of the world of Israel's ancestors.

If Genesis 12–50 in its present form reflects the time of the biblical
writers (that is, the time of the monarchy or later) rather than the time
of the patriarchs, is it possible to look behind the present, literary form
of the biblical narrative to examine the traditions upon which this material is based? Such a procedure might shed light on the development of
the traditions and, ultimately, provide information about the history of
the patriarchal age. Modern scholars, therefore, have developed methods for studying the preliterary history of the stories in Genesis.

*Searching for
the social
context of the
patriarchs*

One such method, which was especially popular in the middle
decades of the 20th century, was based largely on archaeology. The
scholars associated with this method took a generally positive view of
the historical value of Genesis 12–50. They acknowledged that the
patriarchal narratives in their present form were composed no earlier
than the United Kingdom (tenth century B.C.E.). Nevertheless, they
argued that these materials were based on historically reliable traditions deriving from earlier periods. Excavations had provided extensive new data, including a substantial amount of written material.
After studying these texts, many scholars were convinced that the
biblical patriarchal stories contained authentic details preserved from
the time of their origin. It seemed reasonable, therefore, to suppose
that there was a historical patriarchal period and to hope that it might
be identified.

This point of view is associated most closely with the work of
William F. Albright and his students.[1] It was also developed and promoted by other prominent scholars, especially Ephraim A. Speiser.[2] In
brief, the argument of this "school" was as follows: Certain details in the
biblical patriarchal stories—including personal names, social customs,
legal practices and aspects of lifestyle—correspond to known features
of second-millennium culture in Mesopotamia, Syria and Canaan.
Many of the same details, moreover, do not fit into the culture of the
Israelite monarchy, the time when the stories were written down. In the
judgment of Albright and those who shared his viewpoint, it seemed
likely that these details preserved authentic elements of the civilization
of the patriarchal period; by studying them and comparing them to
surviving second-millennium materials outside the Bible, we should be
able to determine the original historical context of the patriarchal traditions. As Albright himself put it,

> So many corroborations of detail have been discovered in recent
> years that most competent scholars have given up the old critical
> theory according to which the stories of the Patriarchs are mostly
> retrojections from the time of the Dual Monarchy [late tenth cen-
> tury B.C.E. and later].[3]

He wrote elsewhere,

> As a whole, the picture in Genesis is historical, and there is no
> reason to doubt the general accuracy of the biographical details
> and the sketches of personality which make the patriarchs come
> alive with a vividness unknown to a single extrabiblical character
> in the whole vast literature of the ancient Near East.[4]

In general, Albright's students did not express this viewpoint quite
so strongly. As they acknowledged, archaeology cannot be expected
to corroborate biographical details or specific references to private
events. Nevertheless, archaeology might be able to shed light on the
general historical context of the patriarchal stories. And this is primarily what was claimed by Albright and his students. They argued
that the general cultural milieu of the patriarchal stories—as indicated by the details of social, economic and legal customs mentioned
in the Bible—could best be identified with an early period and, more
particularly, with the early second millennium B.C.E. According to
G. Ernest Wright:

> We shall probably never be able to prove that Abram really
> existed, that he did this or that, said thus and so, but what we can
> prove is that his life and times, as reflected in the stories about
> him, fit perfectly within the early second millennium, but imper-
> fectly with any later period.[5]

The reconstruction of patriarchal history achieved by Albright,
Speiser and others has had far-reaching consequences. It remains
widely influential today. Recent research, however, has cast substantial
doubt on many of its arguments, and the confidence these arguments
inspired in scholars a generation ago has dissipated. To understand
why this change has taken place, we must look more closely at their
reconstruction and the evidence upon which it was based.

An urban culture flourished in Syria and Canaan during the Early
Bronze Age, which spanned much of the third millennium B.C.E.
During the last quarter of the third millennium, however, this civilization collapsed and was replaced by a predominantly nonurban,
pastoral culture. The factors that produced this change are not fully
understood. The third dynasty of the city of Ur held sway in Mesopotamia at the time, and the records of the Ur III rulers complain of
chronic trouble with nonurban peoples who were laying claim to
lands previously controlled by the city. Scholars long supposed,
therefore, that a chief factor in the urban collapse was an invasion—
or at least a massive immigration—of nomadic peoples from the
desert fringes of the region. These peoples, called *Amurru*—that is,
"Westerners" or "Amorites"—in the Mesopotamian sources, gradually gained ascendancy in the settled portions of both Syria-Canaan
and Mesopotamia, so that in the early second millennium they took
the leadership in reestablishing urban centers.

The theory that an invasion or immigration of Amorites was responsible for the radical cultural changes that characterized the transition from the Early to Middle Bronze Age is sometimes called "the Amorite hypothesis." A corollary of this hypothesis identifies the biblical patriarchs as Amorites. Albright associated Abraham's wanderings with the Amorite movements and dated the Abraham phase of the patriarchal period to the end of the third millennium. He called this period, which he dated to 2100–1900 B.C.E., Middle Bronze I (MB I), since it represented a break from the preceding Early Bronze Age and was characterized by the arrival of the people who would assume cultural leadership later in the Middle Bronze Age.

The succeeding period, which Albright called MB II A, was an age of unwalled villages in Syria and Canaan. The strong XIIth Dynasty kings of Egypt encouraged the gradual development of a system of city-states in Syria and Canaan. Then, as Egypt began to weaken at the end of this period, the new urban centers entered a period of independence, prosperity and high cultural attainment. Albright identified this period, which he called MB II B, as the time of the patriarch Jacob. This was the Old Babylonian period in Mesopotamia, when Hammurabi and his successors ruled. In Syria it is sometimes called "the age of Mari," after a city on the Upper Euphrates that attained a position of ascendancy in Syria and western Mesopotamia at the time. The life and history of Mari are recorded in a major cuneiform archive found at the site, called Tell Hariri, on the Syrian side of the modern Syro-Iraqi frontier. Local leadership for the process of reurbanization came from the previously nomadic Amorite population. We know this because the new ruling dynasties in the city-states of Syria and Mesopotamia have characteristically Amorite names. There remained, however, a substantial nomadic population, which was also Amorite. The royal archives of Mari provide ample illustration of the coexistence of the two groups.

Many scholars—including several of Albright's own students—were reluctant to be as precise as Albright in dating the Abraham phase of the patriarchal period to MB I and the Jacob phase to MB II B. They preferred a more general date, contending "simply that the Patriarchal stories are best understood in the setting of the early second millennium."[6] This position had the advantage of avoiding one of the problems of the Amorite hypothesis in its original form: Although MB I (to which Albright assigned the Abraham phase) was a strictly nonurban period, the Abraham narratives in the Bible do mention several cities.* Moreover, none of the archaeological sites associated with these biblical cities has yielded any substantial MB I remains.[7] It seemed better, therefore, to identify the patriarchal age with the subsequent period of reurbanization in MB II and, more particularly, MB II B. Throughout

*These include the various cities of the Jordan Valley (Genesis 14:2), the Philistine city of Gerar (Genesis 20:1), the fortified city of Hebron (Genesis 23:2), etc.

Genesis, Abraham, Isaac and Jacob are depicted as living in tents in proximity to urban centers, a situation that may be compared with the coexistence of nomadic and urban peoples at Mari and other cities in MB II B. Thus it was argued that the patriarchal way of life as depicted in the Genesis narratives was especially compatible with what we know of the civilization of the early second millennium.[8]

In addition to general observations of this kind, two arguments were developed to support the association of the patriarchs with the early second millennium. The first was based on the analysis of the personal names found in Genesis 12–50; the second, on studies of the social customs and legal practices mentioned in the patriarchal narratives.

Let us consider the personal names first. As indicated above, Amorite names form a distinctive group. They may be identified by a number of peculiar linguistic features. Names of this type are common in materials from the first half of the second millennium. Advocates of a similar date for the patriarchal age pointed out that the names in the patriarchal narratives are largely of the same type. A form of the name "Jacob," for example, occurs several times in early-second-millennium materials, and the name "Abram" is said to be attested for the same period.[9] No examples of "Isaac" or "Joseph" have survived, but both of these names are of the Amorite type. The argument, therefore, was that the biblical names from the patriarchal period fit well in the historical context of the early second millennium but could not have originated later, that is, at the time of the biblical writers.

Second, Albright, Speiser and others cited numerous parallels between social and legal practices mentioned in extrabiblical texts from the second millennium and social and legal practices referred to in the biblical patriarchal narratives. Cuneiform texts from Nuzi in Upper Mesopotamia were especially important to this part of the discussion.[10] The Nuzi tablets reflect the practices and customs of the Hurrians, a people who flourished in the eastern Tigris region in the middle of the second millennium. Although no one attempted to associate the patriarchs directly with the Hurrian kingdom of Mitanni, it was well known that Hurrian influence was widespread in Syria and even Canaan in this period. Thus, numerous connections between the Hurrians and the Bible were proposed. According to the terms of a Nuzi marriage contract, for example, a barren wife is required to provide a slave woman to her husband to bear his children.[11] In Genesis 16:1–4, the barren Sarai sends her maid Hagar to Abram to bear children. The parallel is obvious. At Nuzi, if this union produces a son, the slave woman's child may not subsequently be expelled; compare Abraham's unwillingness to send away Hagar and her son, Ishmael, in Genesis 21:10–11. Further, as interpreted by Speiser,

> In Hurrian society a wife enjoyed special standing and protection when the law recognized her simultaneously as her husband's

sister, regardless of actual blood ties ... This dual role conferred on the wife a superior position in society.[12]

According to Speiser, this custom lies behind those episodes in Genesis in which Abraham (12:10–20, 20:1–18) and later Isaac (26:6–11) introduce their wives as their sisters.

The story of Sarai and Hagar and the wife-sister episodes are only two of the numerous details of the patriarchal narratives that were interpreted in light of Middle Bronze Age texts (dating to about 2000–1550 B.C.E.). The general argument was that many social and legal customs referred to in Genesis have parallels in middle- or early-second-millennium practice, but that the same customs are without parallel in later times. From this it was concluded that the presence of these references in Genesis was an indication of the early-second-millennium origin of the biblical traditions.

A scholarly failure   Despite its attractions, this reconstruction has proved vulnerable to criticism of various kinds.

Doubts about the application of the Amorite hypothesis to the problems of the patriarchal period have led to a serious modification and abandonment of many of the positions cited above. It now seems unlikely that an invasion or immigration of nomads was a primary factor in the collapse of urban civilization in the last part of the third millennium.[13] The pastoral peoples so prominent in this period were present in earlier times as well, living alongside the established urban centers. Instead, overpopulation, drought, famine or a combination of such problems may have exhausted the resources necessary to the maintenance of an urban way of life. When the cities disappeared, the nomadic encampments remained. Other nomads, originally living on the fringes of the desert, probably took advantage of the new situation to infiltrate previously settled areas; but there was no widespread immigration, and most of the cultural changes detected by archaeology can best be explained as indigenous, not produced by the arrival of outsiders. The period called MB I by Albright, therefore, was really the last, posturban phase of the Early Bronze Age, and an emerging consensus of scholarship now prefers to call it Early Bronze IV (EB IV).*

*Many scholars also now believe that Albright's dates for this period were about a century too low. Our dating and periodization of the Middle Bronze Age, in contrast to the scheme developed by Albright, are shown in the following chart. In general we follow William G. Dever (see endnote 13):

Date	Archaeological Period	Albright's Scheme	Albright's Date
2250–2000	EB IV	MB I	2100–1900
2000–1800	MB I	MB II A	1900–1750
1800–1630	MB II	MB II B	1700–1600
1630–1550	MB III	MB II C	1600–1550

If no invasion or widespread migration took place in EB IV, there is no reason to associate Abram's wanderings with the events of that period, especially in view of the difficulty, already noted, created by the absence in this period of the urban centers mentioned in Genesis 12–25.

On the other hand, the circumstances of what we now call late MB I (Albright's MB II A) and MB II (MB II B), during which nomads and urban dwellers lived side by side in Syria and Canaan, do provide a suitable context for the patriarchal stories.[14] Also, as we have seen, a modified version of the Amorite hypothesis located the patriarchal period more generally in the early second millennium. Yet it is becoming increasingly clear that this "dimorphic" pattern—of city dwellers and tribal peoples (including both pastoralists and villagers) living contiguously—has been typical of the Middle East from ancient until modern times.[15] This pattern prevailed even in the third millennium; after the interruption of EB IV, it resumed in the Middle Bronze Age, as the archives from Mari show.[16] Although we do not have archival evidence for later periods, as we do for the earlier period at Mari, there is no reason to doubt that the pattern persisted throughout the Late Bronze Age and beyond. The archaeological evidence and modern anthropological studies seem to confirm this.[17] That this dimorphic lifestyle is a fitting background for the stories about the patriarchs provides no basis for locating them in MB I and II in preference to other periods.

The other criteria urged in favor of an early second-millennium date for the patriarchal age have also been challenged. In almost every specific instance, the proposed parallels between details of the patriarchal stories and information found in surviving second-millennium documents have now been disputed.[18] Many of the parallels are no longer regarded as valid. In several other cases, the phenomena in question have been identified in texts from one or more later periods, thus diminishing the importance of the parallels for dating the patriarchal tradition. More particularly, the Nuzi evidence, which once figured so prominently in the discussion, has been vitiated by the discovery that the information it provides about private life reflects widespread Mesopotamian practices rather than distinctively Hurrian customs that might be assumed to have penetrated into Canaan.[19]

We can no longer argue, for example, that the patriarchal names fit best into the early second millennium. Names similar or identical to the names found in Genesis are attested from a number of different periods. The identification of the name "Abram" or "Abraham" in Middle Bronze materials is uncertain or dubious, whereas forms of this name ("Abram," "Abiram") occur several times in texts from the Late Bronze Age (1550–1200 B.C.E.) and later.[20] Moreover, names with the same structure are exceedingly common, attested in almost all periods.[21] Similarly, the name type to which "Isaac," "Jacob" and "Joseph" belong is widely distributed across the history of the ancient

Near East. It is especially well known from Middle Bronze sources and, in fact, is the most characteristic type of Amorite name.[22] But there is no reason to believe that its use diminished significantly after the Middle Bronze Age;[23] in the Late Bronze Age, it is well attested in Ugaritic and Amarna Canaanite names;[24] and in the Iron Age it occurs in Hebrew inscriptions as well as in the Bible.[25] While it is true that the name "Jacob" is very common in the Middle Bronze Age, it is also found in Late Bronze sources,[26] and related names occur in both Elephantine (fifth century B.C.E.) and Palmyrene (first century B.C.E. through third century C.E.) Aramaic.[27]

Similar difficulties arise with the proposition that the legal practices and social customs referred to in the stories in Genesis support a Middle Bronze date for the patriarchs. Reexamination of the second-millennium parallels proposed by Albright, Speiser and others has shown that many cannot be restricted to a single, early period. The Nuzi parallel to Genesis 16:1–4, for example, in which the barren Sarai provides her husband with her bondwoman, is not unique: The responsibility of a barren wife to provide a slave woman to her husband to bear children is cited in Old Babylonian, Old Assyrian and Nuzi texts (all from the Middle Bronze Age), but also in a 12th-century Egyptian document and a marriage contract from Nimrud, dated 648 B.C.E.[28] As for the biblical "wife-sister motif," it now seems doubtful that relevant parallel material is to be found in the Nuzi archives. In the contracts cited by Speiser, the adopting "brother" is usually not the future husband of the adopted woman.[29] Although in one instance a "brother" does subsequently marry his "sister," this is a special case requiring a document of marriage to replace the earlier document of adoption. In the biblical stories, moreover, the designation of the wives of the patriarchs as sisters is a trick to protect the patriarchs from men who might lust after their wives, not a legal procedure intended to confer status. Speiser recognized this, suggesting that the "original" meaning was lost; but Speiser's assumption is highly questionable in view of the inapplicability or at least ambiguity of the Nuzi parallels.[30]

The search for the history of tradition

A second and very different attempt to trace the preliterary history of the patriarchal stories—undertaken at about the same time that Albright and the others were investigating the archaeological materials—is associated with the names of Martin Noth and his teacher Albrecht Alt. These two scholars sought to penetrate to an early stage in the patriarchal tradition through a critical analysis of the biblical literature itself.

On the basis of his study of the biblical materials pertaining to the premonarchical period, Noth was convinced that the larger entity of Israel had been formed by an amalgamation of various clans and tribes, a process that took place gradually during the period of settlement in Canaan.[31] From Noth's viewpoint, therefore, it seemed impossible that all of these clans and tribes could have known *all* of the traditions about the presettlement period—about the patriarchs, the captivity in Egypt and the Exodus, the wanderings in the wilderness, the revelation at Sinai and the conquest of Canaan. Instead, individual elements of these traditions must have been passed down within individual tribes or clans. As these groups were absorbed into the larger association of Israel, the various elements of tradition were combined and incorporated into a common heritage.

Drawing on the form-critical method devised by Hermann Gunkel,[32] Noth tried to reconstruct the history of discrete units of tradition from their origin within a particular tribe or clan to their integration into the larger story.[33] This method has been described as the "history of traditions."

A major clue to the origin of a particular element of a tradition is its connection with a region, place or other geographical feature. The narratives about the individual patriarchs have certain clear geographical connections. Abraham is generally associated with southern Canaan, and his principal residence is at the "oaks of Mamre" near Hebron (Genesis 13:18, 14:13, 18:1). Isaac dwells at the oases of Beersheba (Genesis 26:32–33) and Beer-lahai-roi (Genesis 24:62, 25:11). Jacob is most closely identified with Shechem (Genesis 33:18–19) and Bethel (Genesis 28:18–19, 35:1–8), though he also has important associations with the region of Gilead, east of the Jordan River (Genesis 31:43–50, 32:2–3, 32:30, 33:17). It therefore seemed likely to Noth that the traditions about Abraham came from the Judean hills, those about Isaac from southwestern Judah and the Negev and those about Jacob from the central Ephraimite hills. Noting that the immediate ancestor of the Israelites, Jacob (whose name is also Israel), is linked with the heartland of the country, Noth concluded that the Jacob tradition was the oldest component of the patriarchal lore. As Israel expanded southward, absorbing Judah and the northern Negev, Abraham and Isaac entered the tradition and then were linked by genealogy with Jacob. The priority eventually assigned to Abraham (the first patriarch) is an indication of the southern development of the tradition as it has come down to us.

When did this blending of patriarchal traditions take place? That is, when were the stories about Abraham and Isaac combined with those about Jacob? It is obvious that this development was completed during the time when the stories were being transmitted orally, that is, before the composition of the so-called J source,* the earliest of the literary

---

*According to the documentary hypothesis, the Pentateuch is an amalgam of at least four strands or sources: the J source (the Yahwist); the E source (the Elohist); the P source (Priestly material) and the D source (Deuteronomistic material). J and E were combined before the introduction of D and P. Many scholars now doubt that E had an independent existence apart from J.

strands in Genesis, in which Abraham, Isaac and Jacob are represented as members of the same family. The dates biblical scholars assign to J differ widely, however, ranging from the tenth to the sixth century B.C.E. A better clue to the date when the northern and southern patriarchal traditions were combined, therefore, is the priority that was assigned the southern patriarchs when the combination took place. The fact that a southern patriarch (Abraham) was regarded as the eldest suggests that the combination occurred at a time when Judah was in ascendancy over Israel. Such a political situation cannot have existed, however, before the establishment of the Davidic monarchy. Indeed, it is unlikely that Judah was incorporated into Israel before the reign of David.[34] And even if Judah was a part of Israel when David came to the throne, it had not been so for long, since the earliest tribal list makes no mention of the southern tribes (cf. Judges 5:14–18).

It is not likely, therefore, that patriarchal figures from the newly incorporated regions of Hebron and Beersheba, in the south, would have been accorded priority over the old Israelite patriarch Jacob before the radical realignment of power that took place when David the Judahite became king of Israel. The combination of traditions preserved in the patriarchal stories cannot have been complete before the end of the 11th century B.C.E. We must not forget, however, that this combination was one of the last phases of a lengthy and complex development that must have gone on for centuries. Noth believed that the development of the tradition was coeval with the development of Israel itself. That is, the process that shaped the patriarchal tradition was concurrent with the long series of clan and tribal alliances by which Israel grew from the earliest group that bore the name to a larger tribal association and, finally, to a kingdom.

Although Noth believed that the history of traditions allows us to trace the preliterary development of the *traditions* about the patriarchs, it provides only very indirect information about the patriarchs themselves. Noth did not deny that the patriarchs may have actually lived, but he believed that even if they did, they were now inaccessible as historical figures. Because the patriarchal traditions as we know them are products of the settlement period, he argued, they may not be relied upon to preserve authentic historical information about the patriarchal period itself.[35]

Another scholarly failure   Noth assumed that the patriarchal tradition grew from small, originally independent literary units into its present complex pattern. In this assumption he followed Gunkel, who believed that folk literature evolved from short, simple units into extended, discursive complexes. Thus, for Noth, a story with a complex structure was necessarily late, whereas a simple narrative unit was likely to be early. Subsequent improvement in our understanding of oral literatures, however, has exposed the error of this view.[36] We now know that in the preliterary, oral stage of transmission, long stories with complex structures were routine in most traditional literatures. Homer, for example, was almost certainly an oral poet; the Ugaritic* myths and epics, if they are not actual transcriptions of oral performances, stand very close to the stage of oral composition. Both the Homeric and Ugaritic literatures are characterized by extended narratives with complex structures.

Recent analysis of the patriarchal tradition itself shows that Noth's account of its evolution from isolated units to interconnected patterns requires revision. As we noted at the outset of our discussion, the story of the biblical patriarchs is a family story. The traditional complex that underlies the narratives of Genesis expresses, among other things, an elaborate account of kinship relationships that existed (or were believed to exist) between the ancestors of Israel and their neighbors. Modern anthropological research has shown that kinship patterns are very often the central factors in the social structure and self-definition of a community. In other words, the final constellation of stories is not just a magpie's nest of individual brief stories contributed by various clans and tribes, but has its own coherence as a complex genealogical narrative through which Israel defined herself and her relationships with her neighbors.[37]

Did this genealogical pattern influence the evolution of the stories in Israelite oral traditions? To be sure, these stories are not mere "etiologies" of ethnic relationships, as some have maintained. The conflicts and personal relationships in the stories are so closely tied to the genealogical relationships that the two aspects—genealogy and story—were very likely intertwined in the oral traditions. Analogies from Arabic, Greek and other traditional literatures show this is to be expected in stories about a culture's ancestors. Therefore, it is reasonable to suggest that the genealogical structure of the stories is a feature not only of the final literary form, but also of the preliterary development of the stories.

If there is such an organizational structure inherent in the genealogical framework of the stories (though genealogies, too, are changeable over time), and if the length or complexity of a story has no intrinsic bearing on its date of origins, then the chief pillars of Noth's history-of-traditions method fall to the ground. This is not to say that all of Noth's conclusions are invalid, but a more adequate method would be needed to substantiate any of them.[38]

In contrast to the confident scholars of an earlier generation, today's historians of ancient Israel approach the prehistory of Israel with extreme caution. Most remain convinced that the stories about

A kernel of history

---

*Ugarit was the name of a city on the northern coast of Syria that flourished in the 14th and 13th centuries B.C.E. A large cuneiform archive has been found at the site, modern Ras Shamra.

Abraham, Isaac and Jacob contain a kernel of authentic history. Recognizing the complexity of the oral and literary development of the narratives in Genesis 12–50, however, they are reluctant to designate individual features as historically authentic. The best hope for success probably lies in the selective application of the methods used in the past (archaeology, philology and tradition history), supplemented or modified according to the results of more recent research, including studies using the methods of sociology and anthropology.

In this effort, we must always be aware that the patriarchal narratives are ideology, not history. They were cast into literary form in the first millennium B.C.E. by authors with varying political, theological and literary motivations. They cannot be approached as historiography in anything like the modern sense. If we tried to do so, we would not only arrive at a spurious prehistory of Israel but would also overlook the authentic information the patriarchal narratives provide.

It does not follow from this that Genesis 12–50 has no value for the reconstruction of the prehistory of Israel. It is safe to assume that the Israelites, like almost all other peoples, had traditions about their own past, and it seems likely that the biblical writers were drawing upon and interpreting these traditions.

Is it possible to separate the older from the more recent traditions in the current form of the literary compositions? We saw that Noth's approach was flawed, but, by heeding a principle stressed by Hermann Gunkel, we may be able to gain some reliable insights into the history of tradition.

In one of his early works, Gunkel formulated a still-viable rule for identifying old traditions:

> Certain features, which once had a clear meaning in their earlier context, have been so transmitted in their newer setting as to have lost their meaningful context. Such ancient features, fragments of an earlier whole, are thus left without context in their newer setting and so appear hardly intelligible in the thought-world of the narrator. Such features betray to the investigator the existence of an earlier narrative.[39]

A feature in a narrative that is anomalous in its present literary context, but which is intelligible in an earlier context, may be a relic of an earlier stage of the tradition. This principle is clearly illustrated by such anomalous stories in Genesis as the account of the sexual escapades of the Sons of God and the daughters of men in Genesis 6:1–4, where the brevity and obscurity of the story points to a fuller context in the preliterary oral tradition, perhaps even in pre-Israelite Canaanite tradition where the Sons of God (literally Sons or Children of El, the high god of the Canaanite pantheon) are prominent figures.[40]

By such means we are able to probe the preliterary traditions of the stories and discern aspects of their history that might otherwise be unnoticed. But to detect features that belong to an earlier historical context, we must first determine the historical context of the final form of the stories.

The story of the patriarchs in its final form reflects the self-understanding of the community at the end of the period of settlement, about 1000 B.C.E. (A few details suggest that the stories were first written down some generations later, perhaps in the ninth or eighth century B.C.E.)[41] Israel is represented as a 12-tribe entity with the southern tribes, and notably Judah, in full membership, something that probably did not occur until David's time. This scheme reflects considerable southern development: The eldest patriarch (Abraham) is especially associated with Hebron, the traditional capital of the Judean hill country in the southern part of the country; the second patriarch (Isaac) is at home even farther south, in the northern Negev. The patriarchal stories are not likely to have existed in this form before the institution of the Davidic monarchy in about 1000 B.C.E.[42] The priority of Abraham as the eldest patriarch suggests the intertribal relationship that existed during the reigns of David and Solomon and, in any case, reflects a Judahite point of view.

The patriarchal history as self-understanding

To a limited extent, the evolution of the tradition can be reconstructed from biblical and extrabiblical evidence. The 12 sons of Israel who appear in the current form of the stories about Jacob and Joseph reflect the tribal roster as it stood at the end of the process. A somewhat different list is preserved in Judges 5:14–18, part of an ancient poem describing the victory of the Israelite tribes over a Canaanite foe: Here there is no mention of the southern tribes, Judah and Simeon, suggesting that southern Canaan had not yet been incorporated into Israel. Moreover, Manasseh and Gad are also missing in this old poem, while two tribes are cited that do not appear in the later list, namely, Machir (Judges 5:14) and Gilead (Judges 5:17).[43] This list in Judges 5 provides us with a glimpse of the tribal association as it stood about the middle of the 12th century, say 1150 B.C.E.[44] Moreover, we know that a group named Israel already existed, at least in rudimentary form, by about 1207 B.C.E., when the Egyptian king Merneptah boasted, on an inscribed stele, of having defeated a people named "Israel."[45]

It follows that tribal Israel existed in the central hills before 1150 B.C.E. and probably as early as 1207 B.C.E. Though this community may have been newly formed, it already had a sense of ethnic identity: Its members were Israelite or "Hebrew" and not something else.[46] This identity found expression in and, at the same time, derived its authority from the ancestral tradition preserved in the patriarchal narratives of the Bible.

The insistence upon ethnic separateness is one of the most conspicuous features of this tradition. The stories uniformly assert that the ancestors of Israel were foreigners, not natives of Canaan. They came from "beyond the River," that is, beyond the Euphrates (cf. Joshua 24:2–3), in the region we call Mesopotamia (modern Iraq and eastern Syria). Whatever the ultimate origin of the term "Hebrews," this was the meaning it came to have in the tradition: The 'Ibrîm, "Hebrews," were those who came from 'ēber, "beyond," the Euphrates.

As explained in Chapter III, the early Israelites were probably of diverse origin, and many or most seem to have been indigenous to Canaan. The strong insistence in the patriarchal narratives that the ancestors of Israel were *not* Canaanites is a reflection of the process of ethnic boundary-marking by which the early Israelite community was defined and by which its identity was subsequently maintained. This kind of boundary-marking is well known to modern students of the social phenomenon of ethnicity.[47] In this case, it probably derives from the early conflict between the hill-dwelling people from whom Israel emerged and the population of the cities of the plains and valleys controlled by Egypt in the Late Bronze Age. Through the tradition of Mesopotamian origin, as well as through the biblical genealogical materials, the Israelites acknowledge ethnic solidarity with the peoples of the East, the Transjordanians and the Arameans, but deny any link with the peoples of the Egypto-Canaanite West.

The basic genealogical structure of the patriarchal tradition, therefore, emerged at the end of the Late Bronze Age, contemporary with the early formation of Israel. This conclusion, however, pertains only to the patriarchal tradition, not to the patriarchs themselves. We must now attempt to discover the extent to which the tradition was based on historical people and events.

This is a difficult task. As we have seen, the structure of the tradition came into existence at the same time as the community itself. A careful investigation of this structure and its purposes might help us understand the circumstances under which the community first coalesced in central Canaan, but this structure cannot be expected to shed light on an earlier period.

If we accept the genealogical self-understanding of the stories as stemming from the period of Israel's emergence as a nation (c. 1200–1000 B.C.E.), then, following the principle enunciated by Gunkel, we may ask whether any features that are anomalous in their current setting might be more intelligible in an earlier cultural or historical context. This is the most reliable procedure for detecting traces of the preliterary history of the tradition.

In the patriarchal narratives, the personal names and geographical references provide the best clues for tracing historical memories. Two bodies of evidence provide the strongest indications for the roots of the tradition in pre- and early Israelite times, perhaps reaching back to the mid-second millennium B.C.E. These are (1) the divine elements in the patriarchal names* and (2) the location of the patriarchal homeland in the Middle Euphrates region of Syro-Mesopotamia.[48]

Personal names and geographical references provide clues

In his groundbreaking essay of 1929, "The God of the Fathers," Albrecht Alt observed that the name Yahweh does not appear as part of patriarchal and tribal names. This indicates that the origins of the patriarchal tradition lie in early or pre-Israelite traditions. Two of the literary sources of the Pentateuch, E (the Elohist source) and P (the Priestly Code), explicitly date the revelation of the name Yahweh to the time of Moses (E in Exodus 3, and P in Exodus 6). As Alt observed:

> The well-known restriction of the name of Yahweh to the period from Moses on, in the Elohist and Priestly treatment of the sagas, can hardly be explained as simply the result of later theories about Israel's prehistory without any basis in the tradition, although there is no doubt that it was quite consciously seized on by the authors of these narratives in order to mark off different eras in the past ... The names of the tribes and their forefathers do not give a single reliable indication of [Yahweh's] existence.[49]

By these arguments, Alt traces the origin of the pattern of divine names to early Israelite tradition, prior to the time of the Pentateuchal writers.

These arguments can be made even stronger, however. If we consider the position of the J source in this pattern, we find a systematic anomaly. After the creation story, J consistently refers to the Israelite deity as "Yahweh." (Alt plausibly explains the J [Yahwist] source's departure from this pattern as a function of J's universalistic theology reflected in the creation story.) But the personal names in the patriarchal narratives in J (as elsewhere) retain the divine element *-el* (as in the names Ishmael, Israel and Bethuel) rather than the divine element based on Yahweh. Not until the era of Moses do personal names contain the divine element derived from Yahweh (as in Joshua [*Yehoshua*] and Jochebed [*Yochebed*], Moses' mother). How then are we to explain the absence of Yahweh as a divine element and the presence instead of *-el* in the patriarchal names? As noted, E and P explicitly state that the name Yahweh was not known to the patriarchs. We would therefore not be surprised to find *-el* names in the patriarchal narratives in E and P. But these *-el* names also show up in J *despite* J's overt use of only the name Yahweh to designate the Israelite God from the beginning of his patriarchal narrative. This is a clear indication that

---

*Personal and tribal names often incorporated elements of divine names, called theophoric elements, as in *Yeho*-shua (which includes a divine element based on Yahweh) and Isra-*el*.

on one level J is drawing on the same traditions as E and P, even though J is trying on another level to reject that tradition. Despite J's use of the name Yahweh to designate the Israelite God, the personal names in J nevertheless preserve a tradition that the patriarchal God was not Yahweh, but El. Although J would have it otherwise, the God of the (patriarchal) fathers is El, as revealed by the divine element in the names in J's patriarchal narratives. According to Gunkel's principle, "Such features betray to the investigator the existence of an earlier narrative." Here we detect a clear trace of the history of the tradition in which the patriarchs worshiped El.

Is there an earlier historical or cultural context within which this preservation of an El tradition is intelligible? Canaanite religious texts from ancient Ugarit, dated to about 1400 B.C.E., tell us that the high god of the Canaanite pantheon was indeed named El.[50] Moreover, Frank Moore Cross has demonstrated that several of the titles of the deity named El in the patriarchal narratives (such as El-Shaddai, God of the [Sacred] Mountain) have close parallels in the titles and descriptions of Canaanite El.[51] We may conclude that the use of divine names in the patriarchal narratives preserves an early tradition of the patriarchal worship of the god El. This tradition, understood by the biblical writers as describing pre-Mosaic times, finds its intelligible context in the culture of Canaan in the second millennium B.C.E. and in Israel (note the name El in Isra-*el*) of the premonarchic period.[52] In other words, the presence of El and the absence of Yahweh in the patriarchal names preserve memories of pre- and early Israelite times of the second millennium B.C.E.

A second body of evidence, the geographical references to the patriarchal homeland in the region of Haran, corroborates the evidence of personal names and points us to the mid-second millennium B.C.E. The Amorite hypothesis advanced by Albright and others has been justly criticized and generally abandoned (see above). But amid the wreckage of this hypothesis, some features remain that require us to consider an early date. The region of Haran in the Middle Euphrates region of Syro-Mesopotamia was the home of the Arameans, not the Amorites, from the 12th century B.C.E. onwards. If the region of Haran is where the patriarchs go to live with—and marry—their kin (Genesis 24 and 29), then for Iron Age Israelites this designates the patriarchs as Aramean. Hence the prayer in Deuteronomy 26:5: "My father was a wandering (or perishing) Aramean," referring to the patriarchal homeland. The problem with this tradition is that it clashes with the cultural context of the first millennium B.C.E.; from the time of David, the Arameans were enemies of Israel. No group would trace its ancestral homeland to the home of its enemies unless the tradition was so well established that it had no choice but to do so.

Following Gunkel's principle, we should look for a historical context within which this anomalous tradition is intelligible. For this we must look to the period prior to the 12th century B.C.E., back when the region of Haran was the homeland of a rural people we call the Amorites.[53] The Amorites of this period were pastoralists and agriculturalists living in a tribal society. They spoke an early Northwest Semitic dialect (or dialects). What we know of their lifestyle and religion is comparable to the picture of the patriarchs in Genesis.[54] The divine name El is found commonly in Amorite personal names, and in Akkadian texts this god is referred to as "El Amurru," El of the Amorites.[55] Thus the tradition of the patriarchal homeland in the region of Haran is intelligible in the context of Amorite culture in the Middle and Late Bronze Ages, but its Aramean context would be exceedingly strange in the Iron Age (the time when the narrative was written). The first-millennium identification of the patriarchs with the hated Arameans makes sense only as a revision (according to the then-current ethnic map) of a much older tradition.[56]

Neither of these arguments constitutes definitive proof that the patriarchal traditions stem from Canaanite or Amorite culture of the mid- to late second millennium B.C.E. But our application of Gunkel's principle suggests that this derivation is plausible. These traces of the history of the patriarchal traditions point to earlier oral narratives in Israel and pre-Israelite Canaan that told of the ancestors' migration from the Amorite homeland in Syro-Mesopotamia to Canaan, and their devotion to the ancestral god El.

This historical reconstruction has several intriguing implications. It indicates that some early Israelites traced their ancestry to Syro-Mesopotamia and felt an ethnic kinship to that region. It also means that a strong substratum of El-worship merged with or transformed itself into the worship of Yahweh. El was worshiped in the Amorite region of Syro-Mesopotamia as well as in the Canaanite region farther west. The spread of El-worship was probably a contributing factor in the formation of a common Israelite identity among the diverse groups in the hill country during Iron Age I (1200–1000 B.C.E.). The equivalence between El and Yahweh was perhaps made by another group, the Moses-group who recounted their momentous escape from Egypt via Midian (see Chapter II). The merging of El and Yahweh in the religion of Israel corresponds to the merging of different groups in early Israel—some with stories of Syro-Mesopotamian origins, and some with memories of slavery in Egypt and Yahweh's revelation at Mt. Sinai. Somehow—and the details elude us—these different groups coalesced into a single ethnic identity, and the stories coalesced into the complex epic traditions that join together Syro-Mesopotamia, Egypt and Sinai, with all paths leading to the Promised Land.

Are the   The invention of ancestors is a common way of establishing the kin-
patriarchs   ship bonds that are necessary for the cohesion of a community. The
genealogical   practice is known among modern Bedouin, and it is well attested in
fictions?   antiquity. The "Amorite" dynasties of Hammurabi of Babylon and
                  Shamshi-Adad I of Assyria shared a common tradition about their
                  tribal origins, and many of the names of their early ancestors are also
                  known as names of West Semitic tribes.[57]

                  Similar fictitious heroes are frequently encountered in biblical
                  genealogies, and often their origins can be traced. Jerahmeel, for exam-
                  ple, was the name of a non-Israelite tribe living somewhere in the
                  Negev in the time of David (1 Samuel 27:10, 30:29). In the course of
                  time, however, the Jerahmeelites were incorporated into Judah, and the
                  new relationship was expressed genealogically by the identification of
                  Jerahmeel as a great-grandson of Judah in a line collateral to that of
                  David (1 Chronicles 2:9,25–27).

                  There is no question that the patriarchal genealogies contain the
                  names of many individuals who originated as fictitious eponyms.*
                  Moab and Ben-ammi, the sons of Lot and ancestors of the Moabites
                  and Ammonites (Genesis 19:37–38), are obvious examples, as is
                  Shechem son of Hamor, the prince of the city of Shechem (Genesis
                  34:2). Sometimes these figures play prominent roles in the story, as
                  in the case of Ishmael, the ancestor of the Ishmaelites (cf. Genesis
                  16:10–12, 17:20, 25:12–16). The Edomite genealogy recorded in
                  Genesis 36 contains a mixture of personal and tribal or clan
                  names. Esau's (Edom's) eldest son, for example, bears the name
                  "Eliphaz," which has the form of a personal name. Eliphaz was
                  probably a hero of the past rather than an eponym (cf. Job 2:11),
                  but his sons' names (Genesis 36:11–12) include eponyms of well-
                  known tribes or places, including Teman, the home of the Eliphaz
                  of the Book of Job. This, then, is what we expect from the early
                  genealogies: a few names of traditional heroes sprinkled among a
                  preponderance of eponymic names derived from clans, tribes,
                  places or regions.

Abraham   Abraham seems to belong in the former category. His name (in con-
                  trast to those of Isaac, Jacob, Israel and Joseph) appears only as a per-
                  sonal name in the Bible, never as a tribal or local designation. Thus
                  it seems fairly certain that he was not an eponymous ancestor. He
                  may have been a historical individual before he became a figure of
                  tradition and legend. If so, however, it seems impossible to determine
                  the period in which he lived. "Abram," at least in the form "Abiram,"
                  is a very common type of name, known in all periods. It is especially

---

*To repeat, an eponym is a person, real or imaginary, from whom the name of a later group
is derived or is supposed to be derived.

well attested in the Late Bronze Age (1550–1200 B.C.E.),[58] though this may be no more than a coincidence. The variants "Abram" and "Abraham" arose in different languages and dialects.[59]

Nor can we determine whether any of the biblical stories told about Abraham has a historical basis. The claim that Abraham came to Canaan from Mesopotamia is not historically implausible. Such a journey could have taken place in more than one historical period. As we have seen, however, the insistence that the Israelites were not Canaanite in origin was so pervasive that the belief that the first patriarch came from a foreign land could have arisen as part of the ethnic boundary-marking that characterized the development of the tradition. Still, the connections between the family of Abraham and the city of Haran in northern Mesopotamia (Eski Harran or "Old Haran" in modern Turkey) are very precise in our earliest narrative source (J, or the Yahwist). Terah, Nahor and Serug—Abraham's father, grandfather and great-grandfather (Genesis 11:22–26)—seem to be the eponymous ancestors of towns in the basin of the Balikh River, near Haran. All three names appear in Assyrian texts from the first half of the first millennium B.C.E. as the names of towns or ruined towns in the region of Haran, namely, Til-(sha)-Turakhi (the ruin of Turakh), Til-Nakhiri (the ruin of Nakhir) and Sarugi. Earlier, in the second millennium B.C.E., Til-Nakhiri had been an important administrative center, called Nakhuru. The patriarchal connection with this region may be rooted in historical memories of Amorite culture of the second millennium B.C.E.

Abraham is represented as the founder of religious sites in the regions of Shechem (Genesis 12:7), Bethel/Ai (Genesis 12:8, cf. 13:4), Hebron (Genesis 13:18), Mount Moriah (Genesis 22:2) and Beersheba (Genesis 21:33). As Benjamin Mazar has noted, all these sites lie within the boundaries of early Israelite settlement in Iron Age I (1200–1000 B.C.E.).[60] These stories present Abraham as the founder of major cultic sites both in Manasseh-Ephraim and in Judah, the dominant tribes of the north and south. Here we see Abraham functioning as the founder of a common social and religious identity, uniting northern and southern tribes.*

The earliest reference to Abraham may be the name of a town in the Negev listed in a victory inscription of Pharoah Shishak I (biblical Sheshonk). The campaign occurred in about 925 B.C.E. during

---

*Amos's references to Beersheba (in the south) as a pilgrimage shrine for northerners (Amos 5:5, 8:14) is consistent with the connection between Abraham and Beersheba in the E source, and must derive from some prior northern religious association with Beersheba. (On the affinities between E and Amos, see recently Karel van der Toorn, *Family Religion* [see endnote 52], pp. 261–264.) In the J source, Abraham's southerly home is Hebron, not Beersheba (which is founded by Isaac in J), an address that points to Hebron's importance in Judah in the Davidic period (2 Samuel 5:1–5, 15:7–10).

HERSHEL SHANKS

Beersheba well. *According to Genesis 26:18–25, "Isaac dug again the wells of water that had been dug in the days of his father Abraham; for the Philistines had stopped them up after the death of Abraham ... [Isaac] went up to Beersheba ... [and] Isaac's servants dug a well." Dated by the excavator to the 13th century B.C.E., this 100-foot-deep shaft at Beersheba may be the well the author of this passage had in mind.*

the reign of Rehoboam (1 Kings 14:25–26; 2 Chronicles 12:2–12). A place-name in the Negev section of the inscription is *pa' ḥa-q-ru-'a 'i-bi-ra-ma*, which is best read "the fortification of Abram" or, more simply, "Fort Abram."[61] The location and chronological context of this site make it plausible that the Abram after whom the site was named was the Abram of biblical tradition. Although we cannot be certain of this identification, the place name probably indicates the presence and importance of the Abram/Abraham tradition in the tenth century B.C.E.

Isaac   The biblical Isaac has clear geographical associations with the northern Negev, and particularly the oases of Beersheba and Beer-lahai-roi (Genesis 24:62, 25:11, 26:32–33). The archaeological record indicates that this area was not settled before the end of the Late Bronze Age. Expansion into the Negev from the north began no earlier than the latter part of the 13th century B.C.E. Archaeological excavations at Beersheba have shown that a deep well associated with the sanctuary was dug at about this time.[62] Apparently, this is the well mentioned in Genesis 21:25 and 26:25. The settlement of the Negev spread southward and was complete by the 11th century.[63] This shows that the attachment of the patriarchal tradition to the Beersheba region cannot have preceded the 12th century and, in fact, may have occurred later as a part of the southern development of the tradition in the time of David and Solomon.

As we have noted, "Isaac" is structurally suitable as a personal, tribal or geographical name. We might expect the meaning of the name to indicate which of these possibilities is most likely. Though it is unattested outside the Bible, we assume that "Isaac" is a shortened form of a name like "Isaac-El," which may mean "May [the god] El smile," that is, "May El look favorably upon."[64] If this is correct,* the name then seems equally acceptable as the designation of an individual, group or place. In referring to the northern kingdom in the eighth century, moreover, Amos twice uses the name Isaac as parallel to Israel (Amos 7:9,16). This usage must reflect a recollection of the name Isaac as a designation for the northern tribal region.[65] In this light, it is intriguing to note that J depicts Isaac as the founder of the religious site at Beersheba (Genesis 26:23,25), a southern shrine to which northerners made pilgrimage (Amos 5:5, 8:14).

Jacob

According to Genesis, the events of Jacob's birth and childhood take place at Beersheba, Isaac's home; but after returning from Haran, Jacob lives in the region of Shechem in the central hill country. He is the founder of the religious site of Bethel (Genesis 28:10–22, 35:1–15), and like Abraham he builds an altar at Shechem (Genesis 33:18–20). Both sites are in the north. It is not surprising that Jacob dwells in the central hill country, since at this point Jacob *is* Israel. The historical association of Israel with the central hills was strong, as its persistence during the time of David and beyond shows. In contrast to Abraham and Isaac, therefore, Jacob was never thought of in close association with the southern part of the country.

It is generally agreed that the biblical name "Jacob" is a shortened form of "Jacob-El" or something very similar. An early form of "Jacob," constructed with "El" or another divine name, was a common West Semitic personal name of the Middle Bronze Age and the Hyksos period, when Egypt was ruled by Asiatic princes (c. 1675–1552 B.C.E.).[66] It is also attested at Ugarit (in Syria) in the Late Bronze Age, but it does not appear again (outside of the biblical patriarchal narratives) until the Persian period. "Jacob-El," however, was also a Late Bronze Age place-name. It occurs in lists of enemies conquered by Thuthmosis III (c. 1479–1425 B.C.E.) and other kings of Egypt.[67] Most of the identifiable names in these documents refer to cities, though some designate districts and even tribal groups. Because of the loose organization of the lists, the precise location of

---

*Our uncertainty about this meaning arises from the fact that the verbal element does not have quite this sense elsewhere; it ordinarily means "laugh, laugh at, sport, jest."

Jacob-El cannot be determined. It is clear, however, that it was in central Canaan,[68] most probably in the general vicinity of Rehob and Beth-Shean, both of which lay north of Shechem.[69] In view of the proximity of both time and place, therefore, it does not seem reckless to conclude that the Jacob-El conquered by Tuthmosis had something to do with the biblical Jacob tradition.

We must ask, then, which had priority, the patriarch Jacob or the place Jacob-El. The name probably means "Let El protect,"* and this seems equally suitable as the name of a person or a place. It is possible that there was an early hero called Jacob-El who gave his name to the town or district mentioned in the Egyptian lists.[70]

Archaeologist Aharon Kempinsky suggested, on the basis of a scarab of Jacob-Har found in a tomb at Shiqmona, Israel, dating to the 18th century B.C.E., that the later Hyksos king of Egypt named Jacob-Har may be the descendant of a local Palestinian king of the same name. This local ruler may be the Jacob for whom the place was named.[71] Although this argument is speculative, it offers an intriguing possibility for the origin of the Jacob tradition in the central hills of Palestine in the second millennium B.C.E.

In the Bible, Jacob has two names. According to the earliest written account, Jacob was given the name Israel after wrestling with a divine being on the bank of the Jabbok River (Genesis 32:28–29).** In the latter part of Genesis, the two names Jacob and Israel are used more or less interchangeably. Modern biblical scholars have explained this in a variety of ways. Noth concluded that Israel, the collective name of the tribes, was assigned to the patriarch Jacob at a fairly late point in the development of the tradition.[72] On the other hand, the elaborate genealogical structure of the tradition was itself an early feature; the purpose of this structure was to give a social definition to Israel. Jacob, the eponym of the people or district of Jacob-El, was the key figure in the genealogical scheme. It is very likely, then, that he was identified as Israel, the eponym of the newly emerging community, when the kinship tradition was devised at the time of the formation of the tribal alliance.

This is not to suggest that the name "Israel" was invented at this time. Several scholars have attempted to identify a distinctive group of traditions around a patriarch Israel, whom they would distinguish from Jacob,[73] and it is possible that there was some kind of early tribal group in the central hills called Israel.[74] In fact, however, our sources give us no hint of the use of the name in Canaan before the time of Merneptah (c. 1207 B.C.E.), which, as we have seen, must have been very close to

---

*The verb is known with this meaning in Ethiopic and Old South Arabic but not in biblical Hebrew.

**According to the later account in Genesis 35:6–10, the renaming took place at Bethel.

the time of the formation of the community itself. Since we know that the population of the hill country was growing steadily at this time,[75] we must also consider the possibility that the name "Israel" was brought into the region by one of the arriving peoples.

Finally, Jacob's relationship with Esau may predate the identification of the two brothers with Israel and Edom in the genealogical structure. As Gunkel noted, Esau's name and personality have little to do with Edom, which had a reputation for wisdom in biblical tradition.[76] Gunkel associated the conflict of the two brothers with a cultural memory of the ascent of herders over hunters in Palestinian history, which Noth localized to the history of Gilead.[77] It is doubtful, however, that a socioeconomic history of the region can be derived from the rivalry between the two brothers. The relationship is more adequately characterized as a conflict between civilization and nature. Note the consistent series of contrasts between Jacob and Esau in Genesis 25 and 27: man of the tents (civilized habitat) vs. man of the steppe (wild habitat); cooking (characteristic of human culture) vs. hunting (common to humans and predatory animals); cunning intelligence vs. stupidity; smooth skin vs. hairy skin; domestic animals (as meal and disguise) vs. wild game; and, finally, the culmination in blessing and political dominance vs. curse and subjection. (Compare the way Gilgamesh and Enkidu are contrasted in the Mesopotamian Gilgamesh epic.)[78] The fraternal relationship, therefore, falls into the category of ethnic boundary-making, as one's own ancestor is identified with civilization in contrast to another's ancestor, who is wild and uncivilized (compare the characterization of Ishmael, as opposed to Isaac, in Genesis 16:12 and 21:20, and the parentage of Ammon and Moab in Genesis 19). In other words, the relationship between Jacob and Esau is best comprehended as an expression of cultural and ethnic self-definition. This feature may predate the identification of the two with Israel and Edom, but it continues to function in this identification.

Turning finally to the sons of Israel, we begin by recalling that the name "Joseph" belongs in the category of "Isaac," "Jacob" and "Israel," as noted earlier. We assume that it is a shorter form of "Joseph-El," which means "May El increase," and this too seems equally suitable as a personal, tribal or geographical designation.* Thus it is possible that Joseph was a hero of the past or the fictitious eponym of a group or district. The latter possibility is suggested by the use of "the house of Joseph" as a collective designation for the northern tribes in the literature of the early monarchy (2 Samuel 19:21) and elsewhere. A strong

Joseph

---

*That is, it might be a wish for another child (cf. Genesis 30:24) or for the increased fertility or prosperity of a tribe or town.

case can be made, however, that this expression was coined after the unification of Judah and Israel as a term parallel to "the house of Judah."[79] References to a tribe of Joseph, moreover, are rare and appear only in late materials (Numbers 13:11, 36:5). It thus seems more likely that "Joseph" was a personal name belonging to a local hero of the past.[80] During the period of the formation of the Israelite community, Joseph was identified as a son of Jacob and the father of the tribal eponyms Ephraim and Manasseh.

The special prominence of Joseph in the biblical narrative must be, at least in part, a reflection of the eminence of "the house of Joseph" at the end of the settlement period (about 1000 B.C.E.) and the continuing historical importance of the Manasseh-Ephraim region. Scholars believe that the long story about Joseph and his family in Genesis 37 and 39–47 originated independently of the other patriarchal narratives. This story depicts Joseph as preeminent among his brothers and as the favorite of his father, Jacob (Israel). The story was probably passed down orally among the inhabitants of the region around Shechem and Dothan (cf. Genesis 37:12 and 37:17), in the heart of the traditional territory of Ephraim and Manasseh, the two "half-tribes" of Joseph's sons. In an early form, this story may have eulogized Joseph, the tribal patriarch, as a man who went to Egypt as a slave and rose to a position of authority in the Egyptian court.

Many scholars believe that the events described in the story of Joseph have an ultimate basis in historical fact. It has often been supposed, especially by those scholars who believe that Abraham, Isaac and Jacob lived in the Middle Bronze Age (about 2000–1550 B.C.E.), that Joseph lived during the so-called Hyksos period (c. 1675–1552), when Egypt was ruled by two dynasties of Asiatic princes. The scholars who hold this view argue that since Joseph was himself an Asiatic, he would have been most likely to find a favorable reception from an Asiatic king of Egypt. Moreover, the capital of Egypt during the Hyksos period was located in the eastern Delta, which is generally agreed to have been the site of the biblical "land of Goshen," where the family of Joseph settled (Genesis 45:10, 46:28–29, 47:1).[81]

But even if the general outline of the Joseph story is based on the life of a historical individual, it is unlikely that much of the information found in Genesis 37 and 39–47 is historically factual. The biblical Joseph story has more in common with a historical romance than a work of history. Its carefully planned story line is fashioned from narrative motifs that were widespread in the literature and folklore of the ancient Near East. The episode of Potiphar's wife, who accuses Joseph of attempted rape after she fails to seduce him (Genesis 39:6b–20), has numerous parallels in the literature of the ancient world,[82] including the popular "Tale of Two Brothers" of XIXth-Dynasty Egypt (13th century B.C.E.).[83] The motifs of dreams and dream interpretation are found in literature, folklore and myth throughout antiquity.[84] The convention of the seven lean years is known from Egyptian, Akkadian and Canaanite literature.[85]

Further, the author of the biblical Joseph story displays only a limited knowledge of the life and culture of Egypt.[86] Recalling the hot wind that blows across the Transjordanian plateau into Israel, he writes of the *east* wind scorching pharaoh's grain (Genesis 41:23,27), but in Egypt it is the *south* wind that blights crops.[87] The titles and offices the author assigns to various Egyptian officials have closer parallels in Syria and Canaan than in Egypt.[88]

There are a number of authentic Egyptian details in the Joseph story, but these details correspond to the Egyptian way of life in the author's own day, not in the Hyksos period. The king of Egypt is called "Pharaoh," an Egyptian phrase meaning "great house," which was not used as a title for the king before the reign of Thutmosis III (c. 1479–1425 B.C.E.). In Genesis 47:11, the area in which the family of Joseph settles is called "the region of Rameses," a designation that could not have been used earlier than the reign of Ramesses II (c. 1279–1213 B.C.E.).*

Some of the personal names in the story are Egyptian. Joseph's wife is called Asenath (Genesis 41:45), which could correspond to one of several Egyptian names from the second and first millennia B.C.E.[89] The name of Asenath's father is Potiphera (Genesis 41:45), and this name has been found on an Egyptian stele dating to the XXIst Dynasty (c. 1069–945 B.C.E.) or later.[90] The name of Joseph's Egyptian master, Potiphar (Genesis 37:36), is probably a shorter form of the name Potiphera. Joseph's own Egyptian name, Zaphenath-paneah (Genesis 41:45), has no exact parallel in extant Egyptian records, but names with a similar structure are attested from the XXIst Dynasty and later.[91]

It is unlikely, therefore, that the Joseph story as we know it in the Bible was composed before the establishment of the United Kingdom (that is, before about 1000 B.C.E.). Many of the elements of the plot and most of the narrative details are fictional. It does not follow from this, however, that the tradition upon which the story is based is unhistorical. We cannot exclude the possibility that there was a historical Joseph who went to Egypt as a slave and rose to a position of power there.

Egyptian records from the Middle Kingdom to the Roman period cite numerous individuals of Syrian, Canaanite and nomadic origin who rose to high positions in the Egyptian government.[92] An especially interesting parallel to the story of Joseph is that of an Asiatic named Irsu, who seized power in Egypt during a period of hardship (probably famine) at the end of the 19th Dynasty (c. 1200 B.C.E.).[93]

---

*It is possible, however, that "in the region of Rameses" in Genesis 47:11 is a scribe's gloss, intended to harmonize the account of the Israelites' entry into Egypt with the statement in Exodus 1:11 that locates the Israelites in "Pithom and Raamses."

Many Egyptologists believe that Irsu was another name for Bay, the powerful chancellor who ruled Egypt during the minority of the last king of the XIXth Dynasty and who may have come from Palestine.[94]

Clearly, then, the biblical description of Joseph's career is historically plausible in its general outline. We might surmise that Joseph was the leader of a group of people from the vicinity of Shechem and Dothan who migrated to Egypt seeking pasturage during a time of drought in Canaan. Such groups are amply attested to in Egyptian records. In a text from the reign of Merneptah (c. 1212–1202 B.C.E.), for example, a frontier official reports:

> [We] have finished letting the Bedouin tribes of Edom pass the Fortress [of] Mer-ne-Ptah ... which is (in) Tjeku* ... to the pools of Per-Atum** ... which are (in) Tjeku, to keep them alive and to keep their cattle alive.[95]

Alternatively, the people of the central hills may have preserved memories of Hyksos kings of local origin (perhaps even from the line of a local king named Jacob) and combined these memories with the tradition of the Exodus of slaves from Egypt. By this means the patriarchal stories may have been joined with those of the Exodus, yielding a coherent epic tradition, uniting all the tribes. Of course these are mere speculations about the history of the Joseph tradition. We have few clues from the narrative itself.

Jacob's other sons The names of most of the other sons of Jacob (Israel) do not have the form of personal names. Several are geographical names. "Asher" was a name by which the Egyptians knew the coastal region north of Carmel in the Late Bronze Age.[96] "Judah," "Ephraim"[†] and "Naphtali" seem first to have been the names of ranges of hills (cf. Joshua 20:7); the people who inhabited the hill country of Judah were called *běnê yěhûdâ*, "the children of Judah," or "Judahites"; and so on.[97] The name "Benjamin" probably arose from the location of the tribe's territory; it lay to the south of the other (northern) tribes, so that the people were called *běnê yāmîn* "the children of the south," or "Benjaminites."[98]

On the other hand, the names of a few of the sons of Jacob (Israel) do take the form of personal names. "Simeon" and "Manasseh," for example, are most easily understood in this way,[99] and the corresponding tribes may have been named after tribal heroes or even patriarchs. In the genealogical structure, the 12 sons of Israel are eponyms of the 12 tribes of Israel, created in the course of the evolution of the Israelite tradition during the period of settlement. The process of community formation, which began in about 1200 B.C.E., at the end of the

---

*"Tjeku" is the Egyptian name for the land called Goshen in the Bible.

**Per-Atum is biblical Pithom (Exodus 1:11).

[†]Ephraim and Manasseh were sons of Joseph and grandsons of Jacob (Israel). According to Genesis 48:5, however, they were adopted by their grandfather.

Late Bronze Age, presupposes the existence of the tribes with established names. The origin of the various tribal names—whether derived from geographical associations, ancestral traditions or something else— was already in the remote past. When the tribes were joined together into the larger entity of Israel, their kinship was expressed in terms of brotherhood; and a group of 12 sons, the eponyms of the 12 tribes, was assigned to the patriarch Jacob (Israel).

It follows from all this that the setting of the prehistory of the Israelite community was the central hill country, between the valley of Aijalon and the Beth-Shean corridor, in the Late Bronze Age. This region was very sparsely populated before 1200 B.C.E.,[100] suggesting that the people among whom the Israelite tradition germinated were pastoralists, as the patriarchal stories would lead us to expect. They venerated a local hero called Abram or Abraham, who was probably already regarded as a patriarchal figure; that is, he was identified as the ancestor of one or more of the groups in the region. Jacob and Isaac may also have been revered as ancestors in local tribal lore.

These proto-Israelites were hill people and shepherds, and they must have seen themselves as distinct from the peoples of the cities, which, in this period, were situated on the coastal plain and in the major valleys.[101] This was the period of Egypt in Canaan, but the remoteness of the highlands from the population centers and the major trading routes sheltered Israel's forerunners from the full influence of Egypt. These circumstances were favorable to the creation of a national community larger than the city-states of the Bronze Age,[102] a development that needed only an increase in population to make it possible. This requirement was fulfilled at the end of the Late Bronze Age when new peoples penetrated into the forests of the Ephraimite plateau and the saddle of Benjamin to the south. At this time a larger tribal alliance was formed, and the old relationships were formalized genealogically. Abraham was identified as the father of Isaac and Isaac of Jacob. Jacob became the father of a large group of sons, eponyms of the various groups and districts that made up the new alliance. A core group of this alliance (to which the Merneptah Stele refers) bore the collective name "Israel." Thus the eponym Israel had an equal claim to the status of tribal father, and he was identified with Jacob.

T W O

Israel in Egypt
The Egyptian Sojourn
and the Exodus

NAHUM M. SARNA
revised by Hershel Shanks

ACCORDING TO THE BIBLE, A FAMINE OF UNUSUAL SEVERITY AND duration in the land of Canaan brought the patriarch Jacob and his family to Egypt. They settled in the region of Goshen, in the Nile Delta, through the influence of Jacob's son Joseph, who was a high official in the Egyptian administration (Genesis 41:1–47:12). This Hebrew migration was intended to be temporary (Genesis 46:4, 50:24) but soon extended itself.

After the death of Joseph and his brothers, a change of fortunes occurred when a new pharaoh "who did not know Joseph" came to the throne (Exodus 1:8). The Israelites' proliferation and prosperity were perceived as a threat to Egyptian security. The new pharaoh introduced drastic measures to curb the Hebrews' population growth, and the Israelites were pressed into corvée service (Exodus 1:9–13). As the biblical text describes it: "They set taskmasters over them to oppress them with forced labor; and [the Israelites] built garrison cities for Pharaoh: Pithom and Raamses" (Exodus 1:11). The harsh labors to which they were subjected did not have the anticipated results: "The more they were oppressed, the more they increased and spread out, so that the [Egyptians] came to dread the Israelites" (Exodus 1:12). New repressive measures were instituted. In addition to intensifying the various physical labors imposed on the Israelites, the king ordered midwives to kill the newborn males at birth. Motivated by compassion, however, the midwives resisted the infamous decree. Pharaoh then ordained that all male Hebrew babies were to be abandoned to the Nile (Exodus 1:15–22).

A married couple from the tribe of Levi attempted to thwart this royal edict by hiding their infant son, but after three months this was no longer possible, and the mother was forced to yield him to the river. Placing him in a waterproof basket, she set him among the Nile reeds and appointed his sister to keep watch over him. The basket was soon discovered by Pharaoh's daughter. At the suggestion of the baby's sister, the Egyptian princess hired the baby's Hebrew mother to nurse the child. Of course, the relationship was not disclosed. When the boy was sufficiently grown, he was taken to the palace and adopted by Pharaoh's daughter, who named him Moses (Exodus 2:10).[1]

The Bible relates practically nothing about Moses as a young man. The few recorded incidents testify to his hatred of injustice. On one occasion Moses struck down and killed an Egyptian whom he saw beating a Hebrew. Later the deed became known and Moses was forced to flee from Egypt. He found refuge in the land of Midian, and there, by a well, he saw another injustice. Male shepherds were taking advantage of their female counterparts who were waiting their turn at the well. Moses saved the shepherdesses from maltreatment. The upshot was that he eventually married one of the women, thereby becoming the son-in-law of Jethro, priest of Midian, who employed Moses to tend his flocks (Exodus 2:11–21).*

One day, while grazing the sheep deep in the wilderness, Moses caught sight of a bush that was all aflame yet remained unaffected (Exodus 3:1–22).[2] Fascinated by the scene, he approached the burning bush, only to hear himself addressed by a voice disclosing that he was standing on holy ground. Here Moses experienced his first encounter with God. Moses was informed that the divine promises that had been made to the patriarchs of Israel—Abraham, Isaac and Jacob—were now to be realized. God designated Moses to assume the leadership of Israel and to wage the struggle for liberation from Egyptian bondage. Moses' instinctive reaction was to shrink from the task. "Who am I," he asked, "that I should go to Pharaoh and free the Israelites from Egypt?" (Exodus 3:11). After considerable resistance, Moses finally agreed when his brother Aaron was appointed his spokesman.

Moses returned to Egypt to rally his people and to engage the obdurate monarch. His initial efforts were ineffective. Pharaoh was unyielding. Pharaoh said to Moses: "Who is the Lord that I should heed him and let Israel go? I do not know the Lord, nor will I let Israel go" (Exodus 5:2). Pharaoh imposed even harsher measures on the Israelites, and their situation deteriorated further (Exodus 5:1–22).

---

*Moses' father-in-law is also called Reuel (Exodus 2:18; Numbers 10:29) and, perhaps, Hobab (Judges 4:11; but see Numbers 10:29).

A series of ten plagues was then visited upon the land and people of Egypt. Man and beast, the soil and the ecology, were all severely affected.[3] In the course of these plagues, Pharaoh repeatedly made concessions, only to withdraw them at the last moment. Finally, his will was broken. He summoned Moses and Aaron in the middle of the night and capitulated. The Israelites assembled at Raamses and marched to Succoth, the first stopping place on their route out of Egypt. From there they entered the wilderness, headed for the land of Canaan (Exodus 7:14–11:10, 12:29–37).

The shortest route would have taken them up the Mediterranean coastal road, but they deliberately avoided it, following instead a roundabout course that led far into the wilderness. The Egyptians interpreted this to mean that the fleeing Israelites were hopelessly lost. Pharaoh mustered his forces and went after them in hot pursuit. The Israelites suddenly found themselves hemmed in by the Sea of Reeds (Red Sea) on one side and the Egyptian army on the other. At that critical moment, they were told by God to advance into the sea. As they did, the waters parted, allowing the Israelites to cross over to the other shore. Just as the Egyptian forces were halfway across in pursuit, the waters returned to their normal state. The entire Egyptian infantry and chariotry were drowned, and Israel was free at last (Exodus 13:17–14:31). Then Moses and the Israelites sang the Song of the Sea in praise of God, and Miriam led the women in a dance (Exodus 15:1–21).* Forever after, the event has been celebrated annually in the Passover festival (Exodus 12:1–28,43–50, 13:1–10).

Placing the Exodus account in historical context

It is extremely difficult to fit this narrative, set forth in the first 15 chapters of Exodus, into the framework of known history. On the other hand, rarely, if ever, can archaeology confirm the occurrence of individual events portrayed in narratives like this. Events of this sort are not "likely to have left marks in the archaeological record, or even in contemporaneous monuments."[4]

Moreover, the biblical writers were not concerned with the objective recording of details or even with the processes of historical change, as a modern historian would be. The biblical writers were not consciously engaged in what we would consider history writing, or historiography. Their concern was with the didactic use of selected historical traditions for a theological purpose. Exclusive concentration on the criterion of literal historicity tends to obscure the purpose and message of the text, which, after all, are the enduring qualities of scripture. Finally, the miracles—divine intervention—are not the stuff of history, but of faith.

*Many scholars now attribute the Song of the Sea to Miriam. See Phyllis Trible, "Bringing Miriam Out of the Shadows," *BR*, February 1989, pp. 14–25, 34.

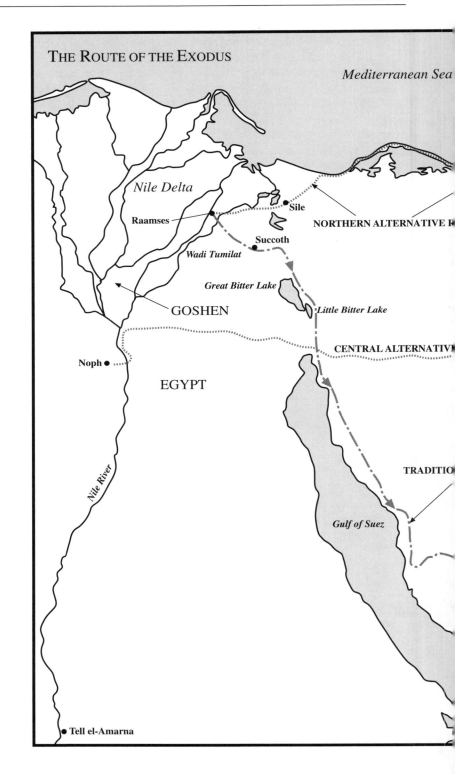

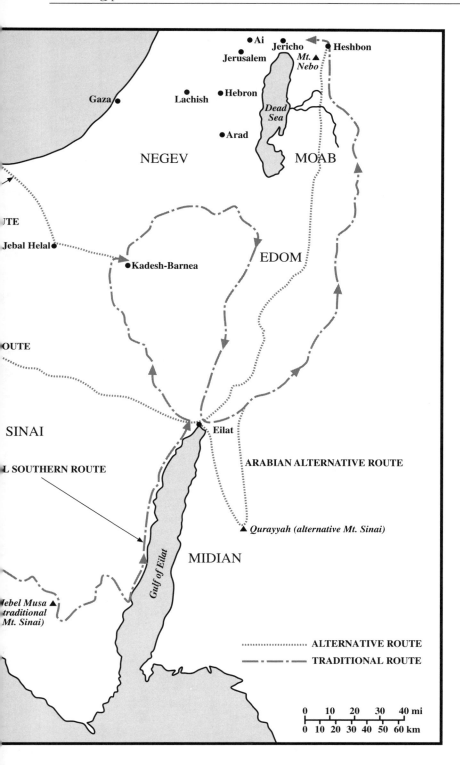

Ai

Jericho Heshbon

Jerusalem Mt. ▲
Nebo

Gaza

Lachish Hebron

Dead
Sea

NEGEV MOAB

Arad

ITE

Jebal Helal

Kadesh-Barnea EDOM

OUTE

SINAI

Eilat

ARABIAN ALTERNATIVE ROUTE

L SOUTHERN ROUTE

▲ Qurayyah (alternative Mt. Sinai)

Gulf of Eilat MIDIAN

Jebel Musa ▲
traditional
Mt. Sinai)

.... ALTERNATIVE ROUTE
—·—·— TRADITIONAL ROUTE

0   10   20   30   40 mi

0 10 20 30 40 50 60 km

The Egyptian sojourn cannot be fictional

With all these limitations what can we ask as historians? Actually, quite a lot. First, was there a sojourn and an enslavement in Egypt? The answer must be yes. This answer does not depend so much on an analysis of the text or on archaeological finds, but on common sense. No nation would be likely to invent for itself, and faithfully transmit century after century and millennium after millennium, such an inglorious and inconvenient tradition unless it had an authentic historical core.[5] Many peoples have fashioned foundational narratives recounting how they came to be, some with more, some with less historical value. But none, so far as we are aware, has ever suggested that its origins were as slaves.[6]

Though archaeology cannot confirm the Israelite sojourn in Egypt, it can provide a context. In general, archaeology can sometimes contradict—or suggest problems with—a biblical narrative. But it cannot confirm it. If the biblical account had said that the Israelites were forced to cut *stones* to build the store-cities of Pithom and Raamses (see Exodus 1:11), we would question the authenticity of the account because we know that mudbricks were the standard construction material in the Nile Delta but stones were not (they had to be shipped in, usually by water). If, on the other hand, the account says, as it does, that the Israelites were forced to make mudbricks, this does not confirm the historicity of the account. It merely provides a plausible context. Indeed, a 15th-century B.C.E. tomb painting shows Semitic slaves making mudbricks at Thebes. A text complains of not enough straw, just as the Israelites complained. Especially significant is the fact that straw was not typically used to make mudbricks in Canaan.[7] The account seems even more plausible when we consider that stone was the building material of choice in Jerusalem hundreds of years later when the account was written down. Still, confirmation eludes us.

Finding a suitable context for the Exodus

Indeed, much of what we know about life in Egypt in the second millennium B.C.E. provides a plausible context for the Egyptian sojourn. For example, there is considerable evidence of Asiatic slaves serving in Egypt. One papyrus lists more than 40 female slaves with Semitic names.[8] One of these female slaves is named Shiphrah, the name of one of the midwives in the Exodus narrative whom Pharaoh called to account because they were not following orders to kill male Israelites as soon as they were born (Exodus 1:15–18). We certainly do not mean to suggest that the two Shiphrahs were the same. We are talking about plausibility, not confirmation.

Or take geography. The region of Israelite settlement in Egypt is consistently designated as Goshen (Genesis 45:10, 46:28,29,34, 47:1,4,6,27, 50:8; Exodus 8:22, 9:26). This territory surely lay in the eastern Nile Delta. In a text known as "The Instruction for Merikare" (c. 2040 B.C.E.), an Egyptian ruler speaks to his son:

The east [the Nile Delta] abounds with foreigners ... Now speaking about these foreigners, as for the miserable Asiatic, wretched
is the place where he is ... Food causes his feet to roam about ...
But as I live and will be what I am, these foreigners were indeed
a sealed wall, its gates were opened when I besieged it. I caused
the Delta to attack it. I plundered their inhabitants, having captured their cattle. I slaughtered [the people] among them so that
the Asiatics abhorred Egypt.[9]

Here, according to an Egyptian record, Asiatics have roamed into the
eastern Delta (Goshen) to find food, just as the Israelites are said to
have done hundreds of years later.

Another Egyptian ruler at about the same time is advised to deal
with the Asiatic infiltrators by reinforcing Egypt's border defenses "to
prevent Asiatics from going down into Egypt. They beg for water in
the customary manner in order to let their flocks drink."[10] Apparently
there was a drought where they lived. The famous "Admonitions of
Ipuwer" describes Egyptian border defenses designed "to repulse the
Asiatics, to trample the Bedouin."[11]

A text known as Papyrus Anastasi 5, which dates to the 13th century B.C.E., contains a report from an Egyptian officer on the eastern
frontier who is trying to track down two runaway slaves who have
escaped into the wilderness. A scout has seen them near Migdol (one
of the sites mentioned in Numbers 33:7 on the route of the Exodus).
The Egyptian report has a dramatic immediacy that rivals the Bible:
"When my letter reaches you, write to me about all that has happened
to [them]. Who found their tracks? Which watch found their tracks?
What people are after them? Write to me about all that has happened
to them and how many people you send out after them."[12] This surely
does not confirm the Israelite Exodus. But it does provide a context for
the Israelite escape, and perhaps even makes the story more plausible.

A famous painting on a tomb wall at Beni Hasan in middle Egypt
portrays Asiatic traders in a donkey caravan coming down to Egypt
with their families and their wares in about 1890 B.C.E.

We have already mentioned mudbricks, which the Bible says the
Israelites were forced to manufacture. A well-known painting in the
tomb of Rekhmire (15th century B.C.E.) shows slaves making mudbricks. The Bible indicates that a brick-making quota was imposed
on the Israelites. At one point, they were required to find their own
straw, but the quota remained the same (Exodus 5:6–18). There is
evidence from Egypt that such quotas did exist; the Louvre Leather
Roll (1274 B.C.E.) reports the shortfalls of the assigned quotas,[13] just
as the Bible reports that the Israelite foremen were beaten because
their charges failed to meet the quotas (Exodus 5:14). This same
Egyptian text indicates that workers were granted time off for their
religious holidays. Similarly, a text discovered in the workmen's village of Deir el-Medineh states that workers had gone "to offer to

Brick-making in Pharaoh's Egypt. *"The Egyptians became ruthless in imposing tasks on the Israelites," the Book of Exodus 1:13–14 recounts, "and made their lives bitter with hard service in mortar and brick." The Hebrews' labors for Pharaoh were no doubt similar to these realistic scenes painted on the walls of the tomb of Rekh-mire, the Egyptian vizier (or prime minister) in the mid-15th century B.C.E. Two workmen with hoes (bottom left) knead clay moistened with water; a third, kneeling figure (lower right) tightens his hoe. Other workers pass buckets of wet clay to two brick makers (upper right), who use molds to form the bricks. At top left, a worker constructs a wall with the newly manufactured bricks. The accompanying inscription declares that the workers are "making bricks to build anew the workshops in Karnak."*

their god."[14] This of course is reminiscent of the Israelites' request to take off three days to go into the wilderness to worship their God (Exodus 3:18, 5:3).

If an Egyptian sojourn is so plausible, why then do some scholars deny it?

Denying the Exodus   It must be admitted that there is no direct evidence of Israel in Egypt. No existing Egyptian source even hints at Israel's presence there. This, combined with what has been called a "hermeneutic of suspicion,"[15] has produced extreme skepticism, if not denial of the value of the biblical text for reconstructing ancient Israel's history. This stance is often associated with a group of scholars known as biblical minimalists. The following statement by Thomas Thompson of the University of Copenhagen is typical: "Israel's own origin tradition is radically irrelevant to writing such a history."[16] Or consider this statement by Robert Coote of San Francisco Theological Seminary: "The writers of the Hebrew Scriptures knew little or nothing about the origin of Israel ... [The] period [of the Exodus] never existed."[17]

Some of the skepticism about Israel's sojourn in Egypt relates to the difficulty of dating it. No synchronism exists between any event recorded in the Book of Exodus and a dated occurrence documented in extrabiblical sources.[18] The Egyptian evidence for plausibility set forth above comes from a variety of periods. For the most part, this does not detract from the plausibility argument because it suggests the conditions existed over an extended period of time. Even if these conditions existed at a single period, however, this would not provide a date for the Egyptian sojourn, unless, as is almost never the case, these conditions were absent at other periods. And even if we could date the conditions to a particular period, this still would not confirm the biblical narrative, only make it somewhat more plausible.

The biblical chronology itself is problematic. The pentateuchal texts do not agree with one another as to how long the sojourn in Egypt lasted. Various biblically preserved traditions mention four generations (Genesis 15:16), 400 years (Genesis 15:13) and 430 years (Exodus 12:40–41). The first-century C.E. Jewish historian Flavius Josephus records a tradition of 215 years,[19] and an ancient rabbinic source gives 210 years.[20] The confusion is reflected in the case of Machir, grandson of Joseph. Machir's sons were born in the lifetime of Joseph, yet, according to the Bible, they participated in the conquest of Canaan and the settlement of the land (Genesis 50:23; Numbers 32:39–40; Joshua 13:31, 17:1). If this is true, then the Hebrew enslavement was limited to one generation. How, then, could it be that the Israelites in Egypt had, as the opening words of Exodus declare, "multiplied and increased very greatly, so that the land was filled with them" (Exodus 1:7)? Indeed, how could this occur in four generations?[21]

Questions of chronology

Calculating backward from a relatively secure date in biblical history produces no better results. The only biblical reference that provides a chronological hook is found in 1 Kings 1:6, which states that King Solomon began to build the Temple 480 years after the Israelites left Egypt. It is generally agreed that Solomon came to the throne in about 960 B.C.E., so that according to this reckoning the Exodus would have occurred in about 1440 B.C.E. (or 1436 B.C.E., since he started to build the Temple four years after he became king [1 Kings 6:1]). Most scholars question the accuracy of the number 480, however. It bears the marks of a symbolic rather than literal number. It equals 12 generations of 40 years each, a conventional figure in the Bible. The wilderness wanderings lasted 40 years (Numbers 14:33–34, 32:13; see also Deuteronomy 2:7, 8:2, 29:4; Joshua 5:6; Amos 2:10, 5:25; Psalm 95:10); 40 is used repeatedly in the period of the Judges (Judges 3:11, 5:31, 8:28, 13:1; see also Judges 3:30 [80 = twice 40]); and it also determines the incumbency of Eli the priest (1 Samuel 4:18) and the reigns of David (2 Samuel 5:4; 1 Kings 2:11; 1 Chronicles 29:27) and Solomon (1 Kings 11:42; 2 Chronicles 9:30). Exactly 480 years also elapsed from the commencement of the building of the Temple to the end of the Babylonian Exile, according to the data given in Kings.[22] All this suggests that we are dealing with a schematized chronology that dates the Temple from the

Exodus (and we try to work backward). The biblical writer wanted to place the Temple at the center of biblical history.

Scholars have defended two principal possibilities for the date of the Exodus: (1) the 15th century B.C.E., as the Bible seems to indicate, and (2) the 13th century B.C.E. The latter is far more likely.

Problems with a 15th-century Exodus

In the 15th century, Pharaoh Thutmosis III (1479–1425 B.C.E.) and his son Amenhotep (Amenophis) II (1425–1401 B.C.E.) conducted extensive campaigns in Canaan. It would be very unlikely for the Exodus to have occurred during the reigns of these powerful kings. Egypt is not even mentioned in the biblical accounts of Joshua's conquest of Canaan. This would be most unlikely if the escape to Canaan took place when Egypt controlled Canaan in the 15th century.

Another difficulty with a 15th-century Exodus is that it appears to conflict with the archaeological evidence. As is clear from the next chapter, Israel makes its first appearance in the archaeological record in the central hill country of Canaan in about 1200 B.C.E. This would place the Exodus in about 1240 B.C.E., assuming 40 years in the desert. If the Exodus occurred in the 15th century, we would expect to find much earlier evidence of the settlement in Canaan.[23]

A 13th-century Exodus?

The emergence of Israel in the hill country of central Canaan at the beginning of the 12th century is one of the reasons that most scholars have opted for a 13th-century Exodus. As we will see in more detail in the next chapter, far-reaching changes occurred in Canaan around 1200 B.C.E., with the close of the Late Bronze Age and the beginning of the Iron Age. The landscape of the central highlands underwent a major transformation. New settlers appeared in sizable numbers. Villages were founded on the hilltops, and extensive deforestation took place. Large-scale terracing of the slopes was undertaken to create areas for agricultural cultivation so that the needs of the enlarged population could be met. Throughout the central highlands, cisterns were constructed, distinguished by waterproof linings of lime plaster that rendered them impermeable.[24]

There is no direct evidence to prove that the new arrivals who were responsible for these changes were the tribes of Israel. But this is a thoroughly reasonable assumption. This is just where the Bible tells us the Israelites settled (Joshua 17:14–18, 20:7, 21:11,20).

The absence of any mention in the conquest narratives of Egyptian military might in Canaan is also understandable in the 13th century B.C.E., when Egyptian hegemony waned.

Ramesses II

The area of the Israelite settlement in Egypt is called the region of Rameses (Genesis 47:11). A city built by the Israelites is named Raamses (Exodus 1:11), and this was the rallying point for their departure from Egypt (Exodus 12:37; Numbers 33:3,5). This strongly suggests a connection with Pharaoh Ramesses II (1279–1213 B.C.E.), who shifted the administrative center of Egypt to the northeast Delta and named the capital that he had built there after himself.[25] This long-lived pharaoh was famous for his extensive and massive building program, which he executed by conscripting large numbers of civilians, especially foreigners.

The city that Ramesses built is called Pi-Ramesses (meaning "House of Ramesses") in Egyptian records.[26] It has recently been identified in the course of excavation of a site now called Tell ed-Daba. (During an earlier period, when an Asiatic people known as the Hyksos ruled Egypt, Tell ed-Daba was known as Avaris, the Hyksos capital. More about the Hyksos later.) A record (Leiden Papyrus 348) of construction work at Pi-Ramesses has survived. In it an official of Ramesses II instructs the foreman to distribute rations to the 'Apiru. Some scholars[27] connect the 'Apiru, referred to in numerous Egyptian documents, with the biblical 'Ibrî (meaning Hebrew; plural 'Ibrîm).[28] (In cuneiform sources the term appears as "Habiru" or "Hapiru.") These people are referred to in more than 200 West Semitic inscriptions. The 'Apiru or Habiru are generally regarded as a kind of renegade, foreign population; one scholar has called them "uprooted migrants," people who "lived for awhile as foreigners in another country."[29] Sometimes they are identified as mercenaries. If the term "'Apiru" is indeed related to "Hebrew,"[30] then Hebrews—or, more accurately, proto-Hebrews—may well have been part of the Egyptian corvée, or forced labor crew, who built Ramesses' capital in the 13th century B.C.E., just as the Bible says.[31] The term "'Apiru" clearly referred to people of low social status; it is a derogatory term. In the Book of Exodus, "Hebrews" is not used by the Israelites in reference to themselves, but by foreigners speaking of the Israelites (see, for example, Exodus 1:16, 2:6), and by the narrator in the context of Egyptians vis-à-vis the Israelites (for example, Exodus 1:19, 2:7, 3:18, 5:3, etc.). We should not conclude that all 'Apiru became Hebrews; but, if the etymological equation is correct, it would seem likely that some 'Apiru were among the workers at Pithom and Raamses and perhaps through them the name 'Ibrîm (Hebrews) began to be applied to this people as an ethnic term.[32]

Egyptian history also suggests Ramesses II as the pharaoh of the oppression. Toward the end of Ramesses' long reign, Egyptian national power declined. Apart from a raid into Canaan by his successor, Merneptah, the Egyptian hold on Asian lands weakened appreciably. Around 1200 B.C.E., the XIXth Dynasty came to an end, amidst anarchy and chaos. The political situation at this time provide the most appropriate background for the events of the Israelite oppression and liberation.

The situation in Transjordan also figures in the equation. In Numbers 20:14–21 and 21:21–35, we are told that Moses was in contact with the kingdoms of Edom, Moab and Ammon. Archaeological surveys have shown that these settled kingdoms did not come into existence before the 13th century B.C.E., at the earliest.[33] Assuming the biblical references are accurate, this would eliminate a 15th-century date for the Exodus.

The Bible is clear that Pharaoh* pursued the Israelites with chariots pulled by horses (Exodus 14:6–9, 15:1–4). Both horses and chariots were extremely rare in the 15th century B.C.E. They begin to appear in significant numbers only in the 13th century B.C.E.[34] If these are historical references, the Exodus most likely did not occur before the 13th century B.C.E. Another possibility is that the references to horses and chariots are anachronistic; that is, the biblical author, writing when horses and chariots were common, assumed, contrary to fact, that horses and chariots were used in pursuit of the Israelites.

The Merneptah Stele

The famous Merneptah Stele is also relevant, if inconclusive, at this point.[35] The Merneptah Stele, or Israel Stele as it is sometimes called, is a hieroglyphic account of Pharaoh Merneptah's military campaigns, including one in Canaan. Merneptah (1212–1202 B.C.E.) boasts that he has destroyed several named cities as well as "Israel": "Israel is laid waste and his seed is not." An Egyptian sign called a determinative is attached to the name Israel. It tells the reader that Israel is a people. Different signs are used to indicate a city or a state. The campaign described in the stele can be confidently dated to 1205 B.C.E., give or take a year or two. About all this there is universal agreement. Some have used the Israel Stele as support for a 13th-century Exodus, in about 1250 or so. Those who deny that there was an Exodus argue that the Israel referred to in the Merneptah Stele is different from the Israel of the Bible.[36]

A centuries-long Exodus

Another recent suggestion from a leading Israeli historian, Abraham Malamat of Hebrew University, is that we should not look for a specific date for the Exodus because it involved "a steady flow of Israelites from Egypt over hundreds of years. If the Exodus was a durative event, as seems likely, the search for a specific date for it is futile."[37] Malamat argues that, based on historical circumstances in Egypt, the outflow probably peaked in the 12th century B.C.E. with the collapse and exhaustion of the Near East's two superpowers, the Hittite and Egyptian empires.

---

*According to Exodus 2:23, the pharaoh of the oppression died, so the pharaoh of the Exodus is a successor.

Although the Exodus cannot be fixed with certainty at any particular time, this does not necessarily mean there was no Exodus. It simply means we cannot date it precisely.

We have already noted the presence of what are apparently Israelites in the hill country of central Canaan beginning in about 1200 B.C.E., a subject that will be treated at length in the following chapter but that must also be considered in connection with the Exodus. Various historical models have been proposed to account for the hundreds of new settlements in central Canaan at this time. Initially, scholars asked whether these settlers came by way of conquest or by way of peaceful infiltration. More recently, it has been argued that these people who became Israelites were actually Canaanites fleeing from the declining cities to the central hill country at the end of the Late Bronze Age (1550–1200 B.C.E.). As this contention became more widely adopted, the debate centered largely on whether the Israelites came from outside Canaan or from inside. The best scholarship today suggests that the emergence of Israel involved all of these things: There must have been some military confrontations; surely some people infiltrated peacefully; and just as surely many Canaanites accreted to the emerging Israelites.[38] Biblical support can, in fact, be found for all these theories. What seems increasingly clear, however, is that at least some Israelites came from Egypt. Otherwise, how can we account for the adoption of this epic as Israel's foundational narrative? Indeed, no other event figures as prominently in the Bible as Israel's liberation from Egyptian bondage. It is pervasive not only in the historical narratives, but even in the Prophets and the Psalms.

Settlement in Canaan

Had Israel really arisen in Canaan and never been enslaved in Egypt, a biblical writer would have had no reason to conceal that fact and could surely have devised an appropriate narrative to accommodate that reality. We are simply at a loss to explain the need to fabricate such an uncomfortable account of Israel's disreputable national origins. Nor can we explain how such a falsity could so pervade the national psyche as to eliminate all other traditions and historical memories, let alone become the dominant and controlling theme in the national religion.[39]

How large the Exodus was is another matter. Surely the biblical claim of 600,000 able-bodied men (and their families, for a total of approximately 2,000,000) (Exodus 12:37–38) is a gross exaggeration,[40] but the historical core of an Exodus of some sort seems highly likely. If they were slaves in Egypt, they must have gotten out somehow.

Another objection to a historical Exodus relates to the fact that the biblical version was written centuries after the events it purports to describe. According to this objection, what we can glean from the biblical text relates only to the time when the account was written, not to the time it describes.

Evaluating the historicity of the biblical narrative

The composition of the Pentateuch is admittedly a complicated process that extended over centuries. Not surprisingly, scholars disagree considerably about the details of this process. It is widely recognized, however, that embedded in the text are four authorial strands identified as J (for Yahwist or, in German, *Jahwist*), E (the Elohist), P (the Priestly Code) and D (the Deuteronomist). The intertwining of these four sources was the work of an editor or editors referred to as R (the Redactor). This is a vastly simplified description of a nuanced and, in its broad outlines, convincing explanation of how the Pentateuch developed. Scholars sometimes disagree as to what passages are to be ascribed to which source, as well as how the process occurred. Some posit an oral element in the text that developed side by side with its written composition.[41] But there is general agreement on the overall process.

Quite naturally, there are also disagreements as to when the various strands were composed. J is generally thought to be the earliest, E next, then J and E were combined to form JE, which was subsequently combined with P. D is a separate book, Deuteronomy. Exodus is a combination of JE and P. Some scholars date J as early as the tenth century B.C.E. A better date is probably a century or two later. The date of P is the most controversial. Some date it before the Babylonian Exile (sixth century B.C.E.); others date it during or after the Exile.

Scholars who deny any historicity to the Exodus account date the text late, some as late as the Hellenistic period (third to second century B.C.E.). They argue that the biblical account cannot be relied on to reveal any historical information because the text was composed so long after the events. This question must be addressed regardless of when the texts were composed. Even the earliest date proposed by scholars is still hundreds of years after the events described.

It is difficult to believe that these stories were simply concocted out of whole cloth. Whoever first wrote the accounts, regardless of when they lived, must have had sources. What these sources were is hard to determine. Some were probably written; the Bible itself refers to a number of books that have not survived. The Chronicles of the Kings of Judah is mentioned 15 times. The Chronicles of the Kings of Israel is mentioned 18 times. Collections of even earlier accounts may have been contained in such titles as the Book of Jashar (quoted in Joshua 10–12) and the Book of the Wars of Yahweh (Numbers 21:14). Other sources may have been oral, a part of the developing tradition of the people Israel.

For those who reject the Bible as a source for the history of Israel, the Exodus account is sheer fiction,[42] a myth[43] created to provide Israel with a past that never occurred. Even mainstream scholars recognize legendary elements in the story. But, in addition to the legendary additions and exaggerations, there is also a historical core that can be excavated, as it were, much as an archaeologist excavates the layers of a tell. So even though centuries separate the events described from the compositions, this in itself is no reason totally to reject the history they report. Sometimes we can even demonstrate that a late account is quite reliable.

Excavating the historical core of the Exodus account

An example: In the third century B.C.E., Manetho, an Egyptian priest, wrote a history of Egypt in Greek in which he described the Hyksos rule of Egypt in the mid-second millennium B.C.E. No copy of Manetho's history has survived. What we do have are extracts quoted by the first-century C.E. Jewish historian Josephus, who apparently did not know Manetho's work firsthand but only from other accounts.[44] Extracts from Manetho are also preserved in the writings of Eusebius (third to fourth century C.E.), but he too worked without a copy of Manetho's work, relying instead on the secondhand account of Julius Africanus.[45] As even a skeptical modern historian concedes, however, "Manetho is still an important source in the reconstruction of Egyptian history. Whatever the difficulties with using his work—whatever the lateness and textual corruption of the surviving manuscripts—Egyptologists would regard it as rather foolish to allow these to prevent the use of Manetho."[46] Historians must make use of what evidence is available. That a text was written long after the event it describes does not necessarily mean it is inaccurate. Nor is a contemporaneous account necessarily accurate. In both cases the text must be critically examined. In the case of Manetho, for example, inscriptions bearing the names of some of the kings he mentions have recently turned up in excavations, confirming Manetho's account.[47]

The Hyksos period in Egypt has another relevance: As noted, even late accounts of Hyksos rule—1,500 years after the event—have some reliability. The flip side of this is also worth noting: We would know almost nothing about the Hyksos period if we depended on contemporaneous Egyptian records. As the distinguished Egyptologist John Wilson long ago noted, "It was not in character for an ancient people to enlarge on defeat and subjection at the hands of others. Only the victorious elimination of peril would enter the literature."[48] Might this suggest why extant Egyptian documents, fragmentary though they are, contain no hint of an Israelite presence?

Other problems with the biblical account may affect our view of the historicity of the narrative—for example, the difficulties in tracing the route of the Exodus. When the Israelites left Egypt they sensibly

The route of the Exodus

avoided the shortest and best route to Canaan (Exodus 13:17–18)—along the Mediterranean coast. That route, unfortunately for the Israelites, was heavily defended with Egyptian forts. The 15th-century B.C.E. reliefs carved by Pharaoh Thutmosis III on the outer wall of the hypostyle hall of the Temple to Amun at Karnak display a chain of forts, way stations and wells along this route. Excavations have uncovered ancient Egyptian citadels strung all the way from the Nile Delta to Gaza.[49] Surely it was the better part of valor for the fleeing Israelites to have taken a different route to Canaan.

Numbers 33 contains an itinerary that includes a lengthy list of place-names tracing the route of the Exodus all the way from the Israelites' departure to their arrival in Canaan. Most of these sites, however, cannot be identified. Does this mean that they were made up centuries later, or does it mean that the names have simply been lost to the historical record?

Some of the sites east of the Jordan mentioned in Numbers 33 have been identified in Egyptian sources. The reliefs of Thutmosis III at Karnak mentioned above also contain an extensive list of place-names, presumably in geographical order. Four of the names on the Karnak list can be identified in the same order and in the same general location as the names in Numbers 33.[50] Does this mean that the still unidentified sites in Numbers 33 are fictional or that they simply have not yet been found?

The Red—or Reed—Sea Other sites in the Exodus account are problematic, among them the so-called Red Sea. Even the name is a crux. The Hebrew name is "Yam Suf." *Yam* indeed means "sea." But the word for "red" is *adam*. For some unknown reason, Yam Suf was translated in the early Greek translation of the Bible known as the Septuagint (made for Greek-speaking Jews of Alexandria) as "Erythra Thalassa" (Red Sea); from there it got into the Latin Vulgate as "Mare Rubrum" and "Mare Erythraeum"; and from there into English translations as Red Sea. But "Yam Suf" really means "Sea of Reeds," and that is the more customary English translation today.

In some biblical passages, it is clear that the body of water referred to as the Yam Suf is the modern Red Sea or one of its two northern fingers, the Gulf of Suez or the Gulf of Eilat (or Aqaba) (see, for example, Numbers 21:4; 1 Kings 9:26; Jeremiah 49:21). Perhaps the Red Sea was known by that name even in ancient times; the Septuagint translators knew that the body of water referred to in some passages was the Red Sea, so they simply translated all the occurrences of the term as Red Sea.

Although Yam Suf does sometimes refer to the Red Sea, that cannot be the case for the body of water that the Israelites supposedly crossed dry-shod (Exodus 15:4). The Red Sea is a very large body of water. Besides, there are no reeds there.

In Exodus 14:2 the location of the Yam Suf is given fairly precisely—in relation to Pi-hahiroth, Migdol and Baal-zephon. Unfortunately, none of these sites can be located with any certainty. Many bodies of water have been suggested as the biblical Yam Suf, but no identification is much more convincing than any other. We simply cannot identify with any assurance the body of water referred to in the Bible.

Among the suggested possibilities are Lake Bardwil (the Gulf of Serbonitis) and other gulfs in the northern Delta, Lake Menzaleh, Lake Timsah, the Bitter Lakes, the Gulf of Eilat (the Gulf of Aqaba) and the Gulf of Suez. The last two would seem to be ruled out by the absence of reeds or, more accurately, papyrus marshes.

Some scholars have argued that Yam Suf is a mythological body of water. In this scenario, Yam Suf should be read "Yam Sof." "Sof," which is spelled the same as "Suf" in biblical Hebrew, means "end"; the Yam Sof in this hypothesis would be the Sea of the End, or the sea at the end of the world, or the sea that lay beyond. The principal proponent of this view, Bernard Batto, contends that Yam Suf/Sof can sometimes refer to the Red Sea and sometimes to this mythical body of water at the end of the world. As the Red Sea, it is simply the sea at the end of the world, as the ancients regarded it. As a mythological body of water, the Sea of the End is associated with the chaos existing before God formed the universe (see Genesis 1:1–2). The Exodus is thus a second creation, this time of the Israelite nation instead of the world. The Sea of the End is the chaos out of which the Israelites emerged; the Egyptians perished in this sea at the end of the world.[51]

Mt. Sinai presents some of the same kind of difficulties as Yam Suf. It, too, cannot be located with any certainty. Many sites have been suggested—from the traditional Mt. Sinai, Jebel Musa (a tradition that goes back only to the fourth century C.E.), to other mountains in southern Sinai to a mountain in northwestern Saudi Arabia to a site near the present Egyptian-Israeli border.[52] Often the site is chosen to conform to a particular hypothetical route of the Exodus, which is equally uncertain.[53] In the case of the traditional Mt. Sinai, this particular mountain in southern Sinai may have been so designated because it became associated with traditions of sanctity when early monasteries were established in the area. The monks, however, apparently settled here because of favorable environmental conditions, rather than out of any conviction that the site was Mt. Sinai.[54]

Searching for Mt. Sinai

Does this mean there was no Mt. Sinai? Not necessarily. It only means that neither the historian nor the archaeologist can identify it. It seems likely that the Israelites (or what emerged as the Israelites) had some kind of religious experience in connection with a mountain.* We have the biblical account of it. Yet it is difficult to say anything more from a historical viewpoint.

The case of Kadesh-Barnea

In some ways the case of Kadesh-Barnea is instructive. According to the biblical account, after the Israelites received the law at Mt. Sinai, they camped for 38 years at Kadesh-Barnea. Most scholars accept the identification of the site as modern Ein el-Kudeirat. Its location, the impressive tell, the availability of water and other environmental conditions make it by far the best candidate—in some ways the only candidate—for Kadesh-Barnea. There is one problem, however. It has been extensively excavated and no remains have been found earlier than the tenth century B.C.E., several hundred years after the Exodus.[55] What are we to conclude? That the correct site has not been identified? That the area of the site with earlier remains has not yet been discovered? That the Israelites were there but left no remains? That this aspect of the story was simply made up?

Before deciding, consider the case of Dibon. The Israelites encamped at Dibon-gad (Numbers 33:45), east of the Jordan, where presumably there was a settlement if not a city. The site is confidently identified as Tell Dhiban, which, like Kadesh-Barnea, has been extensively excavated. No settlement from the Late Bronze Age (1550–1200 B.C.E.), when the Israelites encamped at Dibon, has been found there. Since this is the invasion route of the Israelite tribes, one might expect to find a destroyed Late Bronze Age settlement of some sort. Yet from the archaeological viewpoint, Dibon did not exist then. That is not the end of this particular story, however. The 15th-century B.C.E. list of cities in this area carved by Thutmosis III on the wall of the Temple of Amun in Karnak includes a site named Dibon![56] According to Thutmosis, there *was* a city at Dibon at this time even though it is not attested archaeologically! What does this tell us about the absence of early remains at Kadesh-Barnea?

To summarize: The biblical account is complex and contains many different kinds of assertions. At one end of the spectrum are facts we can be relatively certain of. At the other end are theological assertions that historians cannot deal with; by definition, miracles are outside the historians' ken.[57] They are matters of faith to be addressed by theologians.

What we can know about the Exodus

We can confidently assert, however, that a group of people who later became Israel went down to Egypt from Canaan, eventually settling there. At some point they were conscripted in a corvée and were oppressed as foreigners. Some of them later escaped and had a theophanous experience in the desert. Still later, they or their

---

*In the book of Deuteronomy, the mountain is called Horeb rather than Sinai.

descendants entered Canaan, where, joined by other peoples, they became Israel.

Did they have a leader named Moses? This is not the kind of information that we can expect to cull from the archaeological record. It is certainly highly likely that they had a leader of some sort. And Moses is an Egyptian name.[58] In the biblical narrative, the name was chosen by Pharaoh's daughter (Exodus 2:10).[59] The name Moses derives from the Egyptian verb meaning "to give birth" and is a common element in Egyptian names such as Ramesses (which means "born of Ra"), Thutmosis, Amenmosis, Ptahmosis and numerous others.[60] That Moses had an Egyptian name, however, does not mean that all the events of his life as described in the text are historically accurate. On the other hand, it does make his existence as an Israelite leader more plausible.

In short, the overall authentic Egyptian coloration of the story and its background certainly lends plausibility to the broad sweep of the account, especially because we would expect some major gaffes if the story were made up centuries later. But this authentic coloration does not confirm the biblical account.

Some traditions in the stories have the undeniable feel of folklore rather than history. In cuneiform texts dating to the seventh and sixth centuries B.C.E., but relating to King Sargon of Akkad who ruled in the mid-third millennium, the story is told that Sargon's mother, for reasons that are not entirely clear, tried to conceal her son's birth and placed him in a reed basket waterproofed with bitumen and set him adrift, not in the Nile, but in the Euphrates. The similarity to the story of Moses' birth (Exodus 2:3) is clear. Was this element in the story simply incorporated from the cuneiform account or, perhaps, from a common tradition?

Sometimes there may be a historical core to a story that we cannot identify with any assurance. Between the 18th and 16th centuries B.C.E., an era Egyptologists call the Second Intermediate Period, a motley population of Asiatics infiltrated Egypt in increasing numbers, eventually taking control of Lower Egypt. These Asiatics seem to have come mainly from Canaan. The governing class of these Asiatics became known as Hyksos, which means "Rulers of Foreign Lands."[61] Hyksos rulers formed the XVth and XVIth Egyptian dynasties (c. 1675–1552). Their chief base was Avaris, in the eastern Delta, the same site later to be known as Raamses. The Hyksos were ultimately expelled from Egypt and chased back into Canaan—in about the middle of the 16th century B.C.E. Freed of Hyksos domination, the Egyptians established a new dynasty, the XVIIIth Dynasty,[62] with which the New Kingdom began. What relevance has the Hyksos period to a consideration of the historicity of the Exodus narrative? It surely provides a relevant background to Joseph's rise to

The Hyksos

power. It even makes that event plausible. It counters the argument that surely would have been made without such background that the story was fiction because no foreigner could rise to such a position. On the other hand, just as surely it does not confirm that a Hebrew named Joseph in fact rose to this position. But knowledge of the Hyksos period and Asiatic rule in Egypt may well have inspired the Israelites who wrote the Joseph story. The Joseph episode (Genesis 37–50) in many respects reads like a novel and could be what we would call historical fiction—a melding of history and fiction. The Hyksos rule and expulsion could be the background for Joseph's rise to power and the Israelite escape into the wilderness. One leading scholar, Baruch Halpern, has indeed made this argument, even claiming to have archaeological evidence for it. It is a somewhat complicated but fascinating story, involving an Egyptian monument known as the 400-Year Stele.

Inspiration for a Genesis tradition   A tradition preserved in Genesis 15:13 states that Abraham's descendants will be "strangers in a land not theirs and they shall be enslaved and oppressed 400 years." This tradition, Halpern suggests, may have been inspired by an Egyptian monument known as the 400-Year Stele. Follow the thread.

When Moses sends spies into Canaan to scout the land, they travel through the Negev and finally come to Hebron. At this point there is an interpolation in the text. "Hebron was founded," we are told, "seven years before Zoan of Egypt" (Numbers 13:22). In a labyrinthine way, this notice may tell us that the Hyksos era was indeed connected with the Joseph story.

We start out with a question: What were the biblical authors referring to when they stated that Hebron was founded just seven years before Zoan?

We know that the biblical authors were eager to establish the antiquity of Hebron. Remember that David ruled in Hebron before conquering Jerusalem and transferring his capital there (2 Samuel 2:11), so the date of the city was important to the authors. That is why they described Hebron as being even older than the Egyptian city Zoan.

But how did they know the date of Zoan? Well, actually, they did not: Hebron is not seven years older than Zoan. (Indeed, Hebron, a Middle Bronze Age city [1800–1550 B.C.E.], is far older than Zoan, which dates to the 11th or 10th century B.C.E.) But we can learn from their mistake: Their error allows us to determine precisely what source (the 400-Year Stele) they used to arrive at this date. It also allows us to see why they described the sojourn in Egypt as lasting for 400 years.

The Hebrew Zoan is equivalent to the Egyptian Djanet, which is transcribed in Greek as Tanis, and which also appears in English translations of Egyptian inscriptions as Tanis. We will henceforth refer to the city as Tanis, rather than using the biblical equivalent Zoan.

Now let us look at the inscription known as the 400-Year Stele. Erected by Pharaoh Ramesses II in the early 13th century B.C.E., the stele celebrates the inauguration of the cult of the deity Seth 400 years earlier—in the 17th century B.C.E. Both the date and the god Seth indicate that this is a Hyksos inscription: The Hyksos became the rulers of Egypt in about 1675 B.C.E.; moreover, the Egyptians equated the Hyksos god with the Egyptian god Seth. So, although the text does not explicitly mention the Hyksos, scholars recognize that it refers to them *sub silentio*.

If there is any doubt that this monument refers to the Hyksos, it is dispelled by the scene carved on the stele: Seth is portrayed as an Asiatic deity in distinctively Asiatic dress. We should not expect the Hyksos to be mentioned more explicitly. As one commentator noted, "It was, of course, out of the question that the Egyptians should mention the hated Hyksos in such a commemoration."[63]

Ramesses II originally erected the stele in his capital city, Pi-Ramesses (modern Tell ed-Daba). In the stele, Seth is referred to as Seth of Ramesses. Ramesses II had built his capital on the site of (more precisely, adjacent to) the former Hyksos capital Avaris. Ramesses II was aware of the Hyksos connection with the site; he had specifically moved his capital from Thebes to the site of Avaris.

The 400-Year Stele was not discovered at Tell ed-Daba, however. It was found at Tanis—biblical Zoan! How did this happen?

Sometime in the 11th or 10th century B.C.E., the Egyptian capital was again moved, this time from Pi-Ramesses to Tanis, and the stele traveled with it. The stele was in Tanis at the time the biblical author wrote about a 400-year sojourn. The cryptic reference to the founding of Tanis and Hebron within seven years of each other (Numbers 13:22) tells us that the biblical author was familiar with the stele inscription. The biblical author no doubt thought that the 400-Year Stele marked the 400th anniversary of the founding of Tanis (Zoan) because that is where the inscription stood in his day. Therefore, the author (J) mistakenly identified Zoan as a city as ancient as Hebron.

Further, the biblical author linked the 400th anniversary of Hyksos domination commemorated in the stele—that is, the 400 years between the rise of the Hyksos and the rule of Ramesses II, who erected the stele—to the 400-year enslavement of the Israelites (Genesis 15:13). In short, in Halpern's words, "The idea of a four-century span between the Hyksos (and Joseph) and the pharaoh who built the city Raamses [Pi-Ramesses] using Israelite labor must be traced, directly or indirectly, to that [400-year Egyptian] monument. Overall, the Joseph story is a reinterpretation of the Hyksos period from an Israelite perspective."[64]

Halpern's point is not that the Joseph story is historically accurate. He simply wants to tell us how the Hyksos period, when Semites ruled Egypt, provided the inspiration for the Joseph story and also provided a context for it. Halpern deals not with the historicity of the narrative but with the history of the tradition. In his own words, "Israelite tradition associated the descent into Egypt with the Hyksos period."[65] "Israel came to identify itself with the Hyksos."[66]

This illustrates yet another way that history may be incorporated in the biblical tradition. Whether the tradition itself is historical is a different question and one that is more difficult to answer. The tradition often deals with individual events that cannot be expected to find their way into the archaeological record or into surviving contemporaneous records, in this case, of the Egyptians. And the supernatural, by its nature, cannot be affirmed or denied by the natural.

Nor was the biblical author concerned with history in the way a modern historian is. The theological perspective dominates. And in the end the narrative takes its meaning on a nonhistorical plane. It is not whether it all really happened just as the Bible describes it that justifies the story, although it is a fascinating, important and relevant endeavor to ask whether it did; it is the power and inspiration of the tale as it comes down to us that gives the text its ultimate meaning.

THREE

The Settlement in Canaan
The Period of the Judges

JOSEPH A. CALLAWAY
revised by J. Maxwell Miller

How the Israelites acquired their territories in the hill country of Canaan, and what their first settlements were like, continue to be among the most unsettled issues in Israelite history. Yet a casual reading of the Book of Joshua leaves the impression that there is no problem: Joshua and the Israelites entered the land from east of the Jordan River, captured Jericho with the aid of divine intervention and took the rest of Canaan in a series of lightning military campaigns. The various peoples of Canaan were defeated and, as in the case of the inhabitants at Jericho, were "utterly destroyed ... both men and women, young and old, oxen, sheep, and asses, with the edge of the sword" (Joshua 6:21). "So Joshua defeated the whole land, the hill country and the Negev and the lowland and the slopes, and all their kings; he left none remaining, but utterly destroyed all that breathed, as the Lord God of Israel commanded" (Joshua 10:40). "There was not a city that made peace with the people of Israel, except the Hivites, the inhabitants of Gibeon; they took all in battle" (Joshua 11:19).

The biblical description is so graphic and direct that many people have never thought of Israel's acquisition of Canaan in any other way: The land was acquired by military conquest in fewer than five years of struggle (Joshua 14:7,10) and was divided among the nine and one-half tribes that did not receive territorial allotments east of the Jordan River (Joshua 13:8–19:51). The Israelites displaced the various peoples that occupied the towns and villages, and all Israel was involved in taking the land and in settling the portions allotted to the various tribes. Joshua 21:43 summarizes this view: "Thus the Lord gave to Israel all the land which he swore to give to their fathers; and having taken possession of it, they settled there."

Joshua vs. Judges
However quite a different view of the "conquest" and the settlement in Canaan emerges in the Book of Judges. The events related in that book purportedly come "after the death of Joshua" (Judges 1:1), but the picture of Israel in Canaan is not at all what one would expect from reading the Book of Joshua. For instance, the sequence of "conquest followed by allotment of land" is reversed in Judges; in Judges, the land is allotted first, then conquered. Thus, Judah says to Simeon, his brother, "Come up with me into the territory allotted to me, that we may fight against the Canaanites; and I likewise will go with you into the territory allotted to you" (Judges 1:3). Most of Judges 1 describes scattered struggles undertaken by individual tribes or related tribes trying to gain a foothold in the central hill country of Canaan; here we find no unified effort by "all Israel" to possess the land, as the Book of Joshua seems to describe.

Furthermore, in contrast to the sweeping statements in Joshua that Israel wiped out the inhabitants of the land, Judges 1 concludes with a list of 20 cities in which the people were not driven out by the newcomers (Judges 1:21,27–33). The list includes some of the most strategically located and influential cities in the later history of Israel: Jerusalem, Beth-Shean, Taanach, Dor, Ibleam, Megiddo, Gezer and Beth-Shemesh. In the summary of Israel's victories in Joshua 12:7–24, however, it is expressly stated that Jerusalem, Gezer, Taanach, Megiddo and Dor were defeated by "Joshua and the people of Israel."

The Book of Judges, therefore, unlike the Book of Joshua, preserves a tradition that the ancient Israelites gained possession of the land of Canaan over a long period of time, with individual tribes or groups of related tribes acting independently. Also, according to Judges, the land was acquired in various ways. Judah and Simeon, as noted above, conducted small military operations "against the Canaanites" for their allotments. The Kenites, on the other hand, who descended from Moses' father-in-law, "went up with the people of Judah from the city of palms into the wilderness of Judah, which lies in the Negev near Arad; and they went and settled with the people" (Judges 1:16), apparently peacefully. Still other tribal groups seem to have coexisted with Canaanite enclaves, such as the Jebusites, who are said to "have dwelt with the people of Benjamin in Jerusalem to this day" (Judges 1:21).

The Hebrew Bible is our main written source for understanding how the Israelites came to be settled in the land of Canaan, and the view that the Israelites conquered the land by force, as related in Joshua 1–12, is often taken as the biblical view. As seen above, however, there is apparently more than one biblical view. Whereas Joshua 1–12 presupposes a rapid "conquest followed by settlement" of the land, the traditions in Judges preserve memories of peaceful intermingling over a period of time as well as isolated fighting for certain regions. The Joshua account concludes with a list of the cities conquered, which includes the major cities of the land; in Judges, we find the Israelites coexisting with the inhabitants of some 20 major cities that apparently did not come under Israelite control until much later. So the question arises: What is the biblical view? Or, is there a biblical view?

Yet another qualifier must be added. The traditions preserved in both Joshua and Judges were passed down through the generations. They reached their current form long after the Israelites came to possess the land. In other words, they are not eyewitness reports and do not claim to be. As Abraham Malamat, the eminent Israeli biblical scholar and historian, explains, "The tradition of the conquest that the Bible records crystallized only after generations of complex reworking and, in certain respects, reflects the conceptions ... of later editors and redactors."[1] The resulting biblical historiography "explained historical events theologically," in a fashion that "accentuated the role of the Lord of Israel and submerged the human element."[2] Thus, the canonical, or "official," tradition of the conquest emerged. According to this tradition, all 12 tribes of Israel acted together in military operations on both sides of the Jordan. "Thus," Malamat writes, "the divine pledge to the Patriarchs (see for example Deuteronomy 30:20) that Canaan would be occupied in its entirety was redeemed."[3]

The biblical conquest tradition reflects generations of reworking

The Joshua account of the conquest provides signals here and there that it was composed long after the events described. For instance, Joshua 8:28 states that "Joshua burned Ai, and made it forever a heap of ruins, as it is *to this day*." The site of Ai was a village from about 1200 to 1050 B.C.E., after which it was abandoned and never rebuilt.[4] Joshua 8:28, therefore, reflects a time when Ai was in ruins, that is, after 1050 B.C.E., and not the time of the conquest some centuries earlier. In Joshua 10:12–13, the Book of Jashar is cited as a source of information about the sun standing still in the battle between the Israelites and the Amorites at Gibeon. The Book of Jashar has not survived, but it is mentioned again in 2 Samuel 1:18 as containing the lament of David over the deaths of Saul and Jonathan at the battle on Mt. Gilboa. If this Book of Jashar is the same as that mentioned in Joshua 10:12–13, then it dates at least as late as the time of David. This also would place the current composition of the Book of Joshua hundreds of years after the settlement in Canaan.

What we have, then, in the Book of Joshua is the "official" view, to use Malamat's term, of later editors who had access to traditions and documents that do not exist today. They had theological reasons for selecting only short sections of documents such as the Book of Jashar that suited their purposes and for leaving out the rest. This was a common practice in history writing in the biblical period, evident in passages such as 1 Chronicles 29. The account of David's rule is concluded in verse 28, and the sources used by the writers, who lived at a later time, are cited in verses 29–30. These sources are "the Chronicles of Samuel the seer ... the Chronicles of Nathan the prophet ... and the Chronicles of Gad the seer." Not one of these sources, which belong to the time of David, exists today, and we have only the parts selected by the later editors to present their view of David's history.

The "official" view of Israel's history writers, who lived hundreds of years after the settlement in Canaan, favored the notion of a divinely directed military conquest of the land. This view is spelled out dramatically in the Book of Joshua and, as we have noted, this is often regarded as the biblical view. Yet the biblical narrators also preserved and transmitted in the Book of Judges traditions that assume a different understanding of how the Israelites came to be settled in the land. The Judges narratives, as we have seen, assume a longer process in acquiring the land through isolated fighting, infiltration and coexistence. This Judges perspective clearly was secondary to the official view. Nevertheless, it too is a biblical view on two counts. First, this perspective apparently was held by some during biblical times, as is evidenced by its survival in the Judges narratives; and second, Judges is of course as much a part of the Bible as is Joshua.

Did Israel take the land by conquest?

If there were different perspectives during biblical times regarding the circumstances under which the Israelites came to possess the land, it is hardly surprising that 20th-century scholars hold different views on the matter. To understand current trends in the discussion, we need to review two alternate approaches to the conquest-settlement issue that were articulated during the 1930s and 1940s and tended to dominate the discussion through the early 1970s. Both of these approaches recognized that the materials in the books of Joshua and Judges were compiled and shaped long after the events reported and thus were not to be regarded as historically accurate in every detail. At the same time, both approaches presupposed that the biblical traditions preserved kernels of authentic historical memory. An important difference between the two approaches is that, while one of them focused on the conquest perspective and attempted to correlate the Joshua 1–12 account with archaeological evidence, the other regarded the notion of an early military conquest as very unrealistic historically and developed a scenario for Israel's settlement of the land more in keeping with

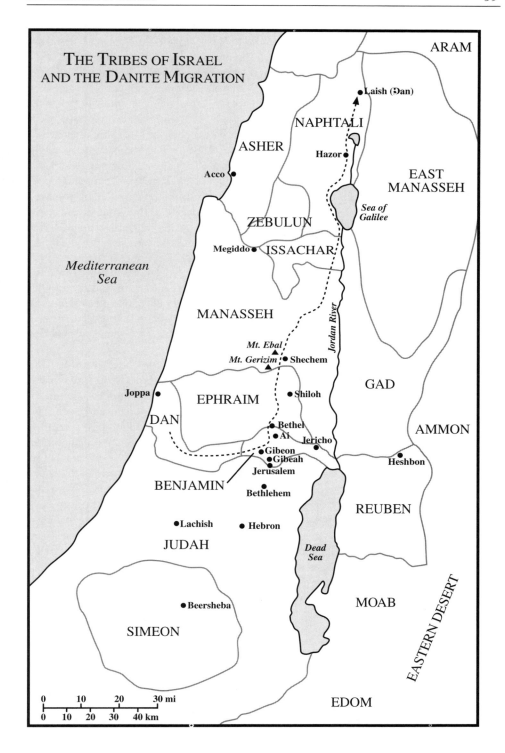

THE TRIBES OF ISRAEL
AND THE DANITE MIGRATION

ARAM

Laish (Dan)

NAPHTALI

ASHER

Hazor

EAST
MANASSEH

Acco

ZEBULUN

Sea of
Galilee

Mediterranean
Sea

Megiddo

ISSACHAR

MANASSEH

Jordan River

Mt. Ebal

Mt. Gerizim

Shechem

GAD

Joppa

EPHRAIM

Shiloh

DAN

Bethel

Ai

Jericho

AMMON

Gibeon

Gibeah

Heshbon

Jerusalem

BENJAMIN

Bethlehem

REUBEN

Lachish

Hebron

JUDAH

Dead
Sea

Beersheba

MOAB

SIMEON

EDOM

EASTERN DESERT

0   10   20   30 mi

0   10   20   30   40 km

the traditions preserved in the Book of Judges. Let us review these two approaches, beginning with the one that favored a military conquest.

This approach, articulated very successfully by William F. Albright and his students,[5] placed the Exodus from Egypt and conquest of Canaan at the end of the Late Bronze Age. The close of that age, approximately the 13th century B.C.E., was marked in Palestine by a pattern of city destructions, and Albright attributed these destructions to the invading Israelites. Two other important spokespersons for this approach were archaeologists Yigael Yadin and Abraham Malamat. "The fact is," argued Yadin as late as 1982, "that excavation results from the last 50 years or so support in a most amazing way (except in some cases ...) the basic historicity of the Biblical account."[6] Yadin noted that "the Biblical narrative in broad outline tells us that at a certain period nomadic Israelites attacked the city-state organization of the Holy Land, destroying many cities and setting them on fire. Then, slowly but surely, the Israelites replaced these cities with new, unfortified cities or settlements."[7] Yadin went on to say that this account "is exactly the picture which the archaeological finds present to us: a complete system of fortified cities collapsed and was replaced by a new culture whose material aspect can be defined as the first efforts of seminomads to settle down."[8]

Both Yadin and Malamat recognized that the actual events of the conquest and settlement were more complex than they appear in the Book of Joshua. "But at the core," Malamat contended, "a military conquest remains."[9] This is reflected in "an intimate and authentic knowledge of the land, and a knowledge of its topography ... as they relate to military strategy."[10] Examining the military strategy reflected in the Joshua account, Malamat considered how the Israelites could have managed to conquer a land with strong fortified cities. One factor that worked to the Israelites' advantage, he explained, was disunity on the part of the inhabitants of the land. The Canaanite city-states and ethnic groups "had no unified, overall military organization with which to confront the [invading Israelites]. Their [the Canaanites'] absence of political cohesion was matched by the lack of any Canaanite national consciousness."[11] As a result, no effort was made to keep the Israelites from fording the Jordan.

Canaan's city-states During the century or so before the close of the Bronze Age (when these scholars dated the conquest), the land was organized politically into small city-states. Occasionally these city-states were clustered in small alliances; often they were in conflict with each other. Joshua 1–12 reflects a similar situation.

Jericho, the first city encountered in the conquest account (Joshua 6:1–21), seems to stand alone, not allied with any other city. It is located on the western edge of the Jordan Valley, a few miles south of the Wadi Makkuk, a deep network of valleys that cuts an opening into the hill country.[12] The second city, Ai (Joshua 7:2ff.), is on the plateau of the hill country, about 10 miles in distance and 3,500 feet in elevation from Jericho. Located about 2 miles southeast of Bethel, Ai (modern et-Tell) sits on the eastern limit of cultivated land, at the edge of the wasteland that reaches down to Jericho. In the biblical account, Ai seems to be allied with Bethel; according to one tradition, the men of Bethel fought with the men of Ai in defense of Ai (Joshua 8:17). Whatever the association was, Bethel and Ai appear in later references together (cf. Nehemiah 7:32; Ezra 2:28), and Nehemiah 11:31 describes Bethel as having "its villages," which would make it the center of a small city-state.

Shechem, the third city Joshua appears in, would have been the center of a larger city-state. During this period, the ruler of Shechem extended his power as far north as Megiddo and controlled a large territory of villages that must have reached as far south as Shiloh. The biblical account does not name the villages allied with Shechem, but Joshua 12:7–24 lists among the captive kings the rulers of Tappuah, Hepher, Aphek and Tirzah, all located in the vicinity of Shechem.

Evidence of a fourth city-state alliance is found in the negotiations between Joshua and the Hivites from Gibeon (Joshua 9:3–27). (Gibeon has been identified with modern el-Jib, located about 5 miles north of Jerusalem.) The Hivites possibly were related to the Hittites or Hurrians, who originated to the north of Canaan. They settled four cities named in Joshua 9:17—Gibeon, Chephirah, Beeroth and Kiriath-jearim—and seem to have maintained a separate identity from the Amorites, who lived south of Gibeon.

Jerusalem seems to have been the head of an Amorite alliance that included the major cities of the southern hill country. Joshua 10:5 names five cities: Jerusalem, Hebron, Jarmuth, Lachish and Eglon. Hebron is the southernmost city, 17 miles from Jerusalem. Lachish guards one of the classic routes from the southwest into the hill country. Jarmuth and Eglon are in the foothill region near Lachish. The Amorites generally are associated with the "Amurru" of extrabiblical texts, a West Semitic people whose Bronze Age origins may be traced to northeastern Syria.[13]

Hazor, the last major city featured in the Joshua account of the conquest, was the head of an alliance that included Madon (possibly Merom), Shimron, Achshaph and some unnamed villages around southern Galilee and in the hills of northern Galilee (Joshua 11:1ff.). Hazor itself is on the west side of the fertile Huleh Valley and on the route that runs north-south on the western side of the Sea of Galilee. It appears to have been the leading city of a Canaanite alliance whose origins may be traced to the Phoenician coastal region.

The Israelite conquest of the land of Canaan, therefore, would have involved military penetration and then settlement of a politically fragmented land. Specifically, the Israelites would have encountered (1) an Amorite alliance of cities that included Jerusalem and other cities to the south; (2) a Hivite alliance that united four villages north and west of Jerusalem, with Bethel and Ai sitting alone on the east side of the Hivites; (3) Shechem and its allied towns and villages in the central hills, known later as Samaria; and (4) a league of Canaanite towns and villages in Galilee, headed by the king of Hazor. Jericho, not allied with any of the city-states, was alone in the Jordan Valley.

Israel's military stratagems

Both Yadin and Malamat characterized the Israelites as seminomads, "emerging from the desert fringes."[14] Facing the chariots and trained forces of Canaan's strongly fortified cities, Israel's "unmounted horde" would have been at a definite disadvantage. However, Malamat explained, this disparity was compensated by maximum use of reconnaissance, clever stratagems such as ambush and preemptive strikes, and the convenient recruitment of defectors, such as Rahab, the Canaanite harlot of Jericho who collaborated with Israel against her own people. Furthermore, considerable attention was given to "logistics," that is, to organizing support services for fighting men in the field and timing campaigns to enable the army to live off the land. For instance, before crossing the Jordan, Joshua commanded his officers to order the people to "prepare [their] provisions; for within three days [they] are to pass over this Jordan" (Joshua 1:10–11). The crossing itself occurred on "the tenth day of the first month" (Joshua 4:19), in early spring, when crops had begun to ripen in the Jordan Valley.[15]

Joshua dispatched two men to spy out Jericho (Joshua 2:1), and they went forth and found lodging at the house of Rahab, which was the nearest thing to a hotel in those times. Rahab's friendly reception enabled the spies to dodge the king of Jericho, who was trying to capture them, and to return safely to the camp at Shittim. The Israelites placed Jericho under siege, and the city gate was shut (see Joshua 2:5) so that "none went out, and none came in" (Joshua 6:1). In the biblical account, the Israelites marched around the city seven days, and on the seventh day the priests blew their trumpets, the people shouted and the wall of Jericho "fell down flat" (Joshua 6:20). A hint of more military action than this ritualistic account indicates is found in Joshua's farewell address: "And you went over the Jordan and came to Jericho," he said, "and the men of Jericho fought against you" (Joshua 24:11).

The stratagem of marching around besieged cities until the enemy inside relaxes its defenses is known from ancient military annals, as Malamat noted. In one case, Frontinus, a Roman military strategist of the first century C.E., cited a Roman general who "marched his troops

Ai. *Stone ruins in the center of the photograph mark the excavations at modern et-Tell, which has been identified with biblical Ai. The Bible attributes the destruction of this city to invading Israelite forces: "Joshua burned Ai, and made it forever a heap of ruins" (Joshua 8:28). But archaeological excavations reveal that Ai was in ruins by 2400 B.C.E., long before the Israelites arrived on the scene.*

regularly around the walls of a well-fortified city in northern Italy, each time returning them to camp; when the vigilance of the defenders waned, he stormed the walls and forced the city's capitulation."[16]

The biblical account of the conquest of Ai, located 10 miles west of Jericho on the plateau of the hill country, also displays sound military strategy, in Malamat's view. Spies sent from Jericho to assess the strength of the city returned with a report that the people "are but few" and that a large force was not needed (Joshua 7:2–3). Some local realism stands out in the spies' request: "Do not make the whole people toil up there." The route to Ai would have been along the deep, rugged Wadi Makkuk, which snakes relentlessly upward from the vicinity of Jericho, 700 feet below sea level, to the hilltop site of Ai, about 2,800 feet above sea level. Based on the spies' report, Joshua sent about 3,000 men from Jericho to Ai, and they were chased back down the valley toward Jericho with a loss of 36 men (Joshua 7:3–5).

As Malamat recognized, theology then takes over in the biblical account of the capture of Ai. The Israelite defeat is attributed to the sin of Achan, who disobeyed the command that everything in Jericho was to be destroyed in a kind of sacrifice to the Lord of Israel of the first fruits of the military campaign. When Achan, his household, his possessions and the items he had salvaged from Jericho were destroyed to eradicate the sin, Joshua prepared another expedition to Ai. Nothing is said about the spies underestimating the strength of the defenders at Ai; the defeat of the first expedition is laid to the sin of Achan. However, Joshua led 35,000 men the second time in an elaborate ambush. This second expedition succeeded: The defenders of Ai were drawn out of the city into the deep valley by a feigned retreat of Joshua and a force of 5,000 men. Meanwhile, 30,000 Israelites lying in ambush rose up and took the city. Joshua's decoy force then helped destroy the men of Ai, who were trapped between the two Israelite forces (Joshua 8:10–23).

Considering the lay of the land Malamat's analysis of the military strategy employed is not entirely convincing, however, even if one agrees with him that the Book of Joshua reflects "a basic element of Israelite consciousness ... that Canaan was 'inherited' by force."[17] In the first place, if we take seriously Malamat's acknowledgment that the present biblical account of the conquest took shape long after the Israelites already were settled in the land, the question emerges whether this "Israelite consciousness" of taking the land by force, to say nothing of the military stratagems narrated, may not also be a product of later times. Moreover, our knowledge of the lay of the land around Jericho and Ai raises further questions regarding the practicality of these stratagems.

According to Malamat, the Wadi Makkuk, leading up from Jericho to the north side of Ai, was chosen as the point of entry. However, the Wadi Makkuk is very narrow, deep and rugged in this region of Ai. It is lined with caves and small branch wadis, including the Wadi Asas, which defines the steep north side of the site of Ai. Actually, the Wadi Makkuk and the Wadi Asas are better suited to infiltration by small bands than by an army of thousands, which would be strung out in such a thin column that superior numbers would not give superiority in fighting ability. Even 3,000 men (Joshua 7:3) in the Wadi Makkuk, and especially in the Wadi Asas, would have been strung out half the distance from Jericho to Ai; 30,000 men (Joshua 8:3) would have had to find another route to the Bethel-Ai plateau.[18]

The general lay of the land in the vicinity of Ai does lend itself in part to the strategy described in Joshua 7–8. Ai is "east of Bethel" (Joshua 7:2); also the site is 3,500 feet in elevation above Jericho, or "up" from Jericho (Joshua 7:2–4); and there is a mountain "behind" Ai, between it and Bethel (Joshua 8:2,9). But again, the numbers of people involved would have been too many for managing an ambush in the terrain. These, admittedly, are the kinds of details that Yadin and Malamat would not press, but they do jeopardize the claim of a military operation that involved all Israel and that placed an army of thousands in a valley too narrow and steep for it to operate.

Actually Malamat himself had difficulties with the biblical narrative of the capture of Ai on yet another point. He noted that the stratagem described in Joshua 8:1–23 is almost identical to that of the internecine battle at Gibeah, reported in Judges 20:18–44. In the latter, the people of Israel went up against the Benjaminites at Gibeah twice and were driven back with heavy casualties (Judges 20:18–28). On the third attempt, an ambush was set "round about Gibeah" (Judges 20:29), and the Benjaminites were drawn out of the city and trapped between the main force of the people of Israel and the ambush, which rose up and cut them off from the city. Malamat notes that this similarity of stratagems "has led many commentators to believe that one of the two accounts served as the literary model for the other."[19] Malamat, yielding to the archaeological record at Ai (see below), concluded that "if indeed there was interdependence the capture of Ai (et-Tell) is more likely the copy, for the archaeological evidence there is quite negative, indicating no destruction level during the period of the Israelite conquest and settlement."[20]

The most serious difficulty with the concept of a military conquest is in fact the negative archaeological evidence. Even when Albright first proposed a connection between the Israelite conquest and the Late Bronze Age (13th century) city destructions, scholars recognized that the theory had rough edges. As additional archaeological data became available, these problems became increasingly evident.[21]

Archaeologists at Jericho

Both Jericho, whose wall it is reported "fell down flat" (Joshua 6:20), and Ai, which is said to have been burned (Joshua 8:19–21), should have identifiable traces of destruction dating to the time of the conquest. The kidney-shaped mound of ancient Jericho still has about 70 feet of occupation layers intact, dating from the earliest settlement at the site, in about 9000 B.C.E., beside a spring known today as Ain es-Sultan. During the 1930s, John Garstang discovered collapsed mudbrick walls under the ruins of houses, which he identified as evidence of the destruction by the Israelites. The walls had fallen outward, down the slope of the mound. Up to 3 feet of ashes from burned houses had accumulated on top of the mound.[22]

Garstang's conclusions were challenged, however, by Kathleen Kenyon, who excavated the site extensively from 1952 to 1958.[23] Using improved techniques for controlling the removal of layers of ancient remains, she reconstructed the actual phases of occupation from the first crude shrine, built on bedrock, to the last fragmentary corner of a small 14th-century B.C.E. hut on top of the mound. The prehistoric phases (from 9000 to 3200 B.C.E.) were dated by radiocarbon

(carbon 14) analyses of wood, grain and other organic remains, while the phases after 3200 B.C.E. were placed in their chronological context by comparative studies of finds as well as by radiocarbon dating.[24]

Kenyon concluded that Garstang's collapsed mudbrick wall, which he dated to about 1400 B.C.E., actually dated to about 2300 B.C.E., a thousand years before the close of the Late Bronze Age. In fact, Kenyon found evidence of many collapses of mudbrick walls at Jericho between 3200 and 2300 B.C.E., which she attributed mostly to frequent earthquakes in the area. Jericho sits on top of the fault line along the west side of the Jordan Valley. Formed in geological ages past by parallel faults on each side of the valley, this fault line allowed the entire valley to settle down almost 3,000 feet below the level of the plateaus on either side.

Kenyon also found a city wall from the Middle Bronze Age (about 1560 B.C.E.) built on top of the Early Bronze Age walls dating to the third millennium. The city that was enclosed by this Middle Bronze wall had been burned. The part of this city on the top of the mound (including fortifications) had eroded away—so it was impossible to reconstruct the city's history after 1560 B.C.E.

Does this mean that a walled city from Joshua's time existed on top of the present ruin, and that its remains have eroded away over the past 3,000 years? That is not very likely. If a city had existed between 1400 and 1200 B.C.E., then surely some pottery sherds or other artifacts would be found on the slopes of the mound, washed by rain or blown by wind off the summit. Yet the only evidence of any occupation from the closing centuries of the Late Bronze Age is the remnant of one corner of a small mudbrick house, built on top of the ruins of the city destroyed in about 1560 B.C.E. A juglet found on the packed earth floor of the 3-foot-square remnant can be dated to about 1325 B.C.E.[25] The location of the hut on the mound's eastern slope suggests that squatters lived on top of the ruins of the ancient city.

Another possibility, favored by Yigael Yadin, is that the Late Bronze Age settlement at Jericho reused the earlier (Middle Bronze Age) fortifications, and that it is these walls that appear in Joshua 6. This is not very likely either. The houses destroyed in about 1560 B.C.E. were not reoccupied, and no artifacts from the period after this destruction were found, except the remnant of the squatter's hut. And since the squatter's hut was located on an eroded slope unfortified even by the 1560 B.C.E. city walls, Yadin's view that the Late Bronze Age inhabitants reused the earlier fortifications lacks support. Thus, we are confronted with negative archaeological evidence of a walled city at Jericho, despite the highly descriptive account of a conquest of the city in the biblical tradition.

At Ai (modern et-Tell) John Garstang excavated eight trenches in 1928. In 1931 he wrote that "a considerable proportion" of Late Bronze Age I (ending about 1400 B.C.E.) wares were found, including "a Cypriote wishbone handle," and that they were left "in the collection of the American School (now the Albright Institute)."[26] This pottery apparently has been lost, and nothing in the one box of material from Garstang's excavation, now in possession of the Israel Antiquities Authority, comes from the Late Bronze Age. Thus none of Garstang's "Late Bronze" evidence is available for a "second opinion" of his interpretation.

Judith Marquet-Krause led three seasons of excavation at Ai from 1933 to 1935 and was preparing for a fourth season when she died in the summer of 1936, at the age of 29. Although she was apprenticed to Garstang at Jericho for her first field experience in 1932, she later concluded that the city at Ai was destroyed and abandoned at the end of the Early Bronze Age, about 2400 B.C.E., and not resettled until about 1200 B.C.E. At that point, an unfortified village of about three acres was built on the acropolis of the earlier city. Accordingly, Marquet-Krause concluded that the site lay unoccupied from about 2400 B.C.E. until about 1200 B.C.E.[27]

Nine seasons of excavations at Ai led by Joseph Callaway, from 1964 to 1976, confirmed the results of Marquet-Krause's excavations.[28] There was no walled city at Ai after about 2400 B.C.E., and the only evidence of occupation afterward was a small unfortified village built over the earlier ruins on the acropolis. This village was constructed in about 1200 B.C.E. and was abandoned in about 1050 B.C.E.—prior to the emergence of the Israelite monarchy under David in about 1000 B.C.E.

Malamat discussed at length the stratagem of surprise used by the Israelites at Gibeon (Joshua 10:1–14). "So Joshua came upon them [the Amorites] suddenly, having marched all night from Gilgal [to Gibeon]. And the Lord threw them into a panic before Israel, who slew them with a great slaughter at Gibeon and chased them by the way of the ascent of Beth Horon" (Joshua 10:9–10). "Taking advantage of the hours of darkness," Malamat writes, "the Israelites made a lightning march from Gilgal to Gibeon (el-Jib)—a distance of about 20 miles, involving a climb of over 3,000 feet. The attack upon the astonished enemy apparently took place at dawn."[29] This seems to be corroborated by the quotation from the now-lost Book of Jashar about the sun standing still (Joshua 10:12–13). Actually, Joshua commanded the sun to "be silent," or not shine, according to Malamat, so that the darkness of the early morning would be extended while Israel followed up the surprise attack in hot pursuit of the fleeing enemy. Malamat observes that "utilization of the veil of darkness in achieving surprise was ingrained in Israelite tactical planning, from the days of the Conquest to the beginning of the Monarchy."[30]

Problems with Ai and Gibeon

Yet the problem again is that we do not have a Gibeonite city during the time that Albright, Malamat and Yadin would place the event. Excavations at Gibeon by James B. Pritchard in the 1960s produced a small amount of Late Bronze materials in some reused tombs, but no evidence of a city dating to that period.[31] An extensive surface survey of Khirbet Kefire, probably biblical Chephirah of Joshua 9:17 (one of the Hivite cities allied with Gibeon), provided no evidence of a 13th-century B.C.E. city there either.[32]

Other "conquered" cities

The trend set at Jericho, Ai and Gibeon continued with excavations at Arad, Heshbon, Hormah (that is, the sites that are considered candidates for Hormah) and Jarmuth. One after another, they "have taken their place alongside Jericho, Ai, and Gibeon as cities which the Bible associates with the period of the conquest but which offer little or no evidence of having been occupied during the thirteenth century."[33] The archaeological evidence for some of the other "conquered" cities is more ambiguous, partially because of uncertainty over the location of the ancient sites.

Following the defeat of the Amorite alliance and the execution of its kings at Makkedah (Joshua 10:16–27), Joshua is reported to have led a mop-up operation against the cities of the executed kings: Makkedah, Libnah, Lachish, Eglon, Hebron and Debir. J. Alberto Soggin has observed that Joshua's itinerary is a traditional one; it was followed by the Assyrian king Sennacherib in 701 B.C.E. (2 Kings 18:13) and by the Babylonian leader Nebuchadnezzar in 587 B.C.E. (Jeremiah 34:7).[34] Thus this segment of the conquest account may also be a retrojection from a later time.

Albright identified Debir with the ruins of present-day Tell Beit Mirsim, which he excavated between 1926 and 1932. Finding that Tell Beit Mirsim had been destroyed during the 13th century, he attributed the destruction to the Israelites.[35] However, Albright's identification of Tell Beit Mirsim is no longer generally accepted. Debir is more likely to be identified with Khirbet Rabud, the largest Bronze Age site in the region south of Hebron, and one that was occupied in the Late Bronze Age.[36]

Lachish[37] was excavated extensively from 1932 to 1938 under the direction of John Leslie Starkey, with the conclusion that the city met with a massive destruction in about 1230 B.C.E. More recent excavations, conducted by David Ussishkin from 1973 to 1987, have advanced the date of this destruction by at least a hundred years. It appears that Lachish was an unwalled city during the Late Bronze Age, and that this city was destroyed at least as late as the reign of Pharaoh Ramesses III in the mid-12th century and possibly later.[38] Finally, we have a city destruction that could be attributed to the Israelites; but it is at least a century late for the Israelite "conquest of Canaan" as dated by Albright, Yadin and others who championed this notion. Moreover, as some have observed, the conquerors did not leave calling cards. Other predators known to have been active in the region may have been responsible for the destruction of Lachish, including Ramesses III himself. Also, the Sea Peoples, among whom the Peleset, or Philistines, are numbered, were active along the coastal region at about this time.[39]

Whereas Ussishkin's work calls for advancing the destruction of Lachish into the 12th century, contemporary archaeologists are inclined to date the destruction of Late Bronze Age Hazor even earlier in the 13th century than did Yadin. According to Yadin, who extensively excavated this 200-acre site, Hazor was a major Late Bronze Age city that was destroyed no later than 1230 B.C.E. After an indefinite period, a poor settlement of about 15 to 20 acres, characterized by pits but no substantial walls, was established on the upper citadel area.[40] Contemporary archaeologists tend to date the destruction of the Late Bronze Age city slightly earlier, perhaps around 1250 B.C.E.[41] New excavations conducted at Hazor under the direction of Amnon Ben-Tor may clarify this matter further.[42] In the meantime, it would appear that Lachish and Hazor, the only two "conquest cities" that actually show evidence of having been destroyed near the end of the Late Bronze Age, are not in sync with each other.

Hazor

The case of Hazor raises even further questions, moreover, because we have two biblical accounts that report early Israelite encounters with Jabin, the king of the city; one appears in Joshua 11:1–5 and the other in Judges 4:1–5:31. According to the Book of Joshua, Jabin was the head of an alliance of Canaanite kings. He seems to have been threatened by the successes of Joshua in the south; in response he pulled together an army of chariots from the member cities of the alliance. Represented were the northern lowland cities of Hazor, Madon, Shimron and Achshaph (Joshua 11:1). But the account loses credibility when the narrator introduces contingents from all the foes Israel encountered in Canaan, from the Jebusites in the south to the Hivites at the foot of Mt. Hermon. The great host of troops, "in number like the sand ... upon the seashore" (Joshua 11:4), apparently was introduced to extol the greatness of the Lord in giving the victory to Joshua and the Israelites.

Details of the resulting battle "by the waters of Merom" (Joshua 11:7) are unclear. There is a memory of the tactic of hamstringing the enemy's chariot horses, that is, hacking the tendons of the hind legs (Joshua 11:6), and of burning the chariots with fire. This kind of strategy requires, first, that the Israelite foot soldiers outrun the chariot horses and, second, that they immobilize the dangerous archers in the chariots. We are not told how this was accomplished, but presumably the sudden surprise attack (Joshua 11:7) panicked the charioteers, and the horses were disabled in the resulting confusion.

This victory was followed, according to Joshua 11:8, with the extermination of the entire population from Sidon (in the extreme northwest) to Mizpeh (in the extreme northeast). Israel put to the sword all that breathed, until the cities were "utterly destroyed." Hazor was burned with fire (Joshua 11:11).

The Judges story, on the other hand, reports how Deborah encouraged Barak to lead Israel against Jabin, king of Hazor, and concludes with a poetic song celebrating the victory. Some scholars believe only one military episode involving a single Jabin has been described in the Bible three times: first in connection with Joshua (Joshua 11:1–15), and then twice in Judges (the prose account in Judges 4:1–23 and the poetic rendition in Judges 5:1–31). All three passages include details that seem to describe the same war, and the war constructed from the details of the three traditions is in character with the other wars of the Israelites. If the three traditions are connected with the same war of liberation, however, the war in question may have been fought, not for the initial conquest of the land, but during the time of the Judges.

Yigael Yadin, acknowledging the problem of the three traditions, nevertheless attributed the destruction of the 200-acre Late Bronze city of Hazor to Joshua as described in Joshua 11:11–13. His solution was that Judges 4, the prose description of the battle of Deborah and her general Barak against "Jabin king of Hazor," was "a late editorial gloss ... added to a basically authentic historic text." "If Hazor had already been destroyed in Joshua 11," he asked, "how could Deborah and Barak be fighting against its king in Judges 4?" He added, "My own solution is that the reference to 'Jabin king of Hazor' in Judges 4 is an editorial gloss by a later editor." He acknowledged, however, that "we should not be dogmatic [about the details of the biblical account] ... We can pick and choose based upon the evidence in each case," he noted, but "it is not necessary either to accept each detail of the Biblical account, on the one hand, or to reject the basic historicity of the conquest, on the other." On this basis, he concluded that "archaeology broadly confirms that at the end of the Late Bronze Age [13th century B.C.E.], semi-nomadic Israelites destroyed a number of major Canaanite cities; then, gradually and slowly, they built their own sedentary settlements on the ruins, and occupied the remainder of the country."[43]

Was there a military conquest? Does archaeology even broadly confirm a military conquest of Canaan that is anything like the one described in Joshua 1–12? By 1982, when Yadin published the comment quoted above, a dwindling number of scholars and archaeologists was prepared to argue that it did. That trend has continued, so that today only a small circle of scholars would attempt to make an archaeological case for a military conquest of the sort described in Joshua; and they usually do it by redating the supposed conquest on the one hand and revising the archaeological chronology on the other. The two most articulate spokespersons for this approach are John Bimson and Bryant Wood.[44] Their solution is to lower the date of the Middle Bronze Age to the late 15th century B.C.E. and to place the Israelite conquest of Canaan at that point rather than at the end of the Late Bronze Age. This resolves the problem of Jericho, but not of Ai; so they argue that archaeologists have misidentified the site of Ai. The real Ai, in other words, is not et-Tell but remains to be discovered. The biblical traditions clearly place Ai east of Bethel (which is normally identified with Beitin). So this means Bethel has been misidentified as well. Not surprisingly, their proposals have been dismissed by mainstream biblical scholars and archaeologists alike.

Perhaps the most lasting impact of Albright's argument for a 13th-century military conquest is the current consensus that, however the Israelites came to possess the land, the process probably occurred near the close of the Late Bronze Age. The whole of the Middle East seems to have experienced social and political upheaval in approximately 1200 B.C.E. This was followed, during the opening centuries of the Iron Age, by what amounts to a "dark age"—dark both in the sense that the ancient world underwent sociopolitical fragmentation and decline, and in that surviving written sources are scarce. The first reference to Israel in any written source outside of the Bible—the so-called Israel Stele from the reign of Pharaoh Merneptah—dates from the very end of the Late Bronze Age, to about 1207 B.C.E. The stories in the Book of Judges reflect circumstances that fit well with what one would expect to have been the situation in Palestine during the early Iron Age.

More about this later. First, we need to look at another view of how the Israelites came to settle in Canaan, a perspective that likewise has been seriously challenged in recent years yet has also left a strong legacy in contemporary thinking about Israel's origins.

In 1925, Albrecht Alt published (in German) "The Settlement of the Israelites in Palestine," which set forth his view of the seminomadic Israelites' infiltration of the central highlands of Canaan.[45] Working primarily with Egyptian sources from the Late Bronze Age, Alt concluded that the central highlands were only sparsely settled at the time. At the end of the Amarna period, around 1350 B.C.E., Shechem was the only significant city-state in the hill country between Jerusalem and the Jezreel Valley.[46] A century later, when the power of the XIXth Dynasty pharaohs collapsed, the hill country still seems to have been relatively free of occupation.[47] This is the region where biblical traditions locate the initial settlements of the Israelites.

An alternative perspective: peaceful infiltration

Alt's view of how the Israelites acquired this thinly populated region is trenchant: Since little resistance would have been encountered in the wide gaps in the city-state system, a gradual settlement resulted from seminomads following their flocks year after year from east of the Jordan River into the hills west of the river. Eventually these seminomads began to build villages and become sedentary. Thus, the settlement occurred relatively peacefully, rather than by military conquest as indicated in Joshua 1–12.

Alt's pupil, Martin Noth, developed this "gradual settlement" approach further, spelling out a more detailed scenario. Noth contended that tribes developed over time as the various seminomadic elements settled down in different parts of the hill country. Eventually, some of these tribes formed an alliance; and the alliance was expanded in stages until there were 12 tribes. In this way, 12-tribe Israel came into existence. By closely analyzing the tribal lists in the Pentateuch, Noth attempted to trace the stages by which the tribal confederacy expanded to 12. He was guided also by what he believed to be similar alliances in the Greek world (known there as *amphictyonies*).

According to the Alt-Noth model, therefore, "Israel" was a tribal confederacy, with Yahweh as the God of the confederacy and the Ark of the Covenant its central (mobile) shrine. The people who composed the 12 tribes, or at least their ancestors, had entered the land from beyond the Jordan River. But Israel itself, the tribal confederacy, came into existence only after the people were in Canaan.[48] Manfred Weippert, Noth's pupil, summarized the Alt-Noth view as follows:

> This tribal confederacy did not exist at the time when those who later became the Israelites entered Palestine ... One must suppose, rather, that it was a question of individual clans or confederacies of clans of nomads with small cattle (sheep and goats) who, during the winter rainy season and the spring, lived with their herds in the border territory between the desert and the cultivated land and who were forced, when the vegetation in that area ceased in the summer, to penetrate further into the cultivated land and to come to an understanding with the owners of the land about summer pasturage in the harvested fields and in the woods.[49]

Weippert continues:

> The clans who entered the country in this way in the course of regular change of pasture then gradually settled in the relatively thinly populated wooded areas of the uplands, areas which were not directly exposed to the reach either of the Canaanite city-states or of Egyptian sovereignty, and began to practice agriculture once they had turned these wooded areas into arable land. This peaceful process of transition on the part of nomads to a sedentary

> life was, according to Alt, the real process of settlement and it was, in the nature of things, a peaceful development, since the interests of any landowners there might be would not be harmed by it."[50]

Military encounters, Alt and his students believed, occurred in a second stage of Israelite settlement, which Alt characterized as "territorial expansion." However, this was late in the period of the Judges and the early monarchy, when Israel expanded into the plains and valleys that had long been occupied by groups of Canaanites. Also it was a long process during which the Israelites won some fortified cities but also lost some battles. Presumably, the memory of these wars would account for what Abraham Malamat characterizes as "a basic element of Israelite consciousness ... that Canaan was 'inherited' by force."[51] In any case, the military confrontations came at the end of the 11th century B.C.E., when the tribes were beginning to coalesce into a monarchy, instead of at the end of the 13th century B.C.E., when they first entered into Canaan.[52]

Alt's view, which fits better with the Book of Judges than the Book of Joshua, sparked more than a half-century of controversy with Albright, his pupils, and other scholars, such as Yadin and Malamat, who favored the military conquest approach. Some parts of Alt's arguments were very persuasive, however, and still are. As we shall see below, for example, the gradual settlement approach seems in keeping with the available archaeological evidence. During the first two centuries of the Iron Age (beginning in about 1200 B.C.E.), some two or three hundred small settlements were planted in the more or less empty hill country of central Palestine.

The major weakness in the Alt-Noth position was its dependence on the sociological theories of Max Weber, who drew a sharp distinction between the lifestyles of villagers and those of nomads. Alt characterized the earliest Israelites as nomads who, like modern Bedouin, followed their flocks seasonally into the highlands after harvest and exploited any weakness they found in the control of the territory. Lacking specific evidence, Alt and his students worked from analogy based on the sedentarization of Bedouin in this century and conjectured that the same process occurred in the Israelite settlement. More recent sociological theory recognizes, however, that agriculture and seminomadism probably were not such sharply divided lifestyles during ancient times. As we shall see below, it may well be, in fact, that the early Iron Age settlers of the central hill country were primarily farmers and only secondarily herdsmen.

Concluding that the early Iron Age settlers were primarily farmers would not necessarily preclude a gradual settlement process rather than military conquest. But another interesting hypothesis that commanded serious attention for a time does in fact presuppose settlement under less than peaceful circumstances.

Peasants'   The hypothesis, namely, was that Israel emerged not as a result of out-
revolt   siders entering into the central Palestinian hill country from the
Transjordan, but as the outcome of an internal peasants' revolt against
Canaanite overlords. Advocated by George E. Mendenhall and developed by Norman K. Gottwald,[53] this view rejected the characterization
of the Israelites as either military conquerors or as seminomadic herdsmen who infiltrated the highlands in search of pasturage.[54] Instead,
Israel emerged from the melting pot of Canaanite culture in a revolutionary social movement among the peoples already in Canaan. For
Mendenhall, it was a peasants' revolt against Canaanite overlords in
the cities, an internal uprising pitting the villages against the cities,
"ignited by Hebrews who advocated commitment to, and covenant
solidarity with, Yahweh, the liberating God of the Exodus."[55] This revolution began in Transjordan "where Yahweh-worshiping fugitives
from Egypt joined with discontented elements of the population to
overthrow the Amorite kingdoms of Sihon and Og, ... and spread across
the Jordan to the west bank, where the rural population, restive under
the Canaanite city-state system, 'rejected the old political ideologies in
favor of the covenant community of Yahweh.'"[56]

     The model for this view was based on Mendenhall's interpretation of
Habiru activities in the same region a century earlier, during the
Amarna age. The Habiru rebelled against the city-states of Canaan then
ruled by vassal princes appointed by Egypt. According to Mendenhall,
they sought to overthrow Egyptian rule in what was essentially a political struggle between oppressed villagers and Canaanite rulers. There is
no mention of a religious dimension to the struggle in the famous
14th-century B.C.E. Amarna letters, which document this rebellion.

     Gottwald, like Mendenhall, saw early Israel as an alliance of sup-
pressed and disenfranchised elements of Canaanite society, "including
peasants, farmers, pastoralists, outlaws, mercenaries, and adven-
turers."[57] Gottwald's model, however, is the historical cultural materialism of Karl Marx, which gives priority to materialism over religion.[58]
Mendenhall proposed that the social revolution sparked by the
Hebrews was to some extent "created by the new Yahwistic religion";
Gottwald, on the other hand, contended that Yahwism was created to
support the social ideals of early Israel and "arose as a function of the
revolution."[59] For this reason, Mendenhall vehemently denied that he
was the "father" of Gottwald's theory.[60] In both views, however, the so-
called conquest of Canaan is seen as a revolution effected by populations that, with perhaps a few exceptions, were already there. There
was no unified military campaign conducted by outside forces, and
there was no mass killing of the inhabitants of the land.

     The social revolution hypothesis is attractive because it has some
parallels with movements in this century. However, both versions of
the hypothesis lack tangible supporting evidence. The Hebrew Bible

knows nothing of a peasants' revolt, for example, and it would be difficult to corroborate such an event with archaeology. Thus the hypothesis is heavily dependent on social theories, which themselves may be more up-to-date than the theories upon which Alt and Noth depended but still are highly speculative.

We have seen above how mainstream archaeologists have, over the past two or three decades, gradually given up on attempts to match up the stratigraphy of the major tells in Palestine—particularly those representing the "conquest cities"—with the Joshua account of the Israelite conquest of Canaan. Actually this has not been entirely a matter of failed effort but also of significant changes that have occurred over these same decades in the field of archaeology. Archaeologists have begun to concentrate less exclusively on the major tells, for example, while doing more open-country survey work. This reveals the settlement patterns and lifestyles of the smaller villages and hamlets that once surrounded the cities. Also archaeologists are now less focused on historical questions (such as the historicity of the Israelite conquest) and more interested in anthropological and sociological questions: How did people live—in terms of sociological structures as well as in terms of sustenance?

New archaeological evidence

Extensive archaeological surveys of the central hill country reveal that this area was sparsely settled during the Late Bronze Age.[61] There were some towns in the hill country during this period, and perhaps two or three (Shechem, Jerusalem, Hebron) were large enough to be considered small cities. But these were spaced rather far apart, and there seem to have been few settlements in between. During the first centuries of the Iron Age, numerous small villages began to emerge in the hill country. These were very small settlements whose inhabitants engaged in agriculture; by the end of Iron I (in about 1000 B.C.E.), some two or three hundred of these small settlements had cropped up. While the picture is not yet fully in focus, it is clear that all of the hill country was not settled simultaneously. Settlement of the southern hill country, the tribal area of Judah south of Jerusalem, for example, seems to have lagged behind that of the Ephraimite area north of Jerusalem.

Naturally, we wish to know where these early Iron Age hill-country villagers came from and why they settled here. Unfortunately, this is not yet clear either. Lawrence Stager of Harvard University has observed that the villagers were primarily farmers and secondarily herders of sheep and goats who brought with them fixed cultural patterns of village life.[62] The implication of this is that the settlers expanded into the hill country from the lowland regions of Palestine, where there was a long-standing agricultural tradition. In Stager's view, followed by Joseph Callaway[63] and more recently by William Dever,[64] two new subsistence technologies—rock-hewn cisterns and hillside terraces—would have enabled them to establish villages in marginal and even inhospitable areas of the semi-arid hill country where villages had not been located before. Houses on hilltop sites in the Bethel-Ai region had their own bell-shaped cisterns hewn out of solid rock with metal chisels to provide water for the home. Tell en-Nasbeh, southwest of Bethel, has been characterized as "truly a place of cisterns" because 53 were excavated there.[65] Likewise, agricultural terraces for the cultivation of wheat, barley and vegetables were constructed on the contours of steep hillsides never before planted with crops. For instance, the Iron Age I village houses at Ai (et-Tell) were founded on terraces that provided a relatively level foundation on the steep east slope of the acropolis area; one terrace system discovered in the cultivated area just below the village extended more than 325 feet.[66]

Israel Finkelstein, who surveyed in the Ephraimite area and also excavated two important Iron Age sites in that area ('Izbet Sartah and Shiloh), claims, however, that the new settlers were in the hill country all along, but previously followed a nomadic lifestyle. The appearance of villages does not signal the arrival of a new population group from Transjordan or the Palestinian lowlands, therefore, but rather a change in lifestyle.[67] Neither terraces nor cisterns were new technologies, he observes. Instead, the resettlement of the hill country during Iron I should be seen as part of a cyclic process of "alternative demographic expansion and decay." The cyclic process can be observed unfolding over two millennia and involved "three waves of settlement (in the Early Bronze I, Middle Bronze IIB-C and Iron I), with two periods of severe settlement crisis between them (Intermediate Bronze Age and Late Bronze Age)."[68]

A third position has been advanced by Adam Zertal, who argues that the settlers must have come from the direction of the Transjordan because, in his view, the settlements fan out from the northeast toward the southwest.[69] Yohanan Aharoni gave a similar interpretation to the earliest Iron Age settlements in the vicinity of Beersheba and Tel Masos. Aharoni concluded that settlements were established in the Beersheba region at the very beginning of the Iron Age and then, over the next 200 years, spread northward into the hill country and southward across the southern Negev. This penetration and settlement of the region from the south "occurred mainly in unoccupied or sparsely settled areas," Aharoni noted, "a picture that corresponds to the description in the Book of Judges, contrasting to the picture of unified conquest reflected in the Book of Joshua."[70]

Archaeological evidence thus indicates a complex process of settlement during the opening centuries of the Iron Age, a process that may have involved to some degree all of the explanations summarized above.

Throughout the eastern Mediterranean area, this was a time of political upheaval caused by the demise of Egyptian authority; the fragmentation of the Hittite Empire in north Syria and Asia Minor into small warring city-states; and the Dorian invasion of the Greek mainland, which caused uprooted Sea Peoples from the Aegean area to migrate eastward to the Syrian coast, southeastward to the Palestinian coastal area, and across the sea to North Africa and Egypt. The Sea Peoples in turn pushed the less militant "Canaanites" inland toward the mountains of Lebanon and the central hill country of Palestine, where they found "a refuge and redoubt" in inaccessible hilltop villages such as Khirbet Raddana and Ai (et-Tell) north of Jerusalem. Hittites and Hivites also settled in the region of Gibeon, possibly in Jerusalem (where they may have been known as the Jebusites) and north to the slopes of Mt. Hermon. People of Aramean background moved southward into northern Transjordan and perhaps also into the hills of Canaan. And on we could go. When one adds to this mix whatever number of Hebrew refugees from slavery in Egypt may have been involved in an Exodus (or more than one), we have a "melting pot composed of diverse elements living under various 'ad hoc' political and religious circumstances"[71] out of which biblical Israel emerged.

A time of upheaval

Any discussion of how Israel came to be settled in the Land of Canaan must take into account the Merneptah Stele. This intriguing Egyptian monument dating to about 1207 B.C.E. mentions Israel, spelling it in hieroglyphic signs. Known as the Merneptah Stele after the pharaoh whose reign it commemorates, the inscribed stone provides us with the earliest extant reference to Israel. For that reason, it is also known as the Israel Stele. Merneptah's victory ode proclaims in part,

The Merneptah Stele

> The princes are prostrate, saying "Peace!"
> Not one is raising his head among the Nine Bows.
> Now that Tehenu [Lybia] has come to ruin, Hatti is pacified;
> The Canaan has been plundered into every sort of woe:
> Ashkelon has been overcome;
> Gezer has been captured;
> Yano'am is made nonexistent.
> Israel is laid waste and his seed is not;
> Hurru is become a widow because of Egypt.[72]

Unpronounced hieroglyphic signs called determinatives are sometimes attached to a word to indicate the category of the word. Thus, in this inscription the determinative for a city-state is attached to the words for Ashkelon, Gezer and Yano'am. The determinative for a foreign land is attached to Canaan. By contrast, the determinative for a foreign people is attached to the hieroglyphic signs for Israel.

Much ink has been spilled interpreting the Merneptah Stele. Was this the Israel of the Exodus and conquest? If so, was Israel already

The Merneptah Stele.
After defeating a coalition of Libyan tribesmen and Sea Peoples, in about 1207 B.C.E. Pharaoh Merneptah commissioned a victory ode to be carved on this 7.5-foot high, black granite stele from Thebes. At top, the stele depicts Merneptah receiving a scimitar from Amun, the god of Thebes.

The hieroglyphic text recounts the pharaoh's earlier campaign in Canaan. In the earliest known reference to Israel, the inscription states, in the second line from the bottom (closeup, below), that "Israel is laid waste and his seed is not." This suggests that a people called Israel had emerged in Canaan by the end of the 13th century B.C.E. But scholars today are divided about whether the "Israel" in the inscription refers to the people of the Exodus or to a group whose roots were in Canaan long before the time of Merneptah.

established in Canaan, so that Merneptah could—albeit with obvious exaggeration—claim that he had "laid [him] waste and his seed [was] not"? Many have argued this. If it is true, the Exodus and conquest must have occurred before 1207 B.C.E.

Another, more recent view that has been garnering support is that the "Israel" referred to in the Merneptah Stele is not the Israel of the Exodus, but instead Israel whose roots were in Canaan long before the time of the Merneptah Stele. Lawrence Stager focused on the last two lines of the victory ode, the meaning of which, he claimed, can be understood in terms of its parallel poetic construction:

> Israel is laid waste and his seed is not;
> Hurru is become a widow because of Egypt.[73]

"Hurru and Israel form a distinct complementary pair in the ode," says Stager, "viz. husband (Israel) and wife/widow (Hurru)."[74] Since the term "Hurru" usually referred to the region of Syria-Palestine, or to a lesser area within the region, the parallel construction with Israel indicates an entity larger than the city-states of Ashkelon, Gezer and Yano'am, also named on the stele. Hurru is spelled with the determinative for land. Israel, however, is spelled with the determinative for a people rather than a land or a state. Thus Israel apparently was a population group in Hurru (Syria-Palestine or some part of it) capable of fielding a sizable fighting force against pharaoh's chariots.[75]

Gösta Ahlström reached a similar conclusion based on a different interpretation of the inscription's literary structure. The inscription pairs Hatti with Hurru and Israel with Canaan, Ahlström contended. Hatti and Hurru both refer to the whole area of Syria-Palestine, while Canaan and Israel were the two main subdivisions of Palestine. "Remembering that in its extended meaning Canaan referred to the cultural and urban areas of the country, the name Israel logically refers to the remaining sparsely populated hill country area where few cities were located."[76] Too much has been made of the determinative, Ahlström explained. "Egyptologists attach little significance to the choice of determinative here, recognizing that determinatives were generally used rather loosely by scribes, especially when a people was called by the name of the territory they inhabited."[77]

Merneptah's inscription verifies the presence of a people known as Israel on the scene in Palestine at the very end of the Late Bronze Age. And whether or not the inscription places them specifically in the central hill country as Ahlström contended, the biblical traditions clearly understand the core of Israelite settlement to have been in that area during premonarchical times. Moreover, there is undisputed archaeological evidence that new settlements emerged in the central hill country at the beginning of the Iron Age, and there is a clear continuity of material culture from these early Iron Age settlements to the later centuries of the Iron Age, when the central hill country was the center of an Israelite monarchy. So is this not

Who were the Israelites?

enough evidence to conclude that the early Iron Age hill country settlements were Israelite settlements?

In a general sense, one can draw this conclusion. As an analogy, consider how all of those who immigrated from various parts of the world
to what later became the United States, along with the native
Americans who were already here, may be lumped together as early
Americans. Thus Finkelstein titled the English edition of his masterful
study of the early Iron Age settlements *The Archaeology of the Israelite
Settlement* and explained,

> The formation of the Israelite identity was a long, intricate,
> and complex process which, in our opinion, was completed only
> at the beginning of the Monarchy ...
>
> Accordingly, an Israelite during the Iron I period was anyone
> whose descendants—as early as the days of Shiloh (first half of
> the 11th century BCE) or as late as the beginning of the
> Monarchy—described themselves as Israelites. These were, by
> and large, the people who resided in the territorial framework of
> the early Israelite Monarchy, before its expansion began ... Thus
> even a person who may have considered himself a Hivite,
> Gibeonite, Kennizzite, etc., in the early 12th century, but whose
> descendants in the same village a few generations later thought of
> themselves as Israelites will, in like manner, also be considered
> here as an Israelite.[78]

Although Finkelstein's definition may be about as good as we can
come up with at the moment, it is not totally satisfying because the biblical narratives conspicuously distinguish between the Israelites and the
other peoples who were settled in the hill country during premonarchical times. The narrator of Judges 19–21 (see especially 19:10–15)
clearly presupposed a distinction between Israelite and non-Israelite
villages, for example. Finkelstein's definition itself recognizes that "the
formation of the Israelite identity" involved a "long, intricate, and complex process." What sort of designation was "Israelite" at the earliest
stages of this process? Was it primarily a kinship designation, pertaining to clan and tribal affiliations? Or was it primarily a geographical
designation as Ahlström contended? Perhaps it was more of a religious
designation as Mendenhall proposed—an Israelite was a worshiper of
Yahweh. Finkelstein sees the monarchy as the "cut off" time for deter-
mining who was and was not an Israelite. Yet a close reading of the biblical account of David's reign suggests that even then distinctions were
made between the Israelites and other constituents of his realm, including the Judahites (2 Samuel 19:8–13).

This question has been addressed by Baruch Halpern in an important study, *The Emergence of Israel in Canaan*,[79] and also by J. Maxwell
Miller in *A History of Ancient Israel and Judah* (cowritten with John H.
Hayes).[80] Both Halpern and Miller are confident that historical
memory is embedded in the biblical narratives and lists, in Joshua as

well as in Judges, although very deeply embedded indeed; and both conclude that premonarchical Israel, regardless of where the name came from, was a group of tribes (using the term rather loosely) that, having lived in close proximity to each other over time, came to regard themselves as ethnically related. These Israelite tribes exchanged sons and daughters in marriage, shared cultic practices and occasionally came to each other's defense. Therefore, both Halpern and Miller regard Israel as an entity that emerged from the pluralistic population of the land, although Halpern places more emphasis on the concept of a core group entering Palestine from the Transjordan than does Miller, and Halpern envisions a full 12-tribe Israelite confederacy in place before the rise of the monarchy whereas Miller does not.

Halpern rejects the traditional notion of a comprehensive military conquest, but suspects that there was some sort of invasion from the east. Also he rejects the idea of a peasants' revolt but suspects that disenchantment with social conditions led many indigenous Canaanites to attach themselves to the newly arrived Israelites. Working with the various tribal lists in the Hebrew Bible, Halpern concludes that a ten-tribe confederation had emerged by the time of Deborah and is presupposed by the Song of Deborah (Judges 5). This expanded to a 12-tribe confederation by the eve of the monarchy. Halpern writes:

> At any rate, in the present state of research, it seems safest to postulate that some Israelite Hebrew group did enter Canaan by way of the Aijalon Pass. Entrenching itself particularly in the central hills, this group attracted both by coincident interest and by the nature of the terrain and agricultural climate some proportion of the Canaanite population, which had a history of sporadic petty revolt against Egypt. What proportion of the population was thus assimilated, and what proportion of Israel consisted of Canaanites, one simply cannot say. However, over the course of the 13th and 12th centuries, an ethnic consciousness and solidarity dawned on this Israel. No later than the late 12th century, the time of the song of Deborah (Judges 5:13–18), a full-blown confederacy of tribes existed.[81]

Miller, less confident of the antiquity of the Song of Deborah and the tribal lists, prefers to search the biblical narratives and geographical lists for clues as to which tribal groups seem central to Israelite affairs. He notes that the Book of Judges tends to focus on the tribe of Ephraim and three neighboring groups—the Benjaminites, the Manassites and the Gileadites—all three of which appear to have been dominated by or closely aligned with Ephraim in some fashion.[82] Ephraim covered that part of the hill country between Shechem and Bethel. Benjamin, which means "sons of the south" or "southerners" (from the perspective of Ephraim), was in the Bethel-Ai region, reaching south toward

Jerusalem and centering around Gibeah. Manasseh, north of Ephraim, between Shechem and the Jezreel Valley, spilled over into Transjordan. Gilead was opposite Ephraim in Transjordan.

Miller notes that these tribal groups of the hill country on opposite sides of the Jordan River, all settled in relatively close proximity to each other, were "loosely associated" in a satellite or client relationship dominated by Ephraim. He continues: "Probably this loose alliance of tribes was the premonarchical 'Israel' to which the Merneptah inscription refers."[83] Later these Ephraim-Israel tribes of the central highlands north of Jerusalem and across the Jordan would form the core of Saul's "Israelite" monarchy; and still later, after Solomon's death, they became the core of the northern kingdom called variously Ephraim, Israel or Samaria. In other words, there was no 12-tribe Israel before the Davidic monarchy; and even then, under David and Solomon, the Israelites (that is, Ephraim and client tribes) were joined together only temporarily with other groups, including the Judahites.[84]

In any case, earliest Israel probably was a loose confederation of tribes and clans that "emerged" gradually from the pluralistic population of the land. Accordingly, Israel's ancestors would have been of diverse origins. Some may have been immigrants from Transjordan, possibly even from Egypt. But basically Israel seems to have emerged from the "melting pot" of peoples already in the land of Canaan at the beginning of the Iron Age. Accordingly, their lifestyle and material culture were essentially "Canaanite." Their sense of kinship with each other and separateness from other groups resulted from living in proximity with each other and from patterns of marriages and mutual support over time. Their emergence from tribal society into a nation with a national religion also was the result of a long process of struggle shaped internally by dynamic leaders we know as judges, and externally by political pressures exerted primarily by the Philistines. This scenario, admittedly, is more complex than one might suppose from a casual reading of Joshua and Judges, but it finds support from a more careful reading of the biblical text as well as from archaeological research.

Social organization   Both the Book of Judges and the results of archaeological excavations indicate that the village was the basic form of social organization among the Israelites and their neighbors in the Palestinian hill country during the period of the Judges, corresponding to what archaeologists call Iron Age I (about 1200 to 1000 B.C.E.). As attested by archaeology, these villages shared layouts, features of house design, and an economy of dry farming supplemented by animal husbandry. Before 1200 B.C.E., permanent settlements were located near natural water sources; but with the settlement of the central hills of Canaan, villages subsisted on rainwater captured in rock-cut cisterns. Hillsides around village sites were terraced to slow and capture runoff water, thus allowing for the cultivation of wheat, barley, vegetables and olive trees at sites that lacked natural water sources, such as streams.

The village was an economic entity in itself, independent of other villages and, for the most part, not subject to any market or trade system. It featured a subsistence system dependent more on the vagaries of nature than on political or economic influences. Anthropologists characterize this aspect of village life as "isolation,"[85] but to some extent this is a misnomer. Although we find very few imported artifacts in excavated villages, there are exceptions, including bronze tools obtained in trade or the ingots from which these tools were made, which were bartered or purchased. Thus the isolation was not complete, although it was the village's predominant characteristic.

The village's self-sufficiency and pragmatic isolation had implications for the larger social structure of the people and their political organization: They fostered a natural tendency to resist political unification and social conformity as threats to the integrity of the village unit.

The dominant socioeconomic unit within the village was the household. A household consisted of an extended family compound separated from other compounds by dividing walls or space. Stager has noted that these household compounds "probably reflect the socioeconomic unit known from biblical sources as the *bêt 'āb*" (plural, *bêt 'ābōt*), the house of the father.[86] Gottwald has observed that "a *bêt 'āb* "customarily includes the family head and his wife (or wives), their sons and unmarried daughters, the sons' wives and children ... as far as the biological and affinal links extended generationally."[87] The biological link was not the sole determinant, however, because slaves and strangers who shared the mutual dwelling were also considered part of the *bêt 'āb*.

The *bêt 'ābōt* were grouped together in what the biblical text refers to as the *mishpahah*, or clan. The concept of *mishpahah* can extend, as Gottwald has noted, not only to a group of related families but also to a more neutral characterization of a "protective association of extended families."[88] In the case of small Iron Age I villages, the village itself could be the equivalent of the biblical *mishpahah*. Indeed, the concept of clan and village often coincided.[89]

Tribes were made up of a group of clans, and, as Miller has noted, they were essentially territorial in character. "Thus," he says, "the name 'Ephraim' probably originated with reference to the people living in the vicinity of Mt. Ephraim."[90] The same would be true of Gilead, Benjamin (which means "sons of the south"), Naphtali, etc. The names of places, on the other hand, were also closely related to the names of constituent clans, so that the tribe was not purely territorial in nature but also had a proto-ethnic context.

Political leadership among the tribes seems to have been clan- or village-oriented. The isolation of village life encouraged a highly individualistic kind of leadership, allowing the emergence of a diversity of leadership types. Local affairs were managed by elders of the clans, probably made up of the heads of different expanded families.

The tribal leader is exemplified by Jephthah in Judges 11:1, who is referred to as a "mighty warrior, but the son of a harlot." When the elders of Gilead were threatened by the Ammonites, they went to Jephthah in "the land of Tob," apparently a place of exile where the warrior's half-brothers had driven him because he was a harlot's son. Jephthah initially responded, "Did you not hate me, and drive me out of my father's house (*bêt 'āb*)? Why have you come to me now that you are in trouble?" (Judges 11:7). However, in the end he relents when the elders promise to make him head of the tribe if he fights the Ammonites.

Also certain leaders, such as Deborah, seem to have risen above the tribal level. Deborah is said to have sat under a palm tree between Ramah and Bethel in the hill country of Ephraim, "and the people of Israel came up to her for judgment" (Judges 4:5). When the Israelites were threatened by an alliance of Canaanites, Deborah issued a call to all the tribes to join forces; six of ten Israelite tribes responded, according to Judges 5. Evidently she had acquired a reputation as a wise arbitrator who transcended clan and tribal limitations.

The tribal allotments   Although Joshua 13–22 presupposes 12 discrete tribes that were allotted territory after the conquest, a close reading of Joshua and Judges indicates an evolution in the relationships of tribes and groups of tribes that spanned most of the period of the Judges and possibly more. As noted above, Halpern sees the Song of Deborah in Judges 5 as evidence of a ten-tribe stage in this evolution. Miller, on the other hand, supposes that premonarchical Israel consisted essentially of Ephraim and at least three "client" or "satellite" tribes: Manasseh, Gilead and Benjamin.[91] The patriarchal narratives, in Miller's opinion, appear to support this view. The stories about Jacob, also named "Israel" (Genesis 32:27–28, 35:10), "have their setting primarily in the territory of these Ephraimite-dominated tribes." Joseph and Benjamin are depicted as favorite sons of Jacob/Israel, with Benjamin as the younger. Manasseh and Ephraim are identified as Joseph's sons, with Ephraim as the one destined to dominate (Genesis 48).[92] In the Book of Joshua, Miller writes, occasional references to "the house of Joseph … pertain to these three related tribes—Ephraim/Benjamin and Manasseh" (see Joshua 17:14–18).[93] And "after the death of Solomon, the territory of these same tribes became the core of the northern kingdom, which in turn is referred to interchangeably as 'Ephraim,' 'Israel' and 'Samaria' (after the capital city)."[94]

The Galilee-Jezreel tribes of Asher, Zebulon and Naphtali are described in Judges 1:30–33 as living among Canaanites, whom they dominated and subjected to "forced labor." These tribes were involved in two battles against oppressors in which the Ephraimite tribes took the initiative. First, Gideon of Ophrah, a Manassehite village, led an attack on Midianites and Amalekites from the east who had taken over part of the Valley of Jezreel. Asher, Zebulon and Naphtali responded to the call (Judges 6:35), and the raiders from east of the Jordan were defeated. Second, when the Canaanites led by Sisera of Harosheth-ha-goiim (Judges 4:2) oppressed the Galilee tribes, Deborah of Ephraim-Benjamin summoned Barak of Naphtali to lead an army against the oppressors. Zebulon joined forces with the men from Naphtali, and apparently a contingent from Ephraim was involved. In any case, the Ephraim group seems to have taken the initiative, and the Canaanites were defeated. In the victory ode of Judges 5:12–18, ten tribes are mentioned, although not all of them took part in the battle. These accounts suggest circumstances in which the concerns of the Ephraim-Israel tribes overlapped those of the Galilee tribes, and the former assumed the leadership role.[95]

The tribes of Dan, Judah, Reuben and Gad were located peripherally to the Ephraim-Israel tribes and do not figure significantly in leadership roles. The Danite clans, located along the Mediterranean coast, were pressed back into the edge of the hill country of Ephraim by the Amorites (Judges 1:34–35), and to find relief from oppression, migrated to Laish (later Dan) at the foot of Mt. Hermon in northern Galilee (Judges 17–18).

Gad and Reuben, associated with the Transjordan in the patriarchal narratives (Genesis 29:31–32, 49:3–4) and allotted territory east of the Jordan according to Joshua 13:15–28, are rarely mentioned in the Book of Judges. The same is true of the Judahite clans that occupied the southern hill country. They were separated from the tribes of the northern hill country (Ephraim, Benjamin and Manasseh) by the alliances of Hivite and Jebusite villages in the vicinity of Jerusalem. Judah apparently did not begin to play a significant role until the time of David.

Thus, regardless of whether premonarchical Israel was a full 12-tribe confederation that covered much of Palestine, or a less extensive confederation composed of Ephraim and a few client tribes, it seems that the Ephraim-related tribes were the focus of leadership during the period of the Judges and were the historic center of the Israel that emerged as a monarchy during the time of Saul. The focus of leadership changed during the emergence of David and the reign of Solomon, but reverted to local leaders when Solomon died and rival monarchies were established in Samaria and Jerusalem.

Early Israelite religion The Book of Judges reflects considerable diversity in the pre-monarchical religion of Israel, and this is confirmed by archaeology. The final editors of the book had a rather idealistic view of religious conditions—the Levites led the other tribes in the worship of Yahweh, which contrasted sharply with the idolatry of the Canaanites. Once we get behind the editorial framework of the compilers, however, we find a far more complex situation. For instance, when Gideon was called upon to deliver Israel from the Midianite oppression, an angel of Yahweh appeared before him at Ophrah and commanded him to "pull down the altar of Baal which your father has, and cut down the Asherah that is beside it; and build an altar to the Lord your God on top of the stronghold" (Judges 6:25–26). Apparently, the altar to Baal served as a village shrine. Gideon pulled down the altar by night to escape the notice of his family and the men of the town; he built the altar to Yahweh and offered a bull upon it. When the men of the town discovered what he had done, they went to the house of Gideon's father and demanded that he be brought out so they could execute him. Joash, Gideon's father, interceded and saved his son from the townspeople.

After Gideon defeated the Midianites, he received from the Israelites the loot taken from the Midianites (Ishmaelites)—golden earings, crescents and pendants, as well as purple garments worn by the kings of Midian. Gideon proceeded to make from this material (the Hebrew word is "it," so we cannot be sure if the antecedent is the gold or the robes) an ephod. An ephod can be a decorated priestly garment, as in Exodus 28:4, or it can be an image clothed in a cultic garment, as appears to be the case in the Gideon incident, because it "became a snare to Gideon and to his family" (Judges 8:27).

In another episode, Micah, an Ephraimite, steals 1,100 pieces of silver from his mother, for which she curses him (Judges 17:2ff.). Repentant, Micah restores the silver; his mother then gives him 200 pieces of silver, which he turns over "to the silversmith, who made it into a graven image and a molten image; and it was in the house of Micah" (Judges 17:4). The account continues: "And the man Micah had a shrine, and he made an ephod and teraphim, and installed one of his sons, who became his priest" (Judges 17:5).

This description of a household shrine finds an echo in Iron Age I houses excavated by Joseph Callaway at Khirbet Raddana, two of which had small platforms built up of stones beside the roof support pillars of the great room. In one house, two offering stands were recovered. The account of Micah's household shrine suggests, as does this excavation, that the religion of Yahweh that we meet later in the Bible went through a process of development. We cannot trace this development to an imageless Yahweh with any certainty.

A collection of ancient Hebrew and Phoenician inscriptions from a later period was recovered in 1975 and 1976 at Kuntillet 'Ajrud, in the desert southwest of Kadesh-Barnea. Although they date to the eighth century B.C.E., they have implications for the period of the Judges as well. These inscriptions contain the names of El and Yahweh (spelled YHWH as in the Hebrew Bible), suggesting to the excavator, Ze'ev Meshel, that the site was a religious center, or shrine.[96] The inscriptions and some primitive drawings were found on large storage jars and on the plaster from a building. One Phoenician inscription, apparently written on the plaster of a door jamb, reads "... blessed be Baal in the day of ..."[97] It refers to Baal rather than Yahweh, but its appearance on a door jamb recalls the injunction in Deuteronomy 6:9 to write a biblical passage on "the doorposts of your house and on your gates." One of the storage jars at Kuntillet 'Ajrud was inscribed with poorly preserved drawings and a blessing that reads: "Amaryau said to my lord ... may you be blessed by Yahweh and by his Asherah. Yahweh bless you and keep you and be with you."[98] (See Chapter V.)

The reference to Asherah in this inscription is highly controversial, as, indeed, is the meaning of the term *Asherah* in the Hebrew Bible.[99] Asherah appears in Canaanite literature as the female consort of Baal. In the Bible, she is always condemned as a pagan deity. But here, in the eighth century B.C.E., the time of the classical prophets, we find Asherah, at least according to some interpreters, mentioned as a consort of Yahweh. What we seem to have here is a grassroots cultic pluralism that inspired periodic religious reforms throughout Israel's history. Examples are King Hezekiah's reform of the eighth century B.C.E. and King Josiah's reform of the seventh century B.C.E. (See Chapter V.) If this cultic pluralism, with Yahweh worshiped alongside Baal and Asherah, persisted until the time of Kuntillet 'Ajrud, then it certainly existed in the period of the Judges.

We do not know the origins of Yahweh worship. Exodus 6:3 attributes the revelation of Yahwism to Moses in the land of the Midianites, south of Canaan. Moses married a Midianite woman whose father is called "the priest of Midian" (Exodus 18:1); Moses' father-in-law officiated at a cultic celebration of Yahweh's deliverance of Israel from Egypt (Exodus 18:10–12). Miller points out that "certain poetical texts associate Yahweh in a special way with the south, and speak of Yahweh coming from that area to aid Israel in warfare," as in Judges 5:4–5 and Deuteronomy 33:2.[100] If Yahwism did have its origins among the desert peoples of the south, its acceptance among the tribal groups in Canaan apparently occurred over a long period of time, during which different factions competed. These different factions were associated with various cult symbols. The Ark of the Covenant may have been a symbol of southern origin; other symbols, such as the brazen serpent finally removed from the Temple during

Hezekiah's reform (2 Kings 18:4), seem to have Canaanite origins. The evolution and triumph of Yahwism in Israel must have come about through intense internal struggles.

The Judges—
prelude to
monarchy

The period of the Judges, when "there was no king in Israel; [and] every man did what was right in his own eyes" (Judges 21:25), lasted about 200 years—from around 1200 to 1000 B.C.E. When, however, the periods of time given for each episode in the Book of Judges are added together, the total far exceeds 200 years. It even exceeds the 480 years the Bible says elapsed between the Exodus and the founding of Solomon's Temple (1 Kings 6:1). This is because the episodes are not to be joined as consecutive events; some undoubtedly occurred simultaneously. Further, the recurrence of the highly symbolic numbers 20, 40 and 80 suggests that these figures are not necessarily to be taken literally. Numbers in the biblical world often have more sophisticated vocations than counting.

The stories of the Book of Judges have been arranged in a theological pattern in which historical detail often yields to theology. The theological pattern is given in Judges 2:11–23:

(1) turning from Yahweh to Baal;

(2) incurring the wrath of Yahweh, who allows an enemy to oppress Israel;

(3) raising up judges to deliver the people from oppression; and

(4) allowing a time of peace before the next apostasy.

Miller notes that "the basic assumption behind this theological pattern is that fidelity to Yahweh was the determinative factor in the vicissitudes of ancient Israelite history."[101] The writer's or editor's purpose is religious instruction, not history. As a result, the modern historian must interpret the text accordingly.

The transition from the period of the Judges to the beginning of the monarchy under Saul occurred during the priestly career of Samuel, the last of the judges. According to 1 Samuel, Samuel's father was an Ephraimite from the town of Ramah, south of Bethel, who went on annual pilgrimages to the sanctuary at Shiloh. On one of these pilgrimages, Hannah, Elkanah's barren wife, was promised a child. The birth of her son Samuel is described as a miraculous event. In gratitude to Yahweh, Hannah entrusted Samuel to Eli, the priest at Shiloh, to rear and educate. Samuel became an exemplary man of God, and was recognized widely as a prophet and a judge. He worked an annual circuit that took him to Bethel, Gilgal, Mizpah and back to Ramah where he built an altar to Yahweh (1 Samuel 7:3–17).

Samuel's sons, however, were not of Samuel's caliber, and the elders of Israel called on Samuel to appoint a king to rule over them. Samuel's position on this matter is unclear, because 1 Samuel preserves conflicting traditions. In 1 Samuel 8:6–22, Samuel is instructed by Yahweh to oppose the appointment of a king; in 1 Samuel 9:15–24, Samuel is instructed to anoint Saul secretly as king. Perhaps Samuel was of two minds on the question. In any event, Samuel played a decisive role in the creation of the monarchy.

Thus the era of the settlement and Judges ended. Israel was embarked on the road to nationhood.

FOUR

The United Monarchy
Saul, David and Solomon

written and revised by
ANDRÉ LEMAIRE

T HE UNITED KINGDOM WAS THE MOMENT OF ISRAEL'S GLORY ON THE international scene—a moment to be remembered and recalled for millennia. What led to the creation of the Israelite monarchy? In the words of William E. Evans, "The impetus ... [was] the Philistine threat."[1] As most historians recognize, this is certainly part of the truth. However, external pressure came not only from the Philistines: An Ammonite threat also played a role in bringing an end to the loose tribal confederacy—if indeed that is what it was—by which Israel had been led and protected. Moreover, internal (social, economic and demographic) pressures must be taken into account.[2] Charismatic tribal leaders who arose as needed were no longer enough to lead the emerging nation. The United Kingdom of Israel lasted for about a century (c. 1030–931 B.C.E.). Three strong personalities occupied the throne: Saul, David and Solomon. Then the United Kingdom split in two, with Israel in the north and Judah in the south.

Under Saul, the Israelite monarchy controlled a small, petty territory. Under David and then Solomon, Israel was transformed into a larger, unified kingdom with vassal states subject to it. As the monarchy assumed an international role, other powers in the ancient Near East, mainly Phoenicia and Egypt, were required to give due regard to Israel.

The historian of this period is fortunate: The biblical record is copious because this period was later conceived of as a kind of golden age.

The Bible probably devotes more space to this century than to any other in ancient Israel's history. Accounts of this period appear in both of the Bible's parallel histories—1 Samuel 8 to 1 Kings 11 and 1 Chronicles 3 to 2 Chronicles 9.

The principal difficulty in reconstructing the history of the period, however, is that we are dependent almost exclusively on the Bible. The assurance that comes from a variety of sources is missing here, and the biblical account is often tendentious and includes traditions that are not completely reliable as history. It also tends to idealize this period. As underlined by J. Maxwell Miller: "The important question is not whether we should use the Hebrew Bible in our attempts to understand the origin and early history of Israel, but how we should use it. In my opinion, it should be approached critically, examined with the careful attention to its internal typology and stratigraphy that archaeologists give to their data, and then used very cautiously, alongside other kinds of evidence."[3]

To understand this period of Israel's history, we must therefore consider questions of literary criticism, as well as differences in the various traditions preserved in the Bible. Finally, we must consider the light archaeology sheds (or fails to shed) on the monarchy—not an easy task, as exemplified by the contemporary controversy over the archaeology of the tenth century B.C.E.[4] Two divergent views of this century have recently emerged, one known as the maximalist viewpoint, the other as the minimalist. The former group contends that the biblical account of the United Monarchy has a historical core, while the latter tends to deny that the biblical traditions of this period have any basis whatsoever in history.[5] The ensuing debates remind us that the results of literary criticism and the interpretation of archaeological discoveries are seldom clear-cut. One must therefore be very careful to distinguish what the biblical record says from the historical interpretation of it based on archaeology. Each reign presents different aspects of the problem.

Saul (c. 1030?–1009 B.C.E.)

The Philistine threat   The Bible depicts Saul as a study in contrasts. Although he was Israel's first king, he was ultimately rejected (1 Samuel 15:10–11). His dark, fitful personality suffers by contrast with the two legendary figures between whom he seems wedged—Samuel, the prophet-priest, and David, Saul's hero-successor. The Bible describes Saul rising to the throne in the face of the Philistine military threat. The Philistines are known both from the Bible and from extrabiblical sources.[6] Egyptian inscriptions mention them as one of the so-called Sea Peoples. Apparently, they originally came from the Aegean area or from southern Anatolia. Other Sea Peoples include the Tjekkar,

Philistine warrior. *The Philistines and other Sea Peoples inhabited several cities on the eastern Mediterranean coast in the early 12th century B.C.E. A large-scale sea battle between the Sea Peoples and Egyptian forces is depicted in wall reliefs from Ramesses III's mortuary temple at Medinet Habu, in Thebes. This plaster cast (made by Sir William Flinders Petrie) of a detail from one relief showcases the Philistines' characteristic battle headdress, which included a headband and upright strips that may be feathers, reeds, leather strips, horsehair or an unusual hairdo. The military threat posed by the warlike Philistines was one of the factors leading to the creation of the United Kingdom of Israel.*

the Sheklesh, the Danuna and the Weshesh. The Sea Peoples destroyed a number of cities on the Syro-Phoenician coast at the beginning of the 12th century B.C.E. and even tried to subdue Egypt. However, they were stopped in a large-scale battle, fought both on land and on sea, in the eighth year of the reign of Pharaoh Ramesses III (c. 1177 B.C.E.). Reliefs and hieroglyphic accounts of this battle appear on the walls of Ramesses III's temple at Medinet Habu in Thebes.[7] The Sea Peoples settled in various parts of the Egyptian province of Canaan, probably with Egypt's agreement: The Philistines occupied the coastal plain between Gaza and Jaffa; the Tjekkar occupied the Sharon plain around the city of Dor; the Cherethites (Cretans?), perhaps another Sea People, settled the so-called Negev of the Cherethites (1 Samuel 30:14).

In the coastal plain, the Philistines organized themselves into a pentapolis, a confederation of five cities: Gaza, Ashdod, Ashkelon, Gath and Ekron. Each city was ruled by a *sérèn*. (The only Philistine word that is known with certainty, *sérèn* [Joshua 13:3; Judges 16:5,8,23,27; 1 Samuel 5:8,11] may be related to the Greek term *tyrannos*.)[8]

Eventually, the Philistine military expansion near Aphek brought the Philistines close to the territory occupied by the Israelite confederation.[9] The Philistines were apparently skilled warriors who used the most advanced military equipment of their time. Their weapons were made of both bronze, the predominant metal until about 1200 B.C.E., and iron, which was becoming increasingly available.[10]

According to the biblical record, the Israelites mustered in the hill country overlooking Aphek. A two-stage battle between the Israelites and the Philistines ensued. In the first phase of the battle, "Israel was defeated by the Philistines, who slew about four thousand men on the field of battle" (1 Samuel 4:2). In desperation, the Israelites brought the Ark of the Covenant, which had been installed at Shiloh, to lead them in battle. In the second phase of the battle, the Israelites were again defeated, and the Ark was captured by the Philistines. After the battle of Ebenezer (1 Samuel 4), the Philistines occupied at least part of the Ephraimite hill country. After their victory at Ebenezer, the Philistines installed garrisons (or governors) in the hill country of Ephraim and Benjamin, the most important of which was at Geba (1 Samuel 13:3–5).

Like the Habiru/'Apiru of the Late Bronze Age, hundreds of years earlier, and the Jews of the Maccabean revolt, hundreds of years later, some Israelites took to the hill country and hid in natural caves (1 Samuel 14:11,22).

The choice of Saul

Facing these dire circumstances, the Israelite tribes determined that they must have a king. The story of the choice of Saul as king appears in three different traditions: In the first, Saul is looking for his father's lost she-asses when he meets Samuel, who anoints him prince (*nasi*) over Israel (1 Samuel 9:3–10:16). In the second tradition, Saul is hiding among baggage at Mizpah when Samuel casts lots to choose the king (1 Samuel 10:17–27); in the third and probably most reliable tradition,[11] Saul, at the head of Israelite columns, has rescued Jabesh-Gilead from an Ammonite attack, and the people, with Samuel's agreement, proclaim their allegiance to Saul at Gilgal (1 Samuel 11–15). In each of these accounts, Saul is installed and anointed as king by Samuel, now an old man.[12]

Samuel was regarded as the last of the judges (1 Samuel 7:6,15, 8:1–3), the charismatic leaders who emerged at times of crisis. Another tradition, probably a later one, regarded Samuel as a prophet (1 Samuel 3:20). He also officiated at the tabernacle at Shiloh, where the Ark was kept, which means he was a priest. But Samuel's leadership was regarded as insufficient. The tribal elders apparently felt that the appointment of a king was a historical necessity: "Now appoint for us

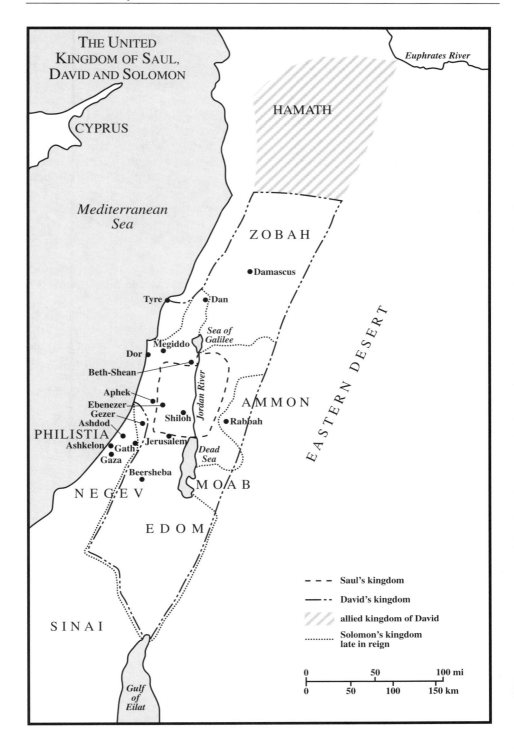

THE UNITED
KINGDOM OF SAUL,
DAVID AND SOLOMON

Euphrates River

CYPRUS

HAMATH

*Mediterranean
Sea*

ZOBAH

•Damascus

Tyre• •Dan

*Sea of
Galilee*

Megiddo

Dor

Beth-Shean

Jordan River

EASTERN DESERT

Aphek
Ebenezer
Gezer
Ashdod

Shiloh

AMMON

•Rabbah

PHILISTIA

Ashkelon• •Jerusalem
Gath
Gaza

*Dead
Sea*

Beersheba

NEGEV

MOAB

EDOM

SINAI

*Gulf
of
Eilat*

– – – Saul's kingdom

– · – David's kingdom

▨▨▨ allied kingdom of David

··········· Solomon's kingdom
late in reign

0   50   100 mi
0   50   100   150 km

a king to govern us like all the nations," they told Samuel (1 Samuel 8:5). Saul, a Benjaminite, seems to have been chosen because he was tall and strong and well qualified to wage war against Israel's enemies.

Like earlier charismatic leaders, Saul's principal task was to conduct a war of liberation. Saul's successful expedition against the Ammonites at Jabesh-Gilead (1 Samuel 11:1–11) was no doubt an important consideration in his selection.[13] Now he was called upon to lead the people against the Philistines, a people who were well organized, well equipped and motivated by an expansionist ideology that included plans to bring the whole country west of the Jordan under its control.

The first battle—at Michmash—was a victory for Israel (1 Samuel 13:5–14:46). The decision to appoint a king seemed to have been a wise one. But this was by no means the last battle of the war.

Saul the   "There was hard fighting against the Philistines all the days of Saul;
warrior   and when Saul saw any strong man, or any valiant man, he attached him to himself" (1 Samuel 14:52).

The Philistine war thus became a guerrilla war, characterized by ambushes and surprise attacks against enemy posts. Generally, it did not involve great numbers of fighters. Saul had only "about six hundred men with him" near Gibeah (1 Samuel 14:2). Unfortunately, the Bible gives only brief intimations of the details of the continuing wars with the Philistines. Saul probably succeeded in driving the Philistines out of the central part of Israel. But the Philistines did not give up. They apparently attacked from the south, threatening Judah in a confrontation in which a young Judahite named David distinguished himself (1 Samuel 17).

Saul seems to have been generally successful as long as he fought in the hills, but his troops could not win a battle in the open plain. Witness what happened near Mt. Gilboa (1 Samuel 28–31). The Philistines attacked from the north through the Jezreel Valley. The Israelites should never have come down into the plain to fight.

> The Philistines fought against Israel; and the men of Israel fled before the Philistines, and fell slain on Mt. Gilboa ... Thus Saul died, and his three sons, and his armor-bearer, and all his men, on the same day together. And when the men of Israel who were on the other side of the valley and those beyond the Jordan saw that the men of Israel had fled and that Saul and his sons were dead, they forsook their cities and fled; and the Philistines came and dwelt in them.
>
> (1 Samuel 31:1,6–7)

This sober presentation of an Israelite disaster has a ring of truth even though, beginning in David's time, there were divergent traditions concerning the details of Saul's death (compare 1 Samuel 31:3–5 with 2 Samuel 1:6–10).

Ammonite king. *This life-size limestone head, with plaited hair, curled beard, earrings and crown, is said to have been discovered near Amman, Jordan, a city whose name preserves its Ammonite origins. According to the Bible, the Ammonites, who lived east of the Jordan during the Israelite monarchy, were one of Israel's most important adversaries, second only to the Philistines.*

Other than the Philistine war, which seems to have been the principal feature of Saul's reign, the biblical text mentions wars against the Moabites, the Ammonites, the Edomites, the king of Zobah and the Amalekites (1 Samuel 14:47–48).

The main battle of the war with the Amalekites is described in 1 Samuel 15. The Amalekites were the Israelites' special enemies because they were the first to confront Israel in the wilderness after the Israelites left Egypt. Without provocation, the Amalekites had attacked Israel from the rear (Exodus 17:8–16).

Samuel instructed Saul and his men to kill all the Amalekites and their animals, according to the tradition of *hérèm* (compare Joshua 6:18 and 7), which allotted the fruits of victory to the Lord alone. However, Saul spared the Amalekite king Agag and the best of the Amalekites' domestic animals. For this sin, Samuel denounced Saul and declared that the Lord had irrevocably rejected him. Samuel, the Bible tells us, "never saw Saul again ... And the Lord was sorry that he had made Saul king over Israel" (1 Samuel 15:35).

Tentative evaluation of Saul's reign

We do not know how long Saul ruled. According to the traditional Hebrew text (the Masoretic text), which unfortunately is badly preserved at this point, Saul became king when he was one year old (!) and his reign lasted only "two years" (1 Samuel 13:1).[14] This of course seems improbable, and several commentators correct the text to read "twenty-two years"; but this remains conjectural.

Although the length of Saul's reign is uncertain, two biblical passages offer some information about the general economic and political conditions under Saul:

> Now there was no smith to be found throughout all the land of Israel; for the Philistines said, "The Hebrews must not make swords or spears for themselves"; so all the Israelites went down to the Philistines to sharpen their plowshare, mattocks, axes, or sickles; and the charge was a pim [two-thirds of a shekel] for the plowshares and for the mattocks, and a third of a shekel for sharpening the axes and for setting the goads. So on the day of the battle, neither sword nor spear was to be found in the possession of any of the people with Saul and Jonathan; but Saul and Jonathan his son had them.
> (1 Samuel 13:19–22)

This first passage reflects a nonspecialized society of peasants and shepherds in which even iron implements were rare.

The second passage describes Saul's family:

> Now the sons of Saul were Jonathan, Ishvi, and Malchishua; and the names of his two daughters were these: the name of the firstborn was Merab and the name of the younger, Michal. The name of Saul's wife was Ahinoam daughter of Ahimaaz. And the

name of the commander of his army was Abner son of Ner,
Saul's uncle.

(1 Samuel 14:49–50)

This passage demonstrates that Saul's kingship was essentially a family
matter. The principal specialized responsibility, leadership of the army,
was in the hands of Saul's cousin Abner.

It is difficult to give a balanced historical assessment of Saul's
reign.[15] In the biblical tradition, he seems to be presented as the typical bad king,[16] in contrast to his adversary and successor, David. This
contrast is the central theme of the stories in 1 Samuel 16–27, the
bulk of which seems to have been written by David's companion and
priest Abiathar (cf. 1 Samuel 22:20) or someone close to him.[17] These
chapters may contain some reliable information,[18] but it is presented
in a one-sided and tendentious way. They describe, in sometimes
divergent traditions, the stormy relationship between Saul and the
young David. David had distinguished himself in the Philistine wars
and had been given Saul's second daughter, Michal, in marriage. Saul
became increasingly jealous of David, accusing his son-in-law of conspiring against him. On several occasions, Saul tried to kill David.
David fled to Judah, but Saul pursued him. Finally, David took refuge
in Philistine territory. Written from David's viewpoint, the stories in 1
Samuel 16–27 tend to depict David as right in rebelling against Saul
and seeking refuge in Philistine territory.[19] But they also reveal that
people from Bethlehem in Judah joined Saul in battle when the
Philistines tried to invade the central hill country from the southwest
(1 Samuel 17:1). Saul obviously exerted some political influence south
of Jerusalem in the northern mountains of Judah, preparing the way
for the federation of Israel and Judah under David.[20]

The historicity of many of Saul's other wars, however, is doubtful.
The wars against the Moabites, the Edomites, the king of Zobah and
even the Amalekites (1 Samuel 14:47–48, 15) may simply be a trans-
position from David to Saul made by the Judahite historian because he
had so little information about Saul. Such wars far from Saul's home
base seem improbable, especially when the Philistine threat was so
strong and Saul's army was so poorly organized.

Unfortunately, we are left with little solid information about Saul or
his reign. All that can be said with confidence is that Saul seems to have
been named king so that he would lead the Israelites in their wars
against the Philistines.

Saul's "kingdom" was not very large. It probably included Mt.
Ephraim, Benjamin and Gilead. He also exerted some influence in the
northern mountains of Judah and beyond the Jezreel Valley. Instead
of having a capital city or a palace, Saul set up his tent "in the out-
skirts of Gibeah under the pomegranate tree which is at Migron"
(1 Samuel 14:2) or in Gibeah, where he sat "under the tamarisk tree

on the height with his spear in his hand, and all his servants [i.e., ministers] were standing about him" (1 Samuel 22:6).[21]

Saul's "kingship," as might be expected from the biblical record, left hardly a trace archaeologically speaking. Surveys and excavations in the hill country of Manasseh,[22] Ephraim[23] and Benjamin,[24] and at sites like 'Izbet Sartah,[25] have revealed farms, small villages and open-air cult places on hilltops. To the south, in northern Judah, settlement was even sparser.[26] The fortified site of Khirbet ed-Dawwara, northeast of Jerusalem, had perhaps a hundred inhabitants,[27] and this was large for Saul's kingdom. The principal Israelite site of the previous period, Shiloh,[28] seems to have been destroyed in the mid-11th century B.C.E.[29] by an intense conflagration. This destruction is often attributed to the Philistines as a follow-up operation after their victory over the Israelites at Ebenezer (1 Samuel 4). Shiloh is mentioned only once in the stories of Saul and David (1 Samuel 14:3).

Archaeology seems to confirm that until about 1000 B.C.E., the end of Iron Age I, Israelite society was essentially a society of farmers and stockbreeders without any truly centralized organization and administration.[30] Recent population estimates set "a figure of about 50,000 settled Israelites west of the Jordan at the end of the eleventh century B.C."[31]

By contrast, Philistine urban civilization was flourishing in the 11th century B.C.E., as revealed by recent excavations at Ashdod, Tel Gerisa, Tel Miqne (biblical Ekron) and Ashkelon.[32]

Saul's reign ended in total failure with his tragic death. After the rout on Mt. Gilboa, the Israelite revolt against Philistine domination seemed hopeless. Under the leadership of Saul's adversary, David, however, the fight for independence from the Philistines—the *raison d'être* of Saul's kingship—was taken up once again.

David (c. 1009/1001–969 B.C.E.)

With David's reign, we begin to see Israel emerge as a national entity. The loose confederation of tribes has been transformed into a strong chiefdom. Israel's political existence is confirmed by its king, its army, its royal cabinet, its extended territory and its relations with neighboring countries. Even historians like Mario Liverani[33] and J. Alberto Soggin,[34] who hesitate to say anything about the early history of Israel, agree that from about 1000 B.C.E. "the History of Israel leaves the realm of pre-history, of cultic and popular traditions, and enters the arena of history proper."[35]

This does not mean, however, that everything is clear and that no historical questions remain. Indeed, a few scholars have recently gone so far as to deny that David really founded the kingdom of Jerusalem as a political power.[36] According to Ernst A. Knauf, "Archaeologically speaking there are no indications of statehood being achieved before the ninth century B.C.E. in Israel and the eighth century B.C.E. in Judah."[37] Although it may be true that Israel was more of a powerful chiefdom than a well-administered state or a centralized empire, it is wrong to deny the historicity of David's kingdom as *some* sort of political power. The methodological weakness of this extreme position is highlighted by two monumental ninth-century B.C.E. inscriptions written by enemies of Israel—Mesha of Moab[38] and Hazael of Damascus[39]—who designate the kingdom of Judah as *Be(y)t Dawid*, "the House of David," probably the official diplomatic name for David's dynasty in this period.[40]

The Bible tells the story of David's reign in detail (1 Samuel 16 to 1 Kings 2:11), reflecting its importance as well as its length. David "reigned over Israel for forty years, seven and a half in Hebron and thirty-three in Jerusalem" (c. 1009/1001–969 B.C.E.). His long reign was later regarded as Israel's "golden age"; David himself was seen as the model king.   **A model king**

David's later glorification may seem paradoxical in light of the fact that he was a Bethlehemite, from the tribe of Judah, and not from any of the original, northern tribes (Ephraim, Manasseh and Benjamin). Furthermore, David was one of Saul's adversaries, who had been banned because he was considered the personal enemy of the first Israelite king. Moreover, at the time of Saul's death, David was serving as a mercenary in the army of the Philistines, Israel's bitter enemy.

According to 1 Samuel 16:1–13, David was the youngest son of Jesse. The prophet-priest Samuel "anointed him in the midst of his brothers; and the Spirit of the Lord came mightily upon David from that day forward."

The Bible offers two accounts of how David became part of Saul's household. In the first, Saul takes David into his service as his "armor-bearer" (1 Samuel 16:14–23). In the second version, David, having killed the Philistine champion Goliath in single combat (1 Samuel 17), is officially presented to Saul as a hero. The biblical account of David's rise to power may well represent an amalgamation of different traditions concerning the early relationship between David and Saul.

In any event, with the support of his friend Jonathan (Saul's son), David was "made ... a commander of a thousand; and David marched out and came in, leading the army. David had success in all his undertakings; for the Lord was with him" (1 Samuel 18:13–14).

This happy situation did not last. David was soon accused of conspiring against Saul (1 Samuel 22:8). David decided it would be prudent to flee to the hill country:

> David departed from there and escaped to the cave of Adullam; and when his brothers and all his father's house heard it, they went down there to him. And every one who was in distress, and

every one who was in debt, and every one who was discontented
gathered to him; and he became captain over them. And there
were with him about four hundred men.

(1 Samuel 22:1–2)

Among them were Abiathar (the son of Ahimelech the son of Ahitub
the priest of Nob, descendant of Eli the chief priest at Shiloh) and
the prophet Gad (1 Samuel 22:5,20). That these religious personalities joined David suggests the importance of Yahwism among
David's partisans.

After some time hiding in various locations throughout Judah as Saul
pursued him, David sought refuge in Philistine territory:

So David ... and the six hundred men who were with him [escaped
to the land of the Philistines] to Achish son of Maoch, king of
Gath. And David dwelt with Achish in Gath, he and his men, every
man with his household and David with his two wives.

(1 Samuel 27:2–3)

After a while "Achish gave him [David] Ziklag" (1 Samuel 27:6).[41]

During this period, David attempted to maintain good relations with
the leaders of the territory of Judah by fighting Judah's enemy, the
Amalekites (1 Samuel 27:8, 30:1–31). His efforts proved fruitful. After
Saul's death at the battle of Mt. Gilboa,

David went [to Hebron in the territory of Judah] and his two
wives also, Ahinoam of Jezreel, and Abigail the widow of Nabal of
Carmel. And David brought up his men who were with him,
every one with his household; and they dwelt in the towns of
Hebron. And the men of Judah came, and there they anointed
David king over the house of Judah.

(2 Samuel 2:2–4)

This does not seem to have provoked the Philistines, who, at first,
were apparently pleased that one of their vassals controlled the territory of Judah.

The same was not true, however, of Saul's descendants:

Now Abner the son of Ner, commander of Saul's army, had taken
Ishbosheth the son of Saul, and brought him over to Mahanaim;[42]
and he made him king over Gilead and the Ashurites and Jezreel
and Ephraim and Benjamin and all Israel. Ishbosheth, Saul's son,
was forty years old when he began to reign over Israel; and he
reigned two years.

(2 Samuel 2:8–10)[43]

King David   A "long war" ensued between the house of Saul and the house of David
(2 Samuel 3:1). But in the meantime a disagreement soon split Abner
and Ishbosheth (Eshbaal). Both of them were killed, apparently as a
result of personal vengeance (2 Samuel 3–4).[44] The way was open for
David to become the king of all Israel:

> All the elders of Israel came to the king at Hebron; and King
> David made a covenant with them at Hebron before the Lord, and
> they anointed David king over Israel.
>
> (2 Samuel 5:3)

The Philistines could no longer remain indifferent in the face of the unification of their longtime enemy. They attacked twice in the central hill country, once near the Valley of Rephaim and probably once near Gibeon. But David defeated them both times (2 Samuel 5:17–25).[45] The Philistines then gave up their efforts at military expansion.

After driving off the Philistines, David was free to attack the Jebusites of Jerusalem and take the city, which until then had remained in Canaanite hands: "And David dwelt in the stronghold [of Jerusalem] and called it the City of David" (2 Samuel 5:9).

Jerusalem soon became not only the political capital of Judah and Israel, but also the religious center of all Israel. To accomplish this, David brought the Ark of the Covenant to the City of David (2 Samuel 6). This was the Ark that, according to tradition, had accompanied Israel in the Sinai, that had rested in the tabernacle of Shiloh before being captured by the Philistines and that had remained in storage at Kiriath Yearim after being returned by the Philistines. When David brought the Ark to Jerusalem, the religion of Yahweh became a unifying factor, strengthening the bond between Judah and Israel.

From the beginning of his career, David showed himself to be a fervent Yahwist. His religious devotion was confirmed by the presence in his retinue of the priest Abiathar and the prophet Gad. David's devotion to Yahweh probably made it easier for the leaders of Israel to accept him as their king.

David cemented his relations with various political and national groups through marriage. His wives included Abigail of Carmel; Ahinoam of Jezreel; and Maacah, daughter of the Transjordanian king of Geshur (2 Samuel 3:2–5).[46]

Militarily, David had already developed a cadre of well-trained troops when he fled from Saul. These devoted soldiers were ready to follow him anywhere, and, in fact, did follow him from the wilderness of Judah to Gath, Ziklag, Hebron and, finally, Jerusalem. These troops became his personal guard and the core of his regular army. His nephew Joab served as chief of the army (2 Samuel 8:16).

After checking the Philistine advances on Israel's western border, David was free to expand his kingdom to the east. There he defeated the Moabites, who then became a vassal state, paying tribute to David (2 Samuel 8:2). As discussed below, David also fought with the Ammonites, although the precise sequence of these wars is unclear. He also led a campaign to Edom, where he won a battle in the Valley of Salt. David then appointed "garrisons (or governors) in Edom;

throughout all Edom he put garrisons, and all the Edomites became David's servants" (2 Samuel 8:14).

In the biblical tradition, after the Philistines, the Ammonites were Israel's most important adversary. The Ammonite war began as a result of a diplomatic incident. Nahash, the king of the Ammonites, had been David's friend. When Nahash died, David sent condolences to his son and successor, Hanun. But Hanun treated David's messengers with contempt: He cut away half of their beards and half of their garments, accusing them of being David's spies (2 Samuel 10:1–5). Hanun probably thought he could get away with this because of an alliance he had made with the Aramean kingdoms of northern Transjordan and southern Syria (2 Samuel 10:6).[47]

In retaliation, David's general, Joab, led an attack near the Ammonite capital. An Ammonite ally—Hadadezer the Rehobite, king of Zobah—summoned other Arameans from "beyond the Great Bend of the Euphrates" to join forces against David (2 Samuel 10:16). David met and defeated this Aramean army at Helam (2 Samuel 10:17–18). He "took from him [Hadadezer] a thousand and seven hundred horsemen, and twenty thousand foot soldiers; and David hamstrung all the chariot horses, but left enough for a hundred chariots" (2 Samuel 8:4). (Apparently, chariots were not used much in David's army; otherwise, he would not have crippled so many horses.)

As a result of this enormous victory, David was able to conquer Rabbah, the Ammonite capital. David then "took the crown of their king (or of Milkom) from his head ... and it was placed on David's head" (2 Samuel 12:30). The Ammonites became David's subjects. In addition, the kingdom of Zobah, headed by Hadadezer, became David's vassal: "David put garrisons (or governors) in Aram of Damascus; the Syrians [Arameans] became servants to David and brought tribute" (2 Samuel 8:6). Finally, "All the kings who were servants of Hadadezer ... made peace with Israel and became subject to them" (2 Samuel 10:19). Among them was Toi, the king of the important kingdom of Hamath (2 Samuel 8:9–10). David thus extended his direct or indirect political control from the Red Sea to the bend of the Euphrates.

By gaining control over international trade routes, the Israelite kingdom became an economic power. David became rich from the spoil and tribute brought to Jerusalem. Even the Phoenician king of Tyre, Hiram, started trading with him, especially after David made Jerusalem his capital (2 Samuel 5:11–12).

The inchoate nature of the early state   The expansion of David's kingdom altered the status of Jerusalem.[48] From a small declining Canaanite city-state with a territory of a few square miles, it became—probably with little physical change—the capital of the united Israelite and Judahite kingdoms. These kingdoms, after David's victories, extended far and wide. The borders of the United Kingdom stretched from Dan to Beersheba, but its many administrative territories and vassal states reached far beyond. David's kingdom may have been a strong chiefdom or a kind of empire at this point, but it was still not well organized with a strong central administration.

At least toward the end of David's reign, there was a kind of royal cabinet in Jerusalem in which David's general Joab played an important role:

> So David reigned over all Israel; and David administered justice and equity to all his people. And Joab the son of Zeruiah was over the army; and Jehoshaphat the son of Ahilud was recorder, and Zadok the son of Ahitub and Ahimelech the son of Abiathar were priests; and Seraiah was secretary; and Benaiah the son of Jehoiada was over the Cherethite and the Pelethites; and David's sons were priests.
>
> (2 Samuel 8:15–18; cf. 2 Samuel 20:23–26)[49]

The spoils of war, the levies from the administered territories, the tributes of vassal kings—all flowed into David's royal treasury. Further, the produce of the royal lands filled the royal coffers (1 Chronicles 27:25–31). Justice was administered at the local level by the elders of the cities, but appeals could now be taken directly to the king (2 Samuel 14:15).

David planned to build a new Temple in Jerusalem (2 Samuel 7) and organized a census, probably as a basis for administration, taxation and conscription (2 Samuel 24:1–9). Both the Temple project and the census met internal opposition. Even the prophet Gad, one of David's oldest and most loyal companions, opposed the census; he did, however, support the construction of an altar on the threshing floor of Araunah the Jebusite, the site David purchased for the Temple (2 Samuel 24:18).

The guiding principles of the United Kingdom were organization and centralization. But the process of centralization really only began toward the end of David's reign. It was later applied more broadly by his son and successor, Solomon.

Internally, the problem of David's legitimacy as successor to Saul loomed large. It was doubtless exacerbated by the unstable union of the houses of Israel and Judah. This problem is treated at great length in the Bible. Indeed, this is the principal subject from 2 Samuel 6 through 1 Kings 2, often called the "History of the Succession."

The problem of succession

Initially, David tried to gain the goodwill of Saul's house.[50] He even married Michal, Saul's daughter. David also welcomed to his table on a regular basis Meribbaal (Mephibosheth), a cripple who was Saul's heir. True, this seeming act of kindness permitted David to control Meribbaal's activity (2 Samuel 9). And in the end David more or less abandoned Michal, who "had no child to the day of her death"

(2 Samuel 6:23). When David allowed the Gibeonites to take revenge on seven of Saul's descendants, reconciliation between the two houses was no longer possible (2 Samuel 21:1–14).[51]

David's own house was also beset with rivalries and jealousies among his sons. His eldest son, Amnon, was killed by order of David's third son, Absalom (2 Samuel 13). Absalom himself was killed by Joab, the general of David's army, after leading an almost-successful revolt against his father (2 Samuel 15–19). Absalom's revolt was connected with the rivalry between Israel and Judah and with Benjaminite opposition to David (compare the roles played by Shimei and by Sheba son of Bichri, both Benjaminites [2 Samuel 19:16–23, 20:1–22]).

After Amnon and Absalom were killed, Adonijah became David's heir apparent. David's old retainers, including his general Joab and the priest Abiathar, were ready to support Adonijah (1 Kings 1:5–7). However, according to 1 Kings 1, the aged David promised Bathsheba that their son Solomon would become king. With the help of the prophet Nathan, the priest Zadok and the chief of the guards Benaiah, Solomon was recognized as king while David was still living. David himself died peacefully some time afterward (1 Kings 2:10–12).

Assessing the biblical text

In the absence of any text contemporary with the biblical account, a historical appreciation of David's reign is difficult. A literary analysis of the biblical tradition seems to indicate, however, that a good deal of it was written either in David's or Solomon's time, close enough to the events to be reliable witnesses,[52] although there are doubtless later additions and glosses reflecting the influence of the so-called Deuteronomistic historians of later centuries.[53]

Of course, even early traditions can be tendentious, and it does seem that most of the account of David's reign was written to glorify David and his son Solomon. This is particularly true of the stories concerning David's accession, which reflect the most attractive side of his personality and try to justify his claim to the kingship.[54] This is also true of the account of Solomon's accession, which explains how Solomon, one of David's younger sons, could be his legitimate heir. The aged David's promise to Bathsheba to make her son king sounds more like literary artifice than history. Or perhaps Bathsheba, with the help of the prophet Nathan[55] and the priest Zadok, succeeded in convincing an old and weakened David to support their conspiracy to elevate Solomon and thus to legitimate what was in effect a *coup d'état*.[56]

The account of David's external policies also bears the marks of tendentiousness. The biblical text emphasizes David's military victories rather than his political control of the conquered territories. But even if David was victorious against the invading Philistines, he was probably unable to control the Philistines' territory. The biblical statement that David "subdued" the Philistines (2 Samuel 8:1,11–12) is ambiguous. Further, 2 Samuel 5:25 tells us that David defeated the Philistines only as far as Gezer, which lay on the eastern border of Philistine territory. Gezer itself did not become part of Israel until Solomon's reign (see below).

David's relations with Hiram, king of Tyre, must also be looked at critically. The Phoenicians were technologically superior to the Israelites, and David's relationship with them was essentially commercial; there was no vassal submission. Moreover, even this commercial relationship probably dated to the end of David's reign, or even more likely, to the beginning of Solomon's.[57]

After the Ammonite war, if indeed David did take for himself the Ammonite crown, he probably dismissed the ruling Ammonite king only to put in his place another son of Nahash: "Shobi the son of Nahash from Rabbah of the Ammonites," who supported David during Absalom's revolt (2 Samuel 17:27–29). In the Aramean territories that David administered (Zobah and Damascus),[58] the governors were probably chosen from local leaders. In the vassal kingdoms (like Moab), their own kings continued to rule, although they paid tribute to David. Sometimes it is difficult to tell the difference between a vassal state and an allied kingdom—for instance, Toi, king of Hamath, probably considered himself as much an ally as a vassal (see 2 Samuel 8:9–10).

Even if David's influence did extend from the Red Sea to the Euphrates, we must realize that there are varying degrees of political control.[59] For example, David's influence over the outlying areas was sometimes only nominal, mainly dependent on the fear inspired by his soldiers. As stated earlier, David's political sphere should probably be characterized as a strong chiefdom rather than an "early state" or "empire." Only at the very end of his reign did he begin seriously to organize and centralize his power. According to biblical tradition, David's reign was characterized by wars (cf. 2 Samuel 8, 10; 1 Kings 5:17); the few buildings attributed to him are more likely to be connected with Solomon (2 Samuel 5:9–11).

As would be expected, the archaeology of David's reign is sparse, aside from the possible destructions of Canaanite cities.[60] In the 1970s, Yohanan Aharoni argued that Dan and Beersheba were rebuilt by David and that the Iron Age gates of these cities could be dated to the beginning of the tenth century B.C.E.,[61] but few archaeologists today support his conclusions. More recently, Eilat Mazar has proposed identifying monumental archaeological fragments found south of the Ophel, in Jerusalem, with King David's palace.[62] However Solomon's palace would be a better candidate. Moreover, the date of the "Jebusite ramp," or Stepped-Stone Structure, built on the eastern slope of the City of David is still hotly debated (see below). It appears therefore—both from the texts and from archaeological excavations— that Jebusite Jerusalem did not change much during David's reign.[63]

The best candidates for archaeological remains that may be dated to David's reign lie in Hebron and in the Judean Hills: Avi Ofer's excavations in Hebron and his survey of the hill country of Judah reveal a "breakthrough in the settlement history of the Judean Hills."[64] However, it is difficult to date any artifact or architecture to the *beginning* of the tenth century. Most of the building activity in the tenth century probably occurred later, during King Solomon's reign.

Despite all these reservations, David's reign represents a glorious achievement. Seizing the opportunity occasioned by the weakness of Assyria and Egypt,[65] a strong and brilliant personality[66] joined the houses of Israel and Judah, made Jerusalem the capital of both and used this unification as the basis of his dominion. With this favorable international situation, David created what was for a short time one of the most important powers in the ancient Near East. He also laid the foundations of religious institutions that would support the worship of the Hebrew God Yahweh for millennia.

Solomon (c. 970/969–931 B.C.E.)

David was occupied chiefly with fighting wars and with expanding his kingdom by both military and political means. Solomon was concerned mainly with consolidating the lands acquired by David and organizing the administration of the kingdom. But before he could turn to this, Solomon had to strengthen his position as king.

Threats to Solomon's rule During the first years of his reign, Solomon was confronted first with an internal and then an external threat. As long as Adonijah, David's oldest surviving son, lived, this apparent Davidic heir was a danger; there was always the possibility that he would present himself as the legitimate successor to David. Solomon seized an early opportunity to rid himself of this threat: Adonijah was executed as soon as he was suspected of scheming against Solomon. David's powerful general Joab, one of Adonijah's supporters, was also executed, and Abiathar the priest, another of Adonijah's chief supporters, was exiled to his own estate in Anathoth (1 Kings 2:13–35). Solomon also put to death Shimei, a supporter of the house of Saul (1 Kings 2:36–46). In this way, the Bible tells us, "the kingdom was established in the hand of Solomon" (1 Kings 2:46).

Outside of Israel, the Egyptian pharaoh, probably Siamun, tried to take advantage of the change in rulers to intervene.[67] He organized a military expedition that seized and destroyed Gezer (1 Kings 9:16), a destruction that now seems confirmed by archaeological excavations.[68] Apparently the pharaoh did not go further, however; that is, he did not enter Solomon's territory. On the contrary, perhaps because he was aware of Solomon's power, he made an alliance with Solomon[69] and gave one of his daughters to Solomon as a wife, with the city of Gezer as her dowry (1 Kings 3:1, 7:8, 11:1). Such an unusual marriage reflects Egypt's weakness at the time.[70] Perhaps Solomon had promised in return not to attack the Philistine territory, which was, at least theoretically, under Egyptian sovereignty.

Except for the addition of Gezer, Solomon's kingdom was probably the same as David's kingdom, at least at the beginning of his reign. No significant change in external policy occurred except, perhaps, a development in commercial relations with Hiram, king of Tyre (1 Kings 5:1–18).

Like David, Solomon entered diplomatic marriages to ensure the fidelity of neighboring kingdoms. He probably married "Naamah the Ammonitess," whose son later became King Rehoboam (1 Kings 14:21).[71] According to 1 Kings 4:21 (Old Testament), Solomon, like his father, "ruled over all the kingdoms from the River [the Euphrates] to Philistia, as far as the Egyptian frontier; they were bringing gifts (or tribute) and were subject to him all his life." But this general assertion needs to be qualified, especially for Philistia (see above) and for Damascus's kingdom (see below), as well as more generally for northern Syria and the Phoenician coast north of Tyre.

Solomon also reorganized the administration of his kingdom, a task to which he devoted very considerable effort and for which biblical tradition accords him the title "wise" (hakam)—that is to say, he was both a clever politician and a good administrator. Various areas of administrative organization or reorganization can be distinguished.[72] First was the central government, in which a new royal cabinet was nominated:

> And these were his high officials: Azariah the son of Zadok was the priest; Elihoreph and Ahijah the sons of Shisha were secretaries; Jehoshaphat the son of Ahilud was recorder; Benaiah the son of Jehoiada was in command of the army; Zadok and Abiathar were priests;[73] Azariah the son of Nathan was over the officers; Zabud the son of Nathan was priest and king's friend; Ahishar was in charge of the palace; and Adoniram the son of Abda was in charge of the forced labor.
>
> (1 Kings 4:2–6)

In comparison with David's royal cabinet (2 Samuel 8:16), Solomon's appointments reflect a certain continuity, a son often inheriting his father's position. We can also detect Egyptian influence in the bureaucratic structure.[74] There are new officials such as the man over the officers/governors, the man in charge of the administration of the palace and the man in charge of the forced labor levy. In general, the bureaucracy became more complex and more pervasive.

Two sons of the prophet Nathan were made members of this cabinet, probably because of the prominent part their father played in the designation of Solomon as king (1 Kings 1:11–38).

Israelite territory now included a number of annexed Canaanite city-states, such as Dor, Megiddo and Beth-Shean. As it expanded, Israel was divided into 12 administrative districts or provinces.[75] Each province had at its head a prefect or governor appointed by the king. Administration was thus centralized. In 1 Kings 4:8–19 (Old Testament) we find a list of the governors with their territories and principal cities, which presents a good parallel to other ancient Near Eastern administrative lists.[76] At least two governors married Solomon's daughters (1 Kings 4:11,15), another way of centralizing and controlling the government administration.

Each administrative district was required to provide for the king and his palace for one month a year (1 Kings 4:7; 4:27–28 [Old Testament]). This was a heavier economic responsibility than it might at first seem. It included the expenses of maintaining the royal harem, of providing for a number of functionaries and of equipping the army with horses and chariots (1 Kings 4:28 [Old Testament] = 1 Kings 5:8 [Hebrew Bible]). As in David's reign, the royal treasury also received income from royal properties. Although the royal treasury did not receive as much booty in Solomon's reign as in David's, Solomon's treasury was supplied regularly with tribute from administered territories and from vassal lands (1 Kings 4:21 [Old Testament] = 1 Kings 5:1 [Hebrew Bible]).

Trade and construction during Solomon's reign

Solomon also developed an important new source of income from the international trade that became so important during his peaceful reign.[77] The government operated this trade, and the royal treasury profited from it in various ways: Trade with Phoenicia provided timber (cedar and pine) and technical aid (mainly for the construction of Solomon's official buildings). In exchange, Israel supplied agricultural produce (wheat and olive oil) (1 Kings 5:8–11 [Old Testament] = 1 Kings 5:22–25 [Hebrew Bible]). In cooperation with the Tyrians, Solomon sent trading expeditions to Ophir[78] through the Red Sea.[79] These expeditions brought back gold, precious stones and tropical products (*almug* wood, apes and baboons) (1 Kings 9:26–28, 10:11,22). Caravans through the Arabian desert returned with spices (1 Kings 10:1–10).

Although Solomon's reign was comparatively peaceful (David had been almost continually at war), he nevertheless took care to modernize his army.[80] He equipped it with large numbers of chariots imported from Egypt, for which he imported horses from the kingdom of Que (Cilicia) (1 Kings 10:26–29).[81] Solomon also built special garrisons in various administrative districts for his chariots and their horses (1 Kings 4:26–28 [Old Testament] = 1 Kings 5:6–8 [Hebrew Bible]; 9:19).

Solomon is also famous for his building activities. He constructed a wall around Jerusalem and built three fortified cities, Hazor,

Megiddo and Gezer (1 Kings 9:15). These building activities can be related to military defense (see 1 Kings 9:17–18).[82] Solomon's public works in Jerusalem were major accomplishments. It took him seven years to build the Temple (1 Kings 6:37–38) and 13 years to build his royal palace (1 Kings 7:1, 9:10). He also built a structure in Jerusalem known as the *millo*. No one today is certain what the *millo* was. The most likely suggestion is that it was some kind of terracing, since the word seems to be related to the Hebrew term for "fill."[83]

To plan and construct these official buildings, Solomon needed the technical aid of the Phoenicians, who provided assistance not only with the basic architecture and structure, but also with the decoration of the buildings and the acquisition of the raw materials (wood, ivory, gold). These imports were expensive. Indeed, during the second part of his reign, "King Solomon gave to Hiram twenty cities in the land of Galilee" (1 Kings 9:11–13), that is "the Land of Cabul"[84] (Asher with the rich plain of Acco),[85] to balance the trade deficit between the two kings. To cast the many bronze objects decorating the Temple and the royal palace, Solomon used his metalworks in the Jordan Valley "between Succoth and Zarethan." The casting seems to have been supervised by a Phoenician who specialized in bronze craftsmanship (1 Kings 7:13–47). The origin of the metal is not specified, and Solomon's copper mines—if indeed they existed—have not been found.[86]

The Bible's detailed description of Solomon's public buildings, especially the Temple (1 Kings 5–6), reflects not only the importance of these monuments to the king's glory but also to the people. Jerusalemites, as well as pilgrims, were no doubt proud to see such achievements, which helped to legitimize the new political organization.[87] However, to build and maintain them Solomon needed a reservoir of cheap manpower. His solution was the corvée, forced labor required not only of non-Israelite peoples (1 Kings 9:20–21) but of Israelites as well. The statement in 1 Kings 9:22 that "of the people of Israel Solomon made no slaves" seems contradicted by several statements in Kings (1 Kings 5:13–18 [Old Testament] = 1 Kings 6:27–32 [Hebrew Bible]; 11:28; 12:4). The corvée and the conscription of Israelites into Solomon's army (1 Kings 9:22) were probably the two principal sources of popular dissatisfaction with Solomon's reign.[88]

As often happens during long reigns, internal discontent grew in the latter half of Solomon's rule; at the same time, serious external threats surfaced. The biblical tradition gives us a few hints of the dissension inside Israel, as well as of disturbances in the vassal states (1 Kings 11).[89]

The text speaks of two foreign adversaries (*satan*) of Solomon: The first was "Hadad the Edomite [Aramean]." A member of the royal house of Edom (Aram),[90] Hadad sought refuge in Egypt and even married a sister of the queen (Tahpenes) before trying to go back to his country (1 Kings 11:14–22). The second adversary of Solomon was "Rezon the son of Eliyada," who fled from his master Hadadezer, king of Zobah, and took to the hills as the chief of a small troop: "They went to Damascus, and dwelt there and made him king in Damascus" (1 Kings 11:23–24). (Actually, as we will discuss below, these two enemies might have been one and the same: "the Aramean Prince/*Rezon* Hadad son of Eliyada.")

In Israel itself, internal dissatisfaction led to a revolt spearheaded by Jeroboam, an Ephraimite who had the support of the prophet Ahijah from Shiloh: "Solomon sought therefore to kill Jeroboam; but Jeroboam arose and fled into Egypt, to Shishak king of Egypt and was in Egypt until the death of Solomon" (1 Kings 11:29–40).[91]

The dissatisfaction with Solomon's rule probably had many sources, but the biblical tradition insists principally on the people's objections, based on religious grounds, to Solomon's many foreign wives.

> For when Solomon was old his wives turned away his heart after other gods ... He went after Ashtoreh, the goddess of the Sidonians, and after Milcom, the abomination of the Ammonites ... Then Solomon built a high place for Chemosh the abomination of Moab, and for Molech (Milcom)[92] the abomination of the Ammonites, on the mountain[93] east of Jerusalem.
>
> (1 Kings 11:4–7)

The biblical account of Solomon's reign closes by again mentioning the wisdom of Solomon (1 Kings 11:41; see previously 1 Kings 4:29–34 [Old Testament] = 1 Kings 5:9–14 [Hebrew Bible] and 1 Kings 10:1–13) and by fixing the length of his reign at 40 years (1 Kings 11:42).

Biblical text vs. history   As with David, it is difficult to assess as history the biblical traditions regarding Solomon's reign. In the absence of contemporary Hebrew texts or references to Solomon in ancient Near Eastern texts, we must depend almost exclusively on the Bible and archaeology.

The principal parts of 1 Kings 1–11 contain an early literary tradition that appears to have been taken from a now-lost account of Solomon's reign, referred to in the Bible as "the Acts of Solomon" (1 Kings 11:41), which was probably written not long after Solomon's death. The lost account presented Solomon as a typically wise king since it could not speak about his glory at war.[94] However, this early tradition is often mixed with later Deuteronomistic additions and with emendations by later editors.[95] For instance, two different literary traditions seem to have been combined in 1 Kings 9:26–10:13, concerning the journey to Ophir and the visit of the Queen of Sheba. Part of the early tradition preserved in Kings tries to justify and exalt Solomon. This is even truer of later traditions. For example, 2 Chronicles 8:3–4 refers to Solomon's expedition to northern Syria: "And Solomon went to Hamath-Zobah and took it. He built Tadmor [Palmyra] in the wilderness and all the store-cities which he built in Hamath." However, the Hebrew text of 1 Kings 9:15–18, which lists Solomon's building projects, does not mention Hamath-Zobah or Tadmor. These names are probably a conforming alteration of 1 Kings 9:15–18 by the author of Chronicles.[96] In the same way, the Hebrew text of 1 Kings 9:19 mentions "Lebanon," in addition to Jerusalem, as a place where Solomon conducted building activities; however, "Lebanon" is missing in some manuscripts of the Greek translation known as the Septuagint and probably has no historical basis.

Nonetheless, if we put aside overstatements and later additions, and discount for the flattering style of most of the texts, the principal points of the biblical tradition seem generally trustworthy. We can rely most heavily on passages that are close in style to contemporaneous annals and administrative texts.[97]

Our extrabiblical knowledge of the history of the region during this period provides information regarding several aspects of Solomon's reign, especially in connection with his relations with Egypt,[98] but also with Phoenicia and Sheba. And archaeology helps us to understand Solomon's reputation as a builder, as well as the social transformation that took place during his reign.

Although Egypt is hardly mentioned as a political power in the biblical accounts of David's reign, several pharaohs did play an important role in Solomon's day. At the beginning of Solomon's reign, a pharaoh attacked Gezer. This pharaoh, as earlier mentioned, was probably Siamun, one of the last pharaohs of the XXIst Dynasty.[99] Although Egyptian texts thus far discovered do not confirm the matrimonial alliance between Solomon and the pharaoh's daughter, several studies have tried to show that there was a strong Egyptian cultural influence at Solomon's court. As evidence, these studies cite the design of the royal cabinet[100] and Solomon's organization of the country into 12 administrative districts.[101] Regarding the 12 administrative districts, however, some scholars contend that the influence went in the opposite direction.[102] That the same type of administrative organization appears at about the same time in Israel as in Egypt is probably not a mere coincidence, although the direction of influence is not entirely clear. It is also quite possible that the literary tradition of the 12 sons of Jacob and of the 12 tribes of Israel finds its origin in this organization into 12 administrative districts, as Gösta W. Ahlström has suggested.[103] The notion of 12 tribes of Israel would thus be a retrojection from this period to the patriarchal age.

Another pharaoh mentioned in the biblical account of Solomon's reign (in connection with Jeroboam's revolt [1 Kings 11:26–42]) is called "Shishak." This is Pharaoh Sheshonk, the founder of the XXIInd Dynasty. Shishak was a strong personality who wanted to restore

*Relations
with Egypt*

Egyptian power, especially in the ancient Egyptian province of
Canaan. His accession to the throne (c. 945 B.C.E.) probably marks a
turning point in Solomon's reign. Instead of an ally and friend,
Shishak was hostile to the Israelite king and supportive of all his
opponents. Finally, in the fifth year of the reign of Solomon's successor and son, Rehoboam, Shishak organized a military expedition
against the kingdoms of Judah and Israel (1 Kings 14:25–28).[104]

It is therefore not surprising to find Shishak supporting Jeroboam's
revolt. This political and military threat—and the independence of
Damascus—probably increased the financial strains on Solomon. He
received less tribute and had to spend more money on defense.

*Relations
with
Phoenicia*

A literary tradition sheds some light on the relationship between
Israel and Phoenicia at this time. Preserved in Phoenician annals, the
tradition has been transmitted to us second- or thirdhand through
Menander of Ephesus, Alexander Dius Polyhistor and Josephus.[105]
Although we must read these works with some caution, because
they evolved indirectly via two or three Greek intermediaries, they
are part of a serious literary tradition; they reflect the use of actual
Tyrian archives or annals telling about the principal military expedi-
tions and building activities of the Phoenician kings.[106] Some kind of
Solomonic annals probably existed as a contemporaneous parallel—
and may well have been partly inspired by the Phoenician annals.
Thus Josephus quotes Dius Polyhistor, probably from his history of
Phoenicia:

> On the death of Abibalus [Abibaal], his son Hirom came to the
> throne. He leveled up the eastern part of the city with embank-
> ments, enlarged the town, united it by a causeway to the temple
> of Olympian Zeus, which was isolated on an island, and adorned
> it with offerings of gold; he also went up to Libanus and had tim-
> ber cut down for the construction of temples.[107]

Menander of Ephesus, as quoted by Josephus, writes of a similar tradition.[108] Even if these texts present historical problems of
their own and differ in detail, they were probably originally based
on the same annals of Tyre and thus shed some light on the cultural and commercial relations between Hiram and Solomon.
Furthermore, other late traditions as well as some Phoenician
inscriptions confirm the important part played by the Phoenicians,
mainly the Tyrians, in the maritime trade of the Red Sea during the
first millennium B.C.E.[109]

*The Queen
of Sheba*

Although in the Bible the story of the Ophir expedition through the
Red Sea is now intertwined with the expedition of the Queen of
Sheba (1 Kings 9:26–10:22), these two events should not be con-
fused. The Queen of Sheba did not come on Phoenician-Israelite

ships plying the Red Sea but traveled instead on camels and brought with her primarily spices. These two features are characteristic of the Arabian peninsula. Although the story of the Queen of Sheba contains various literary and legendary themes and was clearly written to glorify Solomon, Assyrian texts of the eighth and seventh centuries B.C.E. do mention a kingdom of Sheba in Arabia and several queens of northern Arabian kingdoms.[110] Other Assyrian texts, connected with Hindanu on the Middle Euphrates, show that the international South-Arabian trade was already in place in about 890 B.C.E.[111] In light of these texts, we know that an official mission of Sheba could well have come from southern Arabia to Jerusalem in the second half of the tenth century B.C.E.

The confused story of Hadad the "Edomite" and "Rezon the son of Eliyada" (1 Kings 11:14–22) probably represents a distorted image of a historical tradition concerning the first king of Damascus: the Aramean Prince (*Rezon*) Hadad, son of Eliyada,[112] whose revolt Solomon apparently did not dare to crush by a military expedition, which means that Solomon probably did not control any Aramean country.

Relations with Edom— or Aram?

Epigraphic discoveries from the period of the United Kingdom are still very rare. An exception is the famous Gezer calendar, a small limestone tablet containing a list of the 12 months with the agricultural work performed in each month. However, this inscription may well be Philistian Semitic rather than Hebrew.[113]

Writing

Despite this paucity, the period of David and Solomon was probably an important period of literary creation, much of it composed to support ideological and political goals of the government. Although a matter of considerable scholarly dispute, Israelite historiography probably began at this time.[114] It is likely that its development paralleled that of Phoenician historiography (see above). It may have begun with a history of David's accession written by Abiathar the priest or by someone close to him.[115] David and, even more so, Solomon probably promoted the writing of a history that brought together the early Israelite traditions originally connected with different sanctuaries (Shechem, Hebron, Beersheba, Shiloh, etc.).[116] The original unification of these early traditions may have been the work of the famous and much discussed Yahwist.[117] The Yahwist (also called J) is the earliest strand of tradition in the Pentateuch, according to the so-called documentary hypothesis, which divides the Pentateuch into four different strands, the others being E (for Elohist), P (Priestly Code and history) and D (Deuteronomist). J probably established the tradition of the 12 sons of Jacob and was the first to present Abraham, Isaac and Jacob as members of the same family.

Gezer calendar. Inscribed in soft
limestone in the tenth century
B.C.E., this tablet is the oldest
known Hebrew inscription of
significant length. Small enough to
be held in one hand, it lists by month
a farmer's duties—planting, reaping,
vine-tending, and so on.

ERICH LESSING

Solomon's complex state administration required officials who could
read and write. The development of national historical and legal traditions, as well as a new royal ideology, also required literate scribes. We
may therefore assume that there were scribes and probably schools in
Jerusalem[118] and in the capitals of the administrative districts[119] as well
as in some of the ancient Canaanite city-states. The tradition of
Solomon "the wise ... who declared 3,000 proverbs and 1,005 songs"
is clearly an exaggeration (1 Kings 4:32 [Old Testament] = 1 Kings 5:12
[Hebrew Bible]); nevertheless, the Solomonic period, probably in part
under Egyptian influence (note the use of hieratic ciphers in later
Hebrew epigraphy), no doubt saw the birth of an important stream of
Hebrew literature connected with royal ideology.

Solomon and   Archaeology also sheds some light on the activities of Solomon as a
archaeology   builder and on the contemporaneous transformation of Israelite society. According to William G. Dever, the tenth-century B.C.E. architectural remains "are not only the earliest evidence we possess of
monumental architecture in ancient Israel but [the buildings] are
among the most impressive."[120]

The Solomonic Temple was probably completely destroyed by the
Babylonians in 586 B.C.E. After the Israelites returned from the

ZEV RADOVAN, JERUSALEM

The Stepped-Stone Structure. *Located on the eastern ridge of the City of David, this massive stone structure originally stood nearly 90 feet tall and 130 feet wide at top. It is preserved to a height of 50 feet, making it one of the most imposing structures to have survived from ancient Israel. The Stepped-Stone Structure may have been built to support a public building or as part of a fortification system. Although scholars agree that the structure incorporates several centuries of building, the dating of the various elements is contested. The most recent excavations date its core to pre-Davidic times, suggesting it may have been part of the fortress that defended Jebusite Jerusalem when King David successfully assaulted the city, in about 1000 B.C.E.*

Babylonian Exile, a second Temple was built. This Temple was rebuilt by Herod the Great in the first century B.C.E. and subsequently burned by the Romans in 70 C.E. According to Ernest-Marie Laperrousaz, however, part of the Solomonic retaining wall of the Temple Mount (the platform on which the Temple stood) can still be seen on the eastern side of the Temple Mount as it exists today.[121] (This particular part of the wall begins north of the so-called straight joint on the eastern wall of the Temple Mount, 105.5 feet north of its southeast corner.)

The recent excavations in the City of David (a spur south of the present Temple Mount), led by Yigal Shiloh, have uncovered a huge Stepped-Stone Structure probably built to support an enlarged platform on top of the northern part of the City of David. The platform may have supported a public building—perhaps the royal palace; or the Stepped-Stone Structure may be the famous *millo* mentioned in 1 Kings 9:15. However this last interpretation is conjectural and the dating of this structure is disputed (13th/12th or 10th century B.C.E.), as is the date of the monumental archaeological fragments

(10th or 9th century B.C.E.) found north of the Ophel that could be connected with Solomon's palace.[122]

Other remains from the City of David that have been dated to the tenth century B.C.E. include a few walls discovered by Yigal Shiloh and a wall fragment excavated by Kathleen Kenyon. Further, Jane Cahill, who is preparing Shiloh's excavation for publication, has recently argued that the Stepped-Stone Structure (which she dates to the 13th/12th century B.C.E.) was partially dismantled in the tenth century to accommodate the construction of houses on top.[123]

As noted, in 1 Kings 9:15–17 we are told that Solomon rebuilt three Canaanite cities that became part of his kingdom—Hazor, Megiddo and Gezer. Major excavations have been conducted at each of these three cities. Yigael Yadin, followed by many others, tried to demonstrate that these three cities were probably rebuilt in about the middle of the tenth century B.C.E. (the time of Solomon).[124] Yadin and other archaeologists have based their conclusions on the presence of almost identical fortification plans at all three sites. Each city is surrounded by a casemate wall* and has a gateway with three chambers on each side (that is, with four pairs of piers) of nearly the same dimensions. Furthermore the ashlars (hewn stones) of these three gateways are dressed the same way. All these similarities in design can best be explained as having been the work of the same architect or school of architects during Solomon's reign.[125] These dates and this interpretation have been corroborated by later excavations at Gezer by William Dever[126] and at Hazor by Amnon Ben-Tor.[127] The dating of the gate of Megiddo, however, is still a matter of dispute.[128]

The stratigraphy of Megiddo at the beginning of Iron Age II (beginning in about 1000 B.C.E.) is not at all clear. So, for instance, the structures identified by early American excavators as Solomonic stables[129] were redated by Yadin to the ninth century B.C.E.[130] Furthermore, their identification as "stables" is still a matter of dispute.[131] However, Graham I. Davies has shown that a similar, earlier building at Megiddo might well have been the Solomonic stables.[132] Most archaeologists date level VA-IVB at Megiddo to the tenth century, corresponding to the Solomonic period.[133] This dating has recently been questioned by David Ussishkin, who argues that, at least for the "Solomonic" gate, this level must be dated to the ninth century;[134] moreover, G.J. Wightman[135] and Israel Finkelstein[136] propose a general shift in the dating, lowering what have been thought of as tenth-century B.C.E. remains to the ninth century. This proposal, however, is beset with major problems and has been rejected by many excavators at other sites.[137] We can only hope that the renewed excavations at Megiddo will clarify the dating there.

---

*A casemate wall consists of two parallel walls crossed by short perpendicular walls that form internal rooms for storage, etc.

Gezer gate. In 1 Kings 9:15, we read that Solomon fortified "Hazor, Megiddo and Gezer." In this view from inside Gezer, we see six chambers (three on each side) of a monumental gate dated to the tenth century B.C.E. Nearly identical gates have been discovered at Hazor and Megiddo, and for decades, archaeologists have believed that all three gates were evidence of Solomon's handiwork—mighty public works constructed by a powerful central authority. Recently, however, excavators at Megiddo have redated the gate at their site to the ninth century B.C.E., nearly 100 years after Solomon. In renewed excavations at Hazor, the excavator confirms the tenth-century date of that gate.

Another town mentioned in 1 Kings 9:18 is "Tamar in the wilderness," which has been identified with 'En Hazeva. Excavations led by Rudolph Cohen and Yigal Yisrael at this site have revealed a tenth-century B.C.E. level (stratum VI), which seems to match with Solomonic building.[138]

More generally, many archaeological sites in ancient Israel appear to have been built or rebuilt around the middle of the tenth century.[139] These sites include new cities as well as fortresses. Indeed a network of early Iron Age fortresses in the Negev may be connected with Solomon's reign.[140] Some of them were later destroyed by Pharaoh Shishak's military expedition in about 925 B.C.E.

From the point of view of archaeology, the general picture of the mid-tenth century B.C.E. seems to be that of a booming, transitional society. Israelites areas were inhabited not only by farmers and stock-breeders in villages but also, beginning in the tenth century, by craftsmen, merchants and functionaries who served in the army and in the government administration and lived in royal fortified cities.

Archaeology attests to the beginning of a process of reurbanization typical of an early state.[141] This social change, from a tribal society to an early state under a central administration probably accounts for the appearance of public buildings in the new fortified cities—governors' palaces, storehouses and administrative buildings.[142] At about this time, we also begin to find many small precious objects. As Yohanan Aharoni notes, "The change in material culture during the tenth century is discernible not only in luxury items but also especially in ceramics," which are of a higher quality.[143] The economic growth and development of new cities was probably connected with a population boom, natural in a period of peace and prosperity. In the area inhabited by Israel, the population could well have doubled in the century that extended from the beginning of Saul's reign to the end of Solomon's.[144] By this time, the sedentary population of the Judahite hills (not including the Shephelah and the Negev) made up probably only 3 percent of the total population of the country.[145]

Social and political tensions

This transformation of Israelite society into an early state and the requirements of the new state's administrative structures[146] were resisted by many levels of Israelite society.[147] This was especially so among the "house of Israel" (the northern tribes), which wanted to retain its own religious and political traditions. Social tensions were also produced by the mixing of the populations in Solomon's military conscription and the forced levy (the corvée). All this certainly served to sharpen the antagonisms between Israel and Judah.[148] No doubt, members of the House of Israel resented the Judahites, who probably held the better positions in the civil government and in the military. Solomon's death and the political errors of his successor soon revealed the unstable base on which he and David had set their achievements, and probably delayed the further evolution of Israelite and Judahite society into a well-organized national state. Moreover, that evolution would now occur in two separate states.

Plate 1. The Sinai peninsula. *This view of the "great and terrible wilderness" (Deuteronomy 8:15) traversed by the Israelites on their Exodus wanderings was taken by a NASA satellite miles out in space. (See Chapter II.)*

HERSHEL SHANKS

Plate 2. Tomb painting from Beni Hasan, Egypt. *Leaning over his ibex, a figure named Abisha and identified by the title Hyksos leads brightly garbed Semitic clansmen into Egypt to conduct trade. Dating to about 1890 B.C.E., the painting is preserved on the wall of a tomb carved into cliffs overlooking the Nile at Beni Hasan, about halfway between Cairo and Luxor.*

Foreign groups often sojourned in Egypt, especially in pursuit of trade. In the early second millennium B.C.E., numerous Asiatics infiltrated Egypt, some of whom eventually gained control over Lower Egypt for about a century and a half. The governing class of these people became known as the Hyksos, which means "Rulers of Foreign Lands." Knowledge of this period of Asiatic rule in Egypt may have affected the biblical account of Joseph's rise to power. (See Chapter II.)

COLLECTION ISRAEL ANTIQUITIES AUTHORITY/
EXHIBITED AND PHOTOGRAPHED ISRAEL MUSEUM

Plate 3. Philistine pottery. *The fine craftsmanship of these pitchers and bowls challenges the traditional characterization of the Philistines as a boorish, warlike people devoid of an aesthetic sensibility. Known as bichrome ware because it was decorated with two colors—black and red—this pottery displays typical Philistine designs, including birds (visible on the wine decanter, at right), checkerboards, spirals and other geometric patterns. (See Chapter IV.)*

ISRAEL MUSEUM

Plate 4. Canaanite cult stand from Taanach. *Four tiers of cryptic scenes ornament this tenth-century B.C.E. pottery stand from Taanach (about 5 miles southeast of Megiddo). A shallow basin—presumably for offerings or libations—crowns the 21-inch-high stand. The bottom register depicts, in high relief, a nude female figure, perhaps the mother-goddess Asherah, holding the ears of two lions. Winged sphinxes flank the opening in the second register. Lions appear again on the third register; between them, two goats nibble on a stylized tree—perhaps a "tree of life"—a motif associated with Asherah. Two columns frame the top scene, which depicts a horse or calf with a winged sun-disk above its back.*

Although the images are often identified as the Canaanite deities Baal (represented as a bull) and Asherah, it has recently been suggested that they actually represent the Israelite deity Yahweh (represented by the horse and by the empty space in the second register) with Asherah as his consort. (See Chapters III and IV.)

Plate 5. Ivory cherub. *Modeled in ivory, this 5-inch-tall ivory plaque, dating to the ninth or eighth century B.C.E., depicts a winged creature with an exquisite human face, the forequarters of a lion and what may be the hindquarters of a bull. Such composite creatures, like the Egyptian sphinx, were common in the ancient Near East, where they were often associated with divinity. This ivory, probably from Arslan Tash in northern Syria, recalls the cherub described by the prophet Ezekiel as combining characteristics of humans, lions, bulls and eagles (Ezekiel 1:10). Mentioned more than 90 times in the Hebrew Bible, cherubim guarded the gates of the Garden of Eden and stood over the Ark in the Holy of Holies in the Temple.*

Solomon's "great throne of ivory," described in 1 Kings 10:18, may have been decorated with such ivory plaques. Ornamenting thrones and beds with ivory was a well-known specialty of the Phoenicians, Solomon's trading partners. (See Chapter IV.)

COLLECTION ISRAEL ANTIQUITIES AUTHORITY/PHOTO BY ZEV RADOVAN

Plate 6. Israelite bull figurine. *Dating to about 1200 B.C.E., this 4-inch-tall bronze statue was discovered at a cult site near biblical Dothan, in the heart of the hill country that was then being settled by the Israelites.*

Although the biblical writers consistently condemn the iconography of young bulls, archaeological finds such as this indicate that the bull was an early Israelite symbol of divinity. This figurine may resemble the bull statues erected by Jeroboam (c. 930–908 B.C.E.) at Bethel and Dan (1 Kings 12:26–33). (See Chapter V.)

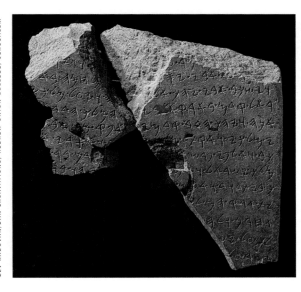

ZEV RADOVAN/DAN EXCAVATIONS, HEBREW UNION COLLEGE, JERUSALEM

Plate 7. Tel Dan Stele. *An Aramean king—probably Hazael of Damascus—boasts of his victories over "[Jo]ram son of [Ahab], king of Israel," and "[Ahaz]iah son of [Jehoram, ki]ng of the House of David," in this Old Aramaic inscription from Dan. The dates of the reigns of the biblical kings Joram of Israel (c. 850–841 B.C.E.) and Ahaziah of Judah (c. 841 B.C.E.) provide a mid-ninth-century B.C.E. date for the inscription. The reference to "the House [or dynasty] of David" suggests that Judahite kings traced their descent back to an actual David who lived a century earlier. It is the earliest appearance of the name of David outside the Bible. (See Chapter V.)*

Plate 8. Ivory pomegranate from Solomon's Temple. *This exquisite carving may be the only surviving artifact from Solomon's Temple in Jerusalem. A small hole bored into the bottom of the ivory indicates that it served as the decorative head of a ceremonial scepter carried by Temple priests.*

The fragmentary inscription around the neck reads "Holy to the priests, belonging to the H[ouse of Yahwe]h." The paleo-Hebrew script dates to the late eighth century B.C.E., around the time of King Hezekiah (727–697 B.C.E.), who attempted to centralize all Israelite worship in the Jerusalem Temple. (See Chapter V.)

Plate 9. Herodium. *To protect himself in case of insurrection, Herod the Great (37–4 B.C.E.) built a string of palace-fortresses—including this volcano-like structure that he named after himself—in the Judean wilderness. At Herodium, Herod started with a natural hill and then created an artificial mountain over it. Inside he fashioned a palace that included living rooms, a reception and dining hall, a colonnaded courtyard, cisterns and a bathhouse. Four massive towers and a double wall protected the intimate palace. At the foot of the mountain, a 135-foot by 21-foot basin (visible in the left foreground) served as a reservoir, a pool and a lake for small sailboats; picnickers may have enjoyed the circular pavilion at the center of this desert oasis. (See Chapter VIII.)*

GARO NALBANDIAN

BARON WOLMAN

Plate 10. Masada. *This imposing citadel—built by Herod the Great (37–4 B.C.E.) on an isolated plateau at the edge of the Judean wilderness—is associated with a legendary act of defiance. According to the first-century C.E. Jewish historian Josephus, a band of Jewish fighters, unwilling to concede defeat during the First Jewish Revolt against Rome, held out at Masada for more than three years against a large imperial army after the fall of Jerusalem in 70 C.E. Masada fell in 73 or 74 C.E., when the Romans built a ramp on a spur on the western side of the plateau. (See Chapter VIII.)*

F I V E

The Divided Monarchy
The Kingdoms of Judah and Israel

SIEGFRIED H. HORN
revised by P. Kyle McCarter, Jr.

The Early Years

WHEN SOLOMON DIED, HIS SON REHOBOAM (C. 930–913 B.C.E.) succeeded him as king of Judah, apparently without incident (1 Kings 11:43). Rehoboam then traveled north to Shechem to lay his claim to the throne of Israel as well. The account of the ensuing negotiations preserved in 1 Kings 12 suggests that the leaders of the northern tribes were prepared to accept Rehoboam's rule, as long as the new king mitigated the harsh labor policies of his father. Historians assume that part of their concern was the tax burden required to support Solomon's building projects and to maintain his palace, as detailed in the description of revenue collection in the administrative districts he established (1 Kings 4:7–28), but the only grievances expressed in the account of the Shechem parley are "the hard service of your father and the heavy yoke that he placed on us" (1 Kings 12:4). According to 1 Kings 9:15–23, Solomon imposed *corvée*, or conscript labor, only on the foreign, non-Israelite population, while the Israelites involved in his work projects served as overseers and officers (1 Kings 12:22–23). Nevertheless, the language of the northern leaders' complaint indicates that they felt enslaved by Solomon's labor policies, and it is noteworthy that when the secession movement found a leader, he was a dissident officer in Solomon's labor force and a fugitive from the king's justice.

The schism at the death of Solomon

As a young man from Zeredah (a town west of Shiloh in the Ephraimite highlands), Jeroboam son of Nebat had come to Solomon's attention because of his administrative skills and energy. Solomon placed him in charge of the *corvée* labor of the House of Joseph—that is, the conscript labor battalions of the territories of the half-tribes of Ephraim and Manasseh (1 Kings 11:26–28). Despite this high-ranking appointment, Jeroboam proved not to be a loyal member of Solomon's administration and, in circumstances not explained, he "lifted his hand against the king" (1 Kings 11:26), that is, he led some kind of insurrection. With Solomon's police seeking his life, Jeroboam fled to Egypt and found refuge with Pharaoh Sheshonk I (c. 945–924 B.C.E.), the biblical Shishak, in whose safekeeping he remained until Solomon's death.

Shishak, a Libyan nobleman, was the founder of the XXIInd Egyptian Dynasty, superseding the weak XXIst Dynasty, which, under Pharaoh Siamun (978–959 B.C.E.), seems to have made common cause with Israel and Judah against the Philistines. (See Chapter IV.) Shishak's hospitality to Jeroboam, however, may be an indication that Egypt, invigorated and ambitious after the rise of the XXIInd Dynasty, no longer felt the need for a policy of accommodation with Jerusalem. On the contrary, Shishak may have viewed the burgeoning power of Solomon's dual kingdom as a serious threat to Egyptian interests in Canaan.

After Solomon's death, Jeroboam returned to Israel. According to the account in 1 Kings 12, he exercised a leadership role in the parley at Shechem. As already noted, Rehoboam might have been able to win over the northern tribal leaders if he had dealt with them respectfully and assured them of less oppressive treatment. Indeed, his senior advisors recommended this course of action (1 Kings 12:7). But Rehoboam followed the advice of more junior advisors, his contemporaries, and replied to the petition of Jeroboam and his companions with hostility and even vulgarity: "My little finger is thicker than my father's loins" (1 Kings 12:10). Having been threatened by Rehoboam with policies even harsher than Solomon's, the northern leaders took up the slogan of Sheba's revolt—"What share do we have in David?" (compare 2 Samuel 20:1 with 1 Kings 12:16)—and withdrew from Shechem. When Rehoboam sent Adoram (or Adoniram; compare 1 Kings 4:6), his chief *corvée* officer, to raise a work levy, the Israelites stoned him to death (1 Kings 12:18), and the division of the kingdoms became an accomplished fact. Rehoboam was obliged to flee to Jerusalem for his own safety (1 Kings 12:18).

What role, if any, was played by Egypt in these events is difficult to say. A strong Israelite state, unified and including Judah, would be a threat to Egypt's interest in freely accessing, if not controlling, the trade routes along the coastal highway—the Via Maris or, as the Egyptians called it, the Way of Horus—and through the corridor running from Jezreel to Beth-Shean. Jeroboam must have used the time he spent in

Egypt to prepare for his role in the schism, and we may suspect that he did so with Shishak's encouragement if not his active tutelage. After the Israelites embraced Jeroboam as their king (1 Kings 12:20), however, there is no reason to think that he ruled as an Egyptian puppet or even with active Egyptian support. The earlier pharaoh Siamun may have been content to forge alliances with Israelite kings, but Shishak's ambition was greater.

Not long after the separation of Israel and Judah, Shishak led a large Egyptian army across the Sinai Peninsula into Canaan. Our knowledge of this campaign comes from brief accounts in 1 Kings 14:25–26 and 2 Chronicles 12:1–12, where it is dated to the fifth year of Rehoboam's reign (c. 926 B.C.E.), and from the hieroglyphic text that accompanies Shishak's triumphal relief on the so-called Bubastite Portal[1] on the south wall of the first forecourt of the Great Temple of Amun at Karnak in Thebes (modern Luxor). The biblical account gives the impression that the incursion was directed at Jerusalem (1 Kings 14:25) or at Jerusalem and the fortified cities of Judah (2 Chronicles 12:4), as if Shishak, who had given asylum to Jeroboam when he was a refugee, was now acting on his behalf in his ongoing conflict with Rehoboam of Judah (cf. 1 Kings 14:30; 2 Chronicles 12:15b). The list of conquered cities in the Karnak relief, however, shows that Shishak attacked cities throughout Canaan, north and south. In fact, many northern, or Israelite, cities appear on the list, but few Judahite cities. The Egyptian army marched through the heartland of the northern kingdom, subduing many of Jeroboam's own cities as well as the adjoining regions. Though the sequence of cities attacked is unclear in the Karnak list,[2] the itinerary included cities in the Plain of Sharon (Socoh, Yahma, Borim, Aruna), through the Jezreel corridor (Megiddo, Taanach, Shunem, Beth-Shean, Rehob) and east of the Jordan (Succoth, Penuel, Mahanaim, Adam). This shows that Shishak's campaign was not aimed at Judah in particular but was intended instead to reassert Egypt's ancient interests in Canaan and to reestablish some measure of influence, if not control, along the major trade routes. Both the organization of the campaign and the rhetoric of its memorialization at Karnak suggest that Shishak was nostalgically emulating the style of the great conqueror Ramesses II.[3]

Shishak's invasion

Even if Shishak cannot be said to have been acting on behalf of Jeroboam, however, it seems probable that his *initial* target was Jerusalem. The hieroglyphic text on the Bubastite Portal asserts that the campaign was undertaken in response to attacks by Asiatics, who were threatening Egyptian frontier settlements,[4] and it is possible that Shishak viewed Solomon's construction of fortresses in the southern Negev[5] as a provocation. After leaving Egypt and Sinai and entering Canaan, Shishak marched north through Gaza and began the assault at Gezer; from there he turned east into the southern Ephraimite hills and made his way

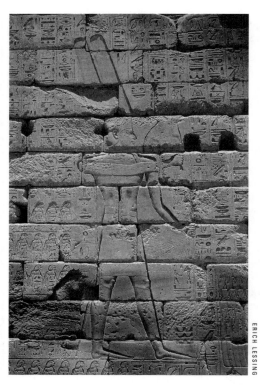

ERICH LESSING

The Bubastite Portal. *In the fifth year of the reign of Rehoboam, "King Shishak of Egypt ... took the fortified cities of Judah and came as far as Jerusalem" (2 Chronicles 12:2–4). Scenes depicting the military exploits of Pharaoh Sheshonk I (c. 945–924 B.C.E.)— biblical Shishak—decorate a doorway in the forecourt of the Great Temple of Amun at Karnak, in Thebes.*

towards Jerusalem along the usual northern approach, via Aijalon, Beth-horon, and Gibeon.[6] It was probably at this point, with the Egyptian army encamped in the hills north of Jerusalem, that Rehoboam paid Shishak the heavy tribute described in 1 Kings 14:26: "He took away the treasures of the house of the Lord and the treasures of the king's house; he took everything." Shishak, evidently satisfied with this payment, turned north, sparing the principal cities of Judah and Jerusalem itself. Later in the campaign, when the Egyptian army came south again, Shishak gave his attention to the region south of Judah; the Karnak list contains an extensive roster of places conquered in the Negev.

Shishak's invasion is especially important as a source of information for reconstructing the history of Israel. It provides our earliest clear connection between the history of Israel and the history of Egypt. The Egyptian materials in the Joseph story and the Exodus narrative, though rich and suggestive, are much more difficult to control as historical sources. In addition, Shishak's invasion gives us a conspicuous point of reference in the archaeological record. The techniques of siege warfare, which the neo-Assyrian conquerors would perfect a century later, were already well enough developed for Shishak to be able to capture and destroy cities throughout the region.[7] Excavators have found evidence of violent conflagrations in strata corresponding to the late tenth century at a number of sites along the itinerary recorded in the Bubastite Portal reliefs. Shishak's army has been posited as the agent of destruction at a large number of these sites, including some named in the extant portions of the itinerary and many others that are not.[8] The former group includes Arad, Gezer, Taanach and Megiddo, where a fragment of a stele erected by Shishak was found.

Two aspects of the archaeological record that emerge from an examination of the Shishak destructions are especially impressive and noteworthy.[9] One is the wide distribution and high quality of the tenth-century fortifications and other architecture, lending credence to the assumption that Solomon's later reputation as a great builder, as reflected in the biblical account of his reign (1 Kings 6–7, 9:15–23), was well deserved. The other noteworthy aspect of the archaeological record is the rapidity and thoroughness with which the destroyed cities were rebuilt, sometimes to an even higher standard.[10] This suggests that Shishak's incursion, as devastating as it was, had little lasting impact on the region.[11]

Shechem, where Rehoboam had failed to win the allegiance of the northern tribes, became the site of Jeroboam's government, but he soon moved his base of operations to Penuel, a town in Gilead that he is said to have fortified (1 Kings 12:25). Although historians have speculated that Jeroboam withdrew to Transjordan to seek refuge at the time of Shishak's incursion, the biblical narrative provides no reasons for the

The religious policies of Jeroboam

move. Nor is there any explanation why he eventually returned west and established a capital at Tirzah, as is implied by 1 Kings 14:17. In any case, Tirzah (now usually identified with the extensive tenth-century ruins at Tell el-Far'ah [North], northeast of Shechem) was the capital during the reigns of his successors, Baasha (1 Kings 15:33; cf. 1 Kings 15:21), Elah (1 Kings 16:8) and Zimri (1 Kings 16:15), until the sixth year of Omri, when Samaria was founded (1 Kings 16:23; cf. 1 Kings 16:24).

The paucity of information about Jeroboam's political headquarters in the biblical account contrasts sharply with the extended report on the national religious centers he established at Dan and Bethel (1 Kings 12:26–33; see also 1 Kings 13:1–14:18). This contrast is an indication of the interests of the writers whose work is preserved in the Books of Kings, our principal biblical resource for the history of the monarchy. This literature was given its primary shape by a historian whom scholars describe as Deuteronomistic, because his perspective on the history of Israel is based on religious ideas preserved in the Book of Deuteronomy. Many scholars believe that the Deuteronomistic historian wrote during the reign of King Josiah of Judah (640–609 B.C.E.) in support of the king's program of religious reform and cultic centralization.[12]

In any case, the historian placed special emphasis on Jerusalem as the divinely ordained central sanctuary for all Israel and the only place where sacrifice could legitimately be offered to the God of Israel. It was, in his view, "the place that the Lord your God will choose," foretold by Moses as the one acceptable place of sacrifice after the conquest of Canaan (Deuteronomy 12:13–14). From this perspective, Jeroboam's installation of national sanctuaries at Dan and Bethel was a fundamental breach of religious law and a flaunting of the divine will.

As the Deuteronomistic historian saw it (1 Kings 12:26–33), Jeroboam established these two cult centers because he feared that if his people continued to make regular pilgrimages to Jerusalem, they might eventually renew their allegiance to Rehoboam. He therefore established northern sanctuaries to replace Jerusalem in direct violation of Yahweh's instructions to Moses in Deuteronomy 12, and instituted a festival at Bethel beginning the fifteenth day of the eighth month—"a month that he alone had devised" (1 Kings 12:33), that is, without divine authorization—to rival the authorized festival of Sukkoth, which was celebrated in Jerusalem one month earlier (Leviticus 23:34; cf. Deuteronomy 16:13–17). He compounded this crime by fashioning two golden calves to be worshiped at the two sanctuaries and installing nonlevitical priests to officiate.

It is unlikely, however, that the people whose allegiance Jeroboam was trying to win, his contemporary Israelites from the northern tribes, viewed his actions as arbitrary innovation. For them, Jerusalem held no special claim to religious authority. A Canaanite enclave conquered by David, Jerusalem was the city of the Judahite kings Solomon and Rehoboam, and as such it represented outside rule and oppression. By contrast, Bethel was an ancient Yahwistic sanctuary, strongly associated with Israel's patriarchs (Genesis 12:8, 28:10–22). Dan, too, was a long-established center of Yahwism.[13] Even the bulls were probably old and authentic Yahwistic symbols.* In any case, there is no suggestion, even in our hostile Deuteronomistic account, that Jeroboam introduced any

---

*The iconography of the young bull is consistently condemned by the biblical writers, and it may never have had a place in the Jerusalem cult. Nevertheless, there is considerable evidence to suggest that it was an Israelite symbol of divinity with a venerable pedigree. A bronze bull figurine was found at a probable 12th-century B.C.E. cultic site, in the heart of the region that was then being settled by Israelites in the hill country of Samaria (Amihai Mazar, *Archaeology of the Land of the Bible 10,000–586 B.C.E.*, Anchor Bible Reference Library [New York: Doubleday, 1990], pp. 350–351; and "Bronze Bull Found in Israelite 'High Place' from the Time of the Judges," *BAR*, September/October 1983, pp. 34–40). The depiction of "Yahweh of Samaria" in *bovine* form on a *pithos* from Kuntillet 'Ajrud shows that bull iconography was still a viable form of religious expression at the beginning of the eighth century B.C.E. (P. Kyle McCarter, Jr., *Ancient Inscriptions: Voices from the Biblical World* [Washington, DC: Biblical Archaeology Society, 1996], pp. 106–108; Ze'ev Meshel, "Did Yahweh Have a Consort?" *BAR*, March/April 1979, pp. 24–35; and André Lemaire, "Who or What Was Yahweh's Asherah?" *BAR*, November/December 1984, pp. 42–51). Hosea's diatribes against "the calf of Samaria" (Hosea 8:5,6) and "the calf of Beth-aven" (Hosea 10:5, where Beth-aven, "House of Wickedness," is a pejorative distortion of Bethel, "House of God") show that it was still a part of the northern cult later in the eighth century B.C.E.

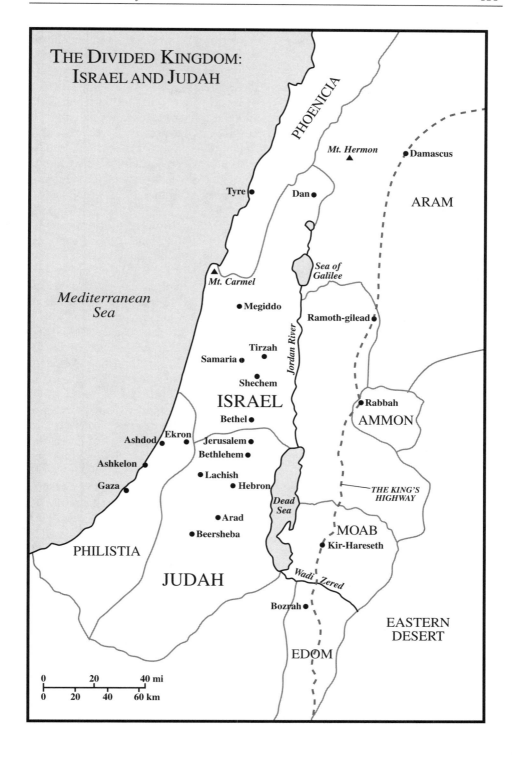

THE DIVIDED KINGDOM:
ISRAEL AND JUDAH

PHOENICIA

Mt. Hermon ▲ ● **Damascus**

Tyre ● **Dan** ● **ARAM**

*Mediterranean
Sea*

▲
Mt. Carmel

*Sea of
Galilee*

● **Megiddo** **Ramoth-gilead** ●

Jordan River

Tirzah
Samaria ● ●

● **Shechem**

ISRAEL

Bethel ● **Rabbah** ●

AMMON

Ashdod **Ekron** **Jerusalem** ●
● ● **Bethlehem** ●

Ashkelon ● ● **Lachish**
Hebron ●

Gaza ● *Dead
Sea* *THE KING'S
HIGHWAY*

● **Arad**
● **Beersheba**

PHILISTIA **MOAB**
● **Kir-Hareseth**

JUDAH
Wadi Zered

Bozrah ● **EASTERN
DESERT**

EDOM

```
0        20        40 mi
0    20    40    60 km
```

kind of non-Yahwistic cult. Nevertheless, from the Deuteronomistic perspective that shapes the larger biblical narrative of the early Divided Monarchy, Jeroboam's installation of the golden calves at Dan and Bethel was a heinous crime ("This thing became a sin," 1 Kings 12:30), for which his kingship would be divinely rejected and his family condemned (1 Kings 14:9–11). In the Deuteronomistic interpretation of history, moreover, the disastrous consequences of Jeroboam's crime spread beyond his own reign. "The sin of Jeroboam," as the Deuteronomistic historian called it, was perpetuated by his successors (1 Kings 15:26,34, etc.), and it eventually led to the fall of the northern kingdom and the exile of its people (2 Kings 17:21–23).[14]

The wars of the early Divided Monarchy

The early years of the Divided Monarchy were characterized by almost constant warfare between Israel and Judah. When Rehoboam died after a reign of some 17 years (1 Kings 14:21), he was succeeded by his short-lived son, Abijam (c. 913–911 B.C.E.) or Abijah (as he is called in Chronicles), about whom little is said except that he was victorious over Jeroboam in a major battle fought on the southern boundary of Ephraim (2 Chronicles 13:3–20; cf. 1 Kings 15:7).

Jeroboam died a few years later, and his son, Nadab (c. 908–907 B.C.E.), after only a couple of years rule, was assassinated by Baasha son of Ahijah, a member of the tribe of Issachar and one of Nadab's senior officers (1 Kings 15:25–31). The coup took place during an Israelite siege of the Philistine-controlled fortress of Gibbethon. This may be taken as an indication of ongoing border disputes between Israel and Philistia in this period, especially in view of the fact that Gibbethon (usually identified with Tell el-Malat, just west of Gezer) was under Israelite siege again a generation later when Baasha's son was unseated in another military coup (1 Kings 16:8–10). Baasha, having quickly secured his position by a massacre of the remaining members of the family of Jeroboam (1 Kings 15:29), was able to stabilize the situation and establish himself in Tirzah as the new king. He ruled for a substantial number of years (c. 907–884 B.C.E.), though we are told in 1 Kings 15:16 that his reign was troubled by constant warfare with Judah, which was now ruled by the even more long-lived Asa (c. 911–870 B.C.E.), Rehoboam's grandson.

At some point in the long reigns of these two kings (Baasha in the north and Asa in the south)—the year is uncertain and disputed—a series of events drew Damascus into the hostilities between Israel and Judah (1 Kings 15:17–22 = 2 Chronicles 16:1–6). Baasha's forces had captured and fortified the border fortress of Ramah (modern er-Ram) and imposed an embargo on Jerusalem, a few miles to the south. Asa sought the help of Ben-hadad, the king of Damascus.[15]

Asa, appealing to a former or still-existing treaty between Jerusalem and Damascus, asked Ben-hadad to invade Israel. He enticed the

Israel's Kings

The United Monarchy

Saul   c. 1030?–1009 B.C.E.
David   c. 1009/1001–969 B.C.E.
Solomon   c. 970/969–931 B.C.E.

The Divided Monarchy

Kingdom of Judah c. 930–587/6 B.C.E.		Kingdom of Israel c. 930–722 B.C.E.	
Rehoboam	c. 930–913	Jeroboam I	c. 930–908
Abijam (Abijah)	c. 913–911	Nadab	c. 908–907
Asa	c. 911–870	Baasha	c. 907–884
		Elah	c. 884–883
		Zimri	c. 883
		Omri	c. 883–872
Jehoshaphat	c. 870–846	Ahab	c. 872–851
		Ahaziah	c. 851–850
Jehoram	c. 846–841	Joram	c. 850–841
Ahaziah	c. 841	Jehu	c. 841–818
Athaliah	c. 841–835		
Jehoash	c. 835–801	Jehoahaz	c. 818–802
Amaziah	c. 801–783	Joash	c. 802–787
Azariah (Uzziah)	c. 783–732	Jeroboam II	c. 787–748
		Zechariah	748–747
		Shallum	747
Jotham	750–735	Menahem	747–738
		Pekahiah	738–737
Ahaz	735–727	Pekah	737–732
		Hoshea	732–724
Hezekiah	727–697		
Manasseh	697–642		
Amon	642–640		
Josiah	640–609		
Jehoahaz	609		
Jehoiakim	609–598		
Jehoiachin	598–597		
Zedekiah	597–586		

Aramean king with a large gift of silver and gold collected from the Jerusalem Temple and his own royal palace. Although Ben-hadad seems also to have had a treaty with Baasha (see 1 Kings 15:19), he accepted Asa's invitation and sent an Aramean army south to ravage Israelite cities in the region north of the Sea of Galilee. Thus, Asa's strategy was successful, and Baasha was forced to withdraw from Ramah and lift the embargo. The Israelite withdrawal gave Asa the opportunity to strengthen the northern border of Judah. According to 1 Kings 15:22, the Judahites took the building materials with which the Israelites had fortified Ramah, transported them to Geba and Mizpah[16] and fortified those places, thus shoring up the Judahite frontier against Israel.

Although the silver and gold with which Asa is said to have bribed Ben-hadad might have been enough to entice him into action, it is also clear that the region he attacked had strategic importance to Damascus. The cities listed in 1 Kings 15:20 as having been conquered by Ben-hadad, "Ijon, Dan, Abel-beth-maacah," lie at the northern extreme of Israelite territory, on or beneath the western slope of Mt. Hermon in the direction of the watershed of the Litani River. Control of this region provided Damascus with passage into the river valley and thus to the Phoenician port city of Tyre, situated only 6 miles south of the mouth of the Litani. Having access to Tyre without having to negotiate with Israelite intermediaries was a major advantage for the merchants of Damascus in the ongoing struggle for control of the important trade routes of northern Palestine.

Baasha's son and successor, Elah (c. 884–883 B.C.E.), succumbed to a coup early in his reign (1 Kings 16:8–20). He was assassinated in his palace at Tirzah while his army, commanded by Omri, was away from the capital besieging the Philistine city of Gibbethon. The assassin, a chariot officer named Zimri, quickly massacred the rest of Baasha's family, as Baasha himself had done to the family of Jeroboam.* When word

---

*The repeated pattern of royal assassinations in the early history of the northern kingdom creates an impression of political turmoil in Israel that contrasts with the stability that the Davidic dynasty gave Judah. Neither Jeroboam nor Baasha was able to establish a dynasty, since in each case the son and successor was removed in a coup early in his reign.

Many historians have interpreted this as indicating that the northern kingdom had embraced a tradition of "charismatic" kingship, according to which leaders were expected to arise in times of crisis, receiving divine designation and popular acclamation. The paradigm for this kind of leadership is found in the stories of the premonarchical period, when Israel was ruled by "judges" who were divinely appointed to office in times of need. The transitional figure was Saul, who was appointed and subsequently rejected as king by the prophet Samuel, acting on behalf of Yahweh. This is the pattern in the biblical account of the early years of the northern kingdom, where kingship is repeatedly bestowed and removed by prophetic decrees. Thus Jeroboam is designated (1 Kings 11:29–39) and rejected as king by Ahijah the Shilonite (1 Kings 14:6–16; cf. 1 Kings 15:29), and Baasha is designated (cf. 1 Kings 16:2) and rejected (1 Kings 16:1–4; 1 Kings 16:12) by Jehu son of Hanani. Omri does succeed in establishing his dynasty, but its rule is prophetically condemned and, during the reign of Ahab, formally rejected by Elijah (1 Kings 21:20–24). Scholars disagree whether this is only a literary phenomenon, with later interpretation of the events being expressed by prophetic speeches composed *ex post facto*, or an indication of a distinctly northern ideal of kingship that differed from the dynastic principle that became entrenched early in Judah.

reached Gibbethon, however, the Israelite army proclaimed Omri king and set out for Tirzah. Zimri, after only a week's rule, took his own life. There followed a brief struggle for the crown when Omri's followers were challenged by a group who favored a certain Tibni son of Ginath (1 Kings 16:21–22), but the Omri party prevailed and he became king of Israel in Tirzah.

The Dynasty of Omri

The biblical account of Omri's reign is cryptic (1 Kings 16:23–28). The writers are more interested in his son Ahab, whom they hold up as an example of a bad ruler. Nevertheless, though Omri ruled only 12 years (c. 883–872 B.C.E.), he seems to have accomplished quite a bit, founding a dynasty and restoring Israel to its position as an important trading nation. In the records of the Neo-Assyrian Empire, Israel came to be known as *māt Bit-Ḥumri*, "the (land of) the House of Omri." Though this practice is only known––ironically and probably by accident of survival—in Assyrian texts from the period following Omri's dynasty, it indicates how Omri's achievement was assessed internationally. The biblical account mentions only one of his accomplishments, the founding of Samaria.

King Omri and the restoration of Israel as a trading power

Tirzah's location permitted easy communication with the Jordan Valley via the Wadi Far'ah. (This may have been of paramount importance when Jeroboam moved the capital there from Transjordanian Penuel.) Otherwise, Tirzah was isolated, surrounded by hills that made access to the principal international trade routes difficult. After six years, Omri founded a new capital at Samaria, northwest of Shechem, a choice that favored communication and trade. The site, a strategically located and easily defended summit in a fertile part of the Ephraimite highlands, overlooked one of the main roads into the hills from the coastal highway and the Mediterranean, about 25 miles to the west. Perhaps most important, the location permitted extensive contact with Phoenicia. In many respects, the most salient characteristic of the Omride dynasty was its close relationship with Tyre.

Omri entered into amicable relations with King Ittobaal of Tyre, the biblical Ethbaal, and secured the alliance by marrying his son Ahab to Ethbaal's daughter Jezebel. This couple, reviled by the biblical writers for being corrupt leaders and for promoting the worship of a foreign god, became notorious in biblical tradition. Nevertheless their marriage cemented a diplomatic and commercial relationship with the prosperous mercantile cities of the Mediterranean coast that brought substantial wealth to the landlocked cities of Israel. What was at stake for Phoenicia was a passage through the central hill country into Transjordan, where caravans arrived from the south transporting luxury items along "the King's Highway" (cf. Numbers 20:17, 21:22), the name given to the north-south road that ran along the edge of the entire Transjordanian plateau from the northern tip of the Gulf of Aqabah to Damascus. The caravans were a source of immense wealth, and it was in the interest of Tyre and the other Phoenician ports to divert them west before they reached Damascus. The topography of the region determined the best route for this. It diverged from the King's Highway somewhere near Ramoth-gilead (possibly Tell er-Ramith, near the modern border of Jordan and Syria), descended through the Wadi Yabis into the Jordan Valley, continued on the other side through the Beth-Shean and Jezreel Valleys, and came out on the Plain of Acco with Tyre and the other Phoenician ports dead ahead.[17]

Phoenician expansion eastward along this route in the tenth and ninth centuries B.C.E. is illustrated archaeologically by characteristically Phoenician pottery found at a series of sites extending from Horvat Rosh Zayit[18] on the Plain of Acco to Tel 'Amal, just west of Beth-Shean, to Tell el-Ḥamma in the Jordan Valley.[19] The presence of these sites does not imply direct Phoenician control of the region but rather political amity and commercial cooperation with Israel, within whose borders the route lay. The same pattern is in evidence at northern Israelite sites of the same period, which have yielded a substantial amount of imported Phoenician pottery as well as architectural remains showing the use of building materials imported from Phoenicia and Phoenician building techniques, including ashlar masonry,* Proto-Aeolic capitals** and especially ivory carving. Elegant ivories, Phoenician in style and probably in manufacture, have been found at a number of Israelite and Judahite sites of the tenth to eighth century. The royal palaces at Samaria yielded a hoard of some 500 pieces of carved ivory inlay, bringing to mind "the ivory house that [Ahab] built" in Samaria (1 Kings 22:39) and the "houses of ivory" and "beds of ivory" in Amos's oracles against Samaria (Amos 3:15, 6:4).

This commercial arrangement with Phoenicia brought Israel into conflict with its immediate neighbor to the north, the Aramean state of Damascus. Though we have no biblical or extrabiblical report of Omri's foreign wars, there are strong indirect indications that he successfully pursued the struggle against Damascus begun in the reign of

---

*Ashlars are square-cut stones smoothed on all sides and cut precisely enough to fit together tightly without mortar. To give additional strength, the long and short sides of the rectangular blocks are sometimes laid parallel to the face of the wall in an alternating pattern—a technique known as "header and stretcher." The use of ashlar masonry is characteristic of both Solomonic and Omride architecture and, for that matter, later periods in which Israel or Judah were actively engaged in international trade. The techniques of ashlar stoneworking are believed to have radiated out of Phoenicia.

**A characteristic feature of ashlar construction was ornamentation with a type of engaged pillar capital called "Proto-Aeolic" or "Proto-Ionic" because it anticipates in some respects the capitals of those orders of later Classical architecture. A typical Proto-Aeolic capital consists of a pair of palmette volutes (spiral ornaments) flanking a central triangle.

Baasha, when much of the northern Galilee fell to the depredations of Ben-hadad son of Tabrimmon. Excavations at sites like Dan and Hazor, where archaeologists have found destruction levels they associate with Ben-hadad's raid, indicate that the cities were rebuilt quickly, often to a higher standard and exhibiting the Phoenician-influenced building techniques noted above.[20] This restoration probably corresponds to the rise of Omri, when the region was returned to Israelite control. Eventually, however, the conflict between Samaria and Damascus ended as the two states made common cause against the Assyrian threat, as explained below.

Ahab succeeded Omri as king and ruled 22 years in Samaria (872–851 B.C.E.). Generally speaking, his reign seems to have been a prosperous period for the northern kingdom, although much of its history must be reconstructed from the archaeological record and extrabiblical texts. The biblical account of the Omride dynasty has been shaped by writers whose primary interest was to express a distinctive religious viewpoint that was suspicious of kingship as an institution. Most of the episodes narrated involve the public and private affairs of the royal family, especially their conflicts with opposition groups. The result is that, despite the extensive treatment of the period in the biblical text, relatively few of the events reported there can be associated with external history and evaluated by the historian. This is especially true of the account of Ahab's reign (1 Kings 16:29–22:40), which is similar in spirit to the stories of Saul's kingship in 1 Samuel, which are dominated by the figure of the prophet Samuel, and to stories of certain abuses of power by both David, in which the prophet Nathan is prominent, and by Solomon. The point of view of this type of literature may be called "prophetic," since it places emphasis on the authority of prophets who are shown to be divinely inspired.[21] Kings of Israel are depicted as abusive of the rights of their subjects and dangerous to the religious integrity of Israel since they are often involved in foreign alliances, leading to the worship of foreign gods in Israel.

The reign of Ahab

Ahab in particular is presented as a paradigm of the bad king. He acquires the throne by inheriting it from his father, Omri, rather than by divine choice and prophetic selection. He is married to a foreign woman, Jezebel of Tyre, who aggressively promotes the worship of Baal in Israel. Together, Ahab and Jezebel abuse and exploit their Israelite subjects—the story of Naboth's vineyard (1 Kings 21) is the parade example. Ahab's adversary is the prophet Elijah. Their story is presented as an extended struggle between Yahweh, the God of Israel, for whom Elijah speaks, and Baal, the biblical term for any foreign god. We might understand this as reflecting a historical situation in which the

God of Israel was being challenged by Jezebel's god—presumably Melqart, the god of Tyre—but this seems an unlikely scenario. There is little question that Yahweh was recognized in Samaria as the national God of Israel, even though his worship was conducted in ways that the biblical writers, from their perspective in later Jerusalem, found abhorrent. Ahab's allegiance to Yahweh is demonstrated by the fact that the three of his children whose names we know all had Yahwistic names—two sons, Joram and Ahaziah, both of whom eventually became king, and one daughter, Athaliah, who became queen of Judah. The religious conflict in Samaria was not between Yahwists and non-Yahwists, but rather between the adherents of exclusivistic Yahwism (the prophetic party) and the adherents of an inclusivistic religion (the Samaria aristocracy), which recognized the preeminence of Yahweh as the God of Israel but did not exclude the worship of foreign gods (the policy that Solomon is said to have adopted).

In any case, the literary character of the biblical account of the Omride dynasty makes it less useful than we would hope (in view of its length) for the reconstruction of ninth-century history. There are only a few allusions to Ahab's substantial building projects and little reliable information about his foreign relations. Most striking, there is no reference at all to his participation in the great anti-Assyrian coalition of 853 B.C.E. (see below), despite the major role he is known to have played, as shown by the Assyrian records. Nevertheless, it is possible to give a general description of his reign based on a critical reading of the biblical text and drawing heavily on extrabiblical documents and the archaeological record of the period.

As already noted, the first half of the ninth century is characterized archaeologically by extensive building projects throughout Israel. While these are likely to have begun during Omri's reign, it seems safe to assume that his son Ahab brought them to completion. This is true in particular of the Samaria acropolis, where excavations have shown the ninth-century royal palace to have been an architectural achievement of the highest order, with its finely dressed header-and-stretcher ashlar masonry, Proto-Aeolic capitals and ivories. This is the palace described in the summary of Ahab's reign in 1 Kings 22:39 as "the ivory house that he built." The same passage refers to "all the cities that he built" throughout Israel, and monumental structures have been found at sites like Dan, Hazor, Megiddo, Jezreel (where the Omrides seemed to have maintained a royal estate, if not a subsidiary capital) and many others.

Ahab also perpetuated the essentials of Omri's foreign policy. Since his queen was the Tyrian princess Jezebel, the alliance with Phoenicia remained strong, and Israel continued to benefit from the relationship. In the ongoing conflict with the Aramean kingdom of Damascus, including the contest for control of the east-west trade routes to the

Mediterranean port cities, Israel probably maintained ascendancy during most of Ahab's reign. In his latter years, however, he found it expedient to enter into a defensive alliance with King Hadadezer of Damascus to counter the threat posed by Assyria, a situation reviewed in detail below.[22]

During the dynasty of Omri, Israel seems generally to have held sway over Judah. Jehoshaphat (870–846 B.C.E.), who had succeeded his father Asa as king of Judah early in Ahab's reign, is said in 1 Kings 22:44 to have "made peace with the king of Israel," and we learn in 2 Kings 8:26 that this peace was sealed by the marriage of Ahab's daughter Athaliah to Jehoshaphat's son Jehoram.

Omri and Ahab, like David and Solomon, exercised control east of the Jordan, at least in Gilead and as far south as the region north of the Arnon River, which was disputed with Moab. According to 2 Kings 3:4–5, King Mesha of Moab brought tribute (sheep) during the reigns of Omri and Ahab, then rebelled when Ahab died. A major inscription of Mesha, found at Dhiban (about 20 miles south of Amman), ancient Dibon, Mesha's capital,[23] indicates that "the land of Medeba" (the region surrounding modern Madeba, about 18 miles southwest of Amman) was under Israelite sway "during [Omri's] days and half the days of his son," seeming to indicate that the revolt began earlier than the time of Ahab's death. A reasonable interpretation would be to assume that Ahab maintained firm control of central Transjordan until the latter part of his reign, when his participation with Damascus in the coalition against Assyria diverted his attention to the north.[24] As explained below, a final, unsuccessful attempt to reimpose Israelite control over Moab was made by a later Omride, Joram (c. 850–841 B.C.E.).

After a long period of weakness at the beginning of the first millennium, the Upper Mesopotamian kingdom of Assyria, with its capitals on the east bank of the Tigris at Calah and Nineveh, arose to become a leading factor in the history of the Near East during the ninth to seventh century B.C.E. The Assyrian kings were motivated first by a desire to control the trade routes through northern Syria into the mineral-rich mountain country of Anatolia, but eventually their ambition spread south into the middle Orontes region, southern Syria and even Palestine. By the time Ahab ascended the throne in 872 B.C.E. it was already clear that the growing power of Assyria was a threat that would have to be reckoned with. Ahab must have quickly realized that he could not avoid becoming embroiled in the affairs of imperial Assyria.

Shalmaneser III and the rise of imperial Assyria

A major factor in the resurgence of Assyria was the enormous wealth accumulated by the campaigning of Assurnasirpal II (884–859 B.C.E.), a contemporary of Omri and the early Ahab. A ruthless warrior and master tactician, he conquered Upper Mesopotamia, including numerous

Mesha Stele. *Erected by Mesha, king of Moab in the mid-ninth century B.C.E., this black basalt stele stands about 40 inches high and 24 inches wide. The inscription in Moabite, which is closely related to Hebrew, expresses Mesha's gratitude to his god Chemosh for delivering the Moabites from Israelite rule. Mesha claims he conquered Israelite territory east of the Jordan and humiliated the tribe of Gad. Among the towns mentioned is Dhiban (biblical Dibon), the site, about 20 miles south of Amman, where the stele was discovered. The Book of Kings also tells of a ninth-century Moabite rebellion; but the Bible and the stele may or may not refer to the same conflict. Each paints a different outcome from the other.*

    André Lemaire has recently argued that the inscription, which is poorly preserved in places, may have contained one of the earliest extrabiblical references to "the House of David," that is, the dynasty of David.

Aramean states; campaigned in the West through Syria and the mountains of Lebanon; and washed his weapons in the sea, receiving tribute from Byblos, Sidon, Tyre and several other coastal cities.[25] Despite his success in amassing plunder, however, Assurnasirpal was less talented than his successors at military strategy and diplomacy; he campaigned without a master plan and had little impact on the states of the southern Levant.

By contrast, Assurnasirpal's son and successor, Shalmaneser III (859–824 B.C.E.), was an accomplished strategist who campaigned with tenacity and purpose, if not always with success. He established a pattern, continued by his successors, of annual campaigns by the king or his representative. His repeated forays into Syria seem to have been driven by a master plan to subdue the West, either by outright annexation or, in the case of territories more distant from the Assyrian homeland, by the imposition of regular payments of tribute. That he was never entirely successful in achieving this goal was probably, at least in part, the ironic result of his father's successes. Rankled and impoverished by the strictures that Assurnasirpal's raids had put on the trade routes west of the Euphrates, a number of states in north Syria and the eastern Taurus (Bit Adini, Carchemish, Hattina, Sam'al) formed a coalition that opposed Shalmaneser almost immediately after his accession. In his first year he marched west to reassert Assyrian control of the major routes across northern Syria into the Amanus, the Cilician highlands and the approaches to the mining areas of the Taurus. His advance was finally checked by the combined forces of the coalition in a battle at Lutibu, near Zinjirli in southeastern Turkey (ancient Sam'al).[26] Shalmaneser's response was to focus his attention on Bit Adini, which, lying between the Balikh River and the Euphrates, was the coalition state that lay nearest the Assyrian homeland. He marched west every year for three years (857–855 B.C.E.) until he had conquered Bit Adini and annexed it as an Assyrian province, refounding its riparian capital city, Til Barsib (modern Tell Ahmar), as Kar-Shulman-asharidu, "Shalmaneser's Landing."

After the subjugation of Bit Adini, most of the states of north Syria regularly paid tribute to Assyria. Quickly, however, a new anti-Assyrian coalition was formed by states farther to the south, who now felt threatened by Shalmaneser's relentless campaigns. The new alliance extended from Arvad, Byblos and other Mediterranean coastal cities as far south as Ammon in Transjordan and even Arabia.[27] The ringleader of the coalition—and the target of Shalmaneser's retaliation—was Irhulena of Hamath, a state situated in the rich agricultural lands of the middle Orontes region. Among the 12 kings allied with Irhulena, the most important, in terms of the size of the forces they committed to the cause, were Hadadezer of Damascus and Ahab of Israel. So began Samaria's conflict with the empire that would eventually destroy it.

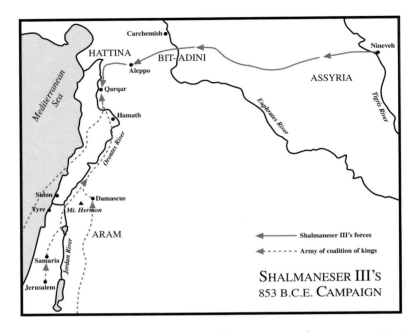

SHALMANESER III's
853 B.C.E. CAMPAIGN

The showdown began during Shalmaneser's sixth-year campaign (853 B.C.E.), when the Assyrian army marched into central Syria for the first time, subduing three of Irhulena's towns and capturing the fortress of Qarqar (probably Tell Qarqur in the northern Gab or Orontes Valley, northwest of the capital city of Hamath, modern Hama). After the fall of Qarqar, the Assyrian army was confronted by the full forces of the coalition. According to Shalmaneser's own records, the main contributors to the opposition force were Irhulena of Hamath (700 chariots, 700 horsemen and 10,000 footsoldiers), Hadadezer[28] of Damascus (1,200 chariots, 1,200 horsemen and 20,000 footsoldiers) and Ahab of Israel (2,000 chariots and 10,000 footsoldiers).[29]

After a brief respite when the Assyrian army was campaigning close to home from 852 to 850 B.C.E., Shalmaneser resumed his assault on the coalition in his tenth year (849 B.C.E.), marching west repeatedly in 848, 845 and 841 B.C.E. The persistence of Shalmaneser's attacks suggests that the alliance was effective, at least during the lifetime of Hadadezer of Damascus, who seems to have assumed the role of coalition leader after the 853 B.C.E. devastation of the domain of Irhulena of Hamath. Hadadezer died during the 845 B.C.E. campaign or shortly afterwards, and the throne of Damascus was seized by Hazael, a usurper.[30] The usurpation is described in detail in 2 Kings 8:7–15, a prophetic narrative in which Elisha foretells the later depradations of Israel by Hazael, who is depicted as personally assassinating his predecessor.[31]

The Assyrian records designate Hazael as the sole target of Shalmaneser's 841 B.C.E. campaign, suggesting that the supporting coalition had dissolved with Hadadezer's death. According to the Assyrian account, Hazael amassed his forces in "Mount Senir" (Mt. Seir or Hermon, the highpoint of the Anti-Lebanon range) but was defeated and forced to retreat eastward into Damascus.[32] Shalmaneser besieged the city briefly, destroying its orchards and devastating the Hauran, the agriculturally rich plateau south of Damascus. He then marched west to a point on the Mediterranean coast where he received tribute from Tyre, Sidon and Israel. Israel's role in these events will be discussed below, but the point to be emphasized here is, once again, the isolation of Damascus—all of its former coalition members having chosen to capitulate rather than stand with Hazael against Assyria. Despite this isolation, however, and the devastation of his territory in 841 B.C.E., Hazael was not defeated. Shalmaneser marched against Damascus once more, in 838 B.C.E., and then spent the rest of his reign campaigning in northern Syria to secure Assyrian control of that region. Hazael survived to become an increasingly powerful force in southern Syria and northern Palestine and to expand his territory at the expense of his neighbors, especially Israel.

Israel and Judah Under the Hegemony of Damascus

During most of the time that Shalmaneser was pressing his cause against Damascus, Israel was ruled by Ahab's son Joram (c. 850–841 B.C.E.). Ahab himself does not seem to have lived long after the battle of Qarqar (853 B.C.E.), although Jezebel survived and exercised considerable influence in her role as queen mother. Their older son, Ahaziah, succeeded Ahab as king, but after reigning for only a couple of years (c. 851–850 B.C.E.) he died of injuries sustained in an accident, having fallen through the railing of his balcony at Samaria (2 Kings 1:2–17), and was replaced by his brother Joram. Although the Assyrian records from Shalmaneser's 848 and 845 B.C.E. campaigns do not mention Israel by name, they do indicate that Hadadezer of Damascus was still supported by a 12-king coalition, and we assume that Joram was among the 12, as his father had been before him. The biblical account of Joram's decade-long reign (2 Kings 3) is silent on this issue, alluding to international events only in connection with his unsuccessful campaign against Moab.[33]

During much of his reign, Joram's counterpart in Judah was a king with the same name, Jehoram (846–841 B.C.E.).* As already noted,

Jehes's revolt

*Jehoram and Joram are variants of the same name. In the ninth century B.C.E. this name was pronounced *Yāhū-rām* in Judah and *Yaw-rām* in Israel, both of which mean "Yahweh is exalted." The spellings of these names are not consistent in the Hebrew Bible, and the variations are preserved in most English translations, in which the king of Judah is most often called Jehoram, but frequently Joram, and the king of Israel is called Jehoram and Joram in roughly equal proportion. To minimize the confusion, and for convenience, the king of Judah is always called Jehoram in our discussion and the king of Israel is called Joram.

Jehoram's father, Jehoshaphat, had arranged for him to be married to Athaliah, daughter of Ahab and Jezebel, so that during Jehoram's reign Judah remained allied with Israel, apparently as a sort of junior partner. Our limited information suggests that Jehoram was no more successful in his military efforts than Joram; the account of his reign in 2 Kings 8:16–25 mentions revolts by Edom, which Jehoram tried but failed to suppress, and Libnah (possibly Tell Bornaṭ, north of Lachish), a city on Judah's western border with Philistia. When Jehoram died and was succeeded as king of Judah by his son Ahaziah, Joram was still on the throne in Samaria.

Not long after Ahaziah's accession, Jehu son of Jehoshaphat son of Nimshi, a high-ranking officer in the Israelite army, instigated a bloody purge that resulted in the deaths of the kings of both Israel and Judah. This was another in the series of military *coups d'état* that had brought both Baasha and Omri to the throne of Israel earlier. In this case, however, we have a better understanding of the factors that led to the revolt. From the viewpoint of the biblical writers, the uprising was the inevitable consequence of outrage (both divine and human) over the religious policies and social abuses of the Omrides, especially Ahab (cf. 1 Kings 21:17–26). A prophetic narrative in 2 Kings 9:1–13 depicts Jehu as having been anointed for his task by an anonymous prophet dispatched for the purpose by Elisha. Though many critics think this episode is merely a literary conceit, there is little doubt that the conflict between the prophetic party and the Omride aristocracy that animates the biblical account reflects real religious and political tensions in ninth-century Israel that arose from the reaction of conservative elements in Israelite society to the policies of the court at Samaria. Nevertheless, we can identify other factors, also important but not emphasized in the biblical account, that must have contributed to dissatisfaction with Omride rule. One of the most important of these was the economic setback represented by the successful revolts of Moab against Israel and Edom against Judah. As already noted, these losses greatly diminished the ability of both countries to benefit from the caravan trade that traveled the King's Highway. Another factor that must have undermined confidence in Joram was his conspicuous lack of success in military endeavors— both in his failed attempt to restore Israelite sovereignty over Moab and, more generally, in the ongoing struggle against Assyria. In fact, it was a serious wound that Joram received on the battlefield that created the circumstances in which the insurrection against Omride rule finally erupted. As the biblical account in 2 Kings 8–9 makes clear, however, the enemy on this occasion was not Moab or Assyria, but Israel's old anti-Assyrian ally, Damascus.

According to 2 Kings 8:28, the trouble began when Joram, accompanied by his ally, Ahaziah of Judah, marched into Transjordan "to wage war against King Hazael of Aram at Ramoth-gilead." We have already noted that after the death of Hadadezer in 845 B.C.E. and the seizure of the throne of Damascus by Hazael, the anti-Assyrian coalition seems to have dissolved, leaving Hazael to face Shalmaneser alone. The confrontation at Ramoth-gilead of the allied kings of Israel and Judah against the Damascene monarch Hazael suggests that Israel's Joram not only refused to support Hazael but became his open adversary.[34] Viewed from the perspective of the long-term relationship between Samaria and Damascus, this was less a reversal of policy than a return to normalcy—another flare-up of the smoldering rivalry between the two states like the one that occurred, for example, during the reigns of Baasha of Israel and Ben-hadad son of Tabrimmon of Damascus in the early ninth century B.C.E. As on that occasion, the principal cause of the hostilities between Joram and Hazael is likely to have been conflicting commercial interests involving the control of trade routes—a likelihood underscored by the location of the confrontation at the critical commercial junction of Ramoth-gilead.[35]

The violent sequence of events that the prophet Hosea would later refer to as "the blood of Jezreel" (Hosea 1:4) is described in detail in 2 Kings 8:28–10:28. Joram and Ahaziah led their armies to Ramoth-gilead, where they engaged the forces of Hazael. In the ensuing battle, Joram was wounded and retreated to recuperate in the town of Jezreel,[36] where he was soon joined by Ahaziah. Jehu may have been left in charge of the Israelite forces at Ramoth-gilead; in any case, he was one of the ranking officers who remained at the front. When Joram departed, the army turned to Jehu and proclaimed him king (2 Kings 9:13).[37] He then rode quickly to Jezreel, where he assassinated Joram, then pursued the fleeing Azariah and killed him too. The coup was secured in the usual way, by tracking down and massacring the surviving members of the fallen dynasty, the Omrides. Ahab's descendants ("seventy sons") were executed by the intimidated city leaders of Samaria and their heads were sent in baskets to Jehu in Jezreel (2 Kings 10:1–11). The once-powerful Israelite queen mother, Jezebel, was killed in Jezreel, where she was hurled from the window of her palace into the streets and her corpse was consumed by dogs (2 Kings 9:30–36). The grim account of her death reflects the strong animosity towards this foreign queen on the part of the prophetic tradition and the biblical writers, who interpret her violent end as the fulfillment of Elijah's prediction in 1 Kings 21:23.

The carnage extended to the Judahite kin of Ahaziah (2 Kings 10:12–14), since as the son of Athaliah, daughter of Ahab and Jezebel, Ahaziah of Judah, too, was of Omride descent. Finally, Jehu instigated a wholesale slaughter of "the prophets of Baal, all his worshipers, and all his priests" (2 Kings 10:19), that is, all those Israelites who represented the religious practices inimical to the conservative Yahwism of the prophetic party. This part of Jehu's purge is stressed by the biblical writers (2 Kings 10:18–28), who, as already noted, regarded Ahab as a paradigm of the wicked king and viewed Jehu primarily as a *religious* revolutionary, who "wiped out Baal from Israel" (2 King 10:28). These events probably took place shortly before 841 B.C.E., when the Assyrian army returned to southern Syria after a few years respite. It has even been suggested that Jehu's revolt was timed to curry favor with Shalmaneser towards Israel by wiping out the anti-Assyrian faction— that is, the Omrides.[38] But new evidence—frustratingly incomplete and inconclusive—raises the possibility that in staging his coup Jehu was in league, not with Shalmaneser, but with Hazael. This evidence comes from the fragments of a basalt stele found at Tel Dan in 1993 and 1994.[39]

Not enough remains of the broken monument to reconstruct a continuous translation of its elegantly carved Old Aramaic inscription, but the surviving portions of the text show that it was left at Dan by an Aramean ruler in commemoration of a victory over a large enemy force. Evidently the defeated enemy was Israel, as indicated not only by the erection of the victory stele at the Israelite city of Dan but also by the language of the first part of the surviving text, which seems to refer to earlier hostilities with a king of Israel. In the latter part of the inscription, describing the Aramean victory, two kings, one of Israel and the other of "the House of David"—that is, Judah—are mentioned by name. Though the text is too fragmentary for certainty, it seems likely that the two kings are said to have been killed. Despite the defective condition of the text at this point, only one reconstruction of these names seems possible: "[Jo]ram son of [Ahab], king of Israel," and "[Ahaz]iah son of [Jehoram, ki]ng of the House of David." It follows from this that the Aramean ruler who erected the monument is very likely to have been Hazael, who was the only king of Damascus contemporary with both Joram and the short-lived Ahaziah.[40] This in turn suggests that Hazael claimed responsibility for the deaths of Joram and Ahaziah, and that he may have regarded Jehu as, in some sense, his agent.[41]

The use of "House of David" as a designation for the kingdom of Judah in the Tel Dan stele deserves special attention. It is the earliest occurrence—or one of the two earliest occurrences[42]—of the name of David outside the Bible, and it confirms the intimate association, already clear from the biblical writings, between the kingdom of Judah and the Davidic dynasty. "House of David" occurs 21 times in the Bible as a way of referring to the ruling family of Judah, either during David's lifetime or, more often, later (2 Samuel 7:26 = 1 Chronicles 17:24; Isaiah 7:2,13; etc.).[43]

Hazael's ascendancy   In political and territorial terms, Jehu's revolt was disastrous for Israel. "In those days," we are told in 2 Kings 10:32–33, "the Lord began to trim off parts of Israel." The passage goes on to describe Hazael's seizure of all of the Israelite territories east of the Jordan. If it is true

Black Obelisk. *The reliefs on this 7-foot tall, black stone monolith (left) depict the leaders of territories conquered by Shalmaneser III paying tribute to the Assyrian emperor. In the detail (above), a king of Israel (or perhaps his emissary) kneels before Shalmaneser, who appears to be admiring a vessel he has received. The annals of Shalmaneser III date the event to 841 B.C.E. The cuneiform inscription on the obelisk identifies the kneeling figure as "Yaw, son of Omri," leading scholars to identify the king as Omri's successor Jehu (c. 883-872).*

The obelisk was discovered among the ruins of Nimrud, the royal seat of King Shalmaneser III of Assyria, on the eastern bank of the Tigris.

that Jehu carried out his revolt with the encouragement or even support of Hazael, we may imagine that the two had an understanding that Jehu would receive Hazael's support in return for ceding Transjordan to Damascus. It is also possible that Jehu fell out of favor with Hazael because he capitulated, shortly after the Jezreel revolt, to Hazael's arch-foe, Assyria. As already noted, Shalmaneser III returned to the West in 841 B.C.E. with Damascus as his principal target. After pursuing Hazael to Damascus and conducting a perfunctory siege of the city, Shalmaneser contented himself with marauding Aramean settlements in the Hauran, and then marched west to a headland on the Mediterranean coast called Ba'li-ra'si, probably Ras en-Naqura (Rosh ha-Niqra, about 12 miles north of the Acco spur), one of the peaks of the "Ladder of Tyre,"[44] where he received tribute from a number of regional states, including Israel. The so-called Black Obelisk of Shalmaneser III from Nimrud,[45] which celebrates this campaign, includes a panel in relief depicting an Israelite king identified as "Yaw, son of Omri" (presumably Jehu) prostrating himself in submission before the Assyrian monarch. Whatever the relationship between Hazael and Jehu might have been previously, this gesture would have made Jehu an enemy of Damascus.

Following a final visit in 838 B.C.E., also directed at Damascus, Shalmaneser departed and never returned to the West, though he continued to rule for another decade. His successor, Shamshi-Adad V (824–811 B.C.E.), was greeted by a major rebellion in the Assyrian capital of Nineveh, and although he was eventually able to quell the Great Revolt (827–822 B.C.E.), as it was called, he was left in too weak a position to control territory farther west than Til Barsib on the Euphrates. In fact, Assyria would not return in force to southern Syria and Palestine until the final years of the ninth century (805 B.C.E.), as explained below. Thus in 838 B.C.E., Hazael, having survived the onslaughts of Shalmaneser III, emerged as the dominant figure in the region, free to exact revenge for what he may have regarded as Jehu's treachery and to realize his ambition to expand the hegemony of Damascus at the expense of Israel, Judah and his other neighbors.

When Ahaziah of Judah was assassinated, his mother Athaliah, daughter of Ahab and Jezebel and widow of Jehoram of Judah, seized power for herself (2 Kings 11:1–3). To consolidate her position, she attempted to eradicate the royal family of Judah. This part of her plan was foiled, however, by Ahaziah's sister Jehosheba, who hid her infant nephew, Jehoash* son of Ahaziah, from Athaliah's executioners and then took the young Davidide secretly to the Temple, where she entrusted him to the protection of the high priest, Jehoiada.[46] Jehoash remained in hiding in the Temple during the seven years that Athaliah ruled in Jerusalem (841–835 B.C.E.). The reference in 2 Kings 11:18 to the dismantling of a "house of Baal" after Athaliah's death suggests that she attempted to introduce the Tyrian religion of her mother into Jerusalem (cf. 2 Chronicles 24:7), but otherwise the biblical record provides no information about her reign. It represented an interruption in the continuity of Davidic rule in Judah, and the biblical writers' silence on the subject is probably a reflection of their contempt for Athaliah, which they make clear in their accounts of her ruthless acquisition of power and the disgraceful manner of her removal from office. The latter is described in detail in 2 Kings 11:4–20. When Jehoash was seven years old, Jehoiada, operating under heavy guard, publicly presented him in the Temple and proclaimed him rightful king of Judah. When Athaliah arrived with a cry of treason, she was led outside of the Temple precincts and summarily executed.

The biblical account of Jehoash's reign deals primarily with the relationship between the royal palace and the Temple. The version in Kings

---

*Like the names Jehoram and Joram, Jehoash and Joash are variants of the same name, which in the ninth century was pronounced *Yāhū-'āš* in Judah and *Yaw-'āš* in Israel, both meaning "Yahweh has given." English Bibles use both names for Jehoash son of Ahaziah, king of Judah (c. 835–801 B.C.E.), and for his northern namesake, Joash or Jehoash of Israel (c. 802–787 B.C.E.). The variation arises from inconsistencies in the spelling of the names in the Hebrew Bible. To minimize the confusion, and for convenience, the king of Judah is always called Jehoash in our discussion and the king of Israel is called Joash.

Three shekels ostracon. *This Hebrew inscription appears to be a receipt for a donation of three silver shekels to the "the House of Yahweh," that is, the Jerusalem Temple. The inscription states that King Ashyahu has commanded that the money be given to one Zechariah. Although the Bible mentions no king of Judah named Ashyahu, this name may be a form of Joash or Jehoash. The inscription probably dates to the early years of King Jehoash (835-801 B.C.E.) of Judah, who, according to 2 Kings 12:4, proclaimed that all contributions to the Temple should be turned over to the priests for repairs. Zechariah was a prominent priest at the time (2 Chronicles 24:20).*

(2 Kings 11–12) presents Jehoash in a favorable light and implicates the priesthood in corruption. It gives the impression that during Jehoash's minority, Jehoiada ruled on his behalf, an arrangement that worked to the advantage of the Temple and the priesthood. A proclamation is said to have been issued in the king's name requiring that all contributions of silver brought to the Temple should be turned over to the priests, who were then to use the funds to repair the Temple. As Jehoash matured, however, he became disenchanted with this arrangement, noting that the silver received by the priests was not reaching its intended destination, so that the Temple remained in disrepair. He insisted that arrangements be made for the funds to be channeled directly to the repairmen, thus eliminating the intermediary role of the priests. The Chronicler's version (2 Chronicles 24) exonerates the priests at the expense of the king. There we are told that the Temple restoration proceeded well until Jehoiada died, after which Jehoash fell under the influence of "the officials of Judah" (2 Chronicles 24:17), who persuaded him to abandon the project. When Jehoiada's own son, Zechariah, publicly objected, he was stoned to death.

A recently recovered ostracon (an inscribed potsherd) dramatically illustrates the biblical account of Jehoash's Temple project.[47] It refers to an order in the name of Jehoash (called Ashyahu here)* for a small amount of silver to be contributed to the Temple: "As Ashyahu the king commanded you to give into the hand of [Ze]chariah silver of Tarshish for the House of Yahweh: three shekels." Since Zechariah is the name of a prominent priest of the period—the son of the high priest Jehoiada—the expression "into the hand of Zechariah" suggests that the ostracon reflects the situation early in Jehoash's reign when contributions of silver were made to the Temple through a priestly intermediary.

Though the Chronicler blames "the officials of Judah" for Jehoash's abandonment of the Temple project, the decision may have been forced on him by external circumstances—specifically, by the threat to Judah posed by Hazael of Damascus. As explained above, Assyria ceased to be an active presence in the west after Shalmaneser's 838 B.C.E. campaign, and this left Hazael with a free hand to satisfy his territorial ambitions. We have already noted that he took control of all of Transjordan as far south as Wadi Arnon, the Moabite frontier, during the reign of Jehu (2 Kings 10:32–33). The biblical summary of the reign of Jehu's successor, Jehoahaz (818–802 B.C.E.), refers to a series of battles lost to the Arameans (2 Kings 13:3) and describes a drastic depletion of the Israelite military capability (2 Kings 13:5). Thus Jehoahaz was in no position to resist when Hazael marched past Israelite territory, pressed down the coastal plain and conquered Philistia south of the Israelite town of Aphek in the Plain of Sharon.[48] According to 2 Kings 12:17–18, Hazael, after conquering the Philistine city of Gath, turned east to threaten Jerusalem. Jehoash was able to save the city only by paying the Aramean king a heavy tribute amassed by emptying the treasuries of both the Temple and the royal palace of several generations' accumulation of gold.[49] However rich this extorted treasure may have been, however, it was not the primary economic benefit of Hazael's coastal campaign. His conquests in Philistia and Judah gave him jurisdiction over the Via Maris, the primary coastal highway, and since he already controlled the northern portion of the King's Highway, the principal trade route east of the Jordan, he now had a virtual monopoly on commercial traffic passing through Palestine and direct access to both the Egyptian and the Arabian markets.

---

*The name appears as *'šyhw*, that is, *'āšyāhū*, "Ashyahu," instead of *yāhū'āš*, the ninth-century B.C.E. form of Jehoash. In other words, the divine name (*yāhū*, "Yahu, Yahweh") and verbal (*'āš* "has given") elements are reversed in relation to the biblical form. This phenomenon is well known in Hebrew personal names, including royal names, in both the biblical and epigraphic record. For example, the name of Jehoash's father, Ahaziah (*'āḥazyāhū* also appears in the Bible (2 Chronicles 21:17;25:23) as Jehoahaz (*yĕhô'āḥāz*), and the northern King Joash, called *yô'āš* or *yĕhô'āš* in the Bible, appears on a *pithos* from Kuntillet 'Ajrud as *'šyw*, "Ashyaw." See "What's in a Name?" *BAR*, May/June 1998, p. 18.

Eighth-Century Prosperity

The ascendancy of Damascus over Israel and Judah extended from the 830s B.C.E. until the early eighth century B.C.E. Hazael must have died sometime before 805 B.C.E., when his son Ben-hadad (Aramaic Bir-hadad), also known as Mari', first begins to appear in Assyrian records. During Jehoahaz's reign, Ben-hadad II* seems to have been able to maintain the domination of Israel that Hazael had established (cf. 2 Kings 13:3), and there are other indications that he was a capable successor to his mighty father. He had the misfortune, however, to come to the throne at about the time that Assyria, its long period of weakness ending, began to reassert itself in Syria-Palestine. The revival of Assyrian power was the achievement of Adad-nirari III (811–783 B.C.E.), who, after a six-year period of minority, turned his attention to the West. Although we have no true annals for Adad-nirari's reign, and his surviving inscriptions do not provide full information about his two western campaigns in 805–802 B.C.E. and 796 B.C.E., there can be little doubt that one of his principal targets was Damascus,[50] which had now regained the dominant role in Syria that it had had under Hadadezer.[51] By the time Adad-nirari's second western campaign was over, however, Ben-hadad had been subdued. An inscription found in Iraq in 1967[52] indicates that at that time (796 B.C.E.) Adad-nirari received tribute from "Mari' of Damascus ... Joash of Samaria, the Tyrians and the Sidonians."

The return of Assyria brought an end to the aggressive policies of Damascus, since Ben-hadad and his successors were now obliged either to submit to Assyria and pay tribute on a regular basis or to defend themselves against the Assyrian army. For the kings of Israel, Judah and the other regional states that had suffered at the hand of Damascus, the arrival of Adad-nirari III was a welcome development. The tribute Joash of Israel (c. 802–787 B.C.E.) paid to Adad-nirari in 796 B.C.E. was probably given, at least in part, in a spirit of gratitude; it has even been suggested that Adad-nirari is the unidentified "savior" of Israel who helped the people escape from the Land of the Syrians (2 Kings 13:5). In any case, Joash was subsequently able to defeat Ben-hadad three times in battle and recover Israelite towns lost to Hazael (2 Kings 13:25). The Edomite campaign of Amaziah of Judah (c. 801–783 B.C.E.)—reported briefly in 2 Kings 14:7 with an expanded account in 2 Chronicles 25:5–16—may also have been inspired by the weakening position of Damascus and the consequent hope on Amaziah's part that he could recover the territory—and trade

The resurgence of Israel and Judah

---

*Since he had the same name as Ben-hadad son of Tabrimmon, the nemesis of Baasha of Israel in the early ninth century B.C.E., we will call him Ben-hadad II. If Hadadezer was succeeded briefly by a son named Ben-hadad, a possibility strongly supported by 2 Kings 8:7-15 (see endnote 31), then we should call Hazael's son Ben-hadad III.

Kuntillet 'Ajrud. *Travelers may have stopped for rest and refreshment at this desert way-station halfway between Beersheba and Elath. The ruins of two late-ninth- to early-eighth-century B.C.E. buildings are visible on the isolated hilltop, which overlooks three major routes across northeastern Sinai. Modern archaeologists have discovered abundant evidence here of early Israelite worship, predating the great religious reforms of Hezekiah and Josiah. (See photo and drawing, opposite.)*

access—that had been lost to Edom in the days of his great-grandfther, Jehoram (cf. 2 Kings 8:20–22). In the flush of a victory at the Edomite stronghold of Sela (possibly el-Sela, southwest of Tafila, Jordan), however, Amaziah overreached himself and sent a defiant message to Joash (2 Kings 14:8–14 = 2 Chronicles 25:17–24), apparently believing that the Israelite army was either too weak or too preoccupied with Damascus to respond. This proved to be a catastrophic miscalculation. Joash marched to Beth-Shemesh in the Shephelah and routed the Judahite army, taking Amaziah prisoner. He then proceeded to Jerusalem, where he broke down the northern wall, looted the treasuries of the Temple and the royal palace, and returned to Samaria with hostages. Thus in 783 B.C.E., when Amaziah's son

ZE'EV MESHEL/DRAWING AFTER PIRHIYA BECK

Yahweh and his asherah. *"I have blessed you by Yahweh of Samaria and his asherah" declares the Hebrew inscription on this pithos, or storage jar, from Kuntillet 'Ajrud. The accompanying painting depicts two grotesque figures standing side-by-side with arms akimbo. The larger figure, at left, has a man's torso and posture, but a bovine face, horns and a tail. The smaller figure has a human body with breasts and a bovine face and tail. A seated musician appears at far right. Some scholars identify the two standing figures as Yahweh and Asherah (although others have suggested that both depictions represent the Egyptian deity Bes). A goddess by the name of Asherah is mentioned with contempt in the Bible; this inscription suggests that in the late ninth or eighth century B.C.E., she was conceived of as Yahweh's consort.*

Azariah became king,[53] Judah was virtually a vassal state of Israel, a situation reminiscent of the heyday of the Omride dynasty.

In the 1970s two ruined buildings dating to the early eighth century B.C.E. were excavated at a remote site in the Sinai peninsula called Kuntillet 'Ajrud.[54] The better preserved of the two buildings yielded an unusually large amount of written material, including Hebrew inscriptions written in ink on *pithoi* (large storage jars) and on plastered walls as well as inscribed on large stone bowls. Although its nature and function are not fully understood, the site is located at the junction of three of the principal roads across the northeastern Sinai, and it is tempting to associate it in some way with Amaziah's interest in controlling the trade routes south and east of Judah, as shown by his Edomite campaign. The corpus includes inscriptions written in both the northern (Israelite) and southern (Judahite) dialects of Hebrew, and this suggests that the site should also be understood in the context of Judah's subjugation by Joash, whose name actually appears on one of the *pithoi* as one who bestowed a blessing.[55]

A surprising feature of the Kuntillet 'Ajrud inscriptions is that their content is substantially religious. They shed invaluable light on the nature of Israelite religion at the dawn of the eighth century B.C.E., before the destruction of Samaria and the incorporation of the northern kingdom into the Assyrian Empire—and, more significantly, long before the great reforms of Hezekiah and Josiah, which transformed Yahwism, centralizing it in Jerusalem and giving it many of the features familiar from the Bible. Thus the Kuntillet 'Ajrud inscriptions provide a window on an early form of Israelite religion and offer clues to some characteristics that later disappeared. In view of the movement towards cult centralization in later Judah, for example, it is important to note that at 'Ajrud the name of the God of Israel is always qualified by a geographical designation, so that it appears not simply as "Yahweh" but as "Yahweh of Samaria" or "Yahweh of Teman."[56] Also, when Yahweh is addressed at Kuntillet 'Ajrud, it is often in the accompaniment of "his asherah"; for example, the blessing of Joash mentioned above is invoked "by Yahweh of Samaria and his asherah." Goddesses known as Asherah are known from a number of ancient Near Eastern societies, and a goddess by that name is mentioned several times in the Bible—always with contempt (1 Kings 18:19, etc.). In the Bible, however, the word appears more often as the name of an object used in worship (an asherah; plural, asherim) than as the name of a goddess (Asherah). Though it is clear that an asherah was part of the conventional paraphernalia of a local shrine or "high place" and

that, in form, it was a wooden object of some kind—perhaps a simple pole but also possibly a carved female image (cf. 2 Kings 21:7) or even a sacred tree—its exact function and appearance are never described by the biblical writers, who unanimously condemn its use. The Hebrew word *'ăšērâ* may originally have meant something like "track" or "trace," so that "the asherah of Yahweh" would have signified the presence of the God of Israel, and the cult object may have served as a concrete representation of the divine presence as it was available for worship. Clearly, though, it was also associated with a goddess, presumably the consort of Yahweh. Taken together, all this suggests that Yahweh's asherah, as she is invoked at Kuntillet 'Ajrud, was a concretization of the divine presence—the technical term is hypostasis—which was personified and worshiped, alongside Yahweh, as a goddess and the consort of the national god.[57] On one of the *pithoi* a blessing invoking "Yahweh of Samaria and his asherah" is inscribed immediately above a drawing of two figures standing side-by-side with arms akimbo. Both figures combine human and bovine features—human torsos and posture with bovine faces, horns (at least on the larger figure), tails and hoofed feet. The smaller figure, who has stylized

ISRAEL ANTIQUITIES AUTHORITY/PHOTO ISRAEL MUSEUM

Fertility figurine. *Excavated in the Jewish Quarter of Jerusalem's Old City, this clay figurine may be a household fertility amulet representing the Canaanite goddess Asherah. The pillar-shaped body may represent a tree, a motif connected with Asherah.*

female breasts, stands alongside and slightly behind the larger figure. They are certainly a divine couple—a god with the visage and head-dress of a bull and a goddess with a cow's face—and are almost certainly "Yahweh and his asherah."[58] The depiction of Yahweh with the visage of a young bull brings to mind "the calf of Samaria," as Hosea called the statue that was the focus of the cult of Yahweh in the capital of the northern kingdom (Hosea 8:6; cf. Hosea 8:5 and 13:2).

Joash's policies—and his success in the ongoing conflict with Damascus—were continued by his successor, Jeroboam II (787–748 B.C.E.). The long reigns of Jeroboam II in Israel and Azariah in Judah (783–732 B.C.E.) corresponded to a period of considerable prosperity in both kingdoms. This was possible not only because of the weakness of Damascus, which had dominated the southern Levant for several decades, but also because of the absence of Assyria, which would not again pose a serious threat to Israel until the first western campaign (743–738 B.C.E.) of Tiglath-pileser III. After Adad-nirari's 796 B.C.E. incursion into Syria, the Assyrian armies were generally engaged near home, as a succession of three weak Assyrian kings dealt with a series of local revolts and other domestic problems. For many of these years, the Assyrian Eponym Chronicle indicates, there was no foreign campaign, and, when there was, it was often directed "against Urartu." Urartu, the biblical Ararat, was the region around Lake Van, north of Assyria. The Urartians had been gradually expanding westward since the end of the reign of Shalmaneser III, who had held them in check, and by the beginning of the eighth century they had taken control of much of Anatolia and Syria north of Aleppo. Because of the distractions caused by domestic unrest and the conflict with Urartu, the Assyrian kings of this period seem to have paid little attention to southern Syria. Only five Syrian expeditions are listed in the Eponym Chronicle, and only one of these—a campaign in 773 B.C.E.—is designated as "against Damascus."[59] Nevertheless, the fortunes of Damascus remained in decline. The devastation inflicted by Adad-nirari III seems to have left the once-powerful state broken and vulnerable.

The reigns of Jeroboam II and Azariah

This turn of events worked very much to the advantage of Israel, whose resurgence, begun under Joash, peaked during the reign of his son, Jeroboam II. According to 2 Kings 14:25, Jeroboam "restored the border of Israel from Lebo-hamath as far as the Sea of Arabah"—that is, from the town of Lebo (modern Lebweh), at the southern boundary of the state of Hamath on the Orontes, to the Dead Sea.[60] One of the implications of this assertion is that Damascus was reduced to the status of an Israelite vassal state, a claim that seems to be made explicit in 2 Kings 14:28: "He recovered for Israel Damascus."[61] Jeroboam also extended the southeastern border of Israel "as far as the Sea of Arabah" at the expense of both Damascus and Moab. Jeroboam was reasserting Israelite control over trade along the King's Highway, which had been lost in the time of Jehu and Hazael. It is safe to assume that the western coastal route from Philistia north into the Galilee, which Hazael had also commandeered, was now back under Israelite control as well.

Though Jeroboam II had the longest reign of any Israelite king and presided over one of the most prosperous periods in the history of the northern kingdom, the account of his reign in Kings is remarkably brief—only seven verses (2 Kings 14:23–29)—and its tone is hostile. This is because the summary notices of his achievements (2 Kings 14:25,28) have been set in a negative framework by the Deuteronomistic historian, who looked on Jeroboam's reign from the perspective of the fall of Samaria half a century later. Thus Jeroboam is condemned, in formulaic Deuteronomistic language, for having perpetuated "all the sins of Jeroboam son of Nebat"—that is, Jeroboam I—the crimes that, from the Deuteronomistic point of view, led eventually to the destruction of the northern kingdom by the Assyrians (cf. 2 Kings 17:22–23). With regard to the recovery of territory for Israel and the expansion of its borders, we are told that Jeroboam II was permitted these accomplishments despite his shortcomings because Yahweh had pity for the plight of the Israelites and there was no one else available to do the job (2 Kings 17:26).

Though the Kings account of Jeroboam's reign is, in its final form, the work of the Deuteronomistic historian of the late seventh century B.C.E., it expresses continuity with the hostility towards Jeroboam found in the oracles of his eighth-century contemporary, the prophet Amos,[62] who confirms the prosperity of the period while presenting it as a facade masking social and religious corruption. In Amos's view, the wealthy, the Samarian aristocracy, were very wealthy indeed (note the description of their extravagant and sybaritic lifestyle in Amos 6:4–6) but their wealth was gained at the expense of the poor. Thus his oracles are often addressed at an exploitative ruling class that oppresses the poor and governs corruptly; they are the idle but powerful rich, who "trample on the needy and bring ruin to the poor of the land … buying the poor for silver and the needy for a pair of sandals" (Amos 8:4,6; cf. 2:6–7, 4:1). In Amos's polemic, even the enlarged national boundaries achieved by Jeroboam (2 Kings 14:25) become the basis of a threat of national disaster: "I am raising up against you a nation … and they shall oppress you from Lebo-hamath to the Wadi Arabah" (Amos 6:14).

The oracles of Amos, therefore, provide confirmation—however indirect and grudging—that Jeroboam II's expansion of Israel's boundaries and recovery of control of the principal trade routes of Palestine led to a substantial increase in material prosperity in Israel. In contrast to the insight he provides about social tensions in the kingdom, however, Amos gives few hints about the ways in which the newly gained resources were put to use. The stinted account of Jeroboam's reign in Kings is no help in this regard, since it lacks any reference to his domestic achievements, including building projects and improvements in living conditions. Faced with this scarcity of information in the biblical sources, therefore, we are primarily dependent on the archaeological record for assessing the state of material culture in eighth-century Israel.[63] Excavations conducted at Israelite sites show that the first half of the eighth century B.C.E. was a period of extensive construction, characterized not by the founding of new cities but by the renovation, refurbishment and expansion of existing cities, some with newly built fortifications and most with more evidence of city planning than is found in previous periods. Nationwide, there was a substantial population increase, as indicated by the results of archaeological surveys of small, nonurban sites as well as estimates based on evidence suggesting the enlargement of existing cities (expansions of walls or settlements spilling over city walls into the surrounding countryside).

A good indication that the trade advantage Jeroboam achieved did result in an accumulation of wealth is the discovery of luxury items in eighth-century archaeological strata. Most characteristic of these are the elaborately carved ivory inlays found at various sites in the northern kingdom but especially at Samaria.[64] Carved ivory was an art form of Phoenician and north Syrian inspiration, so that its presence in the archaeological record points to a renewal of Israelite contact and cooperation with Phoenicia, which, as we have seen, was essential to a robust trade economy.[65] An immense hoard known as the Samaria ivories,[66] found in the ruins of the royal palace, provides direct testimony to the wealth of the aristocracy and is suggestive of extreme social stratification.[67] It is not surprising, therefore, that references to ivory play a part in Amos's invective against the excesses of the aristocracy (Amos 3:15, 6:4).

The epigraphic record also sheds light on life in Samaria during the reign of Jeroboam II. The most impressive Hebrew seal dating from the early to mid-eighth century B.C.E. is surely the seal of "Shema', the servant of Jeroboam," who must have been a high official of the Samarian government stationed at Megiddo, where the seal was found in 1904.[68] The largest corpus of Hebrew inscriptions from the northern kingdom dating to this or any other period are the well-known Samaria ostraca,[69] which were found in 1910 in the ruins of an administrative structure on the acropolis immediately to the west of the royal palace. Dating formulae indicate that the ostraca come from the ninth through the seventeenth year of an unnamed king, almost certainly Jeroboam II, so that they fall between the years 779 and 771 B.C.E. They record regional shipments of agricultural goods, thus shedding light on the support given by large estates to the activities of the court in Samaria. An especially interesting feature of the Samaria ostraca is the number of personal names containing the theophoric or divine element Yahweh (in the form *Yaw*) as opposed to the element Baal (*Ba'l*). The ratio is roughly 11:7.[70] It is difficult to assess the significance of this statistic for the religion of Israel in the period. The Baal names might belong to foreigners (perhaps Phoenicians) who owned property in the vicinity of Samaria or to Israelites who worshiped a foreign god, but it is also possible that *Ba'l*, which means "Lord," might have been an acceptable epithet for Yahweh in this period (cf. Hosea 2:16).

Judah, too, was prosperous in this period, under the rule of Jeroboam's contemporary Azariah (also known as Uzziah) (783–732 B.C.E.).* Though Azariah reigned even longer than Jeroboam, the account of his reign in Kings (2 Kings 15:1–7) is, again, very brief, and there is no mention of victories in foreign wars or other international achievements. The Chronicler's account of his reign (2 Chronicles 26:1–23) is somewhat longer; it presents Azariah as an effective military leader who reorganized the Judahite army and greatly increased both its size and readiness (2 Chronicles 26:11–15). It also describes successful military campaigns that he conducted.[71] Keeping in mind that Judah, since Joash's defeat of Amaziah early in the century, had been in the service of Israel as a junior ally if not actually a vassal state, we can assume that Azariah's build-up of the Judahite army and his various military enterprises were probably encouraged and abetted by Israel as part of Jeroboam's overall plan to reclaim control of the major trade routes of Palestine.[72] It is in this light that we should probably interpret Azariah's goals in the wars he is said to have conducted (2 Chronicles 26:6–7) against the Philistines and two Arabian groups, the Arabs of Gurbaal (an otherwise unknown group) and the Meunites.[73] After his Philistine campaign, during which he breached the walls of Gath, Jabneh and Ashdod, Azariah is said to have built "cities" in Philistine territory. These are most likely to have been fortified garrisons positioned to guard trade routes that ran through disputed territory and connected with roads farther south, which he seems also to have secured with protective fortresses—note the reference in 2 Chronicles 26:10 to Azariah's erection of "the towers in the wilderness." These activities brought him in conflict with the Meunites, a northwestern Arabian tribe who seem at this time to have controlled access from the Philistine ports through the Beersheba depression and the Wadi Zered (the modern Wadi el-Hesa) to the southern end of the King's Highway

---

*Both names are used in the Bible. Generally speaking, Azariah is preferred in the account of his reign in Kings and Uzziah elsewhere, but the pattern is not entirely consistent. Scholars usually assume that one of the names was his personal name and the other a throne name, but this is only a guess.

and the Hejaz route. After defeating the Meunites, Azariah evidently left them in place as guardians of this highly lucrative thoroughfare, but diverted its wealth to Judah by imposing tribute on them (2 Chronicles 26:8).[74] It was probably at this point, after he had gained control of the southern trade corridor, that Azariah was able to recover the seaport of Elath[75] on the Gulf of Aqabah from Edom and rebuild it (2 Chronicles 26:2; cf. 2 Kings 14:22).[76]

Although Azariah's domestic accomplishments may have been considerable—the Chronicler's account credits him with assembling large herds of cattles and employing farmers and viticulturists in the fertile parts of Judah (2 Chronicles 26:10)—he is remembered principally for having been a "leper."[77] After his diagnosis it was necessary for him to live in quarantine, and his son Jotham ruled Judah as his coregent (2 Kings 15:5). Since "leprosy" was determined by an examination by priests, who prescribed whether quarantine was required and how long it would last (Leviticus 13–14), Azariah's exclusion from power may have been the result of a continuation of the struggle in Judah between the king and the priesthood that had created turmoil during the reign of Jehoash in the late ninth century B.C.E.[78] In any case, as a "leper," Azariah was apparently assigned a special burial place in the vicinity of—but apart from—the royal tombs (2 Chronicles 26:23; contrast 2 Kings 15:7). A plaque inscribed with his name found in Jerusalem suggests that he was reburied in the late Herodian period. [79]

The rise of the Israelite and Judahite states in the early centuries of the first millennium B.C.E., the emergence of strongly centralized governments based in the capital cities of Samaria and Jerusalem, and the growth of large regional centers, such as Hazor, Megiddo and Dan in the north and Lachish and Beersheba in the south, led to a highly stratified society in both kingdoms. The upper stratum consisted of the king, his family and an aristocratic nobility that maintained the royal estates and ruled the regional centers as governors. Of somewhat lesser stature were artisans and skilled laborers of various kinds. Most of the rest of the population—indeed, the vast majority—were agriculturalists. The lucrative international trade that flourished in those period when Israel enjoyed good relations with Phoenicia and Judah with Philistia, and when the competition with Damascus was successful, was a source of substantial wealth for the king and his aristocratic servants. The everyday livelihood of most of the ordinary citizens of Israel and Judah throughout the history of the monarchy, however, consisted of family-based farming and horticulture, usually supplemented by the maintenance of small flocks of sheep and

Everyday life during the Divided Monarchy

goats.[80] In the lowland areas the staple crops were grain—wheat, barley and millet—while in the higher elevations and the western slopes of the hill country cereal farming was mixed with arbori-culture—the cultivation of figs, pomegranates, dates, sycamores and especially olives—and viticulture. In some areas olive oil or wine could be produced in sufficient quantities to accumulate surpluses that provided a valuable export commodity.

Archaeological evidence indicates that the basis of this production throughout the monarchical period was the extended family or, to use the biblical term, the "father's house" (*bêt 'āb*). This is shown by the widespread persistence throughout the period of the four-roomed house, which consisted of a central courtyard enclosed by rooms designed not only to house the family (usually on a second story) but also livestock, and to provide storage for agricultural produce. The stockpiling of crop surpluses in individual households, rather than communal storage facilities, indicates that agriculture was family-based, with the work being done by individual "father's houses," consisting of three or more generations of an extended family (along with servants or slaves) and comprising perhaps one to two dozen individuals.[81]

The larger structure of social organization described in the Bible parallels that of other agricultural societies investigated in cross-cultural anthropological studies and corresponds to the pattern that has prevailed in the eastern Mediterranean region from antiquity to the modern period.[82] Several families or "father's houses" constituted a clan. The families of a clan typically lived in the same village or at least in relatively close proximity to each other. A group of clans formed a tribe. Justice was ordinarily dispensed at the clan level by a group of elders, the senior men of the clan or village. In periods in which the central government at the state level was strong, however, the intervention of the king and his officers in matters of local justice, especially the allocation of property rights, was common, and the tension that resulted is reflected in the oracles of the biblical prophets, who often expressed the grievances of the citizenry against what they perceived as royal abuses of power (see, for example, Micah 2:2).[83]

The social organization of ancient Israel and Judah was strongly patriarchal, and women had minimal official involvement in public affairs.[84] Women had extensive and varied involvement in the activities of their families, however, and given the central position of the family in the economy and social organization of the two states, the influence of women on society as a whole is assumed to have been pervasive despite their invisibility in the public record.[85] Spinning, weaving and sewing were tasks especially associated with women, but they also took part in the basic economic endeavors of the family—farming and caring for livestock. Within the family structure a woman's ultimate role was that of mother. Childbearing conferred prestige and position on a woman because of the advantage of numerous children to the economic livelihood of her family in its agricultural activities and because of the necessity of offspring to perpetuate the lineage of her husband.

A woman's legal status was subordinated to that of men in the family, so that she was dependent for her legal rights and protection on her father or husband. When women were orphaned, widowed or divorced, they lost these rights and needed special protection—hence the frequency of injunctions in the Bible calling for special provisions for the welfare of orphans and widows (Exodus 21:22 [Old Testament] = 21:21 [Hebrew Bible]); Deuteronomy 27:19; etc.).[86] On the other hand, the inability of women to act on their own behalf in legal and economic matters is called into question by the discovery of a number of personal seals and seal impressions bearing the names of Judahite women.[87] These seals and sealings, which date to the seventh and early sixth centuries B.C.E., raise the possibility that, at least in this period, women were sometimes involved in legal and economic transactions under their own names.[88] Similarly, a woman's name ("Meshullemeth daughter of Elichen") appears in a list of the recipients—or, less likely, contributors—of specified commodities on a recently published ostracon from the early sixth century B.C.E.,[89] and this seems to be another example of a woman transacting business on her own behalf during the final days of the kingdom of Judah.

Israel and Judah Under the Assyrian Empire

Tiglath-pileser III

Following Adad-nirari III's 796 B.C.E. campaign to Syria, a long period of Assyrian weakness began, during which the empire extended no farther west than the province of Bit-Adini on the Euphrates; the Assyrian kings were unable to gain the upper hand in their competition with Urartu for control of Anatolia and northern Syria. With the accession of Tiglath-pileser III (745–727 B.C.E.), however, the situation began to change rapidly. After moving quickly to reorganize the kingdom administratively, Tiglath-pileser embarked on his first western campaign in 743 B.C.E. He broke the power of Urartu almost immediately and laid siege to Arpad, which was the key to the control of northern Syria (as it had been in the time of Adad-nirari). The fall of Arpad in 740 B.C.E. led to a surrender of most of the other states of northern and central Syria, including Hamath, and to their annexation into the empire.[90] Not content with this victory, Tiglath-pileser continued his march westward and extended the boundary of the Assyrian Empire to the Mediterranean coast. In 738 B.C.E., at the end of this first western campaign, he received tribute from, among others, Rezin (*Ra-ḫi-a-nu*) of Damascus and Queen Zabibe of Arabia (see below), as well as Menahem (*Me-ni-ḫi-im-me*) of Israel.[91]

Menahem had attained to the throne after a series of royal assassinations that brought the dynasty of Jehu to an end (2 Kings 15:8–22). Jeroboam II had died about 748 B.C.E. His son Zechariah (c. 748–747 B.C.E.) succeeded him, but was publicly assassinated after a reign of only six months by a certain Shallum son of Jabesh (c. 747 B.C.E.). One month later Shallum himself was assassinated by Menahem son of Gadi, who had marched against Samaria from the old Israelite capital city of Tirzah. Menahem ruled for a decade (c. 747–738 B.C.E.), witnessed the arrival of Tiglath-pileser in the West, and kept his throne by paying tribute to Assyria. Two years after his death, however, his son and successor, Pekahiah (c. 738–737 B.C.E.), was unseated in an anti-Assyrian coup led by Pekah son of Remaliah and an army of Gileadites. Between them, Menahem and Pekahiah had ruled Israel for 12 relatively stable years in very dangerous times, but the price they paid for peace with Assyria was very high, as the account of Menahem's tax collecting in 2 Kings 15:20 suggests, and we can assume that anti-Assyrian sentiment in the kingdom was strong. Even so, it seems very likely that the revolt was stimulated and supported by Rezin of Damascus, who was organizing the resistance to Assyria from Damascus, following in the footsteps of his ninth-century predecessors, Hadadezer and Hazael.[92]

For most of his reign, Menahem's Judahite contemporary was Jotham (c. 750–735 B.C.E.), who was still ruling as coregent for his leprous father, Azariah. The account of Jotham's reign in Kings (2 Kings 15:32–38) provides little information about his achievements, except that "he built the upper gate of the house of the Lord" (2 Kings 15:35), but the Chronicler (2 Chronicles 27:3–4) gives him credit for other construction projects in Jerusalem, where he "did extensive building on the wall of the Ophel" and in the Judean countryside. Jotham's motivation for these building activities (which are reminiscent of Azariah's efforts to fortify Jerusalem [2 Chronicles 26:9])[93] was probably concern over the possibility of an invasion—not by Assyria, which did not yet pose a direct threat to Judah, but by Israel and Damascus. Nor was such a concern ill-founded or premature. At some point, probably late in Jotham's reign, Pekah and Rezin began making incursions into Judah (2 Kings 15:37), anticipating their full-scale assault on Jerusalem in the time of Ahaz. Most historians interpret their later attack on Ahaz as an attempt to force him to join the anti-Assyrian coalition that had formed in southern Syria and Palestine: If this is correct, the hostilities against Jotham should probably be seen as the beginning of this policy of diplomacy by intimidation. Despite the pressure his northern neighbors brought to bear, however, Jotham did not yield, and his determination to remain unaligned, if not pro-Assyrian, is

Bulla of King Ahaz. *"Belonging to Ahaz (son of) Jotham, King of Judah," reads the Hebrew inscription impressed onto this bulla (lump of clay), which was originally used to secure a papyrus scroll. Ancient bullae and seals are not uncommon, but this is one of the first that can be attributed to a Hebrew king: Ahaz, who ruled over Judah from 735 to 727 B.C.E.*

understandable. To Judah, which had not been among the nations that paid tribute to Tiglath-pileser III in 738 B.C.E., the Assyrian threat must have still seemed remote, and no doubt Jotham thought it wise not to antagonize Tiglath-pileser if he could avoid doing so.

After a few years in which the Assyrian army was occupied north and east of Syria campaigning against the Urartians and Medes,[94] Tiglath-pileser set out on his second western campaign (734–732 B.C.E.), which ended triumphantly with the fall of Assyria's old nemesis in Syria, Damascus. The biblical account of this campaign (2 Kings 16:5–9) claims that it was launched in response to a petition to Tiglath-pileser from Ahaz (735–727 B.C.E.), who was now king of Judah.* Rezin and Pekah had joined forces again, as they had during the reign of Jotham, and this time they laid siege to Jerusalem. Since a pioneering study in 1929 by Joachim Begrich, most modern historians have agreed that Damascus and Israel launched the Syro-Ephraimite war, as Begrich called it, to intimidate Ahaz, so that he would renounce his policy of neutrality and join the anti-Assyrian cause.[95] If this was the case, however, the plan backfired. According to the biblical sources, Ahaz was, in fact, intimidated,[96] but instead of joining the resistance to Assyria, he voluntarily entered into Assyrian vassalage. He sent a message of subservience to Tiglath-pileser together with a gift of silver and gold garnered from the Temple and palace treasuries. The biblical account concludes by indicating that the

---

*A clay bulla, or impression, of the personal seal of Ahaz has recently been published: The inscription reads "Belonging to Ahaz [son of] Jotham, king of Judah." It is the first seal or sealing of a king of Israel or Judah from the biblical period to have been discovered. (See Robert Deutsch, *Messages from the Past: Hebrew Bullae from the Time of Isaiah Through the Destruction of the First Temple* [in Hebrew] [Tel Aviv: Archaeological Center Publications, 1997], pp. 49–51 and pl. XVI; and "First Impression: What We Learn from King Ahaz's Seal," *BAR*, May/June 1998, pp. 54-56, 62. See also "We Have a Winner," *BAR*, March/April 1997, p. 8.)

Assyrian king responded favorably and led his forces into Syria, where he captured Damascus, exiled its populatôn and executed Rezin.

Despite the limited perspective of the biblical account of these events, which naturally centers on the involvement of Judah, we know from Assyrian sources that Rezin and Pekah were involved in a larger anti-Assyrian movement in the West, which included Hiram of Tyre as well as the kings of two Philistine cities, Mitinti of Ashkelon and Hanun (or Hanno) of Gaza. Although the Damascene Rezin, as the ringleader of the coalition, was clearly the primary target of the larger Assyrian campaign, Tiglath-pileser's strategy seems to have been to subdue the other coalition members first, progressively isolating Damascus over the three years of the campaign. Thus in 734 B.C.E., which is designated "to Philistia" in the Assyrian Eponym Chronicle, he moved to subdue the western allies of Damascus and the northern kingdom of Israel. Although the annalistic fragments are too incomplete to permit more than an approximation of his itinerary, he seems to have begun by marching down the Phoenician coast, capturing Byblos and other cities until he came face-to-face with Hiram of Tyre (the namesake of the Hiram of Tyre who helped Solomon build the Temple), who capitulated and paid tribute. Tiglath-pileser then proceeded south to Ashkelon, where he accepted the Philistine Mitinti's surrender and an oath of loyalty that Mitinti would later break. When the Assyrian army reached Gaza, Hanun fled to Egypt, from which he would later return to accept vassalage and to rule over the port of Gaza as an Assyrian imperial entrepôt. The southernmost point reached on the 734 B.C.E. march was the "the Wadi of Egypt" (the Wadi el-'Arish, the traditional southern boundary of Palestine), where Tiglath-pileser was obliged to fight the Meunites, whom Azariah had subdued decades earlier after his own Philistine campaign. Having now subdued the entire coastal plain south of Phoenicia, Tiglath-pileser formally annexed the region from Dor and the Plain of Sharon south to Philistia as an Assyrian province with the name Du'ru (Dor), incorporated the Philistine states as vassaldoms and marked the southern boundary of the Assyrian Empire with a stele erected at the Wadi of Egypt. At that time he accepted tribute not only from the kings of the states defeated on the march (Tyre, Ashkelon, Gaza) but also from Kaushmalaku of Edom, Salamanu of Moab, Sanipu of Bit-Ammon, as well as Ahaz (*Ia-u-ḫa-zi*)* of Judah.[97] Note that the three Transjordanian states, like Judah, seem to have bought their safety by offering tribute and by avoiding alliances with Rezin's coalition. They remained semi-independent—vassal states that were not formally annexed and incorporated into the empire.

---

*The spelling in the Assyrian annals corresponds to the longer form of the king's name, "Jehoahaz," of which the biblical "Ahaz" is a hypocoristic (abbreviated) form.

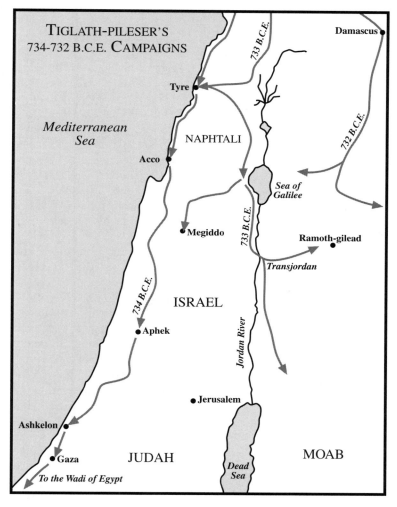

Over the next two years (733–732 B.C.E.), both of which are designated "to Damascus" in the Eponym Chronicles, Tiglath-pileser
turned his attention to Damascus and Israel. Again the fragmentary
nature of the annals permits only an approximation of the sequence
of events, but it seems clear that Damascus was placed under siege
at the beginning of the 733 B.C.E. campaign. Then, leaving part of
his army to carry out the siege, Tiglath-pileser marched through
northern Israel, capturing all of Naphtali and the Upper Galilee, as
well as northern Transjordan (2 Kings 15:29). For the first time
Israelites went into exile under the Assyrian policy of deportations,
as the captives—a total of 13,520 according to a recently published
annal fragment[98]—were led off to Assyria. The rest of Israel was
bypassed and spared when, sometime in 732 B.C.E., Hoshea son of

Elah assassinated Pekah, took his place as king (2 Kings 15:30) and sent a message of fealty to Tiglath-pileser.[99] This ensured that Israel would be spared annexation and survive beyond the reign of Tiglath-pileser, if only as a tiny state in the Ephraimite highlands. Large tracts of former Israelite territory did not survive, however, and they were incorporated into three Assyrian provinces: Du'ru (Dor), which, as noted, had been annexed after the 734 B.C.E. campaign, Magidu (Megiddo), which included the entire Galilee as far south as Megiddo and the Jezreel Valley, and Gal'aza (Gilead), which consisted of Israelite Transjordan as far north as Ramoth-gilead.[100] By this time, Tiglath-pileser's troops had completed the siege of Damascus, which fell in 732 B.C.E. and was incorporated into the empire. Very little information about the fall of Damascus is preserved in Assyrian records,[101] except that Rezin was executed (cf. 2 Kings 16:9) and his hometown of Hadara was destroyed in reprisal.

It is important not to overlook the economic motivations and consequences of Tiglath-pileser's conquests in the West. By incorporating Syria, Phoenicia and the entire Mediterranean coast as far south as the Wadi el-'Arish into the empire, Assyria attained direct control of the major Syrian trade routes and the great coastal highway, the Via Maris, which was the land route to Egypt. Since the Transjordanian states remained semi-independent tributaries (states that paid tribute), Assyria did not directly control the King's Highway with its connection to the lucrative caravan route from the northern Hejaz and farther south. But this hardly mattered, since Assyria's sovereignty over Damascus and the Phoenician and Philistine port cities gave it control of all the regional outlets for this highly profitable traffic. It is thus no surprise that we find an Arabian queen listed as paying tribute after both of Tiglath-pileser's western campaigns: The last name in the 738 B.C.E. tribute list is "Zabibe, the queen of Arabia."[102] When Damascus, Israel and Tyre submitted to Tiglath-pileser of Assyria in 738 B.C.E., this threatened to disrupt the trade from South Arabia to Damascus and from there to Mediterranean ports; hence Zabibe's payment of tribute was probably an attempt to protect her interests and keep the routes open.[103] The 738 B.C.E. tribute list contains an abundance of luxury goods that were bartered in the South Arabian trade, including precious metals and ivory, exotic woods, and the hides of elephants and other exotic animals.

Near its southern end, the principal western bifurcation of the King's Highway ran south of the Dead Sea through the Wadi Hesa-Beersheba depression, then passed through Judahite territory and emerged at Ashkelon or another of the Philistine ports. This route was still free from Assyrian interference after 738 B.C.E., but Tiglath-pileser's 734 B.C.E. incursion into Philistia brought it under Assyrian control. The name of Samsi, who succeeded Zabibe as "queen of Arabia" at this time, has not survived in the damaged tribute list of 734 B.C.E.,[104] but it must have been there, because another annal fragment refers to her violation of an oath she swore to Shamash, the Assyrian god of justice.[105] Mitinti of Ashkelon, who submitted to Tiglath-pileser in 734 B.C.E., later rebelled, and Tiglath-pileser's annals (though, as usual, they are too fragmentary for certainty) seem to associate Samsi's rebellion with Mitinti's.[106] Whether these two acts of defiance were jointly planned or simply simultaneous, they should probably be interpreted as desperate attempts to restore the independence of the spice and incense trade. Both rebellions were quickly suppressed—Mitinti's when he died and his son and successor submitted to Tiglath-pileser, and Samsi's when she surrendered, paid tribute and accepted an Assyrian-appointed overseer—but they serve as good illustrations of what was at stake economically in Tiglath-pileser's Philistine excursion.

Israel enjoyed a brief period of stability after 732 B.C.E., while Hoshea (732–724 B.C.E.) was a loyal vassal of Tiglath-pileser. But in 727 B.C.E., when Tiglath-pileser died and was succeeded by Shalmaneser V (727–722 B.C.E.), Hoshea became embroiled in a revolt that broke out in the western part of the empire. We have no Assyrian historical records from Shalmaneser V's reign, but the general sequence of events can be reconstructed from the Eponym Chronicle, itself poorly preserved at this point, in combination with information that survives third-hand from the annals of Tyre.[107] Evidently Shalmaneser campaigned in Phoenicia in his first regnal year (727 B.C.E.), accepting tribute and then withdrawing. Subsequently, however, a group of Tyrian vassal cities revolted against Tyre and appealed to Assyria for help. In response Shalmaneser marched west again, probably in 725 B.C.E.,[108] and began a siege of Tyre that was lifted without success after five years—after Shalmaneser's reign had ended.

The fall of Samaria

With this framework in mind, we can better understand the brief biblical account of Hoshea's reign and the fall of Samaria (2 Kings 17:1–6). The statement in 2 Kings 17:3 that Shalmaneser marched against Hoshea and accepted his tribute and fealty suggests that Shalmaneser visited Israel on his way to or from Phoenicia or even that Samaria was one of the "Phoenician" cities that, according to the Tyrian annals, paid tribute to the Assyrian king in that year. According to 2 Kings 17:4, however, Hoshea subsequently antagonized Shalmaneser by conspiring against him, communicating with Egypt[109]—presumably in search of support against Assyria—and withholding the annual tribute he had been paying. Shalmaneser responded by arresting Hoshea. Then, with Hoshea in Assyrian custody, Shalmaneser marched to Samaria and laid siege to the city (2 Kings 17:5). It is tempting to associate these developments with the events of 725 B.C.E. and Shalmaneser's attack on Tyre. If this reconstruction is correct, it suggests that Samaria and Tyre had probably formed an alliance against Shalmaneser, reminiscent of the anti-Assyrian coalitions of the past,[110] and that Egypt was encouraging if not actively supporting the alliance.[111] It further suggests that the sieges of Tyre and Samaria probably began at about the same time, in 725 or 724 B.C.E.

At that time, Hoshea's appeal to Egypt having evidently gone unheeded, Shalmaneser "invaded all the land"—that is, overran and devastated Israel as a whole—and put the capital, Samaria, under siege (2 Kings 17:5–6, 18:9–10). The siege lasted three years, concluding in 722 B.C.E.—evidently late in the summer—with the fall of Samaria, and thousands of Israelites were led into exile. The biblical account of these events is telescoped, giving the impression that the same king of Assyria was responsible for the fall of Samaria and the deportation of the Israelites, but this was not the case. Shalmaneser V died only a couple of months after the conclusion of the siege, in the winter of 722 B.C.E., so that the final disposition of Samaria and the exile of the Israelites was left to his successor, the usurper Sargon II (722–705 B.C.E.). In his annals and other inscriptions, Sargon boasts of having besieged and captured Samaria, but the Bible assigns responsibility for the successful siege to Shalmaneser, and this is corroborated by the Babylonian Chronicle (a record of annual events begun in the mid-eighth century B.C.E.).

Sargon was prevented from giving his immediate attention to Samaria by two major revolts in the empire that erupted when he seized the throne. One of these, which took place in Babylon, was an outburst of nationalistic fervor under the leadership of the Chaldean prince Marduk-apla-iddina II—the biblical Merodachbaladan (2 Kings 20:12 = Isaiah 39:1)—who proclaimed himself king of Babylon.[112] Sargon needed 12 years to dislodge him from the throne. The other revolt, which took place in the western provinces, was initiated by Ilu-bi'di of Hamath and Hanun of Gaza, who had also rebelled against Tiglath-pileser in 734 B.C.E. The revolt of Ilu-bi'di and Hanun quickly spread to several other cities including Damascus and Samaria.[113] It was this revolt that brought Sargon west in 720 B.C.E. and gave him the opportunity to complete the incorporation of Samaria into the empire and to initiate the deportation of its citizens. Sargon trapped and destroyed the forces of Hamath in the fortress of Qarqar, where Shalmaneser III had fought Hamath and its allies 133 years earlier. When the region had been pacified and Ilu-bi'di executed, the Assyrian army marched down the coast towards Gaza to deal with Hanun. Like Hoshea a few years earlier, Hanun had appealed to Egypt for help, and in his case the pharaoh[114] responded

SHALMANESER V'S
AND SARGON II'S
CAMPAIGNS

Acco

Sea of Galilee

Dor

Megiddo

Samaria

Jordan River

Mediterranean Sea

ISRAEL

Ashdod

Ekron

Gath

Jerusalem

Gaza

JUDAH

PHILISTIA

Raphia

Dead Sea

Wadi of Egypt

━━━◀━━━ Assyrian forces

◀┄┄┄┄ Egyptian forces

and sent his viceroy (*turtānu*) with a contingent of troops. Sargon met the combined forces of Gaza and Egypt at "the city of the Wadi of Egypt," that is, Raphia (about 15 miles southwest of Gaza), where he won a decisive battle, capturing Hanun and driving away the Egyptian army. With the Assyrian victory, Egypt, for the first time, agreed to pay tribute to Assyria, as did South Arabian leaders[115] who, confronted with another show of Assyrian power in southern Palestine, were anxious to maintain good relations with Sargon in order to protect their trade interests in the region.

It was probably during the first, northern phase of the 720 B.C.E. campaign that Sargon began the deportation of Israelites—one summary inscription indicates that 27,290 people were involved.[116] Although the Assyrian practice of deporting captive peoples had already begun in the ninth century B.C.E., it was Sargon's predecessor,

Beersheba horned altar. _Dating to the eighth century B.C.E., this is the first example discovered of an Israelite horned altar for animal sacrifice. Contrary to biblical law (Exodus 20:25), the 63-inch-tall altar was built of hewn stones. It also has a serpent motif incised on one of its blocks. Sacrifices had apparently been burnt on the altar, for the top stones were blackened. The Beersheba altar provides rare evidence of religious rituals carried out in a Judahite city other than Jerusalem._

Although the altar had been disassembled and its blocks reused in a wall, archaeologists had no trouble distinguishing the calcareous sandstone of the altar blocks from the common limestone of the rest of the wall.

Tiglath-pileser, who gave it its great notoriety, not only by employing it on a much vaster scale than his predecessors but also by introducing the policy of two-way relocations. Conquered peoples from the western portions of the empire were resettled in Assyria and in the eastern provinces, while captives from the eastern and southern regions were resettled in the West. Thus we are told in 2 Kings 17:6 that Sargon transported captive Israelites to Assyria and in 2 Kings 17:24 that he repopulated the cities of Samaria with peoples from Babylonia and Elam (southwestern Iran).[117] More specifically, the Israelites were resettled in Halah (northeast of Nineveh), on the Habor (the Khabur River, a tributary that flows south into Euphrates from the highlands of southeastern Turkey and northeastern Syria), and in the highlands[118] of the Medes (northwestern Iran). Hoshea's former kingdom was reorganized as the Assyrian province of Samerina (Samaria), and the city of Samaria was rebuilt under Assyrian supervision to serve as the provincial capital. The once independent state of Israel, the northern kingdom, which had enjoyed periods of considerable regional power under the Omrides and the last kings of the Jehu dynasty, was no more. In its place were the four Assyrian provinces of Dor, Megiddo, Gilead and Samaria.

King Ahaz of Judah died in about 727 B.C.E. He was succeeded by his son Hezekiah (727–697 B.C.E.), who presided over a critical period in the history of Judah, introducing cultic reforms that charted the course for the subsequent development of Israelite religion, and adopting a bold policy towards Assyria, based first on defiance and then on conciliation, that defined Judah's position in the international affairs of the seventh century B.C.E. Fortunately Hezekiah's pivotal reign is one of the best documented of any king of Israel or Judah, both in biblical and extrabiblical texts. It is extensively reported in both Kings and Chronicles, and it is the setting of a substantial number of the oracles and narratives collected in Isaiah 1–33. The Assyrian annals provide a full account of Hezekiah's rebellion against Assyria and subsequent capitulation. A number of larger and smaller Hebrew inscriptions have survived from Hezekiah's reign, ranging from the famous Siloam tunnel inscription (discussed below) to the extensive corpus of *lmlk* jar handles (also discussed below) to numerous personal seals and seal impressions belonging to the leading citizens of the day. These personal documents permit an especially intimate access to the time of Hezekiah, but none does so more dramatically than a clay impression that has recently come to light of the seal of King Hezekiah himself.[119] It reads "Belonging to Hezekiah (son) of Ahaz, king of Judah."

Sennacherib's invasion of Judah

In the Deuteronomistic historian's summary of his reign (2 Kings 18:1–8, especially verse 4) we are told that Hezekiah "removed the high places" (the local shrines), "broke down the pillars" (standing stones that marked the sacredness of the shrines), "cut down the sacred pole" (the asherah, which seems to have signified the divine presence, sometimes personified as a goddess and consort of the God of Israel) and smashed Nehushtan, "the bronze serpent that Moses had made" (an otherwise unknown but obviously long-venerated cult object). All of these except the last are often-mentioned Israelite cult objects that earlier kings were condemned for failing to abolish, and none of them is Assyrian. It would be a mistake, therefore, to associate Hezekiah's religious reforms with his revolt against Assyria in the closing years of the eighth century.[120] On the contrary, he is more likely to have initiated these reforms early in his reign, before Sennacherib threatened the country and before the elimination of local places of worship might have demoralized the citizenry who lived outside of Jerusalem.[121] The Chronicler states that Hezekiah began to purify the Temple immediately, in the first month of the first year of his reign (2 Chronicles 29:3). This claim seems intended to emphasize the piety of an ancient and revered king, but it may be only slightly exaggerated.[122] The grim example of Samaria gave credence to the voices of prophets like Hosea, who had warned that the gross religious improprieties in the northern kingdom would lead to disaster and exile, and Hezekiah may have hoped that religious reform would help Judah avoid the fate of Israel.

WERNER BRAUN

Arad temple. *Limestone incense altars flank the steps leading into the Holy of Holies, or innermost chamber, of the temple to Yahweh at Arad, in the Negev; at the rear of the niche are two sacred standing stones. Built in the tenth century B.C.E., the Arad temple remained in use until it was destroyed during the religious reforms of either Hezekiah in the late eighth century B.C.E. or Josiah in the late seventh century. When the temple was abolished, the altars were reverently laid on their sides and covered with earth.*

For the first two decades of his reign, Hezekiah seems to have remained a loyal vassal of Assyria. There is no Assyrian record of an attack on Judah by Shalmaneser V or Sargon II during this period. When King Azuri of Ashdod rebelled against Assyria in 714 B.C.E., Hezekiah evidently refused to become involved, despite the seditious messages Azuri is said in Sargon's annals to have sent to Judah.[123] Ashdod had active support from Shabaka (716–702 B.C.E.), the Cushite ruler of Egypt, who had moved to assert the rule of the strong XXVth Dynasty over the entire Nile Valley after the death of the dynastic founder, his brother Piankhy. The "Oracle concerning Ethiopia [i.e., Cush]," in Isaiah 19, with its reference to "sending ambassadors by the Nile," is often taken as an indication that Shabaka contacted Hezekiah, urging him to join the revolt. If so, Hezekiah evidently refused, perhaps swayed by Isaiah's counsel (cf. Isaiah 20:6), and the decision proved to be the safe one, since by 712 B.C.E. Sargon had smashed the revolt in Ashdod and had at least intimidated its Egyptian supporters—this is the background of the threats against Egypt and Ethiopia (Cush) in Isaiah 20.

Hezekiah's policy of compliance with Assyria ended dramatically with the death of Sargon II and the accession of his son Sennacherib (705–681 B.C.E.). Viewed in broad perspective, the reign of Sennacherib was a period of relative tranquillity in the western provinces of the empire. This was partly because the Assyrian army was heavily committed to a long and difficult struggle with Babylon, but it was also because the conquest of the West was now complete. Although Sennacherib's successors would attempt to extend its boundaries to the Nile, the empire had reached its natural limits. Moreover, the imperial administration, to which Sennacherib made a number of improvements, was in place and working, and this brought an unaccustomed stability to Syria-Palestine—the so-called *Pax Assyriaca*. It is somewhat ironic, then, that just as this Assyrian Peace was taking hold in the West, Sennacherib sent an army across the Euphrates—his only western campaign—with Jerusalem as its principal target and final destination.

Bullae of King Hezekiah. *The damaged seal impression (upper right) was published more than ten years ago, but it was too fragmentary to allow scholars to reconstruct the inscription and thus to realize to whom the seal had originally belonged. Recently, a more complete impression (left) of the same seal surfaced in a private London collection. The better-preserved inscription clearly reads: "Belonging to Hezekiah (son) of Ahaz, king of Judah." Above the inscription appears a winged scarab—a symbol found in hundreds of inscriptions dating to the reign of Hezekiah (727–697 B.C.E.).*

Sargon had been killed in battle in Asia Minor, and news of his death sparked hope throughout the empire that Assyrian power would diminish. Almost immediately a rebellion broke out in Babylon, led again by Merodachbaladan, who had also opposed Sargon at his accession (722 B.C.E.). He was supported by a coalition of Babylonian ethnic groups, including his fellow Chaldeans, as well as Arameans and Elamites. Merodachbaladan may also have tried to foment unrest in the West,[124] where, in any case, a major revolt was brewing. The ringleaders were, in the north, Luli, the king of Sidon, and, in the south, Sidqia (*şid-qa-a-a*) of Ashkelon and Hezekiah of Judah. The people of Ekron also joined in, deposing Padi, their pro-Assyrian king, and consigning him to the custody of Hezekiah, who had "attacked the Philistines as far as Gaza and its territory, from watchtower to fortified city" (2 Kings 18:8), evidently attempting to force other Philistine states into the fold. Egypt, hoping to reassert control over the territories and trade routes lost to Tiglath-pileser and Sargon, supported the revolt. Earlier, after Sargon's suppression of the 714–712 B.C.E. revolt in Ashdod, Pharaoh Shabaka had come to terms with Assyria in order to stabilize the position of the XXVth Dynasty in Egypt by reducing the threat from Assyria. Now, however, Shabaka (716–702 B.C.E.) or his successor, Shebitku (702–690 B.C.E.), was ready to support rebellion against Assyria.

In 701 B.C.E., having ousted Merodachbaladan and brought things somewhat under control in Babylonia, Sennacherib marched against the western rebel states, beginning with Sidon.[125] When the Assyrian army arrived, the Phoenician cities surrendered without a fight. Luli fled to Cyprus (cf. Isaiah 23:12), where he later died, while Sennacherib installed Ittobaal (*Tuba'lu*) on the Sidonian throne. The Assyrian annals boast of the submission at this time of the rulers of a number of western states ("all the kings of Amurru"). Some or all of these—including the Transjordanian states of Ammon, Moab and Edom—may originally have supported the coalition, so that their surrender left Ashkelon, Ekron and Judah isolated. Sennacherib stormed down the coast and accepted the surrender of Ashkelon, deporting Sidqia to Assyria and replacing him with Sharruludari, who, despite his Assyrian name, is said to have been the son of a former king of Ashkelon who had been loyal to Assyria.

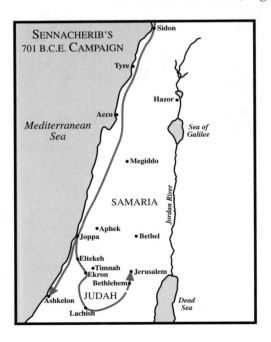

At this point Sennacherib spent some time destroying and looting towns and cities, like Joppa, that had been dependent on Ashkelon. Before he was ready to march on Ekron, he was intercepted at Eltekeh (Tell esh-Shallaf, north of Jabneh) by a very large Egyptian expeditionary force that had responded to a request from Ekron for help.[126] Though the annals claim that Sennacherib defeated the Egyptians, he may have merely escaped them—or at best repulsed them—and their continuing presence in the region was probably a factor in his decision to withdraw permanently from Palestine before consummating his siege of Jerusalem. In any case, he moved on from Eltekeh to Ekron and captured the city, punishing the rebels but sparing those who had remained loyal to Assyria; he would eventually bring Padi back from Jerusalem and restore him to his throne.[127]

After the capture of Ekron, the Assyrian army marched into Judah. For this stage of Sennacherib's campaign we have fairly extensive accounts not only in the Assyrian annals, on which we rely for almost all we know about the earlier stages, but also the Bible. The biblical account, which is found in 2 Kings 18:13–19:37 (= Isaiah 36–37), consists of two distinct sections that are widely recognized as deriving from different sources. The opening section (2 Kings 18:13–16) is a straightforward summary of the events, describing the devastation of the Judahite countryside by the Assyrian army and Hezekiah's payment of tribute to Sennacherib. The businesslike tone of this passage and the absence of ideological or even interpretive expansion suggest that it is a quotation from an early annalistic source. Although much more compact than the Assyrian account, it corresponds closely—sometimes remarkably so[128]—to the picture given there, so that these two annalistic sources, Judahite and Assyrian, tend to corroborate each other. The section that follows in the biblical account (2 Kings 18:17–19:34) is a long discursive narrative detailing demands for the surrender of Jerusalem made by Sennacherib's officers and placing special emphasis on the role of the prophet Isaiah in convincing Hezekiah *not* to surrender. This material probably originated in prophetic circles associated with Isaiah, and its language and ideology indicate it was transmitted in the Deuteronomistic tradition. For these reasons the historical value of this second section of the biblical account of the invasion is sometimes discounted, but a number of studies have demonstrated the presence, especially in the speeches of Sennacherib's ambassadors,[129] of stereotyped elements of style, ideology and language known from Assyrian royal inscriptions. This suggests that this section, too, is based on authentic events—or at least early accounts of events—and therefore has historical value despite its complex literary history[130] and its inclusion of numerous later expansions and interpolations.

According to the Assyrian annals, Sennacherib besieged and captured 46 of Hezekiah's fortified cities (cf. 2 Kings 18:13), turning many of them over to the Philistine states that had been loyal to Assyria. Most of these captured cities, we assume, were on Judah's western frontier, which, with Hezekiah's Philistine allies reduced to vassalage or worse, was vulnerable and unable to resist the Assyrian onslaught. Sennacherib's principal success in this part of the campaign was against the fortress city of Lachish in the Judahite Shephelah, which guarded the southwestern entrance into the passes to Jerusalem. Lachish is not specifically mentioned in Sennacherib's annals—it was presumably one of the 46 captured cities—and the siege is not reported in the Bible (though the presence of the Assyrian army at Lachish is mentioned several times in 2 Kings 18–19). Nevertheless, the siege is very well documented, both by the reliefs depicting the siege found in the ruins of Sennacherib's palace at Nineveh and by the excavation of Lachish.[131] The old annalistic summary at the beginning of the biblical account states that Hezekiah sent a message of contrition to Sennacherib while he was at Lachish, asking the Assyrian king to withdraw and promising that "whatever you impose on me I will bear" (2 Kings 18:14). This suggests that the Assyrian war camp at Lachish, which is depicted in the Nineveh reliefs, was the headquarters for the entire Judahite campaign including the siege of Jerusalem, which must have already been well advanced before Hezekiah dispatched his submissive message.

Despite the arrangement of the biblical materials, it must have been prior to Hezekiah's submission that Sennacherib sent a delegation of three officers to Jerusalem to demand the surrender of the city, as described in 2 Kings 18:17–19:7. The duties of these officers in the normal operations of the Assyrian bureaucracy are well known. Two of the officers, the Tartan (Viceroy) and the Rabsaris (Chief Eunuch), had important military and diplomatic duties,[132] but the third, the Rabshakeh (Chief Cupbearer), who was the highest-ranking *domestic* attendant of the king, ordinarily did not. Yet it was the Rabshakeh who served as the Assyrian spokesman at Jerusalem, and this is best explained by the assumption that he spoke Hebrew.[133] The demand for surrender, though formally addressed to Hezekiah, was also a piece of military propaganda, designed to intimidate and demoralize the citizens of Jerusalem: Rabshakeh refused a request by Hezekiah's delegation that he speak Aramaic (the internationally accepted diplomatic language), and instead shouted a message "in the language of Judah" to the people listening on the city wall, denouncing Hezekiah and offering them favorable surrender terms.

Neither the Assyrian nor the biblical account indicates how long Jerusalem was under siege before Hezekiah submitted, but it was long enough for the Assyrian army to erect earthworks against the city gates and ravage the surrounding countryside while keeping Hezekiah confined, as Sennacherib boasted, "like a bird in a cage."[134]

ERICH LESSING

Wall relief from Sennacherib's palace at Nineveh. *A family from the conquered Judahite city of Lachish walks barefoot into exile. According to the Assyrian annals, Sennacherib (705–681 B.C.E.) besieged and captured 46 of Hezekiah's fortified cities. Sennacherib's greatest success was against Lachish—then the second most important city in Judah—which guarded the southwestern entrance into the passes to Jerusalem. The Assyrian war camp at Lachish, which is depicted in the Nineveh reliefs, became the headquarters for the entire Judahite campaign.*

Sennacherib decorated the central ceremonial room of his Nineveh palace with reliefs like this depicting the conquest of Lachish. Other panels from the series show the Assyrians storming the city, executing the Judahites and carrying off booty.

It may seem surprising, in fact, that the city wall was never breached, but Jerusalem was not as vulnerable as the cities on Judah's western frontier. The four years (705–701 B.C.E.) it had taken Sennacherib to subdue Merodachbaladan had given Hezekiah

Hezekiah's tunnel. Anticipating an attack by Sennacherib of Assyria, the Judahite king Hezekiah (727–697 B.C.E.) built a 1,749-foot-long tunnel to bring the water of the Gihon Spring within the city walls of Jerusalem. This successful building project (with its fresh supply of water, Jerusalem managed to withstand the Assyrian siege) is referred to in 2 Kings 20:20 and 2 Chronicles 32:4.

time to make elaborate preparations, especially in the capital city itself. According to 2 Chronicles 32:5, he had rebuilt and strengthened the city wall of Jerusalem and the *millo*.* He also added "another wall" that was "outside" the first, part of which has been recently uncovered in a Jerusalem excavation directed by Nahman Avigad.[135] Hezekiah's most remarkable achievement in this regard, though, was the construction of a tunnel to protect the city's water supply. The Gihon Spring, Jerusalem's principal source of water, was situated at a vulnerable location in the Kidron Valley outside the city wall. Hezekiah's workers sealed access to the Gihon and the other water sources outside the city (2 Chronicles 32:3–4) and excavated a tunnel, still extant, that diverted the water under the hill to a collecting pool in the western part of the city, within the walls (cf. 2 Kings 20:20; 2 Chronicles 32:30). This remarkable engineering feat—the excavation of a tunnel 1,749 feet long and in places 100 feet beneath the streets of the city—was described and commemorated in an inscription found in 1880.[136] Preceding his reference

*The enigmatic *millo* is first mentioned in connection with the rebuilding of the city after David's conquest (2 Samuel 5:9). It was evidently some kind of fortification, perhaps a filled-earth rampart.

ERICH LESSING

Siloam inscription. *Discovered in 1880, this inscription celebrates the completion of Hezekiah's tunnel. Carved into the wall of the tunnel about 20 feet from its end at the Siloam Pool, the text describes how the workmen tunneled toward each other to build the channel: "While the stonecutters were still wielding the axe, each man towards his fellow, and while there were still three cubits to be cut through, they heard the sound of each man calling to his fellow, for there was a zdh [fissure?] in the rock to the right and the left. And on the day of the breakthrough the stonecutters struck each man towards his fellows, axe against axe, and the waters flowed from the source to the pool, for 1,200 cubits."*

to Hezekiah's tunnel, the Chronicler indicates that Hezekiah maintained numerous storehouses for agricultural goods and places (cities) for quartering livestock (2 Chronicles 32:28–29), and these, too, should probably be seen as part of his preparations for the invasion. The possibility that he reorganized the kingdom fiscally, dividing it into four administrative districts for the distribution of supplies, arises from the study of a large group of stamps found on jar handles and whole vessels—more than 1,200 of them have been found at numerous sites—each of which bears the depiction of a winged scarab[137] and the legend *lmlk*, meaning "Belonging to the king," followed by the name of one of four towns, which may have been central distribution depots.[138]

In the end, the siege of Jerusalem was lifted, and the Assyrian army departed. Although there may have been other factors,[139] Hezekiah's preparations probably made the completion of the siege seem more difficult than it was worth to Sennacherib, especially since he had already achieved his major goals. The revolt in the West had been completely quelled, and all the leading rebel states—Sidon, Ashkelon and Judah—had submitted and accepted vassalage status, the former two with new kings of Sennacherib's choosing. Hezekiah was still on the throne of Jerusalem, but Padi had been freed from his custody and returned to Ekron, and Hezekiah himself had accepted vassalage and paid an extremely high price to keep his throne.[140] To supply the precious metals required by Sennacherib, Hezekiah emptied both the palace and temple treasuries and stripped the gold ornamentation from the entryway of the Temple (2 Kings 18:15–16). True, the Egyptian army was probably still operating somewhere in the region, but, with the size of the force that ambushed him at Eltekeh still fresh in his mind, Sennacherib must have been content to go home and leave the Egypt problem for his successors.[141]

The reign of Manasseh and the Assyrian conquest of Egypt

Hezekiah died in 697 B.C.E. and was succeeded by his son Manasseh (697–642 B.C.E.). Judah was now a very small state, totally under the control of Assyria. Manasseh was a loyal vassal throughout most of his long reign. He is named several times in Assyrian records as one of the western kings required to transport materials to Nineveh or elsewhere for imperial building projects or to supply troops for the Assyrian assault on Egypt.[142] By complying with the demands of the Assyrian administration he managed to reign in peace, at least most of the time, for 55 years (2 Kings 21:1 = 2 Chronicles 33:1), and, to that extent, Judah can be said to have been a beneficiary of the *Pax Assyriaca* in Syria-Palestine. Nevertheless, Manasseh is judged extremely negatively in the Bible, especially in the account of his reign in 2 Kings 21:1–18, where he is condemned not for his loyalty to Assyria, but for his religious policies. The principal author of the account in Kings was an exilic historian of the Deuteronomistic school,[143] thus an advocate of the religious reforms of Hezekiah, Manasseh's father, and Josiah, Manasseh's grandson. The writer was trying to explain why Jerusalem fell despite these reforms, and he fixed on Manasseh because Manasseh was a counterreformer. In 2 Kings 21:10–15, the historian recites an oracle of Yahweh, attributed to unnamed prophets, that lays explicit blame on Manasseh for the fall of Jerusalem and the exile of its people.

It was once assumed that Manasseh's religious policies were the inevitable result of his Assyrian allegiance,[144] but this was not the case. As already noted in connection with Hezekiah's reforms, Assyria imposed no cultic restrictions on vassal states, permitting them to continue their indigenous religious customs.[145] The list of cultic practices for which Manasseh is condemned in 2 King 21:3–7 includes no reference to the worship of Assyrian gods. The cultic changes made by Manasseh were, instead, revivals of old Israelite and Judahite practices that had been accepted in the time of his grandfather, Ahaz, and earlier, but set aside by the reforms of his father, Hezekiah. In particular, "he rebuilt the high places," that is, the local places of sacrifice, "that his father Hezekiah had destroyed" (2 Kings 21:3), thus reversing the movement towards cultic centralization that lay at the core of Hezekiah's reform program. Manasseh's reversion to this and other abandoned practices was harshly condemned by reformers and biblical writers living in the time of Josiah and later.[146] But from another point of view, Manasseh's actions may be understood as a kind of reform in themselves—that is, as a counter-reformation, involving a wholesale rejection of the innovative religious policies of Hezekiah, which, as Manasseh probably saw it, had not succeeded in protecting Judah from Assyria.

Manasseh was a vassal of three Assyrian kings. Sennacherib's last years were spent dealing with unrest in Babylon, which he finally destroyed in 689 B.C.E. Sennacherib was assassinated in 681 B.C.E. by his sons (cf. 2 Kings 19:37), leading to a power struggle that resulted in the accession of his youngest son Esarhaddon (681–669 B.C.E.), who had been Sennacherib's designated heir and not one of his assassins. Much of Esarhaddon's reign was spent in an effort to conquer Egypt, an enterprise that was completed by his own son Assurbanipal (668–627 B.C.E.). Throughout most of this period Egypt was ruled by Taharqa (690–664 B.C.E.), the biblical Tirhakah, whose reign was remarkable for both its achievements and its disasters. It was the high-point of the Cushite Period (the XXVth Dynasty), marked by prosperity and building, especially in the dynasty's homeland of Nubia but also at Thebes; but, as we shall see, the XXVth Dynasty also suffered the first successful invasion of Egypt in a thousand years—that is, since the Hyksos Period.

At the time of Esarhaddon's accession (681 B.C.E.) the Assyrian Empire extended to the border of Egypt; thus, Esarhaddon inherited full control of the coastal trunk road, the King's Highway east of the Jordan, and all the northern outlets available to the South Arabian trade. With the consolidation of Egypt under Pharaoh Tirhakah, however, Assyria had a serious rival for control of commerce, by land and sea, in the eastern Mediterranean. A clash was inevitable. The pattern developed that Assyria became increasingly aggressive towards Egypt while Tirhakah acted covertly or openly to support anti-Assyrian uprisings in the western provinces of the empire.

Before he could turn his attention to the conquest of Egypt, however, Esarhaddon was obliged to spend a few years defending his northern borders against the Medes[147] and the incursions of Eurasian horse nomads, including both Cimmerians[148] and Scythians.[149] He then had to deal with a series of revolts in the West, which can be seen as the opening rounds in his fight with Egypt. Tyre and Sidon, which had been united in the days when Luli had rebelled against Sennacherib, were now rivals. King Baal of Tyre was, like Manasseh, one of Assyria's most submissive vassals, and as a reward Esarhaddon made a treaty with him giving him certain trade privileges such as free entry into all Mediterranean ports. Abdimilkutti of Sidon, provoked by what must have seemed to him unfair advantages for his rival, eventually decided to rebel, most probably with the encouragement and assurances of Pharaoh Tirhakah.[150] In response Esarhaddon marched west in 678 B.C.E. and besieged Sidon; within a year he had captured and beheaded Abdimilkutti and cast the city into the sea, reassigning portions of Sidonian territory to Tyre. Manasseh of Judah was one of several vassal kings required to help in the rebuilding of the ruined city as Kar-Ashur-ah-iddina, "Esarhaddon's Landing."[151]

According to the so-called Babylonian Chronicle, the first major battle between the Assyrian and Egyptian armies in Esarhaddon's reign occurred in his seventh year (674 B.C.E.), when "the army of Assyria was defeated in a bloody battle in Egypt."[152] Nothing more is known of this conflict, but it seems to have been a serious setback for Assyria, since Esarhaddon did not return west until his tenth year (671 B.C.E.). At that time, having accused his old ally Baal of Tyre of conspiring with Tirhakah, Esarhaddon marched past Phoenicia, leaving troops to enforce an embargo on food and water against Tyre, and proceeded south past the now-Egyptian fortress of Ashkelon to the Wadi of Egypt. From there the invasion of Egypt was launched in earnest. The Assyrian army crossed the Sinai, using camels and waterskins provided by "all the kings of Arabia."[153] After arriving in the Nile Delta, Esarhaddon reached Memphis after fighting three battles in 15 days. The city capitulated, and the queen and crown prince were captured, but Tirhakah himself fled south into Upper Egypt, where he still had control, and began to reorganize his forces.[154]

Esarhaddon, probably representing himself as the liberator of Egypt from Cushite rule,[155] accepted the surrender of local rulers of Lower Egypt and departed, leaving the Nile Delta in their hands. As soon as the Assyrian army had withdrawn, however, Tirhakah returned north and seized power again. This provoked Esarhaddon to launch another campaign against Egypt in 669 B.C.E., but the Assyrian emperor died at Haran, shortly after setting out,[156] and it remained for his son Assurbanipal (669–627 B.C.E.) to finish the war with Tirhakah. In 667 B.C.E. Assurbanipal sent an army to Egypt led by his viceroy (*turtānu*).[157] This expeditionary force was supported by ground troops that the Assyrian vassal kings, including Manasseh of Judah, supplied,[158] and it was reinforced by naval fleets launched from coastal vassal states. Again Tirhakah was defeated at Memphis, and again he fled south. This time, however, the Assyrian army pursued his troops up the Nile, establishing control as far south as Aswan. Tirhakah himself escaped to Nubia.

As the Assyrian army withdrew, it again entrusted Egypt to local rulers who had pledged loyalty, and again the local rulers betrayed the Assyrians and conspired with Tirhakah, who in 666 B.C.E. again returned to power. In reprisal, Assurbanipal sent soldiers to seize the disloyal rulers, executing many but bringing two, Necho of Sais and his son Psammetichus, to Nineveh. In 665 B.C.E. he established the former as Necho I (665–664 B.C.E.), the first king of the XXVIth

(Saite) Dynasty. In 664 B.C.E. Tirhakah died, having first named his son Tantamani or Tanwetamani (664–656 B.C.E.) as his successor. When Tantamani attacked the Assyrian troops at Memphis and seized the city, Assurbanipal again sent the Assyrian army into Egypt, where it took back control of Memphis and marched on Thebes. Thebes was captured and sacked in 664/663 B.C.E. (cf. Nahum 3:8–11). Though Tantamani remained at least nominally in power as the Egyptian ruler controlling Upper Egypt from Nubia until his death in 656 B.C.E., Lower Egypt was now governed by Necho's son, Psammetichus I (664–610 B.C.E.), from Sais.

The Assyrian Empire was now badly overextended, and Egypt soon became independent again. After the rebellion of 666–665 B.C.E., Assyria recognized Necho and then Psammetichus as sole king of Egypt on condition that neither would foment rebellion against Assyria. In 656 B.C.E. with the death of Tantamani and the end of the XXVth Dynasty, Psammetichus was able to extend the rule of the XXVIth Dynasty south to Thebes.[159] Meanwhile the Cimmerians, now well established in Asia Minor, continued to threaten Assyria's Syrian holdings. These factors destabilized the empire, but the first really critical blow came from Babylon, where a major revolt erupted in 652 B.C.E. at the instigation of Assurbanipal's own brother Shamash-shum-ukin, whom their father, Esarhaddon, had appointed as vice-regent in Babylon. This revolt soon spread.[160] In the East it was supported by Chaldean nationalists as well as Arameans and Elamites, the same groups who had backed Merodachbaladan earlier. In the West the primary supporters of the revolt seem to have been Arabs,[161] who probably perceived the vulnerability of Assyria as an opportunity to liberate the trade routes of the southern Levant. Though the Assyrian forces were able to contain the various Arab incursions associated with Shamash-shum-ukin's revolt, the victory was only temporary, since at this time much of Transjordan began to be overrun by Kedarites and other Arabian tribes who did not recognize Assyrian sovereignty. By 648 B.C.E. Assurbanipal had quelled the revolt in Babylon, but it was a foreboding of the fate of the empire.

We have no direct evidence of the way the news of the revolt in Babylon, and of Assyria's other troubles in the mid-seventh century B.C.E., was received in Judah. Apart from its polemic against Manasseh's religious policies, the Kings account of Manasseh's reign (2 Kings 21:1–18), with its Deuteronomistic orientation, provides little information about Manasseh's activities.[162] On the other hand, the Chronicler's account (2 Chronicles 33:1–20), though it draws heavily on that of Kings, supplies additional details suggesting that in the last decade of his reign, with Assyria substantially weakened, Manasseh may have begun to move Judah towards independence.

In particular, the Chronicler (2 Chronicles 31:14) credits Manasseh with building "an outer wall for the City of David, west of the Gihon, in the wadi" and assigning military officers to "all the fortified cities of Judah." The Chronicler does not indicate when in Manasseh's reign these things were done, but it seems probable that they began at the time of the revolt in Babylon (652–648 B.C.E.). The activities described are reminiscent on a smaller scale of Hezekiah's preparations for his revolt against Sennacherib, and they sound very much as if they were designed to strengthen Judah in preparation for a declaration of independence against Assyria. Manasseh's "outer wall" may have been identified archaeologically,[163] and, more generally, excavations have found substantial evidence of refortification throughout Judah in the latter part of the seventh century. Most of this building should probably be associated with Josiah, but it may have begun during the last days of Manasseh.

The Final Years of the Kingdom of Judah

The reign of Josiah and the end of the Assyrian Empire

Manasseh's son and successor, Amon (642–640 B.C.E.), died in a court assassination that historians have not been able to explain.[164] According to 2 Kings 21:23–24 (= 2 Chronicles 33:24–25), the assassins were executed by "the people of the land," who set Amon's eight-year-old son, Josiah, on the throne. Since Josiah came to the throne as a minor, Judah was probably ruled at first by a regent or group of regents—perhaps Josiah's mother or one of "the people of the land" who set him on the throne—but we are not told. In fact, the biblical writers, who are interested almost exclusively in Josiah's religious reform, report nothing about his reign before his 18th year (622 B.C.E.), when the reform began. By this time, Assurbanipal had died (627 B.C.E.). After a period of chaos, his son Sin-shar-ishkun (623–612 B.C.E.) succeeded him, but not before Assyria had descended into civil war and permanently lost control of Babylon, which was now ruled by the Chaldean Nabopolassar (625–605 B.C.E.). In short, the Assyrian Empire was in its death throes. This meant that Judah was, in effect, an independent state again, and Josiah was free to institute administrative reforms and even to harbor territorial ambitions.

The overriding interest of the biblical writers, however, was Josiah's religious reform, which is reported in detail in 2 Kings 22:1–23:30. The chief characteristics of this reform, which revived the cultic innovations of Hezekiah and brought an end to the counter-reformation of Manasseh, were, first and foremost, the assertion of the centrality of the Jerusalem Temple and its priesthood. The reform included, as natural corollaries, the elimination throughout the kingdom ("from

Geba to Beersheba" (2 Kings 23:8) of the *bāmôt*, or "high places" (the local places of sacrifice and worship), and the exclusion of the regional priests from priestly service in Jerusalem. Other important measures included the prohibition of certain condemned cultic practices (2 Kings 23:4–7,10–12), such as child sacrifice, and the extirpation from Judah of cults of foreign gods (2 Kings 23:13–14).

According to 2 Kings 22:8 the reform was set in motion by the discovery of "the book of the law in the house of the Lord" by Hilkiah, the high priest. When this scroll was shown to King Josiah, he summoned the people of Judah to the Temple in Jerusalem, where he read them everything that was in the document and vowed to instigate religious reforms in conformity with the rules that were written there. When the Kings and Chronicles accounts of these events are compared, it is not clear whether the reform was initiated by the accidental "discovery" of a scroll as Kings suggests, or whether an already ongoing reform program received its crucial impetus when a scroll was brought forward by the priests. Although 2 Kings 22:3 dates the discovery to Josiah's eighteenth year, 2 Chronicles 34:3 states that he had begun to "seek the God of his ancestor David" in his eighth year, "while he was still a boy," and had begun instituting reforms by his twelfth. It is also true that, even in the account in Kings, Temple repairs were already underway before the finding of the scroll (2 Kings 21:3–7).

For nearly two centuries, most biblical scholars have accepted that Josiah's "book of the law" was the biblical Book of Deuteronomy in its penultimate form. This seems clear from the striking correspondences between the reform measures Josiah is said in 2 Kings 23 to have carried out and the laws of worship and religious devotion recorded in Deuteronomy. Thus, for example, Josiah's instructions to abolish various cultic practices conform to prohibitions in Deuteronomy; these condemned practices include the cult of Asherah and the "asherim," or sacred poles (compare 2 Kings 23:4,6,7,14 to Deuteronomy 7:5, 12:3, 16:21, 17:3); the *maṣṣēbôt*, or "pillars" (compare 2 Kings 23:14 to Deuteronomy 7:5, 12:3); the *bāmôt*, or "high places," of foreign gods (compare 2 Kings 23:13 to Deuteronomy 7:5, 12:2–3), and many others. Compare also Josiah's observation of the Passover in Jerusalem "as prescribed in this book of the covenant" (2 Kings 23:21–23) with the commandment to observe Passover "at the place that the Lord your God will choose" in Deuteronomy 16:1–8.[165]

There were certainly ideological and political dimensions, probably in motivation and certainly in result, to Josiah's religious reform. In terms of national ideals, the assertion of the centrality of Jerusalem served to unify the country and strengthen the central government, and the mandate to return to perceived ancestral customs and values promoted national pride and cultural nostalgia.[166] At the political level, the changes Josiah made represented a vindication for those in the country who still supported the principles of Hezekiah's reform and, by the same token, a repudiation of those who had defended Manasseh's policies. This was not a matter of throwing off the Assyrian yoke, however, since Judah was already free of Assyria when Hilkiah presented the "the book of the law" to the king. And in any case it was not Assyrian imperial policy to interfere with the religious practices of vassals or to require them to worship the Assyrian gods.[167]

On the other hand, the evaporation of Assyrian supervision in the region did permit one aspect of Josiah's reform that would not have been possible earlier, namely, its extension outside of Judah into the territory of the fallen kingdom of Israel. The Deuteronomistic historian gives special attention to the cancellation of the cult established by Jeroboam I at Bethel (2 Kings 23:15–20), and this would not have been possible if Josiah had not been able to expand his influence north into the territory of the former Assyrian province of Samerina (Samaria). While it seems certain that Josiah took advantage of the vacuum created by the Assyrian withdrawal, the existing sources do not provide a clear picture of the full extent of Josiah's territorial expansion.[168] It probably extended to most of Samaria, as 2 Kings 23:19 implies, and may well have penetrated into the Galilee, as suggested by the reference in 2 Chronicles 34:6–7 to his institution of cult reforms there. The possibility of western expansion into former Assyrian-controlled Philistine territory is less clear, especially since we know that this region was now dominated by Egypt, as explained below; but the 1960 discovery of a Hebrew ostracon dating to the end of the seventh century B.C.E. near Yavneh Yam (south of Tel Aviv)[169] provides strong circumstantial evidence that, at least in certain areas, Josiah's westward expansion reached the Mediterranean coast.

After the accession of Sin-shar-ishkun, the failing Assyrian Empire lasted little more than a decade before the critical blow was struck. The agents were the Babylonians and the Medes. The Babylonian Nabopolassar organized the anti-Assyrian forces—Chaldeans, Arameans and Elamites—who had supported the Shamash-shum-ukin rebellion (652–648 B.C.E.) and the rebellions of Merodachbaladan still earlier. By 616 B.C.E. Nabopolassar was ready to begin his advance north and west against Assyria, but at first his results on the battlefield were at best mixed. At about the same time, however, the Medes began their own assault on Assyria from the north. They had found a strong leader in Cyaxares, who had established a major kingdom on the plateau north of Elam with its capital at Ecbatana (modern Hamadan in western Iran, southwest of Tehran). In 614 B.C.E. the Medes captured the ancient Assyrian capital of Ashu, and entered into an alliance with Nabopolassar. Then, in 612 B.C.E., Nineveh, which had been the imperial Assyrian capital since the time of Sennacherib, fell to the combined forces of the Babylonians and Medes. Sin-shar-ishkun seems to have died when the city fell, and Ashur-uballit II (612–609 B.C.E.) became the last Assyrian king, setting up a rump government in Haran, about 100 miles west of Nineveh. Though the Babylonians were not yet secure enough in central and northern Mesopotamia to attack Haran and finish the job, the fall of Nineveh signaled the end of Assyria. It was a major turning-point in the history of the ancient Near East and sent shock waves reverberating throughout the region. The biblical monument to this event is the Book of Nahum, which is entirely devoted to the prophet's "oracle concerning Nineveh" (Nahum 1:1).

Egypt played a prominent and somewhat surprising role in these events. As explained earlier, Egypt had been united since 656 B.C.E. under the XXVIth, or Saite, Dynasty. Psammetichus I (664–610 B.C.E.) had come to the throne as a protégé of Assyria. With the eclipse of Assyria, he became an independent and powerful ruler, not only presiding over the so-called Saite Renaissance at home, but also expanding north to take control of most of Philistia and coastal Palestine as far north as Phoenicia.[170] According to the testimony of Herodotus, Psammetichus took Ashdod by siege[171] and, on another occasion, negotiated the end of an incursion of Scythians into southern Palestine after they had plundered "the Temple of Aphrodite" in Ashkelon.[172] These reports lack direct substantiation in Near Eastern records, but they are plausible and seem to indicate Egyptian domination of Philistia in the latter part of the seventh century B.C.E.[173]

Despite his *de facto* departure from his old vows to Assurbanipal, however, the aging Psammetichus decided to come to the aid of Assyria in its hour of need. Egyptian troops fought alongside the Assyrians against Nabopolassar and his allies in 616 B.C.E., and under Psammetichus's successor, Necho II (610–595 B.C.E.), their support continued as long as there was anything left of Assyria to support—that is, until 609 B.C.E. Historians do not agree about what motivated the Egyptian kings to adopt this policy of attempting to help Assyria survive. Perhaps they envisioned joint Assyrian-Egyptian control of Syria-Palestine. Perhaps they were attempting to position themselves so that when Assyria fell, Egypt would be heir to its empire in the West. It seems likely, in any case, that they wanted to preserve the status quo, as Egypt was beginning to thrive again, and were apprehensive about what future perils a victory for the Chaldeans and the Medes might bring to Egypt.[174]

In 610 B.C.E. the army of the Medes entered Assyria and joined forces with the Babylonians, who already had Scythian support, and in October the Babylonian and Scythian armies advanced on Haran, the last capital of Assyria. Ashur-uballit abandoned the city and fled west to await the arrival of his Egyptian allies. In 609 B.C.E. Necho II set out with a huge expeditionary force and marched north. When the Egyptian army was crossing through the Megiddo pass, Josiah confronted it, and Necho captured and killed him. The circumstances under which this happened are not clear. It is usually assumed on the basis of 2 Chronicles 35:20–24, which describes a battle, that Josiah was trying to intercept the Egyptian army, and it is possible to think of a number of reasons why he might have wanted to do so. If he thought that his own resurgent kingdom was strong enough to wrest control of western Palestine from Egypt, he might have viewed the accession of a new and inexperienced Egyptian king as an opportunity to assert himself. He might have felt an obligation to assist the Babylonians because he regarded Judah as a longtime ally of the Chaldeans, going back to the time of Merodachbaladan and Hezekiah (2 Kings 20:12–13). Or he might simply have wanted to do everything possible to prevent the recovery of Assyria, however unlikely, and the potential for a return to the conditions of subservient vassalage that had prevailed during the reign of his grandfather, Manasseh. On the other hand, the cryptic account of Josiah's death in Kings (2 Kings 23:29) says nothing about a battle. It indicates only that when Necho was on his way to join the king of Assyria, "King Josiah went to meet him; but when Pharaoh Necho met him at Megiddo, he killed him." This raises the possibility that Josiah did not go to Megiddo with a hostile encounter in mind. He might have been seeking an audience or attempting to enter into some kind of negotiation, but the interview became antagonistic and got out of control.

In any case, the Egyptian army proceeded north and, according to the Babylonian Chronicle, crossed the Euphrates in July of 609 B.C.E.; then, joining forces with the Assyrians, they marched against Haran. The results of a four-month siege seem to have been inconclusive—Ashur-uballit may never have reentered the city—but the time was sufficient for the Egyptian army to take control of Syria as far north as Carchemish (cf. 2 Chronicles 35:20), establishing its field headquarters at Riblah in the northern Beqa' (Tell Zerr'a on the Orontes, 21 miles south of Homs).[175] Necho summoned a group of Syro-Palestinian rulers to Riblah to require them to swear oaths of loyalty to Egypt. Among them was King Jehoahaz of Judah (2 Kings 23:33), Josiah's youngest son,[176] whom "the people of the land" had made king when his father was killed (2 Kings 23:30). Necho deposed Jehoahaz and replaced him with his brother Eliakim, changing his name to Jehoiakim (2 Kings 23:31–35), and imposed a heavy tribute on Judah. Judah's brief period of independence—between Assyrian and Egyptian control—was now over.

Egypt seems to have dominated Syria-Palestine, including northern Syria, for a few years, holding the Babylonians at bay until 605 B.C.E., when the Babylonian crown prince, Nabu-kudurri-uṣur (the biblical

Nebuchadnezzar or Nebuchadrezzar), was given charge of field operations in the West. The Babylonian Chronicle reports that under his
leadership the Egyptian army was routed in a decisive battle fought at
Carchemish. Necho fled south, but Nebuchadnezzar overtook him at
Hamath and defeated him again. The Egyptian king then returned to
the banks of the Nile, leaving Syria in Babylonian hands. By that time,
though the fate of Ashur-uballit is unknown, the Assyrian Empire was
a thing of the past. Its former territories were divided between the
Medes and the Babylonians. The Medes took the Assyrian heartland
and northern territories, while the Babylonians took the rest of
Mesopotamia and the western territories. This included rights to not
only Syria but also Palestine, so that a further showdown between
Babylonia and Egypt was inevitable.

Nebuchadnezzar probably intended to follow up his victories at   **The fall**
Carchemish and Hamath by continuing to march south into Palestine,   **of Jerusalem**
but he was prevented from doing so by the death of his father, Nabopolassar, which required him to return to Babylon in August 605 B.C.E.,
and accept the crown as Nebuchadnezzar II (605–562 B.C.E.), the
second king of the Neo-Babylonian Empire. Within a year, however,
Nebuchadnezzar was back in the field, marching through Syria-
Palestine and encountering minimal resis-
tance, since Necho was now back in Egypt
licking his wounds and rebuilding his
forces.[177] In this western campaign of
604 B.C.E. Nebuchadnezzar concentrated
on Philistia, especially Ashkelon, which he
sacked in December 604, capturing its king,
Aga.[178] Judah was understandably intimidated by having the Babylonian army relatively nearby. A fast was proclaimed in
Jerusalem (Jeremiah 36:9), and Jehoiakim,
despite his pro-Egyptian leanings, submitted to Nebuchadnezzar and, according to
2 Kings 24:1, became his vassal for three
years (604–602 B.C.E.).

Nebuchadnezzar suffered one of his few
setbacks in the winter of 601/600 B.C.E.,
when he attempted to invade Egypt[179] and
was repulsed, probably at Migdol (Magdolos,
according to Herodotus),[180] a fortress that
guarded the entry into Egypt at a point not
far south of Pelusium in the eastern Delta.
Nebuchadnezzar was forced to withdraw to
Babylon, where he remained for a full year,

NEBUCHADNEZZAR'S
CAMPAIGNS

rebuilding his army. This gave Necho the opportunity to campaign along the southern coast of Palestine, capturing Gaza (cf. Jeremiah 47). Jehoiakim, sensing that the balance of power had shifted again, ceased to pay tribute to Babylon and tried to restore himself in the favor of Necho, who was attempting to build a coalition against Babylon.

Nebuchadnezzar returned to Palestine in 599 B.C.E. without much show of force, contenting himself with bivouacking at Riblah, as the Babylonian Chronicle seems to imply, and sending out razzias (raiding parties) to attack and plunder the camps of the Kedarites and other Arab tribes (cf. Jeremiah 49:28–33). On his next visit, however, he returned with his forces fully restored. Intent on reprisal against Jehoiakim for having withheld tribute, he marched on Jerusalem in the winter of 598/597 B.C.E. and put the city under siege in January. Not long before this, in 598 B.C.E., Jehoiakim had died, possibly by foul play,[181] and was replaced by his 18-year-old son Jehoiachin. Jerusalem capitulated with no great resistance on the second day of the Babylonian month of Adar in the seventh year of Nebuchadnezzar—that is, March 16, 597 B.C.E. Nebuchadnezzar, apparently content with the removal of Jehoiakim, followed a policy of relative leniency and ordered no general destruction of the city. He did, however, take Jehoiachin into exile, along with much of the royal family, many members of the court and other leading citizens and artisans. According to 2 Kings 24:14, this first deportation from Jerusalem involved 10,000 people; according to 2 Kings 24:16 the number was 8,000 (7,000 prominent people and 1,000 skilled craftsmen); and according to Jeremiah 52:28, it was 3,023, a number that may include only the male heads of households. Nebuchadnezzar made vassalage treaty with a third son of Josiah, Jehoiachin's uncle Mattaniah, whom he placed on the throne, changing his name to Zedekiah.

Over the immediately succeeding years, Nebuchadnezzar conducted repeated campaigns in Syria-Palestine, but with the memory of the Babylonian defeat of 601/600 B.C.E. still fresh, Judah and the other Palestinian states do not seem to have been entirely intimidated. Egypt remained ambitious and formidable under the successors of Necho—Psammetichus II (595–589 B.C.E.) and Apries, the biblical Hophra (589–570 B.C.E.). In these circumstances, anti-Babylonian plotting began almost immediately, and, in 594, probably emboldened by news of an uprising in Babylon in 595/594 B.C.E., Zedekiah seems to have convened an international group of conspirators in Jerusalem to plan a revolt, with representatives from Edom, Moab, Ammon, Tyre and Sidon (cf. Jeremiah 27:3). This conspiracy collapsed quickly when Nebuchadnezzar marched into Palestine in his 11th year (594/593 B.C.E.), and Jehoiachin sent word to him assuring him of Judah's loyalty; but the events foreshadowed what was to come.

Bulla of Jeremiah's scribe. *"Belonging to Berekhyahu, son of Neriyahu, the scribe," reads the inscription on this clay bulla, which appears to have been impressed with the seal belonging to the prophet Jeremiah's scribe and faithful companion Baruch. The Bible recounts that "Baruch son of Neriah ... wrote on a scroll at Jeremiah's dictation all the words of the Lord that he had spoken to him" (Jeremiah 36:4). The biblical names appear on the bulla with the suffix yahu, a form of Yahweh.*

An even more arresting impression appears on the upper left edge of the late-seventh-to early-sixth-century B.C.E. bulla: the whorls of a fingerprint, presumably left by the biblical scribe himself.

In 592 B.C.E., Psammetichus II, flush with a victory in Nubia where he had suppressed the remnant of the XXVth Dynasty, marched into Palestine and conducted a peaceful show of force, encouraging anti-Babylonian sentiment in Judah, Philistia and as far north as Phoenicia. Though a cause-and-effect relationship is difficult to demonstrate, Zedekiah rebelled against Babylon (2 Kings 24:20) soon after Psammetichus's "triumphal progress." Zedekiah's revolt may have occurred as early as 591 B.C.E. and certainly by 589 B.C.E., when Hophra had come to the throne in Egypt and was encouraging anti-Babylonian revolts even more aggressively than Psammetichus. Though Nebuchadnezzar did not respond immediately, he eventually dispatched a Babylonian army, which reached Jerusalem in January 587 B.C.E. There followed an 18-month siege, interrupted only briefly by the arrival of Egyptian aid (Jeremiah 37:5; cf. Jeremiah 37:11).[182]

The walls were breached in July 586 B.C.E. Zedekiah was captured while trying to escape under the cover of night and was led before Nebuchadnezzar, who put the Judahite king's sons to death before his eyes, then blinded the king and sent him into exile. The Babylonian leader commanded that the city and its Temple be razed, and the order was carried out in August 586 B.C.E. According to Jeremiah 52:29, there was an additional deportation of 832 people, a number that may include only male heads of households. There was no immediate plan

Lachish letter. *In 1935, while excavating a burned guardroom beneath a gate tower that had been destroyed by Nebuchadnezzar's army, archaeologists at Lachish found a small archive of wartime correspondence addressed to a certain Ya'ush, evidently the governor or commanding officer of Lachish, from a subordinate named Hawshi'yahu (both names contain forms of the name Yahweh). Written on inscribed potsherds called ostraca, the letters paint an intriguing picture of maneuvers taking place on the southwestern frontier of Judah. Most scholars believe that the ostraca were written on the eve of the destruction of Jerusalem in 586 B.C.E.*

The last four lines of this letter read, "And let [my lord] know that we are watching for the signals of Lachish, according to all the signs which my lord has given, for we do not see Azekah." This recalls Jeremiah's prophecies about a time when "the army of the king of Babylon was fighting against Jerusalem and the cities of Judah—against Lachish and Azekah, for these were the only fortified cities that remained of all the cities of Judah" (Jeremiah 34:7).

to rebuild the city or repopulate it with foreign captives (which was not, in any case, Babylonian policy), and there was no plan for Jerusalem to become a provincial capital, probably because of its long history as a center of rebellion.

Nebuchadnezzar installed a cadre of pro-Babylonian Jews, led by a Judean aristocrat named Gedaliah son of Ahikam, in a governance role at the town of Mizpah, 8 miles northwest of Jerusalem (1 Kings 25:23).[183] The prophet Jeremiah, who had previously been incarcerated for his persistent warnings against resisting Babylon, was part of the new leadership (Jeremiah 40:1–6).

Not surprisingly, Gedaliah's regime was not popular. Many of the Jews who remained in the land regarded him and his colleagues as collaborators. Probably less than a year after his appointment as governor, Gedaliah was assassinated by a Davidide named Ishmael (2 Kings 25:25; cf. the much more detailed account in Jeremiah 41). Though Ishmael seems to have been supported by the Ammonite king Baalis (Jeremiah 40:14, 41:10), the assassination was hardly part of an anti-Babylonian conspiracy, which would have been completely futile; it was a terrorist act of revenge against a man perceived as a quisling. Members of Gedaliah's regime, fearing Babylonian reprisals, fled to Egypt (2 Kings 25:26), taking Jeremiah with them, while Ishmael and his followers fled to Ammon to escape the vengeance of Gedaliah's remaining supporters (Jeremiah 41:15).

Epilogue

The predicament of Judah in the final years before the destruction of Jerusalem was similar to that of Israel before the fall of Samaria. Both were small states swallowed up by great imperial powers, and both had attempted to avoid this fate and maintain some measure of independence by oscillating between policies of appeasement and defiance. In the northern kingdom of Israel this pattern began as soon as Assyria, under Shalmaneser III (859–824 B.C.E.), became a direct threat. Ahab and his Omride successors adopted the policy of defiance. They resisted Shalmaneser's incursions through military action in alliance with Damascus and other regional states. In 841 B.C.E., however, Jehu switched to a policy of appeasement, submitting to Shalmaneser and buying Israel's independence by payment of heavy tribute. The pattern was renewed a century later when Assyria threatened Israel once again under Tiglath-pileser III (745–727 B.C.E.) and his successors. Menahem of Israel chose the safe path of appeasement, paying tribute at the end of Tiglath-pileser's first western campaign (738 B.C.E.), but after the 737 B.C.E. coup of Pekah son of Remaliah, the policy shifted abruptly, and Israel once again took up a position of resistance, based as before on an alliance with Damascus and other local states. This was a dangerous step, and Israel was territorially decimated by Tiglath-pileser's second western campaign (734–732 B.C.E.), in which the anti-Assyrian coalition was crushed and Damascus was captured. Israel survived, however, because of a hasty resumption of the policy of appeasement following the 732 B.C.E. coup of Hoshea, who assassinated Pekah and quickly offered his fealty to Assyria.

The rapidly vacillating policies of Hoshea epitomize the predicament of the northern kingdom in its final years and foreshadow that of Judah a century and a half later. A loyal vassal of Assyria in 732 B.C.E., Hoshea defied Assyria when Tiglath-pileser died in 727 B.C.E. and once again joined neighboring states in revolt. When Shalmaneser V marched west in 727 B.C.E., however, Hoshea shifted positions again, buying a few more years for Israel by submitting and paying tribute. Then in about 725 B.C.E. Hoshea tried again to break free, rebelling against Assyria and seeking safety in yet another alliance of local states. But this time Hoshea had pushed his luck too far. His revolt brought the Assyrian siege engines to the walls of Samaria, and the city fell in 722 B.C.E.

Before the decline of the Assyrian Empire, Judah's policy towards the Assyrian threat was essentially the same as that of Israel in its oscillation between defiance and appeasement. Hezekiah's revolt after the death of Sargon II in 705 B.C.E. followed the Israelite pattern of defiance, a policy of resistance to Assyria secured by an alliance with neighboring states, in this case Sidon and Ashkelon. But when Sennacherib invaded Judah in 701 B.C.E. and placed Jerusalem under siege, Hezekiah was forced to shift to a policy of appeasement, paying a heavy tribute to ensure the survival of his kingdom. This policy continued through most of the long reign of Manasseh (697–642 B.C.E.), whose loyalty to Sennacherib and his successors kept Judah secure.

The Assyrian Empire collapsed in the last decades of the seventh century B.C.E., but the result was that Judah's position became more precarious rather than less. The vacuum left by Assyria's demise was now filled by not one but two great powers. The kings of the XXVIth Egyptian Dynasty, who had been allied with Assyria, asserted their power along the coast of Palestine. At the same time Babylon rose to preeminence under Nabopolassar and Nebuchadnezzar and began to take an interest of its own in the affairs of Palestine. These developments left Judah in the treacherous position of having to conduct its policies of resistance and appeasement in relation to two competing superpowers.[184]

Assyria's demise seemed at first to present Judah with an opportunity to enlarge its territory, but Josiah's expansion of Judah to the north and west brought him into conflict with Egypt and may ultimately have led to his death at the hand of Pharaoh Necho II at Megiddo in

609 B.C.E. Josiah's succession by his like-minded son Jehoahaz signalled a policy in Judah of continued defiance of Egypt. Almost immediately, however, Necho replaced Jehoahaz with his pro-Egyptian brother Jehoiakim. Judah was now an Egyptian vassal state, and a policy of appeasement towards Egypt spared Judah the full measure of Necho's wrath. Soon after, however, Nebuchadnezzar asserted the power of Babylon in Palestine, capturing Ashkelon in 604 B.C.E. Despite his Egyptian leanings, Jehoiakim concluded that it was now Babylon that needed to be appeased, and he began paying tribute to Nebuchadnezzar. When Nebuchadnezzar was repulsed trying to invade Egypt in 601/600 B.C.E., however, Jehoiakim switched allegiances again, withholding tribute in defiance of Babylon. This proved to be a fatal error of judgment. When Nebuchadnezzar returned to Palestine in 598/597 B.C.E., Jehoiakim died—possibly by foul play—and was replaced by Jehoiachin, signalling a return in Judah to a policy of appeasement towards Babylon. Jerusalem capitulated to the Babylonian army, and Nebuchadnezzar followed a relatively lenient policy towards the captured city, exiling Jehoiachin and placing Zedekiah on the throne of Jerusalem.

Zedekiah, however, now faced the predicament that had doomed Jehoiakim, and he made the same mistake. Probably encouraged and pressured by Egypt, he revoked his vassalship to Nebuchadnezzar and rebelled, perhaps in 589 B.C.E. When Nebuchadnezzar returned to Jerusalem he was no longer in a lenient mood, and the Babylonian army besieged and destroyed the city in 587 to 586 B.C.E. In this way the kingdom of Judah suffered the same fate as the kingdom of Israel. Like Hoshea before them, Jehoiakim and Zedekiah were unable to find the right combination of resistance and appeasement that would permit their small kingdom to survive in an international arena dominated by two larger and more aggressive superpowers.

S I X

Exile and Return

From the Babylonian Destruction to the Reconstruction of the Jewish State

JAMES D. PURVIS

revised by Eric M. Meyers

The Exile to Babylonia

The rest of the people who were left in the city and the deserters who had deserted to the king of Babylon, together with the rest of the multitude, were carried into exile by Nebuzaradan the captain of the guard. But the captain of the guard left some of the poorest of the land to be vinedressers and plowmen.

(2 Kings 25:11–12)

T HE CALAMITIES THAT BEFELL JUDAH WHEN KING NEBUCHADNEZZAR of Babylon crushed Zedekiah's rebellion and destroyed Jerusalem in 586 B.C.E. are stated concisely but poignantly in the narrative prose accounts in the books of Kings and Jeremiah. The king's sons were executed before his eyes; then Zedekiah himself was blinded and imprisoned. The Temple was burned; the Temple officials, military commanders and noblemen were executed; and, finally, the survivors were exiled (2 Kings 25:7–21; Jeremiah 39:1–10 and 52:1–16).

Following this, Nebuchadnezzar appointed Gedaliah as governor. Gedaliah established his administrative center at Mizpah. Although the biblical account does not indicate the extent of Gedaliah's authority, there was apparently some hope for peace and economic recovery under his leadership.[1] This hope was thwarted, however, by the assassination of Gedaliah and the flight of his supporters and others to Egypt. Thus, in addition to the destruction of Jerusalem and the exile of its leaders to Babylonia, this dispersion to Egypt further weakened

the nation (2 Kings 25:22–26; Jeremiah 40:1–44:30). All these developments profoundly affected the course of Jewish life in Palestine and
abroad, that is, in the Diaspora.

How many
exiles?   In reprisal for Gedaliah's assassination, the Babylonians deported still
more Jews to Babylon. According to Jeremiah, 745 people were
deported in 582 B.C.E. (Jeremiah tells us that, previously, 832 people
had been deported in 586 B.C.E. and 3,023 in 597 B.C.E., when
King Jehoiachin was defeated [Jeremiah 52:28–30]).

There are several surprises in Jeremiah's figures. First, the number of
deportees to Babylonia at the time of Gedaliah's assassination was not
much smaller than the number of those taken into exile at the destruction of Jerusalem (only 87 fewer). Second, the number deported in the
exile of 586 B.C.E. is itself not very large (832). And third, neither of
these deportations was as large as the exile of 597 B.C.E.: Of the total
number of deportees (4,600), virtually two-thirds (3,023) went into
exile with the captivity of King Jehoiachin in 597 B.C.E.

No figures are given in 2 Kings for the number of deportees in
586 B.C.E. (when Jerusalem was destroyed), and no reference is made
to a deportation following Gedaliah's assassination. Numbers are given,
however, for the first deportation under Jehoiachin. According to
2 Kings 24:14, 10,000 people were exiled at that time (including 7,000
soldiers and 1,000 craftsmen and smiths). This number greatly exceeds
the figure given in Jeremiah. Whatever the true figures, it is clear
enough that it was the leadership of society that was removed and that
about 90 percent of the population remained in Palestine.[2]

The lack of specific figures in 2 Kings for the exile of 586 B.C.E. is
not surprising; the writer wished to stress the destruction of the city
and its Temple and the fate of the survivors. But one thing is clear: For
the writer of 2 Kings, as for the editor of Jeremiah, the Babylonian
Exile began in 597 B.C.E., when Nebuchadnezzar removed and
imprisoned King Jehoiachin and appointed Zedekiah as a puppet-king
to reign in his stead.

Neither is it surprising then that the concluding words of 2 Kings
concern King Jehoiachin. There we learn that in the 37th year of his
exile (561 B.C.E.), the king was released from prison and granted a
position of status by the Babylonian king Evil-merodach (Amel-Marduk
in Babylonian records) (2 Kings 25:27–30; see also Jeremiah
52:31–34). Why was this important to the biblical writers? Because
their hope for the restoration of the Davidic dynasty (the divine elec-
tion of which played such an important role in their theology of history) lay with Jehoiachin, not with Zedekiah. Zedekiah had been
appointed king by the Babylonians only after Jehoiachin had been
taken hostage; Zedekiah's reign was viewed by many as only temporary.[3] In Babylonia, Jehoiachin was regarded as the exiled Judahite king,

both before and after the deportation of 586 B.C.E. It was certainly not accidental that the leader of the first wave of Jewish exiles to return to Jerusalem was Jehoiachin's son, Sheshbazzar, and that the builder of the Second Temple was his grandson, Zerubbabel.[4]

In short, according to the editors of 2 Kings and Jeremiah, the Exile to Babylonia began in 597 B.C.E. when King Jehoiachin was taken hostage by Nebuchadnezzar (2 Kings 24:12–17; Jeremiah 52:28–30). This was the first and largest of three separate deportations; a second deportation occurred at the time of the destruction of Jerusalem in 586 B.C.E. (2 Kings 25:8–12; Jeremiah 52:12–16) and, according to Jeremiah, a third occurred after the assassination of Gedaliah in 582 B.C.E. (Jeremiah 52:30).

The Book of Chronicles presents quite a different picture: Here there is only one deportation, at the time of the destruction of the Temple in 586 B.C.E., and indeed very little is said about it (2 Chronicles 36:20–21). Although the Chronicler records the deportation of Jehoiachin himself in 597 B.C.E. (2 Chronicles 36:10), he does not associate the beginning of the national Exile with that event. Rather, the Chronicler states that "the precious vessels of the house of the Lord" were removed to Babylon with the exile of Jehoiachin; the removal of the Temple vessels is what is important, not the removal of the people.

Second Chronicles is a simplified retelling of the story in which the historian has stressed what he considers most significant. The Temple—its plan, construction, furnishings, administration and service—is of paramount importance throughout the Chronicler's history. In Ezra 1–6 (a continuation of the narrative of 2 Chronicles 36), the Chronicler regards the return of the Temple vessels at the end of the Exile as an important link in establishing continuity between the cultic establishment of the First and Second Temples (Ezra 1:7–11, 5:14–15, 6:5).[5] For the Chronicler, when the Jews returned from Exile, they returned not with a king to reestablish the older political order, but with the Temple vessels to continue the cultic order that had allegedly existed in ancient times.

Equally important for the Chronicler is his claim that the Exile resulted in the land becoming desolate and lying fallow (in effect keeping its own sabbath) (2 Chronicles 36:21). This description of the land seems to have been derived from a tradition (Leviticus 26:1–39) preserved in the Holiness Code; the code states that the punishment for idolatry is banishment to a foreign land, with the result that the land lies fallow:

> And I will scatter you among the nations, and I will unsheath the sword after you; and your land shall be a desolation, and your cities shall be a waste. Then the land shall enjoy its sabbaths as long as it lies desolate, while you are in your enemies' land; then the land shall rest, and enjoy its sabbaths.
>
> (Leviticus 26:33–34)

The Chronicler also made use of Jeremiah's prophecy of an exile of 70 years (Jeremiah 25:11, 29:10), not simply to indicate that this would be the duration of the Exile, but to stress that the land would have a tenfold (seven years times ten) sabbath rest:

> He took into exile in Babylon those who had escaped from the sword to fulfill the word of the Lord by the mouth of Jeremiah, until the land had enjoyed its sabbaths. All the days that it lay desolate it kept sabbath, to fulfill seventy years.
>
> (2 Chronicles 36:21)

The prophet Zechariah also uses the 70-year designation to characterize the period of divine anger (Zechariah 1:12; 7:3,5) and is also certainly dependent on Jeremiah. If the number 70 was important, one had to begin counting at some point. Both Zechariah and the Chronicler chose to begin with the time of the destruction of Jerusalem in 586 B.C.E.,[6] not the captivity of Jehoiachin in 597 B.C.E.

The Chronicler's account of the Exile appears to have been shaped by his editorial concerns. It is thus less useful for historical reconstruction than the traditions in 2 Kings and Jeremiah, especially when Chronicles is in disagreement with these two sources. What does seem fairly certain, however, is that the Babylonian Exile began before the destruction of Jerusalem in 586 B.C.E. When the deportees in 586 B.C.E., and at any subsequent time, reached Babylonia they joined a Jewish community that was already established. Given that the Judahite leaders were among the last to be deported, the task of reestablishing the community began in earnest after 586 B.C.E.

Moreover, in the late eighth century B.C.E., exiles from Israelite Samaria had been settled by the Assyrians in western Syria, Mesopotamia and Media (see 2 Kings 15:29, 17:6; 1 Chronicles 5:26). The annals of Sargon II indicate a deportation/settlement (and also military conscription) of about 27,000 Israelites.[7] The preaching of Ezekiel shows that not all of these communities had been assimilated by pagan cultures; much of this biblical book is concerned with the reunification of the Judahite and Israelite branches of the nation after the destruction of Jerusalem in 586 B.C.E. Indeed, some passages in Ezekiel read as if they were actually directed at specific Israelite—that is, northern—communities in exile. The Jews of the military colony at Elephantine in Egypt (see below) may also have been of northern, Israelite origin.[8]

Thus, while we may date the Babylonian Exile from 597 and 586 B.C.E., this event was but part of a long process of establishing Israelite/Judahite settlements in Mesopotamia and Babylonia, a process that had begun earlier and that would continue. Most of Israel was not deported, and many of the descendants of the exiles never returned; the Jewish people had become a people both in their ancestral homeland and in the Diaspora.

"By the Waters of Babylon":
The Jewish Exiles in Babylonia

The familiar words of Psalm 137, "By the waters of Babylon, there we sat down and wept when we remembered Zion," are often cited as expressing the mood of the Babylonian exiles. This is not surprising; the psalm is a poem of great beauty, in which plaintive lyricism is mixed both with frustration ("How shall we sing the Lord's song in a foreign land?") and with nostalgia and loyalty ("If I forget you, O Jerusalem, let my right hand wither!"). What it expresses was certainly part of the experience of Exile for many of the deportees. But it falls short of conveying all we know of Jewish life in Babylonia and thus ought not to be taken as characteristic of the Exile experience as a whole. A more representative text—certainly of the social and economic dimensions of life by the waters of Babylon—is found in a letter written by Jeremiah to the deportees after 597 B.C.E.:

> Build houses and live in them; plant gardens and eat their produce. Take wives and have sons and daughters; take wives for your sons and give your daughters in marriage, that they may bear sons and daughters; multiply there, and do not decrease. But seek the welfare of the city where I have sent you into exile, and pray to the Lord on its behalf, for in its welfare you will find your welfare.
>
> (Jeremiah 29:5–7)

Indeed, this seems to be how things worked out, though hardly in deference to the prophet's appeal.

Although our knowledge of Jewish life in Babylonia is fragmentary, we are nonetheless able to put together a general picture of the situation from allusions in contemporary biblical texts, from later biblical texts and from extrabiblical sources.

With the exception of some members of the royal Judahite family and aristocracy, the people did not live in "captivity"; they were settled on deserted agricultural land where they were free, as Jeremiah says, to "build houses and live in them; plant gardens and eat their produce." Their status probably did not permit them to be landowners; more likely, they were land-tenants on royal estates.[9] We know that some Jews were settled beside "the river Chebar" (Ezekiel 1:1–3, 3:15,23), an irrigation canal of the Euphrates (Akkadian, *nāru kabari*) that flowed through Nippur. One Jewish settlement beside the Chebar was known as Tel-abib (Ezekiel 3:15); if this settlement was even then a tell, or mound containing a buried ancient city, it might be evidence that the Babylonians settled the Jewish deportees at or near the sites of ruined, abandoned cities, perhaps as part of a program to develop unused land resources. Further support for this suggestion comes from the fact that Jewish exiles were apparently also settled at Tel-melah and

Life in Babylonia

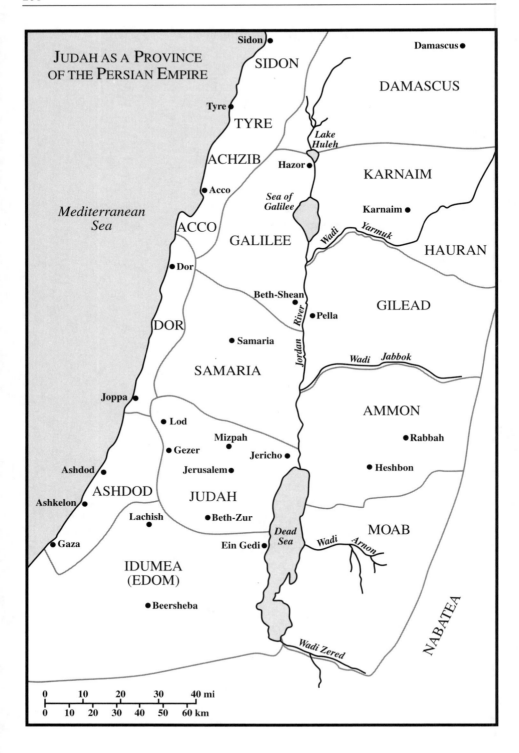

JUDAH AS A PROVINCE
OF THE PERSIAN EMPIRE

Sidon

Damascus

SIDON

DAMASCUS

Tyre

TYRE

Lake
Huleh

ACHZIB

Hazor

KARNAIM

Acco

Sea of
Galilee

Karnaim

*Mediterranean
Sea*

ACCO

GALILEE

Wadi

Yarmuk

HAURAN

Dor

DOR

Beth-Shean

GILEAD

Pella

River

Samaria

Jordan

SAMARIA

Wadi

Jabbok

Joppa

AMMON

Lod

Mizpah

Rabbah

Gezer

Jericho

Ashdod

Jerusalem

Heshbon

ASHDOD

JUDAH

Ashkelon

Lachish

Beth-Zur

MOAB

Dead
Sea

Gaza

Ein Gedi

Wadi

Arnon

IDUMEA
(EDOM)

NABATEA

Beersheba

Wadi Zered

0	10	20	30	40 mi
0	10	20	30	40	50	60 km

Tel-harsha (Ezra 2:59). Other places of Jewish settlement mentioned by name are Cherub, Addan/Addon, Immer (Ezra 2:59; Nehemiah 7:61), and Casiphia (Ezra 8:17). The locations of these cities are not known. Some Jews were probably also conscripted into military and other imperial services, as was the custom both of the Assyrians and of the Babylonians in their dealings with deportees.

Evidence of Jews in the *nâru kabari* (Chebar) region also comes from a number of cuneiform documents discovered in excavations at Nippur. The so-called Murashu texts contain the records of a large Babylonian family banking firm. Copies of contracts made by Jews and other documents concerning Jews testify to the existence of Jewish communities in 28 settlements in the Nippur area. Although dating from the Persian period (fifth century B.C.E.), these records indicate that Jews had prospered in agriculture, trade and banking during the century after their settlement there. There appears to be no discrimination against the Jews even though they were descendants of foreigners. Jews made the same kinds of contracts at the same interest rates as others. Several held positions of prestige, one in the Murashu firm itself, another in government service. One Jew held a military fief, for which he was obliged to render military services or to furnish a substitute.[10]

Indications that some of the Jews of the Exile managed to accumulate wealth also appear in Ezra 1:5–6 and 2:68–69, which speak of contributions in gold, silver and precious goods for the rebuilding of the Temple in Jerusalem. Ezra 2:65 mentions male and female slaves who returned with their Jewish masters. Not only were Jews permitted to own slaves, some were financially able to do so.

The recognized leader of the Jewish community during the Babylonian Exile was the Davidic monarch Jehoiachin. Although his leadership was only titular, it was nonetheless significant. From the very beginning of Jehoiachin's captivity in 597 B.C.E., there was apparently hope for his restoration to power, even though the prophet Jeremiah counseled against a naive optimism in this regard (Jeremiah 28–29). Ezekiel indicated his own loyalty to the hostage king by dating events from the year 597 B.C.E. and expressing the hope that Jehoiachin's family would again shepherd the people in their native land (Ezekiel 34:20–31, 37:24–28). In addition to the biblical texts, two sets of epigraphic data may testify to the status of Jehoiachin in exile: First, a number of seal impressions found throughout Judah bear the inscription "Belonging to Eliakim, steward of Yaukin"; second, a cuneiform document from the official archives in Babylon lists rations of foods to be supplied from the royal storehouses to King Yaukin of Judah, his five sons and other Judahite officials. William F. Albright, who discovered of the first of the Yaukin seals at Tell Beit Mirsim, suggested that Yaukin was a

Jehoiachin, a leader in exile

form of Jehoiachin and that Eliakim was the Judahite administrator of the crown properties of Jehoiachin following the king's deportation. Recently, however, scholars have questioned this identification.[11] Albright argued that Zedekiah, the puppet-king appointed by the Babylonians, decided not to confiscate Jehoiachin's wealth because he was insecure in his own position. Zedekiah was unsure whether Jehoiachin would be restored.[12] As for the significance of the ration for Jehoiachin in the Babylonian cuneiform archives, we may cite Albright:

> Now we know that Jehoiachin was not only the legitimate king of the Jewish exiles in Babylonia from their own point of view, he was also regarded by the Babylonians as legitimate king of Judah, whom they held in reserve for possible restoration to power if circumstances should seem to favor it.[13]

Jehoiachin was released from prison in 561 B.C.E. by Nebuchadnezzar's successor, Amel-Marduk, and thereafter received provisions by royal allowance (2 Kings 25:27–30 and the Babylonian cuneiform archives). Thus, the exiled king and his family enjoyed some measure of freedom in Babylonia. This did not, however, result in Jehoiachin's restoration to power in his native land. We do not know what prompted Jehoiachin's release, and we can only guess at how this action may have related to internal Babylonian politics.[14] All we know is that Jehoiachin spent the remainder of his life in Babylonia as the recognized head of the exiled Jewish community.

The release of Jehoiachin and the attendant hopes at reestablishing the monarchy could well have inspired his contemporary, the incumbent chief priest Jehozadak, to embark on the task of editing the authoritative texts of the emerging Bible: the Pentateuch and Former Prophets (Joshua, Judges, Samuel and Kings).[15] The task of compiling and redacting these texts was certainly the most significant accomplishment of the exiled community. It is impossible to conceive of this activity without the involvement of the learned priestly stratum of Babylonian Jewish society.

Jewish communal leadership in Babylonia appears to have been in the hands of officials known as "elders"—the elders of the Exile, of Judah and of Israel (Jeremiah 29:1; Ezekiel 8:1, 14:1, 20:1). Texts concerning the return to Jerusalem also mention "the heads of families" (e.g., Ezra 2:68, 8:1). The family was apparently the basic unit of social organization in Babylonia. Whether families kept the strict genealogical records indicated in Ezra 2 and Nehemiah 7 is moot; one group of priests was chided (and subsequently disenfranchised) for not having done so (Ezra 2:59–63; Nehemiah 7:61–65). The genealogical tables in Ezra 2:36–58 and Nehemiah 7:39–60 show a keen interest in the families of the cultic orders, that is, the priests, Levites, *nethinim* (temple servants), and a group known as the "sons of Solomon's servants."

A passage in Ezra 8:15–20 indicates that these families were concentrated in particular places; Ezra secured a number of Levites and *nethinim* from "the place Casiphia."

This raises the question of cultic or religious activities among the exiles in Babylonia. From a hoard of papyri known as the Elephantine papyri, we know that a Jewish temple existed in Egypt at Elephantine (Yeb) during the fifth century B.C.E.[16] From Josephus we know that in the Hellenistic period another Jewish temple was built in Egypt at Leontopolis.[17] We also learn from Josephus of a Samaritan temple on Mt. Gerizim.[18] The Deuteronomic restriction on multiple shrines and the command to make pilgrimage to and perform cultic rites at only one place (Deuteronomy 12) was interpreted as applying only to worship in the land of Canaan, not outside. It thus leaves open the question of worship in the Diaspora.

A temple in Babylon

It is sometimes suggested that the synagogue (as a substitute for the temple) came into being at this time. But there is no specific evidence for this, and the question has been debated with no clear resolution.[19] Part of the difficulty stems from the lack of agreement on exactly what is meant by synagogue: Is it the institution known from later times, with clearly defined functions relating to the reading of the law and prayers, or is it simply a meeting place for community activities?[20] Whichever, the origins of the synagogue are obscure. Nor is it clear that its original purpose, functionally speaking, was to provide a place of worship for those who either did not have a temple or found it inconvenient to get to a temple. There were, for example, synagogues in Jerusalem during the Roman period, before the destruction of the Second Temple; such synagogues clearly were not needed as substitutes for the nearby Temple and its rituals. Hence, many of the functions associated with later synagogues (dating after the destruction of the Jerusalem Temple in 70 C.E.), such as Torah study, law, charity and hostelry, may also be associated with the Second Temple equivalent. From the earliest periods (the sixth century B.C.E. to the Hellenistic period), typical gathering places around city gates and other open areas could well have served as models for the later closed and architecturally discrete entity known as the synagogue.[21]

The question of how and where Jews may have worshiped in Babylonia needs to be addressed in the context of the communal character of Jewish prayer. Prayer may be offered in solitude, as was the case with Daniel in Babylon; Daniel prayed three times daily in his chamber, facing a window that opened toward Jerusalem (Daniel 6:10–11). But the experience of prayer in Israel was rooted in community worship. It is through the shared experience of worship that one becomes accustomed to a specific number of daily prayers (the reference in Daniel is the earliest to the thrice-daily practice that later became standard in Judaism), and it is through group conditioning that prayers come to have a standard form: in the case of Daniel's prayer, thanksgiving, petition and supplication (Daniel 6:11).

A shared experience similarly influences religious rites of fasting. It inculcates the custom of observance, determines the dates on which one fasts and sets the standards of what is appropriate for fasting (from what one abstains, conditions of sorrow and mortification, penitential prayers, personal adornment, etc.). We learn from Zechariah 7:1–6 that it had become the custom during the 70 years of the Exile to fast in the fifth and seventh months, that is, in the month in which the Temple had been burned (the seventh day of the fifth month, according to 2 Kings 25:8, although in Jeremiah 52:12 it is the tenth day of the fifth month) and the month in which Gedaliah had been assassinated (the seventh month [2 Kings 25:25; Jeremiah 41:1–2]). A longer catalogue of fast days appears in Zechariah 8:18–19. It includes fasts in the fourth and tenth months, that is, in those months in which the wall of Jerusalem had first been breached by the Chaldeans/Babylonians (the ninth day of the fourth month [2 Kings 25:3–4; Jeremiah 52:6]) and during the previous year, in the month in which the siege of Jerusalem had begun (the tenth day of the tenth month [2 Kings 25:1; Jeremiah 52:4]). Zechariah's consideration of fast days was clearly inspired by a delegation from Beth El, which questioned the appropriateness of fasting during the time of joy and celebration signaled by Cyrus's Edict of Return and the imminence of the rededication of the Second Temple;[22] but the fact that some Judahites were concerned about the continuation of fast days indicates that fast days were observed in many quarters of Judahite society on the eve of the restoration of the Temple.

If Jews in Babylonia observed these fasts, they must have had some place to convene. Esther 4:16 indicates that fasting was a communal phenomenon among Jews in the Exile: "Go, gather all the Jews to be found in Susa, and hold a fast on my behalf and neither eat nor drink for three days, night or day. I and my maids will also fast as you do." But neither a temple with sacred precincts nor a public house of prayer would have been necessary for such gatherings; any open place with adequate space would have sufficed. "The place (*maqôm*) Casiphia," with its concentration of Levites and temple servants, skilled in liturgy, could have been such a place of gathering; if so, it was certainly not the only place. In this connection, Psalm 137 speaks of weeping (rites of mourning) beside the waters (that is, water canals) of Babylon. Ezekiel 1:1–3:15 mentions the banks of the river Chebar (the canal *nâru kabari*) as the place of the prophet's "visions of God" (appropriately so, if it was a place of community worship). Later texts dealing with the Jewish Diaspora of the Greco-Roman world testify to the

NAHMAN AVIGAD, "SEALS OF EXILES," ISRAEL EXPLORATION JOURNAL 15:4

Exilic seal impression. *Made by a sixth-century B.C.E. seal only three-fourths of an inch long, this impression reads "Belonging to Yehoyishma, daughter of Sawas-sar-usur." Yehoyishma, which includes the divine element yeho, a form of Yahweh, is a type of name that originated in Babylonia during the Exile. Sawas-sar-usur is a well-known neo-Babylonian name that means "Shamash [the Babylonian sun-god] protect the king!" Thus, the Jewish woman who owned this seal had a Yahwistic name, but her father had a neo-Babylonian pagan name.*

Israeli archaeologist Nahman Avigad suggested that one of the first exiles in Babylonia gave his son the local name Sawas-sar-usur. By the time this man had a daughter, there was a resurgence of national and religious feeling among the Jews in Exile. Perhaps seeking divine help to return to Jerusalem, Sawas-sar-usur gave his daughter a Jewish name that means "Yahweh will hear."

existence of public places of prayer by the seaside or beside rivers.[23] One such witness comes from the New Testament, in the story of Paul in Philippi:

> We remained in this city some days; and on the sabbath day we went outside the gate to the riverside, where we supposed there was a place of prayer.
>
> (Acts 16:12–13)

Thus, while there may have been special places of public assembly, such as the area around a city gate, where religious rituals were performed, it is clear that there were no buildings associated with these places.

Assimilation

We may assume that not all Jews were faithful to the religion of their parents; some may have assimilated into Babylonian culture. But of this we have no direct evidence. We do know that Ezekiel was concerned with Jews adopting Babylonian cults (Ezekiel 8:14). But his concern was directed primarily at the situation in the Jewish homeland rather than in the Exile. Deutero-Isaiah's oracles against idol worship (Isaiah 44:9–17, 46:1–13), Zechariah's vision of the Woman in the Ephah (Zechariah 5:5–11) and the oracles on the End of False Prophecy (Zechariah 13:2–6) all point to the lure of paganism during the period of the Exile and the severe threat to Yahwism that it represented. The attraction of idols was, and remained, a problem for spiritual leaders in the Jewish Diaspora, as may be seen from later writings, including the letter of Jeremiah and the Wisdom of Solomon 13–15 (from the Apocrypha). In addition, we know that some Jews adopted Babylonian names. Others, while using Hebrew/Aramaic names, replaced the more traditional Israelite/Jewish element *yahu* (a form of Yahweh) with the more general divine element *el*.[24] This indicates a degree of assimilation, but not an abandonment of traditional Jewish religion.

Members of the house of Jehoiachin had Babylonian names, probably out of deference to their royal patrons. Nahman Avigad has published a seal of a woman who had a traditional Jewish name, but whose father bore a Babylonian name, perhaps reflecting the renewal of national aspirations among Babylonian Jews of the second generation in Exile—to which the oracles of Deutero-Isaiah also bear witness.[25] Most notable in this connection are the names of Sheshbazzar (Ezra 1:8, 5:14) and Zerubbabel (Haggai 1:1,14; Zechariah 4:6–10a), both members of the Davidic family and governors of Judah, whose names clearly reflect the pagan milieu of Babylonia.

In short, the Jewish deportees were settled in Babylonia as land-tenants of royal estates in undeveloped areas. As such, they joined other ethnic minorities in the Mesopotamian/Babylonian region, including some previously settled Israelite communities. With the exception of some members of the royal family, the Judahites were not imprisoned or held as captives. They were free to engage in agriculture and commerce and to accumulate wealth, although on a modest scale. They were not coerced to abandon their traditional cultural ways or social organization. The imprisoned (and later freed) king Jehoiachin was their titular head, although *de facto* leadership was in the hands of elders, priests and/or heads of families. Their major pragmatic challenge was compiling their sacred writings, the Torah and the Former Prophets. Their corporate life included religious observances of prayer and public fasting. We have no evidence that they erected public buildings for such communal activities. Some Jews were assimilated into Babylonian culture; others were not. When the opportunity arose, a number of Jewish families returned to their homeland to reconstruct a national life there. Many, however, remained in Babylonia, where the Jewish Diaspora continued as an important cultural phenomenon for more than two millennia.

"And These from the Land of Syene": The Jewish Diaspora in Egypt

The fate of the Jewish exiles in Babylonia would probably be of little concern to us if the restoration of the Jewish state in the late sixth-early fifth century had not been the work of Jewish leaders who came from Babylonia. These leaders led the initial return to Jerusalem, the subsequent rebuilding of the Temple under Zerubbabel and, finally, the cultic/national reforms and the reconstruction of the city under Ezra and Nehemiah. In the books of Ezra and Nehemiah, the local Judahite population (which had not been exiled) is regarded with contempt; the only citizens who seem to matter (and the only Temple personnel allowed to function) are those with proper genealogical records brought from Babylonia. Nonetheless, there were Jews who never left the land, and there were Jewish Diaspora communities in places other than Babylonia—most notably in Egypt.

The books of Ezra and Nehemiah mention no return of Egyptian Jews to Judah during this period. This may have been because there were none, or none worth mentioning, or none the Babylonian Jews wished to acknowledge. Nevertheless, we are reminded of the words of Jeremiah "concerning all the Jews that dwelt in the land of Egypt, at Migdol, at Tahpanhes, at Memphis, and in the land of Pathros ..." (Jeremiah 44:1–14):

> I will punish those who dwell in the land of Egypt, as I have punished Jerusalem, with the sword, with famine, and with pestilence, so that none of the remnant of Judah who have come to live in the land of Egypt shall escape or survive or return to the land of Judah, to which they desire to return to dwell there; for they shall not return, except some fugitives.
>
> (Jeremiah 44:13–14)

On the other hand, Deutero-Isaiah, a prophet active among the exiles in Babylonia, included the Jews of Egypt among those he envisioned as returning to Zion: "Lo, these shall come from afar, and lo, these from the north and from the west, and these from the land of Syene" (Isaiah 49:12).

"The land of Syene" was the southern frontier of Egypt at the first cataract of the Nile (modern Aswan), as in the formulaic expression "the land of Egypt ... from Migdol to Syene, as far as the border of Ethiopia [or Nubia]" (Ezekiel 29:10). Syene was located at the southern border, and Migdol was on the northeastern frontier. The military encampments at both of these sites had settlements of foreign mercenaries and their families.

The existence of a Jewish community at Syene is known from the Elephantine papyri (the major fortress at Syene was on an island in the

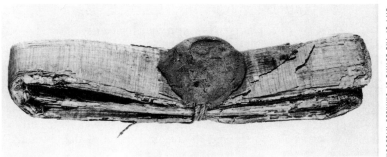

Elephantine papyrus. *Following the destruction of Jerusalem in 586 B.C.E., a Jewish community thrived on Elephantine Island, in the Upper Nile River. This well-preserved papyrus—folded several times, bound with a string, sealed with a bulla and endorsed—was discovered among a hoard of letters, deeds and other documents belonging to the community. According to the papyri, a Jewish temple, oriented toward Jerusalem, stood on Elephantine Island in the sixth and fifth centuries B.C.E.*

Nile later called Elephantine; Jewish troops stationed there referred to it as Yeb).

The existence of Jews in the Migdol area, on the northeastern border of Egypt, may also be alluded to in the Elephantine documents. Jeremiah, as we have seen, speaks of Jews at Migdol and at nearby Tahpanhes (later called Daphni, modern Tel Dafneh) and also at Noph (Memphis) and Pathros (Nubia). According to Jeremiah, Johanan ben Kareah led his group of refugees to the area of Migdol and Tahpanhes after Gedaliah's assassination disrupted the political and social order (Jeremiah 43:8–13).

Archaeological evidence for the Egyptian Diaspora

Excavations east of the Suez Canal under the direction of Eliezer Oren of Ben-Gurion University of the Negev have revealed that, in the early sixth century B.C.E., this area was fertile and densely populated, and had a navigable water system, as well as irrigation and drainage canals. Migdol was not only an Egyptian military center but a commercial and industrial area. Imported pottery types testify to the existence of a large foreign element in the population, which is not surprising because the Egyptians had, since the reign of Psammetichus I (664–610 B.C.E.), come to rely on foreign mercenaries to garrison their border stations and to fill the ranks of their regular army. Nor is it surprising that Jeremiah's catalogue of areas of Jewish residence follows a line of defense systems established by the Egyptians, from the northeast border (Migdol) to Nubia (Pathros). It was in these centers that Jewish soldiers and their families lived, and so it was to these centers that their compatriots would have come when settling in Egypt.[26]

A good deal of information concerning life in the Jewish settlement at the border station of Syene/Yeb during the fifth century B.C.E. comes from the Elephantine papyri. The papyri—Aramaic archival documents, including copies of correspondence, memoranda, contracts and other legal materials—first came to light at the end of the 19th century and were published by numerous scholars over a 60-year period (1906–1966). They have recently been the subject of intensive investigation (with corrections of some mistakes made by earlier scholars) by Bezalel Porten of Hebrew University.[27] The documents date from 495 to 399 B.C.E. and are thus roughly contemporaneous with the reconstruction of the Jewish state under Ezra and Nehemiah; but the Jewish community at Elephantine had existed for at least a century before the earliest Elephantine documents.

The most intriguing aspect of Jewish communal life at Elephantine was a temple dedicated to the Hebrew God Yahu (YHW, a variant form of YHWH). According to the papyri, the temple had been destroyed by the Egyptians at the instigation of the priests of the local cult of Kimura in the 14th year of Darius II (410 B.C.E.). Exactly when the Temple was built is unknown, but it was sometime prior to the Persian conquest of Egypt in 525 B.C.E. Jedaniah, the Jewish communal leader at Elephantine, wrote to Bagohi, the Persian governor of Judah, requesting assistance in rebuilding the Elephantine temple. Jedaniah also wrote to Delaiah and Shelemiah, the sons and successors of Sanballat, governor of Samaria, with the same request. Other correspondence with Jerusalem included requests for information on the correct procedure for observing the Feast of Unleavened Bread (Passover) and on matters of cultic purity.

Although Jedaniah represented his Elephantine temple as a regular Jewish sanctuary, just like the Jerusalem Temple, scholars have tended to regard the cult of Yahu at Elephantine as a syncretistic mixture of Yahwism and Canaanite (especially northern Canaanite) cults of Bethel, Anat-Bethel, Eshem, Eshem-Bethel, Herem-Bethel and Anath-YHW. This is because the names of these deities are referred to in judicial oaths and salutations used by Jews in the Elephantine documents. Accordingly, a northern, Israelite origin of these colonists has been suggested. Porten, on the other hand, contends that "the evidence for a syncretistic communal cult of the Jewish deity dissipates upon close inspection" (although "individual Jewish contact with paganism remains"). According to Porten, the temple was established by priests from Jerusalem who had gone into self-imposed exile in Egypt during the reign of King Manasseh (c. 650 B.C.E.) to establish a purer Yahwistic temple there.[28]

Whether or not the cult of Yahu at Elephantine was syncretistic, or the Jews of Elephantine were themselves syncretistic, one thing remains clear: Pagan religion was more influential in the life of the Jews of

Upper Egypt than it was in the life of Jews in Babylonia. The tradition preserved in Jeremiah 44:15–30 records the worship of a goddess called "the Queen of Heaven" (compare Jeremiah 7:18) by the Jews of Johanan ben Kareah's community in the Pathros-Migdol area of Egypt. Similar tendencies probably prevailed among the Jews in Upper Egypt. This may explain why Jeremiah judges the Jews of Egypt so harshly. This may also be why we read nothing of the Jews of Egypt playing any sort of role in the reconstruction of the Jewish nation during the Persian period.

Return and Restoration Under the Persians

> For we are bondmen; yet our God has not forsaken us in our bondage, but has extended to us his steadfast love before the kings of Persia, to grant us some reviving to set up the house of our God, to repair its ruins, and to give us protection in Judea and Jerusalem.
>
> (Ezra 9:9)

When Cyrus the Great, the Achaemenid ruler of Persia, conquered Babylon in 539 B.C.E., the Persians succeeded the Babylonians as the major imperial power of the Near East. In contrast to their Assyrian and Babylonian predecessors, the Achaemenid Persians presented themselves to their subject states as a benevolent power concerned not just with garnering taxes but also with maintaining peace and order throughout the empire. The territories formerly administered by the Assyrians and Babylonians were reorganized into a system of satrapies and provinces; local governments were strengthened; roads and systems of communication were developed; and—most important for the Jews—displaced and exiled peoples were encouraged to return to their ancestral homelands and to reestablish local religious and political institutions in order to play supportive roles in this new concept of empire.

Cyrus's decree permitting the exiles' return

This is the political background of the decree of Cyrus preserved in 2 Chronicles 36:23 and Ezra 1:2–4:

> Thus says Cyrus king of Persia, "The Lord, the God of Heaven, has given me all the kingdoms of the earth, and has charged me to build Him a house at Jerusalem, which is in Judah. Whoever is among you of all his people—may His God be with him, and let him go up to Jerusalem which is in Judah and rebuild the House of the Lord God of Israel—He is the God who is in Jerusalem; and let each survivor, in whatever place he sojourns, be assisted by the men of his place with silver and gold, with goods, and with beasts besides freewill offering(s) for the house of God that is in Jerusalem."
>
> (Ezra 1:2–4)

Cyrus Cylinder. *The inscription written in cuneiform on this 10-inch-long clay barrel tells how the great god Marduk chose Cyrus (559–529 B.C.E.) to supplant the impious tyrant who was then king of Persia, and of how Cyrus went on to conquer the equally odious king of Babylon, Nabonidas. It then proclaims, "I am Cyrus, king of the world, great king," and describes his new religious policy of toleration, which allowed subject peoples to return to their homelands and repair their ruined sanctuaries.*

The Bible records a similar decree of Cyrus that permitted the Jews to resettle Jerusalem and rebuild their Temple in about 539 B.C.E. (2 Chronicles 36:23 and Ezra 1:2-3).

Although the text of this decree is preserved only in the Bible, it is not dissimilar in spirit and style to an edict of Cyrus known as the Cyrus Cylinder. In this document, Cyrus credits his accomplishments to the Babylonian deity Marduk for the benefit of his Babylonian subjects, just as in the Bible he is said to have acknowledged the assistance of Yahweh; his policy of rebuilding ruined sanctuaries and resettling dispersed populations is also reflected in the Cyrus Cylinder:[29]

> To the cities of Ashur and Susa, Agade, Eshnunna, the cities of Zamban, Metuma, Der, as far as the region of Gutium, the holy cities beyond the Tigris whose sanctuaries had been in ruins over a long period, the gods whose abode is in the midst of them, I returned to their places and housed in lasting abodes. I gathered together all their inhabitants and restored to their dwellings.

The exiled Jewish community of Babylonia greeted Cyrus as a liberator and saw his work as fulfilling a divine purpose in national redemption:

> Thus says the Lord, your Redeemer, who formed you from the womb: "I am the Lord, who made all things, who stretched out the heavens alone ..." who says of Cyrus, "He is my shepherd, and he shall fulfill all my purpose"; saying of Jerusalem, "She shall be built," and of the Temple, "Your foundation shall be laid."

(Isaiah 44:24,28)

But the task of national reconstruction was not without difficulties. The returning exiles found that their hopes conflicted with the new territorial hegemonies that had come into being during their absence—most particularly Samaria, which aspired to exercise control over the Judahite territory.[30]

Rebuilding the Temple

According to biblical sources, there were successive waves of Jewish repatriation under Persian rule. The first was led by Sheshbazzar, the son of King Jehoiachin, who had been taken into captivity in 597 B.C.E. (Sheshbazzar is called Shenazzar in 1 Chronicles 3:18). This first return occurred not long after 539 B.C.E., when Cyrus conquered Babylon and subsequently issued a decree that provided for the rebuilding of the Jewish Temple (Ezra 1:1–11). Sheshbazzar was entrusted with the Temple vessels (Ezra 1:7–8, 5:14–15) and is reported to have laid the foundation for the rebuilt Temple (Ezra 5:16).The rebuilding of the Temple becomes a centerpiece of the Book of Haggai and First Zechariah (chapters 1–8), which presumes that this took place in the time of Zerubbabel (520 B.C.E.), the son of Shealtiel and grandson of Jehoiachin.[31] The nature of the actual work done at the time of the first return, however, remains a mystery. No figures are given for those who returned under Sheshbazzar; it was at best a modest and unpretentious beginning.

A major wave of returning exiles was led by Zerubbabel, and by the high priest Joshua, son of Jehozadak, apparently during the early years of the administration of Darius (522–486 B.C.E.; see Ezra 2:2, 3:2,8, 4:2–3, 5:1–2; Nehemiah 7:7, 12:1,47; Haggai 1:1, 2:2; Zechariah 3:1–4:14). A census of the returnees, who numbered 42,360 people, plus 7,337 servants and 200 singers, is given in Ezra 2:1–67 and Nehemiah 7:6–73.

Zerubbabel and Joshua apparently first established an altar on the Temple Mount in Jerusalem and then began to construct the Temple in the second year of Darius's reign (520 B.C.E.). The foundations of the Second Temple were laid on December 18, 520 B.C.E. to much fanfare and celebration.[32] The involvement of Zerubbabel as a key player in the actual refoundation ceremony no doubt caused intense messianic expectation; he was hailed by Haggai as "servant" and "signet" (Haggai 2:23) and by Zechariah as "my servant the Branch [or shoot]" (Zechariah 3:8).[33] The Temple was completed in the sixth year of Darius (516 B.C.E.), with the encouragement of the prophets Haggai and Zechariah and the support of the Persian court, despite strong local resistance (Ezra 6:1–15).

This repatriation and restoration should be understood against the background of Darius's career. When Darius came to power in 522 B.C.E., he suppressed rebellions throughout his realm, including revolts in Babylon led by Nebuchadnezzar III (522 B.C.E.) and Nebuchadnezzar IV (521 B.C.E.). Darius also reorganized the satrapies and provinces and the command of the armies. He introduced imperial coinage, a road and postal system, and royal building projects. The return of the Jewish exiles and the appointment of Zerubbabel as governor over Judah was part of Darius's reform of the empire's political structure.[34]

Though some of Zerubbabel's supporters saw in these circumstances the opportunity for the restoration of monarchy under Davidic rule, the majority of Judahites clearly understood that the dual leadership of priest and governor was the only form of local rule that would be tolerated by the Persians. The dual messianic sentiments concerning Zerubbabel expressed by the prophet Zechariah ("and he will bear royal majesty, and shall sit upon his throne and rule. A priest will be on his throne, and there will be peaceful counsel between the two of them" [Zechariah 6:13]) unequivocally express the eschatological hopes of the community that were acceptable to the Persians.[35]

It is commonly thought that Darius removed Zerubbabel from office because of the messianic claims that were supported by those who wanted to reinstate the office of kingship. But there is no evidence of this. The argument is based primarily on the low state of Jewish affairs at the next wave of immigration and on the silence of our sources concerning Zerubbabel after the Temple construction began. It is not clear whether he was still in office in 516 B.C.E., when the work was completed. But Zerubbabel was not the only person in the post-Exilic history of Ezra-Nehemiah who vanished from the scene without explanation. True, Zerubbabel was no ordinary figure; he was the last active claimant to the Davidic throne of whom we have knowledge from the Hebrew Scriptures. Naturally, we speculate on what may have happened to him. But the evidence for any clear conclusion is absent.

Equally intriguing, and subject to speculation, is the figure of Joshua, the high priest who led the return with Zerubbabel. He receives as much attention as Zerubbabel (perhaps even more) in Zechariah 3–6. He and Zerubbabel are linked together as "the two anointed who stand by the Lord of the whole earth" (Zechariah 4:14). Joshua's authority was focused primarily on religious affairs; the coronation scene in Zechariah 3 underscores his significance at the center of the Temple. Whether or not his working relationship with Zerubbabel survived the rededication of the Temple, the pattern of leadership involving a high priest and governor survived for many years to come.[36]

Unfortunately, Judah's Samaritan neighbors sought to influence the Persians to limit the development of the renascent Jewish community. Initially, "the adversaries of Judah and Benjamin" (that is, the rulers of Samaria) offered to assist Zerubbabel in rebuilding the Temple of Yahweh, claiming that they too were worshipers of the Hebrew God and had been since they were settled in the land by the Assyrians. Zerubbabel rebuffed the Samaritans' proffered assistance,

Samaritans

however, and this led to their harassing the returning Judahites through correspondence with Persian officials (Ezra 5:1–6:18).[37]

The Yahwistic inhabitants of what was formerly Israel, whose help Zerubbabel rejected, were descendants of Syrian-Mesopotamians. After the Assyrians destroyed the northern kingdom in 722 B.C.E., they sent colonists to settle the district. These Syrian-Mesopotamian colonists subsequently adopted the religion of the land (2 Kings 17:24–41). The biblical writers explain the hostility of the Samaritans, as these people came to be known, as resulting from the petty jealousy of a people whose mixed ethnic background and syncretistic Yahwism precluded participation in a renewed Jewish cult. It is not difficult to see the political agenda, however, in strained relations between the peoples of these two regions. We are told that the "people of the land discouraged the people of Judah" throughout the reign of Cyrus (that is, from 539 to 530 B.C.E.) to the time of Darius I, during the reign of Ahasuerus (Xerxes, 486–465 B.C.E.), and in the days of Artaxerxes I (465–424 B.C.E.; Ezra 4:4–23).

Despite the opposition of the Samaritans, the appointment of a Davidic scion (Zerubbabel), who was raised in Babylonia, with the support and full knowledge of the Achaemenid leadership was a stroke of political genius. It was also consistent with Persia's overall policy of installing loyal representatives of the conquered indigenous populations who could prevent insurrection and foster loyalty to the imperial throne.[38] Pairing the Davidic Zerubbabel with Joshua, the son of Jehozadak, as high priest was a move meant to assuage local concerns and give the newly established subprovince of Yehud (Judah) maximum freedom in invigorating its historic religion while limiting autonomy on the political level. The relative success of such an approach is best observed through the absence of organized opposition to Persia for at least two generations or more. The negative aspect of this was the apparent increase in the appeal of non-Yahwist religious practices in the time of Ezra and Nehemiah. Nonetheless, recent scholarship has attributed to the Persian period an unprecedented flurry of literary activity that surely found its support and inspiration in the reestablished Jewish community of Palestine.[39]

The Greco-Persian Wars

Several political factors emerged in the fifth century B.C.E. to disturb the relative security of the Levant during the reign of Darius I (522–486 B.C.E.). The first and foremost of these were the Greco-Persian wars, which began at the end of the sixth century and ended in 449 B.C.E. with the Peace of Callias between Persia and Athens.[40] Though Persia managed to retain most of its holdings in the Levant during this struggle, the turmoil created among the local population was intense. So uncertain was the outcome of these wars in the fifth century that Egypt and Babylonia both sought to reestablish a degree of independence.[41] The Babylonians succeeded in breaking away from the Persian satrapy of Beyond-the-River (which stretched from the Euphrates river in the east to the Mediterranean in the west and included Judah) in 481 B.C.E., and Egypt began its satrapal revolt in 464 B.C.E., sensing an opportune moment to reassert its power.[42] The Egyptian attempt at independence was unsuccessfully supported by the Greek military.

The end result of these activities was the reassertion in several ways of Persian military control over local areas. First, the Persians constructed numerous fortresses on both sides of the Jordan River to control the major trade routes that linked Mesopotamia and Egypt. The fortresses were maintained by imperial garrisons charged with preventing the local populace from joining the Greek forces.[43] Second, the existing road system was also strengthened to serve the political needs of the Persian government. Some of the most important reverberations of these momentous events are reflected in the oracles of Second Zechariah (Zechariah 9–14) envisioning the destruction of Israel's enemies and the restoration of Zion. In the Greek tragedy *The Persians*, Aeschylus captures the poignant response of the Greeks to these events.

The prophetic responses collected in the books of Second Zechariah, and to some degree in Malachi, also reflect the unusual demographic conditions that predominated in Yehud at least until the mid-fifth century B.C.E., and perhaps until the time of Ezra and Nehemiah. Recent excavations and archaeological surveys have revealed that Yehud was relatively impoverished and modestly settled in the early post-Exilic era (c. 520–450 B.C.E.).[44] This contrasts strongly with the contemporaneous urban settlements along the coastal plain and the Shephelah, which shared in the prosperity generated by the vibrant commercial activity of the day. Such cities as Dor, Jaffa and Shiqmona and the Philistine cities of Ashkelon and Gaza were clearly brought fully into the mainstream of east Mediterranean trade; their material culture reflects the finest imports of Greek origin, attested only a bit later in the interior. The expectations of the restoration community, therefore, were clearly not met in this first period of Persian dominance of the Levant. Hence, Second Zechariah's concerns with the gathering of the dispersed (Zechariah 9:11–17, 10), the repopulation of greater Israel (Zechariah 9:1–10), and the full repopulation of Jerusalem (Zechariah 14) reflect the eschatological yearnings of Israel at a critical time in its history, the first half of the fifth century B.C.E.

Archaeological evidence

These developments bring us down to the time of Ezra and Nehemiah. Ezra came to Jerusalem in the seventh year of the reign of Artaxerxes (458 B.C.E.; see Ezra 7:7). Nehemiah came to Jerusalem in the 20th year of Artaxerxes' reign (445 B.C.E.; Nehemiah 2:1) and was governor until Artaxerxes' 32nd year (433 B.C.E.; Nehemiah 5:14). Nehemiah also served a second term as governor sometime before Artaxerxes' death (424 B.C.E.). This follows the chronological sequence of Ezra and Nehemiah suggested by the current arrangement of the biblical materials.

From the late 19th century until fairly recently, the prevailing opinion had been that Nehemiah actually preceded Ezra (based on the understanding that the Artaxerxes of Ezra 7:7 was Artaxerxes II [404–358 B.C.E.]) and that the two were never contemporaries. An alternative opinion was that Ezra came to Jerusalem during the reign of Artaxerxes (465–424 B.C.E.), but that he was preceded by Nehemiah, of whom he was later a contemporary (the date "the seventh year of Artaxerxes" of Ezra 7:7 being understood as a scribal corruption, probably of "thirty-seven"). More recently these views have been challenged and historical reconstructions proposed in which the traditional order of Ezra and Nehemiah has been restored. These historical reconstructions have resulted, in part, from recent archaeological data, including comparative information on the ruling house of Samaria (the Samaritan papyri of Wadi Dâliyeh).[45] The whole matter remains problematic, however.[46]

Ezra   According to the biblical record, the most dramatic and long-lasting cultural and political changes in the post-Exilic Jewish state occurred during the tenure of Ezra and Nehemiah. From the biblical perspective, Ezra's accomplishments were primarily in the religious sphere, although these should be understood within the larger context of the Persian policy of fostering local religio-legal traditions for the purpose of social stability within the provinces. Ezra arrived in Jerusalem not as a governor but as a "scribe skilled in the law of Moses," with a copy of the law (Ezra 7:6,10) and with a commission from Artaxerxes to establish magistrates and judges in order to enact and teach that law (Ezra 7:11–14,25–26). Ezra was also given funds and precious goods to revitalize religious rites in Jerusalem (Ezra 7:15–20, 8:21–34). This may have required some rebuilding. According to Ezra 6:14, the rebuilding of the Temple was accomplished by the royal decrees of Cyrus, Darius and Artaxerxes, so Ezra may well have participated in it. Nehemiah's rebuilding of the walls of Jerusalem (Nehemiah 3) may also be understood in the larger context of Persian imperial aims to control their Levantine holdings more tightly.[47] Eventually, under Ezra's leadership, and after Nehemiah's arrival (Nehemiah 8:9, 10:1), the law was accepted as the constitutional basis of Jewish life. This was done in a formal public ceremony and by contractual agreement (Ezra 9:1–10; Nehemiah 8:1–10:39). The prohibition of intermarriage

with non-Jews was an especially important dimension of the acceptance of Jewish law. The missions of Ezra and Nehemiah do not
demonstrate that the local community was being rewarded for its
loyalty; rather, their missions represented the efforts of the empire
to develop economic and social relationships that would tie the fortunes of Yehud to the future of the imperial system.[48]

It has been widely assumed that the "law of Moses" that Ezra
brought to Jerusalem was the Pentateuch (the first five books of
the Hebrew Bible) or, if not the Pentateuch in its entirety, then one
of the law codes incorporated in the Pentateuch. One suggestion
is that he brought the so-called Priestly source (P) of the
Pentateuch (P is one of the sources of the Pentateuch according to
the documentary hypothesis, which divides the Pentateuch into
four different narrative strands). Ezra has thus been credited with
a major role in the development of the canon of Jewish Scripture
and/or in the editorial process that produced the Pentateuch in
the form in which it is now known. As noted, however, the
process of editing the major portions of the Hebrew Bible, the
Pentateuch and Former Prophets, had probably begun a full century earlier. It is quite possible that by the end of the fifth century
the Prophets, both major and minor, were organized and promulgated, as were the Chronicler's history (1 and 2 Chronicles) and
the books of Ezra and Nehemiah.[49]

What is curious about the assumption that Ezra played such a
major role in organizing scripture, however, is that not one of the
quotations from Ezra's law code in the books of Ezra and Nehemiah
agrees with any specific passage of the Pentateuch (see, for example, Ezra 9:10–12; Nehemiah 8:14–15). Instead, Ezra's reform measures agree in general with dicta contained in various parts of the
Pentateuch (although Ezra's prohibition against intermarriage is far
more specific than any command in the Pentateuch). Ezra's law
code may have been simply a précis or compendium of Jewish law
in a form suitable for deposit in the Persian court archives. In sum,
we know that Ezra came as a scribe of the law of Moses commissioned by Artaxerxes to be the promulgator and enforcer of that
law. We do not know the particular form of that law, however, or
how that law relates to the Pentateuch as it has come down to us in
its canonical form.

Ezra is frequently referred to as "the father of Judaism," that is, the
father of Judaism as a religious system based upon Torah, or law. He
was certainly an important person in the history of Judaism and played
a significant role in the revitalization of Jewish life based upon Torah.
Without diminishing Ezra's importance, however, we must remember
that he was not the originator of Judaism as a legal system. This legal system can be traced to the religious reforms of King Josiah in 622 B.C.E.

(2 Kings 22–23; 2 Chronicles 34–35). It was Josiah who promulgated a code of law, most likely an edition of Deuteronomy. Ultimately, however, Judaism as a religion of Torah may be traced to the example of Moses and to the role of the levitical priests in the teaching of Torah in early Israelite culture. It is no wonder that Ezra is depicted as a kind of second Moses, emulating the experience of former times through his actions and words.[50]

Against exaggerated claims for Ezra, we may note that when the Jewish sage Ben Sira extolled the great heroes of Judaism from Enoch to Simon the Just in his eulogy "Let us now praise famous men" (Sirach 44–50), he did not even mention Ezra. For Ben Sira, the heroes of the Persian period were Zerubbabel, Joshua and Nehemiah. According to Ben Sira, it was Nehemiah who "raised for us the walls that had fallen, and set up the gates and bars and rebuilt our ruined houses" (Sirach 49:13).

Nehemiah Nehemiah's principal accomplishments are described in the Book of Nehemiah. He rebuilt the gates and walls of Jerusalem, despite the concerted resistance of Sanballat, governor of Samaria, Tobiah, governor of Ammon, and Geshem, the leader of the Arab Kedarite confederacy (Nehemiah 1–4, 6, 12:27–43). Nehemiah also enforced legislation on mortgages, loans and interest for the betterment of the economic life of the Judahite citizens (Nehemiah 5). He repopulated Jerusalem by means of a public lottery in which one-tenth of the Jewish population was moved into the city (Nehemiah 11). He established Jewish control over the cultural and economic life of the city (Nehemiah 13:15–22). He established cultic reforms to ensure that the Levites and Temple singers would not disperse to the countryside (Nehemiah 13:10–14). Finally, he enforced Ezra's legislation concerning intermarriage, especially as it affected the priestly orders (Nehemiah 13:1–9,23–29). Of Nehemiah's varied accomplishments, the greatest attention is given to rebuilding the walls of Jerusalem, and for good reason: This was a major move in the implementation of Persian imperial policy that demonstrated Yehud's continuing cooperation with the powers that be. There is no doubt that Nehemiah's adversaries understood the full import of those actions.

These reforms indicate that during Nehemiah's administrations as governor, he exercised far more control over local affairs than did his predecessors, although he exercised authority within the larger framework of Persian concerns for tighter regulation of local affairs. This is consistent with what we now know about administrative changes allowing more autonomy in the western Persian provinces in the late fifth century B.C.E. The hostility of Nehemiah's neighboring governors also reflects this situation. Each maneuvered for greater control over his own area and entered into alliances (in this case against Judah) aimed at establishing his own hegemony. The positioning of the Samaritan governor Sanballat as leader of the conspiracy against Nehemiah reflects the history of Samaritan desire for hegemony over Judah after its collapse in 586 B.C.E. and the assassination of the puppet governor Gedaliah.[51] Let us survey what is known about this period from archaeological sources.

Until fairly recently, the Persian period was characterized as the dark age of Israelite history. This is no longer true, partly because of the availability of newer materials, but especially because of the work of Ephraim Stern of Hebrew University and other archaeologists in Israel whose surveys and discoveries have opened new vistas for study of this era of profound change and development.[52]

Archaeological evidence from the Persian period

Stern has made a number of pertinent observations: During the Persian period, the land of Israel was divided into two culturally distinct regions. The separation was as definite as that between two countries. One region consisted of the hill country of Judah and Transjordan (and to a lesser extent Samaria); the other included Galilee and the Mediterranean coastal plain. Judah's local culture was a continuation of its earlier culture (as noted by William F. Albright, who called the Persian period Iron Age III), although its culture also reflected Assyrian, Babylonian and Egyptian influence. Galilee and the Mediterranean coast, on the other hand, were influenced by Greek and Phoenician cultures. Strangely, the material culture of the Persian period reflects almost no influence of the ruling Persians—the exceptions being a few pottery types and some Persian-style jewelry manufactured by Phoenicians. The major influence of the Persians on Israelite culture seems to relate to government, military organization, economic life and taxation. The reorganization of the empire by Darius I—who installed local leaders and requested that local laws be collated and religious laws implemented—no doubt greatly influenced the pace and level of literary activities in the conquered territories during his reign.[53] The most direct influence can be seen in coins and seals. Changes in seals impressed on the handles of jars used in connection with the collection of taxes indicate administrative reforms—leading to increased local control—at the end of the fifth century.[54] Imperial Achaemenid motifs in seals and seal impressions gradually are replaced by designs in local Aramaic script. A similar change is noted in coins, where we find the gradual appearance of the province name in Aramaic. Sometimes we even find coins with the governor's name in Aramaic.

The extent of Judahite hegemony in the time of Nehemiah—that is, the borders of the province of Yehud—is reflected in several toponymical references in Ezra and Nehemiah, as well as in the distribution of Yehud seal impressions and coins found in the area. Ezra

The borders of Judah

Yehud stamps and coin. *From Tell en-Nasbeh (biblical Mizpah) in the north to Beth Zur in the south, from Gezer in the west to Jericho in the east, archaeologists have discovered jar handles and coins stamped Yehud, the name for Judah in the Persian period (539-332 B.C.E.). The distribution of these stamps helps modern scholars to establish the borders of Judah at this time.*

A falcon with spread wings shares space with the Yehud stamp on the obverse of a small fourth-century B.C.E. silver coin discovered near Jericho. (A lily appears on the reverse.) The two pottery handles, found at Ramat Rahel and also dating to the fourth century B.C.E., probably came from wine jars. The Yehud impression was literally an official stamp of approval.

(2:21–35) and Nehemiah (7:25–38, 3:2–22, 12:28–29) list names of places in the territory of Benjamin, the Jordan Valley from Jericho to Ein Gedi, the Judahite hills from Jerusalem to Beth Zur, and the districts of Lod and Adulam in the Shephelah. These areas, as Stern has noted, correspond approximately to the region where Yehud seals, seal impressions and coins have been found—from Tel en-Nasbeh in the north to Beth Zur in the south and from Jericho and Ein Gedi in the east to Gezer in the west. Evidence of the borders also comes from archaeological surveys conducted by Moshe Kochavi, Israel Finkelstein and Avi Ofer; these archaeologists have discovered lines of forts erected by the Jews during the Persian period as defenses against the province of Ashdod in the west and Edomite territories in the south.[55] The lines of demarcation of the province of Judah on the south established by these forts correspond to the borders indicated in the biblical lists cited above and to the distribution of Yehud seals and impressions.

A list in Nehemiah 11:23–35, however, gives much wider boundaries for Judah. This may not be a description of the actual borders of Judah, but rather a statement of the territory that Judah considered its own, an idealization based on older biblical boundaries. The actual borders probably were much smaller.[56]

The size of the province of Judah and its capital city, Jerusalem, were limited not simply by the amount of power Nehemiah and his successors could arrogate but also by the available Jewish population. Excavations in Judah and Jerusalem have shown that the city grew significantly in the Persian period, as did the province of Judah. The population nearly doubled to about 17,000 and Jerusalem's size increased approximately fourfold.[57] There is no doubt that the population of Judah decreased significantly in the Exilic period and that in the restoration period the population remained small. By the time of Nehemiah, however, there was significant and important growth and change in the demographics of Judah. The biblical tradition that the land was denuded of its people in the early sixth century B.C.E. is not simply an overstatement by the editors of 2 Kings and Jeremiah or a fiction imposed by the Chronicler to promote the idea of sabbatical rest for the land. The rebuilding of the Jewish population took several hundred years; it was not until the second century B.C.E. that there was a sizable Jewish population in Judah and Jerusalem.

With the work of Nehemiah, biblical historiography ends. Our knowledge of Jewish life during the remainder of the Persian period (until the conquest of the area by Alexander the Great in 332 B.C.E.) is sketchy at best. From the Elephantine papyri we learn that the governor of Yehud in the year 408 B.C.E. was Bagohi and that in the same

Persian period sources

year Samaria was governed by Delaiah and Shelemaiah, sons of Nehemiah's adversary, Sanballat. The Jews of Yeb (Elephantine) wrote to these Samaritan and Judahite leaders seeking assistance in rebuilding their temple. Josephus records an incident from the time of Artaxerxes II (404–358 B.C.E.) in which the Persians "defiled the sanctuary and imposed tribute on the Jews" (and also that "the people were made slaves") for a period of seven years. This, he says, resulted from the interference of Artaxerxes' general Bagoses who tried to appoint Jesus (that is, Joshua/Jeshua) son of Eliashib as high priest and became enraged when Jesus was murdered by his brother, the high priest Joannes (Johanan).[58] Some scholars believe the Bagoses of this story is Bagohi, the governor of Judah known from the Elephantine papyri.[59]

The last Persian period incident recorded by Josephus occurred on the eve of Alexander's conquest of the area. According to Josephus, the Samaritans led by Sanballat built a temple on Mt. Gerizim. The reference is to Sanballat III,[60] grandson of the earlier Sanballat who had opposed Nehemiah's rebuilding of Judah. The building of a Samaritan temple on Mt. Gerizim around 332 B.C.E. is evident not only from Josephus and the sources he used,[61] but also from the archaeological evidence. Foundations of a temple at Tel er-Ras, on Mt. Gerizim, have recently been excavated.[62] Josephus claimed that this temple was built when expelled priests from the Jerusalem Temple and other malcontents from Jewish society took refuge with the Samaritans. This may or may not have been the case. It is more likely that this temple was an expression of the Samaritans' own national identity as a Hebrew people who claimed descent from the old Joseph tribes of the north (Ephraim and Manasseh) and who desired to worship God at the ancient and (from their understanding) true sanctuary at Shechem.

Because Josephus's account bears certain similarities to a brief note in Nehemiah 13:28 concerning Nehemiah's expulsion of a son-in-law of Sanballat I from Jerusalem, some scholars have been inclined to date the building of the Samaritan sanctuary (and the alleged schism) to that earlier time (about 425 B.C.E.). Others have dated the event to the time of Ezra (about 450 B.C.E.), although the biblical traditions on Ezra make no reference at all to the Samaritans, even in cases of intermarriage. In fact, the biblical record does not mention a Samaritan schism during the time of Ezra or Nehemiah. The history of the Samaritans as an autonomous religious community residing at Shechem belongs to a later time, no earlier than 332 B.C.E.[63]

In sum, the restoration of the Jewish nation in the land of Israel following Cyrus's edict of return was accomplished through successive waves of immigration of both leaders and their followers from the Babylonian Exile. We are not told of any role played by those who had remained in the land or by returnees from the Diaspora in Egypt. Although the biblical record covers a period of about 115 years (from

538 to 423 B.C.E.), or longer if Ezra was active during the reign of Artaxerxes II, the reporting of the period is episodic, focusing on the specific actions of five leaders: the return of the Temple vessels under Sheshbazzar; the rebuilding of the Temple under Zerubbabel and Joshua; the renewal of the cult and establishment of Mosaic law as the constitutional basis of society, with the prohibition of mixed marriages, by Ezra; and the rebuilding of the gates and walls of Jerusalem and the development of its economic and religious life by Nehemiah. Of these five leaders, Nehemiah is credited with the greatest specific political and social accomplishments. Resistance to the development of a Jewish state came primarily from Samaria because of cultural differences aggravated by political conditions. The biblical account may be understood against a dual background: the political history of the Persian Empire and the archaeology of the land to which they returned. From the latter, we gain a clearer picture of the political realignments and the development of Judah as a semi-autonomous province in the late sixth century B.C.E., under the leadership of Zerubbabel and Joshua together with subsequent governors and high priests until the leadership of Ezra and Nehemiah in the second half of the fifth century B.C.E. Without these developments, it would be difficult to imagine the subsequent evolution of Judaism as a religion that would survive the loss of the Second Temple and have so great an influence on Western religions.

SEVEN

The Age of Hellenism

Alexander the Great and the Rise and Fall of the Hasmonean Kingdom

written and revised by
LEE I. LEVINE

A LEXANDER THE GREAT CHANGED THE FACE OF JUDEA ALONG WITH the rest of the then-known world. He reigned as emperor from 356 to 323 B.C.E. In 336 B.C.E. he became king of Macedonia and of the Greek city-states conquered by his father, Philip II. Within a decade he defeated the Persians and fell heir to their empire.

Early in that decade, in 332 B.C.E., he conquered Judea, a conquest that was to have profound and far-reaching effects on Jewish history. Conquest itself was nothing new to the Jews; Judea had been subjugated on numerous occasions. This time the conqueror came from the West, rather than the East (as had Assyria, Babylonia and Persia). Two factors made Alexander's conquest indeed historic: The first is cultural; the second, geographic. The Greeks were interested not only in military victories, political expansion and economic gain; they were also committed to disseminating their way of life—their institutions, norms and ideas—to the world of the barbarians (as they called non-Greeks). In addition to political hegemony and imposition of taxes, Greek conquest exposed the eastern Mediterranean lands and beyond to an entirely different way of life—Hellenism.[1]

Perhaps the most effective means by which Hellenism was propagated in new regions was by founding a Greek city, or by reconstituting an already existing city as a *polis*. Either step carried with it political, religious, social and cultural ramifications. The *polis* operated politically under a Greek constitution,* Greek deities were introduced into the city's pantheon, and Greek educational and entertainment institutions were established. Within a century of Alexander's conquest of Judea, Greek cities were founded along the Mediterranean coast, as well as inland at Beth-Shean and Samaria, and to the East in Transjordan. These cities served as centers of Greek life and influence and reinforced one another through joint commercial, cultural and athletic enterprises.[2]

Judea's key location The geographic consequences of Alexander's conquest deeply affected the course of Israel's history. In previous conquests Israel had invariably remained at the periphery of world empires, far from seats of power and authority. Its marginal geographic location assured the Jews a measure of stability and insulation. But with the death of Alexander in 323 B.C.E. and the breakup of his empire, Judea was thrown into the vortex of political and military activity. Geographically sandwiched between two foci of power—the Seleucid kingdom based in Syria and the Ptolemaic kingdom of Egypt, the capital of which was Alexandria—Judea served as a battlefield on which the Seleucids and the Ptolemies faced one another for the next century. No fewer than five major wars were fought between Egypt and Syria during the third century B.C.E., each lasting for at least several years. Garrison troops were posted all over Judea (including Jerusalem), and large armies were stationed throughout the country.

Either factor—exposure to Hellenistic culture or geographic centrality—would have been unsettling under any circumstances. But for the Jews of Judea these factors were wrenching, because in the centuries immediately preceding the conquest these Jews had lived in a kind of splendid isolation. When Persia ruled the world, Cyrus maintained a policy of actively supporting ethnic and religious groups, encouraging them to rebuild their institutions and develop their indigenous traditions. Naturally, Jewish leaders welcomed this policy with open arms. The Persians had demanded only political loyalty and the payment of taxes. The district of Judea, or Yehud, consisted of a small area around Jerusalem that was far removed from the main cities and international highways of the country. Its location guaranteed it relative isolation from the surrounding world—geographically, socially and religiously.[3]

Thus it is not surprising that, following Alexander's conquest, Judea's inundation by Ptolemaic government officials, merchants, soldiers and others was traumatic for many Jews. Jerusalem was no longer able to remain insulated from the outside world.

*A *boule*, or legislative council, met regularly; *archei* (heads) were chosen from this body for the management of day-to-day affairs. A *demos* composed of ordinary citizens met from time to time.

Many of Jerusalem's inhabitants welcomed this change. The opportunities and attractiveness afforded by other cultures were not to be denied. The silver coins minted by the Jerusalem authorities between about 300 and 250 B.C.E. provide a striking expression of the positive response of the city's Jewish political leadership to Hellenistic influence. These coins bear representations of the Egyptian ruler Ptolemy I, his wife Berenike and an eagle—the symbol of Ptolemaic hegemony. The presence of these motifs on Jewish coins is a clear attestation of a desire, at least by some, for successful integration into the new world order.[4]

A further example of the ties between Jerusalem's ruling elite and the wider Hellenistic world is documented in the correspondence between the Jewish High Priest Onias II and Areus, king of Sparta, around 270 B.C.E. According to 1 Maccabees (12:5–23) and Josephus,[5] a bond was forged between the citizens of Jerusalem and the people of Sparta, who saw themselves as descendants of Abraham and who sought to forge an alliance with Jerusalem. The text of the letter, as reported by 1 Maccabees 12:20–23, reads:

> Areus, King of Sparta, to Onias, the High Priest, greetings. A document has been discovered concerning the Spartans and Jews that they are brothers and that they are both of the seed of Abraham. And now, since these matters have become known to us, please write us concerning your welfare. We in turn write to you that your cattle and property are ours, and whatever belongs to us is yours. We have ordered that you be given a full report on these matters.

The practical ramifications of this letter are unknown, but some 125 years later Jonathan the Hasmonean renewed these ties. It is also noteworthy that between these two instances of correspondence, Jason, the former high priest, sought refuge in Sparta (2 Maccabees 5:9), clearly indicating some sort of tie between these cities. While scholars differ as to the authenticity of the third-century B.C.E. epistle, there nevertheless seems to have been some sort of connection between the two cities that would attest to the political-diplomatic integration of Jerusalem into the wider Hellenistic world.

In the various excavations conducted in Jerusalem over the years, more than 1,000 jar handles bearing the official stamp of Rhodes have been discovered. Based on the names of Rhodian priests inscribed on them, these handles are dated from the late fourth to the first century B.C.E., with most dating from the mid-third to the mid-second century B.C.E. These jars were used for wine imported throughout the eastern Mediterranean. Clearly, the inhabitants of Jerusalem imported Rhodian wine for their use; the assumption sometimes made that the wine was intended for the small pagan garrison in the city is most unlikely. On the other hand, it is likewise improbable that these finds attest to a wholesale rejection of the laws of idolatrous wine intended to distance Jews from anything associated with pagan cults. It is much more likely that such prohibitions did not as yet exist, and that many Jerusalemites availed themselves of this luxury commodity. Once again, archaeological remains point to the integration of Jerusalem in the wider Hellenistic world, this time with regard to international trade.

Nevertheless, it should be noted that other wine-jar handles discovered in the city point to a more conservative dimension of Jerusalem society. There were several types of locally made jar handles—one with the inscription *Yehud* in ancient Hebrew script and another with a five-pointed star inscribed with the word "Jerusalem." These stamps emphasize the Jewish component of the city and were probably used for taxed goods and administrative purposes. Or they may indicate the place where the jar or its contents originated.

Assessing the Jewish reaction to Hellenism

It is difficult to assess how Jewish society as a whole responded to this new reality. Did the isolated geographical circumstances of Jews (who lived primarily in the more remote hill country of Judea), combined with ethnic and religious differences, create a buffer between them and the outside world? Or were Jews affected by these changes in the same ways as were their pagan counterparts in the coastal cities, albeit at a somewhat slower pace? Unfortunately, our sources cannot answer these questions adequately. The bits and pieces that have been preserved offer but an inkling of the many and varied Jewish responses to the challenges of the new age. Generally speaking, the divisions in Jewish society deepened as a result of Hellenistic domination, the polarization of political allegiances into factions favoring the north (Seleucids) and south (Ptolemies), the exacerbation of economic and social divergences, and challenges to traditional religious beliefs and practices.[6]

However, the degree of Hellenization among Jews during the Hellenistic period (from Alexander's conquest to the establishment of the Hasmonean monarchy in 141 B.C.E.) remains unclear. Leading scholars have staked out maximalist and minimalist positions; some view the impact of Hellenism as having been profound (Bickerman, Hengel),[7] others see it as having been more negligible and superficial (Tcherikover, Sandmel, Millar).[8] Both positions contain some truth, and the reality was undoubtedly much more complex than either extreme would suggest. Much depends on whom we are referring to (an urban aristocrat or village farmer), the specific time period involved (the fourth or second century B.C.E.) and the particular areas of society under scrutiny (material culture, religious beliefs or social institutions). Much of the Jewish literature written or edited during the early Hellenistic period grapples with ideas from the outside world. The biblical Book of Ecclesiastes (Qohelet)

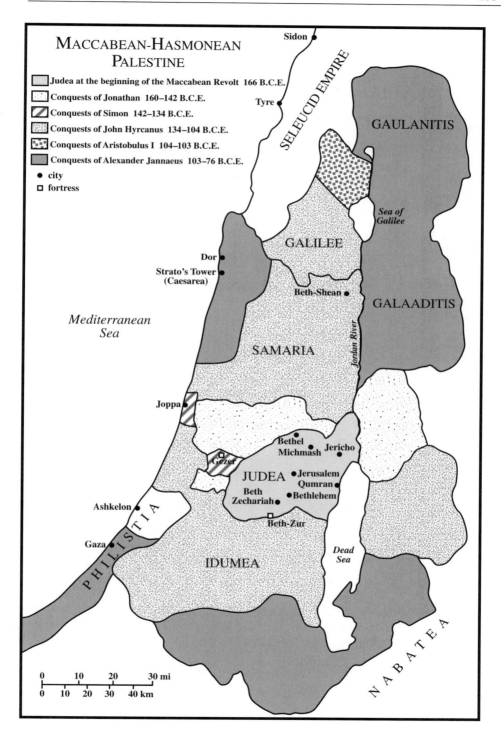

MACCABEAN-HASMONEAN
PALESTINE

Judea at the beginning of the Maccabean Revolt 166 B.C.E.
Conquests of Jonathan 160–142 B.C.E.
Conquests of Simon 142–134 B.C.E.
Conquests of John Hyrcanus 134–104 B.C.E.
Conquests of Aristobulus I 104–103 B.C.E.
Conquests of Alexander Jannaeus 103–76 B.C.E.
● city
□ fortress

Sidon

SELEUCID EMPIRE

Tyre

GAULANITIS

Sea of
Galilee

GALILEE

Dor

Strato's Tower
(Caesarea)

Beth-Shean

GALAADITIS

Mediterranean
Sea

SAMARIA

Jordan River

Joppa

Bethel
Michmash

Jericho

Gezer

JUDEA

Jerusalem
Qumran

Beth
Zechariah

Bethlehem

Ashkelon

PHILISTIA

Beth-Zur

Gaza

Dead
Sea

IDUMEA

NABATEA

0   10   20   30 mi
0   10   20   30   40 km

remains the most explicit and detailed statement that we possess of the disturbing impact of this new environment on a Jew's religious and intellectual commitment.[9] Faith and certainty had been lost, and in their stead came doubt, hesitancy and skepticism. At the turn of the second century, Ben Sira composed a response to this type of thinking, called in Latin *Ecclesiasticus* (the little Ecclesiastes),* which emphasizes loyalty to traditional values, ideas and institutions. The Book of Jubilees at times seems to deliver a polemic in support of such basic commandments as circumcision (Jubilees 15:23–34) and the Sabbath (Jubilees 2:17–33), perhaps in response to a certain laxity in their observance resulting from exposure to the outside world. Finally, the erotic love song that came to be called the Song of Songs was probably edited about this time and reflects themes well attested in Hellenistic poetry.[10]

The apocalyptic literature that originated in this period (for example, the early portions of Enoch) exhibits further indications of outside influences. This literary genre is characterized among other things by descriptions of heavenly journeys, angelic revelations of cosmic secrets to man, visions of the end of days, and the final judgment to be meted out by God on the world. The second half of Daniel (7–12), written in 165 B.C.E., is the best-known example of this type of literature. Nonetheless, scholars are divided as to the source of this apocalyptic literature and worldview. Are these compositions the direct result of earlier prophetic literature from biblical times that underwent a series of transformations between the fifth and third centuries? Or are they the result of new developments in Jewish society relating to exposure to Hellenistic apocalyptic literature and thought? While certitude in this matter is elusive, the parallels with the non-Jewish world are significant enough to warrant some sort of connection with contemporary phenomena.

In this regard, mention should be made of the Letter of Aristeas, which tells of the translation of the Torah into Greek under the auspices of Ptolemy II Philadelphus (285–246 B.C.E.). The translation was reportedly carried out by 72 sages, each knowledgeable in the Torah and well versed in Greek, who were brought from Jerusalem to Alexandria for this express purpose. (This tradition accounts for the common name of the translation: the Septuagint, from the Latin for "seventy.") If there is any truth in this tradition, it would testify to the penetration of Greek thinking into scholarly Jerusalem circles by the third or, at the very latest, second century B.C.E., when this translation was purportedly made.

How much these intellectual and religious currents affected Jewish society at large is hard to gauge; the limited evidence offers conflicting

---

**Ecclesiasticus was included in the Greek translation of the Bible known as the Septuagint and remains a part of the Catholic Bible. For Jews and Protestants it is part of the Apocrypha.

signals. On the one hand, after the Seleucid ruler Antiochus III conquered Jerusalem (about 200 B.C.E.), he granted privileges to the Jews of the city that appear to confirm the traditional status and leadership of the city. The elders, high priest, priests and other Temple personnel were recognized as the leaders of the community and were accorded due privileges. The concerns expressed in Antiochus's edict focus on the Temple, the cult, religious precepts and the welfare of the city, and such issues undoubtedly stood at the forefront of Jerusalem affairs for decades, if not centuries.[11]

On the other hand, this almost idyllic picture becomes clouded when viewed from other perspectives. The Jewish historian Josephus, for example, records a chronicle of the Tobiad family, who represented Jewish interests to the Ptolemaic court in Alexandria and who played a major role in internal Judean affairs as well. The Tobiads underwent a significant degree of acculturation during this period, adopting Greek names, mannerisms and lifestyles.[12]

A second example of a more complex situation is preserved in 2 Maccabees 4. The Seleucid kings were often in desperate need of money to pay their annual tribute to Rome. In 175 B.C.E., Jason, a Jerusalemite of priestly lineage, offered the newly enthroned Seleucid monarch Antiochus IV (Epiphanes) a sum of money to appoint him as high priest in the Jerusalem Temple. Jason then added an additional amount for the right to convert Jerusalem into a Greek *polis*. This probably meant that Jerusalem's inhabitants would be registered as citizens of a *polis*, that the city would be restructured politically, that social institutions would be reorganized in the spirit of a Greek city, and that a *gymnasium* and *ephebium** would be established.[13]

There is no question that this was an extremely bold step. Yet it is not clear to what degree Hellenization had penetrated Jewish society at that time. Phrased differently, did Jason have the backing, either active or passive, of a large segment of the population, or was this program of Hellenization only a superficial mimicry of Greek mannerisms by a small elite of Jerusalem society? Was this a sudden and dramatic step with little forethought or planning, or was it the culmination of a long process? These fundamental questions cannot be answered with any certainty.

Nevertheless it is abundantly clear that by 175 B.C.E. many leading Jerusalemites, especially priests, were committed to a high degree of acculturation. Although we do not know the immediate reaction to Jason's initiative, during the years that followed Jewish society was rocked by a series of events that shook it to its very foundations.

---

*These institutions were traditionally established for the training of Greek citizens. The *gymnasium* was roughly equivalent to today's high school with an emphasis on physical as well as academic subjects; the *ephebium* was a more advanced school specializing in military training.

The heavy hand of Antiochus IV and the rise of the Maccabees

Soon after Jason bought his way into the high priesthood and Jerusalem became a *polis*, the Seleucid overlord Antiochus IV visited Jerusalem (probably in 173 B.C.E.) and was greeted by the populace with a torchlight procession and overwhelming acclamation. At about the same time, the city sent a delegation to participate in the athletic games at Tyre, on the coast of Phoenicia. It is telling that the Jewish members of this delegation felt uncomfortable about offering the customary gift to the local deity at the opening of the games and instead gave their money to the host city's fleet.

In 172 B.C.E., another Jerusalem priest, Menelaus, sought to follow Jason's precedent by bribing the Seleucid king to appoint him high priest in place of Jason. To meet his financial commitment, however, Menelaus was forced to plunder the Temple treasury, an act that enraged the populace. Only with great difficulty was the ensuing violence quelled. Tension remained between the followers of Jason and Menelaus.

Violence flared up again in 169–168 B.C.E., this time provoked by Antiochus IV. First he pillaged the Temple, causing some destruction. He then returned and, with unbridled fury, suppressed the unrest caused by Jason's challenge to Menelaus's authority. Massacre followed pillage, and fire destroyed parts of the city.

This time the Seleucid forces did not leave the city, and Antiochus appointed a military commander over Jerusalem, placed a garrison there and built a fortress called the Akra, which stood in the city for 27 years.[14] Jerusalem churned with discontent, as it was clear that the presence of pagan troops meant the introduction of foreign cults into the Holy City. The Akra was conquered only in 141, after Simon the Hasmonean rose to power.

The precise location of the Akra remains unclear since no remains have been firmly identified. Written sources such as 1 Maccabees and Josephus contradict one another, and at times themselves, with regard to important details. Josephus, for example, claims that the Akra was located in the lower city, that is, the City of David, yet was higher than the Temple Mount—a situation that defies explanation in light of the area's topography.[15] In contrast, 1 Maccabees (13:52) emphasizes the proximity of the Akra to the Temple, noting that after its conquest the Akra was transformed into Simon's palace. But according to Josephus, the Akra and the mountain on which it stood were completely destroyed.

Some have suggested that the Akra was located in the City of David; some have claimed that it was located on the hill of the Temple Mount (in the area of today's Jewish Quarter). Others have suggested that the Akra was northwest of the Temple Mount, where the Herodian fortress, the Antonia, was later built; still others have placed it south of the Temple Mount, either opposite the Ḥuldah Gates or near the Temple Mount's southeastern corner. Just as the question of its location is shrouded in mystery, so too are other important details regarding the Akra—the composition of its population, its size, its economic functions and its political standing, as well as its relations with the rest of Jerusalem.

About a year after Antiochus attacked the city, in the month of Kislev (December), 167 B.C.E., the king issued a decree that banned circumcision, religious study and religious observance (including the Sabbath and festivals), and that forced the Jews to commit what they considered the most unpardonable of sins—worshiping idols and eating forbidden foods. Antiochus proceeded to desecrate the Jews' most holy site by introducing idolatrous worship into the sacred Temple precinct itself.

Why did Antiochus do this? The major sources (1 and 2 Maccabees) differ, as do modern historians. It is clear, however, that Antiochus's decrees were entirely unprecedented. Religious persecution had been hitherto unheard of in the pagan world. A conqueror might impose his deities on a local population, but he would never prohibit the practice of local traditions.

Whatever can be said of Antiochus IV, his personality and quirks, he was educated in the best of Hellenistic traditions. Religious persecution was not part of his cultural or political heritage. Aware of the *sui generis* nature of this policy, historians have sought alternative explanations: The extreme Hellenizers under Menelaus were the real instigators of this upheaval (Bickerman, Hengel);[16] Antiochus was following a policy of religious persecution learned while in Rome (Goldstein);[17] Antiochus's religious persecution was part of an attempt to suppress a revolt that had already broken out in Jerusalem and that had a clear-cut religious character (Tcherikover).[18]

Whatever the causes, these persecutions had enormous consequence for subsequent Jewish history. The immediate reaction was one of confusion. Some Jews saw no way to respond other than to acquiesce passively. A number of Jews fled to the nearby Judean wilderness and perhaps beyond, outside the borders of Judea. Others despaired of worldly measures and took refuge in mystical-messianic aspirations of divine intervention and salvation (see, for example, Daniel 7–12).

In the year following the imposition of these decrees, armed conflict broke out in the remote town of Modi'in in northwestern Judea. It was this response, however, that eventually led to a radical reshaping of Jewish society. The Modi'in uprising was organized and led by a priest named Mattathias and his five sons, Judah Maccabee,* Simon, Johanan, Eleazar and Jonathan. Eventually these sons would reestablish, for the first time in 450 years, a sovereign state and a new dynasty of Jewish kings, the Hasmoneans.**

---

*The additional name Maccabee was given to Judah and was later applied to the entire family as well. Thus far, no satisfactory meaning of this name has been suggested.

**The name Hasmonean refers to an ancestor of Mattathias. It later became a family title of the Maccabees (*Antiq.* 12.265; *War* 1.36).

The struggle
for an
independent
Jewish state

The Hasmonean rise to power, however, was a long and arduous process that succeeded only after a 25-year struggle. This quarter-century may be divided into four distinct periods:

1. *166–164 B.C.E.* These were years of continual guerrilla warfare. Under the command of Judah Maccabee, the Jews attacked the Seleucid armies as they attempted to reach Jerusalem and reinforce their garrison there. Seleucid forces approached the city from almost every direction—north, northwest, west and south—but each time they were defeated and their weapons appropriated to arm the ever-growing Hasmonean forces. The heroic and almost always victorious Hasmonean military efforts are vividly recorded in both 1 and 2 Maccabees.[19] The only inconclusive battle was fought at Beth Zur (south of Jerusalem), in the spring of 164 B.C.E., and a temporary armistice was declared as a result of the joint intervention of Jewish Hellenists and Roman envoys.[20] Six months later, however, Judah Maccabee and his troops surprised the Syrian garrison in Jerusalem, captured the city, purified the Temple and reinstituted the Jewish sacrificial rites. This occurred in the month of Kislev, 164 B.C.E., exactly three years after the persecution of the Jews had commenced. The recapture of Jerusalem, cleansing of the Temple and reinstitution of sacrificial rites are celebrated by Jews to this day with the festival of Hanukkah.[21]

2. *164–160 B.C.E.* These years were marked by a number of dramatic changes in the fortunes of the hitherto victorious Maccabees. Having purified the Temple, the Hasmoneans proceeded to avenge Jews who had been attacked by gentile neighbors. Troops were dispatched to Transjordan, to the Galilee and to the Mediterranean coastal region. Many Jews were brought back to Jerusalem for resettlement. The success of these campaigns won the Hasmoneans unprecedented popularity.

But in 162 B.C.E. the Hasmoneans' fortunes plummeted. Antiochus V sent his Seleucid army to crush the rebels, and at a battle near Beth-Zechariah, south of Jerusalem, the Seleucids were victorious.[22] They were denied the full fruits of their victory, however, when word came of a major crisis in Antioch that required the immediate presence of the commander, Lysias, and his troops. A hasty but, from the Jewish viewpoint, favorable peace treaty was arranged, in which the decrees banning the practice of Judaism were officially revoked. The Jews, for their part, accepted as high priest one Alcimus, a moderate Jewish Hellenist. Most of the population appears to have been satisfied with this compromise, including the Hasidim, a pietist group that had joined the rebellion at its inception.[23] Only the Hasmoneans rejected this arrangement, and they were thus effectively isolated and forced to withdraw from Jerusalem.

In 161 B.C.E. Maccabean political and military fortunes changed once again, this time for the better. Judah Maccabee mustered a sizable

Hasmonean Rulers of Judea, 142–37 B.C.E.

Simon	142–134
John Hyrcanus	134–104
Aristobulus I	104–103
Alexander Jannaeus	103–76
Salome Alexandra	76–67
Aristobulus II	67–63
John Hyrcanus II	63–40
Mattathias Antigonus	40–37

army at Adasa, north of Jerusalem, and defeated the Greek general Nicanor in a major battle. His victory, though impressive, was short-lived. A year later a new Syrian army appeared in Judea, this time under the leadership of Bacchides. In a pitched battle, in which the Jews were badly outnumbered, Judah Maccabee was killed. Any Hasmonean hope of regaining political power was dashed.[24]

3. *160–152 B.C.E.* These were years of ebbing Hasmonean fortune. Few Hasmonean partisans remained in Jerusalem. At first members of the family fled to the region of Teqoa in the Judean wilderness, southeast of Bethlehem. Driven from there, they resettled at Michmash, near Bethel in northeastern Judea, where they lived in semi-isolation, removed from the arena of power and bereft of any titles or privileges.

4. *152–141 B.C.E.* This was a period of Hasmonean ascendancy that culminated in the establishment of an independent sovereign Jewish state. The change came about fortuitously.

In 152 B.C.E. Alexander Balas and Demetrius, both pretenders to the Seleucid throne, sought to win the support of Jonathan, Judah Maccabee's brother and leader of the Hasmoneans, by outbidding one another in the offering of privileges and honors. Finally, Jonathan threw his weight behind Demetrius, an act for which Jonathan was richly rewarded. He was made high priest, permitted to maintain troops and given extensive tax benefits. Thus, despite their quasi-exile during the previous eight years, the Hasmoneans remained the only Jewish element in the country capable of mustering a sizable force. This was ultimately the decisive factor. With the benefits received from Demetrius, Jonathan was soon in firm control of Jewish society and was recognized as the undisputed representative of the Seleucids in Judea.

It is ironic that, less than a quarter of a century earlier, the Hellenizers Jason and Menelaus had acquired the high priesthood by bribing a gentile king. Now the Hasmoneans followed suit; instead of bribes, the Hasmoneans paid with services to be rendered. As Seleucid officials, Jonathan and his brother Simon served the kingdom loyally, at one time even dispatching 3,000 troops at the Seleucid king's request in order to quell an uprising in Antioch. During this decade the Hasmoneans were awarded more territories in northern and northwestern Judea.

However, Jonathan soon fell victim to the same intrigues and political machinations between royal pretenders that he had previously exploited to his own advantage. He was killed in 143 B.C.E. by forces opposed to his patron king.

Simon, the last of the Maccabean brothers, then assumed the high priesthood and political leadership. He immediately drove out the remnants of the Syrian garrison and the Jewish Hellenizers from the Jerusalem Akra. Then, in an impressive public ceremony in 141 B.C.E., he declared his independence from Seleucid rule.

Accounting for the Maccabees' success

Looking back over these 25 years, we must ask ourselves why the Hasmoneans succeeded as they did. Much of their success was undoubtedly due to the charisma of members of the family itself. Their achievements in battle, their purification of the Temple and their willingness to give their lives in defending the Holy Temple and the Holy City accorded them a strong claim to leadership. They were able to consolidate large sectors of the Jewish population. Elders, rural and urban leaders, priests, Levites and others all participated in Simon's coronation ceremony, so vividly described in 1 Maccabees 14. In addition, the Hasmoneans' tenacity in pursuing their political goal, despite all obstacles, put them in a position to take advantage of any opportunities that might—and indeed did—present themselves.

Finally, the Hasmoneans were blessed with good fortune on the international front. The mid-second century B.C.E. saw the decline of the two major Hellenistic powers, the Ptolemies and the Seleucids. The political vacuum in the region was quickly filled by petty ethnic kingdoms (e.g., Itureans, Nabateans) and independent city-states (e.g., Tyre, Sidon, Ascalon). Precisely at this time the Hasmoneans, too, strove for political independence; they took full advantage of these circumstances to reach their end. Only once before in the history of Israel had a similar situation occurred, in the tenth century B.C.E., when David and Solomon carved out their far-flung and powerful kingdom.

Combining political and religious power

With the emergence of the Hasmonean state, the political circumstances of the Jewish people were radically altered. The power and trappings of a self-governing political entity were now introduced into Jewish society. Control of the various societal institutions carried with it enormous authority and influence. From the outset, the Hasmoneans defined themselves as the supreme leaders of the people, both in politics and religion. Having already been appointed to the high priesthood (Jonathan, as noted above, had been appointed high priest with Demetrius's help in 152 B.C.E.), they assumed two more titles in 141 B.C.E.—leader of the people and commander of the army (*strategos*). A generation later, in 104 B.C.E., the title "king" was adopted and from that time several generations of Jewish kings ruled Judea.

Combining the political authority of a sovereign state with the highest religious title in the land (that is, high priest) was indeed an innovation in Jewish history. Earlier, in the First Temple period, the high priesthood stood beside the monarchy; priest and king functioned as two distinctly independent sources of authority. Similarly, in the period following Hasmonean rule, Herod would clearly separate these two realms, reserving the political one exclusively for himself and relegating the religious one, with its decidedly secondary status, to others. The combining of these two realms by the Hasmoneans proved to be explosive, in both a positive and a negative sense, as it provided an ideological component that motivated and justified the most daring of political and military policies.[25]

One of the most remarkable achievements of the Hasmoneans was their radical redrawing of the map of Judea. What had once been a small, isolated subprovince in the Persian period and in the early Hellenistic period (after Alexander's conquest) became, by the end of the Hasmonean era, a major political entity embracing all of modern Israel (except for the southern Negev and the northern coastal area), parts of southern Lebanon and western Jordan.

Expanding Hasmonean rule

Simon, who ruled the new state from 142 to 134 B.C.E., made a major military push to the northwest, toward the sea. He conquered Gezer, expelled its Gentile inhabitants, purified the town and resettled it with observant Jews (1 Maccabees 13:43–48). From Gezer he proceeded to Joppa, which, once taken, served as the major seaport emporium for the Hasmonean state.

Simon's son and successor, John Hyrcanus, ruled for 30 years (134–104 B.C.E.) and, like his father, expanded the country's borders dramatically. Broadening his hold along the coast and even establishing a presence east of the Jordan River, he devoted his major efforts to countering the various ethnic groups living in the hill country—the Idumeans in southern Judea and the northern Negev and the Samaritans to the north.[26] Hyrcanus probably conquered the Galilee as well, although the composition of its population at the time is unknown.

Hyrcanus was succeeded by his son Aristobulus I, the first Hasmonean to adopt the title "king." Although he ruled for only one year (104–103 B.C.E.), he successfully annexed Iturean territory in southern Lebanon.[27]

Aristobulus was succeeded by his brother Alexander Jannaeus (103–76 B.C.E.), the last and perhaps greatest military leader of the

Hasmonean dynasty. Jannaeus annexed new territories in almost every direction. In the northwest, he gained control of Strato's Tower (later Caesarea) and Dor; in the southwest, he took the coastal district, including Gaza, one of the major Hellenistic cities of the time; in the northeast, he overran much of the Golan and Gilead (today's northwestern Jordan); and to the southeast, he conquered large areas of Moab.[28]

The control of neighboring peoples, cities, important trade routes and major ports was an obvious motivation that directed the course and extent of these Hasmonean conquests. The religious-nationalist dimension, however, was no less significant a factor in Hasmonean policy. The Hasmoneans regarded themselves as the successors of the great leaders of the past—the judges and the kings of First Temple times. This is clearly, albeit subtly, reflected in 1 Maccabees, written under Hasmonean patronage toward the end of the second century B.C.E. Both the overall language and the specific terms it uses are reminiscent of the books of Judges and Kings, consciously drawing an analogy between the Hasmoneans, on the one hand, and the development and institutionalization of Jewish political leadership in biblical times, on the other.[29] The book culminates with Simon's coronation, described in 1 Maccabees 14. The carefully crafted account frequently alludes to the glorious days of King Solomon.

Another touch in the same vein: Hasmonean coins bore the ancient Hebrew script that was used in the First Temple period, rather than the square Aramaic script in use at the time. This was undoubtedly a conscious attempt by the Hasmoneans to identify their rule with the earlier Davidic monarchy.

Hasmonean religious ideology

In the religious sphere, the Hasmoneans were committed to ridding their territories of all idolatrous practices. Religious purification of the land became a basic policy. Sometimes this meant driving out pagan inhabitants altogether and then purifying the site; at other times, conversion of the populace was required. Entire populations, both urban and rural, were thus brought into the Jewish fold. The two outstanding examples of this policy were the conversion of the Idumeans by John Hyrcanus and the conversion of the Itureans by Aristobulus I. How smoothly this policy was effected is difficult to determine. No mention of resistance is made in our sources, although undoubtedly some, either active or passive, must have occurred. It is hard to imagine, for example, that the ultimatum of conversion or death offered to the inhabitants of the Hellenistic city of Pella in the Transjordan did not meet with outright hostility and derision.[30]

The ideological component that accompanied the Hasmonean successes was a two-edged sword. On the one hand, it undoubtedly provided a significant additional impetus and motivation for the Hasmoneans' conquests, as well as a transcendent cause firmly rooted in a biblical faith that overshadowed ordinary political concerns. On the other hand, such an anti-pagan attitude was bound to stir up animosity. Hasmonean zealousness might easily be interpreted, perhaps correctly, as an onslaught against gentile values and the pagan way of life. Some of the earliest evidence of pagan anti-Semitism—such as the negative description of Jews and Judaism by Antiochus VII's advisors (as preserved by the Greek historian Diodorus) and the hostility of Posidonius of Syria (as noted by other early writers)—was in large part a reaction to Hasmonean anti-pagan drives. By the first century B.C.E. various anti-Jewish accusations were circulating widely: The Jews were misanthropes, Jewish religious precepts were engendering social animosity and moral perversion, Jewish worship in the Jerusalem Temple was primitive and barbaric, etc. Much of this anti-Jewish hostility seems to have been triggered by political and religious opposition to the Hasmoneans.[31] That many pagans and Jews viewed the Hasmonean conquests as part of a struggle for ultimate control of the country, a struggle in which each side claimed possession of the land, no doubt further exacerbated pagan sentiments.[32]

The Hasmonean combination of political power and religious ideology was equally problematic on the domestic front. Instead of being the art of the possible, politics was fraught with the tensions and passions born of ideological inflexibility. Indeed, the Hasmonean model of combining political and religious leadership was adopted by other elements in their society, particularly by religious groups. In contrast to the later Second Temple period, when the religious character of the various Jewish sects predominated, during the Hasmonean era the political involvement of such groups was paramount. For example, we find leaders of both major sects, the Pharisees and the Sadducees, holding seats in the ruler's inner cabinet. Toward the end of the second century B.C.E., the Sadducees worked hand in glove with John Hyrcanus, who favored the priestly aristocratic classes: The joint political machinations of the Sadducees and the followers of John Hyrcanus finally forced the Pharisees out of government.[33] The Pharisees, however, quickly became an active opposition; in fact, much of the unrest that occurred during the reign of Alexander Jannaeus was supported, encouraged and led by the Pharisees.[34] Open Pharisaic hostility and, at times, insulting behavior toward Jannaeus* finally led to severe countermeasures—including exile, persecution and even mass crucifixion. The opposition, for its part, went to the extreme of inviting the Syrian king Demetrius VI to attack Jerusalem. When the battle was finally joined, the Seleucid side was bolstered by Jewish dissidents and the Hasmonean side was reinforced by pagan mercenaries!

---

*According to Josephus (*Antiq.* 13.372), *etrogim* (small lemon-like fruits used in the Sukkot ritual) were thrown at the high priest on the pilgrimage festival of Sukkot.

Later, Jannaeus's wife and successor, Salome Alexandra (76–67 B.C.E.), reinstated the Pharisees and gave them complete control over the country's internal affairs. They lost little time in avenging themselves against the Sadducees and the wealthy aristocrats who had persecuted them earlier.[35]

The most extreme reaction to this situation was taken by members of another Jewish sect—the Essenes, or Dead Sea sect. In protest against the political and religious leadership of the Hasmoneans, the Essenes left Jerusalem and settled in a remote region of the Judean wilderness, where they awaited the removal of the Hasmonean leadership as part of the messianic drama that, in their opinion, was imminent.

Thus, the political involvement of religious sects in Hasmonean society was endemic. All groups—Sadducees, Pharisees and Essenes—were now organized politically. This injected into the political arena a passion and ideological rigidity that only increased tensions.

A unique synthesis of Hellenism and Judaism

In a quite different realm, the Hasmoneans established a pattern of behavior that deeply affected the cultural and social ambiance of Jewish society; they introduced into Hasmonean Judea a particular synthesis between Jewish and Hellenistic elements. Elias Bickerman has aptly described the Hasmonean attitude as a form of moderate Hellenism.[36] The Hasmoneans were keen to adapt Hellenistic forms to Judaism—rather than altering Judaism to conform to the dictates of Hellenism, as the extreme Hellenizers among the Jews had advocated. Perhaps there is no better indication of the Hasmonean desire to integrate the two worlds than the coins they minted. On these tiny bronze issues, intended as small change and used for propagandistic purposes, we find symbols and inscriptions that convey a clear-cut message: The Jewish and Greek worlds are not irreconcilable. The language is either Greek or Hebrew; only a few issues are in Aramaic, the Semitic language in everyday use at the time. The Greek inscription uses the Hellenistic title of the Jewish ruler (king) and his Greek name (Alexander [Jannaeus]); the Hebrew coins use his Jewish title (high priest) and his Hebrew name (Jonathan). Moreover, the Hebrew script is not the later Aramaic "square" form, but an older style in vogue during First Temple times, but until now not used in Second Temple times.[37]

The symbols on these coins are also an important indication of the Hasmonean attitude to the surrounding culture. None of the symbols is uniquely Jewish. The palm branch, anchor, cornucopia, wheel/star, etc., are found on Ptolemaic coins, Seleucid coins and the coins minted by various cities of the region (such as Gaza, Tyre and Ascalon). The only exceptions to this rule are two issues minted by Alexander Jannaeus's grandson and the last of the Hasmonean rulers, Mattathias Antigonus (40–37 B.C.E.); on these two issues we find the menorah and the table of the shewbread from the Temple. For the most part, however, these Hasmonean coins display symbols of pagan origin, albeit carefully selected. Only the most neutral symbols, those that bore no blatantly pagan overtones, were copied. Thus, a policy of compromise was adopted; Hellenistic symbolism was accepted as long as it was not offensive to Jewish concepts and practices then in vogue.

A similar contrast and synthesis is found at the magnificent Hasmonean winter palace excavated near Jericho.[38] Some of the finest amenities of the Hellenistic world were found there—a large swimming pool, baths, a grand pavilion, frescoed walls with geometric designs, carefully hewn Doric columns and friezes. Between the pool and palace, however, were a number of Jewish ritual baths (*miqva'ot*). These were used by the Hasmoneans who, in their role as priests, were required to be ritually pure before partaking of the free will offerings (*terumah*) given by the people. *Miqva'ot* were unknown in earlier periods; no archaeological remains of such installations have been uncovered at sites of pre-Hasmonean date, nor are they ever mentioned in biblical sources. The Hasmoneans not only adopted Hellenistic architectural styles and associated social-recreational amenities, they also maintained uniquely Jewish institutions such as the ritual bath.

ZEV RADOVAN, JERUSALEM

Hasmonean coin. *Hellenistic and Jewish iconography are blended in this bronze prutah minted by John Hyrcanus I (134–104 B.C.E.). The obverse depicts a double cornucopia, a pagan symbol, but one that was inoffensive to Jews.*

The reverse side of the coin, by contrast, demonstrates Jewish nationalism. The language of the inscription, including the name and title of the ruler, is Hebrew, not Greek: "Jehohanan the High Priest and the council of the Jews." Moreover, the coin is inscribed in an ancient Hebrew script used nearly a millennium earlier, at the time of the Davidic and Solomonic monarchies, as an expression of the Hasmoneans' identification with a glorious past, when Israel was first an independent nation.

Jewish society at large reflected this basic openness to Hellenistic influence, albeit with a significant amount of selectivity and adaptation in the process, which usually meant the rejection of overtly pagan forms.

Let us consider several examples. The funerary remains from the Jerusalem area, which reflect a great degree of outside influence, invariably imitate well-known Hellenistic models. The tomb of Jason, a wealthy Jerusalem aristocrat from the first century B.C.E., had a pyramidal form; the tomb of the sons of Hezir (Bnei Hezir) in the Kidron Valley east of the Old City followed another Egyptian tradition with its columned facade and adjacent funerary monument. The deceased were regularly buried in *kokhim* (*loculi*), small cavities, about the length and width of a human body, cut into the walls of caves. This form of burial was derived from Hellenistic models originating in fourth-century Alexandria. No less Hellenistic in origin were the tomb facades and series of outer courtyards (as at Jason's tomb). Columns, capitals, friezes and architraves of various Greek orders are always found in these tombs, and inscriptions are recorded in Greek, Hebrew and Aramaic. What is uniquely Jewish about these tombs, however, is their artistic expression; here we find a major break with the pagan world. Whereas figural representation is common on pagan tombs in Palestine (for example, at Marissa we find figures in a musical procession) and throughout the Hellenistic world, it is practically nonexistent on Jewish tombs.[39]

This absence of figural representation reflects a significant religious and cultural development in the Hasmonean era. Throughout the previous 1,000 years of Jewish history, figural representations had been common. The cherubs over the Holy Ark, the lions of Solomon's throne, the oxen supporting the huge basin in the Temple courtyard, the bronze serpent for healing used from the days of Moses until King Hezekiah's time, as well as the calves at the sanctuaries of Dan and Bethel all attest to the use of figural art in the biblical period. The innumerable figurines excavated at Israelite sites, not to speak of coins with human and animal depictions minted in Jerusalem in the late Persian and early Hellenistic periods, provide additional evidence of Israelite use of figural art. Commencing with the Hasmoneans, however, and continuing for about 300 years—through the time of Bar-Kokhba (died c. 135 C.E.)—the Jews manifested an almost total aversion to figural art. Josephus's writings and rabbinic literature, as well as archaeological remains from the late Second Temple period, all confirm a widespread adherence to this strict prohibition. Why this happened is not entirely clear. Perhaps it was a traumatic reaction to the decrees of Antiochus IV, who, to the horror of the Jews, introduced idols into the sacred Temple precincts; after all, the Second Commandment's proscription of images was essentially directed against idolatry. Or perhaps it was due to the dominance under the Hasmoneans of a more conservative (Sadducean?) interpretation of the Torah generally and of the Second Commandment of the Decalogue in particular. Instead of banning only figural art for idolatrous purposes (the more lenient position taken earlier in the biblical period and, later, in the talmudic period), the Hasmoneans prohibited all figural depictions. In this reaction against regnant Hellenistic practice, the Jews clearly distinguished themselves from the surrounding culture.

Another illustration of the synthesis of Jewish and Hellenistic cultures—but with a heavy emphasis on Jewish particularism—is preserved in a small apocryphal work known as the Greek Additions to the biblical Book of Esther. These Additions attempt to give the Book of Esther a more pious, Jewish-oriented character. The biblical account as it stands raises some thorny issues. Why is God never mentioned? Why are no expressions of traditional Jewish piety, such as prayer, included? Why does a respectable Jewish girl like Esther marry a gentile king? And sleep with him? And eat from his table? The Additions deal with these issues by supplementing the biblical text with a particularistic religious tone advocating a pro-Jewish and anti-pagan outlook. What is especially fascinating—and indeed ironic—is that the Additions were written in fine Greek literary style, and in Jerusalem; moreover, they were written by a Jewish priest named Lysimachus and were brought to Alexandria by a levite named Ptolemy. For this reason, some highly educated and acculturated Jews (notice their names!) had made a clear bifurcation between their Hellenistic education and their strong Jewish loyalties.

People's names often indicate cultural proclivities. For this reason, in addition to the Hasmonean rulers who bore Greek names (Hyrcanus, Aristobulus, Antigonus, Alexander), many members of the leading political and diplomatic families of the Hasmonean kingdom also bore Greek names.[40]

Hellenistic influence was not restricted only to material culture (art and architecture) or to Greek names and language. It penetrated deeper, even affecting the religious institutions and religious beliefs of Hasmonean society. We have already discussed funerary practices.[41] Rabbinic sources shed light on developments regarding marriage laws. According to tradition, Simeon ben Shataḥ, a leading Pharisaic figure who flourished during the first half of the first century B.C.E., made a major alteration in the Jewish wedding ceremony: the introduction of the *ketubah*, the wedding document specifying the obligation of the groom toward his bride.[42] Previously, the groom had been required to set aside a sum of money or property for the bride's family, with whom he made the contract. This arrangement had its roots in earlier Mesopotamian practice. According to one rabbinic tradition, this arrangement made divorce too easy; the husband had little to lose, for whatever he owed the bride in the case of divorce had already been set aside. In the fourth or third century B.C.E. another arrangement, emanating from Egypt, was introduced into non-Jewish marriage contracts. The contract, negotiated directly between husband and wife, stipulated that in the case of divorce the groom was to pay the settlement from his own property; nothing was set aside at the time of marriage. This was intended to make divorce more difficult. Clearly inspired by Hellenistic models, Simeon ben Shataḥ seems to have introduced this Egyptian practice into the Jewish marriage ceremony some time in the early first century B.C.E.[43]

The impact of Hellenism on Pharisaic tradition was certainly not limited to the *ketubah*. In most cases, however, it is more difficult to trace. For example, as an institution of higher learning the Pharisaic academy (*beth midrash*) had much in common with the Greek philosophical school. The parallels are not so much in the material learned (although in the area of ethics, the overlap may have been quite recognizable),[44] but rather in the nature and organization of this institution. The *beth midrash* was a school of higher learning open to all, with rules governing its operation similar to those of the Greek philosophical schools. The relationship between master and pupil in the *beth midrash* and the principles of exegesis applied there also resembled those of its Greek counterpart.[45] Since no similar institution existed in Palestine before Hellenistic times, and as influences from the Greek academy permeated Pharisaic-rabbinic tradition later on as well,[46] it seems quite probable that the creation of this Jewish institution was inspired by the Greek model.

Several other Pharisaic concepts, such as afterlife in the form of carnal resurrection and the concept of a dual law (written and oral), may also have originated outside of Jewish tradition. Neither has clear-cut biblical roots, and both can be found, in one form or another, in non-Jewish (Greek and Babylonian) traditions.

No discussion of foreign influences on forms of Judaism during the Hasmonean period can ignore the evidence from the Dead Sea caves at Qumran. Time and again it has been demonstrated that the ideology of the Qumran sect was replete with concepts and practices quite different from biblical formulations and remarkably similar to concepts of the surrounding, especially eastern, Hellenistic world.[47] Ideas such as dualism, predestination, astrology, angelology and demonology, the particular notion of wisdom and the spirit, as well as the use of a solar calendar, can all be traced to Hellenistic, especially eastern Hellenistic, models. Other institutions at Qumran— communal living, the concept of "community" (*yahad*), initiation rites, the penal code, celibacy and asceticism—although new to Judaism, have striking parallels elsewhere.[48]

Explaining how such an array of outside influences reached a Jewish sect like the Essenes at Qumran is a formidable challenge. When one considers the fact that, of all groups, the Essene community at Qumran was the most self-consciously isolationist, having physically divorced itself from the rest of society, such massive foreign influence becomes even more perplexing. Several explanations have been offered, yet none seems entirely satisfactory. They all suppose that such influences were early and that the Qumran community for which we have evidence, was probably unaware of the origins of these traditions. One explanation, for example, assumes that the sect originated in the eastern Diaspora (Babylonia) and that by the time it reached Judea it had already absorbed and internalized these concepts.[49] Another suggests that these foreign ideas were current in Judean society of the Hellenistic period and that the forerunners of Qumran adopted them quite early on as an integral part of the legitimate religious and cultural baggage of their environment.[50] Whatever the explanation, the fact remains that such extensive influence on a major Jewish sect of the period is indeed astounding.

In surveying Hasmonean society as a whole, therefore, it becomes evident that no area of society and no sector of the population remained entirely unaffected by Hellenistic culture. The question is only a matter of degree—how much, in what areas, with what intensity, and which parts of the population?

The Hasmonean state has often been portrayed as a reaction against Hellenism, a reassertion of Jewish nationalist and religious will in the face of the demands, temptations and outright coercion of the larger world. This view, however, is only partly true and, as such, a distortion. In a more profound sense, the Hasmonean state must be viewed, at least in part, as a product of Hellenism, as an affirmation of the surrounding culture no less than a rejection of it, an expression of national sovereignty nourished and shaped by its international context. Thus, the Hasmonean state embodied a new Jewish disposition that incorporated a resurgent Jewish identity with varying expressions of Hellenism. Most Jews were prepared to adopt into their lifestyle many forms of Hellenism, albeit in varying degrees and with certain adjustments and changes.

Jerusalem, the Temple and the priests under Hasmonean rule

The creation of the Hasmonean kingdom had a revolutionary effect on Jerusalem, its capital city. Since the beginning of the Second Temple period in the sixth century B.C.E., Jerusalem had occupied a small area that included only the ancient City of David and the area of the Temple Mount. Altogether, the city encompassed some 30 acres; its population numbered only about 5,000 or 6,000. This situation had prevailed for nearly 400 years (c. 540–140 B.C.E.). Then, suddenly, in the short period of Hasmonean rule, Jerusalem expanded more than fivefold, stretching over more than 160 acres and numbering approximately 30,000 inhabitants. It encompassed the entire western hill (Mt. Zion) as far as today's Citadel of David (adjacent to the Jaffa Gate). Remains of the Hasmonean city wall have been discovered in the Jewish Quarter of the Old City, in the Citadel itself and on the slopes of Mt. Zion. In many places this wall followed the same course as the Israelite one of First Temple times; in fact, Hasmonean builders were not only aware of this earlier enceinte, but they even integrated parts of it into their later fortifications.[51]

A precise dating for this wall is almost impossible. Although the literary sources are replete with references to construction of the city's fortifications under various Hasmonean rulers, none ever explicitly mentions any large-scale expansion of the city limits. Moreover, archaeological evidence for dating the wall is scant and inconclusive. Since there were several stages to the Hasmonean wall (as seen most clearly in the Citadel area), it would appear that it was first built in the second century B.C.E., probably under Jonathan or Simon, and subsequently repaired and reinforced periodically.[52]

Jerusalem's population during this period was overwhelmingly, if not exclusively, Jewish: The priests were the leading class within Judean society; they not only controlled the most important institution within the city (the Temple), but they were also an integral part of the local aristocracy. With the rise of the Hasmonean state, priests played a leading role in its religious, political, diplomatic and military affairs. For example, the names of emissaries sent to Rome, Sparta and elsewhere indicate that they were almost always of priestly stock.[53]

Evidence of priestly prominence has also been found in the aforementioned tomb of Jason (almost certainly a priest) and that of the Bnei Hezir family (also of priestly origin; see 1 Chronicles 24:15), and in the abovementioned Additions to Esther, written by a Jerusalem priest.

The priestly caste was undoubtedly a varied group. Some were Hellenistic enthusiasts, such as Jason, Menelaus and others who reportedly flocked to the *gymnasium* instead of performing their Temple duties. On the other hand, Josephus recounts the heroic efforts of the Jerusalem priests during the siege of the city by the Roman general Pompey in 63 B.C.E. Despite near starvation, they faithfully continued to perform their cultic obligations. Some were even massacred by the Romans while fulfilling their priestly duties.[54]

Although the geographical focal point of Jerusalem had been the Temple and the Temple Mount in the First Temple period,[55] power and prestige were nevertheless divided among three different types of leaders—the king, the high priest and the prophets. Each had his sphere of influence and each operated in a different setting: the king from his palace and through his bureaucracy, the high priest in the Temple and the prophet in the marketplace. By the early Second Temple period this power structure had been dramatically altered. Kingship and prophecy had disappeared and were replaced by the wealthy aristocracy (for example, Nehemiah) and the scholar-scribes (such as Ezra). From then until the destruction of the Temple almost six centuries later (in 70 C.E.), the priesthood—with but few exceptions—reigned supreme; the high priest became the religious and political leader of the people, both internally and *vis-à-vis* the ruling authorities.

In the early Hellenistic period, at the time of Ptolemy I (323–285 B.C.E.), the high priest Hezekiah is mentioned as a leader of the people.[56] As noted, in the third century B.C.E., Sparta communicated for diplomatic purposes with the high priest Onias I.[57] The high priest Onias II served as representative of the people before the Ptolemaic court in Alexandria.[58] Another high priest, Simon the Just, was praised by Ben Sira as a leader of his people in the late third century B.C.E.[59] The high priest Jason radically altered the political and cultural institutions of Jerusalem in 175 B.C.E.[60] So the stage was set for the Hasmoneans to culminate this process by combining the high priesthood with the most extensive temporal power enjoyed by a Jewish ruler since 586 B.C.E.—political sovereignty and command of the army.[61]

The importance and prestige of the Temple increased under Hasmonean rule as a result of the enhanced political status of the Hasmonean state. The sanctity of the Temple as the quintessence of Judaism is reflected in a particularly interesting way in 2 Maccabees, which was produced under Hasmonean auspices for political and religious purposes. This book is a summary of a larger, now lost, five-volume work written in the mid-second century (c. 150 B.C.E.) by Jason the Cyrene. It summarizes the events that took place in Jerusalem and Judea between 175 and 160 B.C.E. (until the death of Judah Maccabee). The book was written, however, in the early years of John Hyrcanus's reign (about 120 B.C.E.) to impress the Jews of Alexandria with early Hasmonean military and religious achievements—their triumph over the Seleucids, their purification of the Temple and the celebration of Hanukkah. Aside from the obvious historical value of 2 Maccabees, it is an important statement of Hasmonean propaganda. The sanctity of the Temple is its central theme. The book begins and ends with the preservation of the Temple's purity, focusing on the purification of the Temple in 164 B.C.E. The political message of 2 Maccabees is clear. It was the Hasmoneans who fought and shed their blood for the sake of preserving the sanctity of the Temple, and this fact grants them legitimacy and authority in the eyes of the people.

A number of practices emphasizing the centrality of the Temple had already developed by the first century B.C.E. These practices, which appear to have originated in the Hasmonean period, became widespread and normative in the late Second Temple period. Large-scale pilgrimages to Jerusalem by Jews of the Diaspora, Judea and the Galilee, as well as the half-shekel annual contribution, were nurtured and encouraged by Hasmonean leaders.[62] These practices not only enhanced the political and religious status of the Hasmoneans but also emphasized that Jerusalem—with its Temple—was the spiritual center of world Jewry.

Finally, the most prominent institutions of the period were located in the Temple precincts or on the Temple Mount. It served as the ritual center for the nation's many varied celebrations over the course of the year; it was also the meeting place of the highest courts of the land, and possibly of the *ḥever ha-yehudim* (the governing body of the high council of the Jews), apparently a representative body mentioned on Hasmonean coins. One of the important city markets that served Temple needs operated there, and leaders of the different sects taught their disciples in these precincts.

No other institution in Jewish society rivaled the Temple in its sanctity and importance. Despite the absence of explicit references to the presence of a synagogue in Judea proper, there can be little doubt that this institution had already begun to evolve by the Hasmonean era. Nevertheless, although the synagogue appears to have had a distinctly communal nature with a number of religious functions (such as reading Scriptures, translating them into Aramaic, and giving sermons), it in no way challenged the supremacy of the Temple. This remained true throughout the Second Temple period; only after the destruction of the Temple in 70 C.E. did the synagogue develop its own unique religious profile.[63]

In the Hasmonean period, the religion of the ordinary Jew focused to a large extent on the Temple, its rituals and requirements. Aside from making offerings to priests and Levites, a Jew was obligated to bring the first fruits (*bikkurim*), as well as the first produce of his flocks, to Jerusalem. Moreover, four times every seven years he was to spend a tithe of his earnings within the bounds of Jerusalem. These obligations were in addition to the half-shekel contribution and the requirement (often unobserved by those living at a distance) to be present in the Holy City on each of the three pilgrimage festivals (Passover, Sukkot and Shavuot). As the occasion arose, individual Jews would go to the Temple to offer sacrifices for personal reasons—a sin or guilt offering, a free will offering, an offering in fulfillment of a vow or following childbirth.

Pharisees, Sadducees, Essenes and others

Aside from the Temple, the various sects served as the other major religious frameworks in this period. The term "sect" or "sectarian" requires some comment, however. In Christian terminology, a sect is a group that has severed itself from a mother church because of dissent from policies, personalities or ideologies regnant in a given society. The Essenes were the only Jewish group of this period that seems to fit this definition. The Pharisees, Sadducees, Hasidim and others, however, were associations that operated within the framework of Jewish society and its institutions, accepting the basic premises and parameters of the society while competing for religious and political preeminence.[64] Nevertheless, we will use this term in reference to all religious associations and affiliations during this period.

The growth of such groups was a direct result of the religious revolution introduced by Ezra. With the demise of prophecy and the establishment of the written Torah as the basis of Jewish life, Judaism attained a greater degree of democratization. The word of God was no longer confined to a charismatic personality; now anyone could offer an interpretation of the Torah, and if he commanded a following his group constituted *de facto* a sect within Jewish society.[65] Whether this or that particular group sustained itself in the course of time and developed a unique and appealing ideology and *halakhah* (religious law) was a matter of history. No authoritative body made such a decision. Our sources are completely silent about what kinds of sects, if any, developed in the centuries immediately following Ezra. However, with the rise of the Hasmoneans this situation changed dramatically.

The three sects mentioned specifically by Josephus—the Pharisees, Sadducees and Essenes—appear to have originated and crystallized in the mid-second century B.C.E. All extant sources, literary and archaeological, attest to this dating. The earliest remains of the Dead Sea sect at Qumran are from about 140 to 130 B.C.E. According to rabbinic sources, the earliest Pharisaic sages known by name flourished in the 160s and 150s B.C.E., and these sources likewise claim that the Sadducees emerged some time in the mid-second century B.C.E.[66] Similarly, Josephus's first reference to these sects is in connection with events at the time of Jonathan the Hasmonean,[67] in about 150 B.C.E. While some scholars have tried to find earlier traces of these groups—in the fourth and third centuries B.C.E.—their conclusions are largely speculative and unconvincing. Not only do all available sources point to the second century as the time of these sects' origins, but historical circumstances tend to support such a date. The political upheavals of this period—the transformation of Jerusalem into a *polis*, Antiochus's persecutions, the Maccabean revolt and, finally, the establishment of an independent state—undoubtedly affected the religious life of the society in a profound way. The sects we have mentioned were in large measure a reaction and response to these developments.

The Sadducees

The Sadducees offer a clear example of this phenomenon. With the usurpation of the high priesthood by Jason, Menelaus and, ultimately, the Hasmoneans, the sons of Zadok divided into three separate groups. Around 150 B.C.E., one branch of this family, the adherents of Onias IV, erected a temple in Leontopolis in Egypt under Ptolemaic auspices to rival the Jerusalem Temple then under Hasmonean control.[68] Another branch of the family withdrew to the Judean wilderness and was central in the formation of the Essene sect, as we shall see in more detail below. A third segment remained in Jerusalem, forming an alliance with the Hasmonean ruling power and becoming an integral part of that society for the next two centuries. These were the Sadducees* and they were largely, if not exclusively, a priestly aristocratic party commanding significant wealth and political prominence. Rabbinic literature[69] and Josephus[70] make this point patently clear.

One might have expected that the priestly sons of Zadok regarded themselves as the sole legitimate bearers of the priestly tradition and that they therefore arrayed themselves as implacable enemies of the Hasmoneans. This indeed happened with the first two branches of the

---

*A number of explanations have been offered for the etymology of the Hebrew word "Sadducee"; it probably derives from "Zadok," the name of the high priest in the time of David whose heirs served in that role throughout the Second Temple period.

family described above, those in Egypt and those who retreated to Qumran. With the third branch, however, pragmatism proved decisive; by working closely with the Hasmonean rulers, the Sadducees even succeeded in ousting their rivals, the Pharisees, from all positions of power toward the end of the reign of John Hyrcanus (c. 110 B.C.E.). Sadducean political ascendancy maintained itself right through the era of Alexander Jannaeus (103–76 B.C.E.), and only in the reign of Jannaeus's wife, Salome (76–67 B.C.E.), did the Pharisees again rise to power and remove their opponents from all positions of authority.

Undoubtedly, the basis for Sadducean power lay in their claim to priestly status. As such, they were recognized as the official religious authorities of the people, as servants of the God of Israel in his holy sanctuary and as guardians of the Torah tradition. Josephus claims that the Sadducees found their most loyal adherents among the wealthy, and not the populace.[71] Moreover, members of the priestly class served not only as diplomats but as military leaders.[72]

We are at a distinct disadvantage in our effort to understand the Sadducees, however, because they have left us no written documents. Whatever information we have originated in circles distinctly hostile to them. Rabbinic and New Testament material preserves many traditions about the Sadducees; the Dead Sea Scrolls provide some information and Josephus mentions this group on rare occasion. Each of these sources is openly critical of Sadducean ideology and conduct.[73] What the Sadducees might have said about themselves would have certainly been significantly different. Contrary to popular belief, no consistent halakhic (religious-legal matters) or ideological pattern can be discerned in our sources regarding their positions in disputes with the Pharisees regarding religious law.[74] At times, the Sadducees were more lenient than the Pharisees; at other times, they were more rigorous. Sometimes they adopted a strict constructionist approach toward the biblical text, sometimes they did not. In several disputes, they clearly took positions reflective of their wealthy, aristocratic background; in others, this dimension is not at all evident.

Josephus notes several doctrines associated with the Sadducees: They denied the notion of immortality of the soul, rejected any concept of future reward and punishment, and espoused a doctrine of unlimited free will.[75] Perhaps the most significant tenet differentiating them from the Pharisees was their clear-cut distinction between the Torah of Moses, which they regarded as divine, and all other laws and regulations, which they considered man-made and thus religiously unauthoritative. These nonbiblical laws and regulations were of an *ad hoc* nature and carried no imperative for later generations. For the Sadducees, all laws and regulations, aside from the Torah, merely had the status of decrees, valid for specific times and places, and no more.[76]

The Pharisees, perhaps the best known of the sects at the time and **The Pharisees**
the one destined ultimately to shape Jewish life to our own day, also
crystallized in this period and, as noted, played a central role in
Hasmonean political and religious life.

The name "Pharisee" appears to derive from the Hebrew *parash*,
meaning "separate" or "stand apart." We do not know what the first
Pharisees objected to or what they stood apart from. Many suggestions have been offered: They opposed the dominant priestly class,
the emerging Hasmonean dynasty and its political-military policies,
those who were lax in the observance of purity and tithing laws, and
those overly enamored with Hellenistic influences—or some combination of the above.

Our primary sources also reflect this same vagueness regarding the
basic thrust of early Pharisaism. Josephus, for example, describes the
Pharisees, along with the Sadducees and Essenes, as an essentially
philosophical sect. According to him, Pharisaic beliefs and opinions
were, in the final analysis, not only distinctive, but decisive. It was their
views of reward and punishment after death, their synthesis of free will
and determinism and their belief in the sanctity of the Oral Law that
ultimately prevailed. On the other hand, rabbinic sources emphasize
not the philosophical views of the sect but a plethora of halakhic matters, particularly differences between Pharisees and Sadducees. These
differences ranged from holiday observances and cultic practices to civil
and criminal law, as well as purity and family affairs. Josephus emphasizes the Pharisees' involvement in Hasmonean politics; rabbinic literature, on the other hand, largely ignores this dimension, with the
notable exception of the career of Simeon ben Shataḥ, who lived
toward the end of the Hasmonean era.

Modern theories dealing with Pharisaic origins contrast strikingly.[77]
Louis Finkelstein, for example, views the Pharisees basically as an
urban proletariat whose outlook was dictated by social and economic
circumstances. Isaac (Fritz) Baer, on the other hand, claims that
Pharisaic roots are to be found in rural, pietistic circles that, perhaps
ironically, offer striking analogies with the surrounding Greek world.[78]

When all is said and done, however, we have very little solid evidence
regarding the Pharisees of the Hasmonean era. Josephus treated the sects
only peripherally in his various historical accounts, for he did not regard
them as the primary force in the nation's political events with which he
was preoccupied. Rabbinic literature, too, has preserved very little data
relating to the Pharisaic sages who lived at the time; we know a great
deal more about the Pharisees under Roman rule (63 B.C.E.–70 C.E.)
than we do about their predecessors. The overwhelming majority of
sayings attributed to the Pharisees in rabbinic literature comes from the
later sages, Hillel and Shammai, and their academies (Beth Hillel and
Beth Shammai). We thus have no idea how many of the anonymous

references to the Pharisees actually apply to the Hasmonean period. With but rare exception, it is impossible to date such material confidently. It is no less difficult to understand why so few traditions of these early sages were preserved by the later rabbis. The relatively large time gap between the Hasmonean period and the first redaction of rabbinic sources in about 200 C.E. may in part account for this phenomenon. Perhaps the later rabbis also harbored certain reservations about the political involvements and religious priorities of their distant forebears and thus chose not to include much of their material in the rabbinic corpus. Whatever the reason, this lack of any significant quantity of reliable information about the early Pharisees is a serious obstacle to understanding their place in Hasmonean society.[79] We will thus restrict ourselves to those aspects of early Pharisaism that are relatively well attested and free of controversy.

It seems clear that these early sages constituted a rather diverse group. On the one hand, they looked to the high priest Simon the Just of Zadokite stock as a forebear; on the other hand, an otherwise unknown Jewish savant, the Greek-named Antigonus of Socho, was also numbered among them. Some Pharisees dwelled in cities, others came from rural settings; they hailed from such diverse places as Jerusalem and Zereda in Judea and Arbel in the Galilee. One Pharisee was later recognized as a magician and miracle-worker (Joshua ben Peraḥia); another, Simeon Ben Shataḥ was reported to have been a relative of the royal family and part of the court entourage. The opinions of these Pharisaic sages were equally diverse, some being of an ethical nature, others cultic or narrowly ritualistic. Rarely were opinions voiced on social or political issues, with the striking exception of those expressed by Simeon Ben Shataḥ. Nevertheless, the Pharisees under the Hasmoneans appear to have been highly politicized.

Both Josephus and rabbinic literature claim that the Pharisees enjoyed a significant degree of popularity among the people.[80] Their prestige as religious figures apparently won them their political prominence. Little else seems to have been working in their favor. The Sadducees, as noted, were prominent in diplomatic, military and aristocratic circles, not to speak of their central role in Temple affairs. It is difficult to pinpoint any particular Pharisaic power base, either in the political, social or economic realm. Apart from Simeon Ben Shataḥ, there was no Pharisaic personality who played a major role in the affairs of state. Prominence and acceptance as religious figures were probably the Pharisees' chief political assets.

As noted, one of the basic Pharisaic doctrines distinguishing them from the Sadducees was that they considered their sect's Oral Law the authentic amplification of the Written Law of Moses. As such, the Written and Oral laws stood side by side, and one was incomplete without the other. The Oral Law provided the correct interpretation and application of the Written Law, although the Written Law remained the ultimate authority, the primary text and the basic parameter within which the Oral Law evolved and developed. The crowning recognition of the Oral Law as legitimate and authentic was the Pharisaic claim that it, too, was given at Sinai; God gave the Jews not only the Five Books of Moses but the Oral tradition as well. Armed with this notion, the Pharisees presented themselves to the people as the sole legitimate bearers of Mosaic tradition. This view of the Oral Law ultimately prevailed.

Oddly enough, though he mentions them last, Josephus describes the Essenes in far greater detail than either the Sadducees or Pharisees.[81] Although the Essenes' role in Judean public affairs certainly was not even remotely comparable to either the Sadducees' or Pharisees', it is possible that Josephus presents them in such detail because he thought his readers would be fascinated by a group exhibiting such curious and exotic behavior.

The Essenes

Josephus was probably right regarding the audience of his generation. The archaeological finds from Qumran have certainly increased our amazement at the Essenes. The descriptions of Josephus and Philo, in addition to the almost one thousand scrolls and fragments discovered in the Dead Sea Scroll caves, unfold before our eyes details of a sect unique in the annals of Judaism in late antiquity.[82]

At first scholars debated the identity of the Qumran or Dead Sea sectarians. Although the parallels between them and the Essenes (as described in our literary sources) are extensive and striking, some significant differences are also evident. For example, the scrolls speak of a war-oriented group; the literary sources, of pacifists; the scrolls and archaeological finds offer evidence for the presence of women in the sect; the literary sources speak of a group of celibate men. As a result of these discrepancies, almost every other organized group among the Jews—the Pharisees, Zealots, Sadducees, Boethusians and early Christians—has been mentioned as a candidate for identification with the Dead Sea sect. Nevertheless, a consensus has emerged over the last decades that the Dead Sea sect was indeed the Essenes. Whatever differences there are between the literary descriptions of Josephus and Philo, on the one hand, and the Dead Sea Scrolls, on the other, are to be accounted for in one of the following ways: The different characteristics refer to various subgroups within the Essene sect; the varying characteristics reflect different periods in the sect's history; the differences reflect tendentious presentations by Josephus and Philo, each for his own apologetic purposes.

The Essenes flourished during the last centuries of the Second Temple period and, like the Sadducees and Pharisees, they originated in the mid-second century B.C.E. From about 140 to 130 B.C.E. they moved to Qumran in protest against Hasmonean rule. (Their settlement was destroyed by the Romans in 68 C.E.) Although Qumran served as the group's headquarters, branches existed in other places as well, including perhaps Jerusalem.

The sect was a tight organization with rigorous rules for acceptance and clearly defined penalties and punishments. It was governed by a council of 12 that was headed by an "overseer" (*mevaqer*). Priestly influence was considerable, and the original founder, referred to as the Teacher of Righteousness, was himself a priest, as were the majority of the sects' leaders in each generation.

The sect was organized as a commune. There was no private property, and everything was produced communally and shared equally. Community life focused on meals, scriptural readings, instruction and religious and spiritual observances highlighted by communal prayer. Although marriage was permitted in certain subgroups, members of the Qumran community were generally celibate. The group therefore sustained itself from generation to generation by attracting a continuous stream of newcomers from Jewish society at large.

A crucial and distinctive feature of Qumran was its calendar. In contrast to the rest of Jewish society, which was governed by a lunar calendar (with periodic corrections), the Essenes based their calendar on solar calculations. The year was divided into 12 months of 30 days each. Every three months constituted a season. Seasons were separated from one another by a single day that was not counted in either season. The Essene year thus comprised 364 days. Holidays fell on the same day of the week each year. In addition to using a solar calendar, the sectarians regarded the sun as sacred. Prayer was directed to the east, and members were enjoined never to expose the private parts of their bodies to the sun. It has been suggested that the sect's calendar may have been the basic reason for its withdrawal from Jewish society. Believing that the lunar calculations were false and the holidays were thus not being celebrated at their "appointed times," as commanded by Scripture, the Essenes chose to distance themselves from other Jews to follow the biblical prescriptions in what they assumed to be the right way.[83]

There were other, no less distinctive, aspects of Essene Judaism. For one, the sect firmly believed in a messianic doctrine according to which the world was imminently coming to an end and they themselves would participate in this final drama. To emphasize their high degree of messianic expectation, the sect divided itself into battalions and even wrote a detailed scenario (the War Scroll) of the series of battles that would bring human history to its culmination. Perhaps the most distinctive type of literary genre found at Qumran was the *pesher*, a kind of scriptural interpretation that assumed that all messianic references in the Bible, particularly from the Prophets, were being fulfilled in the sect's own day.

Other components of Qumran ideology included dualism and predestination. The sect viewed the world as being governed by two conflicting forces, good and evil, each at times gaining the upper hand. Only in the end would the forces of good prevail. Even the heavens were divided into opposing camps of angels functioning in the service of these two forces. Just as the final denouement of the world had been carefully programmed in advance, so the life and fortunes of each individual were predestined. For the Essene, there was no room for individual free will.

The recovery of the Essene library at Qumran has greatly facilitated our understanding of ancient Judaism. Because many of the Essenes' ideas and customs seem to be unique within Judaism, they raise intriguing questions as to what the nature of Jewish religion really was at the time. What influence did this group have on Jewish society as a whole? Were Essene practices and beliefs *sui generis*, or did they reflect or, alternatively, have an effect on other segments of Jewish society as well? Given the striking parallels between the Dead Sea doctrines and communal organization, on the one hand, and those of early Christianity, on the other, these questions take on even greater import. No firm answers have been forthcoming to date, but there can be little doubt that future publication and study of these scrolls will have enormous bearing on our understanding of Jewish life in the Hasmonean period.

Popular Judaism

Only a small proportion of Jerusalem's population belonged to organized sects in the Hasmonean period. Many Jews were indeed influenced in one way or another by these sects, yet only a few became full-fledged members, undertaking the full rigors of sectarian life. Most of the populace in this period belonged to that vague group referred to as *'am ha-aretz*, a term used in rabbinic literature to refer to all those who are not Pharisees. According to some scholars, rabbinic tradition as expressed in the sources following the destruction of the Second Temple reflects the way of life practiced by the majority of the people even in the pre-70 C.E. era. However, this perception is romanticized; a Pharisaic-rabbinic tradition became the norm among the people only hundreds of years later, and the process did not peak until the Middle Ages.

What was the brand of Judaism that most of the populace followed in the Hasmonean period? What religious concepts and beliefs did they ascribe to at the time? Little is known about the religious life of the masses in this period. Our sources focus almost entirely on the various sects, whose influence on the majority fluctuated with the changing political and social circumstances. Nevertheless, we shall try to sketch out a number of basic guidelines of Jewish life in Jerusalem in the Hasmonean period.

The most important feature was the belief in one God who chose his people Israel and gave them the Torah. This revelation had a profound effect on the Jew as an individual and as part of a people. Accompanying the Sinaitic revelation was a covenant made between God and his people in which the former swore that Israel would be his chosen nation forever, and the Jews promised to do and to listen to all his precepts. Jews believed that observance of the Torah would bring reward while transgression would be punished. In addition, if the covenant was ever broken, it could be renewed through repentance (*teshuvah*). Based on a monotheistic tenet, Judaism accorded the highest significance to the sanctity of the Torah, the people and the Land, at the center of which stood the Temple and the Temple Mount in Jerusalem.

Jewish observance focused primarily on three areas: (1) Torah commandments, such as laws about forbidden foods and Sabbath observance; (2) agricultural laws, such as first fruits, tithes, etc.; and (3) Temple worship. There can be little doubt that many people set aside offerings of *terumah*, tithes and first fruits (perhaps even observing the sabbatical year laws) and also observed the Sabbath and holidays, in whatever manner; all these stood at the very center of Jewish observance for the masses. Many of these commandments were observed within the confines of the Temple, entrance to which was restricted to those who had purified themselves. In addition, Jews were obligated to donate a half-shekel to the Temple and to make a pilgrimage to the Temple on the three festivals. Many Jews visited the Temple for other reasons, such as offering sacrifices to expiate sin, after giving birth and to fulfill Nazirite vows. Other norms observed by Jewish society at the time included the avoidance of any figural representation as well as the total prohibition of any form of idolatry.

Archaeological finds—especially from the last 30 years—point to other types of behavior that were also widespread in Jerusalem at this time. For example, the Rhodian amphora handles discussed above disappeared in the course of the Hasmonean period. As will be recalled, about a thousand such handles were discovered in Jerusalem primarily from the third and second centuries B.C.E. But it appears that under the Hasmoneans, the prohibition of imported foreign wine was more strictly observed, and this development is reflected in the significant decline in the quantity of Rhodian handles from the late second and early first centuries B.C.E.

As already mentioned, ritual baths made their appearance in this period in Jerusalem as well as Judea. These baths were meant to help the public observe the purity laws. In biblical times, immersion was generally restricted to priests, as prescribed by the Torah.

In the second century B.C.E., however, "purity (concerns) burst forth in Israel," as an early rabbinic text tells us,[84] and thus interest in purity struck root among the populace. As a consequence, ritual installations were in demand throughout the country.[85] Evidence for the punctilious observance of these matters in the Hasmonean period may be found in many sources. The earliest Pharisees who flourished in this period discussed purity matters, and 1 Maccabees emphasizes the importance of purifying the land by eradicating idolatry (see the description of the purification of Gezer and the Akra [1 Maccabees 13:43–54]). Moreover, the Letter of Aristeas (305–306) mentions the custom of ablutions, and Jubilees traces the obligation of purification for a woman who has given birth to the days of Eve (Jubilees 3:9–11).

However, the clearest evidence for the importance of purity in this period is the building of ritual baths beside agricultural installations (wine and olive presses) in both cities and villages. More than 300 such baths have been discovered throughout Judea, half of which were found in the Jerusalem area. Although most of these installations are dated to the Herodian and post-Herodian periods, this custom had already begun in Hasmonean times and spread gradually over the following generations, to the time of the destruction of the Temple. Hasmonean ritual baths have been discovered in Jericho, Qumran and Gezer, and, although we have no evidence, some of the Herodian ritual baths were undoubtedly in use earlier as well.

There is much common ground among the various sectors of society regarding these customs. Nevertheless, there was often a lack of unanimity on how observances should be carried out, and not all precepts were observed by everyone. This is evident in the severe measures taken by John Hyrcanus in ensuring the giving of tithes.[86] Moreover, the *prozbol* enacted by Hillel the Elder later on, in Herod's day, was a measure taken to change the situation wherein many ignored the commandment to lend money to the poor close to a sabbatical year (when debts were considered canceled).[87] This practice was thus an example of laws, even some derived from the Torah, that were changed over time. Changes were introduced in other areas as well; fighting a defensive war on the Sabbath was permissible, and, later, Rabbi Yohanan ben Zakkai suspended the laws of the suspected adulteress (Numbers 5) and of the broken neck of the heifer (Deuteronomy 21). All these resulted from momentous social changes. Finally, in many cases customs differed from region to region within the country, as between the Galilee and Judea.

Despite all these differences, the Jews of the Hasmonean period were undoubtedly a unique and distinct people. What unified them was far greater than what divided them, especially when compared to the surrounding pagan cultures.

The end of
Jewish
sovereignty

Jewish sovereignty was lost to the Romans when Pompey conquered Judea in 63 B.C.E. Was this avoidable? Could the Hasmonean kingdom have averted the Roman conquest? Josephus answers in the affirmative, claiming that all was lost because of the internecine conflict between Hyrcanus II and Aristobulus II. These warring brothers brought ruin to their kingdom through their failure to present a unified front against Rome. Josephus was certainly correct in his appraisal that Hasmonean weakness contributed heavily to the demise of their kingdom. There is no doubt that, had the brothers coordinated their efforts and jointly negotiated with Pompey, they could have avoided such serious losses. However, Josephus is certainly wrong in suggesting that even a unified stand would ultimately have made a difference. Rome was destined to conquer the East irrespective of internal Hasmonean politics. The Hasmoneans could only have hoped to mitigate the conditions of conquest. By demonstrating a unified stand and a willingness to cooperate, their kingdom might have survived much longer and suffered less damage than it in fact did. Their behavior in this regard was a major political failure, one that cost them their independence and hegemony over Jewish society.[88]

EIGHT

Roman Domination

The Jewish Revolt and the
Destruction of the Second Temple

SHAYE J.D. COHEN
revised by Michael Satlow

THE ROMANS ENTERED JUDEAN POLITICS, IRONICALLY, BY INVITATION OF one Jewish faction that was in a power struggle with another. In 76 B.C.E. Alexander Jannaeus, the last great king of the Hasmonean line, died. He was succeeded by his widow Salome Alexandra, who herself died in 67 B.C.E. The royal couple's two sons, Hyrcanus and Aristobulus, then fought each other for succession to the throne. Both Hyrcanus (usually called by scholars Hyrcanus II) and Aristobulus (usually called Aristobulus II) appeared before the Roman legate in Syria, each asking to be recognized as the ruler of Judea. Other Jews appeared as well, asking the Romans to reject the claims of both; by this time many Jews were thoroughly disillusioned with Hasmonean rule.

The Romans at first supported Aristobulus II, but when they realized he was a potential troublemaker, a suspicion amply confirmed by subsequent events, they transferred their support to Hyrcanus II. Aristobulus considered fighting the Romans, but, realizing the overwhelming might of Rome and the hopelessness of his situation, he surrendered in 63 B.C.E. to the Roman general Pompey. The supporters of Hyrcanus opened the city of Jerusalem to the Romans.

But that was not the end of the battle for Jerusalem. Although the city was in Roman hands, many of Aristobulus's supporters garrisoned themselves in the Temple and refused to surrender. After a three-month siege and some fearsome fighting, however, the Temple fell to Pompey's legions (63 B.C.E.).

To punish the Jews for refusing to yield peacefully to Roman dominion, Pompey greatly reduced the territory under Jewish jurisdiction. The empire the Hasmoneans had created through war and struggle was dismembered at a single stroke. The high priest of Jerusalem now ruled only those areas populated by a heavy concentration of Jews, primarily Judea (the district around Jerusalem) and Galilee. Although these Jewish areas were not legally incorporated into the Roman Empire, they were now *de facto* under Roman rule.[1]

Pompey takes Jerusalem

Pompey's conquest of Jerusalem closed one chapter in Roman-Jewish relations and opened another. A hundred years earlier Judah the Maccabee had sought and obtained an alliance with the Romans, who were then just becoming the dominant power in the eastern Mediterranean. At that time, the Romans eagerly supported anyone who would help them weaken the power of the Seleucid kings of Syria. Judah's successors followed the same strategy of seeking Roman support in their struggles for independence from the Seleucids.

Gradually, Rome's power grew; her policy in the region, however, never wavered: Any power that might pose a threat to Roman interests was to be weakened. When the Jews were a useful ally against the Seleucids, they were embraced. When the Hasmonean state expanded, the Romans had no desire to see it become, in turn, a new threat to Roman interests. By the middle of the first century B.C.E., when the Romans at long last decided that the time had come to incorporate the eastern Mediterranean into their empire, the Jews were no longer allies but just another ethnic group that was to be brought into the inchoate imperial system.[2]

Although the struggle for succession between Hyrcanus II and Aristobolus II and their appeals for Roman support provided the occasion for the Roman takeover of the Hasmonean state, we may be sure that in one way or another the Romans would have found a satisfactory excuse to exercise hegemony over the Jewish state.

The three decades (63 to 31 B.C.E.) following Pompey's conquest of Jerusalem were extremely turbulent, not only for the Jews of Judea but for the entire Roman world, especially in the East. This was the period of the decline of the Roman republic, of the struggle between Julius Caesar and Pompey, of Pompey's death and Caesar's ascension to sole power, of Caesar's assassination (on March 15, 44 B.C.E.), and of the struggle between the senate and Caesar's supporters and later between Octavian (Augustus) and Mark Antony. The dust did not settle until the sea battle of Actium in Greece (31 B.C.E.), where Octavian defeated Mark Antony and became the sole ruler of the Roman Empire. During the 20s B.C.E. Octavian consolidated his power and assumed the name "Augustus." He established a pattern of imperial administration that would endure for centuries.

As the Romans were changing their mode of government, so were the Jews. Under the Persian and the Hellenistic monarchies, the Jews had been led by high priests who wielded political as well as religious power. However, during the initial period of Roman rule after Pompey's conquest of Jerusalem, the high priesthood lost virtually all its temporal powers and a new royal dynasty emerged that was not of priestly stock. Its opponents claimed that it was not even wholly Jewish! The Romans, for their part, were delighted to install a dynasty that owed its very existence to Roman favor and therefore could be counted on to provide loyal support.

This new dynasty, usually called the Herodian dynasty after its most famous member, was founded by Herod's father, Antipater the Idumean. The Idumeans, who lived in the area south of Judea, had been incorporated into the Hasmonean Empire and converted to Judaism by John Hyrcanus (Hyrcanus I). Antipater gradually insinuated himself into the circle of Hyrcanus II. When Julius Caesar came to Syria in 47 B.C.E., he conferred various benefits on the Jews. Hyrcanus II was appointed *ethnarch* (literally, ruler of the nation), and Antipater the Idumean was appointed *procurator* (literally, caretaker).

The rise of the Herodian dynasty

A rival soon assassinated Antipater, and his mantle then fell to his son Herod. In 40 B.C.E. the Parthians invaded Syria, captured Hyrcanus II and installed the son of Aristobulus II as king and high priest of the Jews. Herod, now the Roman procurator, fled to Rome and persuaded the senate that only he could restore Roman rule in Judea. With Roman support Herod returned to Judea and, after some severe fighting, reconquered Jerusalem in 37 B.C.E. Herod remained the undisputed leader of the Jews for over 30 years (37–4 B.C.E.).

The vast bulk of what we know about this period derives from the testimony of an ancient Jewish historian, Flavius Josephus. Josephus was a complicated man, and his writings are not always easy to work with. As one scholar notes, "Sometimes the historian working with Flavius Josephus feels like a lawyer forced to build his case in court upon the testimony of a felon. While there may be some truth in what the witness says, the problem always is to separate it from self-serving obfuscation and outright lies."[3] Because so much rests on Josephus's testimony, it is worthwhile to review certain aspects of his life and his works.

The reliability of Josephus

Josephus was a Jewish leader in the First Jewish Revolt (66–70 C.E.) who, in the end, surrendered to the Romans. In 67 C.E. Josephus was the commander of the Jewish revolutionary forces in Galilee. When the

Romans arrived, Josephus and his forces fled to the fortress of Jotapata. After a siege of 47 days, the fortress was taken, and Josephus and some of his men took refuge in a nearby cave. When the Romans discovered them, Josephus's companions argued that they should commit mutual suicide rather than be taken prisoners. But Josephus, remembering the "nightly dreams in which God had foretold to him the impending fate of the Jews and the destinies of the Roman sovereigns," realized that God was on the side of the Romans and that surrender to the Romans was the only legitimate course of action. Since his comrades insisted on suicide, Josephus reluctantly agreed to draw lots with the rest, but as luck would have it, he drew one of the last. After the others had killed themselves, Josephus was left with only one companion and had no trouble convincing him that surrender was a wiser course than death. Upon emerging from the cave Josephus was taken to Vespasian; he predicted that the general would become emperor of Rome, the master of land, sea and the entire human race—a prediction that subsequently proved accurate. Josephus's account of his surrender to the Romans is clearly a mixture of history, fantasy, apology and propaganda.[4]

After the Roman destruction of Jerusalem, Josephus was taken to Rome in the entourage of the Roman general Titus, Vespasian's son. With his newly acquired Roman patrons looking over his shoulder, Josephus wrote his account of the rebellion, *The Jewish War*, completing it in the early 80s C.E.

He wrote it originally in Aramaic, later translating the text into Greek; only the Greek version has survived. Josephus intended *The Jewish War* for an Aramaic-speaking audience, mostly Jews but also other Near Eastern peoples who were under—or on the verge of coming under—Roman domination. The book carries a dual message. To those who might contemplate revolt against Rome, *The Jewish War* advises "don't." Revolt against Rome is both impious and doomed to failure. To the Romans, the message is that the revolt was the work of various hotheads, fanatics and criminals within the Jewish community who in no way represented either Judaism or the Jews and who fomented rebellion for their own selfish and ignoble purposes. Josephus begins this book with the story of the Maccabean uprising (165 B.C.E.). The Maccabean victory established the Hasmonean dynasty, whose internal disputes led to Pompey's entry into Jerusalem, which, in turn, set in motion the chain of events that led to the revolt of 66 C.E. *The Jewish War* ends with a vivid account of the fall of the last Jewish rebels at Masada.

About a decade later, Josephus finished his second work, *Jewish Antiquities*. This is a much more ambitious project, written in Greek and intended to present the entire scope of Jewish history to a Roman audience. *Jewish Antiquities* begins with the biblical account of creation and ends on the eve of the Jewish revolt. Hence, it overlaps with much of the material from *The Jewish War*. Written at a time when the war was less immediate and political fortunes in both Rome and Judea had dramatically shifted, *Jewish Antiquities* is far more nuanced than *The Jewish War*. Shortly after publishing *Jewish Antiquities,* Josephus went on to write two more tracts: *Life*, an autobiography that responds to charges of betrayal (true or not, we do not know) by a rival Jewish historian, and *Against Apion*, an apologetic tract.

Political considerations, self-justification, and apologetic tendencies are not the only factors that make Josephus difficult to use. Like most ancient historians, Josephus was a plagiarist. He freely appropriated the work of others, often without letting his readers know his sources. These sources themselves are often biased. His primary source for his discussion of Herod, for example, was the writing of Nicolaus of Damascus, Herod's "official," thus hardly unbiased, historian.

Bearing Josephus's limitations in mind, let us return to Herod.

Herod is an enigmatic figure.[5] A tyrant, a madman, a murderer, a builder of great cities and fortresses, a wily politician, a successful king, a Jew, a half-Jew, a gentile—Herod was all these and more. He is perhaps best known to posterity as the murderer of several of his wives, children and other relations. The murders were prompted by Herod's suspicions (often justified) of anyone who had an equal or better claim to the throne than he. In the first years of his reign, Herod executed the surviving members of the Hasmonean aristocracy. Since he was married to Mariamme, the daughter of the Hasmonean king Hyrcanus II, Herod thus murdered his own wife's relatives—her brother, her aunt and her father. Finally, he murdered Mariamme too. At the end of his reign, he executed the two sons Mariamme had borne him.

Herod the Great

Herod also executed various other wives, sons and close relations. The Christian tradition of Herod's "massacre of the innocents" (Matthew 2) is based on his unpleasant habit of killing anyone associated with the old aristocracy, including many teachers and religious leaders.

Herod created a new aristocracy that owed its status and prestige to him alone. He raised to the high priesthood men from families that had never previously supplied high priests, including families from the Diaspora (the Jewish communities outside the land of Israel).

Herod was also a great builder. Many of the most popular tourist sites in Israel today were Herod's projects—Masada, Herodium, Caesarea and many of the most conspicuous remains of ancient Jerusalem, including the so-called Tower of David, the Western Wall and much of the Temple Mount. As a result of Herod's works, Jerusalem became "one of the most famous cities of the east"[6] and its Temple, which he rebuilt, was widely admired. In the new city of Caesarea, Herod created a magnificent harbor, using the latest technology in hydraulic cement and underwater construction. Herod also founded several other cities, notably Sebaste (on the site of ancient Samaria). He bestowed gifts and benefactions on cities and enterprises outside his own kingdom. Athens, Sparta, Rhodes and the Olympic games all enjoyed Herod's largesse.

Herod's building program had several purposes.[7] A network of fortresses (Masada, Herodium, Alexandrium, Hyrcania, Machaerus) was designed to provide refuge to Herod and his family in the event of insurrection. Herod rebuilt Jerusalem and the Temple so that his kingdom would have a capital city worthy of his dignity and grandeur and he would win the support of the Jews both in the land of Israel and in the Diaspora. Herod built Sebaste and other pagan cities (even Caesarea was a joint Jewish-pagan city) because he saw himself as the king not only of the Jews but also of the country's substantial pagan population. And last, but not least, the benefactions to the cities of the eastern Mediterranean were prompted by Herod's megalomania. Throughout his life Herod was hungry for power and prestige. He wanted desperately to be recognized as an important personage. He obtained that recognition through his lavish gifts. Even the city of Athens honored him with a public inscription.

Herod tried to win support and recognition from both the Jews and the pagans, both within his kingdom and outside of it. The support of these groups, however, would have meant nothing if Herod had not been supported by Rome. In 37 B.C.E., as we have seen, the Romans made Herod the leader of Judea. In the struggle that developed soon thereafter between Antony and Octavian, Herod supported Mark Antony. This was perhaps because Antony was headquartered in the East. But, as noted above, at the battle of Actium in 31 B.C.E., Octavian defeated Antony, and the entire eastern Mediterranean, including Egypt, came into the hands of Octavian.

Herod had supported the losing side. He was obviously in deep trouble. But, ever the survivor, Herod managed to convince Octavian that everyone's best interests would be served if he remained king of Judea. He had been loyal to Antony, Herod argued, and now would be loyal to Octavian. Octavian accepted Herod's argument and never had cause to regret his decision. Herod was true to his word, and during the course of his long reign was rewarded several times by the emperor (now called Augustus) with grants of additional territory.

Like all other vassal kings subservient to the Romans, Herod was authorized to govern his subjects as he pleased as long as he maintained peace and stability, did not engage in any unauthorized activities outside his kingdom and actively supported Roman administrative and military activities in the area. Herod knew his place and followed these rules. At home he was the tyrant, but in his dealings with the Romans he was ever the dutiful subject. Before engaging in any major enterprise (killing his sons, for example), he consulted the Roman governor of Syria or even the emperor himself.

Herod's popularity during his own lifetime is hard to estimate. Our major evidence, indeed virtually our only evidence, is provided by Josephus. His two books give somewhat varying appraisals. In the earlier work, *The Jewish War*, Josephus paints a portrait of Herod that is basically favorable: a brilliant and successful king who was plagued by personal disaster and calamity. Nevertheless, even here Josephus reports Herod's madness and the fact that he was widely hated. It is in *The Jewish War* that Josephus tells the (true?) story that Herod, fearing that his funeral would be an occasion for rejoicing among the Jews, planned to ensure general mourning by ordering that the distinguished men of the country be assembled and killed upon the news of his death. Nevertheless, as a rule, *The Jewish War* treats the king kindly and regards him as unfortunate rather than mad, and as powerful rather than unpopular. This is probably due both to the biases of Josephus's primary source, Nicolaus of Damascus, and by his desire not to question the wisdom of Augustus, the deified ancestor of Josephus's Roman patron. Here is the final verdict:

> In his life as a whole he was blessed, if ever man was, by fortune; a commoner, he mounted to a throne, retained it for all those years and bequeathed it to his own children; in his family life, on the contrary, no man was more unfortunate.[8]

Although *Jewish Antiquities*, completed in 93/4 C.E., repeats this verdict in almost identical words,[9] its perspective is somewhat different. *Jewish Antiquities* includes much more material unfavorable to Herod. *The Jewish War* either deemphasizes this unfavorable material or omits it altogether.

According to *Jewish Antiquities*, Herod maintained his rule through terror and brutality. His secret police were everywhere and reported to the king any murmurings of discontent. Many citizens were taken to Hyrcania, one of Herod's fortresses, never to be seen again. Herod is even supposed to have prohibited his subjects from assembling in public. These security measures were required because of the general dislike for Herod among the Jews.

Jewish Antiquities broadly recounts two major complaints the Jews had against Herod, aside from his violence and brutality. First was his violation of traditional Jewish laws. He built a theater and an amphitheater in Jerusalem (neither has yet been discovered by archaeologists) where he staged gladitorial games and other forms of entertainment that were foreign to Judaism and inimical to many Jews. He built pagan cities and temples, and seemed to favor the pagan and Samaritan elements in the population over the Jews. Furthermore, many of his judicial and administrative enactments were not in accordance with

Jewish law. Certain elements in the population were offended at his introduction of Roman trophies into the Jerusalem Temple and his erection of a golden eagle over its entrance.

The second reason for the general dislike of Herod was his oppressive taxation. Someone had to pay for Herod's munificent benefactions to the cities of the East, generous gifts to the Romans and extravagant building projects at home. The Jewish citizens of Herod's kingdom had to foot the bill, and they objected.

But if *Jewish Antiquities* condemns Herod in these respects, it also reflects a certain ambivalence. It includes pro-Herodian material as well. Even if in his private life Herod did not follow the traditional Jewish observances (for example, Jewish law does not approve of the murder of one's wife and children), in his public life he often took care not to cause offense. He built no pagan temples or cities in the Jewish areas of the country, and he ordered that only priests were to work on the construction of the sacred precincts of the Temple in Jerusalem. Coins he intended for use in Jewish areas of the country were struck without images. Foreign princes who wished to marry a woman of the Herodian house had to be circumcised first. Moreover, it is in *Jewish Antiquities* that we find reports of several reductions in taxes. Here, too, Josephus notes that Herod was conspicuously generous in the distribution of food to the people during a famine.

Because of the bad press Herod has received, both in Josephus and in the New Testament, he is occasionally vilified by contemporary scholars as a "malevolent maniac" or worse, but he is too complex a figure to be dismissed so easily. As we have seen, even in *Jewish Antiquities*, which is the major source of anti-Herodian material, we find a more nuanced picture. Herod aimed to be both king of the Jews and king of Judea; he benefited the Jews both of the land of Israel and of the Diaspora. But he never forgot that his kingdom consisted of other groups as well.

Perhaps Herod's policy was dictated by the fact that he himself was the offspring of one of these groups, the Idumeans, who had been converted to Judaism only three generations earlier. Herod's court historian, Nicolaus of Damascus, claimed that Herod was a scion of one of Judea's noblest families, which had returned from Babylonia in the time of the Persians; but Herod's detractors called him a "half-Jew," or even a gentile, because of his Idumean extraction.[10] His marginal status in the native Jewish community perhaps explains his eagerness to solicit the support of the Samaritans and the gentiles of the country. Herod was also an astute politician who never forgot that the key to his success lay in the hands of the Romans. Above all else, he was resilient and resourceful. Protected by his paranoia, he succeeded in reigning 33 years in a period of tremendous upheaval and instability.

Herod's death in 4 B.C.E. released the accumulated passions and frustrations of the people who had been kept in check by his brutality. As Herod lay on his deathbed, two pious men and their followers removed the golden eagle that Herod had erected over the entrance to the Temple and hacked the bird to pieces. Immediately after Herod's death, riots and rebellions broke out in Jerusalem, Judea, Galilee and the Transjordan (Perea). The leaders of the riots had diverse goals. Some were simply venting their anger at a hated and feared regime; others were eager to profit from a period of chaos and disorder; still others dreamed of ridding themselves of Roman rule and proclaiming themselves king.

These riots illustrate the underside of Herodian rule. Herod's high taxes and extravagant spending caused, or at least accelerated, the impoverishment of broad sections of the population. A clear sign of social distress was the resurgence of brigands—landless men who marauded the countryside in groups and were either hailed by the peasants as heroes (like Robin Hood) or hunted as villains. Brigandage had surfaced earlier, decades after Pompey's conquest in 63 B.C.E. Although Pompey himself had respected the Temple and the property of the Jews, the governors he left behind (Gabinius and Crassus) did not. They engaged in robbery and pillage; Crassus even plundered the Temple. Perhaps as a result of these depredations Galilee was almost overrun by brigands. In 47/6 B.C.E. Herod routed and suppressed the brigands. Several years later, they resurfaced and Herod again suppressed them. Brigandage reemerged in the years after Herod's death, especially, as we shall see below, in the period from 44 C.E. to the outbreak of the Jewish rebellion against Rome in 66 C.E. The impoverishment of the country and its consequent social distress were an unfortunate legacy of Herod the Great.[11]

From Herod's death to the First Jewish Revolt

During the first half of the first century C.E., the Romans used vassal kings to govern those areas of the eastern empire that, like Judea, were neither urbanized nor greatly "Hellenized" but were home to vigorous national cultures. Administration through a vassal king, a native aristocrat who could understand the peculiar ways of the population, was thought preferable to direct Roman rule. Thus, throughout eastern Asia Minor, northern Syria, and Palestine, native dynasts governed their territories in accordance with the wishes of the Romans. In accordance with this policy, after Herod's death, his kingdom was divided among three of his sons. Antipas received Galilee and Perea; Philip, the Golan heights and points east. Archelaus became ruler of the largest and most important part of Herod's kingdom—Judea. In 6 C.E., however, the Romans deposed Archelaus for misrule and Judea, along with Idumea, Samaria and much of the Mediterranean coast, was annexed to the province of Syria. Henceforth Judea was

Roman-Jewish relations

administered by functionaries in the Roman civil service known as *prefects* or (after 44 C.E.) *procurators*. The rest of the country remained in the hands of Antipas and Philip for another 30 years, but then became the domain of Herod's grandson Agrippa I. In 41 C.E. Agrippa I received from the emperor Claudius the kingship over Judea as well, thereby reigning over a kingdom almost as large as Herod's own. Agrippa I died, however, three years later, in 44 C.E.

After Agrippa's death, all of the Jewish portions of the country were governed by Roman procurators. For a few years, from the middle of the century until the end of the First Jewish Revolt in 70 C.E., a small piece of Galilee was given to Agrippa's son, known as Agrippa II, but otherwise, an overall change in Roman policy and administration was unmistakable. At the beginning of the first century, the land of Israel was governed by vassal rulers—men like Herod and his sons; by the middle of the century it was governed by Roman procurators (with the exception of Agrippa II). This same shift can be found elsewhere in the Roman East.[12]

Judea, on the other hand, was governed by Roman prefects from 6 C.E. Of the six or seven Roman prefects who governed Judea following Archelaus's deposition, most are bare names to us. Even Josephus has little to say about them. The exception is the Roman prefect Pontius Pilate (c. 26 to 36 C.E.). Pilate receives a negative assessment in the Gospels, in Philo, as well as in Josephus. According to the Gospels, Pilate massacred a group of Galileans (Luke 13:1) and brutally suppressed a rebellion (Mark 15:7), quite aside from crucifying Jesus. According to Philo, Pilate introduced into Herod's former palace in Jerusalem some golden shields inscribed with the name of the emperor Tiberius. The Jews objected strenuously, because they felt that any object associated with emperor worship, not to mention emperor worship itself, was idolatrous and an offense to the Jewish religion. Previous Roman governors had respected Jewish sensitivities in this matter, but Pilate did not. After being petitioned by the Jews, the emperor ordered Pilate to remove the shields from Jerusalem and to deposit them in the temple of Augustus in Caesarea, a mixed Jewish-pagan city. Josephus narrates a similar incident (or perhaps a different version of the same incident) involving the importation of military standards (which of course contained images) into Jerusalem. The people protested loudly, saying they would rather die than see the ancestral law violated. Pilate relented and ordered the images to be removed. Ultimately, Pilate was removed from office when the Jews complained to his superiors.[13]

When a procurator like Pilate was brutal or corrupt, the Jews could appeal to the governor of Syria or even to the emperor himself to remove the malefactor. But when the emperor was responsible for actions that were deleterious to the Jewish community, the Jews had nowhere to turn. This was the dilemma that confronted the Jews of both Alexandria and the land of Israel during the reign of the emperor Caligula (37–41 C.E.).

The Romans realized that Judaism was unlike the numerous other native religions of the empire; the Jews refused to worship any god but their own, refused to acknowledge the emperor's right to divine honors, refused to tolerate images in public places and buildings, and refused to perform any sort of work every seventh day. Aware of these peculiarities, the Romans, following the practice of the Seleucids, permitted Jewish citizens to refrain from participation in pagan ceremonies; allowed priests of the Jerusalem Temple to offer sacrifices on behalf of, rather than to, the emperor; minted coins in Judea without images (even if many of the coins that circulated in the country were minted elsewhere and bore images); and exempted the Jews from military service and ensured that they would not be called to court on the Sabbath or lose any official benefits as a result of their Sabbath observances. In many of the cities of the East, the Romans authorized the Jews to create *polituemata* (singular, *politeuma*) autonomous ethnic communities, that allowed the Jews to govern their own communal affairs.[14]

The mad emperor Caligula and his legate in Egypt withdrew, or attempted to withdraw, these rights and privileges. Riots erupted first in Alexandria—the "Greeks" (that is, the Greek-speaking population of the city, most of whom were not "Greek" at all) against the Jews. Exactly who or what started the riots is not clear. The root cause of the conflict, however, was the ambiguous status of the city's Jews. On the one hand, the Alexandrians resented the Jewish *politeuma* and regarded it as a diminution of the prestige and autonomy of their own city. On the other hand, the Jews thought that membership in their own *politeuma* should confer on them the same rights and privileges the citizens of the city had. The result of these conflicting claims was bloodshed and destruction. Aided by the Roman governor of Egypt, the Greeks attacked the Jews, pillaged Jewish property, desecrated or destroyed Jewish synagogues and herded the Jews into a "ghetto." The Jews were hardly passive during these events, and resisted both militarily and diplomatically. The most distinguished Jew of the city, the philosopher Philo, led a delegation to the emperor to argue the Jewish cause.

Riots in Alexandria

While in Rome Philo learned of another, even more serious, assault on Judaism by the state. Angered by the Jews' refusal to accord him divine honors, Caligula ordered the governor of Syria to erect a colossal statue of the emperor in the Temple of Jerusalem. Whether something more than coincidence ties together the anti-Jewish riots in Alexandria with Caligula's assault on the Temple is not clear, especially because of some uncertainty in the relative chronology of the two sets of events.[15] In any case, the rights of the Jews of Alexandria and the sanctity of the Temple in Jerusalem were threatened simultaneously. The Roman governor of Syria, Publius Petronius, realizing that the execution of Caligula's order to erect his statue in the Temple could not be accomplished without riots and a tremendous loss of life, procrastinated. In a letter to Caligula, Petronius explained that the matter should be delayed because otherwise it would interfere with the harvest; in a second letter, he asked the emperor to rescind his order outright. In the meantime, Agrippa II, who was a friend of Caligula's, convinced the emperor to rescind his demand. Caligula did so but was angered when he received Petronius's second letter, which indicated that Petronius had no intention of following the imperial order. In reply, Caligula ordered Petronius to commit suicide. Petronius received this ultimatum, however, only after he learned that Caligula had been assassinated. This brought to an end the potential troubles in the land of Israel. The troubles in Alexandria were settled by Claudius, Caligula's successor, who ordered both the Jews and the Greeks to return to the status quo: The Jews were to maintain their *politeuma*, but were not to ask for more rights than was their due.

Perhaps one of the most significant aspects of these events was the refusal of the Jews even to consider rebellion against the empire. In Alexandria, the Jews took up arms only in self-defense and only with reluctance—at least this is what Philo tells us. The Jews directed their fighting against their enemies, not against the emperor or the Roman Empire. In the land of Israel itself, when Caligula's edict to erect a statue of himself in the Temple became known, the Jews assembled before Petronius *en masse* and declared that he would have to kill every one of them before they would allow the Temple to be desecrated. But the Jews did not threaten rebellion. Instead, in anticipation of Mahatma Gandhi in India in the 20th century, they offered passive resistance. Because Petronius was an ethical man with a conscience, he was convinced by these mass demonstrations not to carry out his assignment. Even a governor with less moral fiber might have been persuaded by these tactics: Pontius Pilate removed the golden shields from Jerusalem after the Jews protested, declaring that they would rather be killed than allow the images to remain in the Temple. At no point in either story do "brigands" or revolutionaries make an appearance.

Agrippa I   Despite the success of this policy of passive resistance, the years after Caligula's reign saw the growth of violent resistance to Roman rule. Caligula's madness seems to have driven home the point that the beneficence of Roman rule was not secure, and that the only way to ensure the safety and sanctity of the Temple was to expel the Romans from the country and to remove those Jews who actively supported them.

This process might have been prevented had Agrippa I been blessed with as long a reign as his grandfather, Herod the Great. Instead, Agrippa I ruled for only three years (41–44 C.E.). Despite his short reign, he was a popular king; both Josephus and rabbinic literature have only nice things to say about him. In some respects he resembled his grandfather. He was a wily and able politician. He sponsored pagan games at Caesarea and bestowed magnificent gifts on Beirut, a pagan city. But, unlike Herod, he was not criticized for these donations, for in other respects he was Herod's superior. He lacked Herod's brutality. Whereas Herod refrained from flouting traditional Jewish laws in the Jewish areas of his domain, Agrippa was conspicuous for observing them. In the political sphere, he tried to attain a modest degree of independence from Rome. He even began the construction of a new wall on the northern side of Jerusalem; had it been completed, Josephus says, the city would have been impregnable during the Jewish revolt that erupted in 66 C.E.

Had Agrippa reigned a long time, perhaps the disaffected elements in Judea would have been reconciled again to foreign dominion. On Agrippa's death in 44 C.E., however, Judea once again became the domain of the Roman procurators. There was no longer a Jewish authority who, despite ultimate subservience to Rome, could satisfy Jewish nationalist aspirations.

Moreover, the procurators after 44 C.E. were incompetent and insensitive at best, corrupt and wicked at worst. A country that, even in the face of Caligula's assault on its religious sensitivities, had maintained peace was brought to rebellion after little more than 20 years of rule by the Roman procurators who followed Agrippa I. Josephus narrates a long string of minor incidents, disturbances, riots, assassinations and lootings, which, in retrospect, were forerunners of the Great Revolt against Rome. The participants in these incidents probably never realized that they were preparing the way for war. Nevertheless, various elements in the population were expressing their frustrations with the status quo, and the procurators were using the power of their office for fun and profit.

In the fall of 66 C.E., after Gessius Florus (who would be the last of the procurators) had stolen money from the Temple treasury (for overdue taxes, he claimed), a particularly violent riot led to the massacre of the Roman garrison in Jerusalem. The governor of Syria intervened, but even he failed to restore the peace. He was forced to withdraw from Jerusalem, suffering a major defeat. The Jews of Judea had rebelled against the Roman Empire.

Before recounting the story of this rebellion and its disastrous consequences, let us pause to look at the religious atmosphere generally and the social texture of Palestine in the first century C.E.

Variegated   Judaism at the time was a remarkably variegated phenomenon.*
Judaism   Above all, Judaism was a *belief* in the God of Moses, who created the
                   world, who chose the Jews to be his special people and who
                   rewarded and punished his people in accordance with their loyalty
                   to him. Judaism was also the *practice* of the laws and rituals that
                   Moses had commanded in God's name, most conspicuously the rit-
                   uals of circumcision, Sabbath and prohibited foods. The Jews vigor-
                   ously debated among themselves the precise meaning and content of
                   their beliefs and practices, but all, or almost all, were in agreement
                   over the general outlines.

Judaism during this period was different from, or at least was not
identical to, the religion of pre-Exilic Israel.[16] Judaism in this period was
a "book religion"; at its center was the recitation and study of a collection of sacred writings, the most important of which was the Torah
(Instruction) of Moses. By this time, many Jews had added two other
categories of sacred literature to the Torah: the Prophets and the
Writings. These three groups of writings together constitute the Bible,
called the Old Testament by Christians and the Tanakh** by Jews. Pre-
Exilic Israel, by contrast, did not have such a sacred book; to be sure, it
preserved in written form many sacred traditions, but it was not a "book
religion." Pre-Exilic Israelites communicated and communed with God
through the sacrificial cult in the Jerusalem Temple and through the revelations of the prophets. By Hellenistic times, however, and certainly by
the first century of our era, the institutional access to God through the
Temple and the charismatic access to God through the prophets were
being supplemented, and to some degree supplanted, by new forms of
piety, especially the regular prayer and study of scripture.

The institutional home of this new piety was the *synagogue* (assembly or gathering) or *proseuche* (prayer-house), which is first attested in
Egypt in the third century B.C.E. By the first century of our era, there
were synagogues not only in every Diaspora settlement but also
throughout the land of Israel. Archaeological remains of synagogues
from this period have been discovered at Masada, Herodium, Gamla
and various Diaspora sites.[17]

Pre-Exilic Israelite religion focused on the group, the community and
the clan; first-century C.E. Judaism, by contrast, focused on the individual Jew. First-century Judaism enjoined the individual Jew to sanc-
tify his (or her) life through the daily performance of numerous rituals. Sanctity was not restricted to the Temple; God's presence was

---

*The word "Jew" derives from the Greek *Ioudaios* and the Latin *Judaeus*, which originally
meant "an inhabitant or a native of the district of Judea; a member of the tribe of Judah."
The English equivalent is "Judean." However, by the Hellenistic period the term began to
have another meaning as well, one that approximates the English term "Jew." The Jews'
manner of life (their religion) was called *Ioudaismos*, "Judaism."
**Tanakh is an acronym for *Torah* (the Five Books of Moses), *Neviim* (the Prophets) and
Ktuvim (the Writings).

WERNER BRAUN

Synagogue at Herodium. *During the First Jewish Revolt against Rome (66–70 C.E.), the reception and dining hall of Herod the Great's former palace-fortress Herodium was transformed into a synagogue. Benches were added around the walls and four columns supported a new roof.*

In Hellenistic times, worship at the Jerusalem Temple was complemented by regular prayer and the study of scripture in synagogues. Following the Roman destruction of the Temple in Jerusalem in 70 C.E., synagogues became the center of Jewish religious life.

everywhere, and the Jew was to be continually mindful of this fact. Every moment was an opportunity for the observance of the commandments, the sanctification of life and subservience to God. Not only were the people of Israel collectively responsible to God, but each individual Jew was as well. The cult of the Temple, therefore, was supplemented by a religious regimen that focused on the individual rather than the group.

Prophecy too no longer was what it had been. Many Jews believed that prophecy had ceased, or at least had so transformed itself that it no longer had the prestige and the authority it had commanded when the classical prophets like Isaiah and Jeremiah of the eighth and sixth centuries B.C.E. spoke. Those Jews who continued to see heavenly visions and hear heavenly voices no longer saw and heard them in the manner of their predecessors. The new literary genre, called by modern scholars *apocalypse* (revelation), assigned a much greater role to complex symbolic visions and angelic intermediaries than did biblical prophecy. Apocalyptic thinking was dominated by a sense that the world was in the throes of a final crisis that would be resolved by the immediate arrival of the end of time. Not only were the *style* and the *atmosphere* of apocalypse different from those of biblical prophecy, but much of its *content* was different as well. In pre-Exilic Israel, the Israelites believed that God rewarded the righteous and punished the wicked in this world, and did so by rewarding or punishing either the actor himself or his children. By the first century C.E., this doctrine had been rejected, and replaced by the idea that every individual received his or her just deserts from God either in this world or in the world to come. Elaborate theories were developed about the rewards and punishments that awaited people after death or at the end of time, or both. Then there would be a resurrection of the dead and a final judgment, and the nation of Israel, the plaything of gentile kingdoms in this world, would finally receive its due; God would send a redeemer, either a human being or an angel, who would restore Israel's sovereignty. The nations of the world would then recognize the Lord and accept the hegemony of the Jews. These new ideas were widely accepted in society, even though apocalyptic literature was so esoteric that it could be appreciated only by a few.

The new ideas, rituals and institutions that gradually emerged were adopted in their most extreme forms by various pietistic groups, but they also had an impressive impact on broad reaches of the population. The evidence for "popular religion,"[18] either in the land of Israel or the Diaspora, is very meager, but the literary evidence of Josephus, Philo and the New Testament shows that popular piety included the study of Scripture and the participation in synagogue services on the Sabbath; observance of the Sabbath, the dietary prohibitions and various other rituals; separation from pagans and anything connected with pagan religious ceremonies; and pilgrimages to the Temple in Jerusalem for the festivals. Many Jews of Jerusalem, rich and poor alike, believed in the ultimate resurrection of the dead. This is demonstrated by their practice of reburial. A year or so after depositing a corpse in a temporary grave, they would dig up the bones, carefully arrange them in a special box known as an ossuary and place the ossuary in a cave or some other safe location. Thus the dead would be ready for the resurrection; all the bones were united safely in one place, awaiting reassembly.[19] In the Diaspora, the most conspicuously observed rituals, to judge from the testimony of pagan writers, were circumcision, the Sabbath and the dietary prohibitions (notably the avoidance of pork).

"Popular religion," at least in the land of Israel, also contained a strong element of the "magical" and the "miraculous." Magic brought divine activity into direct and immediate contact with humans. Teachers and holy men of all sorts roamed the countryside, preaching repentance and performing "miraculous" cures. Jesus spent much of his time exorcising demons and performing faith healings, but he was hardly unique in this respect. Holy men, who often modeled themselves to some extent on the prophet Elisha, answered the immediate needs of the populace, which was more concerned about good health and abundant harvests than about salvation and redemption.[20]

Given the growing tensions and explosive mix of interests in first-century Palestine, this religious ferment is not particularly surprising.[21] The major Jewish "schools"—the Pharisees, Sadducees and Essenes described by Josephus (discussed in the previous chapter)—continued through the Roman period. In addition to these groups, however, several new groups emerged in the first century C.E.: the Sicarii, various other revolutionary groups and, of course, the Christians. Josephus gives the impression that the countryside teemed with teachers and holy men. The diversity of religious movements within Judaism was a sign, and symptom, of the breakdown of social and religious order.

Pharisees, Sadducees and Essenes

Apocalyptic expectations accompanied the increasing number of varieties of Judaism and the authority assumed by charismatic figures. Some of these new groups were revolutionary apocalypticists, who believed that their activities would usher in the new age. Josephus, for example, tells the story of an Egyptian "prophet" who convinced a large crowd to ascend the Mount of Olives, "for he asserted that he wished to demonstrate from there that at his command Jerusalem's walls would fall down, through which he promised to provide them an entrance into the city."[22] The Roman procurator correctly perceived this as a challenge to his authority, and promptly had the crowd imprisoned and/or slaughtered. Josephus, in what he referred to as his "fourth philosophy," asserts that God was Israel's only king; this served as justification for active opposition to Rome. These groups fused their apocalyptic beliefs to their political activities. By opposing Rome they were doing God's will, reforming Judaism in accordance with their view of the divine plan.

Other Jewish apocalyptic groups were isolationist. These groups believed no less than the active ones that the end of time was imminent. But they rejected the idea that human activity would bring it about. The Essenes and Therapeutae fall into this category. As described by classical authors, the Essenes organized themselves in a strict hierarchy and lived a life of purity and Torah study while they waited for the new age. Philo describes the Therapeutae—located in Egypt—in similar terms. Our sources do not tell us when or why these voluntary groups formed.[23]

The scrolls found at the settlement at Qumran (the Dead Sea Scrolls), whether or not they were written by the Essenes or any other group know to us from our sources, reveal both the growing apocalyptic mood and the tendency toward isolationism.[24] Although this group established itself before the Romans entered Palestine, as time went on

Temple Scroll. One of the famed Dead Sea Scrolls, this text is named for its
detailed plans for a temple—perhaps a visionary one—to be built in Jerusalem.
Israeli archaeologist Yigael Yadin, who published the scroll, believed that it was
written by the Essenes, who considered it to be part of their Holy Scriptures, equal
in authority to the Pentateuch.

the group developed strikingly harsh and apocalyptic concepts. From
its beginnings as a group concerned with the impurity of the Temple
and the legitimacy of its priests, the Qumran community metamor-
phosed into the "sons of light" who eagerly anticipated—albeit in the
utopian future—their ultimate bloody triumph over the "sons of darkness." For those at Qumran, the "sons of darkness" included not only
the Romans but also, and perhaps primarily, those other Jews who did
not adhere to the group's legal interpretations. In the meantime, they
too organized themselves as a tightly knit, hierarchical community that
waited in purity for the end of days in their isolated settlement on the
western bank of the Dead Sea.[25]

At some point in the first century C.E., the Pharisees gained the
upper hand over these various groups. Writing on the major Jewish
"schools," Josephus says:

> [The Pharisees are] extremely influential among the townsfolk;
> and all prayers and sacred rites of divine worship are performed
> according to their exposition. This is the great tribute that the
> inhabitants of the cities ... have paid to the excellence of the
> Pharisees.
>
> There are but few men to whom this doctrine has been made
> known, but these [the Sadducees] are men of the highest stand-
> ing. They accomplish practically nothing, however. For whenever
> they assume some office, though they submit unwillingly and

perforce, yet submit they do to the formulas of the Pharisees, since otherwise the masses would not tolerate them.

[The Essenes] send votive offerings to the temple, but perform their sacrifices employing a different ritual of purification. For this reason they are barred (or they distance themselves) from those precincts of the temple that are frequented by all the people and perform their rites by themselves ... The men who practice this way of life number more than four thousand.[26]

Thus, according to Josephus, the Pharisees had the support of the masses, especially the urban masses, while the Sadducees had the support of only the well-to-do. As a result, the Sadducees had to accept the dictates of the Pharisees and conduct all public rituals in accordance with Pharisaic rules. The Essenes, in contrast, distanced themselves from general society and from the Temple and were supported only by their own members, who numbered somewhat more than 4,000.

The characteristics and identity of the Pharisees have long exercised scholars. Were the Pharisees the leaders of Jewish society? Were all public rituals conducted in accordance with Pharisaic rulings? Was—or is—"Pharisaic Judaism" virtually synonymous with "Judaism"? The Gospel of Matthew (especially chapter 23) seems to indicate that they were the leaders of Jewish society and that public rituals were conducted in accordance with Pharisaic rulings. Josephus and rabbinic sources agree. Rabbinic sources, indeed, go further; according to them, the Pharisees provided the "norm" according to which other Jewish "deviations" were measured; in short, Pharisaic Judaism was, for the rabbis, synonymous with Judaism.

Matthew, Josephus and, to a lesser extent, the rabbis give the impression that the Pharisees were the "leading" Jewish group from at least the beginning of the first century C.E. But this impression might be misleading. Although Matthew, Josephus and rabbinic sources provide convergent testimony about the Pharisees, they were written after the destruction of the Temple and may reflect to some extent the conditions of that time—when the rabbis, the heirs of the Pharisees, were on the ascendant. Although in Matthew's field of vision the Pharisees loomed large, this may prove only that his Christian community in the 80s C.E. saw the Pharisees as their chief Jewish competitors; Matthew does not necessarily prove that Jesus and the disciples regarded the Pharisees as Matthew depicts them. Similarly, the testimony of Josephus proves only that in the 90s C.E., Josephus regarded the Pharisees as the most powerful Jewish group; Josephus's testimony does not necessarily prove that the Pharisees were powerful several generations earlier. (Of course, if it could be proven that Matthew and Josephus in their descriptions of the Pharisees were using sources that derived from the Second Temple period, their testimonies would have added weight.)[27]

Rabbinic literature, a third source, provides evidence consistent with Matthew and Josephus. However, the rabbis had a vested interest in presenting their ancestors as the group that controlled Jewish society, a position they themselves strived to attain in the centuries following the destruction of the Temple. Accordingly, we must view our sources on first-century Pharisaism with considerable skepticism.

Christians   Of the groups that emerged in the first century C.E., the Christians are the most famous. Jesus, their leader, was a holy man and a teacher who, like many other such people, attracted admirers and disciples. Like many of his contemporaries, he apparently believed that the end time was imminent and that he was sent by God to prepare the way for its arrival. He therefore prophesied that the Jerusalem Temple would be removed because a new and more perfect temple would be erected by God as part of the new, perfect and permanent order of the end time. The high priests, however, regarded Jesus as a troublemaker and handed him over to the Romans for execution. In a paradoxical way, his death marked not the end but the beginning of Christianity (a development outside the purview of this book).

The earliest Christian community, as described by the book of Acts, shares many features with the Jewish movements surveyed above. The apostles controlled this Christian group, property was held in common, disbursements were made to the faithful from the common till and disobedience to one's superiors was not tolerated (Acts 5:1–11). The group dined and prayed together. New members were "converted" through baptism and repentance (Acts 2:38–42). Like the Essenes, the Christians attempted to create a utopian community. A sense of alienation from the rest of society is apparent in the numerous calls for repentance and in the eschatological fervor of the group.

Although Christianity emerged from a Jewish context, as one among many first-century C.E. Jewish apocalyptic groups, by the end of the century it had separated from its mother religion. Christianity's development of an independent identity was a *process*, however, not a single event. Several early Christian groups abolished circumcision and welcomed non-Jews. This change of ethnic composition alone was enough to make Christianity appear to its Jewish neighbors as a new religion. Religious change accompanied this "gentilization" of Christianity. Primary among the religious changes were the abrogation of food restrictions and the observance of the Sabbath and the elevation of Jesus to a position far higher and more significant than that of any angel or any other intermediary figure in Judaism. At this point, not only the Jews saw Christianity as a distinct religion, but so did the Romans—and, as the Christian martyrs soon discovered, the Romans had a marked distaste for new religions. Curiously, while most

Christians and Christian groups had ceased to identify themselves as Jews by the beginning of the second century C.E., several Christian groups continued to view themselves as Jewish over the next few hundred years. These groups would be rejected by Jews as "gentile" and by Christians as heretical.[28]

In 66 C.E. the Jews of Palestine revolted against their Roman rulers. To this day, the reasons for the "Great Revolt," which ended with the destruction of the Second Temple, are not entirely clear. Josephus is, once again, our primary source. Despite his general unreliability, Josephus does provide enough information to piece together the array of causes that seem to have led to the revolt.

Chief among them were social ferment, Roman misadministration, revolutionary ardor and a leadership vacuum. As we have noted, brigandage, that unmistakable symptom of social distress, increased significantly in the countryside after Agrippa I's death in 44 C.E. Jerusalem too was racked by social turmoil. In the early 60s C.E., work on the Temple Mount, begun by Herod the Great many years earlier, was finally completed. Faced with the prospect of having 18,000 laborers added to the ranks of the unemployed, the priests suggested to Agrippa II that the porticoes be torn down so that they could be rebuilt! Agrippa II wisely remarked that it was easier to destroy than to build such edifices and suggested that the laborers devote their energies to repaving the streets. His suggestion was accepted. The laborers were paid for a full day of work even if they actually worked for only an hour. In short, the city of Jerusalem became, in effect, a welfare state, dependent on "make-work" projects for the maintenance of social peace.[29] The wealthy, in contrast, lived their lives and buried their dead in opulence and splendor. Aristocrats in Jerusalem and throughout the country maintained bands of armed retainers to threaten their opponents and to work for their own interests. Within the priesthood there was strife, and sometimes violence, between the upper and the lower clergy. Peasants in Galilee in 66–67 C.E. wanted nothing more than to attack and loot Sepphoris, Tiberias and Gabara, the three largest settlements of the district. After the Great Revolt commenced in 66 C.E., many peasants of both Galilee and Judea fled to Jerusalem, where they turned on both the city aristocracy and the small, organized priestly elite. These tensions within Jewish society often surfaced violently during the Great Revolt. For many of the participants in the war, the primary enemies were not Roman but Jewish.[30]

According to Josephus, especially in *Jewish Antiquities*, the Roman procurators in the years leading up to the revolt went from bad to worse. Of all these corrupt and incompetent Roman administrators of Palestine, none was worse than the last one, Gessius Florus. Albinus, himself an execrable procurator, is described by Josephus as a "paragon of virtue" when compared to Florus. Florus, according to Josephus, "ostentatiously paraded his outrages upon the nation, and, as though he had been sent as hangman of condemned criminals, abstained from no form of robbery or violence ... No man has ever poured greater contempt on truth; none invented more crafty methods of crime."[31] The Jews ultimately appealed to Florus's superior Celestius Gallus, the governor of Syria, for relief. Not only was the appeal unsuccessful, but it was soon followed by Florus's mishandling of ethnic tensions in Caesarea and then his plundering of the Temple treasury and slaughter of the Jews who sought to prevent him from desecrating holy ground.

The revolutionaries may also have believed that they were living at the threshhold of the end time. Josephus narrates that "what more than all else incited them to the war was an ambiguous oracle, found in their sacred scriptures, to the effect that at that time one from their country would become ruler of the world."[32] In the years immediately preceding the revolt, many "eschatological prophets" were active, predicting the imminent approach of the end time or attempting, by means of a symbolic action (for example, splitting the Jordan River), to hasten or implement its arrival. Although Josephus states that the equivocal prophecy quoted above was the primary inducement for the Jews to go to war, in the body of his narrative he seldom alludes to the eschatological expectations of the revolutionaries. Perhaps some of the revolutionary leaders regarded themselves as messiahs, or were so regarded by their followers, but Josephus nowhere makes this point explicit. Accordingly, while few scholars would deny that eschatological expectations played a role in the motivation of the revolutionaries, the relative importance of this factor remains the subject of debate.[33]

The Jewish aristocracy was just as unhappy with Roman rule as were the lower classes, and they took a leading role in the early stages of the revolt. Although established by the Romans as local leaders, the Jewish aristocrats were systematically deprived of the means to govern. Hence, they were left in the awkward position of being identified with the Romans, but of having no real power to respond to the needs of their compatriots. The way out of this predicament was to oppose the Roman procurator, a choice that put them on the fast track to war.[34]

Yet it is clear that Josephus does not want his readership to conclude that the Jewish revolt was led and embraced by the Jewish aristocracy. Reading his *Jewish War*, one could easily conclude that it was the work of a few fanatics. In his desire to repair Roman-Jewish relations, however, Josephus protests too much. Aristocratic involvement in the revolt was far too prominent to conceal.

Josephus's apologetic for the Romans is also evident from his account of the war itself. Vespasian and Titus, the Roman generals, were perfect gentlemen who gave the Jews every opportunity to come to their senses and surrender. They even commiserated with the poor innocents who had to suffer the tyranny of the revolutionaries and the horrors of war. According to Josephus, Titus did his best to save the Temple (see below) and wept when he beheld the destruction of the city and of the house of God. Josephus is clearly saying that Titus and the Romans bore no responsibility for the destruction of the Temple, and that this unfortunate consequence of the war should not bar the resumption of normal relations between the Romans and their Jewish subjects.

In *Jewish Antiquities*, Josephus writes anew about the prehistory of the war. Here he is much less concerned about war guilt and much more prepared to admit that responsibility for the war should not be ascribed to the revolutionaries alone. In *The Jewish War* Josephus wanted to cover up any connection between the revolutionaries and the "official" representatives of Judaism; in *Jewish Antiquities* he no longer felt constrained to do so. For example, in *Jewish Antiquities*, one procurator even colludes with the assassins in order to remove an opponent; another empties the prisons of all those who were arrested for seditious activity. The emperor Nero, by favoring the pagan element of the city of Caesarea in its dispute with the Jewish citizenry, also bears some responsibility for the ensuing catastrophe.[35] Here the corruption and incompetence of the Roman procurators is far more evident.

Most modern scholars see the war as the result of a complex array of factors, both internal and external. The perspective of modern scholarship resembles that of *Jewish Antiquities* much more than that of *The Jewish War*. Moreover, unlike Josephus, many modern scholars admire the revolutionaries, or at least do not condemn them. For Josephus, even in *Jewish Antiquities*, they are villains and scoundrels, the dregs of society. For modern Israelis and for many others, they are heroes who were trying to reclaim what was rightly theirs.

The rabbis of the Talmud shared the perspective of Josephus in *The Jewish War*: The revolutionaries were crazed fanatics who did not listen to the sage counsel of the rabbis and persisted in their folly. They brought disaster upon the entire house of Israel. In the Talmudic account, the hero of the war is Rabban Yohanan ben Zakkai, a man who fled from Jerusalem, went over to the Roman side and acknowledged the suzerainty of Vespasian, the Roman general and soon-to-be emperor. Isaiah's prophecy that "Lebanon shall fall to a mighty one" (Isaiah 10:34) was interpreted by Yohanan ben Zakkai to mean that the Temple (constructed from the cedars of Lebanon) would fall into the hands of Vespasian (a mighty one). The rabbinic hero thus hailed the Roman general as victor and emperor well before his actual victory and his elevation to the purple. From the perspective of the revolutionaries, this was treason; but from the perspective of the rabbis, viewed with acute hindsight, this was wisdom, a course of action that to their regret had not been followed.

Whether the historical Rabban Yohanan did anything even remotely approximating the deeds ascribed to him in the rabbinic account is, of course, unknown and unknowable. The story probably tells us much more about the political outlook of the rabbis of the third and fourth centuries than about the actions of Rabban Yohanan in the first.[36]

The social tensions and eschatological expectations that impelled Judea to war with Rome were not uniquely Jewish. In fact the war of 66–70 C.E. follows a pattern evident in other native rebellions against the Roman Empire. Tensions between rich and poor, and between city and country, were endemic to ancient society and often contributed to native rebellions. Like the uprising in Judea, other native rebellions were often led by aristocrats, although peasants, day laborers and landless poor formed the bulk of the revolutionary army. As so often happens in revolutions ancient and modern, in its initial phases the struggle is led by aristocratic (or bourgeois) elements, which are later ousted, usually with great violence, by more extreme (or proletarian) groups. Like the Jews, other rebels in antiquity also dreamed of subjugating the universal Roman Empire. The revolt of the Gauls in 69 C.E. was prompted in part by a Druid prediction that Rome would be destroyed and that the rule of the empire would devolve on the tribes of Transalpine Gaul. The Jewish revolt was, therefore, hardly unique in the annals of Rome.[37] What makes it special is its intensity, its duration and, most important of all, the fact that an ancient historian saw fit to write its history in great detail. Because of Josephus's *The Jewish War*, we are better informed about this war than about any other native revolt against Rome.

The course of the First Jewish Revolt
With this background, let us turn to the course of the war itself. In the fall of 66 C.E., no one knew that a war between the Jews and the Romans was imminent. Some revolutionaries, perhaps, were dreaming of a final conflict, but even they had no way of knowing precisely when the conflict would erupt or what form it would take.

The spark was provided by the procurator Florus when he seized 17 talents from the Temple treasury as compensation, he said, for uncollected back taxes. This act was not significantly worse than the depredations and misdeeds of previous procurators, and the riot it provoked was not significantly worse than the riots that had erupted during the tenures of previous procurators.

This riot, however, was the first act of a war, because it came at the end of a period of almost 20 years of unrelieved tension and lawlessness. When Florus brutally suppressed the riot, the people responded with even greater intensity, with the result that Florus had to flee the city.

At this point various revolutionary factions stepped forward. It is difficult to determine the interrelationship of all these groups. Some scholars argue that the anti-Roman forces formed a single "war party," which for purposes of convenience can be called "Zealots" after its most distinctive constituent group. Others argue that no single "war party" ever existed and that each of the groups and figures had a distinctive history. The diverse groups shared a common willingness to fight the Romans, but differed from each other in many other respects, which explains why they spent so much time fighting each other. The latter interpretation is much more plausible than the former.[38]

At the outbreak of the war, an aristocratic priestly revolutionary party, led initially by Eleazar, son of the high priest Ananias, seems to have controlled the revolution. Eleazar suspended the daily sacrifice in the Temple that had been offered for the welfare of the emperor and the Roman Empire.[39] This act was tantamount to a declaration of war. As if to emphasize the point, Eleazar and his supporters turned on the Roman garrisons Florus had left in the city after his retreat and besieged them.

Whether the aristocratic priestly revolutionaries were truly committed to the revolution, or were merely playing for time in the hope of forestalling the emergence of more radical and more dangerous elements, is debated among scholars. Josephus seems to give contradictory answers: Although they probably began as revolutionaries who deeply resented the Roman diminution of their prestige and prerogatives, when they were faced with the opposition of other revolutionary groups whose primary targets were the Jewish aristocracy, it is likely the priestly revolutionaries began to hope for a peace agreement with the Romans.[40]

In any event, these priestly revolutionaries were soon eclipsed by another group, the Sicarii, led by one Menahem. In the fall of 66 C.E., the Sicarii entered Jerusalem. In addition to attacking the Roman forces that remained in the city, the Sicarii also attacked the Jewish aristocracy. They looted the homes of the well-to-do and massacred many of the nobility. The most prominent of their victims was Ananias the high priest, the father of Eleazar, who had led the priestly revolutionaries. The priestly group, headquartered in the Temple, fought back and killed the Sicarii leader, Menahem. Menahem's followers then fled to Masada, one of Herod's great fortresses in the Judean wilderness. There they remained for the rest of the war, doing nothing to help the struggle. Other bands of fighters, however, were already, or would soon become, active in Jerusalem.

Revolutionary ardor also spread outside Jerusalem. In Caesarea and in many other cities of Palestine and Syria, Jews and pagans attacked one another. The hostility toward pagans and paganism that motivated the revolutionaries in Jerusalem seems also to have motivated Jews throughout the country. The pagans, for their part, gave vent to the same animosities that had exploded in the anti-Jewish riots in Alexandria 30 years earlier.

The Roman governor of Syria, Cestius, went to Judea to restore order, but after entering Jerusalem he decided that he was not strong enough to take the Temple from the revolutionaries. In the course of his withdrawal, his troops were beset by the Jews and had to abandon much of their equipment.

After the defeat of Cestius, the revolutionaries, led by the priestly revolutionary party, assigned generals to each district in the country. Most of the commissioned generals were priests. Their task was to prepare the country for war, in anticipation of either negotiations or hostilities with the Romans. The general about whose activities we are best informed is, of course, Josephus. He was sent to Galilee, where he spent the next six months feuding with local leaders, trying to impose his rule on a fractious population that had little desire to fight the Romans. He fortified several key locations, raised and trained an army, brought local brigands into his employ, and intimidated the cities of the district (notably Sepphoris, which supported the Romans, and Tiberias, which was divided).

Josephus had had no military or administrative experience, and was not temperamentally suited to cooperative leadership; it is no surprise that he ultimately failed in his mission. With the appearance of the Roman army, led by the Roman general Vespasian, in the summer of 67 C.E., Josephus's army all but disappeared, and the Romans had little difficulty in subduing the district. Only one location gave them trouble, the fortress of Jotapata, a hilltop town fortified by Josephus, which became the refuge for the remnants of Josephus's army, such as it was. It held out for almost seven weeks before falling to the Roman assault. Josephus himself was captured and delivered his prophecy to Vespasian, as noted above. Galilee was now pacified.

The revolutionaries in the Golan congregated at Gamla, but after some fierce fighting, that fortress too was taken. The entire northern part of the country was once again brought under Roman rule.

After taking a winter break, Vespasian resumed operations in the spring of 68 C.E. and by early summer had pacified the entire countryside; Jerusalem alone (and some isolated fortresses, notably Masada) remained in the hands of the rebels.

A respite in the war is wasted

Everything seemed prepared for an immediate attack on Jerusalem, but during the summer of 68 C.E. Vespasian learned of the emperor Nero's assassination. The death of the reigning emperor meant that Vespasian's commission as general had expired; accordingly, he discontinued his military activities. In the summer of 69 C.E., Vespasian had himself proclaimed emperor. He left Judea and returned to Rome in order to establish his own imperial power. By the end of the year he had succeeded. Some months later, in the spring of 70 C.E., Vespasian once again turned his attention to Judea.

The two-year hiatus should have been a great boon to the revolutionaries in Jerusalem, allowing them time to organize their forces, fortify the city and lay away provisions. But the opposite was the case. As the refugees entered Jerusalem from the countryside, internecine strife intensified. The party of Zealots now emerged, consisting for the most part of Judean peasants. They turned against the aristocratic priests, who until that point had been in charge of the war, and appointed a new high priest by lot. The Zealots enlisted support from the Jews of Idumea, country peasants like themselves who could be counted on to hate the city aristocracy.[41] At first, the Idumeans supported the Zealots in their attacks on the aristocracy, but after a while even they, says Josephus, were disgusted by the excesses of the Zealots and withdrew.

Thus 68 C.E. was spent in fighting between the aristocratic (or "moderate") revolutionary groups and the more radical proletarian ones. The latter triumphed. In 69 C.E. the radical revolutionaries themselves fell to attacking one another. John of Gischala, supported by his contingent of Galileans, turned on his former allies the Zealots and ultimately succeeded in ousting their leader and bringing them under his control. But a new revolutionary faction then emerged, led by Simon bar Giora, a native of Gerasa (a city of the Transjordan). Like the Zealots, he had a radical social program and drew much of his support from freed slaves. The intense fighting among these various groups had disastrous consequences. Large stocks of grain and other provisions were destroyed. When the Roman siege began in earnest in 70 C.E., a famine soon ensued.

The Roman siege of Jerusalem

Vespasian had by then securely established himself as emperor and wanted a resounding success to legitimate his new dynasty. In his propaganda, Vespasian had pictured himself as the savior of the empire, the man who, after a year and a half of political chaos, had restored order and stability. There was no better way to prove this point than to bring to a successful conclusion the protracted war in Judea. In order to emphasize the dynastic implications of the victory, Vespasian appointed his son Titus to command the Roman army in its assault on the holy city of the Jews. In the spring of 70 C.E., the Romans, under Titus, besieged the city and cut off all supplies and all means of escape.

The fighting for the city and the Temple was intense. The major rallying point of the revolutionaries, and consequently the major target of the Romans, was the Temple. The Temple was a veritable fortress, but it still was a temple. The priests maintained all the customary rituals, even with death and destruction all around them. Three weeks before the final catastrophe, the *Tamid*, the "continual sacrifice," which was offered every morning and evening, ceased because of a shortage of lambs. The severity of the famine is illustrated in many gruesome tales by Josephus; but despite their suffering, the Jews were still willing to sacrifice two lambs every day to God. Their only hope for success was through divine intervention, and only a properly maintained cult would convince God to aid the faithful.

Divine help, however, was not forthcoming. The Romans advanced methodically toward their goal. The Jews were weakened by famine and internecine strife and, although Titus made some serious tactical errors in prosecuting the siege, the Roman victory was only a matter of time. Each of the city's three protective walls was breached in turn, and the Romans finally found themselves, by mid-summer of 70 C.E., just outside the sacred precincts.

At this point, according to Josephus, Titus called a meeting of his general staff and asked for advice. What should he do with the Jewish Temple? Some of his adjutants argued that it should be destroyed, because as long as it was left standing it would serve as a focal point for anti-Roman agitation. According to the "rule of war" in antiquity, temples were not to be molested, but this Temple had become a fortress and therefore was a fair military target. No opprobrium would be attached to its destruction. Titus, however, argued that the Temple should be preserved as a monument to Roman magnanimity. Indeed, according to Josephus, during the siege Titus offered the revolutionaries numerous opportunities to surrender or, at least, to vacate the Temple and carry on the fighting elsewhere. Even at the end Titus was eager to preserve the Temple. But Titus's plan was thwarted. On the next day, a soldier, acting against orders, tossed a firebrand into the sanctuary, and the flames shot up, immediately out of control. Josephus insists that Titus did his best to douse the flames, but Josephus's apology for Titus is as unsuccessful as Titus's attempt to halt the conflagration.[42] It is very unlikely that this fantastic account of Roman magnanimity and self-restraint contains any historical truth. Scholars debate whether this portrait of moderate generals was concocted for a Jewish or a Roman audience, but most agree that it is as exaggerated as Josephus's other claim that the Jews were compelled by the revolutionaries to fight a war they did not want.

On the tenth of the month of Ab (in rabbinic chronology on the ninth), late August of 70 C.E., the Temple was destroyed. Titus and his troops spent the next month subduing the rest of the city and collecting loot as the reward for their victory.

Upon his return to Rome in 71 C.E., Titus celebrated a joint triumph with his father, the emperor Vespasian. In the procession were the enemy leaders Simon bar Giora and John of Gischala, and various objects from the Temple (notably the menorah, table and trumpets). Simon was beheaded, John was probably enslaved and the sacred objects were deposited in the Temple of Peace in Rome.[43] Two triumphal arches were erected in the following years to celebrate the victory; one was destroyed in the 14th or 15th century, the other still

ERICH LESSING

Arch of Titus relief. The golden menorah, a pair of trumpets, the golden table and other booty from the Jerusalem Temple are carried aloft in a Roman victory procession, depicted in this marble relief from the Arch of Titus. Erected in Rome in 80 C.E., the arch celebrates the Roman victory over the Jews and conquest of Jerusalem.

stands, the Arch of Titus, with its famous depiction of the sacred objects from the Temple carried in the procession. The destroyed arch bore the following inscription:

> The senate and people of Rome (dedicate this arch) to the emperor Titus ... because with the guidance and plans of his father, and under his auspices, he subdued the Jewish people and destroyed the city of Jerusalem, which all generals, kings and peoples before him had either attacked without success or left entirely unassailed.[44]

To punish the Jews for the war the Romans imposed the *fiscus Judaicus,* the "Jewish tax." The half-shekel that Jews throughout the empire had formerly contributed to the Temple in Jerusalem was now collected for the temple of Jupiter Capitolinus in Rome. The imposition of this tax, which was collected throughout the empire at least until the middle of the second century C.E., shows that the Romans regarded all the Jews of the empire as partly responsible for the war. Dio Cassius, a Roman historian of the third century C.E., records that the Judean revolutionaries were aided by their coreligionists throughout the Roman Empire.[45] Josephus implicitly denies this, but it is perhaps confirmed by the Jewish tax on Diaspora, as well as Judean, Jews.

The Romans did not, however, institute any other harsh measures against the Jews. They confiscated much Jewish land in Judea, distributing it to their soldiers and to Jewish collaborators (like Josephus), but this was a normal procedure after a war. They did not engage in religious persecution or strip the Jews of their rights. On the contrary, Josephus reports that the non-Jewish citizens of Antioch petitioned Titus to allow them to expel their Jewish population, but Titus adamantly refused; the Jews were still entitled to the protection of the state.

Masada   Titus's triumph in Rome in 71 C.E. marked the official end of the war. A few "mopping up" operations remained. Three strongholds, all originally fortified by Herod the Great, were still in rebel hands, but only one of them caused any real trouble for the Romans. This was Masada (which fell in either 73 or 74 C.E.). Archaeological excavations confirm Josephus's description of the magnificence of the site and the difficulty of the siege. The Romans built a ramp against one side of the plateau and pushed a tower up against the wall of the fortress. We may assume that this activity was accompanied by a constant hail of arrows and stones thrown by the rebels, although Josephus does not mention this. (Nor does he mention even a single Roman casualty!)

When the Masada rebels saw that the end was near, they had to decide whether to continue their struggle. At this point Josephus narrates a very dramatic tale. The leader of the Sicarii, Eleazar ben Yair, assembled the "manliest" of his comrades and convinced them that an honorable self-inflicted death was preferable to the disgrace of capture and enslavement. Acting upon his instructions, each man killed his own wife and family. Then ten men were chosen by lot to kill the rest. Finally, one was chosen to kill the remaining nine and then himself. All told, 960 men, women and children perished. When the Romans entered the fortress the next day, they expected a battle, but all they found was silence.

The historicity of this famous account is uncertain. The basic elements of the story are of course accurate and confirmed by the archaeological findings—the remains of the rebel presence at Masada, the Roman siege works, the Roman camps and the Roman ramp are in a remarkable state of preservation. Even the stones hurled by the Romans from their siege tower have been found. Some of the Jews slew their families, burned their possessions and set the public buildings on fire. Some of them killed themselves. That some tried to escape, however, is suggested by skeletons found at the site, which may have belonged to people who were found by the Romans and killed.

Josephus probably invented or exaggerated the use of lots in the suicide process. True, Israeli archaeologist Yigael Yadin found 11 "lots" at Masada, but the first drawing required several hundred lots and the second only ten. Moreover, many of the details in Josephus's account are irreconcilable with the archaeological evidence. For

DAVID HARRIS

Lots cast by Masada's defenders? *The first-century C.E. Jewish historian Josephus tells us that three years after the Roman destruction of Jerusalem in 70 C.E., the remaining Jewish rebels, besieged at Masada, decided to commit suicide rather than succumb to the Roman army. With defeat just hours away, the Jewish commander Eleazar ben Yair convinced his fighters to die with their families rather than become Roman slaves. By lot, the rebels selected ten men who would slay the rest of the community.*

The late Israeli archaeologist Yigael Yadin, who excavated Masada in the 1960s, speculated that these sherds, each inscribed with a different name, were the very lots used by the defenders. The sherd at lower left bears the name "ben Yair." However, some scholars question whether Ben Yair ever made such a speech and even whether a mass suicide occurred.

example, Josephus says that all the possessions were gathered together in one large pile and set on fire, but archaeology shows there were many piles and many fires. Josephus writes that Eleazar ordered his men to destroy everything except the foodstuffs, but archaeology demonstrates that many storerooms that contained provisions were burned. Josephus implies that all the murders took place in the palace, but the northern palace is too small for an assembly of almost a thousand people.[46] More important, the speeches Josephus puts into the mouth of the rebel leader Eleazar ben Yair are incongruous to say the least. Imagine a Jewish revolutionary leader justifying suicide by appealing to the example of the Brahmins of India! It is highly unlikely that there was time for such speeches or that the rebels acted with such unanimity.

As we have seen, the Jewish revolt was not a reaction to an unmistakable threat or provocation by the state. In the fall of 66 C.E.—as the result of social tensions between rich and poor, between city and country, and between Jew and gentile; of the impoverishment of large sections of the economy; of religious speculations about the imminent arrival of the end time and the messianic redeemer; of nationalist stirrings against foreign rule; of the incompetent and insensitive administration of the procurators—the Jews of Palestine went to war against the Roman Empire.

The war was characterized, as we have seen, by internecine fighting. The fighting was not only between revolutionary groups but also between the revolutionaries and large segments of the populace. Josephus is surely correct that many Jews opposed the war. Moreover, the number of people enrolled in the revolutionary parties was quite small. Many Jews had no desire to participate in the struggle. It was one thing to riot against the procurator, quite another to rebel against the Roman Empire. Wealthy and poor alike were afraid that war would mean the loss of everything they had, and since the Romans had not done anything intolerable, there was no compelling reason to go to war. This attitude was widespread. Aside from Jerusalem, only Gamla was the site of fierce fighting. Galilee, Perea (the Transjordan), the coast, Idumea—all these saw some anti-Roman activity, but all were pacified immediately upon the arrival of the Roman forces. Jerusalem was the seat of the rebellion—where it began, where it ended and where the vast majority of the combatants maintained their strongholds.

The causes for the failure of the war are not hard to see. The war began with little advance planning, the revolutionaries were badly divided and the timing was off. Had they rebelled a few years earlier while the Romans were fighting the Parthians, they might have been able to succeed at least to the point of exacting various concessions from the Romans in return for their surrender. Had they waited two years beyond 66 C.E.—after Nero's assassination in 68 C.E.—their odds would have been immeasurably better. At that time, the empire was in chaos; the succession was vigorously disputed; Gaul had risen in revolt. This would have been a perfect moment for revolt, but for the Jews it came too late.

A new beginning The destruction of the Temple did not mean the end of Judaism, however.[47] The theological and religious crisis it caused seems to have been much less severe than that experienced in the aftermath of the Babylonian destruction of the First Temple in 586 B.C.E., perhaps because the Judaism of the Second Temple period had created new institutions and ideologies that prepared it for a time when the Temple and the sacrificial cult would no longer exist. By the time the Second Temple was destroyed, the Temple itself had been supplemented by synagogues, the priests had been supplemented by scholars, the sacrificial cult had been supplemented by prayer, and the study of the Torah—along with the reliance on the intermediation of the Temple priesthood—had been supplemented by a piety that emphasized the observance of the commandments of the Torah by every Jew.

In short, the path to the future was already clearly marked. The sufferings of this world would be compensated by rewards in the hereafter. The disgrace of seeing Rome triumph over the God of Israel and destroy the Temple would be effaced by the glory of the new kingdom that God would establish for his people in the end time. The cessation of the sacrificial cult did not mean estrangement from God, since God could be worshiped through good deeds, prayer, the observance of the commandments and the study of the Torah. Synagogues could take the place of the Temple, and rabbis could take the place of the priests. These were the responses of the Jews to the catastrophe of 70 C.E., and they were greatly elaborated during the following centuries.

For all of the destruction caused by the events of 70 C.E., in many important respects the post-70 C.E. period does not mark a radical break with the past. But in other respects the post-70 C.E. period is discontinuous with the past. The period from the Maccabees to the destruction of the Temple was marked by religious and social ferment, but after 70 C.E. the ferment all but disappeared. Within a generation the Jews ceased to write (or at least ceased to preserve) apocalypses, and they desisted from making detailed speculations about God's control of human events in the present and the future. The Pharisees, Sadducees, Essenes, Sicarii and Zealots are no longer living realities in Jewish society. They are mentioned by sources of the second and third centuries only as figures of the Second Temple period. Instead of sectarian diversity, the post-70 C.E. period is characterized by a peculiar homogeneity. The only group to appear in our documentation is that of the *rabbis*, as a result of which the post-70 C.E. period is often called the rabbinic period.

The origins of the rabbinic group are most obscure. They were led by Rabban Gamaliel, a scion of a prominent Pharisaic family, a fact that implies that the heirs of the Pharisees of the Second Temple period were the dominant element in this new group. Various features shared by the Pharisees and the rabbis also imply some intimate link between them, but there is no indication that all Pharisees became rabbis or that all rabbis were the descendants of Pharisees.

The absence of other organized groups does not, of course, mean that all Jews everywhere instantly became pious followers of the rabbis. The contrary was the case. In Second Temple times most Jews did not belong to any sect or group, but were content to serve God in their own way. This pattern continued in the rabbinic period as well, as the rabbinic texts themselves make abundantly clear. But in the end, the masses recognized the rabbis as the leaders and shapers of Judaism. The rabbis were heirs to the legacy of Second Temple Judaism, but through their distinctive literature and patterns of religion they gave Judaism a new form of expression that would endure to our own day. The destruction of the Temple thus marked not only an end but also a beginning.

Notes

I. The Patriarchal Age

[1] The viewpoint is illustrated very well by the second chapter of William F. Albright's *Yahweh and the Gods of Canaan* (Garden City, NY: Doubleday, 1968), titled "The Patriarchal Background of Israel's Faith." Its fullest expression is perhaps the discussion in John Bright, *A History of Israel* (Philadelphia: Westminster, 3rd ed., 1981), pp. 67–102.

[2] See especially Ephraim A. Speiser, *Genesis*, Anchor Bible 1 (Garden City, NY: Doubleday, 1964).

[3] Albright, *From the Stone Age to Christianity* (Garden City, NY: Anchor/Doubleday, 2nd ed., 1957), p. 241.

[4] Albright, *The Biblical Period from Abraham to Ezra* (New York: Torchbooks/Harper & Row, 1963), p. 5.

[5] G. Ernest Wright, *Biblical Archaeology* (Philadelphia: Westminster, rev. ed., 1962), p. 40.

[6] Wright, *Biblical Archaeology* (see endnote 5), p. 50, note 5.

[7] See William G. Dever, "Palestine in the Second Millennium BCE: The Archaeological Picture," in *Israelite and Judaean History*, ed. John M. Hayes and J. Maxwell

Miller (Philadelphia: Westminster, 1977), pp. 70–120, especially pp. 99–101.

[8] The most forceful and complete statement of this position is probably that of Roland de Vaux (*The Early History of Israel*, trans. David Smith [Philadelphia: Westminster, 1978], pp. 161–287).

[9] See citations in endnote 20.

[10] Speiser, *Genesis* (see endnote 2), passim; Cyrus H. Gordon, "Biblical Customs and the Nuzu Tablets," *Biblical Archaeologist Reader 2*, ed. E.F. Campbell and David Noel Freedman (Garden City, NY: Anchor/Doubleday, 1964), pp. 21–33.

[11] Speiser, *Genesis* (see endnote 2), pp. 120–121; Gordon, "Biblical Customs" (see endnote 10), pp. 22–23.

[12] Speiser, *Genesis* (see endnote 2), p. xi; for Speiser's full discussion, see "The Wife-Sister Motif in the Patriarchal Narratives," in *Biblical and Other Studies*, ed. A. Altmann (Cambridge, MA: Harvard Univ. Press, 1963), pp. 15–28; also in *Oriental and Biblical Studies*, ed. Jacob J. Finkelstein and M. Greenberg (Philadelphia: Univ. of Pennsylvania, 1967), pp. 62–82.

[13] See especially the studies of Dever, "The Beginning of the Middle Bronze Age in Syria-Palestine," in *Magnalia Dei: The Mighty Acts of God—Essays on the Bible and Archaeology in*

Memory of G. Ernest Wright, ed. Frank M. Cross et al. (Garden City, NY: Doubleday, 1976), pp. 3–38; "The 'Middle Bronze I' Period in Syria and Palestine," in *Near Eastern Archaeology in the Twentieth Century: Essays in Honor of Nelson Glueck*, ed. J.A. Sanders (Garden City, NY: Doubleday, 1970), pp. 132–163; "New Vistas in the EB IV ('MB I') Horizon in Syria and Palestine," *BASOR* 237 (1980), pp. 35–64.

[14] See the cautious conclusions of Dever ("Palestine in the Second Millennium" [see endnote 7], pp. 117–120).

[15] This has been shown in several studies by M.B. Rowton, including the following: "Autonomy and Nomadism in Western Asia," *Orientalia* 42 (1973), pp. 247–258; "Urban Autonomy in a Nomadic Environment," *JNES* 32 (1973), pp. 201–215; "Dimorphic Structure and the Problem of the 'Apirû-'Ibrim," *JNES* 35 (1976), pp. 13–20.

[16] See J.T. Luke, *Pastoralism and Politics in the Mari Period: A Re-Examination of the Character and Political Significance of the Major West Semitic Tribal Groups on the Middle Euphrates, c. 1828–1753 B.C.* (Ph.D. dissertation, Univ. of Michigan [Ann Arbor, MI: University Microfilms, 1965]); V.H. Matthews, *Pastoral Nomadism in the Mari Kingdom ca. 1830–1760 B.C.*, ASOR Dissertation Series (Cambridge, MA: ASOR, 1978).

[17] See the literature cited in Dever, "Palestine in the Second Millennium" (see endnote 7), pp. 102–111.

[18] The two studies that were most effective in calling attention to the problems with the early-second-millennium hypothesis were Thomas L. Thompson, *The Historicity of the Patriarchal Narratives*, ZAW supp. 133 (Berlin: de Gruyter, 1974), and John Van Seters, *Abraham in History and Tradition* (New Haven, CT: Yale Univ. Press, 1975). See also Nahum Sarna, "Abraham in History," *BAR*, December 1977, pp. 5–9.

[19] Cf. Barry L. Eichler, "Nuzi and the Bible: A Retrospective," in H. Behrens, D. Loding, and M. Roth, eds., *DUMU-E₂-DUB-BA-A: Studies in Honor of Åke W. Sjöberg* (Philadelphia: University Museum, 1989), pp. 107–19.

[20] Cf. Van Seters, *Abraham in History* (see endnote 18), pp. 40–42, and especially Thompson, *Historicity of the Patriarchal Narratives* (see endnote 18), pp. 22–36, for complete citation of the extrabiblical materials. In the Bible, "Abiram" is the name of a Reubenite who participated in the revolt against Moses in the wilderness (Numbers 16:1) and of the firstborn son of Hiel the Bethelite, who founded Israelite Jericho in the ninth century B.C.E. (1 Kings 16:34).

[21] Compare the name "Ahiram" and its shortened form "Hiram." In the Bible it is mentioned as the name of a son of Benjamin, a clan of Benjaminites (Numbers 26:38); the Phoenician king contemporary with David and Solomon (2 Samuel 5:11; 1 Kings 5); and the craftsman who supervised the building of Solomon's Temple (1 Kings 7:13). It appears in Phoenician inscriptions as the name of a tenth-century B.C.E. king of Byblos and an eighth-century B.C.E. king of Tyre. See also Thompson, *Historicity of the Patriarchal Narratives* (see endnote 18), pp. 29–31, and Van Seters, *Abraham in History* (see endnote 18), p. 41.

[22] Cf. Herbert B. Huffmon, *Amorite Personal Names in the Mari Texts* (Baltimore, MD: Johns Hopkins Press, 1965), pp. 63–86.

[23] *Pace* Kenneth Kitchen in his review of *Ancient Israel*, ed. Hershel Shanks, *Themelios* 15:1 (October, 1989), p. 25. Kitchen's statistical analysis of name-types is dependent on random archaeological finds and cannot claim any kind of scientific consistency. Cf. William G. Dever's criticisms of Kitchen's use of such archaeological data: "Is This Man a Biblical Archaeologist?" *BAR*, July/August 1996, p. 63.

[24] Cf. Frauke Gröndahl, *Die Personennamen der Texte aus Ugarit*, Studia Pohl 1 (Rome: Pontifical Biblical Institute, 1967), pp. 41–42.

[25] For a sample of the inscriptional evidence, see Jeffrey H. Tigay, *You Shall Have No Other Gods: Israelite Religion in the Light of Hebrew Inscriptions*, Harvard Semitic Studies 31 (Atlanta: Scholars Press, 1986), pp. 52–56, 85. For biblical names, see Martin Noth, *Die israelitischen Personennamen im Rahmen der gemeinsemitischen Namengebung*, Beiträge zur Wissenschaft vom Alten und Neuen Testament, III/10 (Stuttgart: Kohlhammer, 1928; reprint Hildesheim: Olms, 1966), pp. 27–28.

[26] As a place name in Palestine, "Jacob-'el," to be discussed below, and as a personal name at Ugarit, *ia-qub-ba'l = ya'qub-ba'l*, "Jacob-Baal." Cf. Gröndahl, *Personennamen* (see endnote 24), p. 41.

[27] Martin Noth, *Die israelitischen Personennamen* (see endnote 25), pp. 45–46. See further, Thompson, *Historicity of the Patriarchal Narratives* (see endnote 18), pp. 43–50.

[28] Van Seters, *Abraham in History* (see endnote 18), pp. 68–71; cf. Thompson, *Historicity of the Patriarchal Narratives* (see endnote 18), pp. 252–269.

[29] Van Seters, *Abraham in History* (see endnote 18), pp. 71–76.

[30] Cf. Thompson, *Historicity of the Patriarchal Narratives* (see endnote 18), pp. 243–248.

[31] Noth, *The History of Israel*, trans. P.R. Ackroyd (New York: Harper & Row, 1960), pp. 53–84.

[32] According to Hermann Gunkel, the critical time in the formation of the patriarchal traditions was the preliterary, oral stage, when the individual units of tradition were expressed in particular genres or forms (*Gattungen*). Thus the history of the traditions can best be studied through the identification of these units by reference to the forms in which they are preserved (form criticism) and the investigation of the manner in which these units were combined into larger narratives. See *The Legends of Genesis: The Biblical Saga and History* [1901], trans. W.R. Carruth (New York: Schocken, 1964).

[33] Noth, *A History of Pentateuchal Traditions* [1948], trans. B.W. Anderson (Englewood Cliffs, NJ: Prentice-Hall, 1972).

[34] This is, of course, the biblical tradition, but there are many reasons to doubt it. In working through the materials for his commentaries for *I Samuel* and *II Samuel*, Anchor Bible 8–9 (Garden City, NY: Doubleday, 1980, 1984), P. Kyle McCarter, Jr., came to the conclusion previously reached by others that it was David who combined Judah with Israel for the first time. See, for example, James W. Flanagan, "Judah in All Israel," in *No Famine in the Land: Studies in Honor of John L. McKenzie*, ed. Flanagan and A.W. Robinson (Missoula, MT: Scholars Press, 1975), pp. 101–116.

[35] Noth, *History of Israel* (see endnote 31), p. 123. Other proponents of the history of traditions method have not been as negative as Noth. According to de Vaux (*Early History* [see endnote 8], p. 180), whose work represents the best attempt to exploit both tradition-historical and archaeological methods, "It is true that the patriarchal tradition was only given its definitive form in the perspective of 'all Israel' after the conquest and settlement in the Promised Land ... However complicated this development may have been, and however obscure it may still be, we should not be justified in concluding that the traditions have no historical value at all, since without evidence it would be wrong to claim that the Israelites had no knowledge at all of their own origins."

[36] Cf. the comments by Frank M. Cross in "The Epic Tradition of Early Israel: Epic Narrative and the Reconstruction of Early Israelite Institutions," in *The Poet and the Historian: Essays in Literary and Historical Biblical Criticism*, ed. Richard E. Friedman, Harvard Semitic Studies (Chico, CA: Scholars Press, 1983), pp. 13–40, especially pp. 24–25.

[37] On the importance of kinship relations in the stories, see Robert A. Oden, "Jacob as Father, Husband, and Nephew: Kinship Studies and the Patriarchal Narratives," *JBL*

102 (1983), pp. 189–205, with the valuable corrections of Naomi Steinberg, "Alliance or Descent? The Function of Marriage in Genesis," *JSOT* 51 (1991), pp. 45–55. On the functions of biblical genealogies generally, see Robert Wilson, *Genealogy and History in the Biblical World*, Yale Near Eastern Researches 7 (New Haven: Yale Univ. Press, 1977).

[38] For more extensive criticisms of Noth's history of traditions method, see Robert Polzin, "Martin Noth's *A History of Pentateuchal Traditions*," *BASOR* 221 (1976), pp. 113–120; on his form-critical presuppositions, see Rolf Knierim, "Old Testament Form Criticism Reconsidered," *Interpretation* 27 (1973), pp. 435–468; and Sean M. Warner, "Primitive Saga Men," *VT* 29 (1979), pp. 325–335.

[39] Gunkel, "The Influence of Babylonian Mythology upon the Biblical Creation Story," *Creation in the Old Testament* (ed. B.W. Anderson; Philadelphia: Fortress, 1984; German original, *Schöpfung und Chaos*, 1895), p. 26.

[40] See Ronald S. Hendel, "When the Sons of God Cavorted with the Daughters of Men," in *Understanding the Dead Sea Scrolls*, ed. Hershel Shanks (New York: Random House, 1992), pp. 167–177; first published in *BR*, Summer 1987, pp. 8–13.

[41] Some references in the J source to Mesopotamian matters indicate a historical context in the Neo-Assyrian period. These include the designation of southern Mesopotamia as Chaldean (Genesis 11:28, cf. Genesis 22:22), and the reference to Nineveh as a major Assyrian city (Genesis 10:11–12). These references indicate a historical context in the mid- to late eighth century B.C.E. Corresponding to these notices is the cultural identification of the Tigris River with Assyria (Genesis 2:14).

[42] Cf. Terry J. Prewitt, "Kinship Structures and the Genesis Genealogies," *JNES* 40 (1981), pp. 97–98.

[43] This refers to a time before Machir had been replaced by Manasseh and reduced to the status of a Manassite clan (cf. de Vaux, *Early History* [see endnote 8], pp. 651–652) and before Gilead had been replaced by Gad south of the Jabbok and the name Gilead had been generalized to include all of Transjordan (pp. 571–572, 574–576).

[44] On the complex problems involved in the dating of the battle described in Judges 5, see Chapter III of this volume and de Vaux, *Early History* (see endnote 8), pp. 789–796.

[45] *ANET*, pp. 376–378.

[46] The emphasis in recent research on the sociological conditions out of which the community emerged has begun to lead to excellent

results. It has created a tendency, however, to overlook the importance of the emergence of an ethnic identity. A valuable balance to this tendency is provided by Baruch Halpern in *The Emergence of Israel in Canaan*, SBL Monograph Series 29 (Chico, CA: Scholars Press, 1983), especially pp. 90, 100.

[47] For an overview of this subject, see the introduction to *Ethnic Groups and Boundaries*, ed. Frederick Barth (Boston: Little, Brown, 1969).

[48] See Hendel, "Finding Historical Memories in the Patriarchal Narratives," *BAR*, July/August 1995, pp. 52–59, 70–72.

[49] Albrecht Alt, "The God of the Fathers" [1929], *Essays on Old Testament History and Religion*, trans. R.A. Wilson (Garden City, NY: Doubleday, 1968), p. 7.

[50] See Cross, *Canaanite Myth and Hebrew Epic: Essays in the History of the Religion of Israel* (Cambridge: Harvard Univ. Press, 1973), pp. 13–43.

[51] Cross, *Canaanite Myth*, (see endnote 50), pp. 44–75.

[52] According to the distribution of personal names in the Bible, El predominates as a divine element during the premonarchic period, with Yahweh becoming popular in the early monarchic period and thereafter. For the statistics and some implications, see recently Karel van der Toorn, *Family Religion in Babylonia, Syria and Israel: Continuity and Change in the Forms of Religious Life*, Studies in the History and Culture of the Ancient Near East 7 (Leiden: Brill, 1996), pp. 237–238.

[53] Hendel, "Finding Historical Memories" (see endnote 48), pp. 59, 70–71; Giorgio Buccellati, "From Khana to Laqê: The End of Syro-Mesopotamia, in Ö. Tunca, ed., *De la Babylonie à la Syrie, en passant par Mari* (Liège, 1990), pp. 229–253.

[54] See the careful comments of Abraham Malamat, *Mari and the Early Israelite Experience* (Oxford: Oxford Univ. Press, 1989), pp. 27–30.

[55] Cross, *Canaanite Myth* (see endnote 50), p. 57.

[56] Arguments that the Aramaic connection stems from the mid-first millennium B.C.E. are exceedingly weak; cf. Van Seters (*Abraham* [see endnote 18], p. 34), who suggests that the Assyrian deportation of Israelites to the Middle Euphrates region after 722 B.C.E. and the resurgence of the trade route through Haran in the Neo-Babylonian period may have been factors in the formation of an ethnic identification with Arameans in this period.

[57] Jacob J. Finkelstein, "The Genealogy of the Hammurapi Dynasty," *JCS* 20 (1966), pp. 95–118, especially pp. 97–98.

[58] See endnote 20.

[59] As pointed out first by Hugo Gressmann ("Sage und Geschichte in den Patriarch-enerzählungen," *ZAW* 30 [1910], pp. 1–34, especially p. 2 and note 4), the longer form of the name "Abraham" occur in Aramaic. See also de Vaux (*Early History* [see endnote 8], pp. 197–198 and notes 73 and 74), who cites evidence for a similar phenomenon in Ugaritic and Phoenician; his examples, however, are not precisely parallel.

[60] Benjamin Mazar, "The Historical Background of the Book of Genesis," in *The Early Biblical Period*, ed. S. Ahituv and B.A. Levine (Jerusalem: Israel Exploration Society, 1986), p. 59; originally published in *JNES* 28 (1969), p. 81.

[61] Hendel, "Finding Historical Memories," pp. 55, 58–59. The importance of this place-name was pointed out by James H. Breasted, "The Earliest Occurrence of the Name of Abram," *American Journal of Semitic Languages and Literature* (1904), p. 36.

[62] Yohanan Aharoni, *The Archaeology of the Land of Israel*, trans. Anson F. Rainey (Philadelphia: Westminster, 1982), p. 168.

[63] Aharoni, *Archaeology of the Land of Israel* (see endnote 62), pp. 162–173.

[64] Cf. Noth, *Die israelitischen Personennamen* (see endnote 25), p. 210.

[65] It is possible that the transferral of the Isaac tradition to Beersheba was partly the result of the historical movement of people from the northern hills into the Negev. Note, for example, the prominent role played by Simeon and Levi, the patriarchs of the tribes of southwestern Judah and the northern Negev, in the story of the rape of Dinah at Shechem (Genesis 34). Cf. Noth, *History of Israel* (see endnote 31), pp. 71 and 76, note 1. Contrast de Vaux, *Early History* (see endnote 8), pp. 532–533.

[66] See Thompson, *Historicity of the Patriarchal Narratives* (see endnote 18), pp. 45–48.

[67] For the citations, see J. Simons, *Handbook for the Study of Egyptian Topographical Lists Relating to Western Asia* (Leiden: Brill, 1937), xxxiv, lists 1a and 1b/102 (Thutmosis III), 23/9 (Rameses II) and 27/104 (Rameses III), and most recently, Shmuel Ahituv, *Canaanite Toponyms in Ancient Egyptian Documents* (Jerusalem: Magnes, 1984), p. 200. Cf. *ANET*, p. 242.

[68] Cf. Shmuel Yeivin ("The Short List of the Towns in Palestine and Syria Captured by Thutmosis III During His First Campaign," *Eretz Israel* 3 [Jerusalem: IES, 1954], pp. 32–38, especially p. 36), who proposes an identification with Tel Melat, west of Gezer, which is often associated with the biblical city of Gibbethon.

[69] Both of these cities are mentioned in the same part of the Thutmosis list, as are a number of nearby places east of the Jordan in the Yarmuk region. See H. Wolfgang Helck, *Die Beziehungen Ägyptens zu Vorderasien im 3. und 2. Jahrtausen v. Chr*, Ägyptologische Abhandlungen 5 (Weisbaden, W. Ger.: Otto Harrassowitz, 1962), p. 128.

[70] This was taken for granted by Albright ("A Third Revision of the Early Chronology of Western Asia," *BASOR* 88 [1942], pp. 28–36, especially p. 36, note 39).

[71] Aharon Kempinsky, "Jacob in History," *BAR*, January/February 1988, pp. 42–47; idem, "Some Observations on the Hyksos (XVth) Dynasty and Its Canaanite Origins," in Sarah Israelit-Groll, ed., *Pharaonic Egypt: The Bible and Christianity* (Jerusalem: Magnes Press, 1985), pp. 129–137; cf. Halpern, ("The Exodus from Egypt: Myth or Reality?" in Hershel Shanks, ed., *The Rise of Ancient Israel* [Washington, DC: Biblical Archaeology Society, 1992], p. 110, note 20), who notes the possibility that the 18th-century Jacob-Har may have been a local ruler in pre-Hyksos Egypt, and that the Shiqmona seal was a sign of trade or other local relations with his dynasty.

[72] Noth, *History of Israel* (see endnote 31), p. 71, note 2.

[73] See, for example, Victor Maag, "Der Hirte Israel," *Schweizerische Theologische Umschau* 28 (1958), pp. 2–28; Horst Seebass, *Der Erzvater Israel*, *ZAW* supp. 98 (Berlin: A. Topelmann, 1966), pp. 1–5, 25–34.

[74] Cf. Siegfried Herrmann, *A History of Israel in Old Testament Times*, trans. John Bowden (Philadelphia: Fortress, 1981), p. 51. Recent proponents of this idea in one form or another include Albert de Pury ("Genèse xxxiv et l'histoire," *RB* 76 [1969], pp. 5–49, especially pp. 39–48) and André Lemaire ("Asriel, šr'l Israel et l'origine de la confédération israelite," *VT* 23 [1973], pp. 239–243); and see P. Kyle McCarter, Jr., "The Origins of Israelite Religion," in Hershel Shanks, ed., *The Rise of Ancient Israel* (see endnote 71), pp. 132–136.

[75] Cf. endnote 100.

[76] Gunkel, *Legends of Genesis, the Biblical Saga and History* (New York: Schocken, 1964), pp. 23–24. Cf. Jeremiah 49:7, Obadiah 1:8, and Job.

[77] Noth, *History of Pentateuchal Traditions* (see endnote 33), pp. 97–98.

[78] Hendel, *The Epic of the Patriarch: The Jacob Cycle and the Narrative Traditions of Canaan and Israel*, Harvard Semitic Monographs 42 (Atlanta: Scholars Press, 1987), pp. 111–131.

[79] Cf. de Vaux, *Early History* (see endnote 8), pp. 642–643.

[80] Noth, *Die israelitischen Personennamen* (see endnote 25), p. 212; de Vaux, *Early History* (see endnote 8), p. 313.

[81] See recently, Halpern, "Exodus from Egypt" (see endnote 71), pp. 92–99.

[82] Theodor H. Gaster, *Myth, Legend, and Custom in the Old Testament*, 2 vols. (New York: Torch-books/Harper & Row, 1975), vol. 1, pp. 217–218; Thompson and Irvin, "The Joseph and Moses Narratives," in Hayes and Miller, *Israelite and Judaean History* (see endnote 7), pp. 185–188.

[83] *ANET*, pp. 23–25.

[84] Thompson and Irvin, "The Joseph and Moses Narratives" (see endnote 82), pp. 188–190.

[85] Seven years of famine are described in an Egyptian text of the Ptolemaic period (perhaps the end of the second century B.C.E.), which claims to derive from King Djoser of the Third Dynasty (c. 2650 B.C.E.); see *ANET*, pp. 31–32. Tablet VI of the Akkadian Gilgamesh epic speaks of "seven years of husks"; see *ANET*, p. 85. The autobiographical inscription of Idrimi, king of the Syrian city of Alalakh in the 16th century B.C.E., refers to two unfavorable periods, each lasting seven years; see *ANET*, pp. 557–558. There is a prediction of seven to eight years of drought in the Ugaritic myth of Áqht; see *ANET*, p. 153.

[86] See Donald B. Redford, *A Study of the Biblical Story of Joseph*, VT supp. 20 (Leiden: Brill, 1970).

[87] Cf. *ANET*, p. 445 and note 10.

[88] See de Vaux, *Early History* (see endnote 8), pp. 301–302.

[89] Herrman Ranke, *Die ägyptischen Personnamen*, 3 vols. (Glückstadt, W. Ger.: J.J. Augustin, 1935), vol. 1, p. 14, names 13–17, and p. 15, name 3. See also Alan R. Schulman, "On the Egyptian Name of Joseph: A New Approach," *Studien zur altägyptischen Kultur* 2 (1975), pp. 238–239; Redford, *Egypt, Canaan, and Israel in Ancient Times* (Princeton: Princeton Univ. Press, 1992), p. 424; and Kitchen, "Genesis 12–50 in the Near Eastern World," in R.S. Hess, P.E. Satterthwaite, and G.J. Wenham, eds., *He Swore an Oath: Biblical Themes from Genesis 12–50* (Cambridge: Tyndale House, 1993), pp. 84–85.

[90] H. Hamada, "Stela of Putiphar," *Annales du Service des Antiquités de l'Égypte* 39 (1939), pp. 273–276 and plate 39.

[91] Ranke, *Die ägyptischen Personnamen* (see endnote 89), pp. 409–412 and Schulman, "Egyptian Name" (see endnote 89), pp. 239–242; cf. the imaginative proposal of Kitchen, "Genesis 12–50" (see endnote 89), pp. 80–84.

[92] Helck, *Die Beziehungen Ägyptens* (see endnote 69), pp. 77–81, 342–369; Jozef M.A. Janssen,

"Fonctionnaires sémites au service de l'Égypte," *Chronique d'Égypte* 26 (1951), pp. 50–62; Albright, "Northwest-Semitic Names in a List of Egyptian Slaves from the Eighteenth Century B.C.," *JAOS* 74 (1954), pp. 222–233; Georges Posener, "Les asiatiques en Égypte sous les XII et XIII dynasties," *Syria* 34 (1957), pp. 145–163.

[93] *ANET*, p. 260.

[94] See Alan H. Gardiner, *Egypt of the Pharaohs: An Introduction* (Oxford: Clarendon Press, 1961), p. 282.

[95] *ANET*, p. 259 (trans. John A. Wilson). The text is a model letter from a scribal school.

[96] See Gardiner, *Ancient Egyptian Onomastica*, 3 vols. (London: Oxford Univ. Press, 1947), pp. 191–193, no. 265. In the present state of our knowledge, we cannot be sure that the equation of the toponym in the Egyptian texts with the name of the Israelite tribe is linguistically valid. Albright associated the name of an Asiatic female slave in 18th-century B.C.E. Egypt with the tribal name ("Northwest Semitic Names" [see endnote 92], p. 229–231 and note 51). The sibilant of the slave name (š=*š) is different from that of the geographical term (š=*t or *ś in the Egyptian texts. It seems to follow that the geographical term can have had nothing to do with the Israelite tribe (cf. Kitchen, *Ancient Orient and the Old Testament* [Chicago: Inter-Varsity Press, 1966], pp. 70–71 and note 53). But it is not certain that Albright's association of the slave and tribal names is correct. The sibilant in the tribal name "Asher" remains unidentified. Thus, despite Kitchen's objections, Shmuel Yeivin is justified in maintaining the possibility of a connection between the Egyptian toponym and the biblical tribal name ("The Israelite Settlement in Galilee and the Wars with Jabin of Hazor," in *Mélanges bibliques rédigés en l'honneur de André Robert*, Travaux de l'Institut Catholique de Paris 4 [Paris: Bloud and Gay, 1957], pp. 95–104, especially pp. 98–99).

[97] See Noth, *The Old Testament World*, trans. V.I. Gruhn (Philadelphia: Fortress, 1966), pp. 55–58. Cf. Noth, *History of Israel* (see endnote 31), pp. 56, 60, 67 and note 1, and the comments by de Vaux, *Early History* (see endnote 8), p. 665.

[98] Noth, *Old Testament World* (see endnote 97), p. 72; in *History of Israel* (see endnote 31), pp. 62–63.

[99] On "Manasseh," cf. Noth, *Die israelitischen Personennamen* (see endnote 25), p. 222.

[100] This is confirmed by the survey of Ephraim currently underway (Israel Finkelstein, "Shiloh Yields Some, But Not All, of Its Secrets," *BAR*, January/February 1986, pp. 22–41, especially

p. 35). Cf. the demographic statistics cited by Lawrence E. Stager, in "The Archaeology of the Family in Ancient Israel," *BASOR* 260 (1985), pp. 1–36, especially p. 3.

[101] The importance of the contrast between the mountains and the plains to the history of this period was first stressed by Albrecht Alt. See "The Settlement of the Israelites in Palestine," in *Essays on Old Testament History and Religion* (Garden City, NY: Anchor/Doubleday, 1968), pp. 173–221, especially pp. 188–204.

[102] Buccellati, *Cities and Nations of Ancient Syria*, Studi Semitici 26 (Rome: Ist. (Institute) di Studi del Vicino Oriente, 1967).

II. Israel in Egypt

[1] On wet-nurses, see Brevard S. Childs, "The Birth of Moses," *JBL* 84 (1965), pp. 109–122. On the name "Moses," see Alan H. Gardiner, "The Egyptian Origin of Some English Personal Names," *JAOS* 56 (1936), pp. 192–194; J. Cerny, "The Greek Etymology of the Name of Moses," *Annales du Service des antiquités de l'Égypte* 51 (1951), pp. 349–354; and Jaroslav G. Griffiths, "The Egyptian Derivation of the Name Moses," *JNES* 12 (1953), pp. 225–231.

[2] See Nahum M. Sarna, *Exploring Exodus* (New York: Schocken Books, 1986), pp. 39–42.

[3] On the plagues, see Moshe Greenberg, "Plagues of Egypt," *Encyclopedia Judaica*, vol. 13, pp. 604–613; Ziony Zevit, "The Priestly Redaction and Interpretation of the Plagues Narrative in Exodus," *JQR* 66 (1976), pp. 193–211; Sarna, *Exploring Exodus* (see endnote 2), pp. 63–80.

[4] Baruch Halpern, "The Exodus from Egypt: Myth or Reality?" in Hershel Shanks, ed., *The Rise of Ancient Israel* (Washington, DC: Biblical Archaeology Society, 1992), p. 87.

[5] Cf. Sir Alan Gardiner, perhaps the best-known and most highly respected Egyptologist of the 20th century, in "The Geography of the Exodus," in *Recueil d'études égyptologiques dediées à la mémoire de Jean-François Champollion* (Paris: Bibliothèque de l'école des hautes études, 1922), p. 205: "That Israel was in Egypt under one form or another no historian could possibly doubt; a legend of such tenacity representing the early fortunes of a peoples under so unfavorable an aspect could not have arisen save as a reflexion, however much distorted, of real occurrences."

[6] This is an application of a more general principle: "Hints in the text which go contrary to its overall bias suggest some authentic information has survived the

editorial process." Lester L. Grabbe, "Are Historians of Ancient Palestine Fellow Creatures—or Different Animals?" in Grabbe, ed., *Can A 'History of Israel' Be Written? JSOT* Supplement Series 245, (Sheffield: Sheffield Academic Press, 1997), p. 30.

[7] Halpern, "The Exodus from Egypt: Myth or Reality?" (see endnote 4), pp. 99–100.

[8] William C. Hayes, *A Papyrus of the Late Middle Kingdom in the Brooklyn Museum [Papyrus Brooklyn 35.1446]* (New York: Brooklyn Museum, 1955). See also William F. Albright, "Northwest Semitic Names in a List of Egyptian Slaves from the Eighteenth Century B.C.," *JAOS* 74 (1954), pp. 222–223.

[9] The translation is that of James K. Hoffmeier, *Israel in Egypt* (Oxford: Oxford University Press, 1997), pp. 54–55.

[10] Hoffmeier, *Israel in Egypt* (see endnote 9), p. 59.

[11] Hoffmeier, *Israel in Egypt* (see endnote 9), p. 60.

[12] *ANET*, p. 259.

[13] Kenneth A. Kitchen, *Ramesside Inscriptions* (Oxford: Blackwell, 1996), vol. 2, pp. 520–522.

[14] Kenneth A. Kitchen, "From the Brickfields of Egypt," *TB* 27 (1976), pp. 145–146.

[15] For a criticism of the hermeneutic of suspicion, see Jon D. Levenson, *The Hebrew Bible, the Old Testament and Historical Criticism* (Louisville: Westminster/John Knox, 1993), p. 116.

[16] Thomas L. Thompson, *The Origin Tradition of Ancient Israel*, vol. 1 (Sheffield: JSOT, 1987), p. 41.

[17] Robert B. Coote, *Early Israel* (Minneapolis: Fortress, 1990), pp. 2–3.

[18] For the problems and different approaches, see C. De Wit, *The Date and Route of the Exodus* (London: Tyndale, 1960); L.T. Wood, "The Date of the Exodus," in *New Perspectives on the Old Testament*, ed. J.B. Wane (Waco, TX: Word Books, 1970), pp. 66–87; B.K. Waltke, "Palestinian Artifactual Evidence Supporting the Early Date for the Exodus," *Bibliotheca Sacra* 129 (1972), pp. 33–47; John J. Bimson, *Redating the Exodus and Conquest*, JSOT Supplement Series 5 (Leiden: Brill, 1978).

[19] *Antiq.* 14.2.

[20] *Seder Olam* 3:2.

[21] For a summary of the chronological problems, see Roland K. Harrison, *Introduction to the Old Testament* (Grand Rapids, MI: Eerdmans, 1969), pp. 164–176, 308–325.

[22] See Charles F. Burney, *Notes on the Hebrew Text of the Book of Kings* (New York: KTAV, 1970), p. 60.

[23] In addition, if the Exodus occurred in the 15th century B.C.E., there would be a 400-year period before the institution of the monarchy at the end of the 11th century B.C.E. This is an unacceptably long time for the period of the Judges.

[24] Lawrence E. Stager, "The Archaeology of the Family in Ancient Israel," *BASOR* 260 (1985), pp. 1–35.

[25] Pierre Montet, *Everyday Life in Egypt in the Days of Ramesses the Great*, trans. A.R. Maxwell-Hyslop and Margaret S. Drower (London: E. Arnold, 1958); Raymond O. Faulkner, "Egypt from the Inception of the Nineteenth Dynasty to the Death of Ramesses II," in *CAH*, vol. 2, part 2, pp. 225–232.

[26] The scholarly debate as to whether the biblical city referred to as Raamses is the same as Pi-Ramesses in Egyptian records has been resolved to the satisfaction of most scholars. Manfred Bietak has shown that the "Pi-" drops off in various grammatical situations. See his "Comments on Exodus," in Anson F. Rainey, ed., *Egypt, Israel, and Sinai* (Tel Aviv: Tel Aviv Univ. Press, 1987), pp. 163–171.

[27] See Manfred Weippert, *The Settlement of the Israelite Tribes in Palestine* (London: SCM Press, 1971), pp. 74–82.

[28] That the two words are etymologically related does not necessarily mean that all the 'Apiru became Hebrews, only that some of them were somehow related to the early Hebrews.

[29] Nadav Na'aman, "Habiru and Hebrews: The Transfer of a Social Term to the Literary Sphere," *JNES* 45 (1986), p. 273.

[30] For an opposing view, see Rainey, "Unruly Elements in Late Bronze Canaanite Society," in David P. Wright, David Noel Freedman and Avi Hurvitz, eds., *Pomegranates and Golden Bells: Studies in Biblical, Jewish, and Near Eastern Ritual, Law and Literature in Honor of Jacob Milgrom* (Winona Lake, IN: Eisenbrauns, 1995), p. 483: "The plethora of attempts to find some way to relate *'apirū* to the gentilic *'ibrî* are all nothing but wishful thinking." Cf. Na'aman, "Habiru and Hebrews" (see endnote 29), p. 278: "The etymological relationship of the term 'Habiru of the ancient Near Eastern texts and the biblical term 'ibri can be established reasonably securely."

[31] For a sophisticated review of the evidence to support the conclusion that Ramesses II was the pharaoh of the Exodus and Merneptah the pharaoh of the oppression (or, more precisely, that Israelite tradition so regarded them), see Halpern, "The Exodus from Egypt" (see endnote 4); and Halpern, "The Exodus and the Israelite Historians," *Eretz Israel* 24 (1993), p. 89*.

[32] Cf. Hershel Shanks, ed., *Frank Moore Cross: Conversations with a Bible Scholar* (Washington, DC: Biblical Archaeology Society, 1994), pp. 21–22.

[33] H.J. Franken, "Palestine in the Time of the Nineteenth Dynasty: Archaeological Evidence," in *CAH*, vol. 2, part 2, pp. 331–337. Halpern, "The Exodus from Egypt" (see endnote 4), p. 101.

[34] Carol Redmount, "Bitter Lives: Israel in and out of Egypt," in Michael D. Coogan, ed., *The Oxford History of the Biblical World* (Oxford: Oxford Univ. Press, 1998), p. 89.

[35] *ANET*, pp. 376–378.

[36] Gösta Ahlström, *Who Were the Israelites?* (Winona Lake, IN: Eisenbrauns, 1986).

[37] Abraham Malamat, "Let My People Go and Go and Go and Go," *BAR*, January/February 1998. See also Malamat, "The Exodus: Egyptian Analogies," in Ernest S. Frerichs and Leonard H. Lesko, eds., *Exodus—The Egyptian Evidence* (Winona Lake, IN: Eisenbrauns, 1997).

[38] See William G. Dever, "Israelite Origins and the 'Nomadic Ideal,'" in Seymour Gitin, Amihai Mazar and Ephraim Stern, eds., *Mediterranean Peoples in Transition* (Jerusalem: Israel Exploration Society, 1998), esp. pp. 231–232.

[39] It will not do, in refutation of this argument, to point to other peoples, such as the Romans, who also reproduced inglorious traditions about their own past. See, for example, J. Alberto Soggin, *A History of Ancient Israel* (Philadelphia: Westminster, 1984), pp. 110–111. On the contrary, such tales may well reflect historical reality, and in any case did not become a central and formative factor in shaping the religion and culture of their respective bearers over thousands of years.

[40] In several biblical passages, the word translated "thousands" (*alafim*) means not thousands but clans. It is sometimes suggested on this basis that the passage in Numbers 1:46 should be understood to refer to 600 families or clans, rather than 600,000 men. It is an ingenious theory, but it founders. For example: The number of the Israelite firstborn sons who went on the Exodus as given in Numbers 3:43 is 22,273. Since the number is exact, the word *elef* cannot be translated as family or clan. Moreover, the context makes clear that the reference is to individuals (firstborn Israelites), not families or clans. If there were 22,273 firstborn Israelites, the total number of families had to be more than 600. See Sarna, *Exploring Exodus* (see endnote 2), pp. 98–100. Sarna writes, "The structures of thought within which the biblical writers operated permitted them to conceive of reality in ways quite different from our own ... [The

account as a whole] is not meant to be history writing in the modern sense of that term, but a historiosophical understanding of a complex of events that happened in historical time" (p. 100).

[41] Susan Niditch, *Oral World and Written Word: Ancient Israelite Literature* (Louisville: Westminster/John Knox, 1996).

[42] See, for example, Niels Peter Lemche, *Early Israel: Anthropological and Historical Studies on the Israelite Society Before the Monarchy* (Leiden: Brill, 1985), p. 412.

[43] Myth, however, does not necessarily indicate a complete lack of historicity. Myth may have a historical core. See Bernard F. Batto, *Slaying the Dragon—Mythmaking in the Biblical Tradition* (Louisville: Westminster/John Knox, 1992), p. 103 and *passim*. Batto contends that "it was the biblical writers' intention to explode the exodus into an 'event' that transcends the particularities of space and time, making it the story of every Israelite in every generation" (p. 103). History has been "mythologized" (p. 109). For Batto, "myth is a sophisticated and abstract mode of thought" (p. 10). It "involves reflective thinking not through syllogistic reasoning or philosophical categories but through the medium of mythic narrative" (p. 40). "[Myth] attempts to express ultimate reality through symbol" (p. 11). "Whatever the historicity of the events that lie behind the biblical narrative, the exodus *as story* has been elevated to mythic proportions" (p. 103).

[44] *Encyclopaedia Judaica*, s.v. "Manetho."

[45] Grabbe, "Are Historians of Ancient Palestine Fellow Creatures?" (see endnote 6), p. 23.

[46] Grabbe, "Are Historians of Ancient Palestine Fellow Creatures?" (see endnote 6), pp. 23–24.

[47] See, in general, James M. Weinstein, "Hyksos," in *ABD*, vol. 3, under "The Fifteenth Dynasty."

[48] *ANET*, p. 230b.

[49] Trude Dothan, "Gaza Sands Yield Lost Outpost of the Egyptian Empire," *National Geographic* (December 1982), pp. 739–768; and "Cultural Crossroads: Deir el-Balah and the Cosmopolitan Culture of the Late Bronze Age," *BAR*, September/October 1998.

[50] Charles R. Krahmalkov, "Exodus Itinerary Confirmed by Egyptian Evidence," *BAR*, September/ October 1994.

[51] See Batto, "Red Sea or Reed Sea?" *BAR*, July/ August 1984; and "The Reed Sea: Requiescat in Pace," *JBL* 102 (1983), p. 27.

[52] Emmanuel Anati, "Has Mt. Sinai Been Found?" *BAR*, July/August 1985. For a chart listing a dozen possibilities, see Itzhaq Beit-Arieh, "The Route Through Sinai," *BAR*, May/June 1988, pp. 36–37.

[53] There were four major routes through the Sinai in antiquity, the northern route along the Mediterranean coast, and three others through wadi systems. See Beit-Arieh, "The Route Through Sinai" (see endnote 52), p. 28; and Redmount, "Bitter Lives" (see endnote 34), pp. 91–94.

[54] Avraham [incorrectly Aviram] Perevolotsky and Israel Finkelstein, "The Southern Sinai Exodus Route in Ecological Perspective," BAR, July/August 1985.

[55] See Rudolph Cohen, "Did I Excavate Kadesh-Barnea?" BAR, May/June 1981.

[56] See Krahmalkov, "Exodus Itinerary Confirmed" (see endnote 50).

[57] As one commentator has observed, "We do the Exodus narrative a profound disservice by uncritically seeking natural interpretations for the clearly miraculous, and it is misguided to supply scientific explanations for such nonhistorical events as the ten plagues of Egypt, the burning bush that spoke to Moses, or the pillars of cloud and fire that accompanied the Israelites in the wilderness." See Redmount, "Bitter Lives" (see endnote 34), pp. 85–86.

[58] Donald B. Redford, Egypt, Canaan and Israel in Ancient Times (Princeton: Princeton Univ. Press, 1992), p. 417.

[59] It is also possible to interpret the verse as stating that Moses' mother named him. But this seems less likely. The text explains the name on the basis of a traditional Hebrew etymology: "to draw out." Pharaoh's daughter explains the choice of name: "I drew him out of the water" (Exodus 2:10).

[60] See Hoffmeier, Israel in Egypt (see endnote 9), p. 140. The divine name seems to have been omitted in the case of Moses. This does sometimes occur in Egyptian records. Or the divine element may have been suppressed by the biblical writer, who would hardly want the name of such a central figure in the development of Israelite religion to suggest allegiance to a foreign god. See Redmount, "Bitter Lives" (see endnote 34), pp. 88–89.

[61] On the Hyksos, see John Van Seters, The Hyksos: A New Investigation (New Haven, CT: Yale Univ. Press, 1966); Redford, "The Hyksos Invasion in History and Tradition," Orientalia 39 (1970), pp. 1–51; William C. Hayes, "Egypt from the Death of Ammenemes III to Seqenenre II," in CAH, vol. 2, part 1, pp. 54–64; T.G.H. James, "Egypt: From the Expulsion of the Hyksos to Amenophis I," in CAH, vol. 2, part 1, pp. 289–312; Yohanan Aharoni, The Land of the Bible: A Historical Geography, rev. and enlarged, trans. and ed. Anson F. Rainey (Philadelphia: Westminster, 1979), pp. 147–150.

[62] The XVIIth Dynasty is an obscure dynasty of Egyptian rulers who ruled part of Egypt from Thebes during the Hyksos era.

[63] ANET, p. 252b.

[64] Halpern, "The Exodus from Egypt" (see endnote 4), pp. 95–98. See also, but less accessibly, Halpern, "The Exodus and the Israelite Historians" (see endnote 31), p. 89*.

[65] Halpern, "The Exodus from Egypt" (see endnote 4), p. 98.

[66] Halpern, "The Exodus from Egypt" (see endnote 4), p. 101. Cf. Redford, Egypt, Canaan and Israel (see endnote 58), pp. 412–413. Redford sees both the Israelite descent into Egypt and the Exodus from Egypt as the Israelite appropriation of the Canaanite version of the Hyksos period in Egypt.

III. The Settlement in Canaan

[1] Abraham Malamat, "How Inferior Israelite Forces Conquered Fortified Canaanite Cities," BAR, March/April 1982, p. 26.

[2] Malamat, "How Inferior Israelite Forces Conquered" (see endnote 1), p. 26.

[3] Malamat, "How Inferior Israelite Forces Conquered" (see endnote 1), p. 27.

[4] Joseph A. Callaway, "'Ai," EAEHL, vol. 1, p. 52.

[5] For William F. Albright's pioneering work on the issue, see especially his "Archaeology and the Date of the Hebrew Conquest of Palestine," BASOR 58 (1935), pp. 10–18; "Further Light on the History of Israel from Lachish and Megiddo," BASOR 68 (1937), pp. 22–26; and "The Israelite Conquest of Canaan in the Light of Archaeology," BASOR 74 (1939), pp. 11–23. His views were developed and widely popularized by his students; see G. Ernest Wright and Floyd Filson, The Westminster Historical Atlas of the Bible (Philadelphia: Westminster Press, 1956); and John Bright, A History of Israel (Philadelphia: Westminster Press, 1959).

[6] Yigael Yadin, "Is the Biblical Account of the Israelite Conquest of Canaan Historically Reliable?" BAR, March/April 1982, p. 18.

[7] Yadin, "Is the Biblical" (see endnote 6), p. 18.

[8] Yadin, "Is the Biblical" (see endnote 6), p. 19.

[9] Malamat, "How Inferior Israelite Forces Conquered" (see endnote 1), p. 27.

[10] Malamat, "How Inferior Israelite Forces Conquered" (see endnote 1), p. 27.

[11] Malamat, "How Inferior Israelite Forces Conquered" (see endnote 1), p. 28.

[12] Malamat, "How Inferior Israelite Forces Conquered" (see endnote 1), map on p. 30.

[13] William H. Stiebing, Jr., "When Was the Age of the Patriarchs?—of Amorites, Canaanites, and Archaeology," *BAR*, June 1975, pp. 17–21.

[14] See Yadin, "The Transition from a Semi-Nomadic to a Sedentary Society in the Twelfth Century B.C.," in *Symposia*, ed. Frank M. Cross (Cambridge, MA: American Schools of Oriental Research, 1979), pp. 57–68.

[15] Cited by Malamat, in "How Inferior Israelite Forces Conquered" (see endnote 1), p. 31.

[16] Malamat, "How Inferior Israelite Forces Conquered" (see endnote 1), p. 33.

[17] Malamat, "How Inferior Israelite Forces Conquered" (see endnote 1), p. 26.

[18] Actually, for a large army, the Wadi Farah, beginning some 15 miles north of Jericho and emerging in the hills at Tirzah, east of Shechem, would have been much more suitable. The Wadi Farah is wide and is currently planted in lush banana and citrus groves.

[19] Malamat, "How Inferior Israelite Forces Conquered" (see endnote 1), p. 33.

[20] Malamat, "How Inferior Israelite Forces Conquered" (see endnote 1), p. 33.

[21] Paul Lapp reviewed the archaeological picture in 1967 with the conclusion that, although the evidence admittedly was ambivalent, on the whole it supported the notion of a 13th-century Israelite military conquest. J. Maxwell Miller reviewed the archaeological evidence again ten years later and concluded that more archaeological evidence had to be "explained away" in order to accommodate the notion of a 13th-century military conquest than could be called upon to support such a notion. See P.W. Lapp, "The Conquest of Palestine in the Light of Archaeology," *Concordia Theological Monthly* 38 (1967), pp. 283–300; and Miller, "Archaeology and the Israelite Conquest of Canaan: Some Methodological Observations," *Palestine Exploration Quarterly* 109 (1977), pp. 87–93.

[22] See Kathleen M. Kenyon and Thomas A. Holland, *Excavations at Jericho III* (Plates) (London: British School of Archaeology in Jerusalem, 1981), pl. 236. This master section of the north side of trench I shows dramatically the successive layers of mudbrick walls that collapsed down the slope of the mound.

[23] Kenyon, *Archaeology in the Holy Land* (New York: Praeger, 1960), pp. 210–211.

[24] Lapp, "The Importance of Dating," *BAR*, March 1977, pp. 13–32.

[25] Kenyon, *Archaeology in the Holy Land* (see endnote 23), p. 210.

[26] John Garstang, *Joshua, Judges* (London: Constable, 1931), p. 356.

[27] William F. Albright, "The Israelite Conquest of Canaan in the Light of Archaeology" (see endnote 5), pp. 15–16; Louis-Hugues Vincent, "Les fouilles d'et-Tell 'Aï," *RB* 46 (1937), p. 256.

[28] Callaway, "The 1964 'Ai (et-Tell) Excavations," *BASOR* 178 (1965), pp. 39–40.

[29] Malamat, "How Inferior Israelite Forces Conquered" (see endnote 1), p. 34.

[30] Malamat, "How Inferior Israelite Forces Conquered" (see endnote 1), p. 34.

[31] James B. Pritchard, *Gibeon Where the Sun Stood Still* (Princeton: Princeton Univ. Press, 1962), p. 136.

[32] Von Carel J.H. Vriezen, "Hirbet Kefire—eine Oberflächenuntersuchung," *Sonderdruck aus Zeitschrift des Deutschen Palästina-Vereins*, vol. 91 (1975), pp. 135–158. Some pottery from the period after 1200 B.C.E. was found; only excavation of the site will reveal what kind of village or city existed here after 1200 B.C.E.

[33] Miller, "The Israelite Occupation of Canaan," in *Israelite and Judaean History*, ed. John H. Hayes and Miller (Philadelphia: Westminster, 1977), p. 272.

[34] J. Alberto Soggin, *Joshua* (Philadelphia: Westminster, 1972), p. 130.

[35] Soggin, *Joshua*, (see endnote 34), p. 131.

[36] Miller, "Biblical Maps: How Reliable Are They?" *BR*, Winter 1987, pp. 32–41.

[37] Lachish is clearly to be identified with Tell ed-Duweir despite objections raised by Gösta Ahlström, "Is Tell ed-Duweir Ancient Lachish?" *Palestine Exploration Quarterly* 112 (1980), pp. 7–9.

[38] David Ussishkin, "Lachish," in *NEAEHL* vol. 3, pp. 897–911.

[39] John A. Wilson, trans., "The War Against the Peoples of the Sea," in *ANET*, pp. 262a–263b.

[40] Yadin, *Hazor: The Rediscovery of a Great Citadel of the Bible* (New York: Random House, 1975), pp. 143–145. See also Amnon Ben-Tor's forthcoming article in *BAR*.

[41] William G. Dever, "How to Tell a Canaanite from an Israelite" in *The Rise of Ancient Israel*, ed. Hershel Shanks (Washington: Biblical Archaeology Society, 1992), pp. 27–56, esp. p. 31.

[42] See Ben-Tor's preliminary reports in *Excavations and Surveys in Israel* 10 (1991), pp. 68–69; 13 (1993); 14 (1994), pp. 9–13; and 15 (1995), pp. 12–13. In a personal communication of October 1998, Ben-Tor estimates that the destruction of Hazor occurred sometime between 1300 and 1275 B.C.E., but adds that he simply does not know and that this estimate may change soon.

[43] Yadin, "Is the Biblical" (see endnote 6), p. 23.

[44] John Bimson, *Redating the Exodus and Conquest* (Sheffield, England: JSOT Press, 1978); Bryant Wood, "Did the Israelites Conquer Jericho? A New Look at the Archaeological Evidence," *BAR*, March/April 1990, pp. 44–59.

[45] Albrecht Alt, "The Settlement of the Israelites in Palestine," in *Essays on Old Testament History and Religion*, trans. R.A. Wilson (Garden City, NY: Doubleday, 1968), pp. 175–221; originally published in German in 1925.

[46] Alt, "Settlement of the Israelites" (see endnote 45), pp. 199–201.

[47] Alt, "Settlement of the Israelites" (see endnote 45), pp. 216–221.

[48] Martin Noth, *Das System der zwölf Stämme Israels*, Beiträge zur Wissenschaft vom Alten und Neuen Testament 4:1 (Stuttgart: W. Kohlhammer, 1930), and *A History of Israel*, 2nd. edition, trans. Peter R. Ackroyd (New York: Harper and Row, 1958).

[49] Manfred Weippert, *The Settlement of the Israelite Tribes in Palestine* (London: SCM Press, 1971), pp. 5–6.

[50] Weippert, *Settlement of the Israelite Tribes* (see endnote 49), p. 6.

[51] Malamat, "How Inferior Israelite Forces Conquered" (see endnote 1), p. 34.

[52] Weippert, *Settlement of the Israelite Tribes* (see endnote 49), pp. 5–6.

[53] George E. Mendenhall, "The Hebrew Conquest of Palestine," *BA* 25 (1961), pp. 66–87; Norman K. Gottwald, *The Tribes of Yahweh* (Maryknoll, NY: Orbis Books, 1979), pp. 210–219.

[54] Gottwald, "Were the Early Israelites Pastoral Nomads?" *BAR*, June 1978, pp. 2–7.

[55] Bernhard W. Anderson, "Mendenhall Disavows Paternity," *BR*, Summer 1986, p. 43.

[56] Anderson, "Mendenhall Disavows Paternity" (see endnote 55) p. 47.

[57] Anderson, "Mendenhall Disavows Paternity" (see endnote 55) p. 47.

[58] P. Kyle McCarter, Jr., "A Major New Introduction to the Bible," *BAR*, Summer 1986, p. 43.

[59] McCarter, "A Major New Introduction" (see endnote 58), p. 44.

[60] Anderson, "Mendenhall Disavows Paternity" (see endnote 55), p. 48.

[61] Most of this recent survey work has been conducted by Israeli archaeologists and overseen by Moshe Kochavi of Tel Aviv University. Raphael Frankel and Zvi Gal surveyed the Upper and Lower Galilee respectively. Adam Zertal covered the central hill country from Shechem northward, and Israel Finkelstein from the Shechem vicinity south to approximately Jerusalem. Avi Ofer has surveyed the hill country south of Jerusalem. For an early report on this work, see Kochavi, "Israelite Settlement in Canaan in the Light of Archaeological Surveys," in *Biblical Archaeology Today* (Jerusalem: Israel Exploration Society, 1985), pp. 54–56. For a more recent and complete account of the survey work by the individual archaeologists, each reporting on the area that he surveyed, see *From Nomadism to Monarchy: Archaeological & Historical Aspects of Early Israel*, ed. Israel Finkelstein and Nadav Na'aman (Jerusalem: Israel Exploration Society, 1994).

[62] Lawrence E. Stager, "Highland Village Life in Palestine Some Three Thousand Years Ago," *Oriental Notes and News* 69 (1981), p. 1.

[63] For example, see the original 1988 version of this chapter by Joseph Callaway.

[64] William G. Dever, "How to Tell a Canaanite from an Israelite" (see endnote 41), pp. 27–60.

[65] Joseph C. Wampler, "Some Cisterns and Silos," in *Tell en-Nasbeh I*, ed. C.C. McCown (Berkeley, CA: Palestine Institute of the Pacific School of Religion, 1947), p. 127.

[66] Callaway, *The Early Bronze Age Citadel and Lower City at Ai (et-Tell)* (Cambridge, MA: ASOR, 1980). See fig. 2 for the location of contour 840 and fig. 145 for a plan of the Iron Age I terrace.

[67] Finkelstein, *The Archaeology of the Israelite Settlement* (Jerusalem: Israel Exploration Society, 1998); "The Emergence of Israel: A Phase in the Cyclic History of Canaan in the Third and Second Millennia BCE," in *From Nomadism to Monarchy* (see endnote 61), pp. 150–178.

[68] Finkelstein, "Response to William Dever," in *The Rise of Ancient Israel* (see endnote 41), p. 68.

[69] Adam Zertal, "Israel Enters Canaan— Following the Pottery Trail," *BAR*, September/October 1991, pp. 28–47.

[70] Yohanan Aharoni, "The Israelite Occupation of Canaan," *BAR*, May/June 1982, p. 18.

[71] Miller and John H. Hayes, *A History of Ancient Israel and Judah* (Philadelphia: Westminster, 1986), p. 78.

[72] Lawrence E. Stager, "Merneptah, Israel and Sea Peoples," *Eretz Israel* 18 (Jerusalem: Israel Exploration Society, 1985), p. 56.

[73] Stager, "Merneptah" (see endnote 72), p. 61.

[74] Stager, "Merneptah" (see endnote 72), p. 60.

[75] Stager called attention to a study by his then-colleague at the University of Chicago, Frank Yurco, of the depiction of the pharaoh's enemies in a battle scene at Karnak. Yurco identified in the battle scene what he thought to be the

people called "Israel" on the Merneptah Stele. Their dress is decidedly Canaanite in style and not that of nomads, such as the "Shasu" depicted elsewhere in the battle scene. Anson Rainey has since challenged Yurco's identification, however, and argued that Merneptah's Israel is in fact represented by the Shasu in the battle scene. Frank J. Yurco, "3,200-Year-Old Picture of Israelites Found in Egypt," *BAR*, September/October 1990; Anson F. Rainey, "Anson F. Rainey's Challenge," *BAR*, November/December 1991, pp. 56–60, 93.

[76] Ahlström, *Who Were the Israelites?* (Winona Lake, IN: Eisenbrauns, 1986), p. 40.

[77] Ahlström, *Who Were the Israelites?* (see endnote 76), p. 40.

[78] Finkelstein, *The Archaeology of the Israelite Settlement* (see endnote 67), pp. 27–28.

[79] Baruch Halpern, *The Emergence of Israel in Canaan*, Society of Biblical Literature Monograph Series 29 (Chico, CA: Scholars Press, 1983).

[80] Miller and Hayes, *History of Ancient Israel* (see endnote 71).

[81] Halpern, *Emergence of Israel* (see endnote 79), p. 91.

[82] Miller and Hayes, *History of Ancient Israel* (see endnote 71), p. 97.

[83] Miller and Hayes, *History of Ancient Israel* (see endnote 71), p. 97.

[84] Callaway, in the original 1988 version of this chapter, proposed a syntheses of the two views: "Since the Merneptah inscription dates to before the time of Deborah (sometime in the 12th century B.C.), we can postulate an evolution in tribal alignments, beginning at least with the four tribes of the loose Ephraimite alignment, i.e., Ephraim, Manasseh, Gilead and Benjamin. By the time of Deborah, there seems to have been an alliance of ten tribes; they are listed in the 'Roll Call of the Tribes' in Judges 5:12–18. Eventually, when the monarchy was established in Jerusalem, there were 12 tribes."

[85] C.A.O. van Nieuwenhuijze, "The Near Eastern Village: A Profile," *Middle East Journal* 16 (1962), p. 300.

[86] Stager, "The Archaeology of the Family in Ancient Israel," *BASOR* 260 (1985), pp. 1–36; and "The Song of Deborah—Why Some Tribes Answered the Call and Others Did Not," *BAR*, January/February 1989, pp. 50–64.

[87] Gottwald, *Tribes of Yahweh* (see endnote 53), p. 285.

[88] Gottwald, *Tribes of Yahweh* (see endnote 53), p. 258.

[89] C.H.J. de Geus, *The Tribes of Israel* (Amsterdam: Van Gorcum, Assen, 1976), p. 138.

[90] Miller and Hayes, *History of Ancient Israel* (see endnote 71), p. 92.

[91] Miller and Hayes, *History of Ancient Israel* (see endnote 71), p. 97.

[92] Miller and Hayes, *History of Ancient Israel* (see endnote 71), p. 97.

[93] Miller and Hayes, *History of Ancient Israel* (see endnote 71), p. 97.

[94] Miller and Hayes, *History of Ancient Israel* (see endnote 71), p. 97.

[95] Miller and Hayes, *History of Ancient Israel* (see endnote 71), pp. 99–100.

[96] Ze'ev Meshel, "Did Yahweh Have a Consort?" *BAR*, March/April, 1979, pp. 29–30; André Lemaire, "Who or What Was Yahweh's Asherah?" *BAR*, November/December 1984, pp. 42–51; William G. Dever, "Asherah, Consort of Yahweh? New Evidence from Kuntillet 'Ajrud," *BASOR* 255 (1984), pp. 21–37.

[97] Meshel, "Did Yahweh Have a Consort?" (see endnote 96), p. 32.

[98] Meshel, "Did Yahweh Have a Consort" (see endnote 96), p. 32.

[99] Lemaire, "Who or What" (see endnote 96), pp. 42ff.

[100] Miller and Hayes, *History of Ancient Israel* (see endnote 71), pp. 111–112.

[101] Miller and Hayes, *History of Ancient Israel* (see endnote 71), pp. 111–112.

IV. The United Monarchy

[1] William E. Evans, "An Historical Reconstruction of the Emergence of Israelite Kingship and the Reign of Saul," in William W. Hallo et al., *Scripture in Context II* (Winona Lake, IN: Eisenbrauns, 1983), pp. 61–78, especially p. 77.

[2] Israel Finkelstein, "The Emergence of the Monarchy in Israel: The Environmental and Socio-Economic Aspects," *JSOT* 44 (1989), pp. 43–74.

[3] J. Maxwell Miller, "Is it Possible to Write a History of Israel Without Relying on the Hebrew Bible?" in *The Fabric of History*, ed. Diana Vikander Edelman, JSOT Supplement Series 127 (Sheffield, UK: Sheffield Academic Press, 1991), pp. 93–102, especially p. 101.

[4] See, for example, Finkelstein, "The Archaeology of the United Monarchy: An Alternative View," *Levant* 28 (1996), pp. 177–187; Amihai Mazar, "Iron Age Chronology: A Reply to I. Finkelstein," *Levant* 29 (1997), pp. 157–167.

[5] See, for instance, Margaret M. Gelinas, "United Monarchy—Divided Monarchy: Fact

or Fiction," in *The Pitcher Is Broken, Memorial Essays for Gösta W. Ahlström*, JSOT Supplement Series 190 (Sheffield, UK: Sheffield Academic Press, 1995), pp. 227–237. See also Hershel Shanks, "The Biblical Minimalists," *BR*, June 1997, pp. 32–39, 50–52; "The Biblical Minimalists Meet Their Challengers," *BAR*, July/August 1997, pp. 26–42, 66.

[6] See Trude Dothan, "The Philistines Reconsidered," in *Biblical Archaeology Today 1984* (Jerusalem: Israel Exploration Society, 1985), pp. 165–176; T. Dothan, "Ekron of the Philistines—Part I: Where They Came From, How They Settled Down and the Place They Worshiped In," *BAR*, January/February 1990, pp. 26–36; T. Dothan and Moshe Dothan, *People of the Sea: The Search for the Philistines* (New York/Toronto: Macmillan, 1992); Ed Noort, *Die Seevölker in Palästina* (Kampen: Pharos, 1994).

[7] *ANET*, pp. 262b–263b.

[8] Franco Pintore, "Sèrèn, tarwanis, tyrannos," in *Studi orientalistici in ricordo di F. Pintore*, ed. Onofrio Carruba et al., Studia mediterranea 4 (Pavia, Italy: GJES, 1983), pp. 285–322.

[9] See Itamar Singer, "Egyptians, Canaanites, and Philistines in the Period of the Emergence of Israel," in *From Nomadism to Monarchy: Archaeological and Historical Aspects of Early Israel*, ed. Finkelstein and Nadav Na'aman (Jerusalem/Washington: Yad Izhak Ben-Zvi and Israel Exploration Society/Biblical Archaeology Society, 1994), pp. 282–338.

[10] In the 12th to 11th century B.C.E., iron technology developed in the Aegean, in Cyprus and in Canaan. In Cyprus and Canaan, this development apparently had an Aegean connection. See James D. Muhly, "How Iron Technology Changed the Ancient World and Gave the Philistines a Military Edge," *BAR*, November/December 1982, pp. 40–54.

[11] See A.D.H. Mayes, "The Period of Judges and the Rise of the Monarchy," in *Israelite and Judaean History*, ed. John H. Hayes and Miller (Philadelphia: Westminster, 1977), pp. 285–331, especially p. 325; Na'aman, "The Pre-Deuteronomistic Story of King Saul and Its Historical Significance," *CBQ* 54 (1992), pp. 638–658. Nahash's way of treating the Israelites (see Frank Moore Cross, "The Ammonite Oppression of the Tribes of Gad and Ruben," in *History, Historiography and Interpretation*, ed. Hayim Tadmor and Moshe Weinfeld [Jerusalem: Magnes Press, 1983], pp. 148–158) is attested in Assyrian tradition (see Albert Kirk Grayson, *Assyrian Royal Inscriptions I* [Wiesbaden, Germany: Harrassowitz, 1972], sec. 530 [especially note 177]; vol. 2 [1976], sec. 549).

[12] See the essay of Volkmar Fritz, "Die Deutungen des Königtums Sauls in den Überlieferungen von seiner Enstehung, I Sam 9–11," *ZAW* 88 (1976), pp. 346–362.

[13] For a possible, not probable, later date of this expedition, see Edelman, "Saul's Rescue of Jabesh-Gilead (1 Sam 11:1–11)," *ZAW* 96 (1984), pp. 195–209.

[14] This number seems to be accepted by J. Alberto Soggin (*A History of Ancient Israel* [Philadelphia: Westminster, 1984], pp. 49–50).

[15] See Joseph Blenkinsopp, "The Quest of the Historical Saul," in *No Famine in the Land: Studies in Honor of John L. McKenzie*, ed. J.W. Flanagan and A.W. Robinson (Missoula, MT: Scholars Press, 1975), pp. 75–79; Na'aman, "Pre-Deuteronomistic Story" (see endnote 11), pp. 638–658; V. Philips Long, "How Did Saul Become King? Literary Reading and Historical Reconstruction," in *Faith, Tradition, and History: Old Testament Historiography in Its Near Eastern Context*, ed. Alan R. Millard (Winona Lake, IN: Eisenbrauns, 1994), pp. 271–284.

[16] See David M. Gunn, *The Fate of King Saul*, JSOT Supplement Series 14 (Sheffield, UK: Sheffield Academic Press, 1980); Edelman, *King Saul in the Historiography of Judah*, JSOT Supplement Series 121 (Sheffield, UK: Sheffield Academic Press, 1991).

[17] See André Caquot and Philippe de Robert, *Les livres de Samuel* (Geneva: Labor et fides, 1994), pp. 19–20; Robert P. Gordon, "In Search of David: The David Tradition in Recent Study," in *Faith, Tradition, and History* (see endnote 15), pp. 285–298, especially p. 298.

[18] See W. Lee Humphreys, "The Rise and Fall of King Saul," *JSOT* 18 (1980), pp. 74–90; "From Tragic Hero to Villain: A Study of the Figure of Saul and the Development of 1 Samuel," *JSOT* 22 (1982), pp. 95–117.

[19] See P. Kyle McCarter, Jr., "The Apology of David," *JBL* 99 (1980), pp. 485–504. On this literary genre in Assyria, see Tadmor, "Autobiographical Apology in the Royal Assyrian Literature," in Tadmor and Weinfeld, *History, Historiography* (see endnote 11), pp. 36–57.

[20] See André Lemaire, "La montagne de Juda (XIII–XIe siècle av. J.-C.)," in *La protohistoire d'Israël*, ed. Ernest-Marie Laperrousaz (Paris: Cerf, 1990), pp. 293–298.

[21] One may be skeptical about the thesis that Saul was "initially … a petty king of Gibeon," as proposed by Edelman, "Saul Ben Kish in History and Tradition," in *The Origins of the Ancient Israelite States*, ed. Fritz and Philip R. Davies, JSOT Supplement Series 228 (Sheffield, UK: Sheffield Academic Press, 1996), pp. 142–159, especially p. 156.

[22] Adam Zertal, *The Manasseh Hill Country Survey* (Haifa: Haifa Univ., 1992); "'To the Land of the Perizzites and the Giants': On the Israelite Settlement in the Hill Country of Manasseh," in *From Nomadism to Monarchy* (see endnote 9), pp. 47–69, especially pp. 57–60.

[23] See Finkelstein, *The Archaeology of the Israelite Settlement* (Jerusalem: Israel Exploration Society, 1988), especially pp. 260–269.

[24] Finkelstein and Yitzhak Magen, eds., *Archaeological Survey of the Hill Country of Benjamin* (Jerusalem: Israel Antiquities Authority, 1993); A. Mazar, "Jerusalem and Its Vicinity in Iron Age I," in *From Nomadism to Monarchy* (see endnote 9), pp. 70–91, especially pp. 70–78.

[25] Moshe Kochavi, "An Ostracon of the Period of the Judges from 'Izbet Sartah," *Tel Aviv* 4 (1977), pp. 1–13; Kochavi and Aaron Demsky, "An Israelite Village from the Days of the Judges," *BAR*, September/October 1978, pp. 19–30; Finkelstein, *Isbet Sartah: An Early Iron Age Site near Rosh Ha'ayin, Israel*, British Archaeological Reports, International Series 299 (Oxford: Oxford Univ. Press, 1986).

[26] Mazar, "Jerusalem and Its Vicinity," in *From Nomadism to Monarchy* (see endnote 9), p. 75.

[27] Finkelstein, "Excavations at Khirbet ed-Dawwara: An Iron Age I Site Northeast of Jerusalem," *Tel Aviv* 17 (1990), pp. 163–208.

[28] Lemaire, "Aux origines d'Israël: la montagne d'Ephraïm et le territoire de Manassé," in *La protohistoire d'Israël* (see endnote 20), pp. 183–292, especially pp. 251–255, 284–286.

[29] "Did the Philistines Destroy the Israelite Sanctuary at Shiloh? The Archaeological Evidence," *BAR*, June 1975, pp. 3–5; Finkelstein and Zvi Lederman, "Shiloh, 1983," *IEJ* 33 (1983), pp. 267–268; Finkelstein, *The Archaeology of the Israelite Settlement* (see endnote 23), pp. 225–226, 322–323. See also, on the destruction of Ai, Joseph A. Callaway, "A Visit with Ahilud," *BAR*, September/October 1983, pp. 42–53.

[30] Baruch Rosen, "Subsistence Economy in Iron Age I," in *From Nomadism to Monarchy* (see endnote 9), pp. 339–351.

[31] Finkelstein, *The Archaeology of the Israelite Settlement* (see endnote 23), p. 82; comments as a respondent in *Biblical Archaeology Today 1984* (see endnote 6), pp. 80–83; "The Emergence of the Monarchy in Israel: The Environmental and Socio-Economic Aspects," *JSOT* 44 (1989), pp. 43–74, especially p. 59.

[32] See "Philistine Temple Discovered Within Tel Aviv City Limits," *BAR*, June 1975, pp. 1, 6–9; A. Mazar, *Excavations at Tell Qasile I: The Philistine Sanctuary, Qedem* 12 (Jerusalem: Hebrew Univ., 1980); *Excavations at Tell Qasile II, Qedem* 20 (1985); T. Dothan, *The Philistines and Their Material Culture* (New Haven, CT: Yale Univ. Press, 1982); T. Dothan, "What We Know About the Philistines," *BAR*, July/August 1982, pp. 20–44; Ze'ev Herzog, "Tel Gerisa," *IEJ* 33 (1983), pp. 121–123; T. Dothan and Seymour Gitin, "Ekron of the Philistines," *BAR*, January/February 1990, pp. 20–36; T. Dothan and Gitin, "Tel Miqne/Ekron—The Rise and Fall of a Philistine City," *Qadmoniot* 27 (1994), pp. 2–28 (Hebrew); Lawrence E. Stager, "When Canaanites and Philistines Ruled Ashkelon," *BAR*, March/April 1991, pp. 24–37, 40–43; T. Dothan, "Tell Miqne Ekron: The Aegean Affinities of the 'Sea Peoples' ('Philistines') Settlement in Canaan in the Iron Age I," in *Recent Excavations in Israel: A View to the West: Reports on Kabri, Nami, Miqne-Ekron, Dor, and Ashkelon*, ed. Gitin (Dubuque, IA: Kendall/Hunt, 1995), pp. 41–59.

[33] Mario Liverani, "Le 'origini' d'Israele progetto irrealizzabile di ricerca etnogenetica," *Rivista biblica* 28 (1980), pp. 9–31.

[34] Soggin, "The Davidic-Solomonic Kingdom," in Hayes and Miller, *Israelite and Judaean History* (see endnote 11), pp. 332–380; "The History of Israel—A Study in Some Questions of Method," *Eretz-Israel* 14 (Jerusalem: Israel Exploration Society, 1978), pp. 44–51; *History of Ancient Israel* (see endnote 14), pp. 19–40.

[35] Soggin, "Davidic-Solomonic Kingdom" (see endnote 34), p. 332.

[36] See Philip R. Davies, *In Search of 'Ancient Israel'*, JSOT Supplement Series 148 (Sheffield, UK: Sheffield Academic Press, 1992), pp. 68–69; cf. Giovanni Garbini, *History and Ideology in Ancient Israel,* trans. John Bowden (New York: Crossroad, 1988), pp. 21–32; Ernst A. Knauf, "From History to Interpretation," in *Fabric of History* (see endnote 3), pp. 26–64, especially p. 39. See also David W. Jamieson-Drake, *Scribes and Schools in Monarchic Judah—A Socio-Archaeological Approach*, Social World of Biblical Antiquity Series 9/JSOT Supplement Series 109 (Sheffield, UK: The Almond Press, 1991) and my critical review in *JAOS* 112 (1992), pp. 707–708.

[37] Knauf, "From History to Interpretation," in *Fabric of History* (see endnote 3), pp. 26–64, especially p. 39.

[38] Lemaire, "'House of David' Restored in Moabite Inscription," *BAR*, May/June 1994, pp. 30–37; "La dynastie davidique (*byt dwd*) dans deux inscriptions ouest-sémitiques du IXe s. av. J.-C.," *SEL* 11 (1994), pp. 17–19.

[39] "'David' Found at Dan," *BAR*, March/April 1994, pp. 26–39; Lemaire, "Épigraphie

palestinienne: nouveaux documents I. Fragments de stèle araméenne de Tell Dan (IXe s. av. J.-C.)," *Henoch* 16 (1994), pp. 87–93; Avraham Biran and Joseph Naveh, "The Tel Dan Inscription: A New Fragment," *IEJ* 45 (1995), pp. 1–18; William M. Schniedewind, "Tel Dan Stela: New Light on Aramaic and Jehu's Revolt," *BASOR* 302 (1996), pp. 75–90; Lemaire, "The Tel Dan Stela as a Piece of Royal Historiography," *JSOT* 81 (1998), pp. 3-15.

[40] See, for instance, Gary N. Knoppers, "The Vanishing Solomon: The Disappearance of the United Monarchy from Recent Histories of Ancient Israel," *JBL* 116 (1997), pp. 19–44.

[41] Ziklag is generally located at Tell esh-Shari'a. See Eliezer D. Oren, "Ziklag—A Biblical City on the Edge of the Negev," *BA* 45 (1982), pp. 155–166, especially p. 163. However, for the identification of Ziklag as at Tell es-Seba', see Fritz, "Der Beitrag der Archäologie zur historischen Topographie Palästinas am Beispiel von Ziklag," *ZDPV* 106 (1990), pp. 78–85; "Where Is David's Ziklag?" *BAR*, May/June 1993.

[42] For the location of Mahanaim at Tulul edh-Dhahab, see Lemaire, "Galaad et Makir," *VT* 31 (1981), pp. 39–61, especially pp. 53–54.

[43] See Na'aman, "The Kingdom of Ishbaal," *BN* 54 (1990), pp. 33–37.

[44] On the problem of David's possible responsibility, see James C. VanderKam, "Davidic Complicity in the Deaths of Abner and Eshbaal: A Historical and Redactional Study," *JBL* 99 (1980), pp. 521–539; Jean-Claude Haelewyck, "La mort d'Abner: 2 Sam 3:1–39," *RB* 102 (1995), pp. 161–192.

[45] See N.L. Tidwell, "The Philistine Incursions into the Valley of Rephaim," in *Studies in the Historical Books of the O.T.*, ed. John A. Emerton, VT Supplements 30 (Leiden: Brill, 1980), pp. 190–212.

[46] See Jon D. Levenson and Baruch Halpern, "The Political Import of David's Marriages," *JBL* 99 (1980), pp. 507–518.

[47] See Édouard Lipiński, "Aram et Israel du Xe au VIIIe siècle av. n. è.," *Acta Antiqua* 27 (1979), pp. 49–102; P.E. Dion, *Les Araméens à l'âge du Fer: histoire politique et structures sociales*, Études bibliques NS 34 (Paris: Gabalda, 1997), pp. 79–84.

[48] Christa Schäufer-Lichtenberger describes this period as the "inchoate early state" ("Sociological and Biblical Views of the Early State," in *Origins of the Ancient Israelite States* [see endnote 21], pp. 78–105, especially p. 92). For the social and political evolution, see also Frank S. Frick, *The Formation of the State in Ancient Israel*, Social World of Biblical Antiquity Series 4 (Sheffield, UK: Almond Press, 1985); Robert B.

Coote and Keith W. Whitelam, *The Emergence of Early Israel in Historical Perspective of the Davidic State*, Social World of Biblical Antiquity Series 5 (Sheffield, UK: Almond Press, 1987), pp. 139–166; Juval Portugali, "Theoretical Speculations on the Transition from Nomadism to Monarchy," in *From Nomadism to Monarchy* (see endnote 9), pp. 203–217, especially pp. 212–217.

[49] However, Gordon J. Wenham ("Were David's Sons Priests?" *ZAW* 87 [1975], pp. 79–82) proposed reading *sknym* instead of *khnym*.

[50] For a literary analysis of these traditions, see François Langlamet, "David et la maison de Saül," *RB* 86 (1979), pp. 194–213, 385–436, 481–513.

[51] See Henri Cazelles, "David's Monarchy and the Gibeonite Claim," *PEQ* 87 (1955), pp. 165–175.

[52] Na'aman, "Sources and Composition in the History of David," in *Origins of the Ancient Israelite States* (see endnote 21), pp. 170–186.

[53] Lemaire, "Vers l'histoire de la rédaction des livres des Rois," *ZAW* 98 (1986), pp. 221–236; Caquot and de Robert, *Les livres de Samuel* (see endnote 17), pp. 19–20; see also Erik Eynikel, *The Reform of Kings Josiah and the Composition of the Deuteronomistic History*, Oudtestamentische Studiën 33 (Leiden: Brill, 1996); Halpern, "The Construction of the Davidic State: An Exercise in Historiography," in *Origins of the Ancient Israelite States* (see endnote 21), pp. 44–75.

[54] See Niels Peter Lemche, "David's Rise," *JSOT* 10 (1978), pp. 2–25.

[55] On the problem of Nathan's personality, see Ilse von Loewenclau, "Der Prophet Nathan im Zwielicht von theologischer Deutung und Historie," in *Werden und Wirken des Alten Testaments, Festschrift C. Westermann*, ed. E. Albertz et al. (Neukirchen/ Göttingen, Ger.: Neukirchener Verlag/Vandenhoeck und Ruprecht, 1980), pp. 202–215.

[56] See Tomoo Ishida, "Solomon's Succession to the Throne of David—Political Analysis," in *Studies in the Period of David and Solomon*, ed. Ishida (Tokyo: Yamakawa-Shuppansha, 1982), pp. 175–187.

[57] See Herbert Donner, "The Interdependence of Internal Affairs and Foreign Policy During the Davidic-Solomonic Period (with Special Regard to the Phoenician Coast)," in *Studies in the Period* (see endnote 56), pp. 205–214.

[58] In 2 Samuel 8:13–14, there was probably a confusion between "Edom" and "Aram," which were written in the same way in the fifth through third century B.C.E. 2 Samuel 8:14a seems to be a doublet of 2 Samuel 8:6a.

[59] See Abraham Malamat, "A Political Look at the Kingdom of David and Solomon and Its Relations with Egypt," in *Studies in the Period* (see endnote 56), pp. 189–205; "The Monarchy of David and Solomon," in *Recent Archaeology in the Land of Israel*, ed. Hershel Shanks and Benjamin Mazar (Washington/Jerusalem: Biblical Archaeology Society/Israel Exploration Society, 1984), pp. 161–172.

[60] These include, possibly, Megiddo (stratum VIA), Beth-Shean (stratum V) and Yoqneam. See Amihai Mazar, "The Excavations at Tel Beth-Shean in 1989–1990," in *Biblical Archaeology Today 1990*, ed. Avraham Biran and Joseph Aviram (Jerusalem: Israel Exploration Society, 1993), pp. 607–619, especially p. 617.

[61] Yohanan Aharoni, "The Building Activities of David and Solomon," *IEJ* 24 (1974), pp. 13–16; see also Shanks, "King David as Builder," *BAR*, March 1975, p. 13.

[62] Eilat Mazar, "Excavate King David's Palace!" *BAR*, January/February 1997, pp. 50–57, 74.

[63] That is part of the truth; see Margreet Steiner, "David's Jerusalem: Fiction or Reality? It's Not There: Archaeology Proves a Negative," *BAR*, July/August 1998, pp. 26–33, 62–63. However, such a small town may still have been the capital of a strong chiefdom: See Na'aman, "The Contribution of the Amarna Letters to the Debate on Jerusalem's Political Position in the Tenth Century B.C.E.," *BASOR* 304 (1996), pp. 17–27; "Cow Town or Royal Capital? Evidence for Iron Age Jerusalem," *BAR*, July/August 1997, pp. 43–47, 67; and "David's Jerusalem: Fiction or Reality? It Is There: Ancient Texts Prove It," *BAR*, July/August 1998, pp. 42–44. See also Jane Cahill, "David's Jerusalem: Fiction or Reality? It Is There: The Archaeological Evidence Proves It," *BAR*, July/August 1998, pp. 34–41, 63.

[64] Avi Ofer, "'All the Hill Country of Judah': From a Settlement Fringe to a Prosperous Monarchy," in *From Nomadism to Monarchy* (see endnote 9), pp. 92–121, especially pp. 104 and 119–121; "Hebron," in *NEAEHL*, pp. 606–609.

[65] Egypt was almost divided between the kingdoms of Tanis and Thebes.

[66] Cf. Siegfried Herrmann, "King David's State," in *In the Shelter of Elyon: Essays on Ancient Palestinian Life and Literature in Honor of G.W. Ahlström*, ed. W. Boyd Barrick and John R. Spencer, JSOT Supplement Series 31 (Sheffield, UK: Sheffield Academic Press, 1984), pp. 261–275.

[67] See Malamat, "The First Peace Treaty Between Israel and Egypt," *BAR*, September/October 1979, pp. 58–61; "A Political Look" (see endnote 59), especially pp. 197–201. Kenneth A.

Kitchen, *The Third Intermediate Period in Egypt (1100–650 B.C.)* (Warminster, UK: Aris and Phillips, 2nd ed., 1986), pp. 280–283.

[68] Cf. William G. Dever, "Further Excavations at Gezer, 1967–1971," *BA* 34 (1971), p. 110; "Gezer," *NEAEHL*, pp. 496–506.

[69] See endnote 67.

[70] This marriage contradicts Amenhotep III's assertion that "from of old, the daughter of an Egyptian king has not been given in marriage to anyone"; see Alan R. Schulman, "Diplomatic Marriage in the Egyptian New Kingdom," *Journal of Near Eastern Studies* 38 (1979), pp. 177–193, especially p. 179; see also Kitchen, *Third Intermediate Period* (see endnote 67), pp. 282–283.

[71] See also 1 Kings 11:1,5,7. Since Rehoboam was 41 years old when he became king, the marriage of Solomon with Naamah must have taken place toward the end of David's reign.

[72] See E.W. Heaton, *Solomon's New Men: The Emergence of Ancient Israel as a National State* (London: Thames and Hudson, 1974).

[73] This mention of Zadok and Abiathar is probably a later addition taken from 2 Samuel 8:17.

[74] Trygve N.D. Mettinger, *Solomonic State Officials* (Lund, Swed.: Gleerup, 1971).

[75] Aharoni, "The Solomonic Districts," *Tel Aviv* 3 (1976); Hartmut N. Rösel, "Zu den 'Gauen' Salomons," *ZDPV* 100 (1986), pp. 84–90; Fritz, "Die Verwaltungsgebiete Salomos nach 1 Kön. 4,7–19," in *Meilenstein, Festgabe für Herbert Donner, Ägypten und Altes Testament* 30 (Wiesbaden: Harrasowitz, 1995), pp. 19–26. However, there is some confusion about the Land of Hepher; see Lemaire, "Le 'pays de Hepher' et les 'filles de Zelophehad' à la lumière des ostraca de Samarie," *Semitica* 22 (1972), pp. 13–20; *Inscriptions hébraïques I: Les ostraca* (Paris: Cerf, 1977), pp. 287–289. For a divergent historical appreciation, cf. Herrmann M. Niemann, *Herrschaft, Königtum und Staat*, Forschungen zum Alten Testament 6 (Tübingen: Mohr, 1993), pp. 17–41, 246–251; Paul S. Ash, "Solomon's? District? List," *JSOT* 67 (1995), pp. 67–86.

[76] See Richard S. Hess, "The Form and Structure of the Solomonic District List in 1 Kings 4:7–19," in *Crossing Boundaries and Linking Horizons: Studies in Honor of M.C. Astour*, ed. G.D. Young et al. (Bethesda, MD: CDL Press, 1997), pp. 279–292.

[77] Moshe Elat, "The Monarchy and the Development of Trade in Ancient Israel," in *State and Temple Economy in the Ancient Near East II*, ed. Lipiński (Leuven, Belg.: Dept. Oriëntalistiek, 1979), pp. 527–546.

[78] On the problem of the identification of Ophir, see Vassilios Christidès, "L'énigme d'Ophir," *RB* 77 (1970), pp. 240–246; Lois Berkowitz, "Has the U.S. Geological Survey Found King Solomon's Gold Mines?" *BAR*, September 1977, pp. 1, 28–33. From comparison with the ancient Egyptian texts, the most probable solution still seems Somalia-Ethiopia.

[79] See Lemaire, "Les Phéniciens et le commerce entre la Mer Rouge et la Mer Méditerranée," in *Phoenicia and the East Mediterranean in the First Millennium B.C.*, ed. Lipiński, Studia Phoenicia 5/Orientalia Lovaniensia Analecta 22 (Leuven, Belg.: Peeters, 1987), pp. 49–60.

[80] On the change of defense strategy under Solomon, see Chris Hauer, "Economics of National Security in Solomonic Israel," *JSOT* 18 (1980), pp. 63–73.

[81] See Yukata Ikeda, "Solomon's Trade in Horses and Chariots in Its International Setting," in *Studies in the Period* (see endnote 56), pp. 215–238.

[82] See Gösta W. Ahlström, *Royal Administration and National Religion* (Leiden: Brill, 1982). For this motive in Assyria, see Sylvie Lackenbacher, *Le roi bâtisseur, les récits de construction assyriens des origines à Téglatphalazar III* (Paris: Ed. Recherche sur les civilisations, A.D.P.F., 1982).

[83] See Eilat Mazar, "Royal Gateway to Ancient Jerusalem Uncovered," *BAR*, May/June 1989; and "King David's Palace," *BAR*, January/February 1997.

[84] Cabul is probably to be identified with Ras Abu Zeitun. See Zvi Gal, "Cabul, Jiphtah-El and the Boundary Between Asher and Zebulun in the Light of Archaeological Evidence," *ZDPV* 101 (1985), pp. 114–127.

[85] See Lemaire, "Asher et le royaume de Tyr," in *Phoenicia and the Bible*, ed. Lipiński, Studia Phoenicia 11 (Leuven: Peeters, 1991), pp. 135–152.

[86] There is a dispute about a possible origin of this copper from the Timna Valley in the Aravah rift. See Beno Rothenberg, *Timna: Valley of the Biblical Copper Mines* (London: Thames and Hudson, 1972); published in the United States as *Were These King Solomon's Mines? Excavations in the Timna Valley* (New York: Stein and Day, 1972); "Nelson Glueck and King Solomon, A Romance That Ended," *BAR*, June 1978, pp. 1, 10–12, 14; Suzanne F. Singer, "From These Hills ...," *BAR*, June 1978, pp. 11–25; John J. Bimson, "King Solomon's Mines? A Reassessment of Finds in the Aravah," *TB* 32 (1981), pp. 123–149; Knauf, "King Solomon's Copper Supply," in *Phoenicia and the Bible* (see endnote 85), pp. 167–186.

[87] Keith W. Whitelam, "The Symbols of Power, Aspects of Royal Propaganda in the United Monarchy," *BA* 49 (1986), pp. 166–173.

[88] See Soggin, "Compulsory Labor Under David and Solomon," in *Studies in the Period* (see endnote 56), pp. 259–267.

[89] Julio C. Trebolle Barrera, *Salomon y Jeroboan* (Valencia, Spain: Institucion San Jeronimo, 1980), especially pp. 364–366.

[90] Actually "Hadad" sounds more like an Aramean name, and Hadad originally was probably an Aramean. In the Hebrew text of the Bible, there are several confusions between "Aram" and "Edom." The Edomites seem to have been independent, with their own king, only from about 845 B.C.E. (cf. 2 Kings 8:20–22). So Solomon's political power over Aramean countries was very short, if it ever existed: See Lemaire, "Hadad l'édomite ou Hadad l'araméen?" *BN* 43 (1987), pp. 14–18; "Les origines de Damas," *Le Monde de la Bible* 98 (1996), pp. 21–23; "D'Édom à l'Idumée et à Rome," in *Des Sumériens aux Romains d'Orient: La perception géographique du monde*, ed. Arnaud Sérandour, Antiquités sémitiques 2 (Paris: Maisonneuve, 1997), pp. 81–103, especially p. 85. For a divergent view, see Na'aman, "Israel, Edom and Egypt in the 10th Century B.C.E.," *Tel Aviv* 19 (1992), pp. 71–93, especially p. 75.

[91] For a literary criticism of these texts, see Helga Weippert, "Die Ätiologie des Nordreiches und seines Königshauses (1 Reg 11:29–40)," *ZAW* 95 (1983), pp. 344–375; A. Schenker, "Jéroboam et la division du royaume dans la Septante ancienne LXX 1 R 12,24 a-z, TM 11–12; 14 et l'histoire deutéronomiste," in *Israël construit son histoire, l'historiographie deutéronomiste à la lumière des recherches récentes*, ed. Albert de Pury, Thomas Römer, and Jean-Daniel Macchi (Geneva: Labor et fides, 1995), pp. 194–236.

[92] The Masoretic text has "Molech," but the context indicates that we must read "Milcom."

[93] Probably the Mount of Scandal or Mount of Perdition (*har hammashit*).

[94] Lemaire, "Wisdom in Solomonic Historiography," in *Wisdom in Ancient Israel: Essays in Honour of J.A. Emerton*, ed. John Day, Robert P. Gordon and Hugh G.M. Williamson (Cambridge: Cambridge Univ. Press, 1995), pp. 106–118; for a different view of "vor-Dtr Weisheitsquelle," see Pekka Särkiö, *Die Weisheit und Macht Salomos in der israelitischen Historiographie*, Schriften der Finnischen Exegetischen Gesellschaft 60 (Helsinki/Göttingen: Finnische Exegetische Gesellschaft, 1994); "Die Struktur der Salomogeschichte (1 Kön 1–11) und die

Stellung der Weisheit in ihr," *BN* 83 (1996), pp. 83–106.

[95] For a general history of the redaction of the books of Kings, see Lemaire, "Vers l'histoire de la redaction" (see endnote 53), pp. 221–236.

[96] Hugh G.M. Williamson, *1 and 2 Chronicles*, New Century Bible Commentary (Grand Rapids, MI: Eerdmans, 1982), pp. 229–230.

[97] See, for instance, Millard, "Texts and Archaeology: Weighing the Evidence: The Case for King Solomon," *PEQ* 123 (1991), pp. 19–27; "Solomon: Text and Archaeology," *PEQ* 123 (1991), pp. 117-118; Miller, "Solomon: International Potentate or Local King?" *PEQ* 123 (1991), pp. 28–31; Millard, "King Solomon's Shields," in *Scripture and Other Artifacts: Essays in Honor of Philip J. King*, ed. Michael D. Coogan, J. Cheryl Exum, and Lawrence E. Stager (Louisville: Westminster John Knox Press, 1994), pp. 286–295.

[98] See Donald B. Redford, "The Relations Between Egypt and Israel from El-Amarna to the Babylonian Conquest," in *Biblical Archaeology Today 1984* (see endnote 6), pp. 192–205.

[99] Albert R. Green, "Solomon and Siamun: A Synchronism Between Early Dynastic Israel and the Twenty-First Dynasty of Egypt," *JBL* 97 (1978), pp. 353–367.

[100] Cazelles, "Administration salomonienne et terminologie administrative égyptienne," *Comptes Rendus de GLECS* 17 (1973), pp. 23–25; Mettinger, *Solomonic State Officials* (see endnote 74).

[101] Redford, "Studies in Relations Between Palestine and Egypt During the First Millennium B.C., I: The Taxation System of Solomon," in *Studies on the Ancient Palestinian World Presented to F.V. Winnett*, ed. J.W. Wevers and Redford (Toronto: Univ. of Toronto Press, 1972), pp. 141–156.

[102] Green, "Israelite Influence at Shishak's Court," *BASOR* 233 (1979), pp. 59–62.

[103] Ahlström, *Royal Administration* (see endnote 82), p. 33.

[104] For the Egyptian list of conquered towns, see *ANET*, pp. 242a–243b, 263b–264a; B. Mazar, "The Campaign of Pharaoh Shishak to Palestine," in *Congrès de Strasbourg*, VT Supplements 4 (Leiden: Brill, 1957), pp. 57–66; Aharoni, *The Land of the Bible: A Historical Geography*, rev. and enlarged, trans. and ed. Anson F. Rainey (Philadelphia: Westminster, 1979), pp. 323–330; Na'aman, "Israel, Edom and Egypt in the 10th Century B.C.E.," *Tel Aviv* 19 (1992), pp. 71–93; David M. Rohl, "Some Chronological Conundrums of the 21st Dynasty," *Ägypte und Levant* 3 (1992), pp. 133–141, especially pp. 134–136;

Ahlström, "Pharaoh Shoshenq's Campaign to Palestine," in *History and Traditions of Early Israel, Studies Presented to Eduard Nielsen*, ed. Lemaire and Benedikt Otzen, VT Supplements 50 (Leiden: Brill, 1993), pp. 1–16.

[105] See Donner, "Israel und Tyrus im Zeitalter Davids und Salomos," *Journal of Northwest Semitic Languages* 10 (1982), pp. 43–52; Green, "David's Relations with Hiram: Biblical and Josephan Evidence for Tyrian Chronology," in *The Word of the Lord Shall Go Forth: Essays in Honor of D.N. Freedman* (Winona Lake, IN: Eisenbrauns, 1983), pp. 373–397; Kitchen, *Third Intermediate Period* (see endnote 67), pp. 432–447.

[106] See Garbini, "Gli 'Annali di Tiro' e la storiogafia fenicia," in *I Fenici, storia e religione* (Naples: Instituto Universitario Orientale, 1980), pp. 71–86; Lemaire, "Les écrits phéniciens," in A. Barucq et al., *Écrits de l'Orient ancien et sources bibliques*, Petite Bibliothèque des Sciences Bibliques, Ancien Testament 2 (Paris: Desclée, 1986), pp. 213–239, especially pp. 217–219.

[107] *Apion* 1.113; cf. H.St.J. Thackeray, *Josephus I: The Life Against Apion*, Loeb Classical Library (London: Heinemann, 1966), p. 209.

[108] *Contra Apion* 1.117–119; Thackeray, *Josephus I* (see endnote 107), p. 211.

[109] See Lemaire, "Phéniciens et le commerce" (see endnote 79), pp. 49–60.

[110] See Israel Eph'al, *The Ancient Arabs* (Jerusalem: Magnes Press, 1984), pp. 28ff.; Garbini, "I Sabei del Nord come problema storico," in *Studi in onore F. Gabrieli*, ed. R. Traini (Rome: Univ. di Roma, 1984), pp. 373–380.

[111] See Mario Liverani, "Early Caravan Trade Between South-Arabia and Mesopotamia," *Yemen* 1 (1992), pp. 111–115.

[112] See Lemaire, "Les origines de Damas," *Le Monde de la Bible* 98 (1996), pp. 21–23.

[113] See Lemaire, "Phénicien et philistien: paléographie et dialectologie," to be published in *IV Congreso Internacional de Estudios Fenicios y Punicos, Cadiz, 2–6 Octubre 1995*, ed. Maria E. Aubet.

[114] See Hannalis Schulte, *Die Entstehung der Geschichtsschreibung im Alten Israel*, BZAW 128 (Berlin: de Gruyter, 1972); Halpern, *The First Historians: The Hebrew Bible and History* (San Francisco: Harper and Row, 1988). According to John Van Seters ("Histories and Historians of the Ancient Near East," *Orientalia* 50 [1981], pp. 137–185, especially p. 185), "Dtr [Deuteronomist] stands at the beginning of historiography," but this is probably too simplistic a view; see Lemaire, "Vers l'histoire de la rédaction" (see endnote 53).

[115] See Caquot and de Robert, *Les livres de Samuel* (see endnote 17), p. 20: "un Ebyataride ... le premier historien de l'antiquité israélite."

[116] On Hebron, see Lemaire, "Cycle primitif d'Abraham et contexte géographico-historique," in *History and Traditions of Early Israel* (see endnote 104), pp. 62–75.

[117] See Werner H. Schmidt, "A Theologian of the Solomonic Era? A Plea for the Yahwist," in *Studies in the Period* (see endnote 56), pp. 55–73.

[118] Na'aman, "Cow Town or Royal Capital?" (see endnote 63).

[119] Lemaire, *Les écoles et la formation de la Bible dans l'ancien Israël*, Orbis Biblicus et Orientalis 39 (Fribourg, Switz./Göttingen, Ger.: Éditions Universitaires/Vandenhoeck und Ruprecht, 1981), especially pp. 46–50; Nili Shupak, *Where Can Wisdom be Found? The Sage's Language in the Bible and in Ancient Egyptian Literature*, Orbis Biblicus et Orientalis 130 (Fribourg, Switz./ Göttingen, Ger.: Éditions Universitaires/Vandenhoeck und Ruprecht, 1993), especially pp. 349–354. The contrary opinion of David W. Jamieson-Drake, *Scribes and Schools* (see endnote 36), is ill-founded methodologically and has an incomplete archaeological basis. Cf. Lemaire, *JAOS* 112 (1992), pp. 707–708.

[120] Dever, "Monumental Architecture in Ancient Israel in the Period of the United Monarchy," in *Studies in the Period* (see endnote 56), pp. 269–306; cf. also Fritz, "Salomo," *Mitteilungen des deutschen Orient-Gesellschaft* 117 (1985), pp. 47–67. For a recent synthesis of Iron IIA (tenth century B.C.E.), see Larry G. Herr, "The Iron Age II Period: Emerging Nations," *BA* 60 (1997), pp. 114–183, especially pp. 120–129.

[121] Laperrousaz, "A-t-on dégagé l'angle sud-est du 'temple de Salomon'?" *Syria* 50 (1973), pp. 355–399; "Angle sud-est du 'temple de Salomon' ou vestiges de l'Accra des Séleucides'? Un faux problème," *Syria* 52 (1975), pp. 241–259; "Après le 'temple de Salomon,' la *bamah* de Tel Dan: l'utilisation de pierres à bossage phénicien dans la Palestine pré-exilique," *Syria* 59 (1982), pp. 223–237; "À propos des murs d'enceinte antiques de la colline occidentale et du temple de Jérusalem," *Revue des études juives* 141 (1982), pp. 443–458; "King Solomon's Wall Still Supports the Temple Mount," *BAR*, May/June 1987, pp. 34–44.

[122] Cf. Yigal Shiloh, *Excavations at the City of David I, 1978–1982*, Qedem 19 (Jerusalem: Hebrew Univ., 1984), especially p. 27: "Stratum 14"; "Jérusalem, la Ville de David (1978–1981)," *RB* 91 (1984), pp. 420–431, especially pp. 428–429. Cf. also Margreet

Steiner, "The Jebusite Ramp of Jerusalem: The Evidence from the Macalister, Kenyon and Shiloh Excavations," in *Biblical Archaeology Today 1990* (see endnote 60), pp. 585–588; "Re-dating the Terraces of Jerusalem," *IEJ* 44 (1994), pp. 13–20; "David's Jerusalem" (see endnote 63), pp. 26–33, 62–63. For a date c. 1200 for the Stepped-Stone Structure, see Jane M. Cahill and David Tarler, "Respondents," in *Biblical Archaeology Today 1990* (see endnote 60), pp. 625–626; "Excavations Directed by Yigal Shiloh at the City of David, 1978–1985," in *Ancient Jerusalem Revealed*, ed. Hillel Geva (Jerusalem: IES, 1994), pp. 30–45, especially pp. 34–35. See also Cahill, "David's Jerusalem" (see endnote 63).

[123] See Tarler and Cahill, "David, City of," *ABD*, vol. 2, pp. 52–67; Kathleen Kenyon, *Digging Up Jerusalem* (London: Benn, 1974), pp. 92, 114–115; G.J. Wightman, *The Walls of Jerusalem: From the Canaanites to the Mamelukes*, Mediterranean Archaeology Supplement 4 (Sydney: Meditarch, 1993), pp. 33–35; Na'aman, "Cow Town or Royal Capital?" (see endnote 63), p. 43; Cahill, "David's Jerusalem" (see endnote 63), p. 39. However, see also Steiner, "David's Jerusalem" (see endnote 63).

[124] Yadin, "Solomon's City Wall and Gate at Gezer," *IEJ* 8 (1958), pp. 82–86; "Yadin's Popular Book on Hazor Now Available," *BAR*, September 1975, pp. 14–17, 32; "A Rejoinder," *BASOR* 239 (1980), pp. 19–23; Valerie M. Fargo, "Is the Solomonic City Gate at Megiddo Really Solomonic?" *BAR*, September/October 1983, pp. 8–13; "Monarchy at Work? The Evidence of Three Gates," *BAR*, July/August 1997, pp. 38–39.

[125] For a divergent view, see D. Milson, "The Design of the Royal Gates at Megiddo, Hazor and Gezer," *ZDPV* 102 (1986), pp. 87–92.

[126] Dever, "Late Bronze Age and Solomonic Defenses: New Evidence," *BASOR* 262 (1986), pp. 9–34, especially 18–20; "Gezer," *NEAEHL*, pp. 504–505.

[127] Ben-Tor, "Tel Hazor," *IEJ* 45 (1995), pp. 66–68.

[128] See the following articles in *BASOR* 277/278 (1990): Wightman, "The Myth of Solomon"; John S. Holladay, Jr., "Red Slip, Burnish, and the Solomonic Gateway at Gezer"; David Ussishkin, "Notes on Megiddo, Gezer, Ashdod, and Tel Batash in the Tenth to Ninth Centuries B.C."; Finkelstein, "On Archaeological Methods and Historical Considerations"; and Dever, "Of Myths and Methods." See also Shanks, "Where Is the Tenth Century?" *BAR*, March/April 1998, pp. 56–60; "San Francisco Tremors," *BAR*, March/April 1998, pp. 54–56, 60–61.

[129] P.L.O. Guy, *New Light from Armageddon*, Oriental Institute Communications 9 (Chicago: Univ. of Chicago, 1931), pp. 37–47.

[130] Yadin, "The Megiddo Stables," in *Magnalia Dei: The Mighty Acts of God, in Memoriam G.E. Wright*, ed. Cross et al. (Garden City, NY: Doubleday, 1976), pp. 249–252.

[131] See, for example, J.S. Holladay, "The Stables of Ancient Israel: Functional Determinants of Stable Construction and the Interpretation of Pillared Building Remains of the Palestinian Iron Age," in *The Archaeology of Jordan and Other Studies Presented to Siegfried H. Horn*, ed. Lawrence T. Geraty and Larry G. Herr (Berrien Springs, MI: Andrews Univ. 1986), pp. 103–165; Ze'ev Herzog, "Administrative Structures in the Iron Age," in *The Architecture of Ancient Israel from the Prehistoric to the Persian Periods*, ed. Aharon Kempinski and Ronny Reich (Jerusalem: Israel Exploration Society, 1992), pp. 223–230. Also see Moshe Kochavi's forthcoming article in *BAR*.

[132] Graham I. Davies, "Solomonic Stables at Megiddo After All?" *PEQ* 120 (1988), pp. 130–141.

[133] See for instance, Kempinsky, *Megiddo: A City-State and Royal Centre in North Israel* (Munich: C.H. Beck, 1989), pp. 90–95.

[134] Ussishkin, "Was the 'Solomonic' City Gate at Megiddo Built by King Solomon?" *BASOR* 239 (1980), pp. 1–18; "Fresh Examination of Old Excavations: Sanctuaries in the First Temple Period," in *Biblical Archaeology Today 1990* (see endnote 60), pp. 67–85; "Notes on Megiddo, Gezer, Ashdod, and Tel Batash in the Tenth to Ninth Centuries B.C.," (see endnote 128), pp. 71–91; "Jezreel, Samaria and Megiddo: Royal Centres of Omri and Ahab," in *Congress Volume Cambridge 1995*, ed. John A. Emerton, VT Supplements 66 (Leiden: Brill, 1997), pp. 351–364, especially pp. 359–361.

[135] Wightman, "The Myth of Solomon," (see endnote 128), pp. 5–22.

[136] Finkelstein, "The Archaeology of the United Monarchy: An Alternative View," *Levant* 28 (1996), pp. 177–187; cf. also Shanks, "Where Is the Tenth Century?" (see endnote 128); "San Francisco Tremors," (see endnote 128).

[137] See A. Mazar, "Iron Age Chronology" (see endnote 4), pp. 157–167.

[138] Cohen and Yisrael, "The Iron Age Fortresses at 'En Haseva," *BA* 58 (1995), pp. 223–235; *On the Road to Edom, Discoveries from 'En Hazeva*, Israel Museum Catalogue 370 (Jerusalem: Israel Museum, 1995), especially p. 17.

[139] For a provisory list, see Herr, "The Iron Age II Period: Emerging Nations," *BA* 60:3 (1997), pp. 114–183, especially p. 121.

[140] Cohen, "The Iron Age Fortresses in the Central Negev," *BASOR* 236 (1980), pp. 61–79; "Excavations at Kadesh-Barnea 1976–1978," *BA* 44 (1981), pp. 93–107; "Did I Excavate Kadesh-Barnea?" *BAR*, May/June 1981, pp. 20–33; "The Fortresses King Solomon Built to Protect His Southern Border," *BAR*, May/June 1985, pp. 56–70. See also Herzog et al., "The Israelite Fortress at Arad," *BASOR* 254 (1984), pp. 1–34, especially pp. 6–8. For a different dating and interpretation, see Finkelstein, "The Iron Age 'Fortresses' of the Negev—Sedentarization of Desert Nomads," *Tel Aviv* 11 (1984), pp. 189–209.

[141] See Fritz, "Monarchy and Re-urbanization: A New Look at Solomon's Kingdom," in *Origins of the Ancient Israelite States* (see endnote 21), pp. 187–195.

[142] See Ussishkin, "King Solomon's Palaces," *Biblical Archaeologist Reader IV* (Sheffield, UK: Almond Press, 1983), pp. 227–247; Shiloh, *The Proto-Aeolic Capital and Israelite Ashlar Masonry*, Qedem 11 (Jerusalem: Hebrew Univ., 1979); B. Gregori, "Considerazioni sui palazzi 'hilani' del periodo salomonico a Megiddo," *Vicino Oriente* 5 (1982), pp. 85–101.

[143] Aharoni, *The Archaeology of the Land of Israel* (Philadelphia: Westminster, 1982), especially p. 239; cf. also Holladay, "The Use of Pottery and the Other Diagnostic Criteria From the Solomonic Era to the Divided Kingdom," in *Biblical Archaeology Today 1990* (see endnote 60), pp. 86–101, especially p. 95: "Red burnish is only introduced well into Solomon's reign, probably around 950 B.C.E. or so"; "Red Slip, Burnish, and the Solomonic Gateway at Gezer" (see endnote 128), pp. 23–70.

[144] John Bright, *A History of Israel* (Philadelphia: Westminster, 3rd ed. 1982), p. 217.

[145] Finkelstein, "Environmental Archaeology and Social History: Demographic and Economic Aspects of the Monarchic Period," in *Biblical Archaeology Today 1990* (see endnote 60), pp. 56–66, esp. pp. 62–63.

[146] See Winfried Theil, "Soziale Wandlungen in der frühen Königszeit Alt-Israels," in *Gesellschaft und Kultur in alten Vorderasien*, ed. H. Klengel (Berlin: Akademie Verlag, 1982), pp. 235–246.

[147] See Tadmor, "Traditional Institutions and the Monarchy: Social and Political Tensions in the Time of David and Solomon," in *Studies in the Period* (see endnote 56), pp. 239–257.

[148] On the distinction between Israel and Judah, see Lipiński, "Judah et 'Tout Israël'": Analogies et contrastes," in *The Land of Israel: Cross-Roads of Civilizations*, ed. Lipiński, *Orientalia Lovaniensia Analecta* 19 (Leuven, Belg.: Peeters, 1985), pp. 93–112.

V. The Divided Monarchy

[1] The name derives from the town of Bubastis in the Nile Delta, which was the capital of the kings of the XXIInd Dynasty, who constructed the first forecourt. For the reliefs and inscriptions, see George R. Hughes and Charles F. Nims, *The Bubastite Portal*, vol. 3 of *Reliefs and Inscriptions at Karnak*, Oriental Institute Publication Series No. 74 (Chicago: Univ. of Chicago, 1954). See also P. Kyle McCarter, Jr., *Ancient Inscriptions: Voices from the Biblical World* (Washington, DC: Biblical Archaeology Society, 1996), pp. 56-57.

[2] For the details and a reconstruction of the route, see Benjamin Mazar, "Pharoah Shishak's Campaign to the Land of Israel," in *The Early Biblical Period*, ed. Shmuel Aḥituv and Baruch A. Levine (Jerusalem: Israel Exploration Society, 1986), pp. 139–150.

[3] Donald B. Redford, *Egypt, Canaan, and Israel in Ancient Times* (Princeton: Princeton Univ. Press, 1992), pp. 314–315.

[4] Hughes and Sims, *Bubastite Portal* (see endnote 1), pl. 3, col. 7.

[5] Rudolph Cohen, "The Fortresses King Solomon Built to Protect His Southern Border," *BAR*, May/June 1985, pp. 56-70. The date that the installations Cohen calls fortresses were established in the southern Negev (the highlands south of the Zered-Beersheba depression) is disputed, but many agree with him that they were built in the Davidic-Solomonic period (Iron Age IIA). Presumably their primary purpose was commercial—to control access from the northern Sinai and Philistia to the Gulf of Aqaba and the Hejaz trade route.

[6] B. Mazar, "Pharaoh Shishak's Campaign" (see endnote 2), p. 145.

[7] See the remarks in Redford, *Egypt, Canaan, and Israel* (see endnote 3), p. 313.

[8] See the list at the end of Amihai Mazar's discussion of Shishak's campaign in *Archaeology of the Land of the Bible 10,000-586 B.C.E.*, Anchor Bible Reference Library (New York: Doubleday, 1990), pp. 397–398.

[9] These conclusions hinge on the identification of the archaeological horizon associated with these destructions as late tenth century B.C.E. Archaeologists Israel Finkelstein and David Ussishkin of Tel Aviv University have recently proposed a redating of the strata in question to the ninth century B C.E. This proposal seems improbable, and it has not received wide support among other leading archaeologists; but if it proves correct, it would eliminate the synchronism with Shishak's

campaign. For an introduction to the archaeological issues at stake, see Hershel Shanks, "Where Is the Tenth Century?" *BAR*, March/April 1998, pp. 56-60. The Shishak stele fragment from Megiddo cannot settle the question since it was found in a nonstratified context.

[10] John S. Holladay, Jr., "The Kingdoms of Israel and Judah: Political and Economic Centralization in the Iron IIA–B (*ca.* 1000–750 BCE)," in *The Archaeology of Society in the Holy Land*, ed. Thomas E. Levy (New York: Facts on File, 1995), pp. 372–375.

[11] Despite Shishak's ambition and aggressiveness, he and the succeeding Libyan rulers of the XXIInd Dynasty were unable to overcome internal divisions within Egypt and muster the resources to sustain a consistent Asiatic policy. For the details, see the discussions of Nicolas Grimal (*A History of Ancient Egypt* [Oxford: Blackwell, 1992], pp. 319–331) and, succinctly, Redford (*Egypt, Canaan, and Israel* [see endnote 3], pp. 315–319), who calls Shishak's reign a "flash in the pan." The last, ill-fated attempt of the XXIInd Dynasty to assert its authority over Judah may have been the debacle described in 2 Chronicles 14:9–15 (Old Testament) = 2 Chronicles 14:8-14 (Hebrew Bible), in which a Cushite general named Zerah, presumably acting on behalf of Shishak's successor, Osorkon I, challenged and was routed by the army of King Asa (c. 911–870 B.C.E.).

[12] The principal formulation of this position is that of Frank M. Cross, *Canaanite Myth and Hebrew Epic* (Cambridge, MA: Harvard Univ. Press, 1973), pp. 274–289.

[13] The Israelite takeover of Dan, formerly the Canaanite city of Laish, is placed in the premonarchical period by the tradition of the migration of the Danites, preserved in an appendix to the Book of Judges (chapters 17–18).

[14] Cross, *Canaanite Myth and Hebrew Epic* (see endnote 12), pp. 279–283.

[15] Ben-hadad was the name of more than one king of Damascus. Here he is further identified as the son of Tabrimmon son of Hezion. Attempts have been made to identify his grandfather, Hezion, with Solomon's contemporary Rezon son of Eliada. According to 1 Kings 11:23-24, Rezon was an officer of David's nemesis, Hadadezer of Aram-zobah, who fled from Zobah and gathered a band of soldiers around him. Sometime after David's conquest of Damascus, Rezon captured the city and declared himself king. (This was probably the time that Damascus supplanted Zobah as the dominant city in southern Syria, as it would remain until its demise in the late eighth century.) According to 1 Kings 11:25, Rezon

caused problems for Israel throughout Solomon's reign and into that of Jeroboam.

The identification of Hezion with Rezon is unlikely on philological grounds, however, though Hezion might well have been Rezon's successor. For a full evaluation of the various arguments, see Wayne T. Pitard, *Ancient Damascus* (Winona Lake, IN: Eisenbrauns, 1987), pp. 101-104.

[16] A massive, 15-foot-thick wall constructed at this time has been found at Tell en-Nasbeh, ancient Mizpah. See Jeffrey R. Zorn, "Mizpah: Newly Discovered Stratum Reveal's Judah's Other Capital," *BAR*, September/October 1997, pp. 28-36, 66.

[17] Denis Baly, *The Geography of the Bible* (New York: Harper and Row, 1974), p. 99.

[18] Cf. Zvi Gal, "Cabul: A Royal Gift Found," *BAR*, March/April 1993, pp. 38-44, 84.

[19] Gal, "The Diffusion of Phoenician Cultural Influence in Light of the Excavations at Hurvat Rosh Zayit," *Tel Aviv* 22 (1995), pp. 89–93.

[20] Holladay, "Kingdoms of Israel and Judah" (see endnote 10), pp. 372–373.

[21] The most successful comprehensive analysis of this material is the monograph of Antony F. Campbell, *Of Prophets and Kings: A Late Ninth-Century Document (1 Samuel 1–2 Kings 10)* CBQ Monograph Series 17 (Washington, DC: Catholic Biblical Association of America, 1986).

[22] Two passages included in the biblical account of Ahab's reign seem to contradict both of these assumptions—that Israel was stronger than Damascus during Ahab's reign and that a mutual defense pact existed between Ahab and Hadadezer late in Ahab's reign. First Kings 20 describes a two-phase assault on Israel near the end of Ahab's reign by "King Ben-hadad of Aram." The first phase was a siege of Samaria that was broken when the much stronger Aramean force was defeated by Ahab's army after the intervention of an anonymous prophet; the second phase included an Aramean assault at Aphek the following spring, when the Arameans were again defeated and Ben-hadad sued for peace, agreeing to return "the towns that my father took from your father." First Kings 22 indicates that three years later Ahab marched with Jeshoshaphat of Judah to Ramoth-gilead to try to wrest its control from the "the king of Aram." The Israelite army was defeated, however, and Ahab died in battle.

Serious problems arise if we accept these passages as accounts of historical events late in Ahab's reign. There is, in the first place, a series of discrepancies with information found in Assyrian inscriptions contemporary with the events. The Assyrian inscriptions represent Ahab as an ally of Damascus—at least in 853 B.C.E., at the end of his reign—while the biblical passages indicate that Samaria and Damascus had been at war for more than three years at the time of Ahab's death. Moreover, though the biblical account depicts Israel as militarily much inferior to Damascus, the Assyrian inscriptions describing the battle of Qarqar in 853 B.C.E. indicate that Ahab was very strong, especially in chariots—he is said to have sent 2,000 to Qarqar in comparison to 1,200 sent by Hadadezer. Also, the Assyrian inscriptions show that the king of Damascus in 853 B.C.E. was Hadadezer, whereas the king of Damascus in 1 Kings 20 and 22 is called Ben-hadad. The references to the towns that Ben-hadad's father took from Ahab's father are also a problem, since, as already noted, we think Omri gained rather than lost territory to the Arameans. The final problem contains a hint of the solution: The name Ahab sits very loosely in the biblical text; most often "the king of Israel" is not named, and the places where he is named vary considerably in the ancient witnesses to the texts (Hebrew, Greek, etc.).

For all of these reasons, many historians, following suggestions by Alfred Jepsen and J. Maxwell Miller (for bibliography and an up-to-date discussion, see Pitard, *Ancient Damascus* [see endnote 15], pp. 114–125), believe that 1 Kings 20 and 22 derive from accounts of the Aramean campaigns of a later king of Israel, a member of the Jehu dynasty and most probably Joash, who is known to have had victories over Ben-hadad son of Hazael. If this is correct, 1 Kings 20 probably reflects the historical situation described in 2 Kings 13:22–25, and Ahab is not likely to have been killed by a randomly shot arrow at Ramoth-gilead, as indicated by 1 Kings 22:34–35, but to have died a natural death, as implied by the language of the notice in 1 Kings 22:40 that "Ahab slept with his ancestors."

[23] McCarter, *Ancient Inscriptions* (see endnote 1), pp. 90–92.

[24] For a full discussion of the issues, see Gösta Ahlström, *History of Ancient Palestine* (Minneapolis: Fortress, 1993), pp. 579–581.

[25] For an account of Assurnasirpal's campaign to "the Great Sea of the Amurru country," where he "cleaned [his] weapons in the deep sea," see *ANET*, pp. 275b–276b.

[26] *ANET*, pp. 277a–278a.

[27] *ANET*, pp. 278b–279a. The participation of Que in Cilicia (southern Turkey) is doubtful; A. Leo Oppenheim's translation in *ANET* was based on what seems to have been a defective cuneiform spelling of Byblos (*qu-e-e*, "Que," is to be corrected to *gu-<bal>-e-e*, "Byblos").

[28] Called *Adad-idri* in the Assyrian text. The Aramean form of his name was *Hadad-'iḏr* and the Hebrew was *Hadad-'ēzer*—Hadadezer in English (cf. 2 Samuel 8:3)—though this Hadadezer, the contemporary of Ahab, is not mentioned in the Bible. Many historians have identified Hadadezer of Damascus with the Ben-hadad mentioned in 1 Kings 20 and 22, but this no longer seems likely; as explained in endnote 22 above, the battles recounted in those chapters probably occurred much later than the reign of Ahab, whose name has been introduced secondarily into the text. For the reference to the Ben-hadad of 2 Kings 8:7–15, see below.

[29] *ANET*, pp. 278b–279a.

[30] The last reference to Hadadezer in the Assyrian records is in 845 B.C.E., and the records from 841 B.C.E. identify the ruler of Damascus as Hazael. Hazael's status as a usurper is shown by the Assyrian inscription on an undated basalt statue from Qal'at Sherqat, ancient Ashur (*ANET*, p. 280b). The text on the front of this statue, which is now in Berlin, contains a summary of Shalmaneser's dealings with Damascus. After referring to a victory over Hadadezer and the coalition at the Orontes—evidently the 853 B.C.E. battle, since subsequent encounters took place farther south—and to the death of Hadadezer, which cannot have taken place before 845 B.C.E., it goes on to say that Hazael, "the son of a nobody," seized the throne, mustering an army and resuming the resistance before being defeated and driven back to Damascus—evidently a reference to the events of 841 B.C.E. The characterization of Hazael as "the son of nobody" shows that when he seized the throne, at some point between 845 and 841 B.C.E., he did so as a usurper, not as Hadadezer's legitimate successor. See further the translation and discussion of the Berlin statue by Pitard (*Ancient Damascus* [see endnote 15], pp. 132–138), who points out the telescoped and summary nature of the text.

[31] In the biblical account the name of the king from whom Hazael seizes the throne is Ben-hadad, not Hadadezer. It is possible that this is simply a mistake, since reports of Israelite encounters with the later Ben-hadad, Hazael's son (!), have intruded elsewhere into the story of Ahab (1 Kings 20 and 22; see endnote 22). It is also possible, however, that Hadadezer died during or soon after the Assyrian campaign of 845 B.C.E. and was succeeded by a son named Ben-hadad (Aramaic Bir Hadad), who reigned for a few years before being overthrown by Hazael.

[32] *ANET*, p. 280.

[33] As noted above, Moab had been subject to Israel under Omri and Ahab but had withheld tribute after Ahab's death. According to the account in 2 Kings 3:6–27, Joram attempted to retaliate. This was a time, as also noted earlier, that Israel and Judah were united in an alliance cemented by the marriage of Ahab's daughter Athaliah to Jehoshaphat's son Jehoram. In planning his Moabite campaign, therefore, Joram was able to summon the assistance of Jehoshaphat, who in turn called out forces from Edom, which was then a vassal state of Judah. Joram led these combined armies into Transjordan territory and invested the Moabite fortress of Kir-haresheth (el-Kerak, about 50 miles north of Petra), but the siege was lifted when the king of Moab sacrificed his firstborn son on the rampart wall. The language of the biblical text ("a great wrath came upon Israel," 2 Kings 3:27) suggests that the sacrifice succeeded in inducing the Moabite god to drive off the Israelite army. Such a concept would, of course, have been unacceptable to the final editors of the Book of Kings, but they may have preserved the report of the incident because they understood the language to mean that the Israelites were so appalled by the barbarity of the rite that they withdrew in disgust. See Baruch Margalit, "Why King Mesha of Moab Sacrificed His Oldest Son," *BAR*, November/December 1986, pp. 62-63, 76.

[34] This seems likely even if we assume, with many historians, that the prophetic narratives in 2 Kings 6 and 7 belong in a later historical context, so that Joram was not the unnamed "king of Israel" in the parts of those chapters that describe war with Damascus.

[35] As noted earlier, Ramoth-gilead was near the point at which goods transported through Transjordan along the King's Highway could be diverted west to the Phoenician ports via the Beth-Shean depression and the Jezreel Valley. For this reason there was a perennial and often bitterly contested rivalry for control of Ramoth-gilead between the Arameans, who wanted the caravans to continue north to Damascus without diversion, and the Israelites, who could exact tolls and other benefits if the traffic passed west through their territory.

[36] From its strategic position at the foot of Mt. Gilboa, Jezreel held a commanding view of the Valley of Jezreel. It seems to have been a royal residence of the Omrides from the time of Ahab (cf. 1 Kings 18:45–46).

[37] In the biblical account, this is reported at the end of a prophetic narrative in which Jehu is anointed king by an anonymous prophet acting on Elisha's instructions (2 Kings 9:1–13). The

reason given for Yahweh's rejection of Joram and selection of Jehu is vengeance against Ahab and Jezebel for their crimes, especially for "the blood of my servants the prophets and the blood of all the servants of the Lord."

[38] See Michael C. Astour, "841 BC: The First Assyrian Invasion of Israel," *JAOS* (1971), pp. 383–398. This is unlikely, however, in view of the evidence already cited that the anti-Assyrian coalition that had opposed Shalmaneser from 853 to 845 B.C.E. had collapsed after the death of Hadadezer of Damascus, so that Damascus, now ruled by Hazael, was the only target of Shalmaneser's 841 B.C.E. campaign. Moreover, when Joram was wounded at Ramoth-gilead, setting off the sequence of events that eventually led to his assassination, he was at war with Hazael, Shalmaneser's enemy. Under these circumstances Jehu's actions can hardly be interpreted as appeasement towards Assyria. (Recognizing this problem, Ahlström [*History of Ancient Palestine* (see endnote 24), pp. 592–595], in an attempt to defend a position similar to Astour's, argued that, despite the biblical report to the contrary, Joram had gone to Ramoth-gilead to fight Shalmaneser rather than Hazael; but this is arbitrary and unconvincing.) It seems improbable, therefore, that Jehu was conspiring, either directly or indirectly, with Shalmaneser when he revolted against the Omrides.

[39] Avraham Biran and Joseph Naveh, "An Aramaic Stele Fragment from Tel Dan," *IEJ* 43 (1993), pp. 81–98; "The Tel Dan Inscription: A New Fragment," *IEJ* 45 (1995), pp. 1–18. See also "'David' Found at Dan," *BAR*, March/April 1994, pp. 26-39.

[40] This conclusion seems unavoidable, even though in the early part of the text of the Tel Dan stele the Aramean ruler claims to have succeeded his father as king. This is surprising in view of the fact that Hazael is depicted as a usurper both in the biblical account of his accession (2 Kings 8:7–15) and in the above-mentioned description of him as "the son of nobody" in Assyrian records. One way to explain these contradictions is to assume that Hadadezer's legitimate successor was the invalid Ben-hadad of 2 Kings 8:7 and that Hazael was a younger, perhaps illegitimate son, who used the pretext of Ben-hadad's infirmity to seize the throne, contending that his kingship was divinely sanctioned—not in his view by the God of Israel acting through Elisha as presented in the Bible (1 Kings 19:15; cf. 2 Kings 8:13) but by the god of Damascus, of whom he says in line 4 of the Tel Dan inscription, "Hadad caused me to become king."

[41] This was first suggested by Biran and Naveh, "Tel Dan Inscription" (see endnote 39), p. 18.

[42] André Lemaire ("'House of David' Restored in Moabite Inscription," *BAR*, May/June 1994, pp. 30-37) has made a strong case for restoring *byt dwd*, "House of David," as a designation for Judah in the text of the stele of the Moabite king Mesha (see Chapter IV). These two inscriptions—the Tel Dan stele and the Moabite stone—are roughly contemporary, mid-ninth century B.C.E. texts. Kenneth A. Kitchen has recently proposed an even earlier occurrence of the name of David in an Egyptian inscription (see "A Possible Mention of David in the Late Tenth Century BCE, and Deity *Dod as Dead as the Dodo?" *JSOT* 76 [1997], pp. 29-44, esp. pp. 39-41; and Hershel Shanks, "Has David Been Found in Egypt?" *BAR*, January/February 1999.) Kitchen suggests the translation "the highland/heights of David" for a place-name in southern Judah or the Negev that appears in the list recorded on the so-called Bubastite Portal at Karnak of places conquered during Shishak's 925 B.C.E. invasion of Canaan (see above and endnote 1). Though there is nothing implausible about this suggestion, it is only a possibility, as Kitchen himself admits, and the equation of the heiro-glyphic text, which is spelled *d-w-t* (!), with "David" is not straightforward.

[43] In the Tel Dan inscription "House of David" seems to be a synonym or substitution for "Judah," but in the Bible it is always clear that it refers to the ruling family or dynasty, not the kingdom as a whole. Why, then, is the southern kingdom called "House of David" in the Tel Dan inscription instead of simply "Judah," which, according to the biblical writers, was the official name of the kingdom from its founding and which is also used in the earliest extrabiblical references to the southern kingdom (in the annals of the eighth-century B.C.E. Assyrian kings)? Parallels for the occasional use of dynastic names like "House of David" instead of national names like "Judah" are known from contemporary Syria-Palestine, but the phenomenon is not well understood and needs further study.

[44] *ANET*, p. 280b. Another Assyrian text, not included in *ANET*, describes the spot as "opposite Tyre," and this better suits Ras en-Naqura than Mt. Carmel, which is otherwise an attractive alternative. For bibliography, see Mordechai Cogan and Hayim Tadmor, *II Kings*, Anchor Bible 11 (Garden City, NY: Doubleday, 1988), p. 121 n. 11.

[45] McCarter, *Ancient Inscriptions* (see endnote 1), pp. 21–22.

[46] According to the slightly expanded version of the events in Chronicles, Jehosheba was Jehoiada's wife (2 Chronicles 22:11).

[47] The ostracon has been published by Pierre Bordreuil, Felix Israel and Dennis Pardee ("Deux ostraca paléo-hébraux de la collection Sh. Moussaïeff," *Semitica* 46 [1996], pp. 49–76; "King's Command and Widow's Plea: Two New Hebrew Ostraca of the Biblical Period," *Near Eastern Archaeology* 61 [1998], pp. 2–13), who assign it to the late seventh century B.C.E. But, despite one or two typologically advanced features, the script belongs to the Hebrew cursive tradition of the late ninth century B.C.E., the time of Jehoash of Judah. Since the ostracon, which is in the private collection of Mr. Shlomo Moussaieff of London, was not found in a controlled archaeological excavation, its authenticity has been questioned, especially in view of several unique or spectacular features in the text—a king of Judah is referred to by name for the first time in the corpus of Hebrew ostraca, the Temple ("the House of Yahweh") is mentioned, and there is a reference to "silver of Tarshish." Nevertheless, the ostracon and its ink have been subjected to a series of scientific tests in leading laboratories (see the sidebar by Chris A. Rollston in "King's Command and Widow's Plea," pp. 8–9) and none of the results has cast doubt on its antiquity. See also Hershel Shanks, "Three Shekels for the Lord," *BAR*, November/December 1997, pp. 28-32.

[48] We learn this from a notice following 2 Kings 13:22, which is preserved in the best manuscripts of the Greek Bible. It reads, "And Hazael took Philistia from [Jehoahaz's] hand from the Western Sea as far as Aphek." This statement has been lost in the Masoretic text of the Hebrew Bible, and it is lacking in most English translations.

[49] Second Kings 12:20–21 indicates that Jehoash was murdered by members of his own government, a crime later avenged by his son and successor Amaziah (2 Kings 14:5). The Chronicler's account of the assassination plot (2 Chronicles 24:25–26) sets it in the immediate aftermath of Jehoash's capitulation to Hazael and attributes the motive of the conspirators to retribution for the death of Zechariah.

[50] The so-called Assyrian Eponym Chronicle, which identified each year by the name of an individual who served as its eponym official and listed a single significant event for the year, indicates that Adad-nirari's destination in 805 B.C.E. was the city of Arpad in northern Syria and that in 796 B.C.E. he marched to an unidentified place in central or southern Syria called Mansuate. There is no mention of Damascus, but Adad-nirari's few extant monuments make it clear that he regarded his victories over Damascus, in addition to the capture of Arpad, as his principal achievements.

[51] This is illustrated by a stele left by a king of Hamath named Zakkur, a successor of Irḥuleni, Ahab's ally in the 853 B.C.E. coalition against Shalmaneser III (*ANET*, pp. 655b–656a). The Aramaic inscription on the stele asserts Zakkur's claim to the small state of Hazrak (Hadrach in Zechariah 9:1 and Hatarikka in Assyrian inscriptions), which bordered Hamath on the north. Evidently Zakkur, who was probably a usurper (his father's name is not mentioned in the inscription), was an Assyrian vassal, since his annexation of Hazrak provoked a violent reaction among the Syrian states that were resistant to Assyrian domination. The leader of this group, according to the Zakkur stele, was "Bir-Hadad the son of Hazael," who assembled a coalition of ten kings. Some of the coalition states bordered Hazrak on the north, but others lay much farther north, beyond the Amanus and the eastern Taurus into northeastern Turkey. This shows that under Ben-hadad II, Damascus had once again assumed the leadership of anti-Assyrian resistance in southern and central Syria, allied at least in this case with like-minded states farther north.

[52] Stephanie Page, "A Stela of Adad-nirari III and Nergal-Ereš from Tell al Rimah," *Iraq* 35 (1968), pp. 139–153.

[53] Amaziah survived the debacle with Joash, but his subsequent death may have been an indirect result of the humiliation he had brought on his kingdom. Like his father Jehoash, he was the victim of a conspiracy in Jerusalem, which obliged him to flee to Lachish, where he was overtaken and killed (2 Kings 14:19 = 2 Chronicles 25:27).

[54] McCarter, *Ancient Inscriptions* (see endnote 1), pp. 105–110. For an early report by the excavator, see Ze'ev Meshel, "Did Yahweh Have a Consort?" *BAR*, March/April 1979, pp. 24-35.

[55] The name appears in the form šyw hmlk, "'Ashyaw the king," that is, "Yaw'ash" or Joash. The theophoric and verbal elements are transposed in the name, exactly as in the case of Jehoash of Judah in the ostracon described above.

[56] "Yahweh of Samaria" was the local form or manifestation of the God of Israel as he was worshiped in the capital of the northern kingdom. "Yahweh of Teman" was probably the local Yahweh of the region around 'Ajrud itself; biblical Teman, which means "Southland," was a region, not a city, and in modern times Kuntillet 'Ajrud has been given the Hebrew name Horvat Teman ("the Ruin of Teman"). For the advocates of cult centralization, these local cults posed a threat to the authority of the priesthood at the central sanctuary (cf. the later polemic against "high places"). For the

advocates of incipient monothesim in the biblical form—those who stressed the oneness of Yahweh and insisted on the exclusiveness of his worship—the local cults posed another kind of threat, since, according to a widespread Near Eastern pattern, the local manifestations of a deity tended to attain quasi-independent status. See further, McCarter, "The Religious Reforms of Hezekiah and Josiah," in *Aspects of Monotheism: How God Is One*, ed. Hershel Shanks and Jack Meinhardt (Washington, DC: Biblical Archaeology Society, 1997), pp. 57-80.

[57] On this and other aspects of the religious characteristics of the Kuntillet 'Ajrud texts, see McCarter, "Aspects of the Religion of the Israelite Monarchy: Biblical and Epigraphic Data," pp. 137–155 in *Ancient Israelite Religion: Essays in Honor of Frank Moore Cross*, ed. Paul D. Hanson, S. Dean McBride and Patrick D. Miller, Jr. (Philadelphia: Fortress, 1987).

[58] Pirhiya Beck ("The Drawings from Ḥorvat Teiman [Kuntillet 'Ajrud]," *Tel Aviv* 9 [1982], pp. 3–68) interpreted the two figures as representations of the Egyptian dwarf-god Bes, whose traditional squat-legged posture is somewhat reminiscent of their bowlegged stance. Otherwise, however, the 'Ajrud figures are not at all like Bes. It is true that Bes is sometimes portrayed as ithyphallic, and Beck interpreted the appendages between the legs of the two 'Ajrud figures as phalli; but the appendages hang *behind* the abdomens, not in front—they are tails, not penises, and certainly are not erect. Moreover, Bes's head is leonine, not bovine, and his most characteristic feature is his protruding tongue, which is lacking in the 'Ajrud drawings.

[59] The text of a stele found in 1982 at Pazarcik, Turkey, shows that in that year the Assyrian king received tribute from a king of Damascus named Hadianu—possibly the same name as that of the grandfather of Ben-hadad I (1 Kings 15:18).

[60] This approached the ideal limits of the Davidic-Solomonic empire; cf. 2 Samuel 8:1–14; 1 Kings 4:21 [Old Testament] = 1 Kings 5:1 [Hebrew Bible]; 1 Kings 8:65.

[61] The verse goes on to say that Hamath was also "recovered," and it is, at best, improbable that Hamath became a vassal state of Israel, especially in view of the statement in 2 Kings 14:25 that the northern extent of the territory controlled by Jeroboam was at the southern border of Hamath. On the other hand, there is some evidence that Hamath had now become independent of Assyria (cf. Pitard, *Ancient Damascus* [see endnote 15], pp. 176–177), and it is possible that it had entered into an alliance with Israel, perhaps for the mutual containment of Damascus. In any case, the Hebrew

text of 2 Kings 14:28 bristles with difficulties. A literal translation of the pertinent part of the verse reads "… and that he returned Damascus and Hamath to Judah in Israel …" The expression "to Judah in Israel" makes no sense, and though scholars have made several ingenious attempts to emend the text, none carries conviction.

[62] The superscription of the book that preserves his oracles (Amos 1:1) describes Amos as prophesying during the reigns of Jeroboam II of Israel and Uzziah (also called Azariah) of Judah. Most scholars think that his brief career as a prophet took place in the mid-eighth century B.C.E., sometime late in Jeroboam II's reign.

[63] For a detailed survey, see Gabriel Barkay, "The Iron Age II–III," in *The Archaeology of Ancient Israel*, ed. Amnon Ben-Tor (New Haven and London: Yale Univ. Press, 1992), pp. 302–373. The section on Iron IIb, Barkay's designation for the eighth century B.C.E., is found on pp. 327–334.

[64] See Barkay, "The Iron Age II–III" (see endnote 63), pp. 320–323; and William G. Dever, "Social Structure in Palestine in the Iron II Period on the Eve of Destruction," in *Archaeology of Society* (see endnote 10), pp. 416–431.

[65] Another indicator of the renewal of contact with Phoenicia is the presence of imported Phoenician pottery at Israelite sites. Careful examination of the ceramic repertoire at one well-stratified Israelite city (Hazor) shows that Phoenician imports constituted as much as 8.5 percent of the pottery in strata associated with the dynasty of Omri, when the Israelite-Phoenician alliance was strong. During the reign of Jehu they dropped to an all-time low (5 percent), as we might expect, but by the early eighth century B.C.E. they had returned to Omride levels or even higher (over 8.5 percent). See the discussion of Holladay ("Kingdoms of Israel and Judah" [see endnote 10], p. 381), who cites a study of Hazor-Sarepta parallels included in W.P. Anderson, *Sarepta I: The Late Bronze and Iron Age Strata of Area II,Y*, Publications de l'Université Libanaise, Section des Études Archéologiques 2 (Beirut: Département des Publications de l'Université Libanaise, 1988), pp. 139–313.

[66] The ivories were found in the debris of the 722/721 B.C.E. Assyrian destruction of Samaria, so that they are technically eighth-century B.C.E. artifacts, and many must have come from the time of Jeroboam II; but dating ivories stratigraphically is somewhat precarious, since we assume they were preserved and reused from generation to generation (the heirloom factor). Thus it is possible—and usually assumed—that

some number of the Samaria ivories were of ninth-century B.C.E. manufacture.

[67] Dever, in his wide-ranging analysis of Israelite and Judahite society during the Divided Monarchy ("Social Structure in Palestine" [see endnote 64]), discusses the special significance of the Samaria ivories in this regard, explaining that they "constitute an especially eloquent witness to social stratification in ancient Israel: first, they are relatively rare in any context, i.e., true luxury items; second, they were found not only at the capital, but in the ruins of the royal palace; and third, they provide clear evidence of both a sophisticated taste for 'exotic' furnishings of foreign derivation, and the means for acquiring such costly items" (p. 425).

[68] Unfortunately, this magnificent seal, which features an elegantly engraved roaring lion, disappeared soon after its discovery, and we have only a bronze cast; see McCarter, *Ancient Inscriptions* (see endnote 1), pp. 144–145.

[69] See McCarter, *Ancient Inscriptions* (see endnote 1), pp. 103–104.

[70] William F. Albright, *Archaeology and the Religion of Israel*, Anchor Books (Garden City, NY: Doubleday, 1969), p. 155.

[71] For the older theory, no longer tenable, that Azariah of Judah was a leader of the resistance to Tiglath-pileser III's first western campaign (743–738 B.C.E.), see endnote 90 below.

[72] On the other hand, Azariah is said to have greatly strengthened the defensive position of Jerusalem, erecting fortification towers at strategic points (2 Chronicles 26:9) and installing ingenious anti-siege devices on the walls (2 Chronicles 26:15). This could be seen as an attempt to render the city invulnerable to another incursion by Israel like that of Joash in the previous generation. Indeed, one of the gates Azariah fortified, the Corner Gate at the city's northwestern angle, was located in the area where Joash had breeched the wall (2 Kings 14:13). This may suggest that Azariah had begun to think of Judah as independent again, and although there is no record of any hostility with Israel in his reign, the notice in 2 Kings 15:37 indicates that Israel, now in league with Damascus, began incursions into Judah in the reign of Jotham, Azariah's son and coregent.

[73] The original homeland of the Meunites was evidently in the vicinity of Ma'an, about 12 miles southeast of Petra. They are first mentioned in the Bible as participants in a raid into Judah conducted by the Moabites and Ammonites in the time of Jehoshaphat (2 Chronicles 20:1, where the second occurrence of "Ammonites" in the Hebrew text should be corrected to "Meunites" following the Greek).

[74] Reading "Meunites" with the Greek text of 26:8 in preference to the Hebrew "Ammonites." The Meunites not only remained in southern Judah but eventually became kin, having been incorporated into the Judahite genealogy (cf. Ezra 2:50; Nehemiah 7:52).

[75] Ancient Elath is sometimes identified with modern Aqabah, which, however, lacks evidence of occupation at this period or at any other time in the Iron Age. Tell el-Kheleifeh, between Aqabah and modern Elath, is usually said to have been biblical Ezion-Geber, though this, too, is disputed (see Gary Pratico, "Where is Ezion-Geber?" *BAR*, September/ October 1986, pp. 24–35), and many scholars think that Ezion-Geber and Elath were two names (perhaps Israelite and Edomite?) for the same site.

[76] If Elath was another name for Ezion-Geber (see the preceding endnote), it had been controlled by Judah since the time of Solomon (1 Kings 9:26, 22:48). It was probably lost in the Edomite revolt against Jehoram in the mid-ninth century B.C.E. (2 Kings 8:20–22). Azariah "restored it to Judah" (2 Kings 14:22), but only temporarily. It was lost again to Edom in the time of Ahaz, when Jerusalem was threatened by the alliance of Samaria and Damascus (2 Kings 16:6).

[77] The biblical term ṣāra'at, conventionally translated "leprosy," refers to a variety of skin ailments and conditions, ranging from the benign to the virulent. It does not necessarily connote true leprosy or Hansen's disease. See Kenneth V. Mull and Carolyn Sandquist Mull, "Biblical Leprosy—Is It Really?" *BR*, April 1992, pp. 32–39, 62.

[78] This likelihood is enhanced by the description in 2 Chronicles 26:16–21 of a conflict between Azariah and the priesthood. As the Chronicler presents it, the high priest, whose name was also Azariah—the king is called Uzziah in this account—and 80 of his colleagues accused the king of usurping priestly prerogatives by making offerings on the altar of incense in the Temple. When the king became angry, his forehead broke out with "leprosy," which the priests immediately diagnosed. They then rushed him into quarantine.

[79] The original location of the plaque and the circumstances of its discovery are unknown, but it was deposited and preserved in the Russian Orthodox Convent on the Mount of Olives. It bears an Aramaic inscription of late Herodian date that reads "To this place have been brought the bones of Uzziah, the king of Judah—do not open!" See McCarter, *Ancient Inscriptions* (see endnote 1), pp. 132–133.

[80] See David C. Hopkins, *The Highlands of Canaan: Agricultural Life in the Early Iron Age* Social World of Biblical Antiquity 3 (Sheffield, UK: Almond Press, 1985); and Oded Borowski, *Agriculture in Iron Age Israel* (Winona Lake, IN: Eisenbrauns, 1987).

[81] Lawrence E. Stager, "The Archaeology of the Family in Ancient Israel," *BASOR* 260 (1985), pp. 1–35; Stager, "The Sons of Deborah—Why Some Tribes Answered the Call and Others Did Not," *BAR*, January/February 1989, pp. 50–64; Hopkins, *Highlands of Canaan* (see endnote 80), pp. 251–261; Holladay, "Kingdoms of Israel and Judah" (see endnote 10), p. 392.

[82] Roland de Vaux, *Ancient Israel*, vol. 1: *Social Institutions* (New York: McGraw-Hill, 1965), pp. 4–8.

[83] See Raymond Westbrook, "The Abuse of Power," in *Studies in Biblical and Cuneiform Law*, Cahiers de la Revue Biblique (Paris: J. Gabalda, 1988), pp. 9–38.

[84] The principal wife of the kings probably exercised considerable power in her role as queen and, after her husband's death, queen mother. This is suggested, for example, by the activities that 1 Kings 16–21, despite its overall hostile tone, attributes to Jezebel. One queen mother, Athaliah, even ruled Judah as its principal sovereign for several years (c. 841–835 B.C.E.). But these cases are exceptional; women ordinarily had very limited roles outside their immediate families.

[85] On the roles and status of women in the biblical period generally, see Carol L. Meyers, *Discovering Eve: Ancient Israelite Women in Context* (New York: Oxford, 1988). Phyllis A. Bird gives a concise summary of the evidence and issues in "Women (OT)," *ABD*, vol. 6, pp. 951–957.

[86] In ancient Near Eastern law and literature, the protection of the orphan and the widow is traditionally the responsibility of the king, and in the Bible this responsibility is usually assumed by Yahweh as the divine king. See F.C. Fensham, "Widow, Orphan and the Poor in Ancient Near Eastern Legal and Wisdom Literature," *JNES* 21 (1962), pp. 129–139, especially pp. 136–137.

[87] Nahman Avigad and Benjamin Sass, *Corpus of West Semitic Stamp Seals* (Jerusalem: Israel Academy of Sciences and Humanities, 1997), pp. 60–65; Robert Deutsch, *Messages from the Past: Hebrew Bullae from the Time of Isaiah Through the Destruction of the First Temple* (Tel Aviv: Archaeological Center Publications, 1997), pp. 65–69.

[88] The possibility is far from certain. In most cases the seals identify their owners as the wives of their husbands or the daughters of their fathers. In the former case, when the women are identified as wives, it seems unlikely that the seals were used by women acting with full independence. But in the latter case, when the women are identified as daughters, it is possible that the seals were used by women acting independently. This would be especially likely if the women were married but used seals identifying themselves as daughters of their fathers, just as men's seals usually identify their owners as sons of their fathers. On the other hand, the seals that identify their owners as daughters of their fathers might have belonged to unmarried women, so that the degree of independence implied is uncertain.

[89] Deutsch and Michael Heltzer, *New Epigraphic Evidence from the Biblical Period* (Tel Aviv: Archaeological Center Publications, 1995), pp. 83–88.

[90] Tiglath-pileser's annals refer to an enemy named Azariah (*Az-ri-ia-a-ú*) who seized control of a large portion of central and coastal Syria in the years prior to 739–738 B.C.E., when the territory was reclaimed by Tiglath-pileser. For the pertinent section of the annals (lines 103–133), see *ANET*, pp. 282b–283a. The opening lines of this section, where Azariah's name is not fully preserved, indicate that his country was *Ia-u-da-a-a*, which many scholars understood as Judah, thus leading to the hypothesis that Azariah of Judah played a major role in the effort to resist the first onslaught of Tiglath-pileser in the West. Research by Hayim Tadmor and Nadav Na'aman, however, has shown that the fragment containing the opening lines (103–119) does not belong to Tiglath-pileser's annals but derives instead from the records of a later Assyrian king. Thus the name of this Azariah's country is not preserved, and it seems very unlikely that he was the king of Judah. One intriguing fact remains unexplained, however. As Cogan and Tadmor point out, the name *Az-ri-ia-a-ú*, is Hebrew, not Aramaic, raising the possibility that he was an expatriot Israelite or Judahite who had gone to central Syria as a soldier of fortune and gained power there—a possibility raised long ago by the historian Eduard Meyer. For bibliography and a fuller discussion of this episode, see Pitard, *Ancient Damascus* (see endnote 15), pp. 180–181 n. 90, and Cogan and Tadmor, *II Kings* (see endnote 44), pp. 165–166.

[91] *ANET*, p. 283a. Menahem's payment consisted of 1,000 talents of silver according to 2 Kings 15:19, where Tiglath-pileser is called "Pul." This shortened form of his name is often said to have been Tiglath-pileser's throne name

as king of Babylon, a position he claimed in his first regnal year. This name has not been found in contemporary sources, however, though Tiglath-pileser was referred to as *Pulu* in much later cuneiform sources. See Cogan and Tadmor, *II Kings* (see endnote 44), pp. 171–172.

92 This likelihood is increased by the fact that the revolt came out of Gilead, Transjordanian Israel, where the influence of Damascus would be strongest. Cogan and Tadmor (*II Kings* [see endnote 44], p. 178) have raised the possibility that Pekah, whose Transjordanian roots are clear because his army consisted of "fifty of the Gileadites" (2 Kings 15:25), may not have been the only Gileadite to stage a successful coup in Israel in this period. Shallum, the assassin of Jeroboam's son, is called "son of Jabesh," but "Jabesh" is not otherwise known as a personal name, and the meaning may be that he was from the town of Jabesh-gilead (Judges 21:8; 1 Samuel 11:1). Shallum's assassin, Menahem, is said to have marched out "from Tirzah," but Tirzah lies on a natural access route into the Samarian hills via the Jabbok Valley and the Wadi Far'ah, and Menahem's designation "son of Gadi" might mean that he was a member of the tribe of Gad, the northern boundary of which was the Jabbok. If, in fact, all three of these usurpers were Gileadites, it raises the possibility that much of the instability in Israel following the death of Jeroboam II was a result of interference by Damascus.

93 See endnote 72.

94 The Medes were an Indo-Iranian people who lived on a plateau corresponding to the north-western part of modern Iran. Traditional enemies of Assyria, they would eventually become the principal ally of the Babylonians in the overthrow of the Assyrian Empire.

95 Joachim Begrich, "Der syrisch-ephraimitische Krieg und seine weltpolitischen Zusammenhänge," *Zeitschrift der deutschen morgenländischen Gesellschaft* 83 (1929), pp. 213–237.

96 See Isaiah 7:1–2. In response to Ahaz's anxiety the prophet does two things in Yahweh's name. First, he assures Ahaz that Rezin and "the son of Remaliah," as he calls Pekah, will never conquer Jerusalem, and, second, he gives a sign to certify the doom of the two nations that have attacked Jerusalem. This is the well-known Immanuel sign, according to which a child by that name will be born and "before the child knows how to refuse the evil and choose the good"—that is, before the child grows up—"the land before whose two kings you are in dread will be deserted" (Isaiah 7:16).

97 *ANET*, p. 282a.

98 Hayim Tadmor, *The Inscriptions of Tiglath-Pileser III* (Jerusalem: Israel Academy of Sciences and Humanities, 1994), annals 24:1'–9'.

99 According to Tiglath-pileser's annals (*ANET*, p. 284a) the Israelites "overthrew their king Pekah (*Pa-qa-ḫa*) Tiglath-pileser] placed Hoshea (*A-ú-si-'*) as king over them." For other references to the installation of Hoshea in the Assyrian annals, see Cogan and Tadmor, *II Kings* (see endnote 44), p. 175.

100 The region north of Ramoth-gilead, long disputed between Samaria and Damascus, became the Assyrian province of Qarnini (Karnaim).

101 Pitard, *Ancient Damascus* (see endnote 15), pp. 187–188.

102 *ANET*, p. 283a.

103 I. Eph'al, *The Ancient Arabs: Nomads on the Borders of the Fertile Crescent 9th–5th Centuries B.C.* (Jerusalem/Leiden: Hebrew Univ./Brill, 1982), p. 83; Holladay, "Kingdoms of Israel and Judah" (see endnote 10), p. 386.

104 *ANET*, p. 282.

105 *ANET*, p. 283b. The section dealing with the rebellions of Samsi and Mitinti (lines 210–240) begins at the top of the second column (on p. 238b). For the other extant account of the suppression of Samsi's rebellion, see *ANET*, p. 284a.

106 See Eph'al, *Ancient Arabs* (see endnote 103), p. 84. For the relevant annal fragment, see the preceding endnote.

107 Nothing of the Tyrian annals survives in the original Phoenician, but they were translated into Greek by an obscure Hellenistic author known as Menander of Ephesus or Pergamon. Menander's work has also been lost, but portions of his translation of the annals of Tyre are cited in the writings of the Jewish historian Flavius Josephus. For the background to the fall of Samaria, the relevant passage in Josephus is *Antiq.* 9.283–287.

108 For this date and a comprehensive evaluation of the sources, see Cogan and Tadmor, *II Kings* (see endnote 44), pp. 198–199.

109 Who was the Egyptian king to whom Hoshea appealed? The Hebrew text of 2 Kings 17:4 identifies him as "So (*sô'*), the king of Egypt," but no king by that name is known. When Shalmaneser V came to the throne of Assyria, Egypt was emerging from a period of weakness under the last kings of the XXIInd and XXIIIrd Dynasties. Although Piankhy, the founder of the strong XXVth Dynasty had already conquered Egypt, at least formally, he was not yet ready to assert full control and had withdrawn for the time being to his native

Nubia. This left the Egyptian Delta under the effective rule of Tefnacht, the very capable king of Sais in the western Delta, which was the dominant city of Egypt in the last half of the eighth century B.C.E. Osorkon IV, the last king of the XXIInd Dynasty, still ruled Tanis and Bubastis in the eastern Delta, and some historians argue that he was the biblical "So, the king of Egypt," pointing out that an Asiatic ruler like Hoshea would be more likely to be in contact with an Egyptian ruler whose realm was in the eastern Delta and that biblical references in Psalms and the prophetic works are common while Sais is never mentioned. This is the view, for example, of Ahlström (*History of Ancient Palestine* [see endnote 24], pp. 672–674), and Kenneth A. Kitchen (*Third Intermediate Period in Egypt [1100–650 B.C]* [Warminster: Aris & Phillips, 1973], pp. 374–375), who speculates that "So" might be an abbreviation of "Osorkon" (though such abbreviations are unknown). Osorkon, however, seems to have accepted the suzerainty of Tefnacht, who founded the XXIVth Dynasty in 727 B.C.E. and was the *de facto* ruler of Egypt at the time of Hoshea's petition. Tefnacht, therefore, is the most likely candidate for "the king of Egypt" of 2 Kings 17:4, and Hans Goedicke's 1963 solution to the crux of "So, the king of Egypt" is still the best. He interpreted *sô'* as the Hebrew rendering of "Sais" (Egyptian *S3w*) and suggested that the original sense of the slightly corrupt biblical description of Hoshea's action was that "he sent messengers to Sais, to the king of Egypt"; see Goedicke, "The End of 'So, the King of Egypt,'" *BASOR* 171 (1963), pp. 64–66; Redford, *Egypt, Canaan, and Israel* (see endnote 3), p. 346.

[110] There is strong indirect evidence that the alliance included other states, from Philistia and perhaps elsewhere; see J. Maxwell Miller and John H. Hayes, *A History of Ancient Israel and Judah* (Philadelphia: Westminster, 1986), pp. 334–335.

[111] Cf. Cogan and Tadmor, *II Kings* (see endnote 44), p. 199.

[112] Merodachbaladan was from Bit-Yakin, the most southerly of the three Chaldean tribes in Babylonia. The Chaldeans, who were closely related to the Arameans, begin to appear in extant cuneiform sources in the ninth century B.C.E., and by the eighth they were vying for leadership in Babylonia. Eventually their name became synonymous with Babylonians (cf. Genesis 11:28). The nationalistic movement that Merodachbaladan led for more than 20 years during the reigns of Sargon and Sennacherib was fired in part by resentment of the Assyrian kings' practice (beginning with Tiglath-pileser III) of claiming

the Babylonian throne for themselves.

[113] See the excerpts from Sargon's annals and Display Inscriptions for his second year in *ANET*, p. 285.

[114] Probably Tefnacht again; see endnote 109.

[115] These included Queen Samsi of Arabia, who had also paid tribute to Tiglath-pileser, and It'amar the Sabaean, chieftain of the powerful trading people of southwestern Arabia from whom the fabled Queen of Sheba of Solomonic lore also came. Their tribute came in the form of gold dust, horses and camels. When Sargon returned west in his seventh year (715 B.C.E.) to resettle captive peoples in the provinces, Samsi and It'amar brought tribute again. For both lists, see *ANET*, pp. 284b–285a, 286a.

[116] *ANET*, pp. 284b–285a.

[117] The list in 2 Kings 17:24 is part of the peroration on the fall of Samaria by the exilic Deuteronomist (see below). It may contain the names of peoples transported to former Israelite territories at different times, thus collapsing several resettlements into a single statement. From Sargon's own records, we know only that he brought captives from a number of Arabian tribes and settled them in Samaria in 715 B.C.E. (*ANET*, pp. 285b–286a). He may well have resettled additional peoples in Samaria in 711 B.C.E., when he made his final visit to Palestine to suppress a revolt in Ashdod, and there were probably still other resettlements of which we have no record.

[118] Reading "mountain country" or "highlands" with the Greek of 2 Kings 17:6 in preference to the Hebrew reading "cities."

[119] An impression of this seal published by Nahman Avigad (*Hebrew Bullae from the Time of Jeremiah* [Jerusalem: Israel Exploration Society, 1986], p. 110 no. 199) was not well enough preserved to be recognized, but a second, legible impression has been recently acquired by the collection of Shlomo Moussaieff of London. It will be published by Frank Moore Cross in *Realia Dei: Essays in Archaeology and Biblical Interpretation*, ed. Prescott H. Williams, Jr. and Theodore Hiebert (Edward F. Campbell Volume) (Atlanta: Scholars Press, forthcoming) and in "King Hezekiah's Seal," *BAR*, March/April 1999.

[120] Many historians of Israel have assumed that the reforms were undertaken as an integral component of the revolt against Sennacherib, involving a repudiation of the Assyrian gods (John Bright, *History of Israel*, 3rd ed. [Philadelphia: Westminster, 1981], p. 282) and expulsion of Assyrian religious practices from the Temple in Jerusalem (Martin Noth, *History of Israel*, 2nd ed. [New York: Harper & Row, 1960], p. 266). Studies of the religious policies of the empire, however, have shown that, in

contrast to the rules for annexed territories where worship of the Assyrian gods was required, it was not Assyrian policy to interfere with the religious practices of vassal states like Judah; see John W. McKay, *Religion in Judah Under the Assyrians,* Studies in Biblical Theology Second Series 26 (London: SCM, 1973); Cogan, *Imperialism and Religion: Assyria, Judah and Israel in the Eighth and Seventh Centuries B.C.,* SBL Monograph 19 (Missoula, MT: Scholars Press, 1974).

[121] In fact, this very point was part of the rhetoric of Sennacherib's spokesman, the Rabshakeh, in his attempt to intimidate Hezekiah's delegation at the beginning of the siege of Jerusalem (2 Kings 18:22).

[122] The Chronicler's account of Hezekiah's reforms, which constitutes the bulk of three chapters (2 Chronicles 29–31), is much more extensive than the three verses assigned to the subject in the Kings account (2 Kings 18:4–6). This is explainable in part as the Chronicler's expansion of subjects in which he had a particular interest (note, for example, the emphasis on role of the Levites in the purification of the Temple in chapter 30). But we must also allow for a tendency on the part of the Deuteronomistic historian, who was responsible for the Kings account, to diminish the extent of Hezekiah's reform. To be sure, the historian admired Hezekiah and praised him highly, asserting that in his trust in Yahweh "… there was no one like him among all the kings of Judah after him, or among those who were before him" (2 Kings 18:5). But if, as many scholars believe, the historian was working in the time of Josiah—indeed, under the patronage of Josiah—it is not surprising that he would minimize Hezekiah's role in the reform movement in order to reserve the primary credit for Josiah.

[123] The annals contain several references to Azuri's sending "messages (full) of hostilities against Assyria, to the kings (living) in his neighborhood," and in one broken prism (*ANET,* pp. 286b–287a), Judah is named explicitly as one of those Azuri had tried to recruit.

[124] Second Kings 20:12–13 (cf. Isaiah 39:1–2; 2 Chronicles 32:31) describes a visit of Merodachbaladan's envoys to Jerusalem, where Hezekiah showed them the Temple treasury. In the current arrangement of the biblical materials about Hezekiah's reign, this visit is placed after Sennacherib's invasion, but it must have occurred earlier, since in 701 B.C.E. Merodachbaladan was no longer in power. It fits nicely into the events of 704–703 B.C.E., when it would have been very much in

Merodachbaladan's interest to cultivate alliances with other Assyrian vassal states and encourage them to rebel. See Noth, *History of Israel* (see endnote 120), p. 267; Bright, *History of Israel* (see endnote 120), pp. 284–285 and n. 44; Ahlström, *History of Ancient Palestine* (see endnote 24), p. 695. Cogan and Tadmor (*II Kings* [see endnote 44], pp. 260–261) place the visit earlier, during Merodachbaladan's first term as king of Babylon (722–710 B.C.E.).

[125] This was the third of the eight campaigns of Sennacherib recorded in the final edition of his annals, preserved in the Taylor and Oriental Institute prisms (see McCarter, *Ancient Inscriptions* [see endnote 1], pp. 24–25), both of which are dependent, for this campaign, on the slightly fuller account in the so-called Rassam cylinder, which was composed shortly after the campaign itself (for a translation, see Cogan and Tadmor, *II Kings* [see endnote 44], pp. 337–339). When the Assyrian records are complemented and supplemented with information concerning the Judean part of the campaign found in the Bible (2 Kings 18:13–19:8; Isaiah 36:1–37:8; 2 Chronicles 32:1–22), and the ample archaeological testimony to the campaign and Hezekiah's preparations for it at sites like Lachish and Jerusalem, the story of the campaign that emerges is one of the most complete in the history of the Assyrian Empire. See David Ussishkin, "News from the Field: Defensive Judean Counter-Ramp Found at Lachish in 1983 Season," *BAR,* March/April 1984, pp. 66–73.

[126] Presumably this huge force ("an army beyond counting," *ANET,* p. 287b) had been dispatched by Shebitku (702–690 B.C.E.), who had just succeeded Shabaka as king of Egypt. The biblical reference in 2 Kings 19:9 (= Isaiah 37:9) to "King Tirhakah of Ethiopia" is evidently a mistake, since in 701 B.C.E. Taharqa (690–664 B.C.E.), the biblical Tirhakah, was still a child living in Nubia and would not come to the throne of Egypt for another decade; see Redford, *Egypt, Canaan, and Israel* (see endnote 3), p. 353 n. 163. This lapse on the part of the Israelite historian has helped give rise to the hypothesis of a second, later campaign by Sennacherib against Judah; see endnote 141 below.

[127] Padi's name appears in a five-line inscription found in 1996 in the ruins of a temple at Tel Miqne, ancient Ekron; see Seymour Gitin, Trude Dothan and Joseph Naveh, "A Royal Dedicatory Inscription from Ekron," *Israel Exploration Journal* 47 (1997), pp. 1–16. The inscription records the dedication of the temple to a goddess by "Ikaysh (*'kyš*) son of Padi." Ikaysh appears as

one who paid tribute to Assyria in inscriptions of Sennacherib's successor Esarhaddon (681–669 B.C.E.), where he is called Ikausu (*ANET*, pp. 291a, 294a). See Aaron Demsky, "Discovering a Goddess," *BAR*, September/October 1998, pp. 53–58.

[128] At certain points the correspondences are remarkably close. At the beginning of the account of the advance against Hezekiah in the Assyrian annals, Sennacherib says, "I laid siege to 46 of his strong cities, walled forts ... and conquered them ..." (*ANET*, p. 288a), while the biblical account opens with the statement that "King Sennacherib of Assyria came up against all the fortified cities of Judah and captured them" (2 Kings 18:13). In the Assyrian account the amount of precious metal in the tribute Hezekiah paid is given as "30 talents of gold, 800 talents of silver" (*ANET*, p. 288a), while the biblical account specifies the amount as "three hundred talents of silver and thirty talents of gold" (2 Kings 18:14).

[129] H.W.F. Saggs, "The Nimrud Letters, 1952: I," *Iraq* 17 (1955), pp. 23–26; Chaim Cohen, "Neo-Assyrian Elements in the First Speech of the Biblical Rab-šaqê," *Israel Oriental Studies* 9 (1979), pp. 32–48; Peter Machinist, "Assyria and Its Image in First Isaiah," *Journal of the American Oriental Society* 103 (1983), pp. 719–737; Cogan and Tadmor, *II Kings* (see endnote 44), pp. 242–243.

[130] The second section describes two visits to Jerusalem by Sennacherib's officer Rabshakeh—one from Lachish and one from Libnah (possibly Tell Bornat, about 5 miles north of Lachish). The prevailing view among biblical scholars is that this second section is a composite of two versions of one round of negotiations. The first version (2 Kings 18:17–19:7) seems to be older, with less elaboration in the prophetic and Deuteronomistic traditions; it reports the Rabshakeh's attempt to intimidate Jerusalem, Hezekiah's reaction and Isaiah's reassurance. The second version (2 Kings 19:8–34) is probably later; it tells the same basic story, but with much more literary elaboration deriving, in the first place, from prophetic tradition—a poetic oracle of Isaiah reviling Sennacherib in 2 Kings 19:20–28, followed by a prophetic sign of reassurance in 2 Kings 19:29–31 and a prose oracle proclaiming the salvation of the city in 2 Kings 19:32–34—and, in the second place, from a Deuteronomistic compiler, whose hand is most evident in the language of Hezekiah's prayer (2 Kings 19:14–19). It is noteworthy, in this regard, that the historically problematic reference to "King Tirhakah of Ethiopia" (2 Kings 19:9) appears in the late version; see endnote 126 above.

[131] See Ussishkin, *The Conquest of Lachish by Sennacherib,* Publications of the Institute of Archaeology 6 (Tel Aviv: Tel Aviv University, 1982), reviewed by Hershel Shanks in *BAR* March/April 1984, pp. 48–65, and updated by Ussishkin, "News from the Field" (see endnote 125).

[132] According to Isaiah 20:1, for example, it was Sargon's Tartan (Hebrew *tartān* from Akkadian *turtānu*) who conducted the 714–712 B.C.E. campaign against Ashdod. A Babylonian Rabsaris is among the officers listed in connection with the fall of Jerusalem in Jeremiah 39:3,13.

[133] It has been speculated that the Rabshakeh was an exiled Israelite who had found a career in the Assyrian court; see Cogan and Tadmor, *II Kings* (see endnote 44), p. 230, and Ahlström, *History of Ancient Palestine* (see endnote 24), pp. 683–684.

[134] *ANET*, p. 288a.

[135] The well-constructed, 20-foot thick wall was discovered in the 1970 Jewish Quarter excavation. See Nahman Avigad, *Discovering Jerusalem* (Nashville: Abingdon, 1980), pp. 46–57. Magen Broshi and others have suggested that the region surrounding Jerusalem, and especially the western hill, became a camp for refugees after the fall of Samaria and during Sennacherib's depradations in the surrounding countryside, especially with the Assyrian reassignment of Judahite cities to the Philistines; see Broshi, "The Expansion of Jerusalem in the Reigns of Hezekiah and Manasseh," *IEJ* 24 (1974), pp. 21–26. If this is correct, it is likely that Hezekiah's "outside" wall was built in order to incorporate the western hill into the city, with the result that the population of the city may have expanded, according to Broshi's estimate, three- or fourfold in the last quarter of the eighth century B.C.E.

[136] Hezekiah's tunnel is commonly known as the Siloam Tunnel, a name derived from the Shiloah or Siloam Channel, an aqueduct that transported the waters of the Gihon along the southeastern slope of the Ophel to agricultural terraces in the Kidron basin; see further, on both the tunnel and the inscription, McCarter, *Ancient Inscriptions* (see endnote 1), pp. 113–115.

[137] Some of the scarabs have two wings, and some have four—a fact that was formerly interpreted as evidence of chronological development. It has now been shown, however, that all of the *lmlk* stamps belong to the time of Hezekiah, and this fact, combined with the vast numbers in which they appear in excavations (more than 1,200 have been found), strengthens the assumption that they had a function in Hezekiah's administration of the

kingdom before the invasion; see Na'aman, "Sennacherib's Campaign to Judah and the Date of the *lmlk* Stamps," *VT* 29 (1979), pp. 61–86. It is interesting to note in this context that King Hezekiah's personal seal, an impression of which has recently come to light (see endnote 119), also bore a two-winged scarab.

[138] Further evidence that the *lmlk* stamps were part of a centralized administrative program comes from the recent determination that they were all manufactured in a single site in the Judean Shephelah, as revealed by analysis of the clay from which they were manufactured. See further McCarter, *Ancient Inscriptions* (see endnote 1), pp. 142–143.

[139] The overall structure of the biblical narrative is designed to show that the survival of the city was the result of divine deliverance in fulfillment of the oracles of Isaiah, especially the oracle in 2 Kings 19:32–34 announcing that Yahweh would defend the city. The night after this prophecy was uttered, we are told (2 Kings 19:35), "The angel of the Lord ... struck down one hundred eighty-five thousand in the camp of the Assyrians ..." This is the biblical language of plague, as correctly interpreted in Ben Sira 48:21, and it might preserve a historical memory of one of the factors leading to the Assyrian withdrawal, namely, the spread of disease among the siege troops. Herodotus (*History* 2.141) relates the story of a similar deliverence of Egypt from "Sennacherib, king of the Arabs [!] and Assyrians," when mice gnawed the weapons of the Assyrians while they were encamped at Pelusium in the eastern Nile Delta. This story has been associated with Sennacherib's siege of Jerusalem by some historians, who regard the reference to mice as an indirect confirmation of an outbreak of plague in the Assyrian camp. But the Herodotus story is not historical in anything like its present form—Sennacherib never invaded Egypt—and, in any case, it makes no mention of Judah or Jerusalem. At best it might be regarded as a distorted recollection of an event in the reign of Esarhaddon, Sennacherib's successor, who did invade Egypt and was assisted in doing so by Arab guides.

[140] The list of Hezekiah's tribute, which is quite substantial in the Taylor and Oriental Institute prisms, is even more so in the older Rassam cylinder (see endnote 125)—indeed, it is the longest in any of Sennacherib's extant inscriptions.

[141] Some historians argue that Sennacherib conducted a second campaign against Judah sometime after the accession of Tirhakah in 690 B.C.E. The two-campaign hypothesis is an attempt to solve the problems created by the reference to "King Tirhakah of Ethiopia" in 2 Kings 19:9 (see endnote 126) and especially the contradiction regarding the outcome of the siege between the Assyrian account, which says that Hezekiah capitulated and accepted vassal status, and the biblical account, which concludes with Sennacherib's army retreating from Judah after having been severely punished by the hand of Yahweh. According to the two-campaign theory, Sennacherib's surviving inscriptions refer to the 701 B.C.E. campaign, which ended in the reduction of Judah to vassalage, while the biblical references to the failure and withdrawal of the Assyrian army and to the involvement of Tirhakah refer to a campaign not mentioned in extant Assyrian sources. The occasion for this second campaign would have been a rebellion in the West, led by Hezekiah and supported by Tirhakah, that broke out after the Assyrian army was defeated by the Babylonians and Elamites in 691 B.C.E., and Sennacherib would have launched it after his capture of Babylon in 689 B.C.E. Though ingenious, the two-campaign theory does not inspire confidence, since the problems being addressed arise only in the final part of the biblical account of the siege, which, as noted earlier, is widely regarded as late in origin, while the opening summary of the biblical account (2 Kings 18:13–16), which is unanimously regarded as early, is in close agreement with the Assyrian account. For arguments in favor of the two-campaign theory, see Albright, "New Light from Egypt on the Chronology and History of Israel and Judah," *BASOR* 130 (1953), pp. 8–11; Siegfried Horn, "Did Sennacherib Campaign Once or Twice Against Hezekiah?" *AUSS* 4 (1966), pp. 1–28; Bright, *History of Israel* (see endnote 120), pp. 296–398; and William H. Shea, "Sennacherib's Second Palestinian Campaign," *JBL* 104 (1985), pp. 401–418. For a thorough critique, see Cogan and Tadmor, *II Kings* (see endnote 44), pp. 248–251.

[142] *ANET*, pp. 291a, 294a.

[143] On the exilic Deuteronomist and his treatment of Manasseh, see Cross, *Canaanite Myth and Hebrew Epic* (see endnote 12), pp. 285–287. For the Chronicler's account of Manasseh's reign, which contains substantially different material, see the discussion below.

[144] Noth, *History of Israel* (see endnote 120), p. 269; Bright, *History of Israel* (see endnote 120), p. 312.

[145] See endnote 120 and the studies of McKay and Cogan cited there.

[146] The rest of the list of practices for which he is condemned in 1 Kings 21:3–6 corresponds very closely to the cultic sins listed in 2 Kings 17:16–17, amid the long Deuteronomistic

sermon on the fall of Samaria in 2 Kings 17:7–23. Thus, he erected altars to a foreign god (Baal; 1 Kings 21:3) and "the host of heaven," astral deities whose rooftop worship was condemned by prophets like Zephaniah (1:5) and Jeremiah (19:13); he reinstituted the "sacred pole" or asherah (1 Kings 21:3); and he made "his son pass through fire" and practiced soothsaying and augury (1 Kings 21:3). In 2 Kings 17:16–17 these are the very sins that, in the view of the Deuteronomist historian who composed the sermon (cf. Cross, *Canaanite Myth and Hebrew Epic* [see endnote 12], p. 281), led to the downfall of the northern kingdom, and it seems clear that the purpose of the exilic Deuteronomist in composing the present list was to accuse Manasseh of bringing similar judgment on Judah (Cross, *Canaanite Myth and Hebrew Epic*, p. 285). This is surely the point of the comparison of Manasseh to "King Ahab of Israel" in 2 Kings 21:3.

[147] The Medes were Indo-Iranian people living on the plateau corresponding to the northwestern part of modern Iran. Traditional enemies of Assyria, they eventually became the principal ally of Babylonia in the overthrow of the Assyrian Empire, as we shall see.

[148] The Cimmerians—called *Kimmerioi* by the Greeks, *Gimirrai* by the Assyrians and *gōmer*, "Gomer," in the Bible (Ezekiel 38:6; cf. Genesis 10:2–3)—were Indo-Aryan nomads, originally from southern Russia. In the eighth century B.C.E., they had been driven south across the Caucasus under pressure from the Scythians and Assyrians into Asia Minor. Sargon II was fighting the Cimmerians in Asia Minor when he was killed in 705 B.C.E.

[149] The Scythians—called *Skythai* by the Greeks, *Ašguzai*, *Išguzai* by the Assyrians and *'aškěnaz*, "Ashkenaz," in the Bible (Jeremiah 51:27; cf. Genesis 10:3)—were a nomadic people who spoke an Indo-Iranian language. In the eighth century B.C.E. they had moved from their homeland in southern Russia (north and northeast of Black Sea) through the Caucasus into the Near East. Originally enemies of Assyria, they became allies briefly, then enemies again.

[150] Anthony Spalinger, "Esarhaddon and Egypt: An Analysis of the First Invasion of Egypt," *Orientalia* 43 (1974), p. 299.

[151] See, for the treaty between Esarhaddon and Baal, *ANET*, pp. 533b–534a; for Abdimilkutti's rebellion, *ANET*, pp. 290b–291a; and for the rebuilding project, *ANET*, p. 290.

[152] *ANET*, p. 302b.

[153] *ANET*, p. 292b. Earlier (c. 677 B.C.E.) Esarhaddon had pacified Arab tribes in the vicinity of the Wadi of Egypt (*ANET*, p. 291b–292a), guaranteeing their neutrality and learning from them the value of the camel and waterskin.

[154] This is according to the Babylonian Chronicle (*ANET*, p. 302b–303a); for the narrative account in the so-called Zinjirli stele from southeastern Turkey (ancient Sam'al), see *ANET*, p. 293a.

[155] In a stele carved on the rock wall of the Dog River near Beirut, he boasts, "I entered Memphis ... amidst (general) jubilation and rejoicing" (*ANET*, p. 292a).

[156] Again, according to the Babylonian Chronicle, *ANET*, p. 303b.

[157] According to the so-called Rassam cylinder from Kuyunjik, ancient Nineveh (*ANET*, pp. 294–296a), Assurbanipal led this expedition himself, but other inscriptions indicate that he stayed home and entrusted the task to his second-in-command, the *turtānu*.

[158] *ANET*, p. 294a.

[159] This was the period of the Saite Renaissance in Egypt, so-called because of the revival of the ancient Memphite traditions of Lower Egypt, which was now ruled from Sais in the north rather than from Thebes in Upper Egypt. The period was characterized by a revival of art and culture, a thorough reorganization of the government and an increasing openness to foreign contacts, including commerce with Greece. All this was possible because of the escalating collapse of Assyria and the corresponding increase in the autonomy of Egypt. It must be kept in mind, however, that Saite kings of Egypt maintained an official posture of allegiance to Assyria; see Spalinger, "The Concept of Monarchy During the Saite Epoch: An Essay of Synthesis, *Orientalia* 47 (1978), pp. 12–36.

[160] The enigmatic biblical tradition of Manasseh's arrest by the Assyrians (2 Chronicles 33:11) is sometimes thought to belong in the context of the Shamash-shum-ukin revolt. Manasseh is said to have been dragged in chains to Babylon (!), then released and restored to power. Apart from the defection just noted of some of Assyria's Arabian allies, we have only scant evidence to indicate that the revolt spread into the western provinces, but if there was more unrest there than our surviving records indicate, it would not be surprising to find that Manasseh had become involved, especially in view of the biblical and archaeological evidence cited below, which suggests he was moving towards independence later in his reign. Certainly there is nothing implausible about the story of his arrest and restoration to power, since it would parallel the experiences of others in the hands of Assurbanipal. In their

overextended empire, Assurbanipal and Esarhaddon before him had little choice other than to try, with the help of intimidation and promises, to find native rulers who would be loyal to Assyria. The experience of Manasseh, as described in 2 Chronicles 33:11, for example, parallels that of Necho in Egypt and the Arab leader Uate' in Transjordan, both of whom rebelled, were captured and brought before the Assyrian king, then sent home to rule again.

[161] For Esarhaddon's campaign against the Arabs, which is also described on the so-called Rassam cylinder (see endnote 157), see *ANET*, pp. 297b–301a.

[162] In 2 Kings 21:16 Manasseh is accused of "shedding innocent blood." The basis of this charge is unknown, although one was supplied in postbiblical tradition. According to a variety of Jewish and Christian sources, Manasseh, again like Ahab (2 Kings 21:3), persecuted the prophets and even had Isaiah sawed in two (Josephus, *Antiq.* 10.38; BT *Sanhedrin* 103b; Ascension of Isaiah 5:1–7; Justin, *Dialogue with Trypho* 120; Jerome, *Comment on Isaiah* 57:2; cf. Hebrews 11:37).

[163] For the principal suggestions, see Dan Bahat, "The Wall of Manasseh in Jerusalem," *IEJ* 31 [1981], pp. 235–236. Bahat calls special attention to a wall "of substantial appearance" found by Kathleen Kenyon, who dated it to the eighth-seventh century B.C.E., on the eastern slope of the City of David; see her *Digging Up Jerusalem* (London: Benn, 1974), p. 83 (Wall NA). The location fits with the biblical designation "west of the Gihon, in the wadi," and Bahat has suggested that it might be Manasseh's "outer wall," On the difficulties in the archaeological interpretation of the walls of Jerusalem during the last part of the Judean monarchy, see Avigad, *Discovering Jerusalem* (see endnote 135), pp. 46–60.

[164] If our assumption is correct that Manasseh was distancing himself from Assyria at the end of his reign, the assassination is unlikely to have been part of an anti-Assyrian coup, especially since there is no known external event with which it might be associated (the last Assyrian incursion into the West was a punitive attack on Acco and Ushu [island Tyre], probably to be dated to 644 B.C.E.). Redford (*Egypt, Canaan, and Israel* [see endnote 3], pp. 440–441) has made an interesting suggestion that would connect the coup with the Scythian invasion of Palestine mentioned by Herodotus (*History* 1.103–106).

[165] For a convenient delineation of these and other major correspondences between Josiah's reform measures and the cultic laws laid down in Deuteronomy, see the table provided in Ernest W. Nicholson, *Deuteronomy and Tradition* (Philadelphia: Fortress, 1967), p. 3. The hypothesis that Josiah's "book of the law" was an early form of the Book of Deuteronomy was first articulated in W.M.L De Wette's 1805 Berlin doctoral thesis, *Dissertatio Critica ...* .

[166] In this regard, it is important to understand that the Judahite reform movement of the late eighth and seventh centuries B.C.E. arose during a period of international neoclassicism in the ancient Near East, a time when classical forms and ideas were being revived or reconstructed in Egypt and Mesopotamia, as well as Judah. In Egypt both the Cushite rulers of the XXVth Dynasty and the Saite kings of the XXVIth Dynasty promoted the return to traditional Egyptian values and revived long-forgotten practices and beliefs, sometimes on the basis of the discovery of ancient documents, such as the so-called Shabaka Stone, which was claimed to have been copied from an ancient papyrus, "a work of the ancestors, but worm-eaten, so that it could not be comprehended from beginning to end"; see McCarter, *Ancient Inscriptions* (see endnote 1), pp. 58–59; and for the text, *ANET*, pp. 4a–6a. In Assyria, Assurbanipal (668–627 B.C.E.) promoted his own form of Mesopotamian neoclassicism, instructioning his officials to scour the countryside of Assyria and Babylonia, poring through the local temple archives for ancient documents that could be copied and added to the royal collection. The result was an extraordinary library, which, since its discovery in the mid-19th century in the mound of ancient Nineveh at Kuyunjik in northern Iraq, has remained our most important source for the "canonical" literature of ancient Mesopotamia.

[167] To be sure, foreign cults *were* outlawed by Josiah, but the deities whose cult places are listed in 2 Kings 23:13–14 as having been defiled were the gods and goddesses of Judah's West Semitic neighbors—Ashtart of Sidon, Chemosh of Moab, Milcom of Ammon—not those of Assyria.

[168] For a detailed statement of the difficulties and the various positions, see Na'aman, "The Kingdom of Judah Under Josiah," *Tel Aviv* 18 (1991), pp. 41–51. In Na'aman's own view, Josiah was probably able to expand into the Samarian hills, but not into Transjordan, the Jordan Valley, or the Galilee, as some have proposed, and no farther west than the northern Judean Shephelah, since the coastal plain was controlled by Egypt.

[169] See McCarter, *Ancient Inscriptions* (see endnote 1), p. 116.

[170] An inscription of Psammetichus, dated 612 B.C.E., boasts of Egyptian control of Phoenicia and its timber trade; see K.S. Freedy and Redford, "The Dates in Ezekiel in Relation to Biblical, Babylonian and Egyptian Sources," *JAOS* 90 (1970), pp. 462–485.

[171] Herodotus, *History* 2.157.

[172] Herodotus, *History* 1.105.

[173] To what extent this created friction with Josiah, who, as noted above, may also have taken control of parts of Philistia, is unknown, but the potential conflict may have been a factor in Josiah's fatal encounter with Psammetichus's successor at Megiddo in 609 B.C.E.

[174] This is essentially the explanation of Redford (*Egypt, Canaan, and Israel* [see endnote 3], p. 446), who describes the Egyptian policy as "at once unexpected yet farsighted."

[175] Riblah had been an Assyrian administrative and military center earlier, and shortly after this it became a Babylonian military center.

[176] Cf. 1 Chronicles 3:15: "The sons of Josiah: Johanan the firstborn, the second Jehoiakim, the third Zedekiah, the fourth Shallum." That Jehoahaz was Shallum is shown by Jeremiah 22:11–12. The reason "the people of the land" chose the youngest of Josiah's sons is not given. The firstborn, Johanan, is not mentioned earlier and may have died before his father. Jehoiakim, with whom Necho supplanted Jehoahaz, may have been passed over by "the people of his land" because of his pro-Egyptian leanings.

[177] In the words of 2 Kings 24:7, "The king of Egypt did not come again out of his land, for the king of Babylon had taken over all that belonged to the king of Egypt from the Wadi of Egypt to the River Euphrates."

[178] On the Babylonian destruction of Ashkelon, see Stager, "The Fury of Babylon: Ashkelon and the Archaeology of Destruction," *BAR*, January/February 1996, pp. 56–69, 76–77. The mood in Philistia at this time is illustrated by a fragmentary papyrus found at Saqqara containing the Aramaic text of a letter from a certain Adon, ruler of a Philistine state (probably Ekron), requesting help from the pharaoh against the Babylonian army, which, he says, had already captured Aphek. See Bezalel Porten, "The Identity of King Adon," *BA* 44 (1981), pp. 36–52.

[179] Édouard Lipiński, "The Egyptian-Babylonian War of the Winter 601–600," *Annali dell'istituto orientale di Napoli* 22 (1972), pp. 235–241.

[180] Herodotus, *History* 2.159.

[181] Bright, *History of Israel* (see endnote 120), p. 327. The final comment on Jehoiakim by his old nemesis, Jeremiah, shows that the king received no more sympathy in death than he had in life from the prophet, who constantly advised compliance with Babylon and deplored Jehoiakim's pro-Egyptian stance. See Jeremiah 22:18–19.

[182] Conditions in the Judahite countryside during this grim period are vividly illustrated by a group of ostraca found in the ruins of the fortress of Lachish, which, because of its position guarding the main access road into the Judahite Hills from the coastal plain, was attacked by Nebuchadnezzar just as it had been by Sennacherib in 701 B.C.E. The 22 Lachish ostraca constitute a small archive of wartime correspondence between the governor or commanding officer of Lachish and a subordinate. One of the ostraca (no. 3) refers to a general named Coniah son of Elnathan, who was passing by Lachish on a mission to Egypt; he may well have been carrying the invitation that brought Hophra's troops briefly to Jerusalem as described in Jeremiah 37:5; see McCarter, *Ancient Inscriptions* (see endnote 1), pp. 116–118. Another Lachish ostracon (no. 4) speaks of the disappearance of the signal fires of the nearby fortress of Azekah, a statement that poignantly brings to mind the reference in Jeremiah 34:7 to the time "when the army of the king of Babylon was fighting against Jerusalem and against all the cities of Judah that were left, Lachish and Azekah; for these were the only fortified cities of Judah that remained"; see *Ancient Inscriptions* (see endnote 1), pp. 118–119.

[183] Zorn, "Mizpah" (see endnote 16).

[184] See Abraham Malamat, "The Kingdom of Judah Between Egypt and Babylon: A Small State Within a Great Power Confrontation," *Studia Theologica* 44 (1960), pp. 65–77; and a forthcoming article in *BAR*.

VI. Exile and Return

[1] On the economic dimensions of Gedaliah's governorship, note Jeremiah 40:10, "As for me I will dwell at Mizpah, to stand for you before the Chaldeans who will come to us; but as for you, gather wine and summer fruits and oil, and store them in your vessels, and dwell in your cities that you have taken." A recent study by J.N. Graham using seal impressions (including a seal of "Gedaliah who is over the household") and other archaeological data argues that Gedaliah was established as governor to oversee a state-managed agrarian system intended to generate tribute for the Babylonians and also contribute to the local welfare. It is further argued that the "vinedressers and plowmen" (2 Kings 25:12 and Jeremiah 52:16) were

[1] technical terms for those in compulsory service in state industries. See Graham, "Vinedressers and Plowmen," *BA* 47 (1984), pp. 55–58.

[2] It is extremely difficult to estimate actual population on the basis of ancient sources. For a general discussion of this and related issues see Magen Broshi, "Demography" in *OEANE* vol. 2, pp. 142–144. Norman K. Gottwald (*The Hebrew Bible: A Socio-Literary Introduction* [Philadelphia: Fortress Press, 1985], p. 423), estimates that 95 percent of the population of Judah remained in Palestine.

[3] Many in Jerusalem viewed Jehoiachin as the legitimate king, as demonstrated by the oracle of the prophet Hananiah ben Azzur of Gibeon (Jeremiah 28:1–4) and other sources. For Jeremiah's alternative, and apparently minority, opinion, see Jeremiah 22:24–30. See especially Martin Noth, "The Jerusalem Catastrophe of 587 B.C. and Its Significance for Israel," in *The Laws in the Pentateuch and Other Studies* (Edinburgh: Oliver & Boyd, 1966), pp. 260–280.

[4] This is based on the understanding that the Shenazzar of 1 Chronicles 3:18 is Sheshbazzar. For a more detailed discussion of this question see Carol L. Meyers and Eric M. Meyers, *Haggai, Zechariah 1–8: A New Translation with Introduction and Commentary* Anchor Bible 25B (Garden City, NY: Doubleday, 1987), pp. 10–11.

[5] See Peter R. Ackroyd, "The Temple Vessels— A Continuity Theme," in *Studies in the Religion of Ancient Israel,* VT Supplements 23 (Leiden: Brill, 1972), pp. 166–181.

[6] The Chronicler was followed in this interpretation by the author of 1 Esdras, who cites only one deportation at the time of the destruction of Jerusalem, with reference to the removal of the sacred Temple vessels and without reference to the exile of Zedekiah (1 Esdras 1:52–58). Josephus, writing at a later time and conflating all of the biblical traditions (including 1 Esdras), gives the three exiles of 2 Kings and Jeremiah (*Antiq.* 10.101,149–150, 181–182) and includes a fourth deportation not mentioned in the Bible: the removal of 3,000 Jews to Babylonia on the death of Jehoiakim and the accession of Jehoiachin (*Antiq.* 10.98).

[7] Several texts from Sargon II refer to this deportation. See *ANET,* pp. 284–285; D.J. Wiseman, "Records of Assyria and Babylonia," in *Documents from Old Testament Times,* ed. D. Winton Thomas (New York: Torchbooks/ Harper and Row, 1961), p. 60.

[8] This was first suggested by A. Von Hoonacker, *Une communauté judéo-araméene à Éléphantine en Égypte, Schweich Lectures, 1914* (London: British Academy, 1915).

[9] Bustenay Oded, "Judah and the Exile," in *Israelite and Judaean History,* ed. John H. Hayes and J. Maxwell Miller (Philadelphia: Westminster, 1977), p. 483.

[10] On the Murashu texts, see especially Elias J. Bickerman, "The Babylonian Captivity," in *CHJ,* vol. 1, pp. 345–348; Michael D. Coogan, "Life in the Diaspora: Jews at Nippur in the Fifth Century," *BA* 37 (1974), pp. 6–12.

[11] See Peter Machinist's review of *A History of Ancient Israel and Judah,* by J.M. Miller and Hayes, *BAR,* November/December 1986, p. 4.

[12] William F. Albright, "The Seal of Eliakim and the Latest Preexilic History of Judah," *JBL* 51 (1932), pp. 77–106.

[13] Albright, "King Jehoiachin in Exile," *BA* 5 (1942), p. 54.

[14] An interesting scenario is presented by James D. Newsome, Jr. (*By the Waters of Babylon: An Introduction to the History and Theology of the Exile* [Atlanta: John Knox, 1979], pp. 92–97).

[15] See also John Bright, *A History of Israel* (Philadelphia: Westminster, 1981), pp. 352–353; and C. Meyers and E. Meyers, *Haggai, Zechariah 1–8* (see endnote 4), pp. 5 and 16. For the effect of the organization of the Bible on these developments, see David Noel Freedman, "The Earliest Bible," *Michigan Quarterly Review* 22 (1983), pp. 167–175; *The Unity of the Bible* (Ann Arbor: Univ. of Michigan Press, 1991).

[16] See Bezalel Porten, *Archives from Elephantine: The Life of an Ancient Jewish Military Colony* (Berkeley: Univ. of California, 1968); "Aramaic Papyri and Parchments: A New Look," *BA* 42 (1979), pp. 74–104; "The Jews in Egypt," in *CHJ,* vol. 1, pp. 372–400. A publishing history of the Elephantine materials is found in Porten's studies and most recently in *OEANE,* vol. 5, pp. 393–410.

[17] *Antiq.* 12.388f.

[18] *Antiq.* 11.346–347.

[19] For a survey of conflicting opinions, see Peter Ackroyd, *Exile and Restoration: A Study of Hebrew Thought of the Sixth Century B.C.* (London: SCM Press, 1968), pp. 32–35. For the most recent discussion of this issue see Lee I. Levine, "The Nature and Origin of the Palestinian Synagogue Reconsidered," *JBL* 115 (1996), pp. 425–448.

[20] Gottwald (*Hebrew Bible* [see endnote 2], p. 427) and Yehezkel Kaufmann (*History of the Religion of Israel, from the Babylonian Captivity to the End of Prophecy* 4:1–2, [New York: Union of American Hebrew Congregations, 1970], pp. 41–43) argue for and against synagogal origins in Babylonia on the basis of the differing criteria of what made a synagogue.

[21] Levine, "Nature and Origin" (see endnote 19), p. 443.

[22] See C. Meyers and E. Meyers, *Haggai, Zechariah 1–8* (see endnote 4), pp. 377ff.

[23] Walther Zimmerli, *Ezekiel*, Hermeneia (Philadelphia: Fortress, 1979), pp. 115–116.

[24] See especially Bickerman, "Babylonian Captivity" (see endnote 10), pp. 355–357; Coogan, "Life in the Diaspora" (see endnote 10), pp. 11–12.

[25] Nahman Avigad, "Seals of Exiles," *Israel Exploration Journal* 15 (1965), pp. 228–230.

[26] See Eliezer D. Oren, "Migdol: A New Fortress on the Edge of the Eastern Nile Delta," *BASOR* 256 (1984), pp. 7–44; "Sinai," in *OEANE*, vol. 5, pp. 41–46.

[27] See endnote 16 and, more recently, Porten, "Egyptian Aramaic Texts" in *OEANE*, vol. 2, pp. 234–236.

[28] See endnotes 16 and 27.

[29] See Thomas Fish, "The Cyrus Cylinder," in *Documents from Old Testament Times* (see endnote 7),. p. 43.

[30] For a summary of the rather complex arguments relating to whether or not Samaria exercised control over Judah in the neo-Babylonian and early Persian period, see Lester L. Grabbe, *Judaism from Cyrus to Hadrian*, vol. 1, *The Persian and Greek Periods* (Minneapolis, MN: Fortress Press, 1992), pp. 79–84. The opinion adopted in this version is one put forward in C. Meyers and E. Meyers, *Haggai, Zechariah 1–8* (see endnote 4); and *Zechariah 9–14: A New Translation with Introduction and Commentary* Anchor Bible 25C (Garden City, NY: Doubleday, 1993), especially pp. 15–29 and *passim*. See also E. Meyers, "The Persian Period and the Judean Restoration from Zerubbabel to Nehemiah," in *Ancient Israelite Religion: Essays in Honor of Frank Moore Cross*, ed. Patrick D. Miller, Paul D. Hanson, and S. Dean McBride (Philadelphia: Fortress Press, 1987), pp. 509–521; "The Shelomith Seal and Aspects of the Judean Restoration: Some Additional Reconsiderations," *Eretz Israel* 17 (1985), pp. 33–38.

[31] C. Meyers and E. Meyers, *Haggai, Zechariah 1–8* (see endnote 4), pp. xlvi, 63–64, 244–255. The relevant verses are Haggai 2:10,20 and Zechariah 4:7–10.

[32] See C. Meyers and E. Meyers, *Haggai, Zechariah 1–8* (see endnote 4), *ad loc.* as indicated in endnote 31, where they draw attention to parallel (re)foundation ceremonies in Mesopotamian literature. Such an approach is also followed by David L. Petersen in *Haggai and Zechariah 1–8* (Philadelphia: Westminster, 1984), pp. 238–244.

[33] See commentaries cited in endnote 32 *ad loc.* and E. Meyers, "Messianism in First and Second Zechariah and the 'End' of Biblical Prophecy," in *"Go to the land I will show you": Studies in Honor of Dwight W. Young*, ed. Joseph E. Coleson and Victor H. Matthews (Winona Lake, IN: Eisenbrauns, 1996), pp. 127–142.

[34] Ephraim Stern, "The Persian Empire and the Political and Social History of Palestine in the Persian Period," in *CHJ*, vol. 1, pp. 71–72.

[35] See C. Meyers and E. Meyers, *Haggai, Zechariah 1–8* (see endnote 4), pp. 336ff; especially notes and comments on verse 13, pp. 357–362 and 366–375.

[36] See endnote 35. In the same volume see also the discussion of "Joshua and the Priestly Vestments" (Zechariah 3:1–10), pp. 178–227, and especially the notes to verse 7, pp. 194–197, which elaborate on the expanded priestly functions added to Joshua's duties as high priest.

[37] See Peter R. Ackroyd, "The Jewish Community in Palestine in the Persian Period," *CHJ*, vol. 1, pp. 141–143. The complicated "opposition" narratives in Ezra convey a sense of the difficulties the Jewish community met in the rebuilding endeavor. The Aramaic source referred to here (Ezra 5:1–6:18) is consistent with the presentation in Haggai and First Zechariah, attributing their composition and dating to the year of the refoundation of the temple in the sixth year of Darius.

[38] See J.M. Cook, *The Persian Empire* (London: J.M. Dent, 1983), pp. 61, 71.

[39] The impetus for such views was surely the pioneering work of Julius Wellhausen, who formulated the "documentary hypothesis," in which significant portions of the Hebrew Bible were assigned to the Exilic and post-Exilic periods, especially D and P, the so-called Deuteronomistic and Priestly strands. In recent times it has become fashionable to assign most of the historical writings to the Persian period too, leading to a strident attack on the whole question of Israelite origins. Typical of these attacks are Philip R. Davies, *In Search of 'Ancient Israel,'* JSOT Supplement Series 148 (Sheffield, UK: Sheffield Academic Press, 1992); and Niels Peter Lemche, "Early History Revisited," *Currents in Research: Biblical Studies* 4 (1996), pp. 9–34. In denigrating the reliability of much of the Hebrew Bible as a source for understanding pre-Exilic Israelite history, they have willy-nilly proposed the Persian period as the most creative epoch in ancient Israel's literary history. While we believe that the intensity of literary activity is great in this period, even inspired by Darius I's call to collect local

traditions (so Cook, *Persian Empire* [see endnote 38], pp. 72ff.), we believe such scholarly attacks are motivated by prejudice and narrow-mindedness. See William G. Dever's response to these debates in "Will the Real Israel Please Stand Up? Archaeology and Israelite Historiography, Part I," *BASOR* 297 (1995), pp. 61–80 and the bibliography there.

[40] See endnote 30, especially C. Meyers and E. Meyers, *Zechariah 9–14*, pp. 15–26.

[41] Cook, *Persian Empire* (see endnote 38), pp. 91ff.; Kenneth G. Hoglund, *Achaemenid Imperial Administration in Syria-Palestine and the Missions of Ezra and Nehemiah*, SBL Dissertation Series 125 (Atlanta: Scholars Press, 1989).

[42] C. Meyers and E. Meyers, *Zechariah 9–1* (see endnote 30), pp. 20–21; Hoglund, *Achaemenid Imperial Administration* (see endnote 41), pp. 143ff.

[43] Hoglund, *Achaemenid Imperial Administration* (see endnote 41), pp. 165ff. and figs. 1–4.

[44] C. Meyers and E. Meyers, *Zechariah 9–14* (see endnote 30), pp. 22–26; C.C. Carter, "A Social and Demographic Study of Post-Exilic Judah," (Ph.D. diss., Duke University, 1991; forthcoming with JSOT Supplement Series).

[45] See especially Frank Moore Cross, "A Reconstruction of the Judean Restoration," *JBL* 94 (1975), pp. 4–18, 279; also in *Interpretation* 29 (1975), pp. 187–203. Shemaryahu Talmon, "Ezra and Nehemiah," in *IDB*, Supplementary Volume, pp. 317–328.

[46] See Geo Widengren, "Problems in Reconstructing Jewish History in the Persian Period: The Chronological Order of Ezra and Nehemiah," in *Israelite and Judaean History* (see endnote 9), pp. 503–509. See also Aaron Demsky, "Who Returned First—Ezra or Nehemiah?" *BR*, April 1996, p. 28.

[47] Stern, *Material Culture of the Land of the Bible in the Persian Period, 538–332 B.C.* (Warminster, UK/Jerusalem: Aris and Phillips/Israel Exploration Society, 1982). See also Hoglund, *Achaemenid Imperial Administration* (see endnote 41), pp. 226ff.

[48] Hoglund, *Achaemenid Imperial Administration* (see endnote 41), pp. 244–247.

[49] See endnote 15.

[50] See Kenneth Koch, "Ezra and the Origins of Judaism," *Journal of Semitic Studies* (1974), pp. 173ff; *The Prophets: The Babylonian and Persian Periods*, 2 vols. (Philadelphia: Fortress, 1986), vol. 2, p. 187.

[51] In his memoirs, Nehemiah describes "the former governors who were before me" as having laid heavy burdens on the people by exacting food, wine and taxes and as having had subofficials who acted in a heavy-handed manner (Nehemiah 5:15). Albrecht Alt suggested that the reference in Nehemiah was to the governors of Samaria who had administered the Judahite territory in the period between Zerubbabel and Nehemiah. Alt was the first major scholar to contend that Samaritan hegemony over Judah, up to the time of Nehemiah, provided the background for Samaritan-Judahite hostilities during the Persian period. See Alt, "Die Rolle Samarias bei der Entstehung des Judentums" and "Judas Nachbarn zur Zeit Nehemiah," in *Kleine Schriften zur Geschichte des Volkes Israel* (Munich: Becksche Verlag, 1953), vol. 2, pp. 316–337. Nahman Avigad, on the other hand, claims that Judahite seal impressions and bullae of the Persian period bear witness to the existence of Jewish governors during this time, three of whom—Elnathan, Yeho'ezer and Ahzai—are known by name (Avigad, *Bullae and Seals from a Post-Exilic Judean Archive*, Qedem 4 [Jerusalem: Hebrew Univ., 1976]). Eric M. Meyers has gone even further and argued that Elnathan was the son-in-law of Zerubbabel (E. Meyers, "The Shelomith Seal" [see endnote 30], pp. 33–38). Stern (*Material Culture* [see endnote 47]) and S. McEnvue ("The Political Structure in Judah from Cyrus to Nehemiah," *CBQ* vol. 43 [1981], pp. 353–364) have been strong in their support of Alt. But see also Grabbe, *Judaism from Cyrus to Hadrian* (see endnote 30).

[52] See Stern, *Material Culture* (see endnote 47); "The Archaeology of Persian Palestine," in *CJH*, vol. 1, pp. 70–88. See also Carter, "Social and Demographic Study" (see endnote 44); and C. Meyers and E. Meyers, *Zechariah 9–14* (see endnote 30), p. 23 and bibliography there.

[53] See Cook, *Persian Empire* (see endnote 38), pp. 72ff.; C. Meyers and E. Meyers, *Haggai, Zechariah 1–8* (see endnote 4), pp. 277–179, 287–292. Zechariah's image of "the flying scroll" (5:1–4) captures the essence of the intensity of literary activity in this period. This unparalleled image surely has to do with the emergence of a fixed body of law in Judah at this time.

[54] Stern, *Material Culture* (see endnote 47), pp. 236–237.

[55] See Hoglund *Achaemenid Imperial Administration* (see endnote 41), pp. 165ff; and Carter, *Social and Demographic Study* (see endnote 44).

[56] Stern, *Material Culture* (see endnote 47), pp. 245–248; "The Persian Empire" (see endnote 34), pp. 82–86.

[57] See Meyers and Meyers, *Zechariah 9–14* (see endnote 30), pp. 24–25.

[58] *Antiq.* 11.297–301.

[59] Others see this story as alluding to the Persians' punitive actions in suppressing a revolt in the satrapy of Abar Nahara during

the time of Artaxerxes III (Ochus as he is surnamed by modern authorities) (358–336 B.C.E.). Specifically, in 351/350 B.C.E. a rebellion led by Tennes, king of Sidon, was put down by Ochus's general Bagoas. The memory of Bagoas's campaign in Syria-Palestine may be preserved in the apocryphal Book of Judith (with Holofernes representing Bagoas). See Dan Barag, "The Effects of the Tennes Rebellion on Palestine," *BASOR* 183 (1966), pp. 6–12.

[60] Cross, "Aspects of Samaritan and Jewish History in Late Persian and Hellenistic Times," *HTR* 59 (1966), pp. 201–211; "Papyri of the Fourth Century B.C. from Dāliyeh: A Preliminary Report on Their Discovery and Significance," in *New Directions in Biblical Archaeology*, ed. David Noel Freedman and Jonas C. Greenfield (Garden City, NY: Doubleday, 1969), pp. 45–69.

[61] *Antiq.* 11.304–347.

[62] James D. Purvis, *The Samaritan Pentateuch and the Origin of the Samaritan Sect*, Harvard Semitic Monographs 2 (Cambridge, MA: Harvard Univ. Press, 1968), pp. 104–109.

[63] Purvis, "The Samaritan Problem: A Case Study in Jewish Sectarianism in the Roman Era," in *Traditions in Transformation: Turning Points in Biblical Faith*, ed. Baruch Halpern and Jon Levenson (Winona Lake, IN: Eisenbrauns, 1982), pp. 323–350.

VII. The Age of Hellenism

[1] See, for example, William W. Tarn, *Hellenistic Civilization* (London: Arnold, 1952); Arthur D. Nock, *Conversion* (Oxford: Clarendon, 1933); Arnaldo Momigliano, *Alien Wisdom* (Cambridge, UK: Cambridge Univ. Press, 1975); Félix M. Abel, "Hellénisme et orientalisme en Palestine au déclin de la periode séleucide," *RB* 53 (1946), pp. 385–402.

[2] Arnold H.M. Jones, *The Cities of the Eastern Roman Provinces* (Oxford: Clarendon, 1971), pp. 226–294, Victor Tcherikover, *Hellenistic Civilization and the Jews* (Philadelphia: Jewish Publication Society, 1959), pp. 90–116; Shimon Applebaum, "Hellenistic Cities of Palestine—New Dimensions," in *The Second Period in Palestine*, ed. Bezalel Bar Kokhba (Tel Aviv: Hakibbutz Hameuchad, 1980), pp. 277–288 (in Hebrew).

[3] John Bright, *A History of Israel*, 3rd ed. (Philadelphia: Westminster, 1981), pp. 360–402; Elias Bickerman, "The Edict of Cyrus in Ezra I," in *Studies in Jewish and Christian History* I (Leiden: Brill, 1976), pp. 72–108; Frank Moore Cross, "A Reconstruction of the Judean Restoration," *JBL* 94 (1975), pp. 4–18; Ephraim Stern and Hayim Tadmor, "The Persian Period," in *The History of Eretz Israel* 2, ed. Israel Ephal (Jerusalem: Keter, 1984), pp. 225–307 (in Hebrew). For the more general picture, see Albert T. Olmstead, *History of the Persian Empire* (Chicago: Univ. of Chicago Press, 1948); John M. Cook, *The Persian Empire* (London: J.M. Dent, 1983); Richard N. Frye, *The Heritage of Persia* (London: Weidenfeld & Nicolson, 1966); Morton Smith, *Palestinian Parties and Politics that Shaped the Old Testament* (New York: Columbia Univ. Press, 1971).

[4] Ya'akov Meshorer, *Ancient Jewish Coinage* 1 (New York: Amphora, 1982), pp. 13–34; Uriel Rappaport, "The Coins of Jerusalem at the End of Persian Rule and the Beginning of the Hellenistic Period," in *Jerusalem in the Second Temple Period: Schalit Memorial Volume*, ed. Aaron Oppenheimer et al. (Jerusalem: Ben Zvi Institute, 1981), pp. 11–21 (in Hebrew).

[5] *Antiq.* 12.225–227.

[6] Tcherikover, *Hellenistic Civilization* (see endnote 2), pp. 117–151; Eugene Taeubler, "Jerusalem 201 to 199 B.C.," *JQR* 37 (1946–1947), pp. 1–30, 125–137, 249–263.

[7] Bickerman, *From Ezra to the Last of the Maccabees* (New York: Schocken, 1962) and *The God of the Maccabees* (Leiden, 1979); Martin Hengel, *Judaism and Hellenism*, 2 vols. (Philadelphia: Fortress, 1974); John J. Collins, "Jewish Apocalyptic Against Its Hellenistic Near Eastern Environment," *BASOR* 220 (1975), pp. 27–36.

[8] Tcherikover, *Hellenistic Civilization* (see endnote 2), pp. 152–174; Fergus Millar, "The Background to the Maccabean Revolution: Reflections on Martin Hengel's 'Judaism and Hellenism,'" *JJS* 29 (1978), pp. 1–21; Samuel Sandmel, "Hellenism and Judaism," in *Great Confrontations in Jewish History*, ed. Stanley Wagner and Allen Breck (Denver: Center for Jewish Studies, Univ. of Denver, 1977), pp. 21–38; Paul Hanson, "Jewish Apocalyptic Against Its Near Eastern Environment," *RB* 78 (1971), pp. 31–58.

[9] Robert Gordis, *The Wisdom of Koheleth* (London: East and West, 1950), pp. xii–xvii, and *Koheleth—The Man and His World* (New York: Jewish Theological Seminary, 1951), pp. 8–57; Hengel, *Judaism and Hellenism* (see endnote 7), pp. 115–130.

[10] Hengel, *Judaism and Hellenism* (see endnote 7), pp. 131–153; Gerson D. Cohen, "The Song of Songs and the Jewish Religious Mentality," in *The Samuel Friedland Lectures 1960–1966* (New York: Jewish Theological

Seminary, 1966), pp. 1–22; M. Rozler, "The Song of Songs Against the Background of Greek-Hellenistic Eastern Poetry," *Eshkolot* 1 (1954), pp. 33–48 (in Hebrew). However, see also Marvin Pope, *Song of Songs*, Anchor Bible 7C (Garden City, NY: Doubleday, 1977), pp. 22–33. For the Hellenistic background to the maxim of Simeon the Righteous at the beginning of the Ethics of the Fathers, see Judah Goldin, "The Three Pillars of Simeon the Righteous," *PAAJR* 27 (1958), pp. 43–58.

[11] Bickerman, "La charte séleucide de Jerusalem," *REJ* 100 (1935), pp. 4–35, and "Une proclamation séleucide relative au temple de Jerusalem," *Syria* 25 (1946–1948), pp. 67–85; Albrecht Alt, "Zu Antiochos' III Erlass für Jerusalem," *ZAW* 57 (1939), pp. 282–285; Hengel, *Judaism and Hellenism* (see endnote 7), pp. 271–272.

[12] *Antiq.* 12.160–234; Tcherikover, *Hellenistic Civilization* (see endnote 2), pp. 126–142; Benjamin Mazar, *Canaan and Israel—Historical Studies* (Jerusalem: Bialik, 1980), pp. 270–290 (in Hebrew); Menahem Stern, "Notes on the Story of Joseph Son of Tobias," *Tarbiz* 32 (1963), pp. 35–47 (in Hebrew).

[13] Tcherikover, *Hellenistic Civilization* (see endnote 2), pp. 160–169.

[14] Bar Kokhba, "The Status and Origin of the Akra Garrison Before Antiochus' Decrees," *Zion* 36 (1971), pp. 32–47 (in Hebrew); Jonathan Goldstein, *I Maccabees*, Anchor Bible 41 (Garden City, NY: Doubleday, 1976), pp. 213–219; Willis A. Shotwell, "The Problem of the Syrian Akra," *BASOR* 176 (1964), pp. 10–19; Bickerman, *God of the Maccabees* (see endnote 7), pp. 42–53.

[15] *Antiq.* 12.252.

[16] Bickerman, *God of the Maccabees* (see endnote 7), pp. 76–92, and *From Ezra* (see endnote 7), pp. 93–111. Hengel, *Judaism and Hellenism* (see endnote 7), pp. 208–303.

[17] Goldstein, *I Maccabees* (see endnote 14), pp. 104–160.

[18] Tcherikover, *Hellenistic Civilization* (see endnote 2), pp. 175–203.

[19] For a detailed description of these battles, see Bar Kokhba, *The Battles of the Hasmoneans: The Times of Judas Maccabaeus* (Jerusalem: Ben Zvi Institue, 1980) (in Hebrew).

[20] Tcherikover, *Hellenistic Civilization* (see endnote 2), pp. 211–220.

[21] The Hanukkah festival is unusual in the Jewish calendar. First of all, it is the only festival not anchored to a biblical event. Second, its duration is unprecedented: The dedication of the wilderness Tabernacle and Solomon's Temple lasted seven days (Leviticus

9:1; 1 Kings 8:65). The talmudic tradition of the miracle of the cruse of oil (B *Shabbat* 21a) is a problematic historical account, both because of the time gap between the purported event and the written source as well as the miraculous nature of this tradition. Another rabbinic tradition, preserved in *Megillat Ta'anit*, explains the eight-day festival as resulting from the time required to purify the Temple. However, 2 Maccabees 1, which describes the events surrounding the purification of the Temple in great detail, claims that the eight-day celebration in 164 B.C.E. was in reality a postponed Sukkot holiday; that is, since the Jews were unable to celebrate Sukkot at its proper time, once the Temple was purified, the Jews immediately proceeded to do so. The difficulty with this last explanation, which on the face of it comes from a rather reputable source, is with regard to the following year, that is, 163 B.C.E., when the Jews had access to the Temple on Sukkot. Why, then, did they continue to celebrate the eight-day festival two months later? Was the precedent of a celebration the year before enough to establish a new festival that had originally been intended only as a postponed Sukkot?

Another explanation for the eight-day duration relates to Hezekiah's purification of the Temple, which was followed by eight days of festivities (2 Chronicles 29:17). Is it possible that the Hasmonean dedication tradition was influenced by this earlier tradition? Mention should also be made of the widespread practice in antiquity—known from Babylonia, Greece and Rome—of holding an eight-day festival of lights in the middle of winter, in December, when the days are shortest. Even the Talmud, much later on, preserves memories of this practice when commenting on the Roman Saturnalia (B *'Avodah Zarah* 8a). Might there be some connection between this widespread practice and the fact that the eight-day Hanukkah festival in December likewise featured a festival of lights? Having reviewed a plethora of possible factors that may have influenced the shape and form of this festival, it may well be that we need not necessarily choose from among these various explanations and that, as often happens with festivals and institutions, a number of factors may well have led to their establishment.

[22] Bar Kokhba, *Battles of the Hasmoneans* (see endnote 19), pp. 225–263.

[23] The attempts to shed light on this elusive group have been many and varied; see, for example, Tcherikover, *Hellenistic Civilization* (see endnote 2), pp. 187ff.; Hengel, *Judaism and Hellenism* (see endnote 7), pp. 175–180;

Otto Plöger, *Theocracy and Eschatology* (Oxford: Blackwell, 1968), pp. 44–52.

24 Bar Kokhba, *Battles of the Hasmoneans* (see endnote 19), pp. 265–307.

25 On reactions to this synthesis of the political and religious realms, see Hengel, James H. Charlesworth and Doron Mendels, "The Polemical Character of 'On Kingship' in the Temple Scroll: An Attempt at Dating 11Q Temple," *JJS* 37 (1986), pp. 28–38.

26 *Antiq.* 13.254–283.

27 *Antiq.* 13.318–319.

28 *Antiq.* 13.320–397; M. Stern, "Judaea and Her Neighbors in the Days of Alexander Jannaeus," *Jerusalem Cathedra* 1 (Jerusalem: Ben Zvi Institute, 1981), pp. 22–46.

29 Goldstein, *I Maccabees* (see endnote 14), pp. 4–26.

30 *Antiq.* 13.397.

31 See *Apion* 2.71–142; Leon Poliakov, *The History of Antisemitism* (London: Vanguard, 1965), pp. 3–16.

32 Johanan Levi, *Studies in Jewish Hellenism* (Jerusalem: Bialik, 1960), pp. 60–78 (in Hebrew).

33 Lee Levine, "The Political Struggle Between Pharisees and Sadducees in the Hasmonean Period," *Jerusalem in the Second Temple Period* (see endnote 4), pp. 61–83.

34 This assumption of Pharisaic opposition has been made by almost all scholars; see, for example, Yigael Yadin, "Pesher Nahum (4Q Pnahum) Reconsidered," *IEJ* 21 (1971), pp. 1–12. Against this commonly held assumption, see Chaim Rabin, "Alexander Jannai and the Pharisees," *JJS* 7 (1956), pp. 3–11.

35 *Antiq.* 13.408–415. Rabbinic sources confirm this sequence of events, focusing on the political activity of Simeon ben Shataḥ in the first third of the first century B.C.E. See Levine, "Political Struggle" (see endnote 33), pp. 61–83; Israel Ephron, "Simeon Ben Shataḥ and King Yannai," *Gedaliah Alon Memorial Volume*, ed. Menahem Dorman et al. (Tel Aviv: Hakibbutz Hameuchad, 1970), pp. 69–132 (in Hebrew).

36 Bickerman, *The Maccabees* (New York: Schocken, 1947), pp. 85–97.

37 Meshorer, *Jewish Coins of the Second Temple Period* (Jerusalem: 'Am Hassefer, 1967) and *Ancient Jewish Coinage* (see endnote 4), pp. 35–47. On Hasmonean coinage, see also Rappaport, "The Emergence of Hasmonean Coinage," *AJS* 1 (1976), pp. 171–186.

38 Suzanne F. Singer, "The Winter Palaces of Jericho," *BAR*, June 1977, p. 1; Ehud Netzer, "The Hasmonean and Herodian Winter Palaces at Jericho," *IEJ* 25 (1975), pp. 89–100;

"The Winter Palaces of the Judaean Kings at Jericho at the End of the Second Temple Period," *BASOR* 228 (1977), pp. 1–13; "Ancient Ritual Baths (Miqvaot) in Jericho," in *Jerusalem Cathedra* 2, ed. Levine (Jerusalem: Ben Zvi Institute, 1982), pp. 106–119.

39 Nahman Avigad, *Funerary Monuments from the Qidron Valley* (Jerusalem: Bialik, 1954), pp. 37–38 (in Hebrew); Levi Y. Rahmani, "Jason's Tomb," *IEJ* 17 (1967), pp. 61–100; *EAEHL*, vol. 3, pp. 782–792; John P. Peters and Hermann Thiersch, *Painted Tombs in the Necropolis of Marissa* (London: Palestine Exploration Fund, 1905).

40 So, for example, the following: Eupolemos, Numenius, Antiochus, Jason, Antipater, Apollonius, Alexander, Dositheus, Diodorus, Lysimachus, Pausanias, Josephus, Mennaeus, Theodorus, Sopatrus, Straton, Theodotus, Aeneas, Aristobulus, Amyntas, Sosipater, Philip (1 Maccabees 8:17, 12:16, 14:22; *Antiq.* 13.260; 14.241,247–248,306–307).

41 M. Stern, *Greek and Latin Authors on Jews and Judaism*, 3 vols. (Jerusalem: Israel Academy for the Humanities and Sciences, 1974), vol. 1, pp. 27–29, 37–40.

42 B *Ketubot* 82b.

43 Markham Geller, "New Sources for the Origin of the Rabbinic Ketubah," *HUCA* 49 (1978), pp. 227–245.

44 Goldin, "A Philosophical Session in a Tannaitic Academy," *Traditio* 21 (1965), pp. 1–21.

45 Bickerman, "La chaine de la tradition pharisienne," *RB* 49 (1952), pp. 44–54; David Daube, "Rabbinic Methods of Interpretation and Hellenistic Rhetoric," *HUCA* 22 (1949), pp. 239–264. See also Saul Lieberman, *Hellenism in Jewish Palestine* (New York, 1962), pp. 47–68; Bickerman, *From Ezra* (see endnote 7), pp. 148–165; Smith, "Palestinian Judaism in the First Century," in *Israel: Its Role in Civilization*, ed. Moshe Davis (New York: Jewish Theological Seminary, 1956), pp. 67–81.

46 Shaye J.D. Cohen, "Patriarchs and Scholarchs," *PAAJR* 48 (1981), pp. 57–85.

47 D. Winston, "Iranian Components in the Bible, Apocrypha and Qumran," *History of Religion* 5 (1966), pp. 183–216. Shaul Shaked, "Qumran and Iran," *Israel Oriental Studies* 202 (1972), pp. 433–446, "Iranian Influence on Judaism: First Century B.C.E. to Second Century C.E.," in *CHJ*, pp. 308–325.

48 Bruno W. Dombrowski, "היחד in 1QS and τὸ κοινόν: An Instance of Early Greek and Jewish Synthesis," *HTR* 59 (1966), pp. 293–307; Hans Bardthe, "Die Rechtsstellung der Qumran-Gemeinde," *Die Theologische Literaturzeitung* 86 (1961), pp. 93–104.

[49] Jerome Murphy-O'Connor, "The Essenes and Their History," *RB* 81 (1974), pp. 215–244.

[50] Hengel, *Judaism and Hellenism* (see endnote 7), pp. 228–247.

[51] Avigad, *Discovering Jerusalem* (Nashville, TN: Thomas Nelson, 1983), pp. 64–81; Ruth Amiran and Avraham Eitan, "Excavations in the Courtyard of the Citadel, Jerusalem, 1968–1969 (Preliminary Report)," *IEJ* 20 (1970), pp. 9–17. See also Kathleen Kenyon, *Digging Up Jerusalem* (New York: Praeger, 1974), pp. 188–204.

[52] Jan Simons, *Jerusalem in the Old Testament* (Leiden: Brill, 1952), pp. 226–281.

[53] Levine, "Political Struggle" (see endnote 33), pp. 61–83.

[54] *Antiq.* 14.64–71.

[55] Mazar, *The Mountain of the Lord* (Garden City, NY: Doubleday, 1975).

[56] *Apion* 1.186–189.

[57] 1 Maccabees 12.

[58] *Antiq.* 121.160–166.

[59] Ben Sira 50.

[60] 2 Maccabees 4.

[61] 1 Maccabees 14:47.

[62] Shmuel Safrai and M. Stern, *The Jewish People in the First Century* 2 (Assen, Neth.: Van Gorcum, 1976), pp. 876–906.

[63] See Levine, "The Second Temple Synagogue: The Formative Years," in *The Synagogue in Late Antiquity*, ed. Levine (Durham, NC: Jewish Theological Seminary and ASOR, 1987).

[64] Marcel Simon, *Jewish Sects at the Time of Jesus* (Philadelphia: Fortress, 1967), pp. 1–16.

[65] Smith, "The Dead Sea Sect in Relation to Ancient Judaism," *NTS* 7 (1960), pp. 347–360; *Palestinian Parties and Politics* (see endnote 3), pp. 57–81, 126–147. Klaus Koch, "Ezra and the Origins of Judaism," *JSS* 19 (1974), pp. 173–197.

[66] Avot de Rabbi Nathan, A, IV.

[67] *Antiq.* 13.371–373.

[68] *Antiq.* 13.62–73.

[69] Avot de Rabbi Nathan, A, IV.

[70] *Antiq.* 13.297.

[71] *Antiq.* 13.298.

[72] *Antiq.* 13.410–415.

[73] *War* 2.166.

[74] Ellis Rivkin, "Pharisaism and the Crisis of the Individual in the Greco-Roman World," *JQR* 61 (1970), pp. 27–53; Levine, "Political Struggle" (see endnote 33), pp. 61ff.

[75] *War* 2.165.

[76] On the Sadducees, see Abraham Geiger, *The Bible and Its Translations* (Jerusalem, 1949),

pp. 69–102 (in Hebrew); Finkelstein, *The Pharisees*, 3rd ed., 3 vols. (Philadelphia: Jewish Publication Society, 1962), vol. 2, pp. 637–753; Jacob Lauterbach, *Rabbinic Essays* (Cincinnati: Hebrew Union College, 1951), pp. 23–83; and most comprehensively, Rudolf Leszynsky, Die Sadduzäer (Berlin: Mayer & Müller, 1912); Jean Le Moyne, *Les Sadducéens* (Paris, 1972). See also, Alexander Guttman, *Rabbinic Judaism in the Making* (Detroit: Wayne State Univ. Press, 1970), pp. 136–176, where the major controversies between the sects are explicated.

[77] Ralph Marcus, "The Pharisees in the Light of Modern Scholarship," *JR* 32 (1952), pp. 155–164; Gedaliah Alon, *Jews, Judaism and the Classical World* (Jerusalem: Magnes, 1977), pp. 18–47; Smith, "Palestinian Judaism" (see endnote 45), pp. 67–81; Levine, "On the Political Involvement of the Pharisees Under Herod and the Procurators," *Cathedra* 8 (1978), pp. 12–28 (in Hebrew); Jacob Neusner, *From Politics to Piety* (Englewood Cliffs, NJ: Prentice-Hall, 1973).

[78] Finkelstein, *Pharisees* (see endnote 76), pp. 73ff.; Fritz Baer, *Israel Among the Nations* (Jerusalem, 1955) (in Hebrew).

[79] See Neusner, *The Rabbinic Traditions About the Pharisees*, 3 vols. (Leiden: Brill, 1971), pp. 301–319.

[80] A point hotly debated among scholars. For a maximalist position, see Alon, *Jews, Judaism* (see endnote 77), p. 22 and note 11; Neil J. McEleney, "Orthodoxy in Judaism of the First Christian Century," *JSJ* 4 (1973), pp. 19–42. For a minimalist position, see Smith, "Palestinian Judaism" (see endnote 45), pp. 67–81; David Aune, "Orthodoxy in First Century Judaism? A Response to N.J. McEleney," *JSJ* 7 (1976), pp. 1–10.

[81] *War* 2.119–166.

[82] Publications on the Dead Sea sect and scrolls are legion. A classic introductory work in this field remains that of Cross, *The Ancient Library of Qumran and Modern Biblical Studies* (Garden City, NY: Doubleday, 1958). The best single volume on the archaeology of Qumran remains that of Roland de Vaux, *Archaeology and the Dead Sea Scrolls* (Oxford: Clarendon, 1973).

[83] Shemaryahu Talmon, "The Calendar-Reckoning of the Sect from the Judaean Desert," *Scripta Hierosolymitana* 4 (1958), pp. 162–199.

[84] B *Shabbat* 13a.

[85] M *Ḥagigah* 3.4.

[86] J *Ma'aser Sheni* 5,9,56c.

[87] M *Shevi'it* 10.3–6.

[88] This point is meticulously documented in the magisterial work of Abraham Schalit, *King*

Herod (Jerusalem, 1960) (in Hebrew); see also Levine, "Roman Rule in Judea from 63 B.C.E. to 70 C.E.," *The History of Eretz Israel*, vol. 4, ed. M. Stern (Jerusalem: Keter, 1984), pp. 11–25 (in Hebrew).

VIII. Roman Domination

Bibliographical Note: In recent years the history of the latter part of the Second Temple period has been surveyed in several large-scale and reliable works in English: Shaye J.D. Cohen, From the Maccabees to the Mishnah *(Philadelphia: Westminster, 1987); Lester L. Grabbe,* Judaism from Cyrus to Hadrian, 2 vols. *(Minneapolis: Fortress, 1992); Peter Schäfer,* The History of the Jews in Antiquity *(Luxembourg: Harwood Academic Publishers, 1995); Martin S. Jaffee,* Early Judaism: Religious Worlds of the First Judaic Millennium *(Upper Saddle River, NJ: Prentice Hall, 1997); Emil Schürer,* The History of the Jewish People in the Age of Jesus Christ, rev. ed., ed. Geza Vermes et al., 4 vols. *(Edinburgh: T.& T. Clark, 1973–1986); Compendia Rerum Judaicarum ad Novum Testamentum, sec. 1:* The Jewish People in the First Century, *ed. Samuel Safrai and Menahem Stern, 2 vols. (Philadelphia: Fortress, 1974–1976); and* The World History of the Jewish People, vol. 6: The Hellenistic Age, *ed. Abraham Schalit (New Brunswick, NJ: Rutgers Univ. Press, 1972);* The World History of the Jewish People, vol. 7: The Herodian Period, *ed. Zvi Baras (New Brunswick, NJ: Rutgers Univ. Press, 1975); E. Mary Smallwood,* The Jews Under Roman Rule *(Leiden: Brill, 1976, reprinted 1981). Interested readers are referred to these works for complete and detailed references to the ancient evidence and to modern scholarship.*

In this chapter I provide only minimal bibliographical annotation. Further bibliography can be obtained from the two useful volumes of Louis H. Feldman, Josephus and Modern Scholarship 1937–1980 *(Berlin: de Gruyter, 1984), and* Josephus: A Supplementary Bibliography *(New York: Garland, 1986). Because of the centrality of Josephus to all modern discussions, Feldman's bibliography covers virtually all aspects of Jewish history of the later Second Temple period. Quotations from Josephus are taken from the Loeb Classical Library edition, 9 vols., edited by H. St. J. Thackeray, Ralph Marcus, Allen Wikgren and Louis H. Feldman (London/Cambridge, MA: Heinemann/Harvard Univ. Press, 1926–1965, frequently reprinted).*

[1] The precise legal status of Judea in this period is obscure.

[2] See Menahem Stern, "The Relations Between Judea and Rome During the Reign of John Hyrcanus," *Zion* 26 (1961), pp. 1–22 (in Hebrew); A.N. Sherwin-White, *Roman Foreign Policy in the East, 168 B.C. to A.D. 1* (Norman, OK: Univ. of Oklahoma, 1984); Erich S. Gruen, *The Hellenistic World and the Coming of Rome*, 2 vols. (Berkeley: Univ. of California, 1984).

[3] Michael Wise, *Thunder in Gemini* (Sheffield: JSOT Press, 1994), p. 51.

[4] Josephus tells his story in *The Jewish War* 3.8.340–408.

[5] The standard modern biography is by Abraham Schalit, *König Herodes* (Berlin: de Gruyter, 1968).

[6] The phrase is from Pliny the Elder, *Natural History* 5.70; see Stern, *Greek and Latin Authors on Jews and Judaism*, 3 vols. (Jerusalem: Israel Academy of Humanities and Sciences, 1974–1984), vol. 1, p. 471, no. 204. For discussion of pagan statements about the glory of Jerusalem, see the article by Stern in *Jerusalem in the Second Temple Period: Abraham Schalit Memorial Volume*, ed. A. Oppenheimer et al. (Jerusalem: Ben Zvi Institute, 1981), pp. 257–270 (in Hebrew).

[7] See the symposium on "Herod's Building Projects," in *The Jerusalem Cathedra* 1 (with contributions by Ehud Netzer, Lee I. Levine, Magen Broshi and Yoram Tsafrir) (Jerusalem: Ben Zvi Institute, 1981), pp. 48–80.

[8] *War* 1.33.8.665.

[9] *Antiq.* 17.8.1.191–192.

[10] On Herod's genealogy, see *Antiq.* 14.1.3.8–10; 14.7.3.121 and 14.15.2.403; cf. Eusebius, *History of the Church* 1.7.11–14. Jews who disliked Herod fastened upon his less-than-perfect pedigree to justify their dislike; Jews who liked Herod were quite willing to overlook his origins; cf. Mishnah *Sotah* 7:8 regarding Agrippa.

[11] Richard A. Horsley and John S. Hanson, *Bandits, Prophets, and Messiahs: Popular Movements in the Time of Jesus* (New York: Winston-Seabury, 1985).

[12] D.C. Braund, *Rome and the Friendly King: The Character of Client Kingship* (London: Croom Helm, 1984).

[13] See, generally, Jean-Pierre Lémonon, *Pilate et le gouvernement de la Judée* (Paris: Gabalda, 1981); Daniel R. Schwartz, "Josephus and Philo on Pontius Pilate," in *Josephus Flavius, Historian of Eretz Israel* (Jerusalem: Ben Zvi Institute, 1983), pp. 217–236 (in Hebrew).

[14] In Books 14 and 16 of the *Antiquities*, Josephus quotes a series of edicts, laws and letters that bestow special privileges upon the Jews in order to allow them to practice their religion. On *politeumata*, see Aryeh Kasher, *The*

Jews in Hellenistic and Roman Egypt (Tübingen, W. Ger.: Mohr-Siebeck, 1985).

[15] See Emil Schürer, *History of the Jewish People in the Age of Jesus Christ*, ed. Vermes et al. (Edinburgh: T & T Clark, 1973), vol. 1, p. 397.

[16] The argument of the following paragraphs is developed at much greater length in Shaye J.D. Cohen, *From the Maccabees to the Mishnah* (Philadelphia: Westminster, 1987).

[17] Levine, ed., *Ancient Synagogues Revealed* (Jerusalem: Israel Exploration Society, 1981); Hershel Shanks, *Judaism in Stone: The Archaeology of Ancient Synagogues* (Washington, DC: Biblical Archaeology Society, 1978).

[18] Recent scholarship has questioned the usefulness of this concept, but this is not the place to enter that debate. I mean by "popular religion" not the religion of an economic or social class, but the religion of the people who were not members or followers of one of the "virtuoso" or "pietistic" groups discussed below.

[19] Eric M. Meyers, *Jewish Ossuaries: Reburial and Rebirth* (Rome: Biblical Institute, 1971); and Pau Figueras, *Decorated Jewish Ossuaries* (Leiden: Brill, 1983).

[20] See Morton Smith, *Jesus the Magician* (San Francisco: Harper & Row, 1978); compare Daniel J. Harrington, "The Jewishness of Jesus," *BR*, Spring 1987, pp. 32–41.

[21] The best general survey is that of Schürer, *History of the Jewish People* (see endnote 15); Marcel Simon, *Jewish Sects at the Time of Jesus* (Philadelphia: Fortress, 1967), is out of date.

[22] *Antiq.* 20.8.6.171.

[23] For an interpretation of early Jewish sectarianism, see A.I. Baumgarten, *The Flourishing of Jewish Sects in the Maccabean Era* (Leiden: Brill, 1997).

[24] On the disputed identity of the authors of the Dead Sea Scrolls, see Lawrence Schiffman, *Reclaiming the Dead Sea Scrolls* (Philadelphia: Jewish Publication Society, 1994), pp. 83–157; see also Shanks, *The Mystery and the Meaning of the Dead Sea Scrolls* (New York: Random House, 1998).

[25] See John J. Collins, *The Scepter and the Star* (New York: Doubleday, 1995).

[26] *Antiq.* 18.1.3–5,15,17,19–20.

[27] See Daniel R. Schwartz, "Josephus and Nicolaus on the Pharisees," *Journal for the Study of Judaism in the Persian, Hellenistic and Roman Periods* 14 (1983), pp. 157–171.

[28] This discussion of early Christianity has been abridged from Cohen, *From the Maccabees to the Mishnah* (see endnote 16), pp. 166–168.

[29] *Antiq.* 20.9.7.219–222. This is the first securely attested instance of a government

"make-work" project. See Gabriella Giglioni, *Lavori pubblici e occupazione nell'antichità classica* (Bologna, Italy, 1974), pp. 171ff., with the comments of Lionel Casson, *Bulletin of the American Society of Papyrologists* 15 (1978), pp. 50–51.

[30] On these social tensions, see Cohen, *Josephus in Galilee and Rome* (Leiden: Brill, 1979), pp. 206–221; Sean Freyne, *Galilee from Alexander the Great to Hadrian*, part II (Notre Dame, IN: Univ. of Notre Dame 1980); Peter A. Brunt, "Josephus on Social Conflicts in Roman Judaea," *Klio* 59 (1977), pp. 149–153.

[31] *War* 2.14.2.277–278.

[32] *War* 6.5.4.312. The Roman historian Tacitus reports the same information; see Stern, *Greek and Latin Authors* (see endnote 6), vol. 1, p. 31, no. 281.

[33] See especially H. Kreissig, *Die sozialen Zusammenhänge des judäischen Krieges* (Berlin, 1970); Tessa Rajak, *Josephus: The Historian and His Society* (London: Duckworth, 1983), chap. 5.

[34] See Martin Goodman, *The Ruling Class of Judea* (Cambridge: Cambridge University Press, 1987).

[35] Cohen, *Josephus in Galilee* (see endnote 30), pp. 152–160.

[36] The Rabban Yohanan ben Zakkai tale appears in four different versions; they are conveniently available in Jacob Neusner, *Development of a Legend* (Leiden: Brill, 1970). The bibliography on these stories is immense: See Horst Moehring, "Joseph ben Matthia and Flavius Josephus," in *Aufstieg und Niedergang der römischen Welt* 2.21.2, ed. W. Haase (Berlin: de Gruyter, 1984), pp. 864–944, especially pp. 917–944; and Cohen, "Josephus, Jeremiah, and Polybius," *History and Theory* 21 (1982), pp. 366–381.

[37] Tacitus, *Histories* 4.54.2. On native revolts see Stephen L. Dyson, "Native Revolts in the Roman Empire," *Historia* 20 (1971), pp. 239–274, and "Native Revolt Patterns in the Roman Empire," in *Aufstieg und Niedergang der römischen Welt* 2.3, ed. H. Temporini (Berlin: de Gruyter, 1975), pp. 138–175. On the patterns of social revolutions, see Crane Brinton, *The Anatomy of Revolution* (New York: Prentice-Hall, 1952); compare the French and Russian revolutions.

[38] See especially Smith, "Zealots and Sicarii: Their Origins and Relation," *HTR* 64 (1971), pp. 1–19.

[39] Ever since the Persian period, the priests of the Temple had been in the habit of paying for the welfare of the reigning monarch; see Ezra 6:10. In addition, upon his accession to office the high priest took an oath of loyalty to the state; see *Antiq.* 11.8.3.318.

[40] For a defense of this view, see Cohen, *Josephus in Galilee* (see endnote 30), pp. 181–206; for another interpretation, see Rajak, *Josephus* (see endnote 33), pp. 65–103.

[41] That the Idumeans were invited to participate in the war, and that they willingly accepted the invitation, shows that their conversion to Judaism during the reign of John Hyrcanus was sincere and real. The Idumean Herod was a "half-Jew" only because he was disliked. See endnote 10.

[42] The question of Titus's motives and actions has been much debated. See the discussion in Stern, *Greek and Latin Authors* (see endnote 6), vol. 2, pp. 64–67, no. 282. See also Zvi Yavetz, "Reflections on Titus and Josephus," *Greek, Roman and Byzantine Studies* 16 (1975), pp. 411–432.

[43] Josephus does not explicitly state John's fate. On the subsequent history of the sacred vessels, see Hans Lewy, "The Fate of the Sacred Vessels After the Destruction of the Second Temple," in *Studies in Jewish Hellenism* (Jerusalem: Bialik, 1960), pp. 255–258 (in Hebrew).

[44] The translation is from Naphtali Lewis and Meyer Reinhold, *Roman Civilization Sourcebook II: The Empire* (New York: Harper & Row, 1966), p. 92.

[45] Stern, *Greek and Latin Authors* (see endnote 6), vol. 2, p. 373, no. 430. The standard discussion of the *fiscus Judaicus* is by Victor Tcherikover, *Corpus Papyrorum Judaicarum*, 3 vols. (Cambridge, MA: Harvard Univ. Press, 1957–1964), vol. 2, pp. 110–116.

[46] D.J. Ladouceur, "Masada: A Consideration of the Literary Evidence," *Greek, Roman and Byzantine Studies* 21 (1980), pp. 245–260; Stern, "The Suicide of Eleazar ben Yair and His Men at Masada," *Zion* 147 (1982), pp. 367–397 (in Hebrew); Cohen, "Masada: Literary Tradition, Archaeological Remains, and the Credibility of Josephus," *JJS* 33 (1982), pp. 385–405. These three articles provide correction to Yigael Yadin, *Masada* (New York: Random House, 1966).

[47] A full discussion of all the aspects of this question obviously is outside the scope of this essay. Here is some bibliography: W.D. Davies, *The Setting of the Sermon on the Mount* (Cambridge, UK: Cambridge Univ. Press, 1964), pp. 259–286; Neusner, "The Formation of Rabbinic Judaism: Yavneh (Jamnia) from A.D. 70 to 100," in *Aufstieg und Niedergang der römischen Welt* 2.19.2, ed. Temporini and Haase (Berlin: de Gruyter, 1979), pp. 3–42; Neusner, *Eliezer ben Hyrcanus* (Leiden: Brill, 1973); Cohen, "The Significance of Yavneh: Pharisees, Rabbis, and the End of Jewish Sectarianism," *HUCA* 55 (1984), pp. 27–53; Baruch M. Bokser, "Rabbinic Responses to Catastrophe: From Continuity to Discontinuity," *PAAJR* 50 (1983), pp. 37–61.

Index